FINAL FANTASY XII

Getting Started

Welcome to the official strategy guide for one of the most breathtaking games not just of this year, but of *any* year. The universe introduced in *FINAL FANTASY XII* is huge, deep, beautiful, rich, and complex. The quests are many, the foes fierce. As always, secrets and mysteries abound. Fortunately, you hold in your hands the ultimate insider's guide to that universe.

Using This Book

Our guide has the level of help you need, whether what you seek is as simple as an overview map or as complex as an in-depth look at the intricacies of the game's battle system. This guide provides a step-by-step walkthrough of the main story, a thorough guide to the game's myriad hunts, secrets, and side quests, and comprehensive data for all the enemies, items, equipment, magicks, and technicks.

Perhaps best of all, though, is that this guide provides an in-depth look at *FINAL FANTASY XII*'s challenging new gameplay elements: licenses, gambits, and an all-new battle system. Before you dive into the main story or tackle any side quests, make sure you check out the coverage of these important topics.

The Story of Ivalice

A great era of peace and prosperity is fading. The stability bestowed upon Ivalice in the founding days of the Dynast-King has been darkened by the likelihood of war between empires. Rozarria and Archadia seem destined to collide, crushing whatever stands between them.

Indeed, the Archadian push west toward Rozarria has already consumed Nabradia and its sibling sovereignty, the small, peaceful Kingdom of Dalmasca. *FINAL FANTASY XII* opens with a quick glimpse of the last throes of pre-Imperial Dalmasca and its desperate fight for freedom, followed by an equally desperate negotiation for peace. In the opening tutorial mission, you participate in a final, fateful attempt to deliver land and king from the clutches of Archadian domination.

Fast forward two years: In the Dalmascan capital city of Rabanastre, a new consul, Vayne Solidor, son of the Archadian emperor, arrives with a message of hope and renewal for the citizens of that subjugated land. However, his silver-tongued speech doesn't fully convince Vaan, an orphaned street boy who sees the Empire as a thieving bully that has robbed his country of wealth and dignity.

Vaan dreams of escape, seeing his future in the skies as a sky pirate. First, though, he wants some measure of revenge. His bold attempt to infiltrate the Royal Palace during the consul's inaugural fete to take back some of the treasure that belongs to Dalmasca leads Vaan straight into the clasp of a destiny none could foresee. It is a destiny that includes an exhilarating adventure in the company of pirates, a princess, and a great fallen Knight of the Order. As such, the tale begins.

Races of Ivalice

HUME

Some call it the race of "dominance." Many Humes have an abiding attraction to power, much more so than the other races of Ivalice. The Hume's insatiable will to power could be a cause of the rising fury that threatens to consume Ivalice.

However, the race's deep-seated curiosity and desire for knowledge has driven the creation of innovative ways and technologies. Sophisticated and stable internal political systems, stunning and nuanced architecture, and the dogged pursuit of a better, more secure life are the culmination of the Hume race.

VIERA

To the Viera, seclusion is a way of life, a given. This nubile race has avoided all political and cultural contact with Humes and other races for hundreds of years. The timeline of their unique history seems uneventful, in an almost monastic way. Over the centuries, the Viera have never migrated beyond the tangled interiors of the forbidding central forests of Ivalice.

Why? Because the Viera see themselves as an inextricable part of "the Wood," almost as a biological component of a greater being. They have long considered interaction with the outside world to be against the will of the Wood. Those rare Viera who do leave the forest become objects of contempt within their race. However, the imperial conflagrations of recent years, with much of the great forest burnt and villages lost, have awakened many more Viera to doubts about their tradition of seclusion.

Special Characteristics

Long Ears. Prominent, highly sensitive listening organs. Worthy of their name "forest hunters," Viera can detect even the most subtle sounds.

Silver Hair. There is no individual hair color in the Viera race, as all Viera have silver hair. Those few who migrate into the world of Humes, though, often dye their locks.

Feet. Viera have pointed feet. These unique appendages make stiletto heels the best footwear for maintaining balance.

MOOGLE

Moogles have a great tradition of expertise in the area of engineering, as the race has long relied on the clever development of machines. An obvious adaptation to their small size, this mechanical skill puts them on equal terms with other races. In particular, Moogles excel at the creation and maintenance of airships, although they are very adept at other types of technology.

Special Characteristics

Pom-Pom. A fluffy fur-ball headpiece is the trademark of the Moogle race. Each individual Moogle has its own color of Pom-Pom.

Wings. Small wings, not unlike those of a bat. Due to the near-vestigial quality of these wings, only a few Moogles can use them to fly.

Hands. Deft, dexterous, highly skilled hands are perfect for delicate technical work or playing instruments. Moogle musicians often provide accompaniment for public ceremonies or parades.

BANGAA

Bangaa body color has many different hues. At one time, many believed that these colors determined the personality and physical abilities of each Bangaa. For example, the yellow skinned "Rugua Bangaa" was said to be friendly and intelligent, while a blue skinned "Fierce Bangaa" displayed a strong sense of justice and great physical prowess. The red "Bista Bangaa" and the steel gray "Sanga Bangaa" featured other social traits of note. However, today there are so many Bangaa of mixed blood that this theory doesn't apply anymore.

Special Characteristics

Face. Highly reptilian facial features with tiny eyes. Because Bangaa don't rely much on their eyesight, some of them actually sport blindfolds as a fashion statement!

Hanging Ears. The characteristic Bangaa ears are split in two and droop downwards. Some individuals have short ears, though.

Physical Frame. Always big and brawny. Even ascetic Bangaa monks are blessed with considerable brawn!

SEEQ

The Seeq are a more primitive race. They don't wear much clothing and display little in the way of intellectual curiosity. What they *do* display is a passion for "shiny things", like jewels and gold, that they love to drape across their bodies. In the eyes of most other races, Seeq exhibit somewhat poor fashion taste and often end up looking unbalanced and, well, comical.

The Seeq also have a strong interest in the acquisition of gil. Because of their fairly low intellect, simple personalities, and penchant to immediately spend whatever gil they get their hands on, very few Seeq ever achieve significant financial success.

Special Characteristics

Mouth. With its upturned nose and narrow oral cavity, the Seeq struggles mightily with verbal pronunciation. Seeq cannot speak quickly and rarely talk for long periods of time.

Skin Color. Although there were originally only three Seeq skin colors (mauve, light yellow and orange), the interbreeding of Seeq with these skin types has created greater variation.

Physical Frame. Seeq have strong and stable frames that are capable of bringing power to bear quickly. Females have a slightly different frame than males.

LVL.	HP	MP	PWR.	MG. PWR.	VIT.	SPD
1	82-84	25-27	23	20	24	24
10	282-316	40-51	28	24	27	25
20	645-742	62-89	33	28	31	26
30	1111-1293	84-127	39	33	35	28
40	1552-1814	111-176	44	37	39	29
50	2257-2650	134-217	50	42	42	31
60	2878-3387	156-255	55	46	46	32
70	3230-3802	172-282	61	51	50	33
80	3637-4281	188-309	66	55	54	35
90	4192-4938	199-325	72	60	57	36
99	4818-5681	204-330	77	64	61	37

Quickenings

NAME	ATT. PWR.
Lv.1 Red Spiral	90
Lv.2 White Whorl	140
Lv.3 Pyroclasm	230

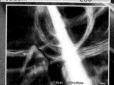

"A boy who sees freedom in the skies."

Vaan

Age: 17

After losing his parents to the plague and his brother Reks to treachery and war, Vaan is now a child of the streets. He's now a leader of a sub-culture of war orphans who roam the slums of Rabanastre.

LVL.	HP	MP	PWR.	MG. PWR.	VIT.	SPD
3	100-106	31-34	22	22	24	23
10	253-284	43-54	26	25	26	24
20	589-679	66-94	31	30	29	25
30	1020-1189	89-135	36	35	33	26
40	1428-1671	117-186	42	40	36	28
50	2081-2445	142-320	47	45	40	29
60	2656-3127	165-270	52	50	43	30
70	2982-3511	182-298	58	55	47	32
80	3359-3955	199-327	63	60	50	33
90	3872-4563	210-344	68	65	53	34
99	4452-5251	216-349	73	69	57	36

Quickenings

NAME	ATT. PWR.
Lv.1 Northswain's Glow	90
Lv.2 Heaven's Wrath	140
Lv.3 Maelstrom's Bolt	230

"A princess who had lost everything."

Ashe

Age: 19

The daughter of the Dalmascan king and heir to the throne, Lady Ashe first loses her newlywed husband Rasler and then her country to the Archadian juggernaut. The official story is that she took her own life in the aftermath of the Imperial conquest. However, resistance is in her blood, as is the legacy of the Dynast-King.

LVL.	HP	MP	PWR.	MG. PWR.	VIT.	SPD
3	138-145	19-22	26	21	20	23
10	306-340	28-37	30	23	22	24
20	673-772	46-68	35	27	25	25
30	1146-1330	64-99	40	31	28	26
40	1593-1858	86-139	46	35	31	28
50	2307-2706	105-172	51	39	34	29
60	2937-3453	122-203	56	43	36	30
70	3294-3873	132-225	62	47	39	31
80	3706-4359	149-247	67	51	42	33
90	4269-5025	157-260	72	55	45	34
99	4903-5778	161-264	77	58	47	35

Quickenings

NAME	ATT. PWR.
Lv.1 Fulminating Darkness	90
Lv.2 Ruin Impendent	140
Lv.3 Flame Purge	230

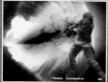

"A loyal knight branded as traitor."

Basch

Age: 36

This great hero of Dalmasca, captain of the Order of Knights, now stands accused of the assassination of his oathsworn liege, King Raminas. Word is that Basch saw the King's attempt to sue for peace with Archadia as a betrayal of the kingdom. But is that word true?

LVL.	HP	MP	PWR.	MG. PWR.	VIT.	SPD
1	65-66	36-37	20	18	23	24
10	244-275	51-62	25	23	26	25
20	570-658	73-100	30	28	30	26
30	989-1153	95-140	35	33	34	27
40	1385-1621	123-189	40	38	38	29
50	2018-2372	146-231	45	43	41	30
60	2577-3035	168-270	50	48	45	31
70	2894-3407	185-297	55	54	49	32
80	3259-3838	201-325	60	59	53	34
90	3758-4428	212-341	65	64	56	35
99	4321-5096	217-346	70	69	60	36

Quickenings

NAME	ATT. PWR.
Lv.1 Intercession	90
Lv.2 Evanescence	140
Lv.3 Resplendence	230

"Vaan's friend."

Penelo Age: 17

Penelo loves Vaan like a brother. Her own parents, who were lost in the recent war, took in Vaan after his loss and raised him as one of their own. She sees the natural leader in him, even if he doesn't quite see it himself.

LVL.	HP	MP	PWR.	MG. PWR.	VIT.	SPD
2	99-103	20-22	25	17	24	24
10	277-311	32-41	29	20	27	25
20	630-725	51-75	34	24	31	26
30	1084-1261	71-109	39	28	34	28
40	1513-1768	95-153	44	32	38	29
50	2198-2581	115-189	50	36	41	31
60	2803-3299	134-223	55	40	45	32
70	3146-3702	149-247	60	44	48	34
80	3542-4168	163-271	65	48	52	35
90	4082-4808	173-285	71	52	55	37
99	4691-5531	177-289	75	56	58	38

Quickenings

NAME	ATT. PWR.
Lv.1 Fires of War	90
Lv.2 Tides of Fate	140
Lv.3 Element of Treachery	230

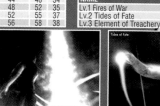

"A dashing sky pirate."

Balthier Age: 22

A man of wit, charm and a mysterious past, Balthier owes allegiance to no crown or council. He prowls the skies of Ivalice with his partner Fran in search of treasure and perhaps something else…

LVL.	HP	MP	PWR.	MG. PWR.	VIT.	SPD
2	85-89	25-27	23	18	20	23
10	256-288	38-49	27	22	23	24
20	594-685	60-88	32	26	26	25
30	1029-1199	83-127	37	30	30	27
40	1440-1684	110-177	42	34	33	28
50	2097-2464	134-218	47	39	36	30
60	2677-3151	156-257	52	43	40	31
70	3005-3538	172-284	57	47	43	32
80	3385-3985	189-312	62	51	46	34
90	3902-4598	200-328	67	55	50	35
99	4486-5290	205-333	71	59	53	36

Quickenings

NAME	ATT. PWR.
Lv.1 Feral Strike	90
Lv.2 Whip Kick	140
Lv.3 Shatterheart	230

"A master of weapons."

Fran Age: unknown

A Viera female with a strong sensitivity to the Mist, Fran is a loyal partner and co-pilot to Balthier. She's quite a formidable warrior and a mechanic to boot. Her adjustment to the greater world since abandoning the forest dwellings of her race is nearly complete. But can one ever completely forsake the voice of the Wood?

Guest Party Members

Vossler
York Azelas

A captain of the Dalmascan Order of Knights and sworn protector of Princess Ashe.

LVL.	HP	MP	PWR.	MG. PWR.	VIT.	SPD
6	211-228	28-36	29	22	21	24
10	323-360	36-49	31	23	22	25
20	715-820	62-95	36	27	25	26
30	1219-1416	89-143	42	31	28	28
40	1696-1979	122-202	47	35	31	29
50	2457-2883	151-252	53	39	34	31
60	3129-3680	177-298	58	43	36	32
70	3510-4128	197-331	64	47	39	33
80	3950-4646	217-364	69	51	42	35
90	4550-5356	230-384	75	55	45	36
99	5227-6160	236-390	80	58	47	37

Reks

Vaan's older brother and a volunteer soldier in the Dalmascan army.

LVL.	HP	MP	PWR.	MG. PWR.	VIT.	SPD
3	112-118	32-35	24	22	23	35
4	129-139	34-39	25	22	24	35
5	148-160	35-42	25	23	24	35
6	168-183	37-45	26	23	24	35
99	4401-5188	233-378	74	67	55	46

Larsa
Ferrinas Solidor

Youngest son of the Archadian emperor.

LVL.	HP	MP	PWR.	MG. PWR.	VIT.	SPD
2	83-87	37-40	21	22	23	24
10	249-280	51-62	25	26	25	25
20	577-665	73-100	30	31	30	26
30	999-1164	95-140	35	36	34	27
40	1398-1636	123-189	40	41	38	29
50	2036-2393	146-231	45	46	41	30
60	2599-3060	168-270	50	51	45	31
70	2918-3435	185-297	55	57	49	32
80	3287-3869	201-325	60	62	53	34
90	3789-4464	212-341	65	67	56	35
99	4356-5137	217-346	70	72	60	36

Reddas

A sky pirate and denizen of the Port of Balfonheim.

LVL.	HP	MP	PWR.	MG. PWR.	VIT.	SPD
5	208-222	35-42	26	23	26	35
10	342-378	45-57	29	25	28	36
20	726-830	70-101	34	30	31	37
30	1221-1414	95-145	39	35	34	39
40	1689-1967	126-201	44	39	38	40
50	2436-2854	153-248	50	44	41	42
60	3096-3636	177-292	55	49	44	43
70	3469-4075	196-323	60	53	47	45
80	3901-4584	215-354	65	58	51	46
90	4490-5281	227-372	71	63	54	48
99	5154-6069	233-378	75	67	57	49

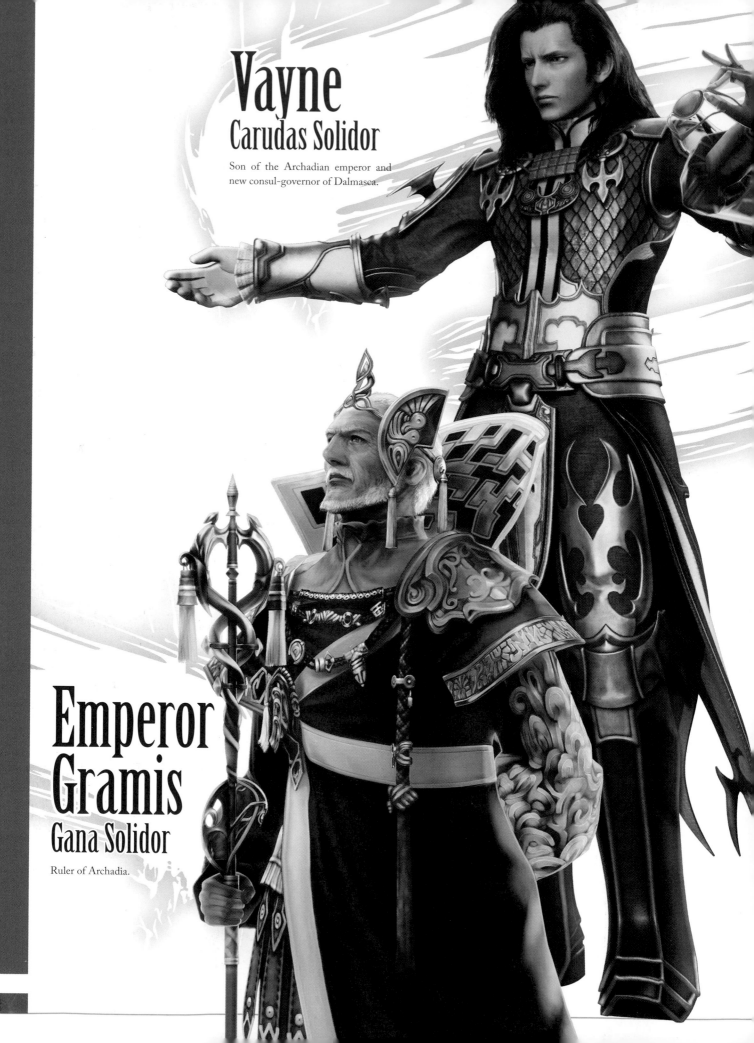

Vayne
Carudas Solidor

Son of the Archadian emperor and
new consul-governor of Dalmasca.

Emperor
Gramis
Gana Solidor

Ruler of Archadia.

Al-Cid
Margrace

A member of the ruling family of Rozarria, Archadia's great rival to the west.

Dr. Cidolfus
Demen Bunansa

Director of Draklor Laboratory, the primary weapons research center of the Archadian empire.

King Raminas

Father of Lady Ashe and benevolent ruler of Dalmasca.

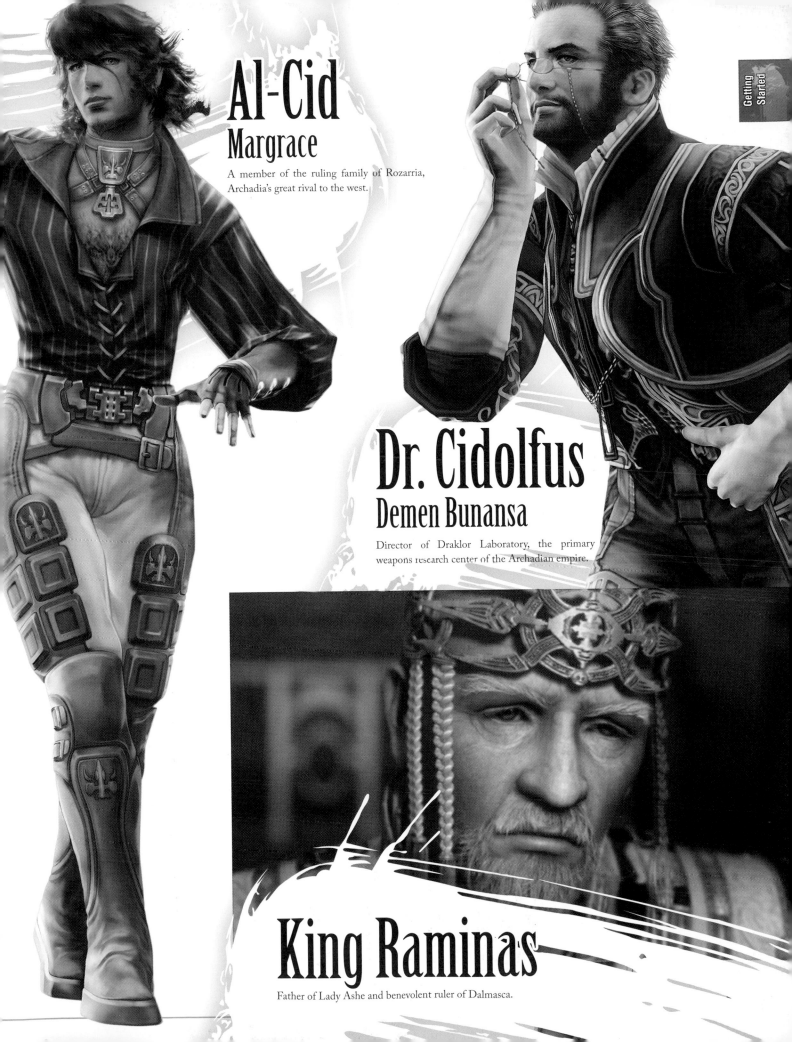

Lord Rasler
Heios Nabradia

Newlywed husband of Lady Ashe and heir to the throne of Nabradia, the sister kingdom of Dalmasca.

Marquis Halim Ondore IV

Head minister of the Skycity of Bhujerba and longtime friend of Dalmasca's King Raminas.

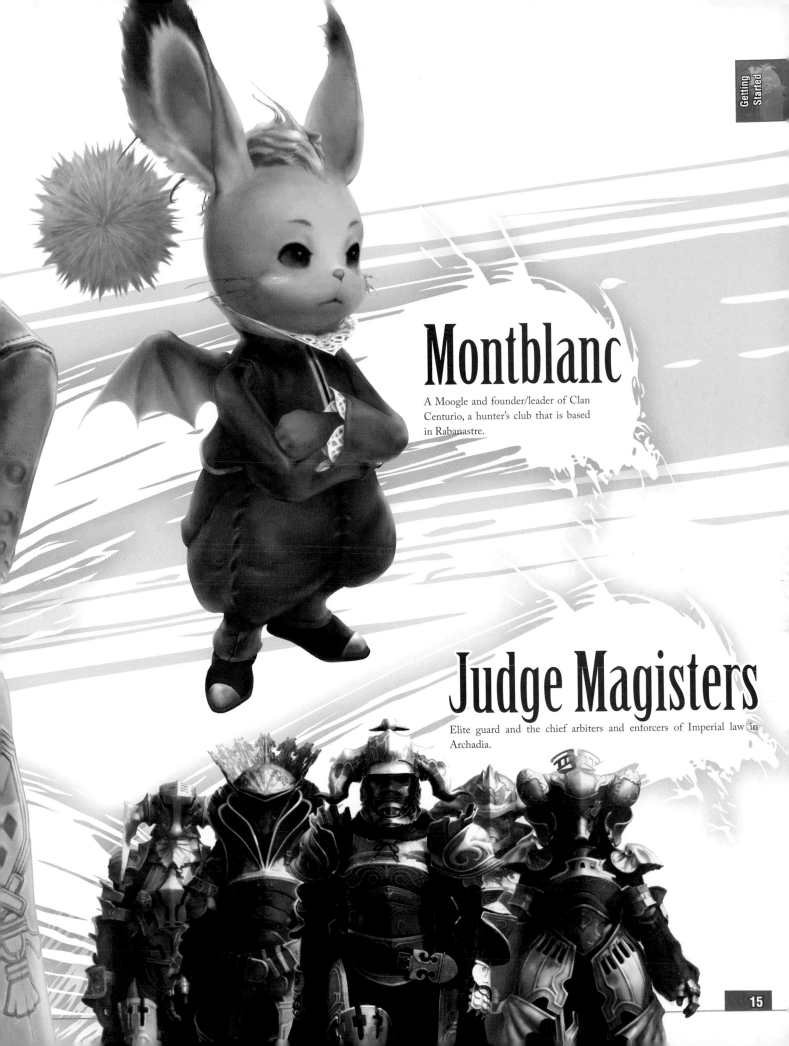

Montblanc

A Moogle and founder/leader of Clan Centurio, a hunter's club that is based in Rabanastre.

Judge Magisters

Elite guard and the chief arbiters and enforcers of Imperial law in Archadia.

Character Relationships

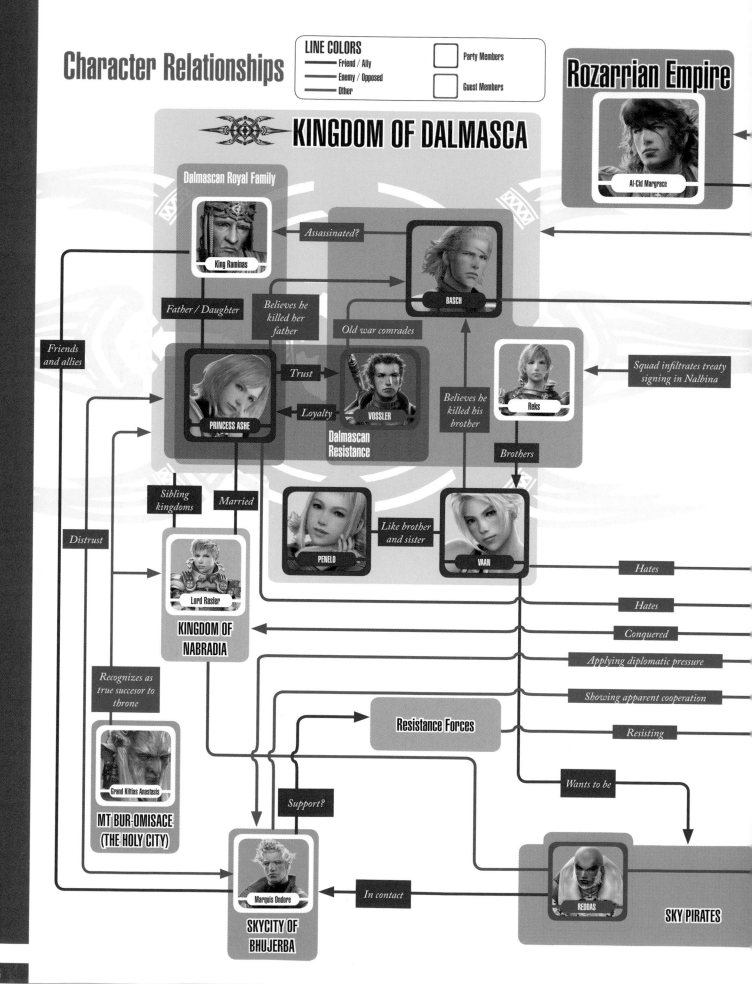

LINE COLORS
Friend / Ally
Enemy / Opposed
Other

Party Members

Guest Members

Rozarrian Empire

Al-Cid Margrace

KINGDOM OF DALMASCA

Dalmascan Royal Family

King Raminas

Assassinated?

BASCH

Father / Daughter

Believes he killed her father

Old war comrades

Trust

PRINCESS ASHE

Loyalty

VOSSLER

Dalmascan Resistance

Believes he killed his brother

Reks

Squad infiltrates treaty signing in Nalbina

Brothers

Friends and allies

Sibling kingdoms

Married

PENELO

Like brother and sister

VAAN

Lord Rasler

KINGDOM OF NABRADIA

Distrust

Recognizes as true succesor to throne

Grand Kiltias Anastasis

MT BUR-OMISACE (THE HOLY CITY)

Hates

Hates

Conquered

Applying diplomatic pressure

Showing apparent cooperation

Resistance Forces

Resisting

Wants to be

Support?

Marquis Ondore

SKYCITY OF BHUJERBA

In contact

REDDAS

SKY PIRATES

16

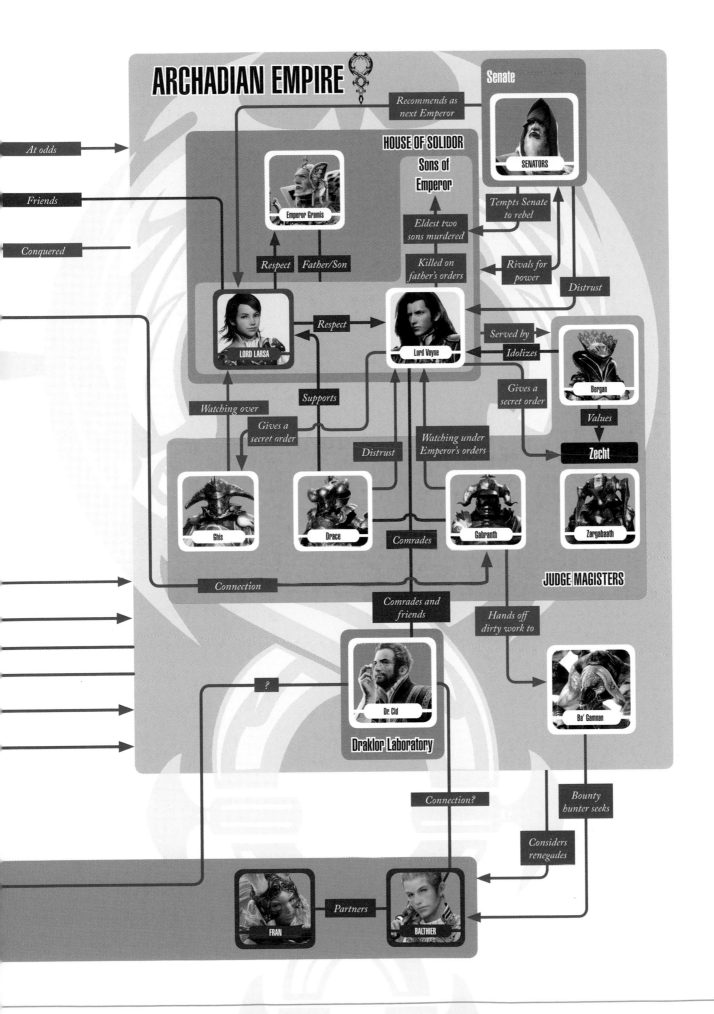

ARCHADIAN EMPIRE

Senate

SENATORS

Recommends as next Emperor

HOUSE OF SOLIDOR

Sons of Emperor

Emperor Gramis

Tempts Senate to rebel

Eldest two sons murdered

Killed on father's orders

Rivals for power

Distrust

At odds

Friends

Conquered

Respect | *Father/Son*

LORD LARSA

Respect

Lord Vayne

Served by

Idolizes

Distrust

Bergan

Gives a secret order

Values

Watching over

Supports

Gives a secret order

Distrust

Watching under Emperor's orders

Zecht

Ghis

Drace

Comrades

Gabranth

Zargabaath

JUDGE MAGISTERS

Connection

Comrades and friends

Hands off dirty work to

Dr. Cid

Draklor Laboratory

Ba' Gamnan

?

Connection?

Bounty hunter seeks

Considers renegades

FRAN

Partners

BALTHIER

Licenses determine a character's growth, abilities, and—ultimately—usefulness throughout the game. Magick, technicks, weapons, armor, and even accessories require a license before a character can wield or equip them. Each character enters the game with a few basic licenses. You can use these "suggested" skills as a basis for growth, or players can break from the mold and develop all six characters in any manner they choose.

How Does It Work?

Licenses are purchased with LP (License Points) earned during battle. Most creatures are worth 1 LP, so it can take a long time to earn the LP needed to unlock some of the best licenses. Check a character's LP by entering the Licenses sub-menu within the Main Menu. Each character can have as much as 99999 LP accumulated; although collecting that much LP would be a highly unlikely scenario, any LP past the amount you need to fill out the characters' license board is wasted.

!! WANDERING BATTLES

Most battles are optional. The party can flee past enemies and avoid combat, if you so desire. The gambit system makes battle less tedious by automating simple battle commands. Let your gambits do the work and take down those lesser enemies. It's worth fighting low-level creatures for LP gains even when the experience earned is minimal.

A character's license board is divided into eight sections. The top half focuses on magick, technicks, accessories, and augmentations. The bottom half is composed primarily of weapons and armor licenses. Expect to spend more time on the top section early on, since weapons and armor are slow to appear and augmentations are extremely valuable from the outset.

At first, most of the board is hidden from view and won't be available until much later in the game. Fortunately, you have this guide to provide a sneak peek of the board and allow for better planning from the beginning. A few panels are already unlocked when a character joins the party. These panels represent the character's experience prior to joining the party. It also enables them to wield basic weapons and armor while using some low-level magicks and technicks too, so they can do a little more than just attack at the start of the adventure.

Next to the unlocked panels are locked panels. These panels are readable, but haven't been purchased with LP. Press the ✗ button over a locked panel and the game will ask you to confirm the purchase if the character has enough LP to complete the transaction. Agree to do so to unlock the locked panel. Any unreadable panels adjacent to the recently unlocked panel are uncovered, becoming readable. These are now available for purchase. Each time a new panel is unlocked, as many as three unreadable panels may become readable.

What Should I Buy?

LP isn't easy to gather, so spend wisely. Come up with a development plan for each character right from the start. Decide who will lead the party into battle and absorb the bulk of the damage. Determine who will play a backup role and act primarily as a caster. Then use these determinations to chart each character's progress throughout the game.

Someone must lead the party into battle. That character should focus on the lower-half of the augmentations section and on swords and heavy armor. Augmentations can rapidly increase a character's HP (Hit Points), ability to block with a shield, and physical attack power. Swords cause reliable damage and heavy armor helps to reduce the damage sustained when fighting.

!! BUILDING THE ULTIMATE FIGHTER

Anyone focusing on physical attacks should collect certain augmentations as early as possible. The three "Shield Block" panels are extremely important. These panels enable the character to deflect many enemy attacks, which drastically reduces the need for healing. The five "Battle Lore" panels increase a character's physical attack damage. The five "+HP" panels are also extremely important, as they greatly increase a character's HP early in the game. This makes it much easier to survive when fighting powerful bosses.

Backup characters, those who rarely fight at close range, should focus more on magicks and the top half of the augmentations section. This area focuses on lowering MP (Mist Point) costs, increasing magick potency, and overall magick proficiency. Characters can wear light or mystic armor and they perform very well with ranged weapons (bows, guns, crossbows, hand-bombs) or mystic weapons (staves, rods, maces, measures). Light armor is best for those who plan to use close-range weapons despite their backup roles (daggers, poles, ninja swords, axes, hammers, spears, katana).

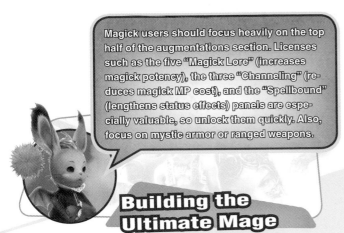

Magick users should focus heavily on the top half of the augmentations section. Licenses such as the five "Magick Lore" (increases magick potency), the three "Channeling" (reduces magick MP cost), and the "Spellbound" (lengthens status effects) panels are especially valuable, so unlock them quickly. Also, focus on mystic armor or ranged weapons.

Building the Ultimate Mage

Be stingy when purchasing licenses for armor, weapons, accessories, and magicks. There's no reason to buy the licenses until the items become available, even if that means diverting from the main story long enough to accumulate the LP when the items arrive in local shops. A little extra combat never hurts!

Technicks are somewhat unusual. They can be useful in some combat situations, however, some are used less often than others. Grab "Steal" and "Charge" early in the game, but wait for others until you purchase more important augmentations.

A FEW THINGS EVERYONE NEEDS

There are certain panels that everyone should have. White Magick is important to every character, as it enables the party to restore lost HP and revive defeated allies. Each member of the party should have these abilities.

The three "Swiftness" augmentations reduce action time and improve the party's efficiency. "Steal" and "Charge" are the only technicks that everyone needs. "Steal" increases the amount of loot the party gathers during their adventures, which is eventually sold for gil and used to unlock new Bazaar items. "Charge" restores a small amount of MP when a character's MP is low, so purchase this one immediately. You will most likely use "Charge" from the start of the game to the very end.

What Are Gambit Slots?

Throughout the augmentations section, there are 10 Gambit Slot panels that increase in cost from 15 LP to as much as 100 LP. Unlocking a Gambit Slot panel adds a gambit slot to that character. This allows for the creation of additional gambits so that you can automate more of a character's actions. Don't invest in these panels at the very start of the game; instead, wait until the gambits are needed. A character can never have too many gambits, but extra HP and quickness are far more important at the beginning of the game.

What's the Deal with Quickenings?

There are 18 Quickening panels scattered around the board. Each character can unlock as many as three Quickening panels. Any of the panels will suffice, but note that once a Quickening panel is unlocked it is immediately and permanently removed from the other characters' license boards. Thus, it's important to plan ahead which characters will go after the different panels to ensure that everyone can unlock three without having to purchase too many undesired abilities.

It pays to go after these panels early in the game, because Quickenings are very powerful attacks. They can often decimate a group of enemies or a boss. Upon unlocking a second and third Quickening panel, the character also gains an additional Mist Charge. The Mist Charge is equal to the character's maximum MP (Mist Points), effectively doubling and then tripling the character's available MP!

Quickening and Esper panels are considered "one-time" panels, since only one character can learn them. Once unlocked, they vanish from the other characters' license boards.

One-Time Panels

Where Are the Espers?

Espers don't appear on the license board until the party finds them and subsequently defeats them. These slots appear as empty spaces until that time arises. Characters can learn any number of Espers, but a character can only summon one Esper at a time. More importantly, only the person who unlocks the Esper may command it.

It requires from one to three Mist Charges to summon an Esper. Try to evenly spread out the Espers amongst the party members, but try to assign the ultimate Esper, Zodiark, to the character used most frequently. Generally, this character should be a melee specialist, since it takes three Mist Charges to summon the beast and a swordsman can quickly restore lost MP by simply attacking.

Breaking Down the License Board

The full license board is shown in this section. Each character has access to the same licenses, so the party can develop in any way you see fit. Feel free to create six melee masters or six menacing magick users. This system is designed in such a way as to give the player absolute freedom to decide the fates of all six main characters.

With that said, there is a recommended approach that involves balance. To really master the game, you must learn to use every advantage available. That requires careful planning and strategic thinking when spending the party's LP. Let's take a look at each section of the license board and discuss the best approach for each piece.

◈ MAGICKS	◈ ACCESSORIES
◈ AUGMENTS	◈ TECHNICKS
◈ WEAPONS	◈ ARMOR
◈ QUICKENINGS	◈ ESPERS

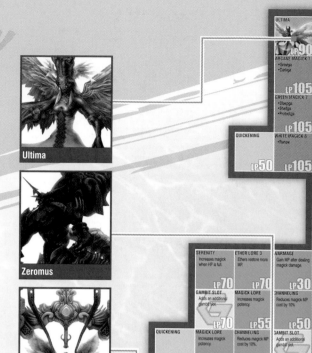

Ultima

Zeromus

Zodiark

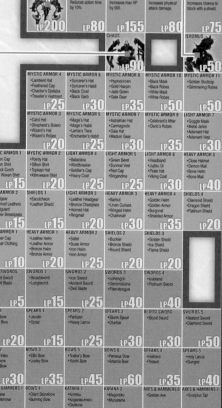

Chaos

Mateus

Zalera

Adrammelech

Hashmal

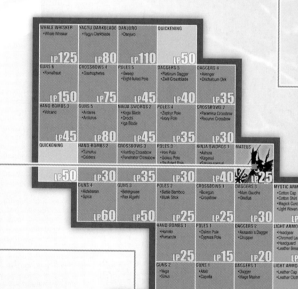

ULTIMA LP90

ARCANE MAGICK 7
•Graviga
•Quriga
LP105

GREEN MAGICK 7
•Stoegga
•Shellga
•Protectga
LP105

WHITE MAGICK 8
•Runew
LP105

QUICKENING LP50

SERENITY
Increases magick when HP is full.
LP70

ETHER LORE 3
Ethers restore more MP.
LP70

WARMAGE
Gain MP after dealing magick damage.
LP30

GAMBIT SLOT
Adds an additional gambit slot.
LP70

MAGICK LORE
Increases magick potency.
LP55

CHANNELING
Reduces magick MP cost by 10%.
LP50

QUICKENING
Increases magick potency.
LP50

MAGICK LORE
Increases magick potency.
LP80

CHANNELING
Reduces magick MP cost by 10%.
LP80

GAMBIT SLOT
Adds an additional gambit slot.
LP50

MAGICK LORE
Increases magick potency.
LP120

BRAWLER
Increases attack power when fighting empty-handed.
LP90

REMEDY LORE 3
Remedies remove Stop, Doom, and Disease.
LP70

SWIFTNESS
Reduces action time by 10%.
LP50

BATTLE LORE
Increases physical attack damage.
LP120

GAMBIT SLOT
Adds an additional gambit slot.
LP100

+200 HP
Increases max HP by 200.
LP100

FOCUS
Increases strength when HP is full.
LP70

ZODIARK LP200

SWIFTNESS
Reduces action time by 10%.
LP80

+500 HP
Increases max HP by 500.
LP155

BATTLE LORE
Increases physical attack damage.
LP80

SHIELD BLOCK
Increases chance to block with a shield.
LP75

CHAOS LP90

ZEROMUS LP50

MYSTIC ARMOR 4
•Lambent Hat
•Feathered Cap
•Chanter's Djellaba
•Traveler's Vestment
LP25

MYSTIC ARMOR 6
•Sorcerer's Hat
•Sorcerer's Habit
•Black Cowl
•Black Garb
LP30

MYSTIC ARMOR 8
•Hypnocrown
•Gold Hairpin
•Jade Gown
•Gaia Gear
LP35

MYSTIC ARMOR 10
•Black Mask
•Black Robes
•White Mask
•White Robes
LP50

MYSTIC ARMOR 11
•Golden Skullcap
•Glimmering Robes
LP50

MYSTIC ARMOR 2
•Calot Hat
•Mage's Bolero
•Mage's Habit
•Wizard's Hat
•Wizard's Robes
LP20

MYSTIC ARMOR 5
•Mage's Hat
•Mage's Habit
•Lamia's Tiara
•Enchanter's Habit
LP25

MYSTIC ARMOR 7
•Astrakhan Hat
•Carmagnole
•Gaia Hat
•Madum Gear
LP30

MYSTIC ARMOR 9
•Celebrant's Miter
•Cleric's Robes
LP35

LIGHT ARMOR 7
•Goggle Mask
•Metal Jerkin
•Adamant Hat
•Adamant Vest
LP30

WHALE WHISKER
•Whale Whisker
LP125

YAGYU DARKBLADE
•Yagyu Darkblade
LP80

DANJURO
•Danjuro
LP110

QUICKENING LP50

GUNS 6
•Fomalhaut
LP150

CROSSBOWS 4
•Gastrapheres
LP75

POLES 5
•Sweep
•Eight-fluted Pole
LP45

DAGGERS 5
•Platinum Dagger
•Zwill Crossblade
LP40

DAGGERS 4
•Avenger
•Orichalcum Dirk
LP35

HAND-BOMBS 3
•Volcano
LP45

GUNS 5
•Antares
•Arcturus
LP80

NINJA SWORDS 3
•Koga Blade
•Orochi
•Iga Blade
LP45

POLES 4
•Zephyr Pole
•Ivory Pole
LP35

CROSSBOWS 3
•Paramina Crossbow
•Recurve Crossbow
LP30

MATEUS LP25

QUICKENING LP50

HAND-BOMBS 2
•Tumulus
•Caldera
LP30

CROSSBOWS 2
•Hunting Crossbow
•Penetrator Crossbow
LP35

POLES 3
•Iron Pole
•Gokuu Pole
LP30

NINJA SWORDS 2
•Ashura
•Kagenui
LP40

MYSTIC ARMOR 1
•Cotton Cap
•Silken Shirt
•Magick Curch
•Light Woven Shirt
LP15

MYSTIC ARMOR 3
•Pointy Hat
•Topknot
•Topkapi Hat
•Kitmurwave Shirt
LP20

LIGHT ARMOR 5
•Balaclava
•Windbreaker
•Soldier's Cap
•Heavy Coat
LP25

LIGHT ARMOR 6
•Green Beret
•Survival Vest
•Red Cap
•Brigandine
LP25

HEAVY ARMOR 5
•Close Helmet
•Demon Mail
•Bone Helm
•Bone Mail
LP40

GUNS 4
•Aldebaran
•Spica
LP60

GUNS 3
•Betelgeuse
•Ras Algethi
LP50

POLES 2
•Battle Bamboo
•Musk Stick
LP25

CROSSBOWS 1
•Bowgun
•Crossbow
LP30

MYSTIC ARMOR 2
•Main Gauche
•Gladius
LP15

LIGHT ARMOR 4
•Headband
•Jujitsu Gi
•Pirate Hat
•Viking Coat
LP30

HAND-BOMBS 1
•Hornito
•Fumarole
LP25

POLES 1
•Oaken Pole
•Cypress Pole
LP15

DAGGERS 2
•Assassin's Dagger
•Chopper
LP20

LIGHT ARMOR 3
•Leather Headgear
•Bronze Chestplate
•Horned Hat
•Ringmail
LP30

HEAVY ARMOR 4
•Barbut
•Linen Cuirass
•Winged Helm
•Chainmail
LP35

SHIELDS 4
•Diamond Shield
•Dragon Shield
•Platinum Shield
LP20

GUNS 2
•Vega
•Sirius
LP40

GUNS 1
•Altair
•Capella
LP30

DAGGERS 1
•Dagger
•Mage Masher
LP15

LIGHT ARMOR 1
•Leather Cap
•Leather Clothing
LP10

HEAVY ARMOR 1
•Leather Helm
•Leather Armor
•Bronze Helm
•Bronze Armor
LP10

HEAVY ARMOR 2
•Sallet
•Scale Armor
•Iron Helm
•Iron Armor
LP20

SHIELDS 2
•Buckler
•Bronze Shield
•Round Shield
LP15

SHIELDS 3
•Golden Shield
•Ice Shield
•Flame Shield
LP20

ZALERA LP25

RODS 2
•Healing Rod
•Gaia Rod
LP25

RODS 1
•Rod
•Serpent Rod
LP15

STAVES 1
•Oak Staff
•Wizard's Staff
•Cherry Staff
LP15

SMALLSWORDS 1
•Mythril Sword
•Mythril Blade
LP5

SWORDS 1
•Broadsword
•Longsword
LP15

SWORDS 2
•Iron Sword
•Ancient Sword
•Zwill Blade
LP25

SWORDS 3
•Lohengrin
•Demonstone
•Flametongue
LP40

SWORDS 4
•Icebrand
•Platinum Sword
LP40

QUICKENING LP50

MACES 4
•Doom Mace
•Zeus Mace
LP25

STAVES 3
•Golden Staff
•Judicer's Staff
LP30

STAVES 2
•Flame Staff
•Glacial Staff
•Storm Staff
LP25

MACES 1
•Mace
•Bronze Mace
LP20

BOWS 1
•Shortbow
•Silver Bow
LP15

SPEARS 1
•Javelin
•Spear
LP15

SPEARS 2
•Partisan
•Heavy Lance
LP25

SPEARS 3
•Storm Spear
•Obelisk
LP30

BLOOD SWORD
•Blood Sword
LP30

SWORDS 5
•Bastard Sword
•Diamond Sword
LP50

ROD OF FAITH
•Rod of Faith
LP120

MACES 5
•Grand Mace
LP50

RODS 3
•Power Rod
•Empyrean Rod
LP30

MACES 2
•Thorned Mace
•Chaos Mace
LP25

MACES 2
•Bhuj
•Miter
LP20

MEASURES 1
•Gift Measure
•Arc Scale
LP20

BOWS 2
•Aevis Killer
•Longbow
•Killer Bow
LP20

BOWS 3
•Elfin Bow
•Loxley Bow
LP35

BOWS 5
•Traitor's Bow
•Yoichi Bow
LP45

BOWS 6
•Perseus Bow
•Artemis Bow
LP60

SPEARS 4
•Halberd
•Trident
LP35

SPEARS 5
•Holy Lance
•Gungnir
LP50

MEASURES 3
•Caliper
•Euclid's Sextant
LP50

RODS 4
•Holy Rod
LP35

STAVES 4
•Cloud Staff
LP30

QUICKENING LP50

ADRAMMELECH LP25

AXES & HAMMERS 2
•Handaxe
•Iron Hammer
LP15

BOWS 4
•Giant Stonebow
•Burning Bow
LP40

KATANA 1
•Kotetsu
•Kogarasumaru
•Osafune
LP35

KATANA 2
•Magoroku
•Murasame
LP40

AXES & HAMMERS 6
•Golden Axe
LP40

AXES & HAMMERS 7
•Scorpion Tail
LP70

STAFF OF THE MAGI
•Staff of the Magi
LP100

MEASURES 2
•Multiscale
•Cross Scale
LP25

HASHMAL LP50

AXES & HAMMERS 1
•Broadaxe
•War Hammer
LP20

AXES & HAMMERS 3
•Slasher
•Sledgehammer
LP25

AXES & HAMMERS 4
•Hammerhead
•Francisca
LP30

AXES & HAMMERS 5
•Morning Star
•Greataxe
LP35

GREATSWORDS 1
•Claymore
LP50

KATANA 3
•Kiku-ichimonji
•Yakei
LP45

QUICKENING LP50

QUICKENING LP50

QUICKENING LP50

GREATSWORDS 2
•Defender
•Save the Queen
LP70

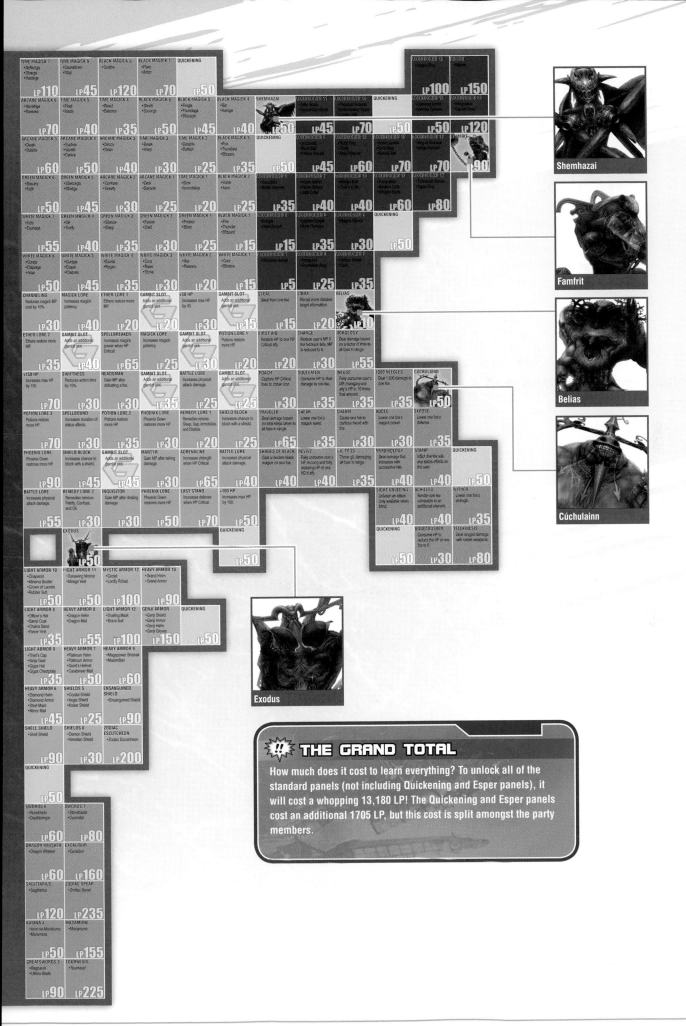

Shemhazai

Famfrit

Belias

Cúchulainn

Exodus

THE GRAND TOTAL

How much does it cost to learn everything? To unlock all of the standard panels (not including Quickening and Esper panels), it will cost a whopping 13,180 LP! The Quickening and Esper panels cost an additional 1705 LP, but this cost is split amongst the party members.

The Top Half

The top of the license board focuses on commands granting magicks and technicks and useful passive bonuses provided by augments and accessories. This portion of the board is split into four sections (refer to the board):

Magicks
Powerful spells used to inflict damage, cure wounds, strengthen the party, and weaken the enemy.

Technicks
Unusual and sometimes useful abilities that don't require MP.

Accessories
Wearable items that provide passive bonuses, immunities, or increase the effectiveness of abilities.

Augments
Passive bonuses that greatly enhance the party's effectiveness in battle.

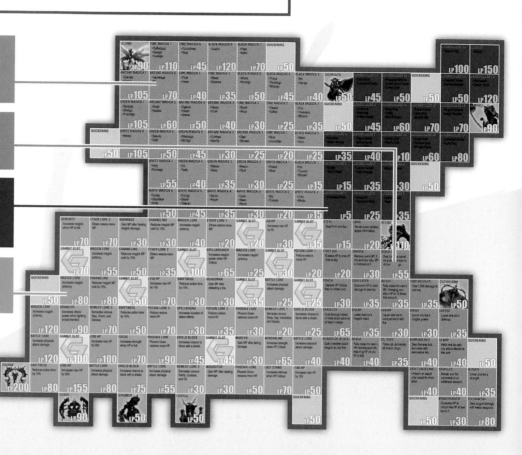

Magicks

Magicks are split into five unique groups:

White
Focuses on healing and restoration.

Black
Largely elemental attacks that allow the party to strike an enemy's weak spot.

Green
Status effects, both positive and negative, that are used to fortify allies or weaken enemies.

Time
Speed-enhancing magick that improves the party's efficiency or slows the enemy and DOT (Damage Over Time) attacks, among other things.

Arcane
Often unpredictable, but very powerful magick.

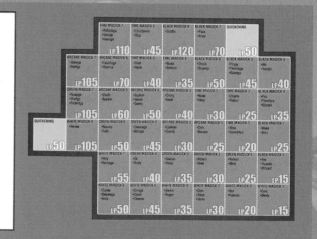

Magicks Explained

White Magick

White magick is all about healing and reviving party members. These spells are critical to all party members. Even those characters who focus on melee should invest in White Magick 1~6. These six provide the basic Cure and Raise magicks along with status restoration magick. The most useful abilities include:

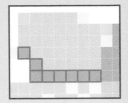

Cure & Curaga

Heal an individual party member. Curaga is an enhanced version of Cure that restores more lost HP. These are absolutely essential; pick them up as early as possible.

Cura & Curaja

These are "group heals" that affect every ally within a small area. These powerful spells will eventually replace Cure and Curaga.

Raise & Arise

You can use these spells to revive a fallen ally. This is essential as the game progresses and enemies become more and more vicious. Players may also use Phoenix Downs to restore downed characters faster, but at an added expense. These spells are the perfect choice in most situations.

Esuna & Esunaga

Negative status effects can cripple party members. These magicks make it easy to erase the negative status. Although they don't affect every status, they take care of the most common ones.

! CURE AND THE UNDEAD

Healing magick has a reverse effect on the undead. Casting Cure on a zombie causes damage equal to the magick's normal healing effect. Likewise, casting Raise can sometimes kill an undead enemy instantly. Thus, Cura and Curaja are powerful area attacks when facing a horde of undead creatures.

Black Magick

Black magick can be a powerful ally in some battles. Enemies with an elemental weakness may suffer critical damage from these magicks when other weapons and magicks seem to bounce right off. Make sure casters are equipped with the following:

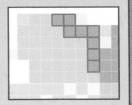

Fire, Blizzard, & Thunder

These are the three basic elemental attacks. Any caster should be ready to use these at a moment's notice.

Scourge

This is a powerful, non-elemental attack that sometimes leaves a Sap effect on its victims. The HP Sap continues to drain HP from the target until the status effect is removed. This is especially effective against targets with a tough physical defense.

Flare

This extremely powerful magick delivers a devastating, non-elemental blow. It's perfect to use when the enemy is immune to the basic elements and tends to absorb magick damage. It's also good to use during some boss fights.

Green Magick

Green magick is all about status effects. These abilities can either protect the party or hamper the enemy. The most essential ones are:

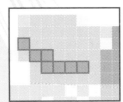

Protect & Protectga

These two improve the party's defense against physical attacks. This is essential when facing a powerful foe in battle. In tough battles, the damage reduction can mean the difference between death and a narrow victory.

Shell & Shellga

Much like the previous magicks, these increase the party's magick defense. It reduces the damage of enemy magicks significantly and can also prove to be a deciding factor in a major battle.

Silence & Silencega

Casters are ineffective when they can't use magicks. Silence robs an enemy of its ability to use magicks until the effect is removed. This effect never runs out on its own, so cast it early and it may last throughout the entire fight.

Blind & Blindga

Blind and Blindga can cripple a character who relies on melee fighting. This type of magick robs the victim of his eyesight, drastically reducing the enemy's chance to hit. This effect never wears off, so use it early in battle.

Time Magick

The status effects found in Time magick increase the party's speed, slow down enemies or stop them altogether, and cause damage over time. These are especially effective, since speed is a huge advantage in any battle. Magicks that damage over time are also an effective way to take down creatures that are otherwise too powerful.

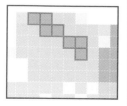

Slow & Slowga

The Slow magicks are key to use when facing tough opponents like bosses or marks. Slowing the target reduces the damage it can cause over the course of the battle and it gives the party more time to react and heal. This effect eventually wears off during long battles, so you may need to recast it.

Haste & Hastega

Haste speeds up the party's actions, allowing them to react and attack much faster. Combine Haste on the party with Slow on an enemy and the party will gain a huge advantage! These spells also eventually wear off during a long fight, so you may need to recast it.

⚡ SPEED EFFECTS

There are three magicks that affect speed: Slow, Haste and Berserk. The following magick combinations result in different bonuses:

Haste + Berserk = 3x Speed

Berserk or Slow + Haste + Berserk* = 2x Speed

Haste = 1.5x Speed

Slow + Haste* or Slow + Berserk = 1x Speed

Slow = 0.5x Speed

Stop = 0x Speed

*Only occurs when one of the effects is provided by an accessory, since Haste removes Slow and Slow removes Haste.

Disable & Stop

These magicks temporarily remove the target from battle. They're most effective when facing large groups of lesser enemies. Note that most bosses are immune to Disable and Stop.

Break

After casting Break, a 10-second countdown begins. If the effect isn't removed in time, the target will turn to Stone. This is a great weapon to use against high-level enemies that are otherwise too strong for the party. Most bosses are immune to Break, but many random enemies aren't.

Float

This magick enables the party to float over traps instead of trying to run around them. It never hurts to set this one up as a gambit, so that it's always in effect while you're exploring areas where traps are very common. It's also a good way to counter Earth magick.

Arcane Magick

Arcane magick is very powerful, but often unpredictable. The status effects found in this group are some of the best and prove vital near the end of the game.

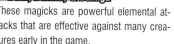

Dark, Darkra, & Darkga

These magicks are powerful elemental attacks that are effective against many creatures early in the game.

Bubble

Bubble magick doubles a character's HP with one cast. Although the effect is temporary, it is crucial when facing the later bosses.

Reverse

This curious magick reverses the effects of attacks, magicks, and techniques. This means that something that would normally cause damage will heal the target instead. Or, things that give life cause death. It's very useful when facing powerful enemies, trying to thwart an enemy's restoration efforts, or overcoming an elemental resistance.

Decoy

Enemies are drawn to attack the character under the effects of this magick. Decoy is a great way to control the enemy and keep casters safe. Try to use this magick from the moment it becomes available until the end of the game.

Syphon

It is sometimes difficult to maintain MP while inside a large dungeon, but Syphon helps. This magick strips the target of some MP and transfers it to the caster. The undead and stronger enemies commonly resist this magick, so don't rely on it all of the time.

Technicks

Technicks are much like magicks except that they typically cause physical damage (except Shades of Black) and they don't require MP to use. Many of these abilities have limited usefulness, since they rely on unusual conditions such as time played and steps taken. A few of the most useful techniks are:

Libra

This handy spell reveals more information about monsters, but more importantly, it also reveals traps. Keep it on a gambit from the very beginning of the game.

Steal

Almost every monster carries loot. Steal enables the party to snatch an extra item from enemies, which greatly increases the amount of loot you can collect. This in turn provides more gil and better weapons, armor, magick and technicks. Steal whenever possible!

Charge

When MP is running low, there's no easier way to earn a few points than to use Charge. The only risk is that a miss reduces the user's MP to zero. Only use this technick when a character's MP is low to avoid misses and wasted MP.

Expose

This technick reduces the target's defense. Expose also works well against most bosses.

1000 Needles

There are few more reliable attacks than 1000 Needles, as it causes 1000 points of damage each time! It's a great attack to use against enemies with high defense, or when a character just can't inflict 1000 points of damage otherwise.

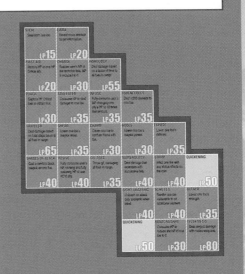

Accessories

The accessories found throughout the game play a huge role. They offer constant effects that are extremely valuable in any fight. Always ensure that characters have a good accessory equipped. These are some of the best available:

Golden Amulet

This item doubles the number of LP earned by the wearer. This is one of the most useful accessories in the game. It's always a good thing to equip it on characters held in reserve, since they earn LP from every battle.

Embroidered Tippet

Need to quickly level up? This item doubles the EXP earned from each monster defeated. It only works on characters in the battle party, though. This is great if you desire to reach Level 99 with your characters, or help a low-level character catch up with the rest of the party.

Bubble Belt

This item has the same effect as the Bubble magick—it doubles the wearer's HP. The difference between the two is that the effect is constant and can't be dispelled or removed by death.

Diamond Armlet

This armlet is essential for finding the rarest treasures in the game.

Cat-ear Hood

This accessory greatly increases the wearer's vitality and speed. Think of it as a constant Haste effect. This is useful at any time during the game.

Sage's Ring

The Sage's Ring cuts the MP cost of magicks in half, rounding down. Improve the efficiency of casters with this handy item.

Ribbon

The Ribbon always has been, and always will be, the ultimate FINAL FANTASY accessory! This accessory prevents all negative status effects, which makes even the toughest battles much easier.

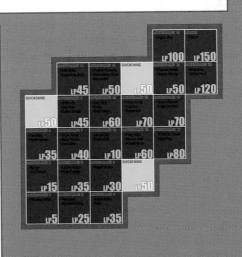

Augmentations

Augmentations provide a character with passive bonuses that remain in effect throughout the course of the game. Purchase these early and use them to truly tailor the party into an effective fighting machine.

+HP

These augmentations provide extra HP. Although the bonuses are initially small, they are worth the investment for every character.

Battle Lore & Magick Lore

These augmentations increase the party's attack power and magic power, respectively. Purchase Battle Lore for melee characters and use Magick Lore for spellcasters.

Swiftness

Speed is everything and these augmentations reduce action time by 10% apiece up to a maximum of 30%. Unlock these as early as possible to drastically improve the party's efficiency in combat.

Channeling

Channeling helps to conserve MP by reducing the cost of magicks by 10% up to a maximum of 30%. These are critical for healers.

Inquisitor, Martyr, Headsman, Warmage

Invest in these augmentations for each character, since they provide additional MP under various circumstances. You can never have too much MP!

The Bottom Half

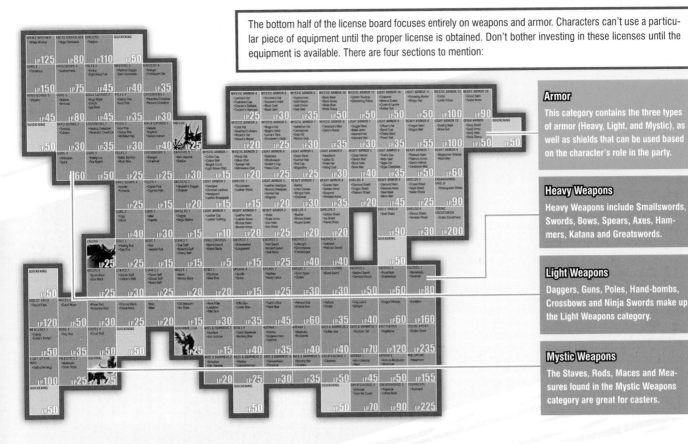

The bottom half of the license board focuses entirely on weapons and armor. Characters can't use a particular piece of equipment until the proper license is obtained. Don't bother investing in these licenses until the equipment is available. There are four sections to mention:

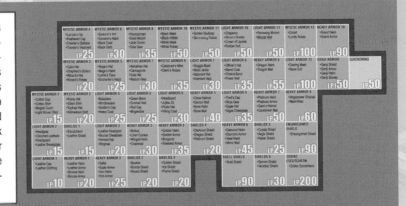

Armor

This category contains the three types of armor (Heavy, Light, and Mystic), as well as shields that can be used based on the character's role in the party.

Heavy Weapons

Heavy Weapons include Smallswords, Swords, Bows, Spears, Axes, Hammers, Katana and Greatswords.

Light Weapons

Daggers, Guns, Poles, Hand-bombs, Crossbows and Ninja Swords make up the Light Weapons category.

Mystic Weapons

The Staves, Rods, Maces and Measures found in the Mystic Weapons category are great for casters.

Armor

Choosing the type of armor a character wears is more important than it may initially seem. Armor affects most attributes except for attack power. Equipping the right type of armor for a character's role is vitally important. Equip the primary melee characters with heavy armor for strength and defense, and equip backup melee characters with light armor for speed and vitality. Equip mystic armor on casters for magick power and resistance. Shields are also essential for the primary melee characters early in the game, since they drastically reduce the damage taken from physical attacks.

OPTIMIZE MANUALLY

The game has a helpful feature called Optimize in the equip menu that automatically selects the best equipment for your character. This is great at the start of the game, but becomes less useful as the game progresses. The reason for that is because the selection is based entirely on equipment stats and not on the overall usefulness. Take the time to manually equip your party members and select the equipment that fits the character's role, not just the strongest gear available.

Heavy Weapons

This section includes Smallswords, Swords, Bows, Spears, Axes, Hammers, Katana and massive Greatswords. Swords, Smallswords, and Greatswords tend to be the most reliable weapons since they cause consistent damage with each swing. These are the best choice for the primary melee character in the party.

Hammers and Axes can cause tremendous damage, but they're quite unpredictable. The number of big hits and little hits tends to balance out in the end, though. Bows serve as great ranged weapons and they are very effective against flying monsters. Katana aren't as powerful as Greatswords, but they are fast and combo often. Spears are powerful, two-handed weapons that are great for a backup melee fighter.

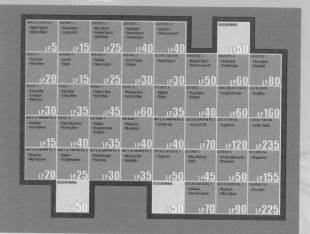

Light Weapons

This portion of the license board includes Daggers, Guns, Poles, Hand-bombs, Crossbows and Ninja Swords. Daggers and Ninja Swords rely heavily on speed and the ability to combo. Hand-bombs are effective ranged weapons, but cause unpredictable amounts of damage. Crossbows are also excellent ranged weapons with a variety of ammunition. Poles are extremely effective against enemies with low magick defense.

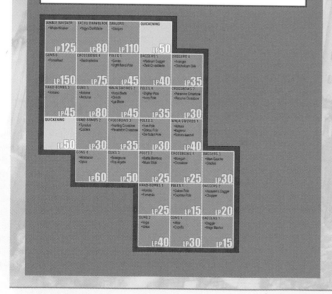

Mystic Weapons

Mystic weapons contain Staves, Rods, Maces and Measures. Staves and Rods are excellent weapons for casters, since they greatly enhance the character's magick power and often strengthen particular elemental attacks. Maces use magick power to determine damage instead of strength.

Measures are unusual weapons that often leave behind beneficial status effects. These are better suited for characters who rarely attack the enemy and focus on supporting the other party members.

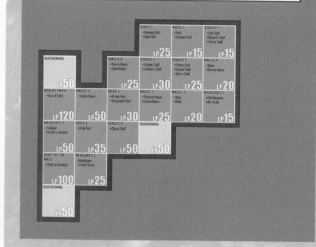

Gambits

Gambits are brand new to the *FINAL FANTASY* series. They introduce a simple way to guide your party in combat without having to micromanage every encounter. A gambit is a programmed command that instructs a character to react automatically in a predetermined manner when faced with a specific situation. Think of it as a user-controlled AI (Artificial Intelligence). Gambits allow you to take as much or as little control in each battle as desired. A carefully crafted set of gambits can handle most battles against common enemies. Bosses and rare monsters often require a more hands-on approach.

Gambit Building 101

Each gambit consists of two separate parts: a condition and a reaction. Thus, the character assesses the situation and reacts in the programmed manner. The gambit conditions focus on an ally(s), a foe(s), or the character (self). You can use them with nearly any learned command from magicks, technicks, and items. As you would expect, the party starts off with very few gambits available, but the commands grow throughout the game as new gambits are found or purchased until nearly anything can be automated.

For example, you can attach simple commands like "Attack" to gambits such as "Foe: nearest visible" to automatically initiate combat whenever a hostile creature wanders within range. Later on, the commands become more complex and specific as magicks like Dispel or technicks like Souleater are added to the equation. For example, a player can dictate that a character always casts Dispel whenever the "Foe: status = Protect," or use Souleater whenever "Foe: character HP > 90%."

⚠ A WORD OF CAUTION

Always test new gambits before going into a major battle. One small mistake can turn a great gambit into a disaster. Make sure everyone is attacking the enemy and not each other.

Also, check for gambits that repeat themselves endlessly, making a character nearly worthless during a fight. This is simple enough to do. Just watch each character closely and ensure that he or she reacts as anticipated. If not, consider rebuilding or reordering the character's gambits or eliminate the problem commands all together.

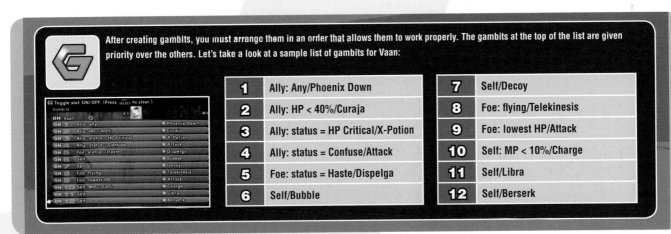

After creating gambits, you must arrange them in an order that allows them to work properly. The gambits at the top of the list are given priority over the others. Let's take a look at a sample list of gambits for Vaan:

#	Gambit	#	Gambit
1	Ally: Any/Phoenix Down	7	Self/Decoy
2	Ally: HP < 40%/Curaja	8	Foe: flying/Telekinesis
3	Ally: status = HP Critical/X-Potion	9	Foe: lowest HP/Attack
4	Ally: status = Confuse/Attack	10	Self: MP < 10%/Charge
5	Foe: status = Haste/Dispelga	11	Self/Libra
6	Self/Bubble	12	Self/Berserk

1	Ally: Any/Phoenix Down	2	Ally: HP < 40%/Curaja

In this case, priority is given to resurrecting a downed ally over all other actions. Vaan always stops other actions, unless manually inputted, to bring someone back to life. Then he checks to ensure that everyone has at least forty percent of their health left. If not, he casts Curaja on the entire party. This can be a little wasteful when only one party member needs healing, but better safe than sorry. Note that reviving takes priority over healing; this doesn't mean that Vaan is always the one who revives a fallen ally. When two or more characters share a gambit, the party leader always acts first. The other characters move on down the list to see if anything else needs doing.

6	Self/Bubble	7	Self/Decoy

The "Self/Bubble" and "Self/Decoy" gambits ensures that Vaan is typically the character taking the brunt of enemy attacks and that he has the HP necessary to survive. Normally it wouldn't be wise for Vaan to cast Decoy on himself, since it has a tendency to miss all too often and may lead to him standing around casting instead of fighting. In this example, though, both gambits are low enough in the chain to ensure that the magick is cast when the primary caster is out of commission due to Silence, Stop, Disable, or even the occasional untimely death.

3	Ally: status = HP Critical/X-Potion

The inclusion of the "Ally: status = HP Critical/X-Potion" helps when the enemies are numerous and hitting hard. Potions are fast, so Vaan may be able to quickly restore a desperate ally's HP before the enemy lands a final blow. Players can also use the First Aid technick for a similar effect without consuming a potion, but the amount of HP restored may not be enough to save the victim. Either way such a gambit helps overcome the lengthy casting times in desperate situations.

MISSING MAGICK

If magicks like Berserk, Decoy, or Reverse miss frequently when cast on your party, it may be due to a high magick resist and magick evade versus a low magick power. Try reducing the target's magick resist and magick evade while increasing the caster's magick power with equipment and Faith to make the spells miss less often.

8	Foe: flying/Telekinesis	9	Foe: lowest HP/Attack

"Foe: lowest HP/Attack" is a very basic battle command. It instructs Vaan to seek out the weakest enemy and fight it until it falls. Early in the game, the same action may require creating two gambits such as "Foe: party leader's target/Attack" and "Foe: any/Attack" and maybe even "Foe: status = HP Critical/Attack." The "Foe: party leader's target" gambit goes first to ensure everyone attacks the same creature. "Foe: any/Attack" follows this gambit to trigger combat whenever a hostile enemy is near. You can place the third gambit, "Foe: status = HP Critical" in front of the other two to ensure that nearly defeated enemies aren't left alone to wander aimlessly and wreak havoc when they could be easily eliminated. "Foe: flying/Telekinesis" overrides the Attack command when flying creatures are near and out of sword's reach.

ITEMS VS. MAGICK

Items are faster than magicks. A gambit for using a Phoenix Down will always take effect before a gambit for casting Raise, so keep this in mind when a character is burning through the party's entire stock of Phoenix Downs or Potions. Try making the gambit a lower priority for that character, or rely on manually triggering item usage. Gambits like "Ally: item AMT ≥ 10" can also limit waste and ensure that the party doesn't run out of a critical item in the middle of a battle.

4	Ally: status = Confuse/Attack

The next gambit focuses on very specific and unusual situations. "Ally: status = Confuse/Attack" only triggers when an ally has been hit with the Confuse status. He immediately strikes the confused ally breaking the effect. It's usually best that the attacker is a player with a weak weapon and attack power, or he may accidentally kill the ally. When used with a Measure (a type of weapon) it becomes even more effective, since it also provides a positive status effect while removing the negative one.

10	Self: MP < 10%/Charge

The tenth gambit isn't effective until the "Self" conditions become available. Charge enables the character to restore a portion of MP. However, there is a risk in that if the technick fails, the character's MP drops to zero. By combining Charge with "Self: MP < 10%," you can ensure that the character rarely wastes MP by using Charge too soon. Note that Vaan isn't used as a caster with this setup; someone focusing on magicks would likely have the Charge gambit much earlier in the list. In fact, if Vaan casts little magick in this scenario, there's no real reason to worry about wasting a gambit slot on Charge in the first place.

5	Foe: status = Haste/Dispelga

The fifth gambit, "Foe: status = Haste/Dispelga" looks for enemies with a specific positive status effect and removes it. Another character in the party may have a more general Dispel gambit like "Foe: any/Dispelga," but this one ensures that Vaan breaks from his normal attack pattern and removes Haste if the other character has been unable to do so. Auto-Dispel gambits are extremely useful in areas where enemies tend to appear with a positive status, or are known for casting them on a regular basis.

⚡ ARTIFICIAL INTELLIGENCE

Characters aren't dim-witted. They make intelligent choices based upon the gambits created. They won't recast a status effect on something already affected by the same status. Don't worry about someone endlessly recasting Protect or Shell on one person and wasting MP.

Unfortunately, some skills don't work the same way. For instance, Steal would be a wonderful thing to automate, but doing so usually means the character steals endlessly even though the enemy's pockets may be empty. Although you can tweak such technicks with conditions like "Foe: HP = 100%," they typically lead to the character running off alone and simply aren't worthwhile. Save such things for manual controls unless there's something specific you want to steal.

11 Self/Libra

The Libra gambit is found near the bottom. During downtime, Vaan casts Libra on himself to ensure the party can see enemy information and traps. It's one of the simplest gambits around and one of the most useful. Placing gambits after the attack command ensures they only occur after combat is completed. This is useful for casting status effects like Protect or Shell, or even topping off the party's HP after a relatively easy fight.

12 Self/Berserk

"Self/Berserk" rounds out the bottom of the list. Rely on another character to cast this magick on Vaan so that he doesn't waste time on misses during battle and let Vaan take care of it outside of battle. Even Bacchus's Wine, an item with the same effect, tends to miss often, so don't let a powerful fighter waste time recasting the same magick over and over until it sticks. Berserk is a great—and often underused—magick that puts the character into a state of rage. Although the affected character's actions are uncontrollable while the effect lasts, his speed, attack power and chance to combo greatly increase. However, you should ensure that there is someone nearby to keep the Berserk character healed, since he can't do it on his own.

In this example, Vaan's primary focus is on resurrection and healing. All characters should start with similar gambits, then you can customize the rest of them to fit your own style. Always try to throw in a few special situations like dealing with flying enemies and eliminating enemy status effects. Remember, though, that the main fighter should primarily focus on attacking the enemy. A caster should center on attacking the enemy's weaknesses and restoring consumed MP. A support character should focus on maintaining the most useful statuses like Haste and Bubble throughout the battle and eliminating negative status effects. This support character should also be the first one to use Healing gambits to recover lost HP. Try to save nonessential gambits like Libra until you're out of combat, as these things slow down the battle and leave the party vulnerable.

Disabling Gambits

Gambits aren't always a good thing. In major battles against extremely tough enemies, it's sometimes best to use only a few simple healing and attack gambits and leave the rest up to manual input. This keeps the party from wasting valuable MP, or accidentally using a technick that has no effect on the enemy. Status attacks are a common issue, as most bosses are immune to several status effects. Unless such Status gambits are disabled for that battle, the caster will stand back and cast an endless stream of worthless magick while expending lots of MP.

Ally Gambits

Gambit	Cost
Ally: any	50
Ally: party leader	50
Ally: Vaan	--
Ally: Ashe	--
Ally: Fran	--
Ally: Balthier	--
Ally: Basch	--
Ally: Penelo	--
Ally: lowest HP	50

Gambit	Cost
Ally: strongest weapon	50
Ally: lowest defense	50
Ally: lowest magick resist	50
Ally: HP < 100%	50
Ally: HP < 90%	50
Ally: HP < 80%	50
Ally: HP < 70%	50
Ally: HP < 60%	50
Ally: HP < 50%	50
Ally: HP < 40%	50
Ally: HP < 30%	50
Ally: HP < 20%	50
Ally: HP < 10%	50
Ally: MP < 100%	50
Ally: MP < 90%	50
Ally: MP < 80%	50
Ally: MP < 70%	50
Ally: MP < 60%	50

Gambit	Cost
Ally: MP < 50%	50
Ally: MP < 40%	50
Ally: MP < 30%	50
Ally: MP < 20%	50
Ally: MP < 10%	50
Ally: status = KO	50
Ally: status = Stone	50
Ally: status = Petrify	50
Ally: status = Stop	50
Ally: status = Sleep	50
Ally: status = Confuse	50
Ally: status = Doom	50
Ally: status = Blind	50
Ally: status = Poison	50
Ally: status = Silence	50
Ally: status = Sap	50
Ally: status = Oil	50
Ally: status = Reverse	50

Gambit	Cost
Ally: status = Disable	50
Ally: status = Immobilize	50
Ally: status = Slow	50
Ally: status = Disease	50
Ally: status = Lure	50
Ally: status =	Protect
Ally: status = Shell	50
Ally: status = Haste	50
Ally: status = Bravery	50
Ally: status = Faith	50
Ally: status = Reflect	50
Ally: status = Invisible	50
Ally: status = Regen	50
Ally: status = Float	50
Ally: status = Berserk	50
Ally: status = Bubble	50
Ally: status = HP Critical	50
Ally: item AMT ≥ 10	100

Foe Gambits

Gambit	Cost
Foe: party leader's target	--
Foe: nearest visible	--
Foe: any	50
Foe: targeting leader	100
Foe: targeting self	100
Foe: targeting ally	100
Foe: furthest	50
Foe: nearest	50
Foe: highest HP	50
Foe: lowest HP	50
Foe: highest max HP	50
Foe: lowest max HP	50
Foe: highest MP	50
Foe: lowest MP	50
Foe: highest max MP	50
Foe: lowest max MP	50
Foe: highest level	50
Foe: lowest level	50
Foe: highest strength	50
Foe: lowest strength	50
Foe: highest magick power	50
Foe: lowest magick power	50
Foe: highest speed	50
Foe: lowest speed	50
Foe: highest defense	50
Foe: highest magick resist	50
Foe: HP ≥ 100,000	50
Foe: HP ≥ 50,000	50
Foe: HP ≥ 10,000	50

Gambit	Cost
Foe: HP ≥ 5,000	50
Foe: HP ≥ 3,000	50
Foe: HP ≥ 2,000	50
Foe: HP ≥ 1,000	50
Foe: HP ≥ 500	50
Foe: HP < 100,000	50
Foe: HP < 50,000	50
Foe: HP < 10,000	50
Foe: HP < 5,000	50
Foe: HP < 3,000	50
Foe: HP < 2,000	50
Foe: HP < 1,000	50
Foe: HP < 500	50
Foe: HP = 100%	50
Foe: HP ≥ 70%	50
Foe: HP ≥ 50%	50
Foe: HP ≥ 30%	50
Foe: status = Petrify	50
Foe: status = Stop	50
Foe: status = Sleep	50
Foe: status = Confuse	50
Foe: status = Doom	50
Foe: status = Blind	50
Foe: status = Poison	50
Foe: status = Silence	50
Foe: status = Sap	50
Foe: status = Oil	50
Foe: status = Reverse	50
Foe: status = Disable	50

Gambit	Cost
Foe: status = Immobilize	50
Foe: status = Slow	50
Foe: status = Disease	50
Foe: status =	Protect
Foe: status = Shell	50
Foe: status = Haste	50
Foe: status = Bravery	50
Foe: status = Faith	50
Foe: status = Reflect	50
Foe: status = Regen	50
Foe: status = Berserk	50
Foe: status = HP Critical	50
Foe: fire-weak	500
Foe: lightning-weak	500
Foe: ice-weak	500
Foe: earth-weak	500
Foe: water-weak	500
Foe: wind-weak	500
Foe: holy-weak	500
Foe: dark-weak	500
Foe: fire-vulnerable	250
Foe: lightning-vulnerable	250
Foe: ice-vulnerable	250
Foe: earth-vulnerable	250
Foe: water-vulnerable	250
Foe: wind-vulnerable	250
Foe: holy-vulnerable	250
Foe: dark-vulnerable	250
Foe: undead	100

Gambit	Cost
Foe: flying	100
Foe: character HP = 100%	100
Foe: item AMT ≥ 10	100
Foe: character status = Blind	100
Foe: character status = Silence	100
Foe: character status = Bravery	100
Foe: character status = Faith	100
Foe: character status = HP Critical	100
Foe: character MP ≥ 90%	100
Foe: character MP ≥ 70%	100
Foe: character MP ≥ 50%	100
Foe: character MP ≥ 30%	100
Foe: character MP ≥ 10%	100
Foe: character MP < 90%	100
Foe: character MP < 70%	100
Foe: character MP < 50%	100
Foe: character MP < 30%	100
Foe: character MP < 10%	100
Foe: character HP ≥ 90%	100
Foe: character HP ≥ 70%	100
Foe: character HP ≥ 50%	100
Foe: character HP ≥ 30%	100
Foe: character HP ≥ 10%	100
Foe: character HP < 90%	100
Foe: character HP < 70%	100
Foe: character HP < 50%	100
Foe: character HP < 30%	100
Foe: character HP < 10%	100

Self Gambits

Gambit	Cost
Self	50
Self: HP < 100%	50
Self: HP < 90%	50
Self: HP < 80%	50
Self: HP < 70%	50
Self: HP < 60%	50
Self: HP < 50%	50
Self: HP < 40%	50
Self: HP < 30%	50
Self: HP < 20%	50
Self: HP < 10%	50

Gambit	Cost
Self: MP < 100%	50
Self: MP < 90%	50
Self: MP < 80%	50
Self: MP < 70%	50
Self: MP < 60%	50
Self: MP < 50%	50
Self: MP < 40%	50
Self: MP < 30%	50
Self: MP < 20%	50
Self: MP < 10%	50
Self: status = Petrify	50

Gambit	Cost
Self: status = Doom	50
Self: status = Blind	50
Self: status = Poison	50
Self: status = Silence	50
Self: status = Sap	50
Self: status = Oil	50
Self: status = Reverse	50
Self: status = Immobilize	50
Self: status = Slow	50
Self: status = Disease	50
Self: status = Lure	50

Gambit	Cost
Self: status =	Protect
Self: status = Shell	50
Self: status = Haste	50
Self: status = Bravery	50
Self: status = Faith	50
Self: status = Reflect	50
Self: status = Invisible	50
Self: status = Regen	50
Self: status = Float	50
Self: status = Bubble	50
Self: status = HP Critical	50

FINDING GAMBITS

You can typically find gambits in shops for a small price. However, urns and chests sometimes contain them as well. The party holds one copy of the gambit no matter how many copies are found. Although finding gambits in the field saves a little gil, shop prices are very reasonable and worth the investment.

Helpful Gambits

The possibilities seem endless, but here are a few useful gambits to get things going in the right direction. Use these as building blocks for more complicated gambits later on in the game. Remember to *always* check your gambits before entering a major battle. One simple mistake can ruin an encounter!

Revive Gambit

Ally:	Any/(Raise, Arise or Phoenix Down)

Make sure each character has this gambit in the number one spot. Reviving downed allies is important in battle. The gambit triggers an immediate response and oftentimes revives the fallen ally before he or she can hit the ground. The negative status effect KO can also be cured by using the Revive technick.

MANUAL REVIVE

Some players may prefer to revive fallen allies manually, especially those who would rather swap out downed characters for reserve characters and worry about reviving later. There are certainly advantages to this strategy, but it does increase the party's overall risk of losing the battle while the player's attention is elsewhere. Figure out which way works best for you.

Healing Gambit

Ally:	HP < ##%/(Cure, Cura, Curaga, or Curaja)

This is perhaps the second most important gambit. Make sure it always follows the Revive gambit. Healing is extremely important in every battle, regardless of what the party is fighting. Unless, of course, you're just fighting weaker creatures for sport or loot! Close to 50% is a good trigger during a fight. Try staggering the percentage between three characters to ensure there's a primary, secondary, and emergency healer. (For instance, use 60%, 50%, and 40%.) Doing so keeps the damage dealers focused on fighting instead of stopping to heal all of the time.

Status Effect Removal Gambits

Ally:	Status = (any status)/(any status remover)

Automating status removal can be a big help. Typically, it's best to refer to the bestiary to see what type of status attacks the enemies are using, or just pay attention while fighting. Find the proper gambit for the status in question and match it up with the cure. Esuna and Esunaga can eliminate most common status effects like Blind and Silence, while others require a specific cure or item. See the following table for a complete breakdown:

Disease
Cleanse/Vaccine/Remedy (requires level 3 license)

Doom
Remedy (requires level 3 license)

KO
Raise/Arise/Phoenix Down/ Revive technick

Oil
Handkerchief/Remedy (requires level 2 license)

Petrify
Gold Needle/Stona/Remedy (requires level 2 license)

Slow
Dispel/Haste/Remedy

Stop
Dispel/Chronos Tear/Remedy (requires level 3 license)

Dispel Gambits

Foe:	Status = (most statuses) / (Dispel or Dispelga)

Some enemies make use of positive status effects like Protect, Shell, Haste, Bravery, Faith and others. Such effects may make battles a bit more challenging, especially when the creature is a boss. Dispel and Dispelga can quickly eliminate such status effects and even wipe out Reflect. The only drawback is that they may also eliminate negative statuses cast by the party such as Slow. The "Foe: any" gambit also works with Dispel, but keep in mind that you will also dispel Slow or Stop.

MP Restoration Gambits

Self:	MP < 10%/Charge
Self:	MP < 90%/Syphon

There are two very effective ways to restore MP without using a Save Crystal or Ether. The first is the Charge technick. A player can take a chance to regain a small amount of MP. The risk is that if the technick fails, the character's MP drops to zero. This is really only effective when the character is extremely low on MP. The risk of failing increases as the character's MP increases, so one to two attempts is usually all that is advisable.

The second gambit involves the use of Syphon magick. With Syphon, a caster can steal a large chunk of MP from most enemies and transfer it to him or her. Most characters can easily restore a third of their MP this way with a single cast of Syphon. Unfortunately, many creatures, especially the undead, are immune to it. Turn off this gambit during such situations to ensure that the character doesn't pointlessly cast Syphon over and over again.

NEARLY UNLIMITED MP

All characters who use a lot of magick should consider using one or both MP restoration gambits. Place the "Self: MP < 10%/Charge" gambit first for maximum effectiveness. Remember to turn off the Syphon gambit when fighting immune creatures or bosses.

Weakness Gambits

Foe:	(Any element)-weak/(matching element)
Foe:	(Any element)-vulnerable/(matching element)

Most enemies have a weakness to at least one element. Casters can take advantage of these weaknesses by using the correct type of magick. For instance, cause extra damage by casting Fire magick on an enemy with a low fire resistance, or Aero on a creature with low wind resistance. Late in the game, gambits will enable you to automatically take advantage of such weaknesses and vulnerabilities. Make sure the caster has an MP restoration gambit before the weakness gambits so he or she never runs out of Mist Points.

WEAK VS. VULNERABLE

The difference between these terms may not be obvious. Creatures that are weak to an element sustain extra damage when hit with such magick. Vulnerability merely suggests that it is possible to damage the enemy with the spell; no extra damage is caused. Some of the toughest enemies lack weaknesses, but they may be vulnerable to more than one element.

Attack Gambits

Foe: (Any or nearest)/(Attack, magick, or technick)

Foe: Party leader's target/(Attack, magick, or technick)

Foe: Lowest HP/Attack, technick)

Attack gambits can change a great deal throughout the game. Early on, for example, it may be tricky to get everyone to focus on the same enemy. To do so, it's best to set up two gambits on the main fighter and one on the two support characters.

The main fighter should use "Foe: any" or "Foe: nearest" to first select a target, but the trick is putting "Foe: party leader's target" prior to the combat initiator. Thus, the leader chooses a target and stays on that target until it is dispatched. All other party members should have the "Foe: party leader's target" equipped, so they always join the leader in dispatching a single enemy. You can use any type of attack (physical, magick, or technick) with these conditions.

Use "Foe: lowest HP/Attack" when the gambit becomes available. Although this has the same basic effect, it takes up less room. Gambits using "party leader's target" can also stop working or become problematic if your party leader falls in battle and you must swap another member in as the leader. "Foe: lowest HP/Attack" does not share this drawback.

Post-Battle/Beneficial Status Gambits

Ally: Any/(positive status)

Ally: HP < 80%/Cura

Ally: Any/(Esuna/Esunaga)

Any gambit placed after the attack gambit is initiated once all nearby enemies are defeated. This is useful for positive status effects such as Haste, Bubble, Faith, Bravery and even Decoy and Berserk. By placing these gambits at the end, it ensures the characters focus on attacking during combat and spend less time protecting. This also means the player must take over during longer battles to ensure that necessary positive status effects remain intact throughout the entire fight.

Gambit Oddities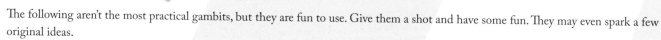

The following aren't the most practical gambits, but they are fun to use. Give them a shot and have some fun. They may even spark a few original ideas.

Ally: (Melee specialist's name)/Berserk

This tricky gambit sacrifices control of one character in favor of drastically increasing his/her attack power, speed, and combos. The character won't consider gambits when acting and may also run from target to target rather than focusing on one. It isn't perfect, but it can be extremely effective.

Self: Status = blind/Sight Unseeing

Sight Unseeing is an amusing technick that only works when the character suffers from the Blind status. You can put this to work by intentionally blinding the character and giving him or her a gambit such as this one. Keep in mind that many enemies are immune to Sight Unseeing (in particular, the undead), so be ready to turn off the gambit when necessary.

Foe: HP = 100%/Charm

This is another technick that can be useful, but more often than not, an enemy will resist it. Placing Charm with the "Foe: HP = 100%" gambit ensures that the caster will try to influence someone *other than* the leader's target. It can be useful when fighting large groups.

Foe: Character HP > 90%/Souleater

Souleater is a powerful technick that consumes the user's HP to damage the enemy. Although it doesn't work well against the undead, it is effective against other enemies. It's especially effective against enemies with a high defense.

Foe: Character MP < 10%/Shades of Black

Low on MP? No worries. Shades of Black enables a caster to fire a random Black magick without consuming any MP. The only drawback is that you never know what will happen! The spell may be extremely powerful, ineffective, or even absorbed by the monster. This is mainly effective against lesser enemies so, unless you feel like taking a risk, don't use it against bosses.

Foe: (Undead/(Cure, Cura, Curaga, Curaja, Raise, or Arise)

The undead may have a bunch of resistances, but they can't stand up against Holy magicks. This includes most restoration spells. Try bombarding a group of undead with Curaja and watch them melt away.

Ally: Party leader/Reverse

Reverse magick is unpredictable at best. It often misses and doesn't last long, but it can be beneficial when facing a particularly difficult enemy. Try casting Reverse on the party leader and watch as the enemy's attacks actually heal that person. This is best used in combination with Decoy. Also, make sure all Healing gambits are turned off while this gambit is active, or someone may actually end up killing the party leader while trying to heal him/her. Alternatively, change the restorative gambits of your non-Reversed party members to "Self: HP < 50%/Curaga" so that they don't undermine your efforts.

Foe: Flying/Telekinesis

This technick comes along very late in the game, but it's incredibly useful. With this gambit, a character equipped with a melee weapon can strike a flying foe for random damage based off the equipped weapon. This is a huge advantage, since melee weapons usually cause more damage than ranged weapons.

The Battle System

FINAL FANTASY XII introduces a new battle system that will seem very foreign to FINAL FANTASY devotees. Don't panic! The new system is more like the battle system of old than it first appears. It may take a little getting used to, but in the end, you'll love it.

ADB: Active Dimension Battle

Perhaps the most notable difference is that there are no longer breaks between battle and exploration. Enemies are visible from a distance, so you choose to avoid or attack them. The party doesn't enter a battle screen that contains and limits the action. This also means that additional enemies may join the battle as it progresses and the party can sometimes use the landscape to its advantage.

Battles take place in real time as before, but you can still select the "Wait" option from the Preferences menu. This grants the player more time to select actions and consider alternatives. Use this option if you're new to the series or until you get accustomed to the new system.

Pressing the ✖ button brings up the Battle Menu. You can then choose actions by pressing up and down on the D-pad and pressing the ✖ button again to confirm. A small timed meter appears next to the character's name in the lower-left corner of the screen (see screenshot). The rate at which the meter rises is based upon the character's speed. When the timed meter fills completely, the character performs the action. You can choose actions individually for each character by bringing up the menu screen and pressing right or left on the D-pad to cycle between the characters.

While the new battle system might seem like a radical departure, it really isn't. With Wait mode on, the game's battle system is virtually identical to that of older titles, just thrown onto a 3-D plane. The main distinction here, then, is the Gambit system. Gambits enable you to automate many actions you would normally have to perform manually.

So Why Fight at All?

Unlike other FINAL FANTASY games, the battles aren't random and you can choose to fight or avoid most enemies. Continuously avoiding enemies has its drawback, though, because battles provide EXP (Experience), LP (License Points), clan points, item drops, gil drops, and additions to the Bestiary for defeating the game's foes. Note, however, that some of the larger enemies—such as bosses, mini-bosses, and certain hunts—will not reward EXP or item drops, but they do offer large amounts of LP.

What's This About Aggro?

It's possible to avoid most enemies while exploring, but as soon as the characters and enemies spot each other, the party enters a battle stance. The battle is then initiated unless you or the enemy decides to flee. Vaan and the rest of the party usually walk around with their swords sheathed. They're in battle stance if their weapons are drawn. Once a battle stance has been initiated, it's usually a good idea to stay in one place and finish the battle, lest you draw more enemies into the fray and be forced to take on several at once.

Most enemies with a green life bar are non-aggressive and will not attack unless provoked; the exception to this rule are Elementals. It can be a good idea to fight these enemies to add them to your Bestiary or collect their dropped items. In some cases, like facing elementals, it's a good idea to just walk past them. If you accidentally target one, it will stay non-aggressive until a hit lands, so there's time to cancel your attack if you accidentally target a creature. There are a few exceptions to this rule regarding foes with green life bars. Elementals, a powerful and unpredictable enemy with a green bar, often appear to be non-aggressive at first, but they will attack if the party casts magic. The other time non-aggressive enemies will attack is if they see your party attacking another one of their kind.

Oh No! What If I'm Seen?

If you initiate a battle that you would rather not fight, hold down the R2 button to trigger a retreat. Holding this button causes your characters to sheathe their weapons, in effect cancelling all actions and disabling all gambits. On occasion, an enemy will continue to chase after the party when they attempt to flee. If other enemies spot the party running away, they may join in the attack. Eventually, some of the foes may give up on the chase, but it's best to find an exit from your current area. Another way out is to run toward a set of enemies/non-

aggressive enemies that are natural enemies of the enemy in pursuit. This sometimes causes the enemies chasing after the party to flee, but may instigate a fight with the new enemies.

The plus side to running away is that the party slowly gains MP (Mist Points). It can sometimes be a good idea to temporarily run away from a winnable battle if the party needs a few more MP.

Restoring HP and MP?

Here are a few ways to solve the problem of restoring HP and MP:

- ▶ Touch a Save Crystal to fully restore all lost HP and MP.
- ▶ Run around to restore MP.
- ▶ Trigger a lucky Rejuvenation trap to gain HP.
- ▶ Hit a lucky Manafont trap to gain MP.
- ▶ Use an item from the Potion family to restore HP.
- ▶ Use an item from the Ether family to restore MP.
- ▶ Use an Elixir item to restore HP and MP.
- ▶ Cast a spell from the Cure family or use the Revive technick to gain HP.
- ▶ Use the Charge technick to restore MP.
- ▶ Use Drain magick on an enemy to steal their HP.

- ▶ Use Syphon magick on an enemy to pilfer their MP, or use it on a berserked character since they restore their MP fast and won't need it while in this state.
- ▶ Let your character get hit by a Magick type that his or her equipment absorbs to restore HP.
- ▶ Cast Regen on a character to slowly restore their HP.
- ▶ Although this rarely occurs, a character may pick up a dropped item that may restore HP, MP, or both. (This happens randomly as a chain combo increases in level.)
- ▶ Unlock certain spots on the license board to reveal other ways to restore MP.
- ▶ Take damage when a character has the Reverse magick cast on them to restore HP equal to the attack's damage.

When a character loses all of his HP, it's not the end of the game. Get the character back in action by casting Raise magick or using a Phoenix Down, or swap them out for reserve characters. The game doesn't necessarily end if all three active party members lose their HP. When this occurs, you can swap in any reserve party members to continue the battle. The game only ends when all of your active and reserve party members have no more HP (hit points).

What Else Is There?

In certain parts of the game, the general rules will be slightly modified to create a more challenging experience. Occasionally, you'll have to fight a battle as your HP or MP slowly seep away, or you may be forced to fight without using items. This is a very rare occurrence, but it's a good idea to know what the icons mean when this does occur.

 HP Sap: The active party's HP decreases as the fight goes on. The effect isn't lethal, though; a character with 1 HP won't die until he gets hit.

 No Attack: This effect disables the Attack command and any gambits that use the Attack command. When this occurs, you must rely on magick and technicks to fight enemies.

 MP Sap: The active party's MP decreases as the fight continues.

 No Magick: This effect prevents the use of all magick or any gambits that cast magick. You must rely on physical attacks and technicks to cause damage and items to heal.

More Icons →

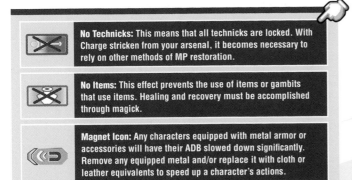

No Technicks: This means that all technicks are locked. With Charge stricken from your arsenal, it becomes necessary to rely on other methods of MP restoration.

No Items: This effect prevents the use of items or gambits that use items. Healing and recovery must be accomplished through magick.

Magnet Icon: Any characters equipped with metal armor or accessories will have their ADB slowed down significantly. Remove any equipped metal and/or replace it with cloth or leather equivalents to speed up a character's actions.

Charge Time Speed	
Status Effects	**Speed**
Haste + Berserk	3x speed
Berserk or Slow + Haste + Berserk*	2x speed
Haste	1.5x speed
Slow + Haste* or Slow + Berserk	1x speed
Slow	0.5x speed
Stop or Stone	0x speed

This effect only occurs if a character has an accessory equipped that automatically provides one of these status effects and the opposite magick is cast on him.

- **Certain areas have no exits:** During most boss battles, there is no chance to exit the zone.
- **Instant game over:** There's just one of these in the game and it occurs when you are fighting the Demon Walls in the Tomb of Raithwall.
- **Battle timer:** A certain battle has a timer that limits the length of the fight. The enemy will have its HP instantly reset when the timer hits zero.

Party

Your party consists of several different types of characters who each play a different sort of role.

- **Battle Member:** A party member who is currently on the battlefield. You are limited to three battle members at a time and any extra party members are forced to sit on the bench as reserve members.
- **Reserve Member:** Reserve members are party members who are not actively fighting, but are members of your party.
- **Guest Member:** A story-related character who joins your party temporarily. This person is not considered a party member, so gambits do not work for them. Other party members can heal these characters and use items on them.
- **Other Member:** A non-story character who joins the party temporarily and does not appear in your party list. This person is also not considered a Party Member.

Charge Time

Every action has a certain time cost associated with it. The charge meter, which measures time for actions, is located in the right-hand corner of the screen next to each character's name. After selecting an action or having a gambit automatically select one for you, the action is displayed above the meter and the meter begins to fill. When the meter is full, the word "action" will appear as soon as you're within range of the target character or enemy. After an action has begun to charge, you can stop it by doing the following:

- Selecting another command
- Entering escape mode
- Changing equipment
- Switching maps (zones)
- Examining a treasure box or speaking to someone
- Having higher priority gambits fulfilling their conditions, which restarts the charge bar in favor of the highest priority action

Watch the information section in the right-hand corner of the screen to notice that the character names change from red to blue depending on what actions are being performed and what actions are being performed against them. If a battle member's name appears in red, this means that you cannot swap out the character for a reserve character. Instead, you must wait until the action is finished to perform the swap.

The Party Leader

One battle member is always designated as the leader. The lead character can be identified by either having their name highlighted or having a red flag attached to their portrait. This is the character who you move around the field. To change the lead character, go to the Party Member screen, change the current battle members, and watch the leader flag jump around between leaders, or simply press the D-pad up or down while exploring. If the lead character runs out of HP, you will be forced to designate a different battle member as the leader before continuing.

Striking a Balance

Reserve party members do not receive EXP when enemies are defeated, but they do receive LP. Depending on your preference, you can choose to focus on a single set of three characters as battle members for most of the game, or continuously swap out battle members and reserve members to keep their levels somewhat even. WARNING! If you focus on a smaller number of characters, you will be more susceptible to defeat when your main group of battle members is defeated.

! BALANCE TO 40

It's best to keep the party at a uniform level throughout most of the game. This is less critical once everyone hits 40. At this point, it's usually best to select a primary battle group and focus on promoting them for the side events to come. It's much easier to raise three characters to 99 than it is to raise all six.

Attributes

Character effectiveness is comprised of several statistics that are altered by things like a character's level and equipment, or negative and positive status effects. Leveling up increases a character's base statistics, but you can also affect these values by equipping certain equipment. The following is a list of things that drastically increase certain attributes:

- ▶ **Increase HP:** Equip Light Armor or unlock +HP slots on the license board.
- ▶ **Increase MP:** Equip a Rod or unlock multiple Quickening panels on the license board.
- ▶ **Increase Attack Power:** Equip weapons and ammunition.
- ▶ **Increase Defense:** Equip armor.
- ▶ **Increase Magick Resist:** Equip hats and helms.
- ▶ **Increase Evade:** Equip a shield.
- ▶ **Increase Magick Evade:** Equip certain shields.
- ▶ **Strength:** Equip Heavy Armor or unlock Battle Lore on the license board.
- ▶ **Magick Power:** Equip Mystic Armor or unlock Magick Lore on the license board.
- ▶ **Vitality:** Equip certain accessories.
- ▶ **Speed:** Equip certain accessories.

EXP Level Requirements

Level	Total EXP	Level	Total EXP	Level	Total EXP	Level	Total EXP
1	0	26	123665	51	1249580	76	5215245
2	51	27	140286	52	1338271	77	5469006
3	169	28	158474	53	1431529	78	5731834
4	386	29	178321	54	1529506	79	6003941
5	735	30	199920	55	1632355	80	6285540
6	1253	31	223368	56	1740233	81	6576848
7	1978	32	248763	57	1853298	82	6878083
8	2950	33	276205	58	1971710	83	7189465
9	4213	34	305798	59	2095633	84	7511218
10	5812	35	337647	60	2225232	85	7843567
11	7796	36	371861	61	2360676	86	8186741
12	10215	37	408550	62	2502135	87	8540970
13	13121	38	447826	63	2649781	88	8906486
14	16570	39	489805	64	2803790	89	9283525
15	20619	40	534604	65	2964339	90	9672324
16	25329	41	582344	66	3131609	91	10073124
17	30762	42	633147	67	3305782	92	10486167
18	36982	43	687137	68	3487042	93	10911697
19	44057	44	744442	69	3675577	94	11349962
20	52056	45	805191	70	3871576	95	11801211
21	61052	46	869517	71	4075232	96	12265697
22	71119	47	937554	72	4286739	97	12743674
23	82333	48	1009438	73	4506293	98	13235398
24	94774	49	1085309	74	4734094	99	13741129
25	108523	50	1165308	75	4970343		

Targeting

When you select an action for a battle member to perform, a target line appears (unless the option is turned off) that shows who the character is targeting. Depending on whether the action is an attack, a curing Magick or a status-enhancing Magick, the line will appear in a different color.

Target Info

The technick Libra enables you to see a lot of useful information about enemies.

1. **Libra:** If Libra is cast on your party, the Libra icon will appear here to show whether the enemy is affected by it or not. If the enemy is not affected by Libra, an "X" will appear over the Libra mark.

2. **Flying:** If the enemy is a flying type, a feather and the words flying type will appear here.

3. **Enemy Level:** If none of your battle members have Libra active, you will see question marks in place of the enemy's level.

4. **Name:** If an enemy's name appears in red, that is an indication that the enemy is three or more levels higher than your character. If the name appears in yellow, the foe is one or two levels higher than your characters. And if the name appears in blue, the enemy is either the same level as yours or lower. This information only appears when Libra is inactive.

5. **Current HP and HP Max:** If none of your battle members have Libra active, you will see question marks in this spot.

6. **Status Effects:** This section indicates any status effects currently in effect.

7. **Weakness:** The enemy's weak point. If none of your battle members have Libra active, you will see nothing in its place.

Target Line

The target line helps to designate whether a character is targeting a friend or foe and with what type of action. Here's a breakdown of the colors and what they mean:

> **Purple:** Monster action (healing)
> **Blue:** Character action (anything aside from healing)
> **Green:** Character action (healing)
> **Red:** Monster action (anything aside from healing)

Target Signal

The target line indicates where your lead character's target is, but there is another arrow next to that character that signifies whether they are actually close enough to the target. This arrow changes color depending on whether or not you are within range.

> **Red Arrow:** Your character is outside of range to attack the monster
> **Yellow Arrow:** Your character is within range to attack the monster.

Switching Targets

Pressing the R1 or L1 button enables you to select a different group of targets. The cursor cycles through target groups in a specific order before coming back around to the original target. If your cursor targets the battle members by default, pressing the R1 button switches to your reserve members, other members, and then enemies. Pressing the L1 button does this in reverse. If no other members are present or performing the action on reserve members is not allowed, these categories will be skipped. Again, that order is as follows:

> Enemy R1 -> battle members R1 -> reserve members R1 -> other members R1 -> back to the enemy

The Battle System

Attacks

Attacks are divided into two categories: regular attacks and magick attacks. The following table breaks down the basic things that affect various aspects of every attack.

Regular Attack	Magick Attack	
Inflict Damage	Attack Power	Magick Power
Reduce Damage	Defense	Magick Resist
Avoid Attacks	Evade	Magick Evade
Dmg. Reduction Mag.	Protect	Shell
Augment Mag.	Bravery	Faith
Negate all/any Dmg.*	Paling	Magick Barrier

*Indicates enemies only.

Critical Attacks and Combos

Weapons don't always hit for the same amount of damage. There are minor fluctuations with most weapons between each hit based on the success of the attack and the enemy's defense. Weapons sometimes make a critical hit, which drastically increases the damage caused. This usually increases the attack power, but it is also affected by elemental weaknesses and strengths that come into play.

Combo attacks are random, but certain weapons are more likely to combo than others. Katana, ninja swords, and daggers combo very often and can create a chain of up to 10 hits at a time. Ranged weapons like bows and guns never combo. Weapons that combo often typically cause less damage per hit, but can bypass the 9999 damage limitation of stronger weapons by hitting multiple times.

> 2H Sword: 9999 damage x 1 hit = 9999 damage
> 2H Katana: 4999 damage x 10 hits = 49990 damage

Keep in mind that combos don't occur with every swing and a 10-hit combo is a very rare occurrence. The damage difference tends to even out over time, so the ability to combo frequently doesn't necessarily make one weapon better than another. However, the Genji Glove accessory will facilitate combo hits, especially with a Katana.

Counters

The Battle Harness accessory enables a character to automatically counterattack upon being attacked. This is a fantastic option early in the game, since it makes it much easier to deal with multiple opponents.

Enemies sometimes counterattack, so beware. The word "Counter" always appears on-screen when a counterattack occurs. You can thwart enemies that counterattack frequently by using Immobilize or Sleep and magicks, since magicks can't be countered.

Elements

Battle members and enemies can use weapons and magicks that are enhanced with the power of the elements. Knowing this and using it to your advantage can give you the upper hand in many battles. Conversely, not paying attention to how these elements can work against you may mean your characters will meet a quick end.

Elemental Armor, Shields, Weapons, & Accessories								
Weak Point	—	Venetian Shield	Adamant Hat, Adamant Vest	—	—	—	Bone Helm, Bone Mail	—
Half Damage	Flame Shield, Adamant Hat, Adamant Vest, Manufactured Nethicite	Manufactured Nethicite	Ice Shield, Manufactured Nethicite	Manufactured Nethicite	Manufactured Nethicite	Windbreaker, Manufactured Nethicite	Manufactured Nethicite	Bone Helm, Bone Mail, Manufactured Nethicite
Immune	—	Zodiac Escutcheon, Rubber Suit	—	Dragon Shield	Viking Coat	—	—	—
Absorb	—	—	—	—	—	—	White Mask, Sage's Ring	Demon Shield, Black Mask
Strengthen Magick	Burning Bow, Flame Staff	Storm Staff	Glacial Staff	—	Six-fluted Pole, Cloud Staff, Fumarole	Cherry Staff	Holy Rod, Staff of the Magi, White Robe	Zeus Mace, Black Garb

> Weak point = 2x damage
> No element changes = 1x damage (normal damage)
> Half damage = 0.5x damage
>
> Not effective = 0x damage (no damage)
> Absorb = -1x damage (healing)

Status Effects

There are two types of status effects: positive and negative. Like their names imply, positive status effects are beneficial to your party. If you have them, good; if not, you may want to think about it. By contrast, negative status effects can change the tide of battle against your party, making things a bit more difficult. You can remove status effects in several different ways. You can use items, magick, or simply wait until the spell wears off.

- ▶ Vitality increases the length of time that positive status effects stay active, while reducing the time that negative status effects are in effect.
- ▶ Save Crystals remove negative status effects, but positive status effects stay active.
- ▶ Unlocking Spellbound on the license board increases the amount of time that positive status effects last, but it has no effect on negative status effects.

Length of Status Effects

The amount of time that status effects stay active on your characters depends upon the effect itself (see the list in this section). Some effects do not go away naturally with time, but most of them do.

> ▶ A higher vitality reduces the amount of time that negative status effects last.
>
> ▶ A higher vitality increases the amount of time that positive status effects last.
>
> ▶ When Stop is cast on your characters, their other status effect timers will not decrease until the Stop wears off or is taken away.
>
> ▶ The status effect time is not effected by modifying the battle speed, or having Slow or Haste inflicted.

Conflicting Status Effects

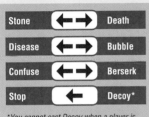

Stone	⬅➡	Death
Disease	⬅➡	Bubble
Confuse	⬅➡	Berserk
Stop	⬅	Decoy*

*You cannot cast Decoy when a player is inflicted with Stop, but a player inflicted with Decoy can still be hit with Stop.

You can remove several status effects by casting an equal but opposite spell on a character. Unfortunately, this doesn't work for everything. See the list to the left for all the details. This list shows pairs of status effects that will not be effective when one has already been cast on the character.

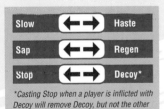

Slow	⬅➡	Haste
Sap	⬅➡	Regen
Stop	⬅➡	Decoy*

*Casting Stop when a player is inflicted with Decoy will remove Decoy, but not the other way around.

The following status effect pairs will overwrite their counterpart when inflicted on an ally or enemy.

Preventing Status Effects with Equipment

Certain equipment can prevent your characters from succumbing to negative status effects, and some will cause your characters to always be inflicted with positive status effects. Examine the equipment section (see page 262) to see the special statuses that equipment and accessories can carry.

Mist Charges

Mist Charges are divisions of Mist Points that you can spend to summon an Esper or use a Quickening. Each character can obtain up to three Mist Charges. The first charge is obtained when the character unlocks his or her first Quickening or Summoning spot on the license board. The second and third charges are obtained when the character unlocks his or her second and third Quickenings on the license board respectively.

Even if you aren't planning on summoning Espers or using Quickenings, it's still a good idea to unlock the Mist Charges as soon as possible. The first Mist Charge simply turns your max MP into a charge, but the second one adds another charge that can hold the same number of MP as your current max, effectively doubling that character's total MP! The third Mist Charge earned adds another charge to your MP Max that is equal in size to the others.

Mist Charge usage is easy to understand. Each Mist Charge requires a percentage of your character's MP to be available before it can be used. If your character has enough MP to fill a Mist Charge, it appears as a yellow bar in the character status section in the right-hand corner. If your character doesn't have enough MP, this bar will be a blue bar instead of a yellow one. If you then restore enough MP to fill a Mist Charge, a subtle chime rings that signals you can use the charge again.

Battle Chain

The basic gist of battle chains is that each time you defeat an enemy that is the same type (classification) as the previously defeated enemy, your battle chain number will increase by one. As you continue to defeat the same type of enemy, the chain continues to grow until eventually the chain level increases. This raises the chance that the fallen enemy will drop valuable items in greater numbers. As the Chain Level increases through each of the four ranks, so too do the rewards.

Easy Money? Sign Me Up!

Unfortunately, fighting the same enemy over and over again can be problematic. There are lots of different enemies in Dalmasca, and the variety of enemies in each area tends to be pretty high. There are three ways to break a Battle Chain:

1. Defeat a monster of a different type.
2. Enter a town.
3. Touch a Save Crystal.

An enemy that has a different name doesn't necessarily mean that it is a different type (classification). If you fight several Wolves and then a few Hyenas, your chain won't break because both are classified as Wolves. If, however, you defeat a Cactuar, the chain will return to zero.

Item Drop Rarity List

Chain Level	Common Drops	Semi-Rare Drops	Rare Drops	Super Rare Drops
0	40%	25%	3%	1%
1	45%	30%	6%	2%
2	50%	35%	8%	3%
3	55%	40%	12%	5%

Intangible Rewards for Chaining

Item rewards are great, but they're not the only rewards for making chains. The items gathered may also restore HP or MP or even cast magick on your characters. Refer to the following chart for all the details:

Chain Level	Bonus	10% HP Restore	10% MP Restore	Protect	Shell
0	0%	0%	0%	0%	0%
1	20%	10%	10%	0%	0%
2	50%	20%	20%	5% (Leader)	5% (Leader)
3	60%	25%	25%	5% (All)	5% (All)

Focus on Useful Accessories

Some accessories offer less useful enhancements. The following accessories are the real deal and offer your characters attractive bonuses that are well worth the cost and effort it takes to acquire them.

Accessory	Effect
Sage's Ring	Half magick cost
Diamond Armlet	Better treasure
Thief's Cuffs	Stealing becomes easier and better loot
Genji Gloves	Improves chance of scoring multiple hits
Nihopalaoa	Reverses effect of potions and status curing items, such that potions cause damage and Antidotes become Poison Potions, etc.
Embroidered Tippet	Double wearer's received EXP
Jade Collar	Improves chance of avoiding attacks
Indigo Pendant	Improves chance for magick to hit
Golden Amulet	Doubles wearer's received LP (excellent for reserve party members)
Bubble Belt	Doubles the wearer's HP
Hermes Sandals	Endows the wearer with the "Haste" status effect
Cat-Ear Hood	Huge Speed and Vitality increase

Battle Advice: Mix Up Your Weapon Types

Allowing the game to automatically select your weapons based on attack power isn't always the best idea. It's often a better idea to mix up your weapon use a bit. Some of the weaker weapons carry specific abilities that can make a character more useful in certain situations. Here are some of the "weaker" weapon groups and their advantages:

- **Bow & Crossbow:** These weapons are primarily for use against flying creatures, but also allow the wielder to keep their distance from ground enemies. The ammunition used also allows for a variety of elemental or status attacks.
- **Gun & Measure:** Guns and Measures completely ignore an enemy's defense, making them a great choice against heavily armored enemies.
- **Axe, Hammer & Hand-Bomb:** These weapons can cause a lot of damage at once, but sometimes hit for very little damage.
- **Rod & Staff:** These magick-user weapons add magick power and MP to their wielders.

Focus on Useful Magick

There are a few spells that are a lot more useful than you may initially think. One of these spell combinations involves casting Reflectga on all of your characters, then attacking them with attack magick.

Another very useful spell is Reverse. When it is cast on your own characters, it converts any damage that the player receives into HP.

- **White Magick:** White Magick can heal your characters and remove nearly any status ailments. Make this a top priority for all characters.
- **Various Attack Magick:** Attack Magick enables you to target a monster's specific weakness. Pure melee characters can ignore these until they have extra LP to spend.
- **Haste & Hastega:** The Haste spells put the status effect Haste on your characters.
- **Reflect & Reflectga:** The Reflect spells put the status effect Reflect on your characters.
- **Protect & Protectga:** The Protect spells put the status effect Protect on your characters. Make sure at least one party member has access to these spells once they become available.
- **Shell & Shellga:** The Shell spells put the status effect Shell on your characters. These aren't as critical as Protect, but come in very handy when facing bosses that use powerful magick.
- **Reverse:** Any damage received is turned into HP, while any cure spells turn into attack damage. This is essential when facing some of the toughest bosses in the game.
- **Decoy:** Decoy draws the attention of the enemy to a specific character. Put this on the primary fighter in the party to keep the support characters safe.

More Magicks →

- ▶ **Bubble:** Bubble doubles your maximum HP for its duration. Use it from the moment it becomes available.
- ▶ **Syphon:** This lets you absorb MP from the target. Some enemies are immune to the effect, especially bosses, but it's far more effective than the Charge technick.

Focus on Useful Technicks

Technicks are nice because they don't require MP to cast. Some are far more useful than others, though. The following technicks are very useful and many become life-saving tools during the course of the game.

- ▶ **Steal:** Steal enables you to take items from enemies. This is a great way to increase cash flow and it is essential to obtaining rare loot that unlocks some of the game's best weapons and armor.
- ▶ **Libra:** Libra enables you to spot traps and view an enemy's stats. Keep it on a gambit at all times.
- ▶ **Charge:** Charge enables you to instantly regain MP. If you miss an attempted charge, your MP will reduce to 0, so be careful!
- ▶ **1,000 Needles:** Deals 1,000 damage to one foe. This can prove useful for a character who uses magick as a primary attack method or a weak weapon that boosts their magick power, but the enemy is temporarily immune to magick damage.
- ▶ **Expose:** Lowers an enemy's defense. You can use this over and over again during a battle to deplete the enemy's defense.

Respawning Treasure Chests

There are three respawning treasure chests inside Barheim Passage Special Op Sector 5 that each contain approximately 3000 gil. To maximize profits, take these three treasure chests, make your way to either the Zeviah Subterrane or the North-South Junction to reset the chests, then return to the Special Op Sector 5 to take them again.

Steal from the King Bomb

King Bomb's Stolen Loot		
Steal Rate	**Item**	**Sell**
Common	Bomb Shell	896 gil
Average	Fire Crystal	160 gil
Rare	Bomb Fragment	1911 gil

The King Bomb battle is one of the rare boss battles during which you can enter and leave as many times as you like. You can then save your game at the Save Crystal just outside of the boss room. You can use this to your advantage in several different ways. First, without touching the Save Crystal between each trip into the room, it's possible to build up a mean battle chain from the endless supply of bombs that King Bomb drops. Second, and perhaps more importantly, you can steal from the King Bomb each time you face him. You can quickly collect up to 99 items that can be sold for a reasonably large chunk of cash.

Reflecting Attacks to Increase Damage

With the right setup, it's possible to hit an enemy multiple times with a single spell. To do this, create a situation where all of your battle members have the status enhancement Reflect cast on them. After doing so, access the magic menu, target each member of your own party, and unleash the elemental attack. The spell will bounce off your party and every individual hit will reflect onto the single opponent, thus magnifying the strength of the attack by three. If you have a guest member and another member in your party, it's possible to increase the number of hits to 5!

Since magic can only be reflected once, it's possible to hit enemies that currently have Reflect cast on them with this as well. Several spells work well with this technique, including Firaga, Blizzaga, Thundaga, and Scathe, which has the power to inflict nearly as much damage as your strongest Quickening combo.

"Last Selection" Cursor Position Damage

In the options screen, there's an option to remember the last-selected action and automatically return your cursor to it when you access the action menu. This option is crucial if you're going to play in Active mode and can be very useful in Wait mode. Regardless of your selected mode, you'll often find yourself needing to perform the same battle action multiple times. "Last Selection" removes the tedium of having to wander through the menu over and over again.

Using Esper License Grid Slots to Gain Mist Charges

If you don't have all three Mist Charges on any of your characters by the time you unlock the Famfrit, Chaos, Ultima, or Zodiark Espers, you can flip over one of these panels to instantly gain access to all three Mist Charges. These Espers require three Mist Charges to cast, so the game will unlock any missing charges when you gain access to the Espers.

"Fishing" for Enemies

When you find a group of difficult enemies that are grouped together and you don't want to fight them all at once, it's possible to lure enemies out one at a time and take them on individually. To do this, make sure your party leader is a ranged character. Approach the enemy from far away and manually select "Attack," targeting the nearest opponent. You'll be too far away to hit the enemy, so slowly creep up to the group until you're within distance to attack and your character will automatically use their attack, drawing its attention to your party. Now that the opponent is aware, hold down the R2 button to run away. The enemy will follow, leaving the rest of his cronies behind to pace back and forth.

Espers

Espers are powerful creatures that characters can summon to aid the party in battle. They take the place of two party members and remain in the battlefield for one minute and thirty seconds or until the summoner or the Esper is defeated. Each Esper has a different set of skills that makes it more useful in some situations than others.

Unlocking the Espers

All of the Espers are locked at the beginning of the game, and they won't become available until the party tracks them down and defeats them. Some of the Espers appear during the normal flow of the game's storyline, but others are more difficult to track down and require a bit of extra adventuring.

Defeated Espers appear on the license board as a panel. A character must then purchase the Esper with LP. These are one-time only panels, so only *one character* can unlock each Esper. There's no limit to the number of Espers one character can command, but it's best to spread them out amongst the party members.

Summoning an Esper

It takes between one to three Mist Charges to summon an Esper. The Esper's cost is a good measure of the creature's power. A single-Mist-Charge beast like Belias doesn't compare to a three-Mist-Charge behemoth like Ultima.

A character can summon an Esper at any time as long as the necessary Mist Charges are available. Also note that Silence has no effect on your ability to summon Espers.

To initiate a summon, select the Mist option from the battle menu and then choose Summon to make a list of available Espers appear. You can summon those names that appear in white, while those names that appear in gray are temporarily unavailable due to cost or a status effect.

LEGEND

Refer to the following legend for a breakdown of the icons used on the following pages:

Fire	Thunder	Ice	Earth	Water	Wind	Light	Dark

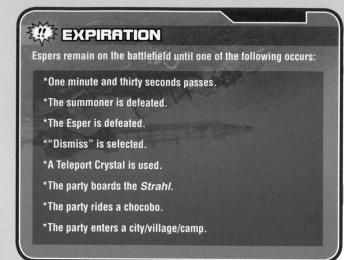

EXPIRATION

Espers remain on the battlefield until one of the following occurs:

* One minute and thirty seconds passes.
* The summoner is defeated.
* The Esper is defeated.
* "Dismiss" is selected.
* A Teleport Crystal is used.
* The party boards the *Strahl*.
* The party rides a chocobo.
* The party enters a city/village/camp.

Restrictions & Notes

Espers respond pretty much like any other guest character, in that the player has no control over the Esper's actions. Each Esper has its own gambits that it follows, which are listed in the following sections.

The summoner's level determines an Esper's level and stats. The effect only determines the Esper's level, not its HP and MP, and these values vary from one Esper to another.

While an Esper is active, the player can't change leaders. The summoner treats the Esper like another party member, so he or she may automatically begin casting things like Haste, Bubble, and Protect if your gambits are set up to do so.

Espers are so powerful that they're immune to many things. For example, most negative status effects won't harm an Esper. There are even some that come equipped with positive effects like Faith and Bravery that cannot be dispelled.

Beware of statuses on an Esper when it is summoned. Some Espers appear in battle with Reflect already cast upon it, which makes it difficult to heal. An Opal Ring really helps out in this situation, since it enables the summoner to cast through the Reflect spell.

Generally, the summoner should focus on healing while an Esper is active. Boost the Esper's power with Haste and Bubble if needed, but keep a Cure ready at all times. Also, try to keep the Esper alive long enough to use its finishing attack.

Belias, the Gigas

Strengths & Weaknesses

Absorb	Half
Half	Half
Weak	Half
Half	Half

LP Cost	10
Mist Charge	1
Attack Pwr.	61
Defense	20
Mag. Resist	15

Scion of darkness and guardian of the Holy Realm, made by the gods in opposition to the Transcendent Loghrif, scion of light. Called the Gigas for his appearance: man and monster fused as one. Considered a mistake upon his making, and receiving not his intended role, the Gigas challenged the gods and lost. Scorned by his masters, he found another: the Dynast-King, whose tomb he swore to protect for eternity.

Belias is discovered within the normal storyline. The first Esper discovered in the game, he's weaker than most. He's still very useful when facing enemies with a weakness to fire magick and comes in handy when challenging the first few hunt marks.

Libra

STATUS EFFECTS

Lvl	Max HP	Max MP	Str.	Mag. Pwr.	Vit.	Spd.
1	890~891	23~25	45	46	26	26
10	1025~1336	50~70	50	51	28	28
20	1270~1336	90~140	56	57	30	30
30	1585~1708	131~212	62	63	33	33
40	1883~2060	181~302	68	69	35	35
50	2359~2625	224~378	74	75	37	37
60	2779~3123	264~448	80	81	40	40
70	3017~3403	294~498	86	87	42	42
80	3292~3727	324~540	91	92	44	44
90	3667~4171	344~578	97	98	47	47
99	4090~4673	353~587	99	99	49	49

Gambit

Number	Description	Name
1	Summon Time Remaining < 10 Seconds	Hellfire
2	If HP < 30%	Hellfire
3	If the enemy can absorb Fire	Attack
4	If the enemy is weak against Fire	Painflare
5	If an enemy is spotted	Painflare

Actions

Name	Range	Scope	Type	Element	Attack Foundation
Attack	3	N/A	Physical	None	61
Painflare	12	N/A	Magick	Fire	60
Hellfire	12	Diameter 8	Magick	Fire	100

Mateus, the Corrupt

Strengths & Weaknesses

Half	Weak

Absorb	Half

Half	Half

Half	Half

LP Cost	25
Mist Charge	1
Attack Pwr.	65
Defense	39
Mag. Resist	25

Scion of darkness ruling and protecting those who live in the underworld, in opposition to Lahabrea, Abyssal Celebrant and scion of light. In the course of his rule, he submitted to avarice, and the darkness took his heart, transforming him until he was both evil and corrupt. Then in his cowardice did he bind a Goddess of the Demesne of Ice, and using her as a living shield, he challenged the gods. Defeated before their might, he fell screaming into the depths of hell, there to be imprisoned for eternity.

Mateus is also encountered during the main storyline. This evil being appears to have entrapped an ice goddess, so it uses a variety of ice magicks. Mateus is more useful when facing creatures that are weak against ice magick. It also has a healing spell that can help keep itself and the summoner alive when facing a group of enemies.

Libra

STATUS EFFECTS

Lvl	Max HP	Max MP	Str.	Mag. Pwr.	Vit.	Spd.
1	1000~1001	23~25	50	46	34	26
10	1135~1158	50~70	55	51	36	28
20	1380~1446	90~140	61	57	38	30
30	1695~1818	131~212	67	63	41	33
40	1993~2170	181~302	73	69	43	35
50	2469~2735	224~378	79	75	45	37
60	2889~3233	264~448	85	81	48	40
70	3127~3513	294~498	91	87	50	42
80	3402~3837	324~548	96	92	52	44
90	3777~4281	344~578	99	98	55	47
99	4200~4783	353~587	99	99	57	49

Gambit

Number	Description	Name
1	Summon Time Remaining < 10 Seconds	Frostwave
2	If HP < 30%	Frostwave
3	If Summoner's HP < 50%	Cura
4	If the enemy can absorb Ice	Attack
5	If the enemy is weak against Fire	Flash-Freeze
6	If an enemy is spotted	Flash-Freeze

Actions

Name	Range	Scope	Type	Element	Attack Foundation
Attack	3	N/A	Physical	None	65
Cura	10	Diameter 10	Magick	None	45
Flash-Freeze	12	N/A	Magick	Ice	66
Frostwave	12	Diameter 8	Magick	Ice	110

Shemhazai, the Whisperer

▶ **Location:** Giruvegan (story-related)

Scion that is both horse and woman, wielding utter control over the souls that wander the underworld, in opposition to the Martyr Igeyorhm, scion of light. Though she once served the gods as a guardian, when Ultima announced her rebellion, Shemhazai went to her, whispering of the gods' hidden weaknesses. She then descended upon the land without leave of the gods, and taught men of destruction and evil. For this was she stricken down and bound.

Shemhazai joins the party as part of the game's normal storyline. She also wields an all-or-nothing attack, which some tougher enemies and bosses can resist. It's best to save her for lesser enemies and rely on other Espers during difficult battles.

STATUS EFFECTS

Haste
Libra

Espers & Quickening

Strengths & Weaknesses

💣 **Weak**	🗡 **Normal**
🧊 **Normal**	🪨 **Normal**
💧 **Normal**	🍃 **Normal**
🌫 **Normal**	⚫ **Normal**

LP Cost	**50**
Mist Charge	**2**
Attack Pwr.	**73**
Defense	**47**
Mag. Resist	**31**

Lvl	Max HP	Max MP	Str.	Mag. Pwr.	Vit.	Spd.
1	2430~2431	23~25	51	46	26	26
10	2565~2588	50~70	56	51	28	28
20	2810~2876	90~140	62	57	30	30
30	3125~3248	131~212	68	63	33	33
40	3423~3600	181~302	74	69	35	35
50	3899~4165	224~378	80	75	37	37
60	4319~4663	264~448	86	81	40	40
70	4557~4943	294~498	92	87	42	42
80	4832~5267	324~548	97	92	44	44
90	5207~5711	344~578	99	98	47	47
99	5630~6213	353~587	99	99	49	49

Gambit

Number	Description	
1	Summon Time Remaining < 10 Seconds	Soul Purge
2	If HP < 30%	Soul Purge
3	If an enemy is spotted	Devour Soul

Actions

Name	Range	Scope	Type	Element	Attack Foundation
Devour Soul	10	N/A	Magick	None	N/A
Soul Purge	12	Diameter 8	Magick	None	N/A

Hashmal, Bringer of Order

Strengths & Weaknesses

Immune	Immune
Immune	Absorb
Immune	Weak
Immune	Immune

LP Cost	50
Mist Charge	2
Attack Pwr.	80
Defense	50
Mag. Resist	33

Scion set by the gods to wield and manipulate the laws of this world, and with holy power lead mankind to order. Created in opposition to Fandaniel the Protector, scion of light. Desiring to bring order to all things, he joined with Ultima in her battle against the gods. He gave his body to the Thousand-Years War, and when his strength was spent, down into the burning inferno he fell.

Hashmal is also encountered during the game's main storyline. His earth attacks are very valuable, since earth is a common weakness among flying foes and yet is unavailable to the party through normal magicks. Triggering his final attack is occasionally difficult, since it requires the summoner's HP to be near critical. This makes Hashmal a good choice when the summoner is already in the critical HP state, so he performs Gaia's Wrath upon entering the battle.

Libra

Lvl	Max HP	Max MP	Str.	Mag. Pwr.	Vit.	Spd.
1	2360~2361	23~25	52	48	26	26
10	2495~2518	50~70	57	53	28	28
20	2740~2806	90~140	63	59	30	30
30	3055~3178	131~212	69	65	33	33
40	3353~3530	181~302	75	71	35	35
50	3829~4095	224~378	81	77	37	37
60	4249~4593	264~448	87	83	40	40
70	4487~4873	294~498	93	89	42	42
80	4762~5197	324~548	98	94	44	44
90	5137~5641	344~578	99	99	47	47
99	5560~6143	353~587	99	99	49	49

Gambit

Number	Description	
1	If Summoner's HP < 10%	Gaia's Wrath
2	If the enemy can absorb Earth	Attack
3	If the enemy is weak against Earth	Roxxor
4	If an enemy is spotted	Roxxor

Actions

Name	Range	Scope	Type	Element	Attack Foundation
Attack	3	N/A	Physical	None	80
Roxxor	12	N/A	Magick	Earth	90
Gaia's Wrath	12	Diameter 8	Magick	Earth	150

Famfrit, the Darkening Cloud

▶ **Location:** The Pharos – Third Ascent (story-related)

Strengths & Weaknesses

Weak	Immune
Immune	Immune
Absorb	Immune
Immune	Immune

LP Cost	**90**
Mist Charge	**3**
Attack Pwr.	**145**
Defense	**56**
Mag. Resist	**37**

The hideous, darkly clouded form of Famfrit, scion in opposition to Holy Queen Emmerololth, scion of light, was anathema even to his creators. Thus, after a great battle, was he broken and sealed within armor laced with wards. The confines of his armor are void of light, so he is called the Darkening Cloud. Men fear the rain that falls from the black clouds that ooze from the giant ewer as a herald of chaos and waste.

Famfrit is encountered during the game's main storyline, although it occurs later in the game. It offers powerful Water attacks that supplement the rather weak Water magick available to the party. Use Famfrit against enemies with weaknesses to Water.

STATUS EFFECTS

Protect
Shell
Libra

Espers & Quickenings

Lvl	Max HP	Max MP	Str.	Mag. Pwr.	Vit.	Spd.
1	3860~3861	23~25	54	53	26	26
10	3995~4018	50~70	59	58	28	28
20	4240~4306	90~140	65	64	30	30
30	4555~4678	131~212	71	70	33	33
40	4853~5030	181~302	77	76	35	35
50	5329~5595	224~378	83	82	37	37
60	5749~6093	264~448	89	88	40	40
70	5987~6373	294~498	95	94	42	42
80	6262~6697	324~548	99	99	44	44
90	6637~7141	344~578	99	99	47	47
99	7060~7643	353~587	99	99	49	49

Gambit

Number	Description	
1	Summon Time Remaining < 10 Seconds	Tsunami
2	If HP < 30%	Tsunami
3	If the enemy can absorb Water	Attack
4	If the enemy is weak against Water	Briny Cannonade
5	If an enemy is spotted	Briny Cannonade

Actions

Name	Range	Scope	Type	Element	Attack Foundation
Attack	2	N/A	Physical	None	145
Briny Cannonade	12	N/A	Magick	Water	140
Tsunami	12	Diameter 8	Magick	Water	200

Adrammelech, the Wroth

▶ **Location:** Zertinan Caverns (side quest, "Paying for the Past")

Strengths & Weaknesses

Immune	Absorb
Weak	Immune
Immune	Immune
Immune	Immune

LP Cost	**25**
Mist Charge	**1**
Attack Pwr.	**63**
Defense	**29**
Mag. Resist	**25**

Emperor among the scions, able to reduce to nothing aught he strikes with a single vengeful blow of his fist, created in opposition to Deudalephon the Benevolent, scion of light. Though he was made by the gods to quell the fiends that raged in the Otherworld, his immense strength and fearsome visage drew the fiends to his side, and turned him against his creators. Adrammelech rose to prominence in the Otherworld, whence he led a fiendish horde against the gods, but in the end, he was defeated.

Adrammelech is found in the Athroza Quicksands section of Zertinan Caverns. He's commonly encountered on the "Paying for the Past" hunt (see page 228 of this guide), which requires the party to search the Zertinan Caverns for the Catoblepas.

This Esper packs a powerful lightning punch that works great against many enemies. This Esper doesn't have much HP, which makes it difficult for it to hang around long enough to use its final attack. Keep it healthy and use Bubble to double its HP right away.

Faith

Libra

STATUS EFFECTS

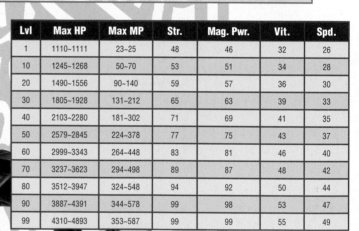

Lvl	Max HP	Max MP	Str.	Mag. Pwr.	Vit.	Spd.
1	1110~1111	23~25	48	46	32	26
10	1245~1268	50~70	53	51	34	28
20	1490~1556	90~140	59	57	36	30
30	1805~1928	131~212	65	63	39	33
40	2103~2280	181~302	71	69	41	35
50	2579~2845	224~378	77	75	43	37
60	2999~3343	264~448	83	81	46	40
70	3237~3623	294~498	89	87	48	42
80	3512~3947	324~548	94	92	50	44
90	3887~4391	344~578	99	98	53	47
99	4310~4893	353~587	99	99	55	49

Gambit

Number	Description	
1	Summon Time Remaining < 10 Seconds	Judgment Bolt
2	If HP < 30%	Judgment Bolt
3	If Summoner's HP < 50%	Curaga
4	If the enemy can absorb Thunder	Bio
5	If more than one enemy present	Thundara
6	If the enemy is weak against Thunder	Flash Arc
7	If an enemy is spotted	Flash Arc

Actions

Name	Range	Scope	Type	Element	Attack Foundation
Curaga	10	N/A	Magick	None	85
Thundara	10	Diameter 6	Magick	Thunder	70
Bio	10	Diameter 6	Magick	None	88
Flash Arc	12	N/A	Magick	Thunder	72
Judgment Bolt	12	Diameter 8	Magick	Thunder	120

Cúchulainn, the Impure

▶ **Location:** Garamsythe Waterway (side quest, "Lost in the Pudding" hunt and "Sluiceway Search")

Strengths & Weaknesses

Half	Half
Half	Half
Half	Half
Half	Half

LP Cost	50
Mist Charge	2
Attack Pwr.	83
Defense	47
Mag. Resist	31

STATUS EFFECTS

- Reflect
- Protect
- Shell
- Brave
- Libra

Scion created to rid the world of its impurities by swallowing them within himself, in opposition to Nabriales the Majestic, scion of light. The world, however, was more filled with impurity and corruption than even the gods dared imagine, and having swallowed it all, the once beautiful Cúchulainn was transformed into a hideous thing, a deity of filth, and so did he turn against his creators. Wherever his feet should fall, there all life withers to dust.

To find this Esper, the party must complete the "Lost in the Pudding" hunt (see page 225 in this guide) to get the Sluice Gate Key. Next, complete the "Waterway Haunting" side quest (see page 224 in this guide) to adjust the water levels and open a path to the boss.

Cúchulainn is an easy Esper to use. He has plenty of HP at his disposal and often heals with Curaja, which enables his summoner to focus more on combat and less on keeping the Esper alive. When paired with a powerful melee character, they can devastate any lesser enemies that crawl around nearly any location.

Lvl	Max HP	Max MP	Str.	Mag. Pwr.	Vit.	Spd.
1	2320~2321	23~25	51	46	26	26
10	2455~2478	50~70	56	51	28	28
20	2700~2766	90~140	62	57	30	30
30	3015~3138	131~212	68	63	33	33
40	3313~3490	181~302	74	69	35	35
50	3789~4055	224~378	80	75	37	37
60	4209~4553	264~448	86	81	40	40
70	4447~4833	294~498	92	87	42	42
80	4722~5157	324~548	97	92	44	44
90	5097~5601	344~578	99	98	47	47
99	5520~6103	353~587	99	99	49	49

Gambit

Number	Description	
1	Summon Time Remaining < 10 Seconds	Blight
2	Undead	Attack
3	If enemy's HP < 100%	Malaise
4	If an enemy is spotted	Attack
5	If own HP < 100%	Curaja

Actions

Name	Range	Scope	Type	Element	Attack Foundation
Attack	2	N/A	Physical	None	83
Curaja	10	Diameter 10	Magick	None	145
Malaise	12	N/A	Magick	None	90
Blight	12	Diameter 8	Magick	None	150

Espers & Quickenings

Chaos, Walker of the Wheel

▶ **Location:** Necrohol of Nabudis (side quest, "Waterway Haunting," "Lost in the Pudding" and "Broken Artifact")

Strengths & Weaknesses

Immune	Immune
Immune	Weak
Immune	Absorb
Immune	Immune

LP Cost	**50**
Mist Charge	**3**
Attack Pwr.	**155**
Defense	**56**
Mag. Resist	**37**

Tutelary deity of the sacred crystals fashioned by the gods at the time of the Great Making. Created in opposition to Mitron the Chastiser, scion of light. Upon entering the world of Man, he was enveloped in the turmoil rampant there. Lost, he died and was reborn countless times, a walker of life's wheel, eventually to rage against the gods that had so fated him. By sitting in meditation upon the Uneh Pedestal does he clear heart and mind until all that has order and reason and thought is made as nothing.

Chaos is located deep within the Necrohol of Nabudis. To reach him, the party must complete the "Waterway Haunting" (see page 224 in this guide) and "Lost in the Pudding" (see page 226 in this guide) hunts. After doing so, you must complete the "Nabreus's Medal" side quest (see page 241 in this guide) that eventually leads into the Necrohol of Nabudis. Defeat the optional bosses, Fury and Humbaba Mistant, to unlock the path to Chaos.

This Esper adjusts well to any situation. It bases its attacks on the enemy's weakness, so it always hits the opponent hard where it hurts the most. Chaos enters battle with Reflect on, which makes it difficult to heal him when the need arises. Equip an Opal Ring before summoning him to prevent this from being an issue.

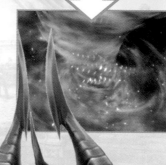

STATUS EFFECT
Reflect
Haste
Faith
Libra

Lvl	Max HP	Max MP	Str.	Mag. Pwr.	Vit.	Spd.
1	4135~4136	23~25	54	53	26	26
10	4270~4293	50~70	59	58	28	28
20	4515~4581	90~140	65	64	30	30
30	4830~4953	131~212	71	70	33	33
40	5128~5305	181~302	77	76	35	35
50	5604~5870	224~378	83	82	37	37
60	6024~6368	264~448	89	88	40	40
70	6262~6648	294~498	95	94	42	42
80	6537~6972	324~548	99	99	44	44
90	6912~7416	344~578	99	99	47	47
99	7335~7918	353~587	99	99	49	49

Gambit

Number	Description	
1	Summon Time Remaining < 10 Seconds	Tornado
2	If HP < 30%	Tornado
3	If the enemy is weak against Light	Holy
4	If the enemy is weak against Dark	Darkga
5	If the enemy is weak against Fire	Firaga
6	If the enemy is weak against Thunder	Thundaga
7	If the enemy is weak against Ice	Blizzaga
8	If the enemy can absorb Wind	Scourge
9	If the enemy is weak against Wind	Aeroga
10	If enemy's HP are high	Whirlwind

Actions

Name	Range	Scope	Type	Element	Attack Foundation
Holy	10	N/A	Magick	Light	157
Whirlwind	10	Diameter 6	Magick	Wind	103
Firaga	10	Diameter 6	Magick	Fire	124
Thundaga	10	Diameter 6	Magick	Thunder	124
Blizzaga	10	Diameter 6	Magick	Ice	124
Scourge	10	Diameter 6	Magick	None	142
Darkga	10	Diameter 6	Magick	Dark	130
Whirlwind	12	N/A	Magick	Wind	—
Tornado	12	Diameter 8	Magick	Wind	—

Zalera, the Death Seraph

▶ **Location:** Terminus No. 7/Barheim Passage (side quests, "Dalmasca's Desert Bloom," "Pursuit of a Cure" and "Missing Ferryman")

Strengths & Weaknesses

Immune

Immune

Immune

Immune

Immune

Immune

Absorb
Immune

Heretic scion who wrapped the world in dark energies, seeking to take the souls of all living things unto himself. Created in opposition to Emet-Selch, Angel of Truth, and scion of light. Originally tasked with the judging of men upon their deaths, his soul was tainted by the curses of those who raged against the heavens, and seizing one of the gods' servants, a shamaness, as a hostage, he rebelled against his creators. Even now, in defeat, he clutches the shamaness to him in his right arm, and with the aid of her death-wail does he summon the soul of darkness to do his bidding.

Zalera appears at the end of a long series of events that lead to the Barheim Passage. It begins with the "Dalmasca's Desert Bloom" hunt (see page 224 in this guide) that prefaces the "Pursuit of a Cure" (see page 231 in this guide) and "Cactaur Family" (see page 239 in this guide) side quests. Complete them all, then dive deep into Barheim Passage to face the Esper and its minions.

Libra

STATUS EFFECTS

LP Cost	25
Mist Charge	1
Attack Pwr.	62
Defense	39
Mag. Resist	25

This Esper is a little different from the others. Its attacks are typically all or nothing, since Kill is an instant death attack. Zalera's attack changes to a devastating magick strike that is less "hit-or-miss" when his HP is less than 80%. Zalera automatically heals himself between battles with Holy, so there's no way to intentionally keep Zalera's HP low to force it to use Shock instead of Kill. Zalera's final attack is triggered by any enemy with critical HP. This may result in a very quick appearance if an enemy with critical HP is already present when the Esper is summoned.

Lvl	Max HP	Max MP	Str.	Mag. Pwr.	Vit.	Spd.
1	1220~1221	23~25	50	46	34	26
10	1355~1378	50~70	55	51	36	28
20	1600~1666	90~140	61	57	38	30
30	1915~2038	131~212	67	63	41	33
40	2213~2390	181~302	73	69	43	35
50	2689~2955	224~378	79	75	45	37
60	3109~3453	264~448	85	81	48	40
70	3347~3733	294~498	91	87	50	42
80	3622~4057	324~548	96	92	52	44
90	3997~4501	344~578	99	98	55	47
99	4420~5003	353~587	99	99	57	49

Gambit

Number	Description	
1	If opponent's HP < 30%	Condemnation
2	If HP > 80%	Kill
3	If an enemy is spotted	Shock
4	If own HP < 100%	Holy*

*Holy used to heal

Actions

Name	Range	Scope	Type	Element	Attack Foundation
Holy	10	N/A	Magick	Light	157
Shock	10	N/A	Magick	None	133
Kill	12	N/A	Magick	None	N/A
Condemnation	12	Diameter 8	Magick	None	N/A

Zeromus, the Condemner

▶ Location: Mt Bur-Omisace (side quest; collect the Stone of the Condemner)

Strengths & Weaknesses

Half	Half
Half	Half
Half	Half
Half	Half

LP Cost	50
Mist Charge	2
Attack Pwr.	103
Defense	53
Mag. Resist	35

Honoring the law more than any other, a scion of holy order and condemner of criminals. Created in opposition to Knight-Star Pashtarot, scion of light. He turns his deep, abiding hatred for those who break the law into living darkness, therein to plunge the guilty in fell judgment. Over time, he came to care less for upholding the law and more for condemnation, and so tainted by hate, he sought to condemn the gods themselves to death. Thus did he earn the title of "The Condemner," and thus did he fall from grace.

To find Zeromus, the party must collect the Stone of the Condemner from the Mt Bur-Omisace region after the area is attacked. The stone is subsequently used in the Stilshrine of Miriam to reach the boss.

Zeromus uses Gravity magick to attack its enemies, which can be devastating or completely ineffective. Ensure that all targets are affected by Gravity before bringing Zeromus into a battle.

Libra

Lvl	Max HP	Max MP	Str.	Mag. Pwr.	Vit.	Spd.
1	2710~2711	23~25	53	46	26	26
10	2845~2868	50~70	58	51	28	28
20	3090~3156	90~140	64	57	30	30
30	3405~3528	131~212	70	63	33	33
40	3703~3880	181~302	76	69	35	35
50	4179~4445	224~378	82	75	37	37
60	4599~4943	264~448	88	81	40	40
70	4837~5223	294~498	94	87	42	42
80	5112~5547	324~548	99	92	44	44
90	5487~5991	344~578	99	98	47	47
99	5910~6493	353~587	99	99	49	49

Gambit

Number	Description	
1	Summon Time Remaining < 10 Seconds	Big Bang
2	If an enemy is spotted	Gravity Well

Actions

Name	Range	Scope	Type	Element	Attack Foundation
Gravity Well	12	N/A	Magick	None	—
Big Bang	12	Diameter 8	Magick	None	—

Exodus, the Judge-Sal

▶ **Location:** Mosphoran Highwaste (side quest; solve floatweed puzzle in Mosphoran Highwaste)

Most ancient of the scions, created in opposition to Halmarut, the Arbiter, and scion of light. Tasked with keeping watch over the world, with the authority to judge the value of all things. As he watched, unseen, unknown, his attachment to the world dwindled and faded until it was as nothing. Fitting that he would desire to make the world, too, as nothing. Yet he fell in the war against the gods, and was thwarted, imprisoned in punishment for his heresy.

You can find Exodus in the Mosphoran Highwaste once the waters begin to flow at the Babbling Vale. Solve the floatweed puzzle to reach the peak where Exodus awaits.

This Esper's final attack is difficult to use. It only occurs at the end of Exodus's summon time, but only if the Esper has been immobilized. This means keeping a close eye on his HP and the time remaining. Cast Immobilize on him at the last second when enemies are near to trigger the meteor attack. It can be devastating, but requires careful timing.

STATUS EFFECTS

- Haste
- Faith
- Libra

Strengths & Weaknesses

Half	Half
Half	Half
Half	Half
Half	Half

LP Cost	**50**
Mist Charge	**2**
Attack Pwr.	**97**
Defense	**53**
Mag. Resist	**35**

Lvl	Max HP	Max MP	Str.	Mag. Pwr.	Vit.	Spd.
1	2820~2821	23~25	53	46	26	26
10	2955~2978	50~70	58	51	28	28
20	3200~3266	90~140	64	57	30	30
30	3515~3638	131~212	70	63	33	33
40	3813~3990	181~302	76	69	35	35
50	4289~4555	224~378	82	75	37	37
60	4709~5053	264~448	88	81	40	40
70	4947~5333	294~498	94	87	42	42
80	5222~5657	324~548	99	92	44	44
90	5597~6101	344~578	99	98	47	47
99	6020~6603	353~587	99	99	49	49

Gambit

Number	Description	
1	Summon Time Remaining < 10 Seconds and Exodus Immobilized	Meteor
2	If an enemy is spotted	Comet

Actions

Name	Range	Scope	Type	Element	Attack Foundation
Comet	12	N/A	Magick	None	—
Meteor	12	Diameter 8	Magick	None	—

Espers & Quickenings

Ultima, the High Seraph

▶ **Location:** Giruvegan (side quest; hidden in Giruvegan's Great Crystal)

Strengths & Weaknesses

Immune	Immune
Immune	Immune
Immune	Immune
Absorb	Weak

LP Cost	**90**
Mist Charge	**3**
Attack Pwr.	**147**
Defense	**61**
Mag. Resist	**40**

Masterpiece among the scions created by the gods, and mastermind of the plot to rise against them. Prior to her betrayal, she was tasked with guiding souls to heaven and aiding in their reincarnation. Called the High Seraph for her angelic wings of glimmering gold, yet it was on wings of deepest black that the tainted angel Ultima rose against the gods. Since her fall, her heart is without light, and impossible to know.

Ultima is hidden deep within the heart of Giruvegan's Great Crystal. Carefully navigate the Way Stones to reach her lair after clearing the city of Giruvegan.

She's very powerful, but has perhaps the single most difficult final attack to trigger. It requires that both she and the summoner have critical HP levels. This is almost impossible to trigger on command, but a blast of Graviga can often help force things. Ultima also enters the battle with Reflect on, so equip an Opal Ring so that the party can heal her.

STATUS EFFECTS

- Reflect
- Protect
- Shell
- Haste
- Libra

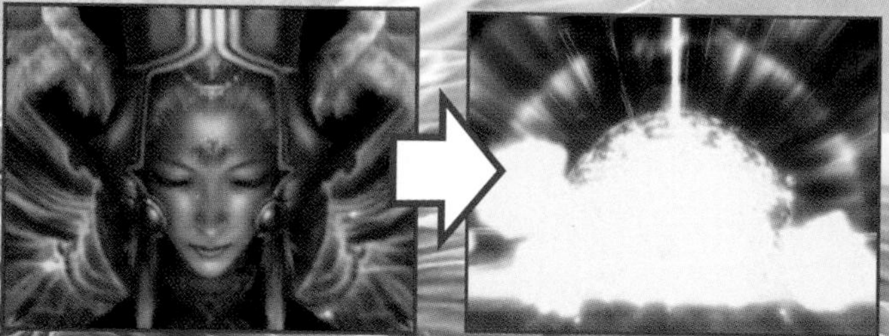

Lvl	Max HP	Max MP	Str.	Mag. Pwr.	Vit.	Spd.
1	4410~4411	23~25	60	46	26	26
10	4545~4568	50~70	66	52	28	28
20	4790~4856	90~140	72	58	30	30
30	5105~5228	131~212	78	64	33	33
40	5403~5580	181~302	84	70	35	35
50	5879~6145	224~378	90	76	37	37
60	6299~6643	264~448	96	82	40	40
70	6537~6923	294~498	99	88	42	42
80	6812~7247	324~548	99	94	44	44
90	7187~7691	344~578	99	99	47	47
99	7610~8193	353~587	99	99	49	49

Gambit

Number	Description	
1	Summoner's and Esper's HP < 30%	Eschaton
2	If the enemy can absorb Light	Flare
3	If the enemy is weak against Light	Redemption
4	If an enemy is spotted	Redemption

Actions

Name	Range	Scope	Type	Element	Attack Foundation
Flare	10	N/A	Magick	None	163
Redemption	12	N/A	Magick	Light	180
Eschaton	12	Diameter 8	Magick	Light	250

Zodiark, Keeper of Precepts

▶ **Location:** Henne Mines (side quest; must acquire at least 10 other Espers)

Strengths & Weaknesses

 Immune
 Immune

Immune	Immune
Immune	Immune
Immune	Immune
Weak	Absorb

LP Cost	200
Mist Charge	3
Attack Pwr.	201
Defense	61
Mag. Resist	40

Strongest of the scions created by the gods, they feared his growth, and so kept him a child. So indomitable is his strength that all things are by him twisted and pressed into oblivion. He alone fashions the laws governing all things, and administers punishment in place of the gods. So is he Keeper of Precepts, and his authority is absolute.

Talk to Geomancer Yugelu in Jahara after the party acquires at least 10 Espers. Yugelu then unlocks the path within the Henne Mines that leads to Zodiark. This is a very difficult road, so be ready for level 65 enemies and some of the nastiest battles yet!

Zodiark is an extremely powerful ally. Its powerful Scathe attacks can wipe out entire enemy clusters in seconds. Zodiark's final attack, Final Eclipse, requires that the summoner be under the stone effect. This is achieved by casting Break on the summoner either before or after Zodiark is summoned. Casting it on the summoner prior to summoning the Esper ensures that Zodiark immediately launches the Final Eclipse upon entering battle. This is especially effective when facing bosses. By the way, Final Eclipse causes approximately 50,000 HP of damage with each use!

STATUS EFFECTS

- Protect
- Shell
- Haste
- Faith
- Libra

Lvl	Max HP	Max MP	Str.	Mag. Pwr.	Vit.	Spd.
1	3090~3091	23~25	60	45	26	26
10	3225~3248	50~70	66	51	28	28
20	3470~3536	90~140	72	57	30	30
30	3785~3908	131~212	78	63	33	33
40	4083~4260	181~302	84	69	35	35
50	4559~4825	224~378	90	75	37	37
60	4979~5323	264~448	96	81	40	40
70	5217~5603	294~498	99	87	42	42
80	5492~5927	324~548	99	93	44	44
90	5867~6371	344~578	99	99	47	47
99	6290~6873	353~587	99	99	49	49

Gambit

Number	Description	
1	If Summoner under Break Effect (Stone)	Final Eclipse
2	If more than one enemy present	Scathe
3	If the enemy can absorb Dark	Flare
4	If the enemy is weak against Dark	Banish Ray
5	If an enemy is spotted	Banish Ray

Actions

Name	Range	Scope	Type	Element	Attack Foundation
Flare	10	N/A	Magick	None	163
Scathe	10	Diameter 6	Magick	None	190
Banish Ray	12	N/A	Magick	Dark	240
Final Eclipse	12	Diameter 8	Magick	None	—

Quickenings

Quickenings are powerful combos that consume the Mist Charges of one to three party members. The power of the attack is based upon the combination of attacks executed to release a devastating finishing attack or "Concurrence." This unique system is much like a slot machine and a little difficult to understand at first, so it's better to break it down and explain just how to get the most out of Quickenings.

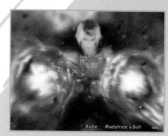

Unlocking Quickenings

Characters begin the game *without* Quickenings. To obtain them, you must unlock the special Quickening panels on the license board. These panels are one-time only panels, which means once a character unlocks a quickening panel, that particular panel is removed from the other members' license boards. Each character can only unlock three panels total. It doesn't matter which panels are unlocked, as Quickenings are based on the character and the number of Quickening panels unlocked rather than the chosen panel itself.

Unlocking one panel earns a character a level 1 Quickening. Unlocking two panels produces the character's level 2 Quickening and a second Mist Charge (it also doubles the character's maximum MP). Unlocking three panels releases the character's level 3 Quickening and adds a third Mist Charge (effectively tripling the character's maximum MP).

Mist Charges

Quickenings consume Mist Charges based upon the level of the Quickening used. Level 1 consumes one Mist Charge; level 2 uses two Mist Charges; and level 3 devours three Mist Charges. Thus, a character with two Mist Charges can use a level 1 or level 2 Quickening.

How It All Works

The Quickening system is much like a slot machine, so there's some luck involved. As the initial attack occurs, up to three lines of text appear in the bottom-right corner of the screen, one line for each character participating in the attack. Think of these lines as the wheels of a slot machine.

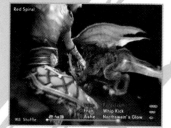

The "wheels" randomly cycle through four possible outcomes. They will display the name of a character's level 1, level 2, or level 3 Quickening or the words "Mist Charge." When they appear in white, the player can activate the command by pressing the button shown to the left of the line of text. Note that lines appearing gray in color aren't available.

With a little luck, there will be a white line or two available from which to choose, but eventually three gray lines will appear. Press the R2 button when this occurs to shuffle the commands again in hopes of getting a white line or two.

The player can initiate as many attacks as possible within the four-second time limit. By achieving certain attack combinations, the party unleashes a powerful Concurrence that delivers a devastating final hit to the target and any nearby enemies. So what makes the white and gray lines appear? This is where things gets tricky. Read on to make sense of it all.

Cost vs. Available Mist Charges

As noted previously, each Quickening costs a certain number of Mist Charges. Characters can only perform an action if they have the Mist Charges to fuel the attack. For example, let's say Vaan enters battle with three Mist Charges and begins his assault with his level 3 attack, Pyroclasm. This will immediately drain all of his Mist Charges, meaning that he can no longer participate in the combo. His teammates, however, likely still have Mist Charges and can perform additional attacks.

Don't count Vaan out just yet, though. Keep an eye on his command line and watch for the words "Mist Charge" to appear. Press the corresponding button when these words appear on-screen to completely refill Vaan's Mist Charges as the commands reshuffle. Now he can use any of his attacks again.

The phrase "Mist Charge" may appear for a character whenever that person has completely drained his or her Mist Charges. Always use the Mist Charge command when it appears, as combos can continue to grow until the timer runs out.

Consider this next example. Vaan begins by using three Mist Charges. He uses Pyroclasm, his level 3 attack, to open a Quickening. "Mist Charge" immediately appears on-screen and is triggered, so his Mist Charge climbs back from nothing to three.

Next, his level 1 attack, Red Spiral, appears and is triggered reducing his Mist Charges to two. As the Red Spiral plays the command for his level 2 attack, White Whorl, appears and is triggered. Now he has performed three attacks and his Mist Charges are back to zero.

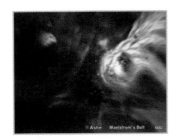

With a little luck, the Mist Charge command will appear again and Vaan can continue to attack, or the timer will run out and a Concurrence will play if it is earned.

Managing the Clock

The clock pauses whenever you trigger an attack command. It doesn't start to move again until the next animation starts to play. Enter the commands quickly to save time, but don't do so in haste. The combination of attacks is very important, so choose the next action carefully and quickly.

The Mist Charge command doesn't stop the clock, but it does reshuffle the commands. Be ready to press another button quickly to avoid wasting time.

Note that a small amount of time is added back to the clock each time a command is entered. As the clock winds down, the bar also speeds up with each successful attack, so eventually there's no time to shuffle or even read the command lines.

Triggering Concurrences

Concurrences arrive at the end of a Quickening when certain conditions have been met. The conditions are based upon the number of level 1, 2, and 3 attacks that are used during the Quickening. For instance, the weakest Concurrence requires that the party perform three level 1 attacks during the Quickening. The toughest, Black Hole, requires four of each level. Obviously, it's easier to perform some Concurrences than others and there's a little luck involved, too. It's usually easy enough to get Ark Blast once everyone in the party has three Mist Charges.

The best combination is always used, too. Say the party uses seven level 1 attacks, five level 2 attacks, and two level 3 attacks. That combination would qualify them for five different Concurrences, but would always result in Ark Blast.

Any damage caused by a Concurrence is non-elemental. The names may make them seem like elemental attacks, but resistances don't come into play. The only creatures that can resist a Quickening are those with an immunity to physical damage.

Concurrence	Power	Requirements		
		Lv 1	Lv 2	Lv 3
Black Hole	253	4	4	4
Whiteout	215	3	3	3
Ark Blast	205	2	2	2
Luminescence	175	—	—	5
Windburst	155	—	5	—
Torrent	130	2	3	—
Cataclysm	110	7	—	—
Inferno	90	3	—	—

Here's your road map through the central storyline of *FINAL FANTASY XII*. If you're new to this style of gaming, jump right in. We start with a step-by-step guide through the opening levels, making no assumptions about your level of experience (we do assume you've read the game manual, but that's all we assume at this point). If you're a veteran Final Fantasy gamer, however, you might want to skip the hand-holding in the first few sections; you're probably deep into the game already.

Please note that this "main story walkthrough" does not include detailed guidance through the myriad side plots in the game—the clan hunts, side quests, and secret areas that make the FINAL FANTASY world so deep and rich and full of life. However, this walkthrough will point out the optimal places to embark on each of those side adventures, and then direct you to the "Hunts," "Side Quests," and "Secrets" chapters in this book.

The Story Begins

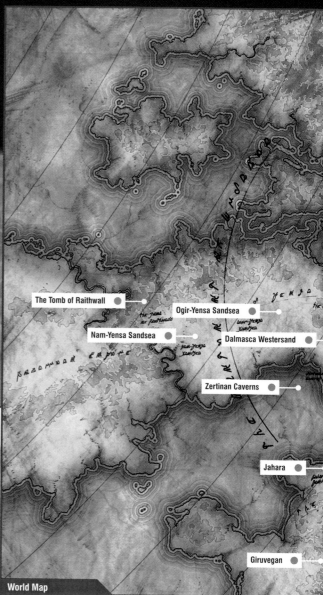

The Tomb of Raithwall

Ogir-Yensa Sandsea

Nam-Yensa Sandsea

Dalmasca Westersand

Zertinan Caverns

Jahara

Giruvegan

World Map

The great saga opens with a happy occasion in Rabanastre, capital of the Kingdom of Dalmasca. Amid great pomp and ceremony, a wedding procession winds through cheering crowds lining the streets of the royal city. The parade celebrates the marriage of Her Royal Highness Princess Ashe (daughter of Raminas, King of Dalmasca) to Lord Rasler (heir to the throne of Dalmasca's eastern neighbor Nabradia).

This is more than a marriage of convenience; Ashe and Rasler are truly in love, a fact that seems to bestow a sacred, joyous air to the proceedings. In the city's great cathedral, the high priest seals the union with the name of the God of Light, Faram. With that, the bordering kingdoms come together in a peaceful union.

But visions of a hopeful future quickly fade. Basch, captain in the Order of the Knights of Dalmasca, soon brings disturbing news to the king's war room: Nabudis, capital of Nabradia, has fallen beneath Archadia's westward surge. Surely Dalmasca is next.

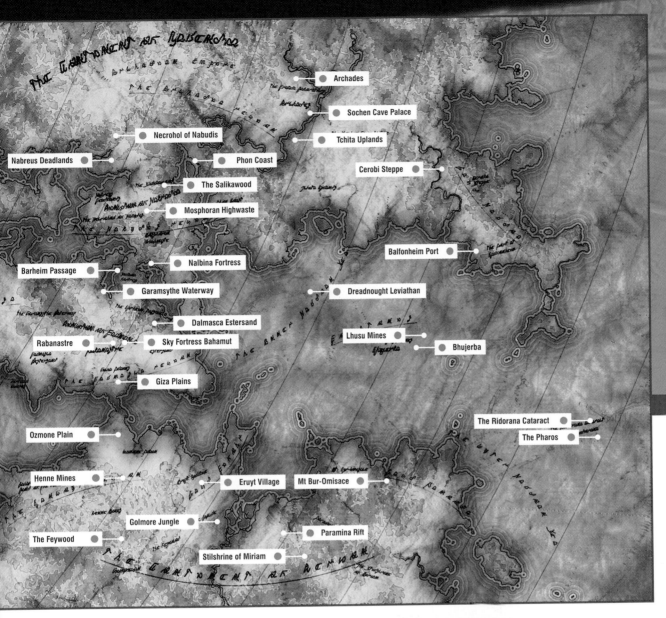

Archades

Sochen Cave Palace

Tchita Uplands

Necrohol of Nabudis

Nabreus Deadlands

Phon Coast

Cerobi Steppe

The Salikawood

Mosphoran Highwaste

Balfonheim Port

Nalbina Fortress

Barheim Passage

Garamsythe Waterway

Dreadnought Leviathan

Dalmasca Estersand

Lhusu Mines

Rabanastre

Sky Fortress Bahamut

Bhujerba

Giza Plains

The Ridorana Cataract

Ozmone Plain

The Pharos

Henne Mines

Eruyt Village

Mt Bur-Omisace

Golmore Jungle

Paramina Rift

The Feywood

Stilshrine of Miriam

King Raminas sends Basch and Lord Rasler to rally Dalmascan defense forces in the border fortress of Nalbina. There, the fight is desperate, furious, and ultimately lost when the stronghold's "paling," a defensive magick barrier, falls. Archadian troops overwhelm the great citadel; in the process, Lord Rasler takes a lethal arrow to the chest. Basch barely manages to escape on a chocobo with the mortally wounded prince.

Back in Dalmasca, Lord Rasler is laid to rest, along with the hopes of the entire region. Here begin the memoirs of the Marquis Halim Ondore IV. Listen carefully to learn how King Raminas agreed to terms with his Archadian conquerors and reluctantly traveled to now-occupied Nalbina Fortress to sign the treaty. The Marquis Ondore's entry ends with some chilling words: "The Treaty would be signed with Steel… and Writ in royal Blood."

OBJECTIVE

Reach the King Before He Signs the Treaty!

World Map

Nalbina Fortress

Action Checklist

1. Complete the basic tutorials.
2. Defeat the Air Cutter Remora.
3. Fight your way to the King.

After completing a few quick tutorials on game basics, fight your way up the Nalbina Fortress to the Highhall where King Raminas is scheduled to sign the peace agreement with Archadia.

Imperial Swordsman

LV	HP	EXP	LP
3	115	24	0

Air Cutter Remora

LV	HP	EXP	LP
10	2200	0	0

Imperial Magus

LV	HP	EXP	LP
7	264	65	1

Nalbina Fortress

LOWER APARTMENTS

THE HIGHHALL

AERIAL GARDENS

Battle

INNER WARD

Battle

UPPER APARTMENTS

TREASURE TABLE	Normal			w/Diamond Armlet Equip.		
No.	App.%	gil %	If gil	50%	50%	gil	90%	10%
1	100%	0%	-	Potion	Potion	-	-	-
2	100%	0%	-	Potion	Potion	-	-	-

Use the following information to determine the contents of the chests. This legend is valid for every map in this walkthrough.

TREASURE TABLE LEGEND:

- = These chests only appear once on the map.
- = This color indicates those chests that only appear once.
- = These chests will reappear on the maps.
- = This color indicates those chests that will reappear on the maps.
- Yellow Text Box = Gambits
- Blue Text Box = *ITEMS THAT CAN BE EQUIPPED*

Learn the Basic Game Controls

As the story begins, you lay unconscious in the Aerial Gardens of the Nalbina Fortress. You are a Dalmascan soldier named Reks, 17, a mere boy orphaned by the war. Your captain, Basch, revives you and checks your condition. Your team includes several soldiers and Vossler Azelas, another esteemed member of the Order of the Knights of Dalmasca.

Note that Reks speaks of his younger brother back in Rabanastre; we'll meet him soon enough. For now, watch Basch decimate a squad of Imperial Swordsmen—he's quite an accomplished warrior—and then follow his directions as you take control of Reks.

As a young soldier named Reks, you join Basch in his attempt to halt the plot against King Raminas.

Remember: Press ✕ to move conversations along. You can also press △ to select Log, which reviews previous exchanges in the current conversation. Press ◯ to exit the log.

Talk and Review

Move the Right Analog Stick to move the camera view around, then use the Left Analog Stick to walk toward Basch. After that, you learn about the Talk Icon. Walk to the Dalmascan soldier posted at the nearby gate and talk to him. Approach the iron gate to learn about the Action Icon, then press ✕ to open the gate.

Take control of Reks and follow Basch's simple commands.

After Reks and Basch climb the stairs to enter the next area, the Inner Ward, you learn about the Party Menu where you can examine your equipment and inventory. Then, prepare for the game's first fight! Basch points out the hostile red Target Line, which indicates that you're being targeted by an attacking enemy—in this case, an Imperial Swordsman.

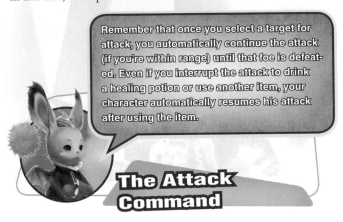

Remember that once you select a target for attack, you automatically continue the attack (if you're within range) until that foe is defeated. Even if you interrupt the attack to drink a healing potion or use another item, your character automatically resumes his attack after using the item.

The Attack Command

Press ✕ to open the Battle Menu. The menu cursor already points to Attack, so just press ✕ to select that action. There is only one target choice, Imperial Swordsman A; the menu cursor already points to that selection, so just press ✕ again. Move Reks toward the enemy guard to initiate the attack and watch the action unfold.

Basch and his squad of Dalmascan soldiers quickly join in and make instant mincemeat of the poor Imperial. Now move forward across the bridge to trigger a quick event showing an approaching airship.

Cross the Inner Ward bridge to trigger the approach of the deadly Air Cutter Remora.

Beat the (Almost) Boss

The health of this airship "boss" is measured by the red bar across the top of the screen.

The Air Cutter Remora is a boss… sort of. Note its red boss health bar across the top of the screen. When you fight any boss-type enemy, a similar bar appears. When you score hits, draining the boss's HP, the health bar drops. Open the Battle Menu and attack the airship.

Of course, this is a tougher fight, so keep an eye on the HP counter next to Reks's name in the lower-right corner. In the unlikely event that it drops below 50 or so, you can replenish HP with a Potion or use a Cure magick spell.

Actually, you don't need to heal Reks at all during the battle with the Air Cutter Remora. One of the Dalmascan Soldiers automatically keeps everyone healthy with Potions.

Someone's Got Your Back

TO DRINK A POTION

Open the Battle Menu and select Items. Then select Potion (you start with 8 of them) and select Reks to restore some of his HP. If your HP gets really low, you can use a Hi-Potion instead. Hi-Potions restore a greater number of HP than regular Potions.

TO CAST CURE

Open the Battle Menu and select Magicks & Technicks. Select White Magicks, then select Cure (the only choice for now). Finally, select Reks; he will cast a Cure spell on himself and restore some HP. This costs 8 MP (Mist Points), so Reks's MP counter will drop from 34 to 26. But you generate MP whenever you run, so you can push your MP back to 34 soon enough.

Sling some Thunder at the Imperial Cutter to practice some magick attacks.

The Air Cutter Remora hovers low enough that regular sword attacks can strike it (this isn't always true of flying foes, but you'll learn more about that later). But you can also sling a magick attack at the craft. Select Black Magicks from the Battle Menu, then select Thunder. Next, select your target, the Air Cutter Remora. Now watch Reks fire a nasty bolt of lightning at the airship.

Once the Remora's health bar drops to about the halfway mark, Basch unleashes a blistering special attack that knocks it silly. (Note: This is a Quickening. You'll get to use these powerful attacks later in the game.) Watch as the Air Cutter Remora disengages and runs. Then prepare for another assault.

Basch gives "Tonberry" a blast of Quickening, chasing it off to its lowly repair hangar.

Climb Through the Fortress

More Imperial Swordsmen descend the stairs directly ahead and attack the group. Your party makes quick work of them with or without your help, but you might as well get in a few good licks for the fun of it. If you exit to the south and reenter the Inner Ward, a few more enemy swordsmen will rush downstairs. You can wait here and practice your combat, if you want; otherwise, ascend the staircase to the next area.

As you reach the area boundary (the dotted blue line across the doorway), Basch gives another tutorial. This time he points out the Minimap and then explains how to access the fuller picture of the Location Map by pressing Select. Try it just for practice. Use the Left Analog Stick to scroll the map, and press the L2 or R2 buttons to zoom in or out.

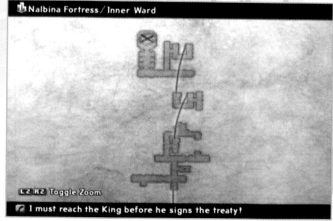

Press Select and check out the Location Map. The red 'X' marks your destination, and your objective is described at the bottom.

Note that your destination is marked by a red 'X' on the map. Also note that your current objective is described just below the map. In this case, it reads: "I must reach the King before he signs the treaty!"

Now move into the next area, the Lower Apartments. This triggers a short event where Basch talks about Vossler and their mission to get the King to safety. He believes that King Raminas is safe until he puts his royal seal to the treaty. Better hurry!

Head north from where you start this area until Basch advises, "Ofttimes retreat is the wiser course." To disengage from a battle and flee, press and hold the R2 button and run away. After you press ✖ to end this conversation, more Imperial Swordsmen will attack from the north and south. Dispatch them and head into the small supply alcove to the east filled with helmets and spears and other equipment. A treasure chest sits in the back corner. Find and open it to obtain a useful item.

Don't miss these treasures scattered throughout many areas in the game. They hold valuable items and gil rewards, all for free!

Exit the alcove and go north, west, and north again, keeping an eye out for more imperial attackers. Don't miss a second treasure in the far north hall tucked behind some crates and barrels. Then return south and veer east to a grand staircase. Turn left and take the staircase leading up to the next level, the Upper Apartments.

Save Your Game!

Turn right and walk up toward the glowing blue Save Crystal in the corner. After Basch explains how it works, approach it and press ✖ to fully restore your HP and MP, then select "Yes" to save your current game. After doing so, turn and climb the stairs to trigger another event.

Save Crystals are always a welcome sight. Touching a crystal replenishes the HP and MP of your entire party, and gives you a chance to save your game.

We strongly recommend that you save your game at every crystal you encounter. This can be a tough game and you never know what's around the next corner.

Save Every Chance You Get!

Fight to the Highhall

More guards spot the party on the staircase. Reks bravely sends Basch and the others ahead to save the King and turns to fight against the imperial pursuers. Here's your first solo fight.

Be patient and stay focused on one enemy at a time.

Just use the tactics you learned before. Nobody will automatically heal Reks now, so keep a close eye on his HP and be ready to use Potions or Cure spells. You should be strong enough to take on the first three Imperial Swordsmen without having to resort to health restoratives.

After the fight, follow the hall west and south to the big Passage Door. Press ✖ to open the door and continue south. Follow the corridor around the corner to another closed door. As you approach it, you trigger a final, disturbing scene as Reks enters the hall.

OBJECTIVE
Help Migelo and Tomaj

World Map

Run an errand for Migelo the shopkeeper and then complete your first monster hunt assignment in the Estersand.

Action Checklist

1	Kill the dire rats.
2	Visit Migelo to get an errand.
3	Find Kytes at the Sandsea and talk to Tomaj.

Dire Rat

LV	HP	EXP	LP
2-4	77	14	1

Rabanastre

NORTH END

Clan Hall

To Lowtown

EAST END

The Sandsea

To Lowtown

MUTHRU BAZAAR

Aerodrome

Migelo's Sundries

To the Westersand

EASTGATE

To the Estersand

WESTGATE

SOUTHERN PLAZA

To Lowtown

SOUTHGATE

To Giza Plains

Rid the Waterway of Rats

The story picks up two years later in the underground waterways beneath occupied Rabanastre. A small boy, Kytes, calls to an older boy named Vaan, who wants to "clean house" in the vermin-infested waterway. Once you gain control of Vaan, slice up the three aggressive Dire Rats in the area to trigger a long event that introduces you to Vaan's life.

Meet Vaan and Kytes, then whack some rats.

ONE WAY OUT

Vaan can't explore other parts of the waterway yet, so just kill the three rats in the area. It's the only way out of the Overflow Cloaca for now.

The Dire Rats will scurry all over the area. To track them, use the game's Minimap. Remember, enemies always appear as red dots.

Minimap Enemies

Kytes suggests that Vaan visit Migelo, the shopkeeper, who might have some errands to run. Vaan, of course, feels like he has more important things to do. The scene then shifts to the streets above. The city, despite the Archadian occupation, bustles with commerce and other activities. Vaan spots a pair of Imperial guards harassing a street merchant and he decides to intervene by plying his own "trade" by stealing the guard's pouch!

As Vaan escapes with his stolen loot, he bumps into his friend Penelo, another street orphan. As they talk, Penelo articulates the creed that Vaan supposedly lives by: the Imperials have robbed the people, so "it's only fair that we take it back." In fact, it's their *duty* as Dalmascans.

As a huge air cruiser passes overhead, Vaan expresses his deepest desire: "One day, I'll fly an airship of my own. I'll be a sky pirate, free to go where I will." Penelo doesn't argue. But for now, she suggests (like Kytes) that he visit Migelo and lend a hand.

Find Migelo

Maybe you should do as the kids suggest: go and see Migelo. A brief map tutorial now adds the World Map to the Party Menu. Press ▲ to open the Party Menu, then select World Map to take a look. The three locations you've visited so far are listed on the map: Nalbina Fortress, Garamsythe Waterway (Vaan's brief rat-killing adventure), and now Rabanastre.

The World Map is a handy accessory that logs maps of every place you visit as well as any unexplored areas for which you may buy or find maps.

If you select Rabanastre, you see its maps broken down further: one for the upper city and one for an area called "Lowtown." We'll explore Lowtown soon enough, but for now, let's find Migelo.

When you open the Rabanastre map, you will find Migelo's location indicated by the flashing red 'X.' Hey, it's nearby. Head due east to the intersection and veer right, bearing south until you trigger another event.

Your starting spot (circled here) is not far from where the red 'X' says Migelo is waiting.

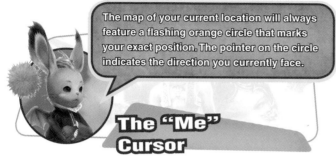

The map of your current location will always feature a flashing orange circle that marks your exact position. The pointer on the circle indicates the direction you currently face.

The "Me" Cursor

Migelo, a bangaa trader, is waiting for some goods to arrive for the palace banquet tonight. Unfortunately, they have not yet turned up, so he has had to order some replacement goods from Tomaj over at the Sandsea, a local tavern. Kytes was supposed to run this errand, but Migelo has seen no sign of him. Your new objective is to find Kytes at the Sandsea and see that the young boy completes his errand.

Migelo sends you to the Sandsea to track down Kytes and get him back on task.

Find Kytes at the Sandsea

Press Select to access the Rabanastre map, then use the directional arrows to highlight your current location, which is the East End. Press ✖ to see a list of all the establishments in East End. Most of Rabanastre's important shops (for your purposes) are in this district, along with the Sandsea. Note that the red 'X' indicating Kytes's location is right on top of the Sandsea.

Head north along the East End street to the Sandsea and enter to trigger an event. Vaan finds Kytes, who points out the Notice Board and says, "This is why Migelo's courier didn't get here on time!" Tomaj comes over and describes the "nastiness" in the Estersand that's harassing the couriers. He's posted a bill offering a reward for anyone who can hunt down the creature.

Go to the Sandsea to find Kytes and learn about the Tomato monster harassing the couriers and disrupting trade in the Estersand.

This first hunt is the only "official" one in the game that is required to progress the story. One of its purposes is to acquaint you with the Notice Boards and the hunt process. You'll find Notice Boards in most towns across Ivalice.

Mandatory Hunt

This "work" is certainly more to Vaan's liking. When the scene ends, Tomaj explains that people post bills on the Notice Board when they need a monster eliminated. Note that when you accept a hunting job, the monster you're tracking is called your "mark."

Tomaj explains the lowdown on the Notice Board and hunting marks.

When Tomaj shows the bill again, select the dialogue choice that asks to learn more about hunts. Tomaj explains how you must contact the petitioner who posted the bill to accept the job and learn where to find the mark. Then, after you complete the hunt, you must report back to that person to claim your bounty. Tomaj also hands over a **Clan Primer** to help keep track of hunts. You can now access the Clan Primer via the Party Menu.

> The Clan Primer is loaded with tips and info of varying degrees of usefulness. After Tomaj gives it to you, open it (from the Party Menu) and read all the topics, especially the Traveler's Tips.

Read the Primer!

Finally, Tomaj relinquishes an **Orrachea Armlet**, a basic accessory that raises a character's Max HP by 25 when the item is both licensed and equipped. Unfortunately, you don't have a license for it yet.

This leads into a quick tutorial on the licensing process in *FINAL FANTASY XII*. You learn that Vaan is currently licensed to use the Steal technick on foes; he also has licenses to equip a Mythril Sword, Leather Clothing (armor that increases Defense), and a Leather Cap (headgear that increases Magick Resist).

You have just 6 License Points (LP) to spend right now, but you can earn more by defeating foes. Luckily, the "Accessories 1" license (which includes the Orrachea Armlet) costs only 5 LP, so go ahead and acquire it, as Tomaj suggests. Note how acquiring the license reveals the licenses on all adjacent squares, making them available for acquisition. Continue the tutorial by pressing ● repeatedly to scroll through Vaan's Action List.

MORE ON LICENSING

For an in-depth look at the licensing process in this game, see "The License Board" chapter of this book. For more on how armor and weapons work, see those respective chapters in this book.

Tomaj gives you a **Writ of Transit** so that you can exit the city gates; he suggests that you leave via the East Gate to find your "mark" in the Estersand. Also note that the Licenses category has now been added to the Party Menu. When Tomaj has finished talking, a graphic flashes onscreen to signify the beginning of the hunt for the Rogue Tomato.

The screen says it all. You get a similar screen each time you accept a hunt from a petitioner.

Before you exit the Sandsea, the game reminds you to equip the Orrachea Armlet. Do it! Open the Party Menu and select Equip, then select Vaan (the only choice right now). Select Equip again, scroll down to the Accessory category, and select that. Finally, select the Orrachea Armlet, the only accessory currently available. Done! Note that Vaan's Max HP jumps from 102 to 127. Now you can exit the Sandsea.

> Tomaj stands at the bar in the Sandsea after your meeting with him. Talk to him any time if you need to review how to hunt marks or how licenses work.

Ask Tomaj

CHECK THE BESTIARY!

Regularly open the Clan Primer and read the Bestiary entries. There is only one creature listed right now, the Dire Rat you defeated in the waterway. Each time you defeat a new foe, information about it will appear in the Bestiary.

Some Bestiary entries have additional pages which contain useful information. Always read these when you get a chance. You can learn about a region's characteristics, get a list of ingredients needed for special items, pick up historical tidbits of interest, or learn other worthwhile info.

Walkthrough

Get to the Dalmasca Estersand

Press Select to open the Rabanastre map and plot your path down to the flashing red 'X' at Eastgate. Before you leave East End, though, we recommend that you explore the shops to see what's available (not much yet), then stop at Migelo's Sundries to purchase a couple of extra Potions just to be safe.

 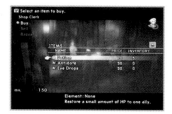

Pick up an extra Potion or two at Migelo's before you head out to face the fearsome tomato.

From East End you must go into the Southern Plaza, then down the eastern stairs to Eastgate to trigger an event. The Imperial guard tries to halt Vaan, but Vaan's Writ of Transit gets him through the gate. Once you're in Eastgate, save your game at the blue crystal and head due east into the Estersand.

Exit the city via the Eastgate to seek the Rogue Tomato. However, save your game at the Save Crystal before you venture out into the dangerous Estersand.

‼ NEED TO GET BACK IN?

See how others are queuing up at the gate to return to the city? If you change your mind and decide to go back inside, you must speak to the Imperial at the back of one of the two lines and then wait your turn to reenter Rabanastre.

Dalmasca Estersand (The Stepping)

Action Checklist

1	Hunt the Rogue Tomato for Tomaj.
2	Return to Tomaj for your bounty.
3	Visit the Clan Hall.

OUTPOST

Rogue Tomato

To Rabanastre (East Gate)

THE STEPPING

Cactite

LV	HP	EXP	LP
4-8	100-136	31-40	1

Cockatrice

LV	HP	EXP	LP
3-5	136-152	11-15	1

Wolf

LV	HP	EXP	LP
2-7	94-134	9-13	1

Rogue Tomato

LV	HP	EXP	LP
2	134	0	3

TREASURE TABLE

No.	App.%	gil %	If gil	Normal 50%	50%	gil	w/Diamond Armlet Equip. 90%	10%
1	70%	60%	~50	Potion	Hi-Potion	~160	Knot of Rust	Ether
2	70%	60%	~50	Potion	Eye Drops	~160	Knot of Rust	Ether
3	70%	60%	~50	Potion	Potion	~170	Knot of Rust	Ether
4	70%	60%	~50	Potion	Potion	~170	Knot of Rust	Ether
5	70%	60%	~120	Potion	Hi-Potion	~430	Knot of Rust	Hi-Potion
6	70%	60%	~45	Potion	Antidote	~155	Knot of Rust	Hi-Potion
7	70%	90%	~80	Potion	Antidote	~200	Knot of Rust	Hi-Potion
8	70%	60%	~45	Potion	Escutcheon	~155	Knot of Rust	Hi-Potion

Hunt the Rogue Tomato

The Estersand is vast and has numerous sub-regions, but for this hunt, you need only explore the first area you enter, called The Stepping. The map shown here indicates where the Rogue Tomato lurks, but explore The Stepping a bit first. Fight a few Wolves and Cactites to earn enough EXP to level up at least once (from Level 1 to Level 2), then heal back up to your max HP by using a Potion or going back to the Save Crystal at Eastgate.

Leave the Big Guy Alone

A massive Wild Saurian roams The Stepping. Note the green health bar over its head. That means it's a neutral creature; it won't attack if you just leave it alone. *Do not try to fight this monster yet!* Vaan doesn't stand a chance. At this early point in your development, it's one chomp and game over!

The Rogue Tomato hangs out on the ledge at the center of the map, near a flowering tree with stunning white blossoms. Use Steal to pilfer an item if you want, then attack the red menace. When the Rogue Tomato's HP drops to roughly half, he takes a running leap off the cliff. You can't jump down after him, so go around the cliff and down the dunes to finish him off.

Look for the Rogue Tomato near the white flowering tree.

Smash this guy into ketchup to get your mark for Tomaj... plus a bonus handful of Galbana Lilies.

When you finally prevail, Vaan picks up a handful of rare Galbana Lilies and then decides to "call it a day." But, before you head back to the city, scour the area to find all eight treasures in The Stepping. Also consider using the Steal technick on a few Wolves and Cactites to gain extra items, too, before attacking them for EXP and LP.

Don't overdo this mop-up fighting, though. You don't want to be caught without Potions in the desert. In particular, watch out for a trio of Wolves near the northern exit of the area. If you attack one, all three will counterattack as a unit. A pair of Cockatrices lurk in the west, too. Tough fight!

The red 'X' on the Location Map now marks the passage

Search for the treasures scattered around the dunes of The Stepping.

back to Rabanastre. Head back to Eastgate where, uh oh, they're not letting anyone back into the city until after the ceremony. Vaan's a resourceful fellow, though. Talk to Kytes, who waits near the gate, and you will trigger an event in which Migelo bribes the gate guards with wine, getting Vaan back in the city.

Next is a long event in which the new Consul appointed to rule Dalmasca, Lord Vayne, son of the Archadian Emperor, is paraded to the foot of the great cathedral. There, he gives a stirring speech that seems to win over the crowd.

Walking the streets of North End with Penelo later, Vaan decides he wants to crash Vayne's banquet tonight. Penelo suggests he goes and sees Old Dalan in Lowtown about gaining entrance to the palace. When you regain control of Vaan, you are now free to enter Lowtown from Rabanastre.

Return to Tomaj for Your Bounty

Before you seek out Old Dalan, however, you should finish up your first hunt properly. Revisit the Sandsea and score that bounty from Tomaj (who is still standing at the bar) for taking out the Rogue Tomato. He also passes on some inside info about a mysterious building in the North End district where a bangaa stands watch.

Tomaj is pleased with your success and pays a generous reward. He also provides a tip about a secret place.

By now you should have accumulated some gil and LP, so this might be a good time to purchase some upgrades. Here's one suggestion: spend 15 LP on the "White Magick 1" license, then go to Yugri's Magicks in East End to buy the Cure spell for 200 gil. Now you can heal Vaan with magick instead of relying entirely on Potions to do the trick.

Heal Thyself

Visit the Clan Hall

Go up to North End and proceed to the westernmost street. (If you check the area map, you can see the mystery building on the North End labeled with question marks, so it should be easy to find.) Approach the entry hall of the mystery building, marked by a green sign, and talk to the "Conspicuous bangaa"; he immediately agrees to let you in. Select "Okay, let me in" to enter the Clan Hall.

If Tomaj gave you a Clan Primer earlier, then the Conspicuous bangaa will let you right into the Clan Hall.

Inside, talk to Clan Centurio members to get a sense of the place, then locate the moogle standing on the banister at the top of the stairs. This is Montblanc, the clan's founder. Talk to him to join the clan and learn how it works. You also learn about the clan shop in the Muthru Bazaar on the west end of town.

Montblanc is the founder of Clan Centurio and the source of all rare hunt information, available only to clan members.

Talk to Montblanc a second time to receive a commemorative gift for joining Clan Centurio. Unfortunately, he has no clan hunts to offer at the moment, so it's time to go and pay Old Dalan a visit.

MONTBLANC'S BOSS BONUSES

Visit Montblanc regularly after you start defeating bosses and rare beasts. He is the source of handsome rewards for each of your major victories.

OBJECTIVE
Obtain a Sunstone for Old Dalan

Rabanastre/Lowtown

World Map

Action Checklist

1	Visit Old Dalan.
2	Explore Lowtown.
3	Buy a map of Giza Plains.
4	Exit Rabanastre via Southgate.

Old Dalan knows a secret path into the palace, but he needs something from the Giza Plains before he can help.

Lowtown

NORTH SPRAWL

To North End

To the Garamsythe Waterway

Traveling Merchant

To East End

To Southgate

Old Dalan's Place

SOUTH SPRAWL

Walkthrough

TREASURE TABLE				Normal		w/Diamond Armlet Equip.		
No.	App.%	gil %	If gil	50%	50%	gil	90%	10%
1	70%	50%	~30	Potion	Eye Drops	~100	Knot of Rust	Ether
2	70%	50%	~20	Red Fang	Phoenix Down	~100	Knot of Rust	Hi-Ether
3	70%	50%	~30	Potion	Potion	~200	Knot of Rust	Ether
4	70%	50%	~30	Potion	Antidote	~100	Knot of Rust	Ether
5	70%	50%	~70	Potion	Potion	~350	Knot of Rust	Ether
6	70%	50%	~40	Potion	Antidote	~150	Knot of Rust	Ether
7	100%	50%	~100	Potion	Eye Drops	~200	Knot of Rust	Ether
8	70%	50%	~30	Potion	Potion	~100	Knot of Rust	Ether
9	70%	50%	~60	Potion	Potion	~250	Knot of Rust	Hi-Ether

Visit Old Dalan in Lowtown

First, go to the Southgate district. After stepping through the gate, turn left (heading east), then open the old freight door to enter Lowtown. Now check the area map to see that you're almost on top of the red 'X'; Old Dalan's place is just to the left!

The old freight door (circled here) next to the south gate (at left) takes you into Lowtown very near Old Dalan's place.

Enter Old Dalan's place to trigger an event in which Vaan asks the old man how to sneak into the palace. Dalan does know of a secret passageway into the palace vaults, including a door that requires "a magicked stone that opens the way." Conveniently, it turns out that Dalan has this object, known as the Crescent Stone.

Old Dalan has the Crescent Stone, but you need to power up its magicks with a Sunstone.

Unfortunately, the Crescent Stone has lost its magicks. It needs the power of a Sunstone to recharge, and the only place to get a Sunstone is from the nomads on the Giza Plains to the south of Rabanastre.

 DON'T TOUCH THAT TREASURE: PART 1

Four treasure chests are connected to a chest found later (in the Necrohol of Nabudis) that holds the most powerful weapon in the game, the **Zodiac Spear**. If any of those first four chests are opened, the Zodiac Spear disappears from its chest in Nabudis.

The first of these is here in Lowtown. If you want the Zodiac Spear later, do *not* open the treasure chest right in front of Old Dalan's place.

Explore Lowtown

Before you head south to Giza, spend some time exploring Lowtown. Find treasure tucked into alleys (see this guide's South and North Sprawl maps) and talk to people to learn about Lowtown's sad history. You can also sell loot to either of Lowtown's Traveling Merchants (one in the northeast part of the North Sprawl and one in the South Sprawl's circular plaza) and stock up on extra Potions and Antidotes.

However, don't overspend on Potions if you have licensed and purchased the Cure spell. You'll need cash for weapon and armor upgrades, too. Make sure you also keep at least 80 gil in reserve so that you can make important purchases when you leave Lowtown.

 You can get cash for the loot you've acquired from treasure chests and enemies. In general, sell everything except Teleport Stones, which are useful for quick travel later in the game. You should note that all merchants in Ivalice will pay the same price for your loot, so it doesn't matter where you sell it.

Sell Your Loot!

Sell any loot you find to Lowtown's traveling merchants (or any merchant in Rabanastre) so you can afford to stock up on Potions and Antidotes before you hit the Giza Plains.

Return to Southgate via the freight door where you entered Lowtown, just around the corner from Old Dalan's. Let's pick up one or two more useful items for the road.

 BUY BAZAAR GOODS

Bazaar goods, available from merchants, can offer excellent value for the money. For example, packages of items that, when purchased individually, usually cost more. It's risky to buy mystery packages, of course, but bazaar items are usually worth it.

Obtain a Sunstone for Old Dalan

Buy a Map of Giza Plains

Maps are always good to have. Go north through the gate into the Southern Plaza and locate the Cartographers' Guild moogle in the yellow suit. You will find him pacing back and forth in the northwest alcove of the plaza. Talk to him to see what maps he has for sale. His maps for Giza Plains (30 gil) and Dalmasca Estersand (50 gil) are quite reasonably priced, so buy both. (The Westersand map is most likely out of your price range for now.) With the Giza Plains map now in the World Map collection, go south downstairs to Southgate and exit Rabanastre.

Buy a Giza Plains map from the Cartographers' Guild moogle in the Southern Plaza to make your upcoming trip a bit easier.

Giza Plains

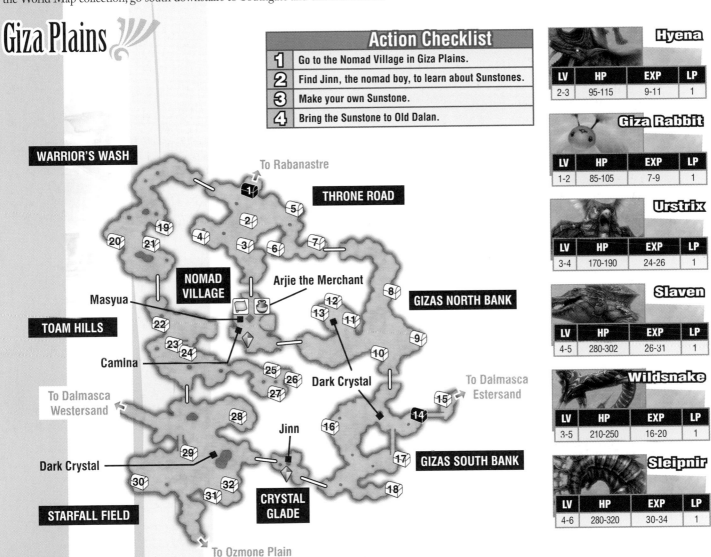

Action Checklist

1. Go to the Nomad Village in Giza Plains.
2. Find Jinn, the nomad boy, to learn about Sunstones.
3. Make your own Sunstone.
4. Bring the Sunstone to Old Dalan.

Hyena			
LV	HP	EXP	LP
2-3	95-115	9-11	1

Giza Rabbit			
LV	HP	EXP	LP
1-2	85-105	7-9	1

Urstrix			
LV	HP	EXP	LP
3-4	170-190	24-26	1

Slaven			
LV	HP	EXP	LP
4-5	280-302	26-31	1

Wildsnake			
LV	HP	EXP	LP
3-5	210-250	16-20	1

Sleipnir			
LV	HP	EXP	LP
4-6	280-320	30-34	1

TREASURE TABLE		Normal		w/Diamond Armlet Equip.		
No.	App.%	gil %	If gil 50%	50%	gil	90%	10%
1	100%	0%	--	Potion	Potion	--	Knot of Rust	Ether
2	72%	50%	~55	Potion	Antidote	~160	Knot of Rust	Ether
3	72%	50%	~55	Potion	Antidote	~160	Knot of Rust	Ether
4	72%	50%	~55	Potion	Potion	~160	Knot of Rust	Ether
5	72%	50%	~60	Potion	Potion	~170	Knot of Rust	Hi-Potion
6	72%	50%	~55	Potion	Antidote	~160	Knot of Rust	Hi-Potion
7	72%	50%	~55	Potion	Antidote	~160	Knot of Rust	Hi-Potion
8	70%	60%	~60	Potion	Eye Drops	~250	Knot of Rust	Ether
9	70%	60%	~70	Potion	Eye Drops	~250	Knot of Rust	Hi-Potion
10	70%	60%	~70	Potion	Ether	~250	Knot of Rust	Hi-Potion
11	67%	70%	~90	Potion	Remedy	~250	Knot of Rust	Hi-Potion
12	88%	70%	~50	Potion	Potion	~250	Knot of Rust	Hi-Potion
13	88%	100%	~100	--	--	~350	--	--
14	70%	30%	550	Potion	Ether	50000	Knot of Rust	Ether
15	85%	50%	~40	Potion	Dark Mote	~50	Knot of Rust	Hi-Potion
16	70%	50%	~80	Potion	Antidote	~300	Knot of Rust	Ether

TREASURE TABLE		Normal		w/Diamond Armlet Equip.		
No.	App.%	gil %	If gil	50%	50%	gil	90%	10%
17	70%	50%	~80	Potion	Ether	~300	Knot of Rust	Ether
18	65%	35%	~320	Potion	Broadsword	~600	Knot of Rust	Ether
19	75%	70%	~50	Potion	Cotton Shirt	~500	Knot of Rust	Ether
20	75%	35%	~70	Potion	Eye Drops	~500	Knot of Rust	Ether
21	75%	35%	~100	Potion	Potion	~1200	Knot of Rust	Hi-Potion
22	67%	45%	~50	Potion	Hi-Potion	~200	Knot of Rust	Hi-Ether
23	67%	45%	~80	Hi-Potion	Ether	~200	Knot of Rust	Hi-Ether
24	67%	45%	~50	Potion	Potion	~190	Knot of Rust	Ether
25	67%	45%	~50	Red Fang	Red Fang	~190	Knot of Rust	Hi-Potion
26	67%	45%	~80	Potion	Potion	~200	Knot of Rust	Ether
27	67%	45%	~50	Potion	Eye Drops	~190	Knot of Rust	Elixir
28	75%	70%	~50	Potion	Eye Drops	~290	Knot of Rust	Elixir
29	75%	30%	~80	Escutcheon	Eye Drop	~290	Knot of Rust	Hi-Potion
30	75%	50%	~60	Potion	Potion	~290	Knot of Rust	Ether
31	75%	66%	~70	Ether	Ether	~320	Knot of Rust	Hi-Potion
32	75%	50%	~70	Potion	Potion	~300	Knot of Rust	Ether

Find the Nomad Village

To find the village, you must travel south across the barren desert. The first area, Throne Road, is loaded with treasure urns, so fully explore the region. Look out for roving Hyenas and the occasional Giza Rabbit. (The bunnies are not aggressive, so you can ignore them if you want.) After plundering all of the treasures lying in the sand, head south to the next area, the Nomad Village.

Beware the hostile Hyenas that roam the southern sand.

Giza Rabbits are docile creatures. Sure they're cute, but if your health is good, whack bunnies for extra EXP, LP, and loot.

There is a blue Save Crystal tucked behind the big center tent in the village. Nearby, a nomad merchant named Arjie has sundry items for sale. Among these is the Bangle, an extremely useful accessory that equips the wearer with the technick Libra. This technick reveals critical information (Level, HP, weaknesses, etc.) about targeted enemies in the field. Remember that you must spend 15 LP to get the Bangle license, which is obtainable under "Accessories 2" on the license board.

Your fight across the desert earns you License Points. Use them! Buy the "Accessories 2" license so you can use a Bangle or "Swords 1" so you can wield a Broadsword.

License Up

Speak to the old woman in front of the central tent. Elder Brunoa speaks about dark crystals and Sunstones and directs Vaan to Masyua, who stands behind the tent. Speak to Masyua and listen to her proposition. She mentions Jinn, a missing child who carries a supply of the Shadestones needed to craft a Sunstone. Her offer: find Jinn and earn a Sunstone in return. Jinn was last seen south of the camp.

Stock up on necessary goods from Arjie, then speak to Masyua to learn your next objective: find Jinn.

The conversation with Masyua also triggers an event: Vaan finds Penelo with the children of the nomad camp. When the scene ends, Penelo joins your party. Speak to the nearby nomad youth, Camina. She says she saw Jinn in the Crystal Glade to the south.

Hey, Penelo's here! Now it's a party.

Now it's time to leave the village via the southwest exit into the Toam Hills. (Don't forget to replenish and save your game at the Save Crystal before you go!) On the way out, Penelo will hand over **3 Potions** and **2 Tufts of Phoenix Down**. Exiting the area also triggers the addition of party commands to your control of characters. Now you can issue specific commands to each party member, and change leaders if you want.

THE COLOR CODE

Even without specific target info (from a Bangle or the Libra technick), you can easily gauge a target's difficulty. When you select a target, the color of its name in the information window will indicate how tough it is. Blue is easy, yellow is formidable but not impossible, and red is *Run awaaaaay! Run awaaaaay!*

Gambits have also been added to the Battle Menu. Gambits are a powerful combat tool, so you will need to understand how they work and develop your own Gambit strategies for every situation. For now, all you can do is toggle them on or off for each character. Our advice: Toggle them on and leave them on. We'll talk more about Gambits later.

By now, you really should have purchased the Cure spell and its license, "White Magick 1". If you haven't, it is highly recommended that you return to Yugri's Magicks in Rabanastre and purchase it. Note that Penelo can use Cure when she joins your party.

Got Cure?

Find Jinn in the Crystal Glade

The party starts in the Toam Hills just west of the village, with the dagger-wielding Penelo following Vaan's lead. (You can make Penelo the leader if you want; just press up or down on the D-pad once to trigger Leader Select, then scroll to Penelo and press ✖ to select her.) Work your way around the area, fighting for EXP, LP, and loot.

It's a welcome change to have a partner who has your back, isn't it? Beware the huge Slaven, the Wildsnake, and the three-dog Hyena pack led by a powerful Alpha Hyena in the eastern extension of the Toam Hills. You can defeat them, but they're tough foes. Heal often! Exit to Starfall Field to the south.

⚡ PHOENIX RISING

Tufts of Phoenix Down raise KO'd characters. If either Vaan or Penelo drops, the other can use a Phoenix Down to revive the fallen ally. Remember that KO'd characters are also revived when you use a Save Crystal.

Now that Penelo's in the party, you can give her attack commands too. You can also switch Gambits on and off for each party member.

Killer Foes

Avoid the powerful Werewolves in the Starfall Field area near the dark crystal. They can KO Vaan or Penelo with a single strike.

In Starfall Field, continue to fight and hunt for treasure, but ensure that you work your way east and don't provoke the powerful Werewolves in the area. Note the "dark crystal" near the center of the area; it has absorbed sunlight and now radiates brilliantly. The eastern exit leads to the Crystal Glade, where you will find Jinn.

Vaan and Penelo are safe here, so you can wait to save your game at the blue Save Crystal until after you complete the conversation with Jinn, the nomad youth who sits next to the dark crystal in the clearing. Talk to him to learn that he has injured his leg. Explain the situation to Jinn and he hands over a **Shadestone** that you can turn into a Sunstone.

*Jinn can't walk very well, so he gives you a **Shadestone** to turn into a Sunstone.*

He explains that you must hold the Shadestone close to the big glowing crystals found in the Giza Plains. The Shadestone will absorb their energies and become a Sunstone. An Energy gauge appears in the upper-right corner to measure your progress. Finally, Jinn marks the dark crystals' locations on the area map, so press Select to see where all four are located.

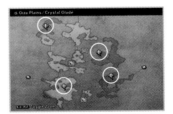

Jinn marks the locations of the four sun-filled dark crystals on the area map, as seen here.

Walkthrough

Make Your Shadestone into a Sunstone

You can visit the dark crystals in any order, but let's take an efficient, circular route that explores new territory (always fun) and runs right past the village Save Crystal at the halfway point. Exit the Crystal Glade east into Gizas South Bank.

Walk up to each glowing crystal and hold the Shadestone up to it.

The shimmering crystals are easy to find. Just walk up to each one, press ✕, and select the option to hold the Shadestone up to the crystal. The Energy gauge indicates what percentage of energy your Shadestone has gained from the transaction. After draining the Gizas South Bank crystal, head north and do the same to the crystal in the Gizas North Bank. Then go west to the Nomad Village and save your game.

Here's a good chance to upgrade your equipment. You should have built up some LP and gathered some loot from your battles, so visit

Keep upgrading your equipment when you get the chance. Remember that you can sell off older equipment, or pass it down to other party members.

Arjie. Sell your loot and see what she has available, including Bazaar items, then spend LP on any corresponding licenses needed to equip what you purchase. You can probably equip Vaan with a Broadsword by now. Get that Bangle licensed and equipped too, if you haven't already.

Now set out west into the Toam Hills again, but this time go north into Warrior's Wash to find and drain the third dark crystal into your Shadestone. Check the Energy gauge and if it hasn't yet reached 100 percent, you must head all the way south, back to Starfall Field, to drain the fourth and final shimmering crystal. Finally, you gain a Sunstone!

Upon reaching 100 percent, the scene automatically shifts to the Crystal Glade, where Jinn examines the Sunstone and pronounces it good. Then the scene shifts again to the Nomad Village where Masyua gives you generous gifts to go with your new Sunstone. Save your game again at this point and head north, back toward Rabanastre.

Jinn likes the Sunstone. Time to go home.

Bring the Sunstone to Old Dalan

Return to Rabanastre's Southgate district, go through the old freight door into Lowtown, and head for Old Dalan's place. As you approach, you trigger an event wherein Penelo leaves your party. Then enter and talk to Dalan, who uses the Sunstone to revitalize his Crescent Stone, then provides directions to the secret palace entrance. Finally, he hands over the **Crescent Stone**, which is used to open a hidden door to the Treasury.

Then he repeats the words: "The signet yearns for Sunstone's strength, to light the clouded way." A signet tile in the palace will light your path with help from the Crescent Stone.

Old Dalan hands over the **Crescent Stone** *and directions for a secret route into the palace.*

⚠ Wolf in the Waste

This is a good place to try hunting another mark. Check the Notice Board in the Sandsea and accept the next hunt listed—the one for Thextera. The petitioner, Gatsly, happens to be sitting on the floor right next to the board!

Thextera is in the Westersand, but the Galtea Downs area isn't too far into the desert. You should be strong enough to handle this by now. For more on this hunt, check out the "Side Quests" chapter in the guide.

SIDE QUEST

OBJECTIVE
Gain Entrance to the Palace

Garamsythe Waterway

World Map

Explore the Garamsythe Waterway to find the secret entrance to the palace.

Action Checklist

1 Reach the underground waterway via Storehouse 5.

2 Follow the waterway to the palace cellar.

Dire Rat

LV	HP	EXP	LP
4-5	212-232	54-56	1

Steeling

LV	HP	EXP	LP
4-5	218-234	57-61	1

Ichthon

LV	HP	EXP	LP
3-4	130-141	17-21	1

Garamsythe Waterway

To the Royal Palace / Cellar Stores

NORTH SPUR SLUICEWAY

NORTHERN SLUICEWAY

CENTRAL SPUR STAIRS

To Storehouse 5

OVERFLOW CLOACA

NO. 10 CHANNEL

TREASURE TABLE				Normal		w/Diamond Armlet Equip.		
No.	App.%	gil %	If gil	50%	50%	gil	90%	10%
1	65%	40%	~50	Potion	Potion	~300	Knot of Rust	Hi-Ether
2	65%	40%	~50	Hi-Potion	Antidote	~300	Knot of Rust	Float Mote
3	65%	40%	~50	Potion	Potion	~300	Knot of Rust	Hi-Ether
4	65%	40%	~50	Ether	Ether	~300	Knot of Rust	Float Mote
5	65%	40%	~50	Remedy	Antidote	~300	Knot of Rust	Hi-Ether
6	65%	40%	~50	Potion	Potion	~300	Knot of Rust	Float Mote
7	65%	45%	~40	Phoenix Down	Phoenix Down	~300	Knot of Rust	Remedy
8	65%	45%	~40	Hi-Potion	Ether	~300	Knot of Rust	Elixir
9	65%	45%	~40	Phoenix Down	Potion	~300	Knot of Rust	Hi-Ether
10	65%	30%	~75	Oak Staff	Potion	~300	Knot of Rust	Hi-Ether
11	65%	45%	~80	Main Gauche	Main Gauche	~300	Knot of Rust	Gold Needle
12	65%	65%	~80	Potion	Potion	~300	Knot of Rust	Vanishga Mote

Get into the Waterway

Use the Location Map to navigate to the flashing red 'X' up in the northwest corner of Lowtown and go through the doors of Storehouse 5 to where Kytes is awaiting. He opens the left waterway door for Vaan, then offers some **Potions** and **Eye Drops**. (This provides a good clue as to what you'll run into below; you might want to find a merchant and buy more Eye Drops.) Go through the left storehouse door to enter the Garamsythe Waterway.

Kytes gets you through the previously locked storehouse door into the waterway.

Find the Palace Entrance

You start in the Central Spur Stairs. Go west and save your game at the blue crystal, then continue up the stairs and around the corner into the next section, the Northern Sluiceway. Continue to move eastward along the corridors. The route is essentially linear, but it's worth checking every alcove for treasure. (Check the map in this section for possible treasure locations.)

It may seem like a maze, but the route through the waterway is fairly straightforward. Look for treasures tucked into alcoves.

The next area, the North Spur Sluiceway, features a tough enemy, a flying fish called the Ichthon. It's easy enough to defeat in a one-on-one battle, but a fight against two of them may be tough because of their multiple-hit attacks. Continue to the final stairway and select "Climb the stairs," then "It's now or never" to enter the palace.

Vaan's climb up the secret stairs triggers a short but spectacular visual introduction to two important characters.

As fireworks punctuate the palace fete, two mysterious strangers arrive via hover bike. Who are they?

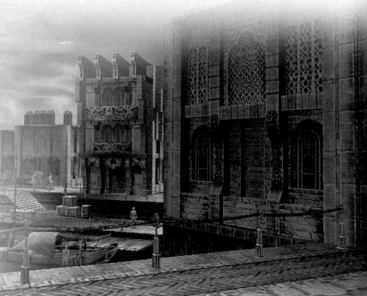

OBJECTIVE
Burgle the Palace Treasury

World Map

Royal Palace of Rabanastre

Walkthrough

Action Checklist

1. Sneak past the guard out of the palace cellars.
2. Maneuver past the maze of Imperial guards in the lower hallway.
3. Use the Crescent Stone on the signet tile.
4. Steal something valuable from the Treasury, then escape from the palace.

Your goal here is to break into the Treasury and "take back what's yours"… for Dalmasca, of course. Unfortunately, Imperial guards are everywhere, so you must use your wiles to sneak past them.

Royal Palace of Rabanastre

THE GARDEN STAIRS

Secret Panel

Switch

SECRET PASSAGE

CELLARS

Lion Signet

Hawk Signet

LOWER HALLS

CELLAR STORES

Map Urn

Start

= Guards (starting position)

TREASURE TABLE				Normal		w/Diamond Armlet Equip.		
No.	App.%	gil %	If gil	50%	50%	gil	90%	10%
1	90%	0%	--	Elixir	Elixir	--	--	--
2	90%	25%	90	Antidote	Antidote	--	--	--
3	90%	25%	100	Remedy	Remedy	--	--	--
4	90%	25%	90	Ether	Ether	--	--	--
5	90%	25%	90	Phoenix Down	Phoenix Down	--	--	--
6	90%	25%	90	Potion	Potion	--	--	--

81

Sneak Out of the Cellars

Open the nearby Map Urn to obtain a full map of the Palace, then save your game at the Save Crystal. Exit the room via the east doors to enter the Cellars, where you find palace workers scurrying about preparing for the fete.

Nab the palace map from the urn and save at the crystal.

> ### DON'T TOUCH THAT TREASURE: PART 2
>
> Here's the second treasure to let stand if you want access to the powerful Zodiac Spear later in the game. Do not open the treasure coffer(s) in the southeast corner of the Cellars.

While you're here, try to find all the treasure chests on both sides of the room for the loot they contain. When you reach the far (north) end of the room, two Imperials give harsh orders to the work crew, threatening to punish anyone who leaves the cellar too soon.

The seeq empathizes with your "hunger" and offers to distract the guard so you can sneak upstairs.

Try to go upstairs. The guard stops Vaan and a seeq palace servant notices the attempt. Go talk to him; he kindly offers to help out. When prompted, press ● to give a shout to the guard— "Hey, bucket head!!" When the guard reaches the seeq and starts talking, rush toward the opposite wall and follow it around to the staircase, then hurry upstairs to the next area, the Lower Halls.

Hurry! The guard is distracted by the seeq! Get up those stairs.

Find the Signet Tile and Maneuver Past the Hallway Guards

Refer to the numbers on the map for the following steps. To find the signet and use the Crescent Stone while eluding the Imperial guards, you need to move *very* precisely. One wrong turn and you could get caught, and have to start over.

From the starting point, walk directly east until you reach the Hawk Signet on the floor (marked as #1 on the map). Note that a pair of guards stands further down this corridor. Press ✖ to examine the signet, then try to use the Crescent Stone. Nothing happens.

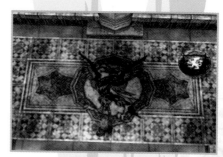

The Hawk Signet is gorgeous but doesn't respond to the Crescent Stone.

Take a few more steps toward the two guards and press ● to call them "bucket heads." Then quickly turn and run back west; turn left at the intersection, heading south. The guards leave their post and give chase as far as the intersection, but then halt and stay put. Turn left again at the next corner, heading east, and left again at the next corner to head north.

Stay on the left side of the hall while running north to the *second* left turn. Take it and go halfway up the hall until you reach the Lion Signet on the floor (see #2 on the map). Note the three guards at the far end of this corridor. Use the Crescent Stone here and it flashes light to a secret passage at the far end of this corridor. Aha!

The Lion Signet lights the way to the secret passage.

Turn around and go back to the intersection, then turn left and head north. At the last corner, turn left again to see the single guard at the far end. Go a little past halfway down the corridor (to #3 on the map), press ● to call the guard, then turn around and sprint away. Remember: Don't get too close to the Imperials!

Turn right at the corner and take the next right to return to the Lion Signet on the floor. Walk west past it a few steps (#4 on the map) and call the three guards. Turn and run away again by sprinting to the corner, turning right, and heading south.

The key is to lure guards down to the west end of the room to clear the path to the Lion Signet, then lure them all back the other way to clear the path to the secret passage.

Take the next right to move up the corridor past the Hawk Signet to #5 on the map and call to the guards at the far end of the hall and run away. The coast is clear to your final destination! Turn right at the next three corners to reach the long hallway running north and south up the west side of the hall. Follow it to the last corner and turn left (to #6 on the map).

Examine the "Faint Light" in the grating, then select "Approach the wall" to enter the secret passage. Oops— the passage door slides shut behind Vaan, locking him in.

Examine the "Faint Light" coming from this grate to gain entrance to a secret passage.

Find the Treasury

Go to the end of the hall and examine the wall on the left (south) side. A switch! Use the switch to unlock the "Suspicious-looking wall" on the opposite side of the hall. Examine the wall to open a secret panel and enter. This triggers an event in which Vaan browses through the Treasury and discovers a gem-like stone.

The two characters introduced earlier, Balthier and Fran, burst in and demand the stone. Vaan refuses to hand it over: "I found it! It's mine!" (Good logic.) It looks like a classic standoff between thieves, but Imperial intruders break up the party.

Escape the Palace via the Waterway

After an event, Vaan ends up at the foot of the Garden Stairs. Climb the stairs to trigger a wild event. A pitched battle is being fought outside! Vaan ends up "escaping" on a hover bike with Balthier and Fran, but they don't get far; the bike breaks down.

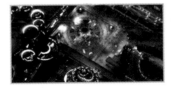 

Balthier comments again on the presence of the powerful Imperial airship, the *Ifrit*. He decides you need to escape "the old-fashioned way," on foot through the waterway. Thus Balthier, a hume sky pirate, and Fran, a viera, now join your party.

OBJECTIVE
Survive the Underground Waterway

World Map

Garamsythe Waterway

Action Checklist

1 Learn how to use the Gambit system.
2 Work through the waterway canals.
3 Pick up a "party guest" and defeat a powerful Imperial force.
4 Fight off a nasty Flan ambush.
5 Defeat Firemane, the game's first real boss.

Venture from the royal palace back to the city via the treacherous underground waterway, defeating deadly foes along the way.

Garamsythe Waterway

To the Royal Palace / Cellar Stores

NORTH SPUR SLUICEWAY

NORTHERN SLUICEWAY

EAST SPUR STAIRS

EAST WATERWAY CONTROL

CENTRAL SPUR STAIRS

To Storehouse 5

OVERFLOW CLOACA

Battle

CENTRAL WATERWAY CONTROL

NO. 10 CHANNEL

NO. 11 CHANNEL

Battle

WEST SLUICE CONTROL

SOUTHERN SLUICEWAY

EAST SLUICE CONTROL

Gigantoad

LV	HP	EXP	LP
5-6	341-361	131-133	1

Imperial Swordsman

LV	HP	EXP	LP
8-9	229-237	65-85	1

Flan

LV	HP	EXP	LP
6-7	280-294	200-207	1

Dire Rat

LV	HP	EXP	LP
4-5	212-232	54-56	1

Steeling

LV	HP	EXP	LP
6-7	282-298	88-92	1

Ghost

LV	HP	EXP	LP
5-7	328-340	136-142	1

Garchimacera

LV	HP	EXP	LP
4-6	287-317	125-137	1

Learn Gambits!

This is a different part of the waterway now: you start at the East Spur Stairs. Save your game at the Save Crystal nearby and head downstairs for a quick Gambit tutorial. Follow it carefully, and take note of Balthier's advice: "Vitality before violence." In general, you should put healing/repair gambits before fighting gambits in your task order. (Again, for a more in-depth look at Gambits, see the "Gambits" chapter in this guide.)

Here's a good opening arrangement of Gambit setups for your three party members. An alternate tactic is to flip-flop Vaan's gambits so his attack gambit is first and the Cure gambit second. That way, he focuses on inflicting damage while Fran and Balthier perform the healing. Note, however, you will have to manually choose the leader's target.

TREASURE TABLE			Normal		w/Diamond Armlet Equip.		
No.	App.%	gil %	If gil	50%	50%	gil	90%	10%
1	75%	30%	~45	Potion	Eye Drops	~300	Knot of Rust	Elixir
2	75%	30%	~45	Potion	Potion	~300	Knot of Rust	Elixir
3	75%	30%	~70	Hi-Potion	Hi-Potion	~500	Knot of Rust	Hi-Ether
4	80%	30%	~45	Potion	Ether	--	--	--
5	65%	30%	~50	Long Sword	Antidote	--	--	--
6	65%	30%	~80	Escutcheon	Escutcheon	--	--	--
7	70%	50%	~80	Leather Armor	Phoenix Down	--	--	--
8	80%	30%	~100	Potion	Eye Drops	--	--	--
9	100%	0%	--	Leather Shield	Hi-Potion	--	--	--
10	100%	0%	--	Dagger	Phoenix Down	--	--	--
11	100%	0%	--	Phoenix Down	Red Fang	--	--	--
12	73%	30%	~100	Potion	Phoenix Down	--	--	--
13	65%	35%	~200	Cotton Shirt	Phoenix Down	--	--	--
14	73%	30%	~400	Foe: targeting self	Potion	--	--	--
15	73%	30%	~300	Hi-Potion	Hi-Potion	--	--	--

After the tutorial, open the Party Menu and check out the party's Gambit setups. Vaan has only one gambit active; create a second one with the condition "Ally: HP<70%" and set the action to "Cure." Then turn that gambit on and move it up into the first slot, ahead of Vaan's attack gambit. Now Vaan will stop fighting and cast Cure on any ally (including himself) whose HP drops below 70 percent. Or, you could just leave the attack gambit first if you want Vaan to focus on fighting, leaving the in-battle healing to others in the party.

Open Balthier's Gambits and change the condition in his second one (an attack Gambit) to "Foe: party leader's target." In general, it's better to have your entire party focus one target at a time because concentrated attacks bring down foes more quickly.

Finally, open Fran's Gambits. Move the first gambit, "Attack the leader's target," down to the second slot. Then change the first slot so she casts Cure whenever an ally's HP drops below 70 percent.

These are just suggestions, mind you. Feel free to experiment with the order and type of gambits in the early going until you get a feel for how they actually work on the ground. And read the chapter in this guide on Gambits!

Move Down the Eastern Waterway

Now examine the fallen soldiers lying nearby. Balthier identifies them as anti-imperial insurgents who infiltrated the area, hoping the Imperial guard would be distracted by the palace fete. He speculates that Vayne used himself as bait to draw them in, then sent in his powerful air brigade led by the *Ifrit* to crush the resistance.

Look at the fallen soldiers to get Balthier's explanation of the night's hostilities.

Head down the waterway into the next area, the East Waterway Control. Turn left to nab the full waterway map from the Map Urn, then continue along the route. As in the west waterway, the eastern route is essentially linear, although there are a few treasures tucked into alcoves and dead ends. (Refer to the maps in this section for possible treasure locations.) Fighting rats and bats is much easier with Balthier's gun and Fran's bow backing up Vaan.

 USE RENEWABLE RESOURCES TO HEAL

Don't use Potions or Hi-Potions for healing unless you need a quick emergency boost of health, or if you've expended all your MP in the heat of battle. Since MP regenerates as you move around, use your party's Cure spells for healing as much as possible.

Continue south through the East Waterway Control into the No. 11 Channel. This is where the party encounters the Gigantoads, formidable Level 5 foes. If you have Libra active, however, you'll see that Gigantoads are weak against the Fire element, so open the Party Menu and set up a gambit to accommodate the situation.

Luckily, Fran can cast the Fire magick, so adjust her attack gambit so that when she targets an enemy, her action is Fire instead of Attack. After you finish off the four toads in the area, switch Fran's "foe" gambit back so its action is a regular Attack.

Switch Fran's Gambit sequence so she attacks with Fire magick instead of her normal bow-and-arrow attack. This will help against the Gigantoads, who are weak against the Fire element.

Upon reaching the East Sluice Control area, your general direction becomes west and, yes, there is a Save Crystal. Save your game and proceed down the stairs to trigger an event. Up ahead, Vaan and the party spot an approaching squad of Imperial soldiers chasing a woman in a red skirt—the same woman you saw earlier in the brief event in the waterway where the resistance forces were rallying for the palace assault.

The woman fights valiantly, but she's outnumbered four to one. The Imperials trap her on a ledge. Her doom looks imminent... until Vaan sprints out into the open, calling for her to jump. She does and Vaan catches her. Saved!

Naturally, the Imperial guard isn't too pleased with this turn of events. Here comes the first serious action against the Empire!

Defeat the Imperial Foursome

The area gates swing shut behind your party as the action begins; no retreat is possible. If your party's gambits are set as suggested earlier, though, you should have no problem with this fight. The woman joins your party in this fight, but she fights independently; you have no control over her.

The rebel woman fights independently, attacking whichever enemy is nearest.

One of the Imperial Swordsmen has a Protect spell cast, so save him for last. When the last enemy falls, the gates reopen followed by another event that introduces the woman as Amalia. Suddenly, the stone Vaan took from the palace treasury starts to glow. What is it?

Fran and Balthier want to move on immediately, so Vaan invites Amalia to join the party. When control returns to Vaan, the gates have reopened, so go back upstairs to the Save Crystal, heal up, and save your game. Then go back downstairs and approach Amalia to trigger one last event. She agrees to travel with the group... but only as a guest, which means you still have no control over her actions.

Fight Off the Flan Ambush

Continue pushing to the west and move into the Southern Sluiceway, which is a big open area just perfect for an ambush. Sure enough, as the party enters, four slimy Flan monsters surround the group. These nasty beasts cast Blind against your party, so prepare to use Eye Drops on anyone afflicted with the Blind status effect. All escape routes are sealed, so you must fight or die.

If you picked up an item called Red Fang, use it to deal Fire damage to all foes within its range. When timed correctly, you can nail all four Flans with one hit of Red Fang.

Red Fang the Flan

Although not technically a boss battle, this fight is long and tough enough that the game displays a congratulations screen when the last Flan finally melts into oblivion. Good work! Now it's time to move on.

The Flan ambush includes one slimy fellow who drops from the ceiling. Keep your eyes clear!

CLEAR YOUR EYES

Remember that Eye Drops will remove the Blind status effect.

This is a tough fight. The Flan beasts cast Cure on each other, so just when you think you've got a gelatin-head on the ropes it may suddenly get a health boost. Don't be dismayed if a party member gets KO'd, however. Just use a Phoenix Down to revive him/her along with a quick Potion to boost HP.

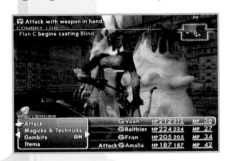

Flans are weak against Fire, so switch Fran's attack gambit action from Attack to Fire.

Get to the Waterway Exit

The passages open back up once you defeat the Flans, so backtrack to the East Sluice Control and use the Save Crystal again. Then go west two areas to the West Sluice Control and start heading northward from there. Watch out for some new enemies, the Ghost (weak against Cure magick) and the Garchimacera (weak against the Water element).

New enemies like the Garchimacera keep things interesting as you push through the underground.

Proceed through the No. 10 Channel until you reach the Central Waterway Control, a semicircular area with a set of four rusted, locked mechanisms used for operating sluice gates. There is also a handy Save Crystal near its north exit. Recharge and save, then go through the door that leads north into the Overflow Cloaca.

Walkthrough

Firemane

LVL	HP	EXP	LP
7	3571	0	3
Steal	Potion, Phoenix Down, Grimoire Togail		

The doors clang shut behind the party. That's never a good sign. Suddenly, a fireball blows into the room and changes into a flaming stallion: Firemane! This boss is weak against the Water element, but you do not have the Water spell at this point in the game, so just launch normal attacks. Do not let Fran attack with Fire magick!

Firemane's super attack is a blistering inferno called Bushfire that inflicts massive damage and sometimes Poison.

If you haven't done so already, you may want to move Vaan's attack gambit above his Cure gambit. All party members will spend a good portion of this battle with less than 70 percent of their normal HP, so Vaan may spend too much time curing and not enough time hitting Firemane with sword attacks.

From time to time, Firemane will teleport around the room so rotate the camera to locate his new position. Amalia is a very valuable ally in this fight; aside from her Potions and attacks, she also automatically uses a Phoenix Down whenever an ally gets KO'ed. So keep Amalia healthy with Cure and Potions if her HP gets too low. With good Cure gambits in place, you can outlast this boss without too much trouble.

The equine beast occasionally rears back and kicks out the powerful Bushfire attack that inflicts Poison in addition to dealing heavy damage. When an ally is poisoned, be quick to administer an Antidote.

Use Those Antidotes

Yes, the victory over Firemane is bittersweet, as Imperial troops under the direct command of Lord Vayne suddenly burst in and seize the entire party, including Amalia. As they are led away in chains, Amalia pleads for their release, but to no avail.

Penelo arrives at the scene and tries to reach Vaan, but Balthier steps into her path and gives her something to keep "just until I bring Vaan back." We also see a bangaa bounty hunter, angry at losing Balthier to the Imperials.

Then the scene fades to a flashback. Here's where the significance of the Galbana Lilies (the ones Vaan picked in the Estersand) is explained.

OBJECTIVE
Escape the Nalbina Dungeons!

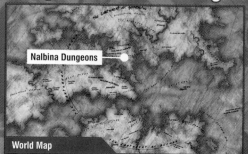

Nalbina Dungeons

World Map

Action Checklist

1. Defeat the three seeq prisoners in the Arena.
2. Fight through the Imperial watch to the magick-sealed door.

Find a way out of this godforsaken oubliette.

Nalbina Dungeons

- 14
- Magicked Door
- 13
- ARENA
- THE BLACK WATCH
- 12
- 11
- 10
- 5 7
- 6
- 9
- 8
- CONFISCATORY
- STOCKADE
- 2
- Battle
- 1
- 3
- 4

Imperial Hoplite			
LV	HP	EXP	LP
5	210	0	2

Imperial Magus			
LV	HP	EXP	LP
5	170	0	2

Imperial Marksman			
LV	HP	EXP	LP
5	180	0	2

Imperial Swordsman			
LV	HP	EXP	LP
5	190	0	2

Imperial Pilot			
LV	HP	EXP	LP
3-5	115-148	0	2

TREASURE TABLE				Normal		w/Diamond Armlet Equip.		
No.	App.%	gil %	If gil	50%	50%	gil	90%	10%
1	100%	0%	-	Knot of Rust	Knot of Rust	--	--	--
2	100%	0%	--	Knot of Rust	Knot of Rust	--	--	--
3	100%	0%	--	Knot of Rust	Knot of Rust	--	--	--
4	100%	0%	--	Knot of Rust	Knot of Rust	--	--	--
5	100%	0%	--	Tourmaline Ring	Tourmaline Ring	--	--	--
6	100%	100%	316	--	--	--	--	--
7	100%	0%	--	Foe: targeting leader	Foe: targeting leader	--	--	--
8	90%	0%	--	Knot of Rust	Aero Mote	--	--	--
9	90%	0%	--	Knot of Rust	Chromed Leathers	--	--	--
10	90%	0%	--	Knot of Rust	Knot of Rust	--	--	--
11	90%	0%	--	Knot of Rust	Ally: HP < 60%	--	--	--
12	90%	0%	--	Knot of Rust	Ether	--	--	--
13	90%	0%	--	Knot of Rust	Foe: targeting ally	--	--	--
14	90%	0%	--	Knot of Rust	Water Mote	--	--	--

Defeat the Seeq Prisoners

Vaan awakens from his dream about Reks to find himself in the infamous Nalbina Dungeons, with Balthier nearby. Not a pretty place—as Balthier explains, "It's not even a proper dungeon. They just sealed off the bottom half of the fortress." If you check your equipment and items, you'll find that you don't have any. The Imperials took your stuff!

Maybe you should just go back to sleep, old chap.

The dungeons are grim, but there is treasure to find… if you like **Knots of Rust**. Explore the Stockade area and search for chests. Each one contains a Knot of Rust. What good is a Knot of Rust? Actually, it makes a decent weapon, so grab all you can. Talk to

your fellow inmates while exploring the area, too. You'll hear a lot about some brutal fellow named Daguza. Important: *Save your game here at the Save Crystal before you go through the next doorway into the Arena!*

*Find the four treasure chests, each of which contains a **Knot of Rust**.*

First, an event shows some vicious seeq prisoners beating a helpless bangaa prisoner. When Vaan protests, he ends up in the Arena for a blood sport event pitting him, unarmed, against three massive, club-wielding seeq bosses. Luckily, Balthier joins the fray in the Arena with the taunt: "I said *you're* the one who stinks, hamshanks. Hear me now?"

Daguza, Galeedo, and Gwitch are three dim bulbs to be sure, but like all seeq they love a good fight. Give them what they want! Try to keep your distance at first (although it's kind of difficult to get separation in the tight arena) and fling a couple of precious Knots of Rust at either Galeedo or Gwitch to take down one of them quickly. Each knot deals a good 30 to 40 points of damage! Or, if you have

unlocked the Black Magick 1 license for Vaan or Balthier, light them up with Fire magick for massive damage. Remember that your gambits are still working, so Vaan's attack (assuming he's your leader) will focus Balthier's fists on that target too.

Sling rust at these bad boys to inflict good damage.

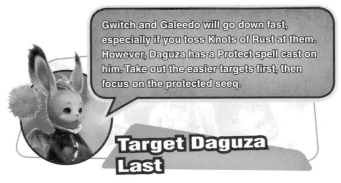

Gwitch and Galeedo will go down fast, especially if you toss Knots of Rust at them. However, Daguza has a Protect spell cast on him. Take out the easier targets first, then focus on the protected seeq.

Target Daguza Last

Remember that your magick and technicks are still available, so use Cure when either Vaan's or Balthier's HP drops below the halfway mark. If you're feeling lucky, try to steal from one of the seeq, but be careful!

A victory over the seeq triggers a long event in which a nasty green bangaa "headhunter" named Ba'Gamnan appears, looking for the sky pirate. It seems Balthier has a price on his head. Fran appears too; she's found a way out of the dungeons. But the magick sealing the exit door is too strong for her.

Vaan and Balthier slip underneath an exit gate just before an imposing new menace makes its appearance: an armored Archadian Judge. Judges are the elite guard and the enforcers of the laws of the Archadian Empire.

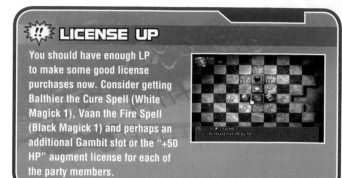

As the event ends, the bangaa headhunter Ba'Gamnan orders his minions to find the sky pirate. Balthier decides to follow the Judge, hoping the Imperials will unwittingly lead the party out of the dungeon.

Find the Dungeon Exit

The party ends up in the Confiscatory near a blue Save Crystal. Walk forward to trigger a short event where the party members recover all their lost items and equipment. The party also receives a handy map of the Nalbina Dungeons. Then save your game at the crystal.

Your stuff is in the Confiscatory, and you automatically get it all back, plus a map.

! DON'T TOUCH THAT TREASURE: PART 3

Here's the third treasure to let stand if you want access to the powerful Zodiac Spear later in the game. Do not open the treasure coffers in the Confiscatory after you recover your lost equipment.

! LICENSE UP

You should have enough LP to make some good license purchases now. Consider getting Balthier the Cure Spell (White Magick 1), Vaan the Fire Spell (Black Magick 1) and perhaps an additional Gambit slot or the "+50 HP" augment license for each of the party members.

Head east into the next area: the Black Watch. A brief event shows the door shutting behind your party and a quick overview of the Imperial-infested corridors up ahead.

There are a number of treasure coffers here, plus 14 patrolling Imperials. You can try to sneak through the watch, but it's probably better to fight your way through, as you will gain valuable EXP, LP, and loot. Plus you'll put together a Battle Chain, since all Imperial soldiers (e.g. Swordsman, Hoplite, Magus, Pilot, and Marksman) are considered the same "type." When a Battle Chain gets high enough, fallen foes may drop better items.

Plenty of Imperial-type soldiers patrol here, so you can string together a good-sized Battle Chain for better items.

Avoid going to the north-central part of the watch area until you've cleared out treasure and foes everywhere else. When you approach the hallway leading to the magicked door (see the map), you trigger an event. Balthier spots the Judge's party, including a mage, moving through the watch; your party silently follows them.

When the Judge's party reaches a sealed door, the mage casts a powerful spell that opens the passage. Thanks, buddy! When control of your party returns to you, lead them through the opening.

This triggers another event in which the party discovers a prisoner held in a brutal isolation chamber. The Judge speaks to him: the prisoner is Basch, former captain in the Order of the Knights of Dalmasca and the man who apparently assassinated the king. The Judge announces that the woman Amalia, a leader of the insurgence, is being brought from Rabanastre.

When the Judge leaves, Balthier leads your party out to the prisoner, Basch. When Balthier calls him a "kingslayer," Basch denies killing Raminas. Fran feels the Mist strongly in this room: "It must be going somewhere," she says. After Vaan vents his anger at Basch, Fran drops the cage and she and Balthier jump aboard.

After a fade to black, you see the cage shattered and Basch freed. Over Vaan's vehement objections, Balthier invites Basch to join the party, saying, "We could use another sword-arm." Basch joins as a guest. Again, this means that you have no control over his actions. You are now in the Barheim Passage.

OBJECTIVE
Navigate the Barheim Passage

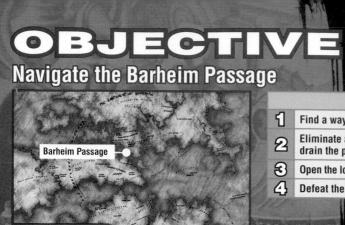

Barheim Passage ●

World Map

Use the tunnels of the Barheim Passage to escape from Nalbina Fortress out into the Estersand.

Action Checklist
1. Find a way into the Barheim Passage tunnels.
2. Eliminate all of the Battery Mimics trying to drain the power conduits.
3. Open the locked gate halfway down the passage.
4. Defeat the Mimic Queen.

Barheim Passage

Power Relay (Needs Fuse)

Gate Switchboard

THE LIGHTWORKS

Burrough

1 2 3

OP SECTOR 37

17 16 B 15 A 14 12 13 A

Gate Switch

OP SECTOR 29

4 A

5 6 A B

SPECIAL OP SECTOR 3

B

NORTH-SOUTH JUNCTION

7

⚡ = Power Conduit

B

GREAT EASTERN PASSAGE

9

10 8

C

11

OPS SECTOR 36

B A

D

GREAT CENTRAL PASSAGE

Locked Gate 18

19

20

22 A C

21 23 24 28

25

26

THE ZEVIAH SUBTERRANE

27 B

Locked Gate

Run through water here

TERMINUS NO. 4 ADJUNCT

Battle

TERMINUS NO. 4

To the Estersand

Tiny Mimic

LV	HP	EXP	LP
7-8	211-217	54-57	1

Tiny Battery

LV	HP	EXP	LP
6-7	120	76	1

Battery Mimic

LV	HP	EXP	LP
7	520	165	2

Zombie

LV	HP	EXP	LP
7-8	280-286	123-126	1

Mimic

LV	HP	EXP	LP
7-8	334-340	135-138	1

Bomb

LV	HP	EXP	LP
6-8	317-347	154-166	1

Seeker

LV	HP	EXP	LP
6-7	535-551	132-136	1

Flan

LV	HP	EXP	LP
6-7	280-294	200-207	1

Suriander

LV	HP	EXP	LP
8-9	410-430	200-202	1

Skeleton

LV	HP	EXP	LP
8-9	557-563	290-293	1

Skull Defender

LV	HP	EXP	LP
8-9	510-516	290-293	1

Steeling

LV	HP	EXP	LP
7-8	446-462	120-124	1

Specter

LV	HP	EXP	LP
8-9	402-408	209-212	1

Fire Up the Power Relay and Open the Gate

Things start out in the Lightworks. Go down the first flight of stairs and turn right into an alcove with three treasure coffers. Open all three to obtain a *lot* of gil. Continue down the next flight of stairs and turn left onto the short ramp that leads to the center column. There, press the switch located on the "Timeworn Device." Nothing happens and Balthier speculates that the fuse must be blown on this central power relay.

The power relay has blown a fuse. Check downstairs with Burrogh for a replacement.

Burrogh has a fuse plus a comprehensive store of equipment and other essential items. Do some shopping before going any further.

Continue downstairs. Go past the Save Crystal for now and talk to Burrogh, the bangaa sitting by the gate. He states that the collapsed cage (the one your party caused) blocked the easy way out of this passage. The only way out now is via the old Barhcim tunnels, which are currently blocked off by a giant gate. However, Burrogh does have something for the power relay; he hands over a "Tube Fuse."

Burrogh also happens to run a little side business, so sell him all your loot (*except* Teleport Stones), then check out his wares and upgrade if possible. Don't forget that you need a license to equip any weapons and armor you purchase. Perhaps the best thing to buy is the **Blizzard** spell; it will be very effective in some upcoming fights. (You need the Black Magick 1 license for Blizzard as well.)

When you're finished with business, go back upstairs and install the Tube Fuse in the power relay. A gauge appears in the right-hand corner of the screen indicating how much of the charge remains. Right now it's at 100 percent. Now save your game at the Save Crystal.

GOOD SPELLS

Blizzard is a *very* helpful Black Magick spell to have in the Barheim Passage. The elemental Ice damage it inflicts is quick and lethal against the Battery Mimics you must eliminate in the tunnels. Buy Blizzard from Burrogh and try to get it licensed for all three of your party members.

Buy Blindna and Poisona, too, then spend LP on their licenses if you can afford it. Whenever possible, you want the power to remove status effects with White Magick, which is renewable, rather than with items like Eye Drops or Antidotes, which can be used up.

Go down and try the Gate Switchboard on the wall next to Burrogh. If you replaced the fuse in the power relay, the gate opens and the charge drops to 70 percent. (If you didn't replace the fuse, the gate doesn't work.) Pay very close attention to what Burrogh says next. He explains that as long as the lights are on, the Barheim Passage isn't so bad. If the charge drops below 30 percent, though, "fierce beasts start comin' out in the dark." Also, if the power drops below 50%, Zombies and Skeletons will appear. If it drops below 30%, Specters and Skull Defenders will emerge. There's even a chance that the Battle Mimics will respawn if the gauge is between 31-50%.

Good news: the gate opens. Bad news: the charge drops to 70 percent.

This is very, very true. The entities that arise in the darkness will overwhelm your party very quickly. Therefore, it is essential that you keep the lights on. Unfortunately, annoying spider-like creatures known as Battery Mimics roam the passages, feeding on energy conduits and draining power from the system. The party's next task is to eliminate these pests to keep the charge above 30 percent. To get started, head through the gate into Op Sector 29.

No.	App.%	gil %	If gil 50%	Normal 50%		w/Diamond Armlet Equip. gil	90%	10%
1	100%	100%	~333	-	-	~5000	-	-
2	100%	100%	~555	-	-	~5000	-	-
3	100%	100%	~777	-	-	5000	-	-
4	80%	30%	~300	Onion Arrows	Onion Arrows	~300	Knot of Rust	Hi-Ether
5	80%	30%	~150	Eye Drops	Antidote	~200	Knot of Rust	Hi-Ether
6	80%	30%	~100	Phoenix Down	Antidote	~200	Knot of Rust	Hi-Ether
7	80%	25%	~150	Antidote	Antidote	~1000	Knot of Rust	Hi-Ether
8	80%	25%	~200	Potion	Onion Shot	~1000	Knot of Rust	Hi-Ether
9	80%	25%	~200	Potion	Ally: HP < 40%	~1000	Knot of Rust	Hi-Ether
10	80%	25%	~200	Potion	Ether	~1000	Knot of Rust	Hi-Ether
11	80%	25%	~100	Remedy	Remedy	~1000	Knot of Rust	Hi-Ether
12	90%	5%	~650	Potion	Onion Arrows	~2000	Knot of Rust	Elixir
13	90%	50%	~350	Potion	Phoenix Down	~650	Knot of Rust	Elixir
14	80%	30%	~200	Potion	Headgear	~500	Knot of Rust	Warp Mote
15	80%	20%	~200	Phoenix Down	Buckler	~500	Knot of Rust	Warp Mote
16	80%	20%	~100	Potion	Leader	~500	Knot of Rust	Warp Mote
17	60%	35%	~500	Mage Masher	Mage Masher	~1200	Knot of Rust	Warp Mote
18	83%	70%	~100	Potion	Leather Helm	~800	Knot of Rust	Elixir
19	83%	20%	~320	Potion	Echo Herbs	~800	Knot of Rust	Elixir
20	83%	25%	~190	Potion	Foe: HP ≥ 50%	~800	Knot of Rust	Elixir
21	77%	30%	~100	Potion	Light Woven Shirt	~500	Knot of Rust	Hi-Ether
22	77%	30%	~70	Phoenix Down	Hi-Potion	~400	Knot of Rust	Hi-Ether
23	77%	30%	~90	Potion	Ether	~400	Knot of Rust	Elixir
24	77%	30%	~180	Water Mote	Antidote	~550	Knot of Rust	Hi-Ether
25	77%	30%	~150	Phoenix Down	Phoenix Down	~500	Knot of Rust	Hi-Ether
26	77%	30%	~120	Potion	Self	~600	Knot of Rust	Elixir
27	85%	15%	~560	Phoenix Down	Oaken Pole	~1800	Knot of Rust	Scathe Mote
28	60%	30%	~200	Potion	Hi-Potion	~660	Knot of Rust	Hi-Ether

Stop the Mimics from Draining Power in Northern Barheim

Two shimmering Battery Mimics lurk in the next area. Balthier provides a quick lesson on the creatures and warns you to stop them from feeding on the power conduits. There are two conduits in Op Sector 29. Refer to the map in this section for their locations, or locate the flashing icons on the area map.

 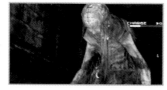

The Battery Mimic will suck power right out of the system if you give it a chance. Knock out this foe before it can drain power to below 30 percent—otherwise, ghastly fiends will arise.

Rush to attack Battery Mimic A, which is feeding on the conduit (see callout "A") just ahead. A second one, Battery Mimic B, scurries away as you attack. It is heading for another conduit downstairs, but let it go for now. Instead, focus your attention on the first Battery Mimic. A Zombie staggers into the fray, but remain focused on the task at hand.

> **Battery Mimics are weak against the Ice element. Sling Blizzard magicks at mimics to take them down fast.**

Ice the Mimics

As soon as the first Mimic gets knocked out, press and hold the R2 button and hurry through the doorway. Sprint downstairs, ignoring any other creature that approaches along the way. Battery Mimic B is greedily draining energy from another conduit (see callout "B"),

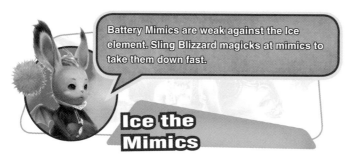

so you need to stop it fast. When you reach the foe, hit it with Blizzard. Once Battery Mimic B goes down, the power charge will stabilize and you can take a bit of time to mop up Op Sector 29.

Just ignore the Zombies and Tiny Mimics until both Battery Mimics in Op Sector 29 are eliminated.

After eliminating all of the monsters and finding the treasures, move into the next section, the Great Eastern Passage. Check the area map to see the four power conduits located in this long sector. Two more Battery Mimics hunker just ahead; as you approach them, one feeds on the nearby conduit (see callout "A") while the other hurries off down the tunnel.

As before, eliminate Battery Mimic A, then press and hold the R2 button and "flee" down the long passage looking for Battery Mimic B, ignoring other creatures for now. When you arrive at the fork in the tunnel, veer up the right fork to find Battery Mimic B gorging on yet another power conduit (callout "B"). After you knock out this mimic, note that a Map Urn rests just below the party, cut off by the break in the tracks.

Retrace your path to the tunnel fork, find the treasure chest in the nearby alcove, then take the other (left) fork in the path. (Or go back north up the tracks and dispose of all the baddies you ignored earlier.) At the next split, take the right fork; you run smack into Battery Mimic C.

After hitting Mimic C, it runs past and down the left fork to another dead-end power conduit (see callout "C"). Chase it down, once you knock it out, return to the split and take a hard left to go southwest.

Don't miss this Map Urn located up one of the side spurs.

Continue until you can curve around a corner to the right and head northeast. This leads back to the Map Urn, plus another treasure hidden in an alcove. At last, a full map of the area! The map reveals one more conduit (see callout "D") here in the Great Eastern Passage, so head down the tracks toward it. Find and defeat Battery Mimic D to wrap up this area.

A door next to the conduit leads west to Op Sector 36. This area is optional, actually; you can skip it if you want, but why would you pass up a chance to knock around more Mimics? There are two more Battery Mimics here feeding at two more conduits—one

upstairs (see callout "A") and one downstairs (see callout "B"). Nail them both, mop up the little spiders, and return to the Great Eastern Passage. Finally, continue south into Special Op Sector 3.

Two more Battery Mimics feed in Op Sector 36. Teach them how power corrupts.

Open the Gate in Central Barheim

You must still find and squash hungry Battery Mimics in the central part of Barheim Passage, so don't forget about that. But you also find a locked gate barring southern passage through Special Op Sector 3. Battery Mimic B will meander to the conduit to the south (see callout "B"), so quickly cast Blizzard on it.

Two Flan creatures block passage into the west chamber of Special Op Sector 3 where a Battery Mimic is draining power. Hit them with Fire spells for quick disposal.

Hurry west toward the next room. Two creepy Flan foes drop into your path; flame-broil them with Fire spells. (Just two shots of Fire should be enough to melt each one.) Then continue downstairs. Another Flan drops in, so dispose of it, then find Battery Mimic A munching away on the electric grid. Cast Blizzard on this fellow. When he drops, explore the area for treasure chests.

Now climb the stairs (watch out for another Flan!) to another doorway that leads to a new area called Op Sector 37. You're looking for a Gate Switch to open that big southern gate, but two more Battery Mimics are feeding in here. One is just inside the entryway to the left (see callout "A" on the Op Sector 37 map) but the other one is downstairs, and another Flan drops from the ceiling to block your path. Fry him quickly and then move through the back hallway to find and eliminate Battery Mimic A.

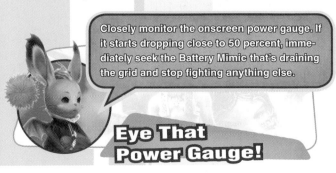

Closely monitor the onscreen power gauge. If it starts dropping close to 50 percent, immediately seek the Battery Mimic that's draining the grid and stop fighting anything else.

Eye That Power Gauge!

After this beast falls, go around the corner heading west and climb up to the Gate Switchboard, burning the pair of Flans that drop in your path. Press the switch to open the gate back in Special Op Sector 3. Nab the treasure just down the corridor, then return to Special Op Sector 3 and move south (through the now-open gate) to the next area, the North-South Junction, to trigger a very interesting event.

Find this gate switchboard in the extreme northwest corner of Op Sector 37 to open the gate back in Special Op Sector 3.

This is where you learn what really happened in the room where King Raminas died. Basch's twin brother, the very same Archadian Judge we saw earlier in the Nalbina Dungeons, engineered the assassination trap and framed Basch. And it was his twin, and not Basch, who put the blade to Vaan's brother, Reks, as well. Complicated? Certainly. But as Balthier says, "The pieces certainly fit."

Vaan is not convinced, but there's no time to debate the past now. Current events are far too perilous. And, as the glib Balthier puts

it: "What's done is done." It's time to move on and leave these dank, dangerous tunnels. However, there is some good news for the team: Basch has picked up a sword and now deals more damage than before.

Before you take a step further, use the Save Crystal in the North-South Junction, then continue south into the next area, the Great Central Passage.

Stop the Mimics in Southern Barheim

Yes, more hungry Battery Mimics lurk in the southernmost four areas of the Barheim Passage. But only one feeds on power in the Great Central Passage; it's just up ahead on the left. Nail him immediately.

Beware of any treasure you find in this area, though. Some Mimics disguise themselves as treasure coffers. It doesn't get any lower than that, so make them pay. These Mimics are weak against Wind damage, but chances are good you haven't purchased Aero (a Wind spell) yet, so save your MP and take them down with conventional attacks.

Some sneaky Mimics disguise themselves as treasure in the southern regions of Barheim. What treachery!

You can't get through the locked gate to the west right now, so continue south down the passage to the next area, the Zeviah Subterrane.

![!] **West Gate to Zalera**

The locked gate on the west wall of the Great Central Passage leads to the Esper Zalera later in the game. It's the final portion of a very long side quest. You can't reach this area until the party obtains the Barheim Key and finds the secret entrance in the Dalmasca Estersand's Murmuring Defile area. For more on this, see the Zalera section in our "Side Quests" chapter.

SIDE QUEST

The Zeviah Subterrane is a large area with three power conduits, each with a power-draining Battery Mimic. More of those annoying Tiny Mimics harass the party, as well as Surianders, huge toad-like creatures. Don't get distracted from your primary task, though. If you let even one Battery Mimic drain the power gauge below 50 percent, Skeletons and Skull Defenders will rise in pairs from the ground. Stay completely focused on finding the three feeding Mimics.

Don't let Tiny Mimics distract you from the task of protecting the conduits.

Battery Mimic A lunges at the party the moment they enter the Zeviah Subterrane, so this one should be easy to knock out quickly. The next one, Battery Mimic B, feeds on a conduit just ahead to the left. But the third Battery Mimic is a bit further away, up the tunnel to the northeast (see callout "C" on the Zeviah Subterrane map).

Like Battery Mimics, the Suriander is weak against the Ice element, so cast Blizzard for a quick defeat.

After eliminating all three Battery Mimics, retrace your route through the area, clear out any enemies and take any treasure. Then return to the northeast passage and proceed into the Terminus No. 4 Adjunct to find a Save Crystal. Prepare for a boss fight! If any of your characters can cast Protect, do so on all members of your party. When you're ready, save your game and rush into the next area, Terminus No. 4.

Mimic Queen

LVL	HP	EXP	LP
10	4073	0	5
Steal	Knot of Rust, Storm Magicite, Rose Corsage		

During this battle, it's best to ignore the smaller Tiny Batteries and focus solely on the queen. Her minions will feed on power and the charge will drop. Don't worry about that, though; the moment the Mimic Queen falls in defeat, the battle ends, so keep your attacks concentrated on her.

The Mimic Queen thrives on electricity, so do not cast Thunder spells as she absorbs lightning. However, she is weak against Blizzard's Ice damage. Don't overdo it, since you want to save some MP for Cure spells. Nine or 10 Blizzard hits should knock down the Mimic Queen's HP to about halfway, but your characters' MP will start to dwindle.

The Queen doesn't like ice, so give it to her. Standard weapon attacks inflict good damage too.

Regular attacks work quite well too, but make sure two of your three party characters (preferably those with ranged weapons) have gambits that heal anyone with HP<70 percent or even HP<50 percent first, with their attack gambits slotted second.

Basch, your guest character, is very effective during this fight, so keep him healed up. When you finally destroy the Mimic Queen, your party automatically escapes from the Barheim Passage out into the Dalmasca Estersand.

OBJECTIVE
Return to Rabanastre

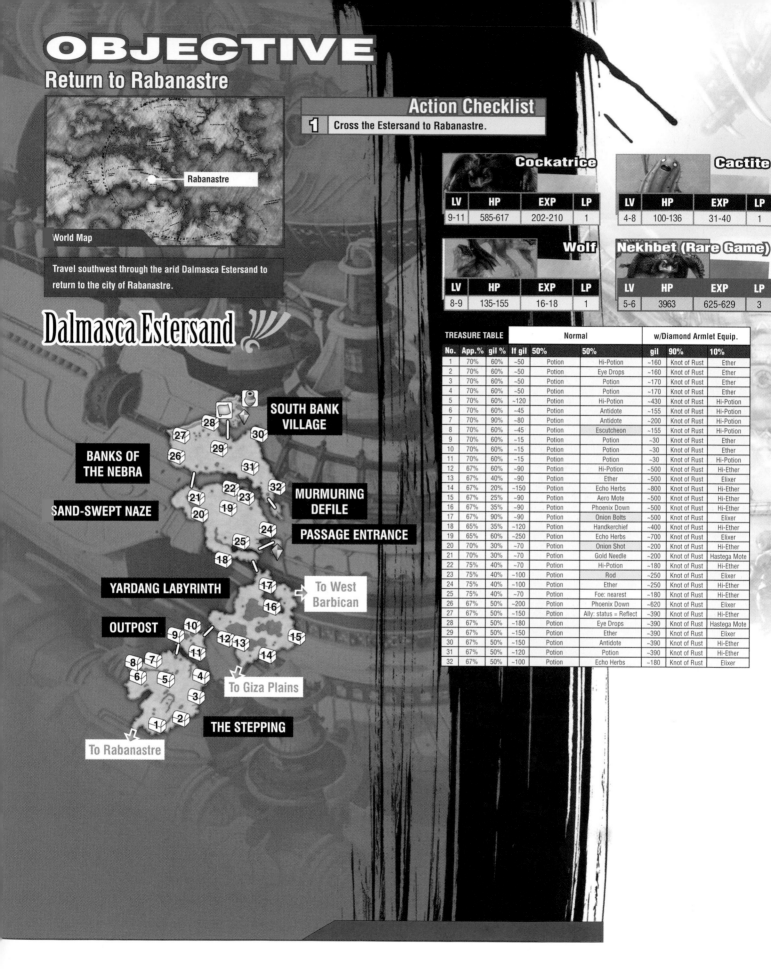

Rabanastre

World Map

Travel southwest through the arid Dalmasca Estersand to return to the city of Rabanastre.

Dalmasca Estersand

Action Checklist

1 Cross the Estersand to Rabanastre.

Cockatrice

LV	HP	EXP	LP
9-11	585-617	202-210	1

Cactite

LV	HP	EXP	LP
4-8	100-136	31-40	1

Wolf

LV	HP	EXP	LP
8-9	135-155	16-18	1

Nekhbet (Rare Game)

LV	HP	EXP	LP
5-6	3963	625-629	3

TREASURE TABLE

No.	App.%	gil %	If gil	Normal 50%	Normal 50%	w/Diamond Armlet Equip. gil	w/Diamond Armlet Equip. 90%	w/Diamond Armlet Equip. 10%
1	70%	60%	~50	Potion	Hi-Potion	~160	Knot of Rust	Ether
2	70%	60%	~50	Potion	Eye Drops	~160	Knot of Rust	Ether
3	70%	60%	~50	Potion	Potion	~170	Knot of Rust	Ether
4	70%	60%	~50	Potion	Potion	~170	Knot of Rust	Ether
5	70%	60%	~120	Potion	Hi-Potion	~430	Knot of Rust	Hi-Potion
6	70%	60%	~45	Potion	Antidote	~155	Knot of Rust	Hi-Potion
7	70%	90%	~80	Potion	Antidote	~200	Knot of Rust	Hi-Potion
8	70%	60%	~45	Potion	Escutcheon	~155	Knot of Rust	Hi-Potion
9	70%	60%	~15	Potion	Potion	~30	Knot of Rust	Ether
10	70%	60%	~15	Potion	Potion	~30	Knot of Rust	Ether
11	70%	60%	~15	Potion	Potion	~30	Knot of Rust	Hi-Potion
12	67%	60%	~90	Potion	Hi-Potion	~500	Knot of Rust	Hi-Ether
13	67%	40%	~90	Potion	Ether	~500	Knot of Rust	Elixer
14	67%	20%	~150	Potion	Echo Herbs	~800	Knot of Rust	Hi-Ether
15	67%	25%	~90	Potion	Aero Mote	~500	Knot of Rust	Hi-Ether
16	67%	35%	~90	Potion	Phoenix Down	~500	Knot of Rust	Hi-Ether
17	67%	90%	~90	Potion	Onion Bolts	~500	Knot of Rust	Elixer
18	65%	35%	~120	Potion	Handkerchief	~400	Knot of Rust	Hi-Ether
19	65%	60%	~250	Potion	Echo Herbs	~700	Knot of Rust	Elixer
20	70%	30%	~70	Potion	Onion Shot	~200	Knot of Rust	Hi-Ether
21	70%	30%	~70	Potion	Gold Needle	~200	Knot of Rust	Hastega Mote
22	75%	40%	~70	Potion	Hi-Potion	~180	Knot of Rust	Hi-Ether
23	75%	40%	~100	Potion	Rod	~250	Knot of Rust	Elixer
24	75%	40%	~100	Potion	Ether	~250	Knot of Rust	Hi-Ether
25	75%	40%	~70	Potion	Foe: nearest	~180	Knot of Rust	Hi-Ether
26	67%	50%	~200	Potion	Phoenix Down	~620	Knot of Rust	Elixer
27	67%	50%	~150	Potion	Ally: status = Reflect	~390	Knot of Rust	Hi-Ether
28	67%	50%	~180	Potion	Eye Drops	~390	Knot of Rust	Hastega Mote
29	67%	50%	~150	Potion	Ether	~390	Knot of Rust	Elixer
30	67%	50%	~150	Potion	Antidote	~390	Knot of Rust	Hi-Ether
31	67%	50%	~120	Potion	Potion	~390	Knot of Rust	Hi-Ether
32	67%	50%	~100	Potion	Echo Herbs	~180	Knot of Rust	Elixer

SOUTH BANK VILLAGE

BANKS OF THE NEBRA

SAND-SWEPT NAZE

MURMURING DEFILE

PASSAGE ENTRANCE

To West Barbican

YARDANG LABYRINTH

OUTPOST

To Giza Plains

To Rabanastre

THE STEPPING

Cross the Desert to Rabanastre

The party starts in the Passage Entrance area just outside the Barheim Passage. Use the Save Crystal and move west into the Sand-Swept Naze. The Naze is a big area with plenty of treasures and enemies, although most of the foes will seem weak after what you faced in Barheim.

One foe is *very* tough, though—a rare beast named Nekhbet. A full party of four can defeat him, but it's by no means easy. The beast casts Slow, a status effect that you can only remove with a Remedy at this point, since you don't have the Haste spell yet. When Nekhbet finally falls, you receive plenty of EXP and LP, so it's worth the effort.

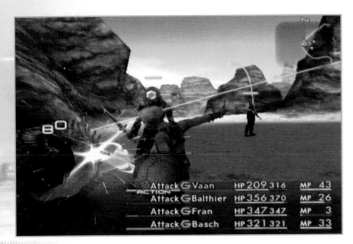

Look for Nekhbet in the Sand-Swept Naze. He resembles a normal Cockatrice, but he's incredibly tough.

The next area to the south is the Yardang Labyrinth. Explore it fully for more treasure and easy fights (Wolves and Cockatrices, mostly) to build up LP. You may encounter a random bangaa hunter roaming the sands too. The green bar above his head indicates that he is non-hostile and the fact that you can't target him outright indicates that he is an "ally." Although you can attack him by selecting Attack from the battle menu and cycling through the target types using the L1 or R1 buttons, it's in your best interest to let him be. NPC allies will occasionally cast beneficial spells on your party and help fight enemies. Continue southwest through the Outpost into The Stepping, the area where you defeated the Rogue Tomato.

The bangaa hunter wandering the desert is entirely neutral; you can target him by selecting battle/attack and pressing the R1 button twice. Note, though, that the bangaa is listed under the header "Allies."

The mighty Wild Saurian still paces in the northern part of The Stepping, and you should carry on avoiding him for now, as he's a level 34 beast. You can fight the Wolves and Cactites, though. At this point, you can decimate them with a single swing of the sword, so you can accrue LP quickly while moving across the desert.

You probably still can't defeat the Wild Saurian, but with the Bangle you can see his awesome Level 34 stats.

Upon reaching Rabanastre, the party splits up. Basch thanks the team and promises to pay his respects to Vaan's brother. Then Fran and Balthier take their leave too, warning you to lay low for a while. They plan to stay in Rabanastre for some time.

Vaan wonders if he can trust Basch and decides he should get rid of the glowing stone he stole from the Royal Treasury. He wants to show it to Penelo first, though, who should be at Migelo's place this time of day.

OBJECTIVE
Make the City Rounds

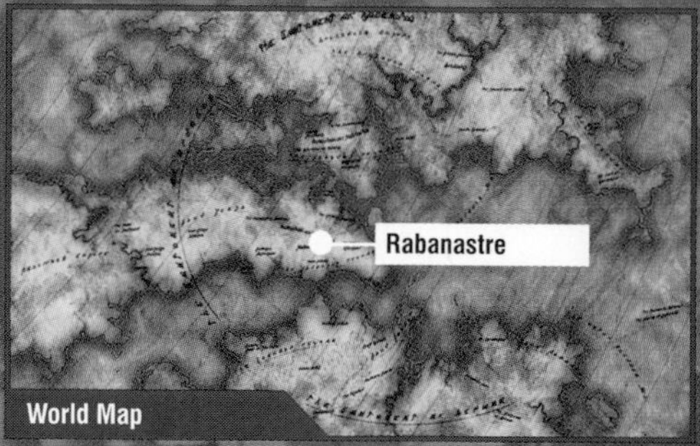

World Map

Rabanastre

Action Checklist

1 Visit Migelo's.
2 Visit Old Dalan and make a delivery for him.
3 Find Balthier and Fran.
4 Go to the Aerodrome.

Vaan wants to show Penelo and Old Dalan the glowing stone he pilfered from the Treasury. But Penelo is missing and Old Dalan sends Vaan on a mysterious errand that leads to a "reunion party."

Rabanastre

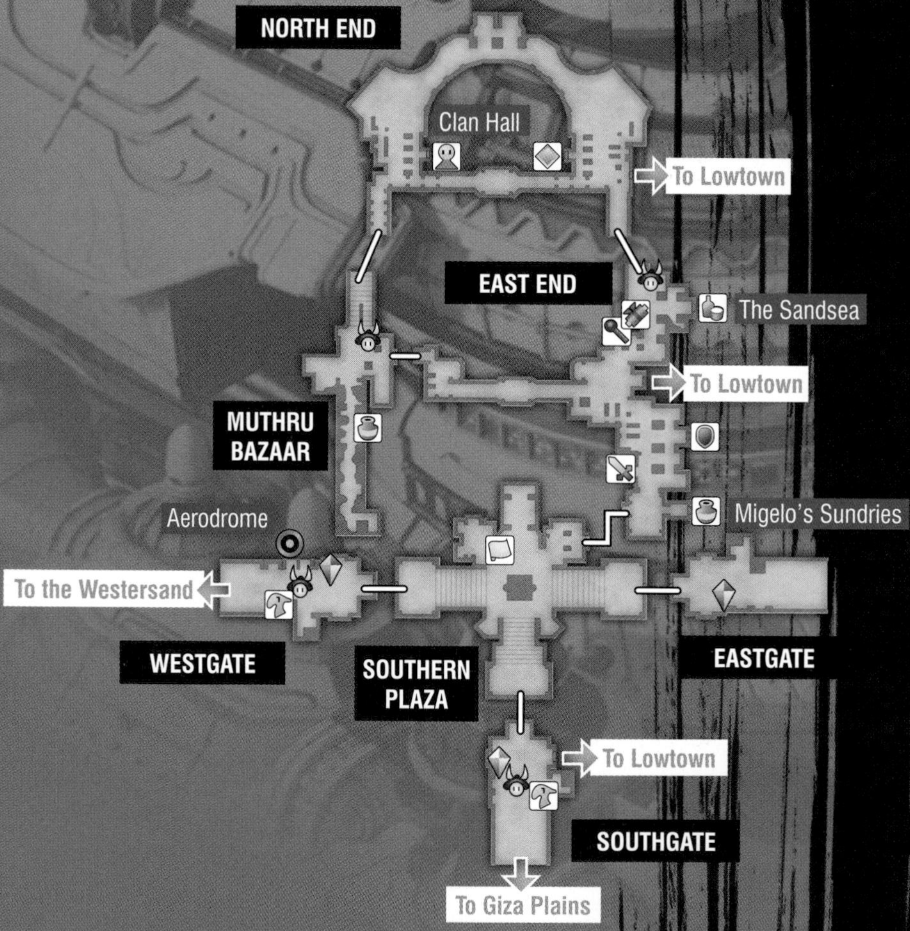

NORTH END

Clan Hall

To Lowtown

EAST END

The Sandsea

To Lowtown

MUTHRU BAZAAR

Migelo's Sundries

Aerodrome

To the Westersand

WESTGATE

SOUTHERN PLAZA

EASTGATE

To Lowtown

SOUTHGATE

To Giza Plains

Visit Migelo's and the Clan Hall

Kytes hasn't seen Penelo, but he says Old Dalan needs errands run. Vaan offers to go see the old man.

The party has disbanded, leaving Vaan all alone. Head up to East End and drop into Migelo's Sundries to trigger an event. Kytes tells Vaan that neither Penelo nor Migelo are around; he also says Old Dalan has an errand to run. Vaan volunteers to run the errand for Kytes, marking a new destination on the area map: Old Dalan's place in Lowtown.

Before you go, sell any loot that you've accumulated and stock up on items that are low in your inventory. Make sure to build a small stock of the new items available (**Echo Herbs** [to remove Silence status] and **Gold Needles** [to remove Stone/Petrify status]). Exit and visit Montblanc in the Clan Hall on the North End to receive rewards for any recent bosses you've defeated. Lastly, go visit other local merchants to see what they have for sale now.

Visit Montblanc at the Clan Hall to receive rewards for defeating the pack of Flans, Fircmanc, and the Mimic Queen.

Always visit the Clan Hall whenever you return to Rabanastre from your latest adventure. Montblanc offers rewards for any bosses or rare game you've defeated.

Montblanc's Largesse

When you're finished shopping (or window-shopping, as the case may be), head down to visit Old Dalan in Lowtown.

> **!! BE A SMART BUYER**
>
> Unless you've been overly active about acquiring loot and LP by obsessively revisiting areas you've already cleared, your resources may be limited at this point in the game, so spend carefully on equipment.
>
> Remember that all party members can share certain purchases with the associated licenses, including those who join up later (except guests). For example, all party members can use licensed magicks and technicks, once purchased. In addition, all party members can use any of the gambits you buy, so you can be somewhat thrifty in this area.

Lowtown

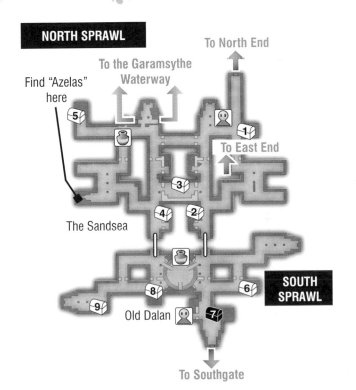

NORTH SPRAWL

To North End

To the Garamsythe Waterway

Find "Azelas" here

To East End

The Sandsea

Old Dalan

SOUTH SPRAWL

To Southgate

Visit Old Dalan and Make His Delivery

Talk to Old Dalan to trigger an event. Vaan shows Dalan the stone, then the old man sends him on an errand. He wants Vaan to deliver a sword to someone named Azelas. Dalan marks his location on the area map; the red "X" isn't far away, just up in the North Sprawl of Lowtown. Vaan asks Old Dalan to help him find out where Penelo is and the old man agrees.

Old Dalan wants Vaan to deliver a Sword of the Order to Azelas in the North Sprawl.

TREASURE TABLE			Normal		w/Diamond Armlet Equip.		
No.	App.%	gil %	If gil 50%	50%	gil	90%	10%
1	70%	50%	~30 Potion	Eye Drops	~100	Knot of Rust	Ether
2	70%	50%	~20 Red Fang	Phoenix Down	~100	Knot of Rust	Hi-Ether
3	70%	50%	~30 Potion	Potion	~200	Knot of Rust	Ether
4	70%	50%	~30 Potion	Antidote	~100	Knot of Rust	Ether
5	70%	50%	~70 Potion	Potion	~350	Knot of Rust	Ether
6	70%	50%	~40 Potion	Antidote	~150	Knot of Rust	Ether
7	100%	50%	~100 Potion	Eye Drops	~200	Knot of Rust	Ether
8	70%	50%	~30 Potion	Potion	~100	Knot of Rust	Ether
9	70%	50%	~60 Potion	Potion	~250	Knot of Rust	Hi-Ether

Follow the path to the "X" on the map and locate a man named Balzac sitting on a crate. Speak to him and he lets you into a secret Resistance hideout. Inside, men argue about the King's assassination. Then Basch emerges… in his Dalmascan uniform. After the event, Basch joins your party.

As Vaan and Basch exit, Basch asks Vaan to take him to Balthier to acquire "wings." Vaan agrees. Basch now joins your party.

Basch joins with some nice equipment and licenses, plus a lot of LP to spend. However, he starts with no shield. Give him one right away if at all possible, or buy one at Panamis's Protectives.

Shield Basch

Back to Rabanastre

Find the Sky Pirate

The map screen provides a clue, pondering where a "tired, thirsty sky pirate" might go in Rabanastre. Answer: The Sandsea, of course! While approaching the tavern, an event occurs during which

Vaan talks about the war orphans in the streets… and his own past.

Vaan tells Basch about losing his parents to the Plague and describes his sibling-like connection to Penelo; her family raised him.

Enter the Sandsea and go upstairs to the balcony to trigger another event. Balthier and Fran sit at a table where Migelo angrily berates

the sky pirate. The bangaa headhunter Ba'Gamnan has kidnapped Penelo and left behind a note telling Balthier to come to the mines in Bhujerba.

According to Balthier, the Imperial Fleet is massing at Bhujerba, a spectacular skycity. Vaan jumps at the chance to save Penelo, even offering the Goddess's Magicite in exchange for passage. Basch offers to join Vaan, saying he has business in Bhujerba too. When the event ends, Balthier and Fran join your party.

Board Balthier's Ship

Balthier sticks around to mention that Ba'Gamnan's note must refer to the Lhusu Mines in Bhujerba, and says to meet him at the Aerodrome. Now that Fran and Balthier have joined your party, you may want to visit the local merchants and upgrade their equipment. After doing so, head for the Aerodrome in the Westgate district of the city. (It's marked on in the area map.)

Fran waits at the entrance to the Aerodrome. Talk to her and head inside to find Balthier.

When you reach the Aerodrome, Fran is waiting outside. Talk to her to learn that Balthier feels responsible for what's happened to Penelo. Enter the Aerodrome and find Balthier waiting in an area near the back of the building, on the left side. Talk to him to learn that Bhujerba is on the sky continent of Dorstonis. The Lhusu Mine is actually a magicite mine located in Bhujerba. He'll also tell you more about Bhujerba, if you want. The skycity is known for its export of magicite and is ruled by Marquis Ondore, a man who has staved off Imperial invasion by maintaining Bhujerba's longtime tradition of neutrality.

Or, you can skip all that and just select "I'm ready" and then "I'm really ready." This triggers an event showing the party boarding Balthier's ship, the *Strahl*, after a team of moogles prep it.

THE BHUJERBA SCRIBE

Note that the man who rules Bhujerba is the same Marquis Ondore whose memoirs appear earlier in the game.

OBJECTIVE
Rescue Penelo!

World Map

Bhujerba

Ba'Gamnan is holding Penelo! Look for her deep in the Lhusu Mines.

Action Checklist

1 Find the Lhusu Mines.

Bhujerba

TRAVICA WAY

Aerodrome

CLOUDBORNE ROW

To the Lhusu Mines

LHUSU SQUARE

KHUS SKYGROUNDS

MINERS' END

KAFF TERRACE

Get to the Lhusu Mines

When you exit the Bhujerba aerodrome, you see a quick event during which a young lad named Lamont asks if he may accompany the party to the Lhusu Mines. Balthier agrees and Lamont joins your party as a guest.

Nice kid, that Lamont. But why is he so interested in the Lhusu Mines?

Proceed due east and climb the staircase. At the top, locate the Cartographers' Guild moogle and buy his maps of Bhujerba and the Lhusu Mines. (If you're a bit short of the steep asking price for the maps, sell a few items at any nearby shop.)

Don't miss the map-seller in the first plaza.

If you have any spare gil, or even if you don't, you can browse a bit in the Bhujerba shops to see what novel items or equipment is available. Next, head for the entrance to the Lhusu Mines from Lhusu Square, in the northeast district of the city. If you talk to people along the way, you learn that the magicite mines are shut down today because of an Imperial inspection party from Archadia.

The entrance to the Lhusu Mines area is imposing. Is Penelo in there?

When you approach the mines, a quick event occurs. Balthier points out that these mines contain one of the richest magicite veins in all of Ivalice. Basch suggests that the mines are probably under Imperial guard, but young Lamont precociously explains that, with but few exceptions, the Imperial army is not permitted in Bhujerba.

Lamont then leads the group into the mines. Basch and Balthier exchange an amused look. Who is this kid?

Lhusu Mines

Action Checklist

1	Work your way into Site 2.
2	Escape Ba'Gamnan and crew!

Steeling

LV	HP	EXP	LP
7-8	446-462	120-124	1

Skull Defender

LV	HP	EXP	LP
8-9	510-516	290-293	1

Skeleton

LV	HP	EXP	LP
8-9	557-563	290-293	1

Slaven

LV	HP	EXP	LP
10-11	780-802	263-268	1

TREASURE TABLE			Normal		w/Diamond Armlet Equip.		
No.	App.%	gil %	If gil	50%	gil	90%	10%
1	85%	50%	~260	Knot of Rust	Dark Mote	~700	Knot of Rust	Hi-Ether
2	85%	50%	~270	Knot of Rust	Onion Arrows	~700	Knot of Rust	Hi-Ether
3	79%	50%	~280	Knot of Rust	Dark Mote	~660	Knot of Rust	Elixir
4	81%	70%	~220	Knot of Rust	Killer Bow	~550	Knot of Rust	Elixir
5	90%	50%	~150	Knot of Rust	Water Mote	~420	Knot of Rust	Hi-Ether
6	75%	50%	~150	Knot of Rust	Dark Mote	~420	Knot of Rust	Hi-Ether
7	80%	50%	~300	Knot of Rust	Dark Mote	--	--	--
8	80%	50%	~250	Knot of Rust	Water Mote	--	--	--
9	80%	50%	~250	Knot of Rust	Self: status = reflect	--	--	--
10	80%	50%	~180	Knot of Rust	Foe: HP ≥ 500	--	--	--
11	80%	70%	~150	Knot of Rust	Assassin's Dagger	--	--	--
12	60%	0%	--	Knot of Rust	Ether	--	Knot of Rust	Elixir
13	60%	0%	--	Knot of Rust	Balance Mote	--	Knot of Rust	Elixir
14	60%	0%	--	Knot of Rust	Ether	--	Knot of Rust	Elixir
15	60%	0%	--	Knot of Rust	Balance Mote	--	Knot of Rust	Elixir
16	100%	0%	--	Knot of Rust	Potion	--	Knot of Rust	Caliper

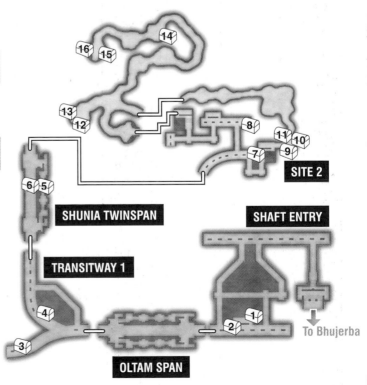

SHUNIA TWINSPAN

TRANSITWAY 1

SHAFT ENTRY

SITE 2

OLTAM SPAN

To Bhujerba

Get to Site 2

Descend into the Shaft Entry to trigger an event in which your party ducks away to avoid an Imperial inspection party led by the Archadian Judge Ghis and the Marquis Ondore.

Imperial inspectors grill Marquis Ondore about the mine's magicite shipments.

After they pass, Lamont emerges and recalls how the Marquis served as the mediator at the negotiations of Dalmasca's surrender. The question now: Are Ondore and Bhujerba still neutral? Or are the rumors true that he's secretly helping the anti-Imperial resistance?

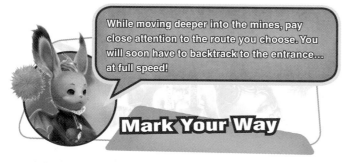

While moving deeper into the mines, pay close attention to the route you choose. You will soon have to backtrack to the entrance... at full speed!

Mark Your Way

Lamont sure knows a lot for a young lad, doesn't he?

Continue into the mines. The path is linear, so just keep moving from sector to sector, battling bats and undead defenders while scoring treasures. Watch out for traps, though! Make sure you move down the westernmost corridor of the Shaft Entry, or else a gate will block the path to the west.

If you locate this gate in the Shaft Entry, head back north and then west to come out on the other side.

Bangle for Traps

Numerous explosive traps line the Lhusu mine shafts. If someone in your party is using the technick Libra, or wearing a Bangle, you can spot them easily, as seen in this screenshot. If you don't have Libra active, the traps will not be visible! You can also create a Libra gambit that automatically keeps the Libra technick active on any party member. This frees up an equipment slot for another accessory.

When you reach Transitway 1, the path splits. An impassable gate (for now) blocks the left path, so take the right fork. Continue north into the next sector, the Shunia Twinspan.

Fight your way through Skeletons and Skull Defenders across the span. There are a *lot* of these skeleton-type enemies here, so this is a great place to build up a good, long Battle Chain and earn some decent loot items. After clearing out all of the skeletons, move north to Site 2.

The Shunia Twinspan is loaded with skeleton enemies. Have the party fight back and forth over the bridge to build up a Battle Chain.

A gate to the west blocks access to the Site 2 tunnel, so work your way through a small storage room (holding a few treasure chests) and into the luminescent blue cavern to the northeast. There you trigger an event in which Lamont explains that the glowing blue stone is something called "manufacted nethicite."

Unlike regular magicite, nethicite absorbs magical energy, making it a very powerful substance. According to Lamont, the Draklor Laboratory has been behind research into the manufacture of nethicite. Balthier starts grilling the boy about his sources and identity, but is interrupted by the appearance of Ba'Gamnan and his bangaa crew. Ba'Gamnan claims he let Penelo loose and she ran off. Lamont leads a rush past the bangaas and the chase is on!

Your party isn't strong enough to take on Ba'Gamnan's crew. Although the fight isn't entirely hopeless, it is very difficult and there's no reward for winning. Therefore, just press and hold the R2 button and retrace your route all the way back to the Shaft Entry. When you cross the boundary into that sector, the pursuers give up and you can relax. Move all the way through the Shaft Entry to the exit into Bhujerba.

Don't try to take on the bangaa boys. Just run!

Back in Bhujerba

The escape from the mines triggers a very interesting event. The boy, Lamont, turns out to be somewhat more than he seemed. After "Lamont" exits with Penelo for the Marquis's estate, Basch says that the entire party now has reason to meet Ondore. But how to arrange such a meeting?

OBJECTIVE
Attract Ondore's Attention

World Map

Bhujerba

Action Checklist

1. Garner enough "notoriety" to get the Resistance's attention.
2. Go to a meeting at Ondore's estate.

Run around town testifying about Captain Basch so the Resistance takes notice, then meet with the Marquis.

Bhujerba

TRAVICA WAY

Aerodrome

Targe's Arms

To Ondore's Estate

CLOUDBORNE ROW

Rithil's Protectives

The Cloudborne

To the Lhusu Mines

LHUSU SQUARE

Street Vendor

Street Vendor

KHUS SKYGROUNDS

Mait's Magicks

Clio's Technicks

MINERS' END

Bashketi's Gambits

KAFF TERRACE

Gain 100 Percent Notoriety!

Climb the stairs from the mines to trigger another event with an answer to the previous question. Balthier suggests that one way to reach Ondore is to "raise a clamor" that Basch is still alive. This will hopefully attract the attention of the Resistance groups that the Marquis is said to fund. Vaan takes up the task. Press the ● button when prompted to hear Vaan practice his idle boasting.

Press the Square button to "testify" that Captain Basch lives!

A "Notoriety" gauge now appears onscreen. The goal is to run around Bhujerba and press the ● button to make loud proclamations to citizens that Captain Basch is still alive. Move quickly because the gauge is constantly dropping; you must fill it up faster than it drops. Testify only to citizens with the Talk Icon above their heads. If you can find groups of such citizens, you can get more than one at a time.

Testify to Bhujerba citizens that Captain Basch lives, but avoid the soldiers in metal helmets.

🔊 SHUN SOLDIERS, SEEK GUIDES

Important: Do not testify near any of the Bhujerban Sainikah, the helmeted soldiers with swords who patrol the streets. If you do, you will get reprimanded and lose 30 percent off the "Notoriety" gauge. On the other hand, parijanah guides with blue books offer extra notoriety.

After filling the Notoriety gauge to 100 percent, another event starts. In this one, Vaan is confronted by Resistance members, then taken to their hideout in the Cloudborne tavern and questioned. Balthier and Fran appear, followed by Basch. Pretty secret hideout, eh? The Resistance now sees that the Captain does live.

From here, the action cuts to a drawing room in the estate of the Marquis Ondore, where Penelo and Lord Larsa discuss Vaan's rescue and the situation in Rabanastre.

❗ Side Quest Central

Bhujerba is a starting and ending point for several side quests. Check out the Cloudborne Tavern's job board for Hunts in the Lhusu Mines once it has been cleared. The Antlion Infestation hunt in particular provides the Site 3 Key, which opens up most of the mine for exploration. Then you can begin opening the large gates by using control panels near each one, and also use mine cars to travel back and forth to the entrance instead of hiking the entire way.

Meet with the Marquis

When the scene ends and control returns to you, exit the Cloudborne tavern and follow the red "X" on the area map to Ondore's estate. Upon reaching the entrance, talk to the Sainikah with the Talk Icon above his head and he will allow you to enter.

Talk to the guard to enter Ondore's estate.

Inside, Ondore reports that Lord Larsa's contingent has rejoined the Imperial detachment, meaning that Penelo is gone too. They

will depart tonight when the fleet arrives... which it soon does, led by its massive flagship, the *Dreadnought Leviathan*.

Ondore and Basch seem to come to some unspoken agreement. Ondore then calls in the guard to arrest everyone and take them to Judge Ghis. What's going on?

Now the scene switches to the Royal Palace at Rabanastre, where Lord Vayne consults with one of his Judges and an associate named Dr. Cid about the Resistance and the situation back in the Archadian Senate. After the event, another event shows Vaan's party being transferred in chains over to the mighty *Leviathan*.

OBJECTIVE
Escape the Leviathan with the Princess

The Dreadnought Leviathan

World Map

Judge Ghis holds a very important prisoner aboard the flagship of the 8th Imperial fleet. Free her and escape.

Action Checklist

1. Proceed to the brig area in the central block of the ship.
2. Defeat a contingent of Imperials led by lesser Judges.
3. Rescue a prisoner from the brig.
4. Defeat the powerful Judge Ghis.

The Dreadnought Leviathan

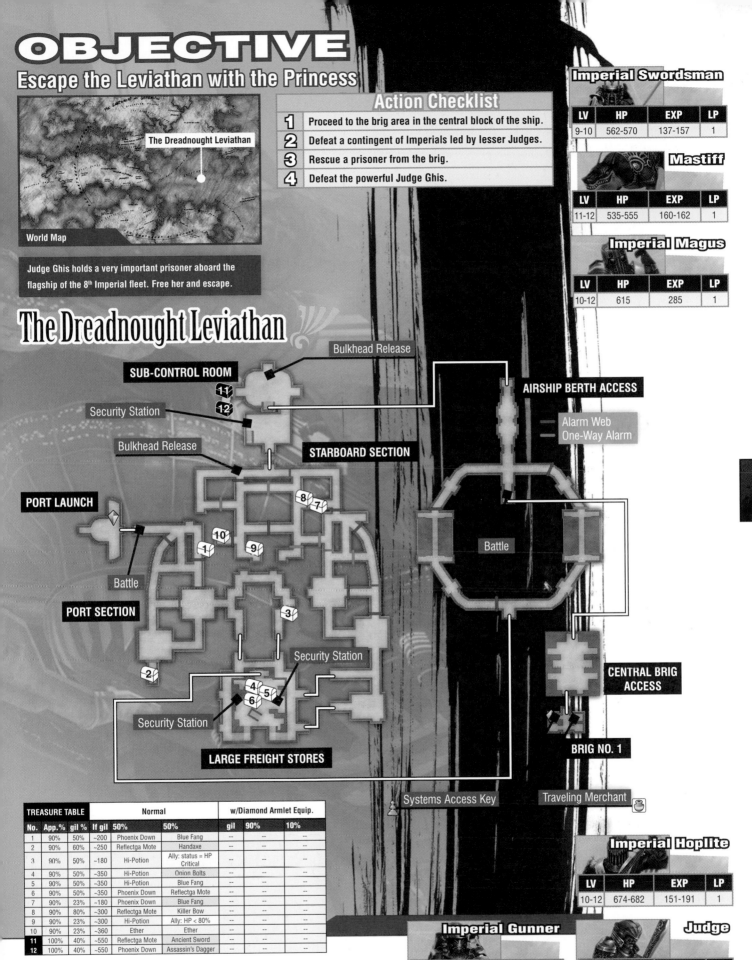

Imperial Swordsman

LV	HP	EXP	LP
9-10	562-570	137-157	1

Mastiff

LV	HP	EXP	LP
11-12	535-555	160-162	1

Imperial Magus

LV	HP	EXP	LP
10-12	615	285	1

Imperial Hoplite

LV	HP	EXP	LP
10-12	674-682	151-191	1

Imperial Gunner

LV	HP	EXP	LP
9	647	164	1

Judge

LV	HP	EXP	LP
11	2245-2445	0	7

TREASURE TABLE				Normal		w/Diamond Armlet Equip.		
No.	App.%	gil %	If gil	50%	50%	gil	90%	10%
1	90%	50%	~200	Phoenix Down	Blue Fang	--	--	--
2	90%	60%	~250	Reflectga Mote	Handaxe	--	--	--
3	90%	50%	~180	Hi-Potion	Ally: status = HP Critical	--	--	--
4	90%	50%	~350	Hi-Potion	Onion Bolts	--	--	--
5	90%	50%	~350	Hi-Potion	Blue Fang	--	--	--
6	90%	50%	~350	Phoenix Down	Reflectga Mote	--	--	--
7	90%	23%	~180	Phoenix Down	Blue Fang	--	--	--
8	90%	80%	~300	Reflectga Mote	Killer Bow	--	--	--
9	90%	23%	~300	Hi-Potion	Ally: HP < 80%	--	--	--
10	90%	23%	~360	Ether	Ether	--	--	--
11	100%	40%	~550	Reflectga Mote	Ancient Sword	--	--	--
12	100%	40%	~550	Phoenix Down	Assassin's Dagger	--	--	--

The Story Continues...

There's one more event before you regain control of your party: a meeting before Judge Ghis with Amalia, AKA the Princess Ashelia B'Nargin Dalmasca. Yes, Amalia is Ashe, the princess said to have committed suicide. Judge Ghis demands her "ministry" in restoring peace to Dalmasca, but Ashe refuses to play puppet to Vayne. Ghis threatens the gallows if she cannot offer proof of her royal claim.

Basch mentions something called the **Dusk Shard**, her birthright as the Dalmascan heir. It's a magic stone that will prove she is of royal blood. But hey, guess who has it? That's right—the "Goddess's Magicite" that Vaan has been carrying, the stone that he stole from the Palace Treasury, is none other than the Dusk Shard! It starts glowing in Vaan's hands.

Ghis demands the stone and Vaan reluctantly gives it to him. The Judge then sends everyone off to be incarcerated…

The scene shifts to a view of the party being marched to the ship's brig. However, a mistake by an overeager Imperial leads to an old-fashioned prison break aided by one of the helmeted guards; it's Vossler! He unlocks everyone's cuffs, explaining that for two full years he has kept Ashe safe, and now he plans to get her out.

Rescue Princess Ashe

At last, control again! Vossler joins your party as a guest, plus you gain a full map of the *Leviathan*. Configure your party the way you want; besides Vossler, who you cannot switch out, you can use three of your four available members. Save your game at the nearby Save Crystal in the Port Launch. Then head through the doors labeled "West Block" into the corridors of the Port Section.

Don't Be Alarmed

The ship is full of light-beam alarm webs. Depending on the route you take, you may have to trip a trap or two to reach the brig area. Don't panic when it happens; the alarm summons a tough, but beatable, Imperial squad to investigate.

The immediate goal is to fight through the Imperial soldiers, mastiffs, and elites to the Large Freight Stores section. While heading down the first hall, Vossler warns about the intruder alarm system. Take the second right to avoid the beams. Then go right, left, and finally south down to the open room with the glazed floor.

Avoid this red web of light beams. It's an intruder alarm.

That treasure looks easy to pluck, but a detection alarm activates after you pass, forcing you to trip the alarm to exit the alcove.

There is a treasure in a dead-end hallway due south. If you go after it, a "one-way" detection web activates behind your party, trapping them in the dead-end; you'll have to trip the alarm to get out. Is the treasure worth it? It's just a handful of gil, but you do get to fight a squad of Imperials.

ONE-WAY ALARMS

Several of the motion alarms are "one-way" activated. In other words, they start out turned off, but activate when your party passes through them.

Exit to the east and follow the corridor until you reach a walkway around an open atrium. You can now take one of two paths south to the next area, the Large Freight Stores.

North or South?

Check the area map. The red "X" marks Brig No. 1. You can take one of two different routes from the Large Freight Stores to reach this area and each way has its advantages and disadvantages.

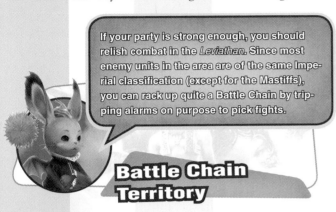

If your party is strong enough, you should relish combat in the *Leviathan*. Since most enemy units in the area are of the same Imperial classification (except for the Mastiffs), you can rack up quite a Battle Chain by tripping alarms on purpose to pick fights.

Battle Chain Territory

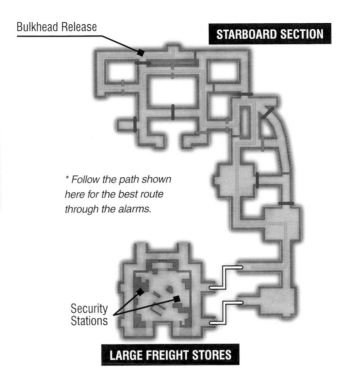

Bulkhead Release

STARBOARD SECTION

* Follow the path shown here for the best route through the alarms.

Security Stations

LARGE FREIGHT STORES

The North Route

Upon entering the Large Freight Stores, go immediately to the east exit via one of two eastern doors and head north through a labyrinth of corridors filled with alarm webs in the Starboard Section and Sub-control Room. This is the much longer way to the Airship Berth Access where the brig is located, but it's actually the easier way—because if you follow the correct route, you can avoid setting off any alarms. (See the blue route on the map of the Starboard Section.) You pass through several one-way alarms that don't activate until after you pass through them, so if you don't backtrack, you won't set them off.

At the north edge of the Starboard Section, use the Bulkhead Release to unlock the door into the Sub-control Room (note that it won't work during an alarm), then proceed through the bulkhead door. In the Sub-control Room, KO the guards at the controls, activate the Bulkhead Release, and proceed downstairs into the Airship Berth Access area. From there, it's a straight shot south to the brig area.

Activate Bulkhead Release stations to unlock doors on the northern route to the brig.

To South Route

You can choose to take the shorter (but more difficult) route downstairs to reach a tough fight on the main floor of the Large Freight Stores. Note the two security stations, one on either side of the room. Raid the treasure chests and exit via the center door to the north. This door takes the party straight to the Airship Berth Access, but forces you through a few alarm webs as you wander around the narrow, circular corridor. The fighting can get pretty intense here!

Move through the crates on the main floor of the Large Freight Stores area. Note the security stations on either side of the room.

STORE AHEAD

A traveling merchant sells a few useful upgrades from a cell within Brig No. 1. You may want to take on as much combat as possible before you get there, accruing gil for purchases and LP for some new licenses.

Walkthrough

Battle Elites and Minions

Whether you go north or south, once you finally reach the Central Brig Access, get ready for a tough fight. A mixed six-pack of Imperials steps into the room ready to fight. A standard approach is to focus on the four lesser Imperials first (three Swordsmen and a Poison-casting Magus), thinning the enemy party quickly to reduce the damage your party takes. But Vossler's advice to focus only on the leaders is well-considered too. The moment both Judges fall, the fight is over, even if the other Imperials are still standing.

When the second Judge falls, the battle ends even if the enemy Swordsmen and Magus are still standing.

The following strategy is based upon fighting the powerful leaders first, the two Judges. However, it may be a good idea to nail the Imperial Magus first to eliminate his spell-casting mischief. Make sure at least two of your characters are set with healing gambit priorities. If anyone in your party falls, switch in your reserve party member right away. Use Phoenix Down as a last resort—for example, if a second character gets KO'd.

Congratulations! Take a few seconds to enjoy it. A tougher fight looms.

After the battle, you receive a congratulations screen and obtain a **No. 1 Brig Key**. Don't pat yourself on the back too much; it's time to move on.

Heal Up and Free Ashe

Proceed to the south exit door and open it to enter Brig No. 1. Open Door C-203 to reach a couple of moogles, one of whom is a traveling merchant. Check out his goods (he has some nice accessories) and buy anything that looks useful.

The moogles in C-203 are grateful and loaded with goods to sell.

*Search for a **Systems Access Key** and a Save Crystal inside C-201. Her Majesty the Princess Ashe is located inside C-202.*

Go across the hall to open C-201. Ah, a Save Crystal! Nab the **Systems Access Key** from the Urn, then heal up and save your game. Now go open C-202 to rescue Ashe. After a short event, she joins your party. Exit Brig No. 1 to set off an alarm and start a wild sprint back to where you started.

Sprint to the Security Terminals

Imperial soldiers will swarm the party if you make a stand, so we recommend that you hold down the R2 button and ignore all attackers. Sprint north, straight through the Central Brig Access into the Airship Berth Access. Turn left at the intersection and sprint along the circular corridor to the southern exit into the Large Freight Stores area.

Run your party to the Large Freight Stores sector and use the security terminals to shut down the alarms.

Check the area map. The Security Terminals are highlighted for good reason. You can use the recently acquired Systems Access Key to reset the security alarm! This silence is good for just 60 seconds—a countdown timer appears onscreen—so immediately run upstairs and exit via the northwest door. Finally, enter the Port Section.

When the party arrives, you meet Larsa and Penelo! Larsa says that Judge Ghis knows about the escape and he tells Vossler (Captain Azelas) to follow him. Then Larsa gives Penelo the blue sample of manufactured nethicite he's been carrying.

Vossler exits with Lord Larsa, thus leaving the party. In his place, Penelo joins the party and the "piece of Manufactured Nethicite" enters your inventory.

There should be a few seconds on the countdown timer before the alarms start wailing again, so make haste to reach the Port Launch where this crazy level began. When the party arrives, their reward for all that quick work is… a meeting with Judge Ghis!

He tells Ashe that she's no longer useful and tries to zap her with a powerful magick spell but, luckily, the manufactured nethicite in Penelo's hand absorbs the magickal energy, rendering the spell harmless. As you may expect, this doesn't sit well with the Judge.

Judge Ghis

LVL	HP	EXP	LP
14	4120	0	22
Steal	Potion, Dark Mote, Jackboots		

Judge Ghis is the first big powerhouse boss in the main story of the game. He hits like he really means it, and his big magick attack can quickly KO any character with less than 50 percent HP remaining. Make sure the party's healers have their Cure or Potion gambits in the top slot, ready to kick in when any ally's HP drops to less than 50 percent—and preferably higher.

Ghis has a fearsome two-blade attack, plus some nasty magick. Quickly pick apart his support screen of Swordsmen, then focus everything on the Judge.

‼ QUICKENING

If any members of your party have licensed a Quickening, consider giving it a try at the beginning of this fight. Wait until Ghis and his Swordsmen move closer together, then target Ghis with a Quickening.

If you manage to chain three Quickening hits, you will trigger a bonus area attack that can quickly flatten the boss and his minions in one shot. It's certainly a risk—you deplete the MP of your Quickening caster(s)—but if it works, this boss battle is much easier.

The Judge's Swordsman minions are nothing special, so try to wipe out all three of them as quickly as possible. Keep your healers back, though; in general, it's good to have ranged fighters (like, say, Balthier with a gun or Fran with a bow) performing the bulk of the healing from a distance. Set the gambits of your close-quarter brawlers to fight first, with healing gambits set for when HP is low or even critical. Needless to say, your melee fighters should also have the heaviest armor you can afford, since they'll be taking the most punishment.

When Ghis finally falls, Vossler bursts into the room and announces that he has secured an Atomos for escape. (Balthier isn't happy about it, but a ship's a ship.) Now sit back and watch a spectacular sequence with Fran calmly piloting the Atomos out of the *Leviathan* and past a fighter wing to safety.

Cut to the Bhujerba Aerodrome. Basch convinces Lady Ashe to meet with Ondore. Vossler then takes his leave to explore other ways to seek Dalmascan freedom and Basch now takes over the role of Ashe's protector.

Visit Ondore's Estate

Exit the Aerodrome and head to the Marquis Ondore's estate again, just up the stairs and to the left. This triggers another event.

Ashe entreats Ondore to stand with her Resistance movement to stop Vayne. However, the Marquis points out that until Ashe regains the Dusk Shard, the Gran Kiltias on Bur-Omisace (a holy man) will not recognize her as the rightful heir. "Without proof of your identity," he tells her, "you are powerless."

Later that night, Vaan catches Ashe trying to hijack Balthier's airship, the *Strahl*. Balthier shows up and Ashe concocts a daring plan. She suggests that Balthier… kidnap her! "You're a sky pirate, aren't you?" she says. In exchange, she will lead him to something called the Dynast-King's treasure in King Raithwall's tomb.

This gets Balthier's attention. He's on board now, as is Basch, who will perform his duty by protecting Ashe. So is Fran, of course; where Balthier goes, she goes. And finally, so are the orphans of Rabanastre, Vaan and Penelo. Your party is now complete.

But before gameplay begins again, there is more story to tell. Far to the north, in the Archadian capital city of Archades, Judge Gabranth stands before Emperor Gramis with reports on the activities at Draklor Laboratories, the Empire's primary weapons research lab.

The Emperor, who is clearly ill, asks the Judge to be Larsa's "shield"—and to keep a close watch on Vayne. Then the scene changes to the Dalmasca Westersand.

OBJECTIVE
Find King Raithwall's Tomb

Ogir-Yensa Sandsea

World Map

Action Checklist
This list is for both sandseas, the Ogir-Yensa and the Nam-Yensa.

1. Cross the Ogir-Yensa Sandsea.
2. Talk to the Sandsea moogle.
3. Defeat the giant tortoise and get the Eksir Berries reward.
4. Cross the Nam-Yensa Sandsea.
5. Enter the Tomb of Raithwall.

Cross the great western sandseas to the Valley of the Dead, seeking the ancient tomb of the Dynast-King.

Ogir-Yensa Sandsea

PRIMARY TANK COMPLEX

EAST JUNCTION

To Zertinan Caverns

To Zertinan Caverns

PLATFORM 1: REFINERY

CENTRAL JUNCTION

To Nam-Yensa Sandsea

PLATFORM 2: REFINERY

YENSA BORDER TUNNEL

To Nam-Yensa Sandsea

Dyce the Merchant

SOUTH TANK APPROACH

Map Urn

PLATFORM 1: EAST TANKS

To the Westersand

PLATFORM 1: SOUTH TANKS

Danbania

LV	HP	EXP	LP
10-13	966-999	290-302	1

Pineapple (Rare Game)

LV	HP	EXP	LP
16-18	4666-4698	639-651	3

Alraune

LV	HP	EXP	LP
10-11	615-627	285-288	1

Urutan Eater

LV	HP	EXP	LP
16	8015	0	8

Urutan-Yensa

LV	HP	EXP	LP
12-14	702-718	345-385	1

Yensa

LV	HP	EXP	LP
13-15	1010-1032	448-456	1

Bagoly

LV	HP	EXP	LP
14-16	1010-1230	490-676	1

Axebeak

LV	HP	EXP	LP
13-15	922-954	375-383	1

Wyvern

LV	HP	EXP	LP
14-16	1493-1713	683-709	1

TREASURE TABLE				Normal		w/Diamond Armlet Equip.		
No.	App.%	gil %	If gil	50%	50%	gil	90%	10%
1	80%	50%	~120	Potion	Bronze Shield	~600	Knot of Rust	Hi-Ether
2	80%	35%	~300	Potion	Phoenix Down	~600	Knot of Rust	Hi-Ether
3	80%	35%	~150	Potion	Ether	~800	Knot of Rust	Hi-Ether
4	75%	30%	~100	Potion	Reflectga Mote	~500	Knot of Rust	Hastega Mote
5	75%	30%	~100	Phoenix Down	Killer Bow	~500	Knot of Rust	X-Potion
6	75%	30%	~150	Hi-Potion	Onion Arrows	~550	Knot of Rust	X-Potion
7	75%	30%	~350	Potion	Mace	~900	Knot of Rust	Scathe Mote
8	75%	30%	~100	Potion	Onion Bombs	~1000	Knot of Rust	Hastega Mote
9	75%	30%	~200	Ether	Ether	~500	Knot of Rust	Scathe Mote
10	75%	30%	~200	Hi-Potion	Handaxe	~600	Knot of Rust	Chronos Tear
11	80%	15%	~500	Cypress Pole	Capella	~600	Knot of Rust	Chronos Tear
12	80%	10%	~500	Spear	Zwill Blade	~1000	Knot of Rust	Scathe Mote
13	75%	30%	~100	Chopper	Ally: HP < 20%	~500	Knot of Rust	Hastega Mote
14	75%	40%	~100	Hi-Potion	Iron Helm	~600	Knot of Rust	X-Potion
15	75%	50%	~100	Potion	Ringmail	~600	Knot of Rust	X-Potion
16	75%	40%	~300	Ether	Ether	~1000	Knot of Rust	X-Potion
17	75%	40%	~100	Hi-Potion	Iron Armor	~600	Knot of Rust	Holy Mote
18	75%	50%	~200	Hi-Potion	Main Gauche	~600	Knot of Rust	Holy Mote
19	75%	40%	~200	Ether	Remedy	~600	Knot of Rust	Holy Mote

TREASURE TABLE				Normal		w/Diamond Armlet Equip.		
No.	App.%	gil %	If gil	50%	50%	gil	90%	10%
20	50%	45%	~700	Potion	Onion Shot	~1300	Knot of Rust	Elixir
21	72%	50%	~150	Phoenix Down	Sallet	~550	Knot of Rust	X-Potion
22	72%	20%	~100	Potion	Hi-Potion	~700	Knot of Rust	Elixir
23	72%	20%	~150	Potion	Ally: MP < 40%	~550	Knot of Rust	X-Potion
24	72%	20%	~150	Phoenix Down	Ally: MP < 60%	~550	Knot of Rust	X-Potion
25	72%	20%	~150	Ether	Sash	~550	Knot of Rust	X-Potion
26	75%	20%	~150	Potion	Ether	~550	Knot of Rust	Elixir
27	71%	15%	~120	Balance Mote	Bronze Shield	~400	Knot of Rust	Elixir
28	80%	30%	~120	Potion	Horned Hat	~400	Knot of Rust	Holy Mote
29	71%	15%	~120	Phoenix Down	Ether	~400	Knot of Rust	Scathe Mote
30	80%	40%	~120	Potion	Wizard's Hat	~400	Knot of Rust	Elixir
31	71%	15%	~200	Potion	Hi-Potion	~600	Knot of Rust	Holy Mote
32	80%	15%	~150	Reflectga Mote	Armguard	~500	Knot of Rust	Scathe Mote
33	71%	15%	~120	Hi-Potion	Battle Harness	~400	Knot of Rust	Elixir
34	76%	20%	~300	Potion	Reflectga Mote	~900	Knot of Rust	Hi-Ether
35	76%	50%	~300	Potion	Spear	~900	Knot of Rust	Hi-Ether
36	76%	20%	~300	Hi-Potion	Gauntlets	~900	Knot of Rust	Hi-Ether
37	76%	20%	~300	Potion	Ally: status = Confuse	~900	Knot of Rust	Hi-Ether

Cross the Ogir-Yensa Sandsea

This section starts in the westernmost area of the Dalmasca Westersand. Balthier has shrouded the *Strahl* in the sky above the desert; the airship can fly no further west because its skystone-powered engines cannot function in the "jagd" in that direction. The party sets off across the sands to seek the tomb of Raithwall, the Dynast-King.

Balthier's airship hovers over the Westersand, waiting for the party's return.

So now the party must trek across the great western sandseas. Actually, they'll be trekking *above* the sandseas; as the brief event implies, you can't walk directly on a sandsea, since its composition is a bizarre granulated liquid. To cross the Ogir-Yensa, and the Nam-Yensa after that, you must use a series of platforms and ramps.

Vaan tests the odd "waters" of the Ogir-Yensa.

Bangle for Traps

Careful! The desert holds its share of explosive traps. Keep a Bangle or a Libra gambit on an active party member to see the traps.

Climb the first ramp and fight through the Alraune while moving across the catwalks of the first three storage tanks. Continue to the next section to trigger an event.

Meanwhile, Fran has some bad premonitions about this place. This is Urutan-Yensa territory and your party has drawn their attention. Better get moving!

Vossler joins your party as a guest. Move around the first tower of the Platform 1 - Refinery and down the ramp to the sand, where the first group of Urutan-Yensa await. The Urutan-Yensa are weak against the Wind element, so if anyone in your party has a Wind-enhanced weapon, get that character out front. These foes occasionally cast Haste on themselves, too, so if you have Slow in your magick arsenal, use it to counteract.

Odd creatures like the Alraune roam amongst the hostile hordes of Urutan-Yensa tribesmen.

Look for rare game like the Pineapple, which resembles a Bomb but is much, much tougher. It casts Reflect on itself, so stick to physical attacks.

Climb the ramp up the tower to the west. On the south side of that tower locate a Map Urn containing a full map of the Ogir-Yensa Sandsea. Next, go back down to ground level and head for the northern ramp that leads up to the huge refinery structure.

> **# MAP EARNED**
>
> Don't miss the Map Urn atop the centermost tower in the Platform 1 - Refinery area.

Proceed across the refinery; on the far side you have a choice of three directions, so take your pick. Each one eventually takes you to where you want to go, the Nam-Yensa Sandsea. For this story walkthrough, let's exit from the southernmost exit, heading to the South Tanks of Platform 1.

Head down the spur extending southwest from the South Tanks to find some treasure, then fight to the west through the Urutan-Yensa along the main platform to the fourth and final tank. Exit northwest to the Platform 2 - Refinery area.

You can follow the north spur past three tanks to find a lot of treasure at the end of the platform. Or, you can take the west spur through the refinery and descend the ramp to the ground on the west side. Then head west into the tunnel to reach the Sandscale Bank of the next region you must cross, the Nam-Yensa Sandsea.

Nam-Yensa Sandsea

Find the Giant Tortoise

Halfway there! Use the Save Crystal at the Sandscale Bank, then approach the Sandsea moogle standing nearby. He states that an Urutan-Yensa warrior just asked him for help. Select "Tell me" to hear about a giant Emeralditan tortoise in Nam-Yensa that is terrorizing the local population. He mentions a possible reward. How could you pass that up?

Talk to the Sandsea moogle near the Save Crystal to learn how you can help the Urutan-Yensa.

Exit west into the Urutan-Yensa Sea. Fight your way through a number of hostile Urutan-Yensa tribesmen and cross the walkbridge into the Withering Shores area.

Defeat the Urutan-Eater

Up ahead, you should spot the giant tortoise mentioned by the moogle. The mighty Emeralditan is named "Urutan Eater," and it battles a handful of Urutan-Yensa warriors. Help them defeat the big beast.

💥 KEEP TURTLES AT RANGE!

Deploy a couple of allies using ranged weapons when you fight any giant tortoise. These armored beasts tend to use close-range area attacks in combat, so party members who stand back and fire guns or bows (or use magick) against a tortoise are likely to sustain less damage.

The Urutan Eater is tough, but the reward is well worth it.

Note that the Urutan Eater is weak against Wind magick. If your gambits are well-organized, it's possible to take him down in just minutes. Remember to swap KO'd party members with new, fresh backups to keep the pressure on the tortoise. When the hard-shelled beast finally falls, return to the Sandscale Bank.

Talk to the Sandsea moogle. He mentions that the Urutan-Yensa warrior who asked for help just went by, headed east back into the Ogir-Yensa Sandsea. Exit east to return to the Platform 2 - Refinery area and climb the refinery ramp to trigger an event.

TREASURE TABLE		Normal			w/Diamond Armlet Equip.		
No.	App.%	gil %	If gil	50%	50%	gil	90%	10%
1	75%	50%	~150	Potion	Lambent Hat	~600	Knot of Rust	Elixir
2	75%	50%	~160	Phoenix Down	Chopper	~800	Knot of Rust	Elixir
3	83%	45%	~300	Potion	Ether	~900	Knot of Rust	Holy Mote
4	65%	50%	~100	Argyle Armlet	Ancient Sword	~300	Knot of Rust	Elixir
5	77%	90%	~700	Hi-Potion	Elixir	~2200	Knot of Rust	Holy Mote
6	60%	55%	~100	Rose Corsage	Vega	~300	Knot of Rust	Elixir
7	65%	40%	~100	Ether	Iron Helm	~300	Knot of Rust	Elixir
8	65%	40%	~100	Potion	Chopper	~300	Knot of Rust	Elixir
9	80%	35%	~300	Phoenix Down	Ether	~300	Knot of Rust	Holy Mote
10	80%	30%	~290	Potion	Ally: status = Sleep	~600	Knot of Rust	Elixir
11	80%	35%	~150	Hi-Potion	Leather Gorget	~800	Knot of Rust	Elixir
12	80%	60%	~400	Potion	Reflectga Mote	~1000	Knot of Rust	Holy Mote
13	60%	40%	~120	Hi-Potion	Killer Bow	~480	Knot of Rust	Elixir
14	77%	23%	~100	Potion	Balance Mote	~450	Knot of Rust	Elixir
15	77%	23%	~300	Foe: flying	Foe: HP ≥ 1000	~600	Knot of Rust	Elixir
16	77%	23%	~100	Potion	Ether	~450	Knot of Rust	Holy Mote
17	77%	23%	~150	Potion	Handkerchief	~500	Knot of Rust	Hi-Ether
18	77%	23%	~100	Potion	Echo Herbs	~450	Knot of Rust	Hi-Ether
19	77%	23%	~150	Phoenix Down	Ether	~450	Knot of Rust	Elixir
20	77%	23%	~150	Potion	Balance Mote	~450	Knot of Rust	Elixir
21	77%	20%	~150	Potion	Foe: HP ≥ 500	~450	Knot of Rust	Elixir
22	77%	23%	~250	Potion	Antidote	~450	Knot of Rust	Elixir
23	60%	50%	~150	Hi-Potion	Iron Armor	~450	Knot of Rust	Holy Mote
24	77%	20%	~150	Hi Potion	Foe: HP < 1000	~450	Knot of Rust	Elixir
25	77%	23%	~200	Potion	Foe: HP = 100%	~500	Knot of Rust	Elixir
26	60%	50%	~120	Phoenix Down	Wizard's Staff	~500	Knot of Rust	Elixir
27	70%	23%	~180	Antidote	Amber Armlet	~600	Knot of Rust	Elixir
28	60%	50%	~160	Phoenix Down	Cypress Pole	~600	Knot of Rust	Elixir
29	77%	20%	~150	Foe: flying	Foe: flying	~500	Knot of Rust	Holy Mote
30	60%	50%	~150	Potion	Windbreaker	~500	Knot of Rust	Elixir
31	65%	10%	~800	Ether	Reflectga Mote	~2000	Knot of Rust	Holy Mote
32	70%	23%	~220	Potion	Balance Mote	~450	Knot of Rust	Elixir

Walkthrough

The moogle talks to the tribesman about the "treasure of the sandsea"… and suddenly the tribesman runs west, back through the tunnel to the Sandscale Bank! Follow him to see a rare gathering of the Urutan-Yensa. The poor tribesman is punished by the Urutan Queen for his plea for help outside the clan. When the dust settles, all that's left is a Rogue Urutan Flower in the sand.

After you regain control, talk to the moogle. Talk to him again to learn about a powerful avion known as the Garuda that hates the scent of this particular flower. Approach the flower and pick its berries to add **Eksir Berries** to the Items list in your inventory.

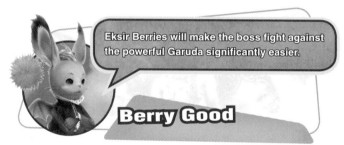

Eksir Berries will make the boss fight against the powerful Garuda significantly easier.

Berry Good

Head back through the Urutan-Yensa Sea into the Withering Shores and head to the east to reach Augur Hill. Once there, cross the bridge on the right to find a Map Urn. Now cross the next bridge and make your way to the southwest exit, which leads to Yellow Sands. (Or, go back across the bridge and head east to the Yensa Border Tunnel to find a merchant and a Save Crystal, and then return; see the tip on this page.)

Cross the Augur Hill bridge to find the Map Urn.

⚠ BUY FROM DYCE

A traveling merchant named Dyce keeps appearing all over the desert area. At first, he camps out near a Save Crystal just east of Augur Hill, in the Yensa Border Tunnel area. Dyce sells the highly useful magick Raise, which will revive KO'd party members without expending a Phoenix Down. He also has Cura, a powerful healing spell that restores HP to all allies within its range.

Yellow Sands has two exits. The southern exit leads into the dangerous Zertinan Caverns, which may be too deadly at this stage. (Two lethal Speartongue toads lurk just inside the entrance!) Instead, go north to the storage tank and exit that way into the Demesne of the Sandqueen. From there, head west across the sands to the Trail of Fading Warmth.

Follow the trail to the northwest, crossing a set of bridges in the process. If you want, you can detour through the tunnel-bridge (guarded by four explosive traps!) up to Simoon Bluff and scour that area for treasure and obtain EXP/LP from combat.

Careful! The bridge to Simoon Bluff is heavily trapped.

Look out for a wild Bagoly ambush near the top of Simoon Bluff. Enemies up here reappear after you dispatch them, so don't linger unless you want lots of combat to level up and build stats.

It's tough up there, though; near the top, a flock of six Bagolys jealously guards some treasure, plus a massive flying Wyvern flaps around nearby. Sling a Water spell at the Wyvern to exploit its weakness, and use party members equipped with ranged weapons.

Birdland

Remember, you can't hit a flying foe like a Wyvern with regular attacks unless you have a ranged weapon like a gun or a bow. Sling magick attacks on a flying enemy; the Wyvern is particularly weak against the Water element.

Now take the Trail of Fading Warmth west to run into Dyce, the traveling merchant. (Even if you met him before back at the Yensa Border Tunnel, he will still be here now.) Stock up if you need to, then exit west to the next area. Here, the game gives you a single opportunity to save your game. Take it, then move on into the Tomb of Raithwall.

Take the free save-game opportunity that the game offers just before the Tomb of Raithwall.

OBJECTIVE
Retrieve the Dawn Shard

World Map

Tomb of Raithwall

World Map

Action Checklist

1. Defeat Garuda.
2. Get past the Demon Walls.
3. Defeat the Esper Belias.
4. Take the Dawn Shard and exit the tomb.

Fight through the foul protectors of Raithwall's legacy to recover the Dawn Shard from the Dynast-King's tomb.

Tomb of Raithwall

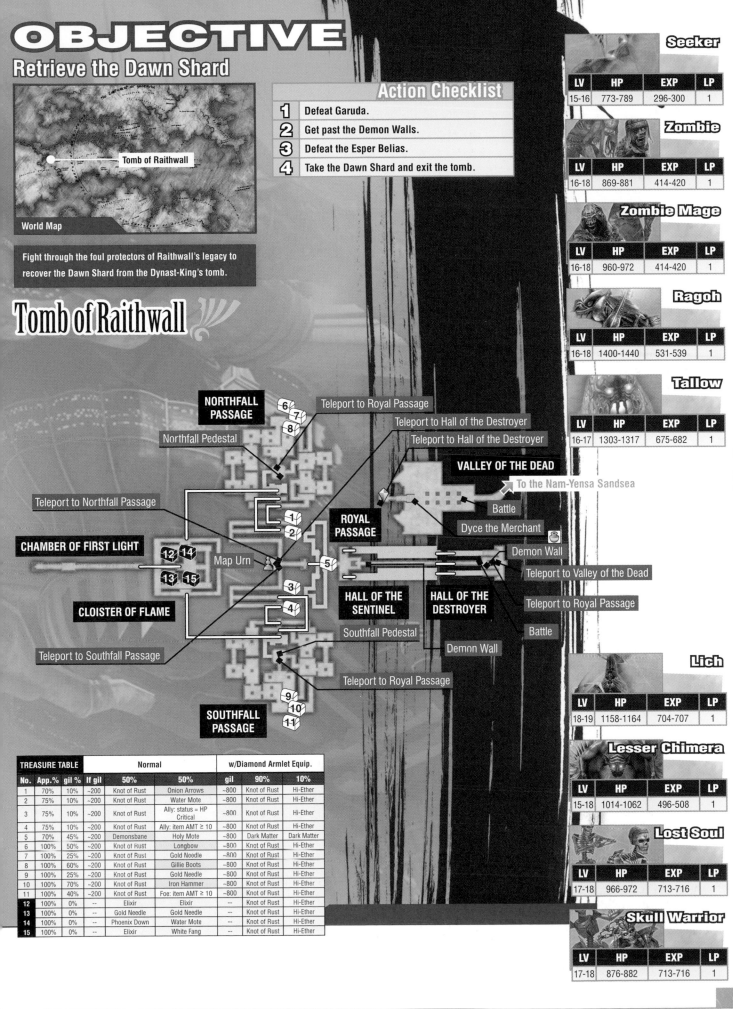

NORTHFALL PASSAGE

Northfall Pedestal

Teleport to Royal Passage

Teleport to Hall of the Destroyer

Teleport to Hall of the Destroyer

Teleport to Northfall Passage

VALLEY OF THE DEAD

To the Nam-Yensa Sandsea

Battle

CHAMBER OF FIRST LIGHT

Map Urn

ROYAL PASSAGE

Dyce the Merchant

Demon Wall

CLOISTER OF FLAME

Teleport to Valley of the Dead

Teleport to Southfall Passage

HALL OF THE SENTINEL

HALL OF THE DESTROYER

Teleport to Royal Passage

Southfall Pedestal

Battle

Demon Wall

Teleport to Royal Passage

SOUTHFALL PASSAGE

TREASURE TABLE

No.	App.%	gil %	If gil	Normal 50%	Normal 50%	w/Diamond Armlet Equip. gil	90%	10%
1	70%	10%	~200	Knot of Rust	Onion Arrows	~800	Knot of Rust	Hi-Ether
2	75%	10%	~200	Knot of Rust	Water Mote	~800	Knot of Rust	Hi-Ether
3	75%	10%	~200	Knot of Rust	Ally: status = HP Critical	~800	Knot of Rust	Hi-Ether
4	75%	10%	~200	Knot of Rust	Ally: item AMT ≥ 10	~800	Knot of Rust	Hi-Ether
5	70%	45%	~200	Demonsbane	Holy Mote	~800	Dark Matter	Dark Matter
6	100%	50%	~200	Knot of Rust	Longbow	~800	Knot of Rust	Hi-Ether
7	100%	25%	~200	Knot of Rust	Gold Noodle	~800	Knot of Rust	Hi-Ether
8	100%	60%	~200	Knot of Rust	Gillie Boots	~800	Knot of Rust	Hi-Ether
9	100%	25%	~200	Knot of Rust	Gold Needle	~800	Knot of Rust	Hi-Ether
10	100%	70%	~200	Knot of Rust	Iron Hammer	~800	Knot of Rust	Hi-Ether
11	100%	40%	~200	Knot of Rust	Foe: item AMT ≥ 10	~800	Knot of Rust	Hi-Ether
12	100%	0%	--	Elixir	Elixir	--	Knot of Rust	Hi-Ether
13	100%	0%	--	Gold Needle	Gold Needle	--	Knot of Rust	Hi-Ether
14	100%	0%	--	Phoenix Down	Water Mote	--	Knot of Rust	Hi-Ether
15	100%	0%	--	Elixir	White Fang	--	Knot of Rust	Hi-Ether

Seeker

LV	HP	EXP	LP
15-16	773-789	296-300	1

Zombie

LV	HP	EXP	LP
16-18	869-881	414-420	1

Zombie Mage

LV	HP	EXP	LP
16-18	960-972	414-420	1

Ragoh

LV	HP	EXP	LP
16-18	1400-1440	531-539	1

Tallow

LV	HP	EXP	LP
16-17	1303-1317	675-682	1

Lich

LV	HP	EXP	LP
18-19	1158-1164	704-707	1

Lesser Chimera

LV	HP	EXP	LP
15-18	1014-1062	496-508	1

Lost Soul

LV	HP	EXP	LP
17-18	966-972	713-716	1

Skull Warrior

LV	HP	EXP	LP
17-18	876-882	713-716	1

Defeat Garuda!

Cross the tomb's entry courtyard, called the Valley of the Dead—not a cheerful name for an area. Soon you learn why. A great avion beast called a Garuda drops from the sky, ready to protect the tomb.

Garuda

LVL	HP	EXP	LP
16	6754	0	11
Steal	Gold Needle, Giant Feather, White Fang		

Immediately use the Eksir Berries on the Garuda. These are the berries you received as a reward for defeating the Urutan Eater back in the sandseas. Their noxious effect knocks a full 15 percent or so off this boss's HP bar in one shot. This gets the fight off to a very, very good start. (Note that you can certainly win the fight without them, but why not make things easier on yourself?)

⚡ BERRY THE GARUDA!

The very first move in this fight should be to nail the Garuda with the Eksir Berries, if you were thorough enough to earn them back in the sandseas.

The Garuda is a flying foe, so ranged and magick attacks are the best way to go. Water

It's amazing how much a few Eksir Berries will degrade the big bird's HP bar.

deals good damage, as does Thunder. Fire away with guns and bows, and keep a close eye on each character's HP. If your party's healing gambits get overwhelmed, step in and manually distribute a few Hi-Potions to get everyone back up to strength.

This boss casts Sleep on occasion, so be ready with the Alarm Clock item to awaken snoozing party members. If you nail this foe with Silence, you can eliminate its magick attacks. (A gun firing Silent Shot works great, too.) Vossler's Telekinesis is also very effective against the Garuda, too, so keep him healed and firing away. When the Garuda finally falls, an "ancient device" stirs inside the tomb. This is a teleportation system, as you'll soon discover.

After the fight, Lady Ashe gives a brief history lesson regarding the Dynast-King and his peaceful, compassionate uses of power. Raithwall's alliance included the city-states of Archadia and Rozarria, and his era of peace and prosperity endured for a long time.

The Dynast-King left three relics to signify his descendants: the Midlight Shard to House Nabradia, the Dusk Shard to the founders of Dalmasca, and the Dawn Shard, which remains hidden inside the tomb.

Get Past the Demon Walls

Revisit the courtyard to see Dyce, the traveling merchant, again. This guy's everywhere! Refill anything you're running low on, then upgrade your weapons and armor. Also, make sure to spend LP on the appropriate licenses for whatever equipment you buy. After doing so, head back upstairs and save your game at the Save Crystal.

Teleport into the tomb via the ancient device.

Now use the nearby "Ancient Device"— a Way Stone that can teleport people to different places. This one teleports the party directly into the tomb. The party arrives in the Hall of the Destroyer. That doesn't sound good either. Another Way Stone nearby doesn't work yet, so move on.

Proceed down one of the center staircases and get ready to run! By stepping onto the main walkway, you bring to life a massive Demon Wall. This boss starts moving toward the party, blocking the walkway, forcing the party to fight or run away.

The first Demon Wall is difficult to defeat, but you can just flee (using R2) through the far doorway to escape.

The best advice here is to *run away*. Just press and hold the R2 button and sprint to the door at the end of the walkway and go through. Uh oh— another Demon Wall! And this time there's no escape. It's time for a boss fight.

You can complete the Tomb of Raithwall level without fighting the first Demon Wall. However, you must fight the second one.

Wall Facts

 DEMONSBANE SWORD!

After defeating the optional Demon Wall, you can go down the secret side stairs that lead to a treasure chest. The powerful sword randomly appears in a treasure chest where the north and south passages meet. It may take several attempts to get the Demonsbane sword, as there is a chance that the chest is holding random loot or nothing at all.

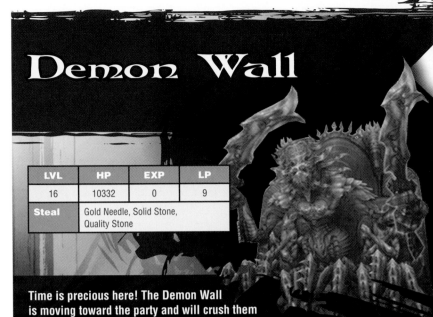

Demon Wall

LVL	HP	EXP	LP
16	10332	0	9
Steal	Gold Needle, Solid Stone, Quality Stone		

Time is precious here! The Demon Wall is moving toward the party and will crush them if you don't defeat it before it pushes them against the far wall. The moment you regain control, sprint immediately toward the wall and start attacking it. Use a party of big hitters. It also helps to have characters with gambits that automatically remove Sleep (with Alarm Clock) and Blind (with Eye Drops or Blindna) status effects, so you don't have to worry about them too much.

BEWARE BANISH!

The Tomb's Demon Walls share a special attack unique to them in the game— Telega! These bosses can remove your characters permanently from the field of battle, completely irretrievable. The only way to bring back a "banished" character is to move to a completely different area—one more reason to act quickly!

If you have any characters with Quickening abilities, use them while you still can, as they will knock a lot of HP out of the wall. Then just start hammering on the monster. Consider lowering or even disabling any Cure gambits that are active. Too much healing takes time away from attacking: remember, time is running out. It may be better to heal manually with Hi-Potions when characters are in a critical condition.

Ethers that restore MP are rare finds, so in general, you want to stockpile them for the final stages of the game. But consider this scenario: The Demon Wall's HP is nearly spent, but he's pushed you inches from the far wall. An effective last-ditch strategy is to use an Ether or two on an ally who has a Quickening in his/her arsenal—enough to restore MP for at least one full Mist Charge. Then quickly unleash the Quickening. It will likely cause enough damage to finish off the boss wall.

 FLAME STOPPERS

Four pairs of torches (called "Altars of Contemplation") burn on the railings along the second Demon Wall's walkway. Touching a torch will either halt or speed up the wall's relentless advance. If the flame extinguishes, the wall stops for a few seconds. If the flame turns blue, though, the Demon Wall actually speeds up! It's risky, but there are more "halt" torches than "speed up" torches, so it's worth a try.

After the victory, head west, climb the stairs, and go through the Ancient Door. Lady Ashe claims to hear the Dawn Shard's call, and so onward they go.

Open the Secret Passage

The next task is to find the secret passage to the Dawn Shard. Descend the stairs leading down to the three Way Stones and a Map Urn. Open the urn to get a full map of the Tomb of Raithwall, then check out the Way Stones:

- *The white Way Stone teleports you back to the Hall of the Destroyer—the arrival area, back before the Demon Wall, thank goodness. From this location, you can use the nearby yellow Way Stone to exit the Tomb and use the Save Crystal, if you want.*

- *The reddish Way Stone connects with a Way Stone in the Northfall Passage, but it doesn't work yet.*

- *The greenish Way Stone connects with a Way Stone in the Southfall Passage, but it doesn't work yet, either.*

The Royal Passage has a map and three Way Stones. Unfortunately, only one Way Stone works and you must activate the other two from elsewhere in the tomb.

Northfall Passage Jewel

Go down the steep north staircase and turn right. Then take the first right, going down another staircase. At the bottom, proceed through the Ancient Door into the Northfall Passage. Follow the corridor around the first corner and knock out the two big Ragohs. Keep moving from room to room, battling through the Zombies, Ragohs, and Lesser Chimeras and descending stairs until you reach a room with a Way Stone.

The crimson jewel lowers the carved stone block halfway into the floor.

Touch the luminous crimson jewel on the Northfall Pedestal to lower the nearby Mystic Altar, a large stone carved with faces blocking a secret passage to the west. The altar only sinks halfway into the floor, however, so you can't enter the passage just yet. As the altar lowers, three Zombie Mages rise and vent their anger at this intrusion, casting Dark magick spells. Wipe them out and use the Way Stone to teleport back to the reddish Way Stone on the Royal Passage platform.

Southfall Passage Jewel

Now repeat the process going south. The Southfall Passage is a mirror image of the Northfall Passage, so follow the same steps as in the last section, only in reverse. You meet new types of undead enemies along the way: the Lich, the Skull Warrior, and the Lost Soul; like Zombies, they are weak against Cure magick.

Upon reaching the Way Stone, note that the Mystic Altar in this room has been lowered halfway already; you did this when you touched the crimson jewel in Northfall. Now touch the glowing beryline jewel set in the Southfall Pedestal to lower the Mystic Altar all the way to the floor. Unfortunately, this also releases a bunch of oil-spewing Liches into the room. Eliminate them and use Handkerchiefs to clean off any lingering Oil status.

Touch the green jewel in the Southfall Pedestal to open the secret passage behind the Mystic Altar.

This might be a good time to use the Way Stone network to teleport back to the Save Crystal in front of the tomb. Save your game! After doing so, return and go through the secret passage now revealed behind the lowered Mystic Altar.

Find the Cloister

Follow the secret passage. The Mini-Map will show the party moving through open, uncharted space. (The guide maps in this book show the parameters of secret areas, however.) Open the Ancient door to trigger an event.

The party enters a foggy area. Fran tells Penelo it is not fog, but "mist." It is dangerous, but dense Mist also allows for the working of powerful magicks, which could be helpful.

When the scene ends, the party stands just inside the south entrance to the Cloister of Flame. Follow the corridor to the left and down the stairs to the main floor. An entity that looks like a statue sits on a throne. But when you approach, something happens.

Belias, the Gigas

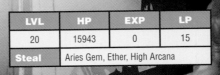

LVL	HP	EXP	LP
20	15943	0	15
Steal	Aries Gem, Ether, High Arcana		

Belias is a powerful Esper who hits hard with physical attacks and Fire spells, including Firaja, a Fire attack with an area effect that sometimes inflicts the Oil status. Start by casting both Protect and Shell (if you have both at your disposal) on all of your frontline fighters. Then start hammering away at Belias.

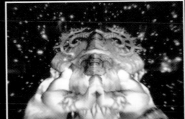

Belias unleashes his fearsome Firaja attack several times. Make sure the party is Oil-free, and keep everyone's HP above the halfway mark at all times.

This Esper is somewhat slow to attack, so it's possible to connect with multiple hits between his attacks. Stick to Cure and Cura to maintain health, but switch to Hi-Potions if you have characters slipping into HP critical conditions. Remember that potions work much faster than healing spells, so they delay your attacks for only a short time.

When Belias finally falls, you obtain his spirit and he appears on the License Board. One of your characters must unlock that spot by purchasing a license on an adjacent square, then spending 10 LP to obtain the Esper Belias for summoning.

Look for Espers like Belias on the License Board after you defeat them.

Find the Dawn Shard and Exit the Tomb

After the fight, Fran and Ashe speak of Espers and their bound relationship to the ones who conquer them. Balthier suggests that Belias has been guarding the Dynast-King's treasure, but Ashe corrects him: "Not so. Belias *is* the Dynast-King's treasure." Balthier, of course, is a bit disappointed.

When control returns, go forward through the door into the Chamber of First Light. Descend the stairs and walk past the Way Stone at the bottom, then climb the stairs on the opposite side. This triggers another event. The party discovers the Dawn Shard. But as Ashe approaches it, she sees a ghostly apparition.

As the apparition drifts away past the party, Lady Ashe is left holding the Dawn Shard. It now enters your inventory, and control returns to you. Return to the Way Stone you just passed at the bottom of the stairs. Use it to teleport back to the Hall of the Destroyer, then use the next (yellow) Way Stone to teleport out of the tomb to the Valley of Death.

Save your game, then proceed down the stairs toward the courtyard to trigger another series of events. An Imperial fleet, led by the *Leviathan*, drops in over the valley.

Soon the party finds itself before Judge Ghis once again. Ghis demands the nethicite—no, not the "base imitation" held by Penelo, which is manufacted nethicite, but rather the real thing: the Dawn Shard, "deifacted nethicite," one of the ancient relics of the Dynast-King. Apparently, Vayne wants all three of the great nethicite shards.

Ashe turns over the stone. The party is sent off to the Light Cruiser *Shiva* while Ghis orders his science staff to assess the Dawn Shard's powers. But as the Imperial nethicite research begins, Fran, sensitive to the Mist, is suddenly stricken.

It becomes clear that Ghis plans to usurp the Archadian throne from Vayne with the aid of this deifacted nethicite. Back on the *Shiva*, Fran, driven into a frenzy by the nethicite experiment on the Leviathan, decimates the guards. The party attempts to escape, but Vossler leaps in their way. And thus begins another boss battle.

Vossler

LVL	HP	EXP	LP
20	9318	0	30
Steal	Potion, Hi-Potion, Black Belt		

What a shame. Vossler seemed like a good guy, but his dreams for Dalmasca have pushed him to the dark side. He's a rugged warrior, and this fight can be very tough. Quickly dispatch his three minions, then focus on the boss. Magick attacks should work at first, but soon Vossler casts both Reflect and Haste on himself. He fights fast, with good combo attacks, and you must respond with pure physical combat.

If you have Quickenings at your disposal, try using them right away. You may wipe out Vossler's trio of guards and damage him significantly if you can put together a Quickening hit chain and trigger Inferno or Cataclysm. Alternately, you may consider summoning the Esper Belias, as he can make short work of Vossler and company.

Fran is still suffering from the effects of Berserk, so she's out of control but she won't attack the party members. Instead, she focuses her attacks on Vossler and his crew.

Fran is berserk as the fight opens, which means you can't control her. That's not a problem though. Just keep her healed, as she can dish out a lot of hurt to the bad guys.

Let Fran Rip

Vossler is all warrior. His magick is directed at himself in the form of Reflect and Haste. Beware his lighting-quick combo attacks.

Vossler unleashes more and faster combinations as his HP drops to critical, but you have six characters' worth of HP and MP to burn through, so you can outlast him. When Vossler falls, victory is bittersweet, for it is clear that he has no personal ambition. He is purely, as he says, "a son of Dalmasca."

Meanwhile, things are going crazy on the bridge of the *Leviathan*. The nethicite is overloading the ship's systems, the power test is spinning out of control and Ghis gets his proof of the Dynast-King's power.

Somehow, Balthier manages to pilot a craft out of the inferno. The Dawn Shard can be seen emerging as well, and soon they are after it.

This segment ends with another excerpt from the memoirs of the Marquis Ondore. He writes of leaving Bhujerba, seeking to bring together scattered pockets of the Resistance throughout Ivalice into a unified movement. Meanwhile, Lady Ashe and crew return to Rabanastre to lay low for awhile and bide their time. The scene shifts to the Imperial City of Archades...

OBJECTIVE

Meet with the Garif

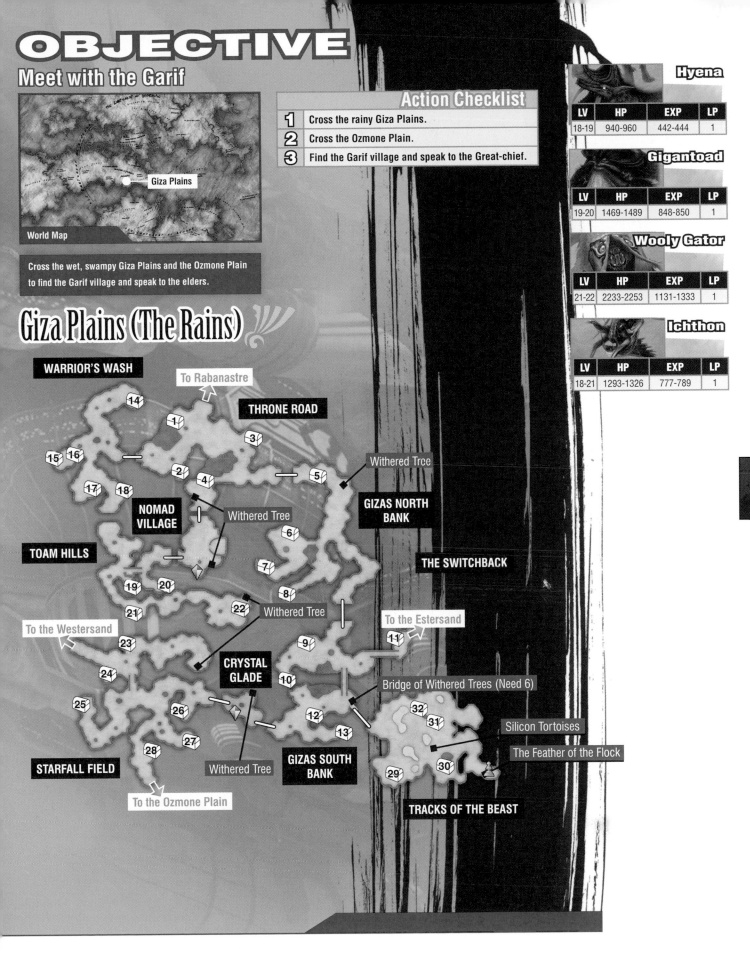

World Map

Giza Plains

Cross the wet, swampy Giza Plains and the Ozmone Plain to find the Garif village and speak to the elders.

Action Checklist

1. Cross the rainy Giza Plains.
2. Cross the Ozmone Plain.
3. Find the Garif village and speak to the Great-chief.

Hyena

LV	HP	EXP	LP
18-19	940-960	442-444	1

Gigantoad

LV	HP	EXP	LP
19-20	1469-1489	848-850	1

Wooly Gator

LV	HP	EXP	LP
21-22	2233-2253	1131-1333	1

Ichthon

LV	HP	EXP	LP
18-21	1293-1326	777-789	1

Giza Plains (The Rains)

WARRIOR'S WASH

To Rabanastre

THRONE ROAD

Withered Tree

GIZAS NORTH BANK

NOMAD VILLAGE

Withered Tree

TOAM HILLS

THE SWITCHBACK

To the Estersand

To the Westersand

Withered Tree

CRYSTAL GLADE

Bridge of Withered Trees (Need 6)

Silicon Tortoises

The Feather of the Flock

STARFALL FIELD

Withered Tree

GIZAS SOUTH BANK

To the Ozmone Plain

TRACKS OF THE BEAST

TREASURE TABLE				Normal		w/Diamond Armlet Equip.		
No.	App.%	gil %	If gil	50%	50%	gil	90%	10%
1	50%	55%	~150	Knot of Rust	Longbow	~500	Knot of Rust	Vanishga Mote
2	70%	40%	~150	Knot of Rust	Dark Mote	~500	Knot of Rust	Reflectga Mote
3	72%	35%	~150	Phoenix Down	Ether	~500	Knot of Rust	Float Mote
4	75%	30%	~150	Knot of Rust	Foe: status = Blind	~500	Knot of Rust	Warp Mote
5	67%	40%	~200	Knot of Rust	Dark Mote	~400	Knot of Rust	Reflectga Mote
6	50%	50%	~200	Knot of Rust	Battle Bamboo	~400	Knot of Rust	Vanishga Mote
7	67%	30%	~200	Echo Herbs	Ether	~400	Knot of Rust	Float Mote
8	67%	40%	~200	Knot of Rust	Foe: status = HP Critical	~400	Knot of Rust	Warp Mote
9	45%	50%	~220	Knot of Rust	Rose Corsage	~400	Knot of Rust	Vanishga Mote
10	67%	40%	~220	Phoenix Down	Dark Mote	~400	Knot of Rust	Reflectga Mote
11	68%	40%	~220	Knot of Rust	Foe: character HP = 100%	~400	Knot of Rust	Float Mote
12	67%	35%	~220	Echo Herbs	Ether	~400	Knot of Rust	Warp Mote
13	35%	60%	~50	Knot of Rust	Jade Collar	~200	Knot of Rust	Knot of Rust
14	67%	40%	~160	Knot of Rust	Dark Mote	~400	Knot of Rust	Reflectga Mote
15	67%	55%	~160	Knot of Rust	Bronze Mace	~400	Knot of Rust	Vanishga Mote
16	50%	35%	~160	Echo Herbs	Ether	~400	Knot of Rust	Float Mote
17	67%	35%	~160	Knot of Rust	Foe: status = Silence	~400	Knot of Rust	Warp Mote
18	50%	40%	~160	Knot of Rust	Onion Bombs	~400	Knot of Rust	Float Mote
19	67%	35%	~250	Knot of Rust	Dark Mote	~400	Knot of Rust	Reflectga Mote
20	50%	55%	~80	Knot of Rust	Main Gauche	~400	Knot of Rust	Vanishga Mote
21	67%	40%	~80	Knot of Rust	Foe: character status = Blind	~400	Knot of Rust	Float Mote
22	67%	30%	~80	Knot of Rust	Ether	~400	Knot of Rust	Warp Mote
23	69%	40%	~210	Phoenix Down	Dark Mote	~400	Knot of Rust	Reflectga Mote
24	50%	50%	~210	Knot of Rust	Heavy Coat	~400	Knot of Rust	Vanishga Mote
25	69%	25%	~210	Rose Corsage	Foe: status = Immobilize	~400	Knot of Rust	Float Mote
26	69%	40%	~210	Knot of Rust	Foe: undead	~400	Knot of Rust	Warp Mote
27	50%	55%	~210	Knot of Rust	Chainmail	~400	Knot of Rust	Vanishga Mote
28	73%	40%	~210	Echo Herbs	Water Mote	~400	Knot of Rust	Float Mote
29	67%	40%	~300	Knot of Rust	Foe: status = Disable	~400	Knot of Rust	Balance Mote
30	67%	40%	~300	Knot of Rust	Foe: lightning-weak	~1000	Knot of Rust	Hastega Mote
31	50%	50%	~300	Knot of Rust	Jackboots	~400	Knot of Rust	Holy Mote
32	50%	50%	~300	Knot of Rust	Black Belt	~400	Knot of Rust	Scathe Mote

The Story Continues...

Back in the Archadian Senate, the Emperor hears reports of Rozarrian war exercises, believed to be a precursor to an actual strike. Some Senators are clearly displeased with what they consider to be Lord Vayne's capricious actions.

Meanwhile, back in Dalmasca, the party discusses the Dawn Shard's awesome destructive force. It is becoming clear to Ashe and the others that Vayne seeks the power of deifacted nethicite for himself, a power that can subjugate all of Ivalice. Vayne most likely already has both the Dusk Shard and the Midlight Shard. Lady Ashe claims she will fight back with the Dawn Shard. She speaks of vengeance—but does she know how to use the stone?

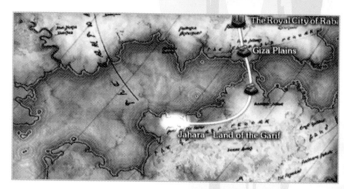

Fran says that the Garif may know. Magicite lore is part of their culture. Ashe asks to be taken there, beyond Ozmone Plain. Finally, everyone moves out into Rabanastre to prepare for the long journey to the Garif village.

Prep for the Journey

Take some time in Rabanastre to visit Montblanc at the Clan Hall for rewards, upgrade equipment, and shop for the latest magicks, technicks, and gambits. This is also a good time to check out the Notice Board at the Sandsea and complete a hunt or two for some extra gil. When you're ready, exit the city via Southgate and head into the Giza Plains.

Check the Sandsea Notice Board for more hunting petitions.

Giza Plains (The Rains)

Cross the Wet Plains

Wow, Giza looks different, doesn't it? The geography alters considerably once the rainy season kicks in; the "wadis" are swollen with the deluge. A new set of monsters roams the swampy plains, and treasure locations have changed. But the general movement from area to area is still the same.

Hey, everything's all wet! Wooly Gators are hopping out of the wash, too.

Beware Elementals!

Watch out for sparkling elementals that drift randomly through certain areas, like the Storm Elemental that appears when it's raining in Giza Plains. An elemental is usually neutral, but if you should cast any magicks within its vicinity, it will immediately turn hostile and cast strong magicks of its own at your party.

In general, it's wise to avoid elementals in the early going. Therefore, if an elemental is nearby, either manually switch off your active characters' gambits to avoid auto-combat and wait until the entity drifts away, or (better yet) just hold down the R2 button and flee, then return after a few seconds.

If other enemies are present near an elemental, you really should just flee. These other foes may notice you and give chase, but keep running! Wait until you are well clear of the elemental before releasing the R2 button to attack the foes that gave chase. If you do attract an elemental's attention, there are usually zone lines nearby and you can always run into the next area.

Of course, you can try to fight these elementals, but make sure your characters are both at a high level and well-equipped.

Fight south through the Hyenas and Gigantoads in Throne Road until you exit into the Nomad Village area. The nomads have packed up and left until the rains end, but the Save Crystal is still here. Talk to the nearby Weary Seeq to learn that the Ozmone Plain is to the south, and the Garif village is on the west end of that plain. He adds, "The creatures there are murder." Uh-oh.

! Withered Tree Bridge

A number of Withered Trees—six, to be exact—sit on the banks of the water in various parts of the Giza Plains. All six locations are marked on the Giza Plains maps in this section.

If you strike a Withered Tree, it falls into the water and floats downstream, snagging at a spot in the Gizas South Bank. When all six Withered Trees are snagged, they form a tangled walkbridge that you can cross into an area called Tracks of the Beast. There, you'll find an Urn that holds an item called the Feather of the Flock. There are also three extremely powerful Silicon Tortoises, all at Level 37 and most likely too tough to fight at this stage of the game.

Obtaining the Feather of the Flock is one part of the Cockatrice side quest. The Tracks of the Beast area is also where a clan mark appears when you take on the Rank III Clan Hunt "Paradise Risen," for the petitioner Nanau. See the "Side Quest" chapter for more details on both of these side events.

You can certainly explore any of the areas not mentioned in this walkthrough, seeking EXP, LP, dropped items, and treasure, all of which are useful and necessary for success. But this is a "story walkthrough," so this section presents the most direct route to Ozmone Plain.

Exit west into the Toam Hills, cross the bridge to the west, then head south and east along the narrow banks of the river to the passage into Starfall Field. Watch for a Wooly Gator and a pair of Ichthons along the way. They are not aggressive, but you can attack them if you want EXP, LP, or the loot items.

You can exit to the south into the Ozmone Plain from Starfall Field. If you feel like exploring, however, you can proceed west into the Crystal Glade to find a Save Crystal, then on to the Gizas South Bank. If you chopped down all six of the Withered Trees in the Giza Plains, you can cross over a bridge of entangled driftwood to the area mentioned earlier, Tracks of the Beast.

A neutral hunter wanders the Giza swamps, taking game trophies.

Ozmone Plain

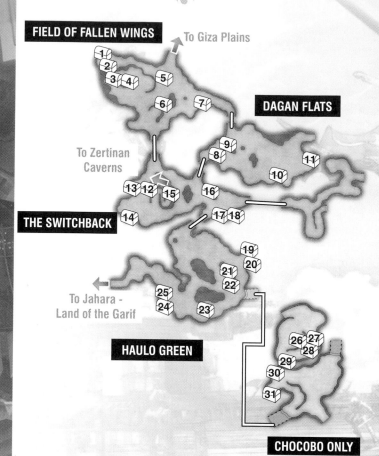

FIELD OF FALLEN WINGS

To Giza Plains

DAGAN FLATS

To Zertinan Caverns

THE SWITCHBACK

To Jahara - Land of the Garif

HAULO GREEN

CHOCOBO ONLY

TREASURE TABLE			Normal		w/Diamond Armlet Equip.		
No.	App.%	gil %	If gil	50%	50%	gil	90%	10%
1	60%	33%	~150	Potion	Hi-Potion	~500	Knot of Rust	Hi-Ether
2	50%	40%	~150	Potion	Sash	~500	Knot of Rust	Elixir
3	60%	33%	~150	Potion	Ether	~500	Knot of Rust	Hi-Ether
4	60%	33%	~150	Potion	Ally with Lowest HP	~500	Knot of Rust	Ruby Bracelet
5	60%	33%	~150	Potion	Phoenix Down	~500	Knot of Rust	Elixir
6	50%	40%	~150	Potion	Argyle Bracelet	~500	Knot of Rust	Hi-Ether
7	60%	33%	~150	Potion	Ether	~500	Knot of Rust	Elixir
8	60%	33%	~200	Potion	Ether	~500	Knot of Rust	Elixir
9	60%	33%	~200	Potion	Ally with "Slow" status	~500	Knot of Rust	Hi-Ether
10	60%	33%	~200	Aero Mote	Hi-Potion	~500	Knot of Rust	Hi-Ether
11	50%	40%	~250	Potion	Survival Vest	~500	Knot of Rust	Gold Shield
12	60%	33%	~150	Potion	Hi-Potion	~500	Knot of Rust	Hi-Ether
13	60%	33%	~150	Aero Mote	Ether	~500	Knot of Rust	Elixir
14	60%	33%	~150	Potion	Ally with "Sleep" status	~500	Knot of Rust	Hi-Ether
15	60%	33%	~150	Potion	Phoenix Down	~500	Knot of Rust	Elixir
16	60%	33%	~150	Potion	Ether	~500	Knot of Rust	Elixir
17	50%	40%	~150	Potion	Black Belt	~500	Knot of Rust	Hi-Ether
18	60%	33%	~150	Aero Mote	Ether	~500	Knot of Rust	Quasimodo Boots
19	60%	50%	~300	Potion	Gladius	~600	Knot of Rust	Elixir
20	60%	33%	~150	Potion	Ether	~500	Knot of Rust	Elixir
21	60%	33%	~180	Potion	Ally with "Confuse" status	~500	Knot of Rust	Hi-Ether
22	60%	33%	~180	Potion	If "Critical" status	~500	Knot of Rust	Feathered Cap
23	50%	40%	~150	Potion	Jackboots	~500	Knot of Rust	Elixir
24	50%	40%	~150	Potion	Flying Helm	~500	Knot of Rust	Hi-Ether
25	60%	33%	~150	Potion	Ether	~500	Knot of Rust	Elixir
26	60%	33%	~200	Aero Mote	Hi-Potion	~500	Knot of Rust	Hi-Ether
27	60%	33%	~200	Phoenix Down	Ether	~500	Knot of Rust	Hi-Ether
28	50%	40%	~200	Potion	Brigandine	~500	Knot of Rust	Elixir
29	60%	33%	~200	Potion	Remaining > or = then ally	~500	Knot of Rust	Magic Gloves
30	50%	40%	~200	Potion	Red Cap	~500	Knot of Rust	Hi-Ether
31	45%	55%	~400	Potion	Gold Amulet	~500	Knot of Rust	Elixir

Cross the Ozmone Plain

The foes grow considerably tougher here in the Ozmone Plain. Massive, brutal Zaghnals, flying Zus, and Mesmenir warhorses will test your party's limits in the Field of Fallen Wings, the northernmost sector of the plain. Try to engage foes one at a time; if they team up, you're in trouble. Zaghnals, in particular, like to trudge around in groups, and these cousins of the Werewolf are very powerful. Don't be afraid to flee if necessary. Always know the location of the nearest area exit.

Zaghnals are brutal beasts. If more than two engage you, run away.

Take the southernmost exit into an area called The Switchback. Herds of Mesmenirs wander this area. Again, be aware that these foes can be challenging when they work in tandem, depending on your characters' levels and quality of equipment.

Except for solitary Vipers, foes on the Ozmone Plain tend to travel in packs. This makes each fight very precarious.

Look out for a dangerous rare beast called the Bull Croc in The Shred area.

A rock ramp in the middle of The Switchback spirals downward into the Zertinan Caverns, but foes are even tougher down there, so leave them alone for now. In any case, it's time to visit the Garif. Leave The Switchback via the south exit into Haulo Green, then exit that area west into Jahara, Land of the Garif.

Zaghnal

LV	HP	EXP	LP
23-24	3157-3179	1201-1206	2

Wu

LV	HP	EXP	LP
20-22	1689-1729	813-817	1

Zu

LV	HP	EXP	LP
21-22	1880-1896	1025-1029	1

Black Chocobo

LV	HP	EXP	LP
19-23	1116-1180	687-703	1

Mesmenir

LV	HP	EXP	LP
20-22	1528-1568	848-852	1

Red Chocobo

LV	HP	EXP	LP
19-23	1116-1180	687-703	1

Viper

LV	HP	EXP	LP
20-21	1410-1430	919-921	1

Bull Croc (Rare Game)

LV	HP	EXP	LP
23-24	13968-14078	2075-2168	5

Hybrid Gator

LV	HP	EXP	LP
21-23	2233-2273	1131-1135	1

Jahara—Land of the Garif

Meet with the Great-chief

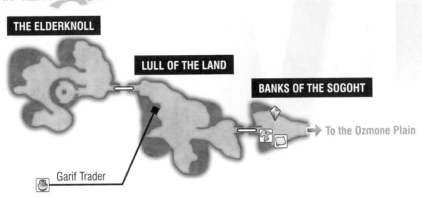

THE ELDERKNOLL

LULL OF THE LAND

BANKS OF THE SOGOHT

To the Ozmone Plain

Garif Trader

Save your game at the Save Crystal and buy maps from the Cartographer's Guild moogle near the chocobo pen if you can afford it—the Ozmone Plain map is pricey. Next, talk to the Garif Warrior at the bridge. He's kind of surly, but another warrior approaches to vouch for you. It's the Garif War-chief, and he lets you pass into the village.

After you cross the bridge, the War-chief introduces himself as Supinelu. He says you must speak to the elders about the nethicite. Now enter the village. Talking to the Garif, it becomes clear that others have been here before you, requesting information about "the stones."

War-chief Supinelu lets you into his village.

Stop at the Garif Trader to sell your loot and upgrade your equipment; he's got some good stuff. Also, consider selling off your old, obsolete equipment for the extra gil. Then go up the hill to the northeast and talk to High-chief Zayalu; he is standing next to two sitting Garif. He says you must speak to the Great-chief to learn of the stones. Then he gives you a **Jaya Stick** to deliver to War-chief Supinelu.

High-chief Zayalu wants you to take a Jaya Stick to the War-chief.

Now head over to the next bridge to the west. Talk to War-chief Supinelu to give him the Jaya Stick. Tell him you want to meet the Great-chief. Ashe joins the conversation and announces her lineage. This seems to be enough for the War-chief and you are granted an audience with the elder chief. Cross the bridge to the Elderknoll. Approach the warrior-guards and request a meeting.

This triggers an event in which the Great-chief examines the used nethicite. He tells of the history of the stones. When the event ends, Lord Larsa makes a surprise appearance with some disturbing news.

Larsa believes that the blessing of His Grace the Gran Kiltias Anastasis at Bur-Omisace may give Ashe the legitimacy she needs to wear the crown and restore Dalmasca. As queen, she can declare peace with the Empire, stop the Marquis, and end the threat of a wider conflagration.

In a final short event, Balthier notes the *Leviathan*'s ability to fly into the heavy jagd of Raithwall's tomb, thus proving that even manufacted nethicite has powers that normal magicite does not. When control finally returns to you, Larsa joins your party as a guest and you have a new objective.

Hop a Chocobo to the Golmore Jungle

But before you tackle this new objective, it's time to backtrack a bit and get across the Ozmone Plain to Golmore Jungle. Many powerful monsters lurk along the route, and you may want to fight them to level up and accumulate LP and loot. Then again, you may want a chocobo ride—just for the fun, convenience, and speed of it.

While exiting the Garif village, War-chief Supinelu hands over the gift of either **Bowgun** or a **Killer Bow**, complete with the appropriate onion ammunition, plus a free ride on a chocobo. Talk to Gurdy, the floating moogle who tends the chocobo in the pen. He confirms the War-chief's one-time offer for a free ride. Go ahead and hire a chocobo. Your mount time is limited to just three minutes, so get going!

Gurdy offers a free chocobo ride, courtesy of the Garif War-chief. Take him up on it for a quick, monster-free trip through the Ozmone Plain to Golmore Jungle.

The party begins in the Haulo Green area of the Ozmone Plain. Check the area map regularly to make sure you're following the most efficient route. Go north to The Switchback, then east into a narrow, winding canyon called The Greensnake. Monsters won't attack while you're astride a chocobo, so that's one less thing to worry about. Now sprint northeast through the Field of Light Winds to the Sunlit Path. When you arrive at the Sunlit Path, you trigger a pair of events.

On one side, we see Ashe and Captain Basch struggling with the notion of making peace with an occupying power. On the other, we see the intrigue at work behind that power: Archadian Judges consult in the Imperial Palace, speaking of Vayne, Larsa, and the wishes and workings of the Senate.

OBJECTIVE

Meet with the Gran Kiltias at Mt Bur-Omisace

World Map

Golmore Jungle (West)

Action Checklist

1 ☐ Find the Eruyt Village.

Mt Bur-Omisace is your ultimate destination. To reach this area, though, you must first complete several sub-tasks and pass through three different areas—the mist-shrouded Golmore Jungle, the dank Henne Mines, and the frigid canyons of the Paramina Rift.

Golmore Jungle (West)

To the Ozmone Plain

= Magick Barrier

PATHS OF CHAINED LIGHT

Map Urn

THE NEEDLEBRAKE

	Panther		
LV	**HP**	**EXP**	**LP**
21-23	1299-1519	900-1086	1

	Malboro		
LV	**HP**	**EXP**	**LP**
22-23	1573-1693	1073-1177	1

	Great Malboro		
LV	**HP**	**EXP**	**LP**
22-23	1630-1750	1141-1245	1

	Gargoyle		
LV	**HP**	**EXP**	**LP**
23-24	1436-1494	894-995	1

	Treant		
LV	**HP**	**EXP**	**LP**
23-24	4274-4384	1089-1242	1

TREASURE TABLE			Normal		w/Diamond Armlet Equip.		
No.	App.%	gil %	If gil	50%	50%	gil	90%	10%
1	75%	20%	~200	Potion	Antidote	~500	Knot of Rust	X-Potion
2	55%	40%	~200	Potion	Jackboots	~500	Knot of Rust	X-Potion
3	75%	20%	~200	Potion	Ether	~500	Knot of Rust	X-Potion
4	75%	20%	~200	Potion	Antidote	~500	Knot of Rust	X-Potion
5	75%	20%	~200	Potion	Eye Drops	~500	Knot of Rust	X-Potion
6	75%	30%	~200	Potion	Foe: item AMT ≥ 10	~500	Knot of Rust	X-Potion
7	75%	30%	~200	Potion	Foe: furthest	~500	Knot of Rust	X-Potion
8	75%	20%	~200	Potion	Sirius	~500	Knot of Rust	X-Potion
9	75%	20%	~200	Potion	Eye Drops	~500	Knot of Rust	X-Potion

Find Eruyt Village

Knock out the pack of Panthers (weak against the Ice element) at the first intersection and go left, then take the first right down the stairs to find the Map Urn with a full map of Golmore Jungle. Follow the path east and defeat the creepy Malboros. After doing so, go south and proceed into The Needlebrake.

Nail Treants with Aero for quicker KOs.

Keep moving along the northernmost route, heading east until you reach a glowing blue magickal barrier that triggers an event. Fran explains that the jungle denies her passage, and opens a secret path to her home, Eruyt Village. When the scene ends, follow the new path to trigger a second event during which Fran tells Vaan to look for Mjrn in the village ahead, and then bring her out. You need Mjrn's help to get past the barriers in the wood.

A magickal barrier blocks the party's access to the east.

Watch Your Status

Magick abounds in Golmore Jungle; its denizens cast a lot of status effect spells. Your party will get hit with Slow, Blind, Petrify, and Sleep, so counter these effects with magicks and items. Esuna is a particularly valuable spell to own and license for this jungle trek, since it removes multiple status effects in one shot.

By now, you should have set up gambits that automatically apply the magick or items necessary to remove status effects. Some gambits are for specific status ailments such as "Ally: status = Sleep." But if you lack a gambit specifically related to the status ailment you want to cure, just set the condition for "Ally: any."

Your character will then use the associated action or item (such as Blindna, Alarm Clock, Vox, etc.) only when an ally has the affliction that can be removed by the action or item.

Fran opens a secret path to Eruyt Village, where she says she is not welcome.

Before entering the village proper, check out the wares of Tetran, the traveling moogle merchant that you helped to escape from the *Leviathan*. If you don't have Esuna yet, buy it and license it for several party members right away! Stock up on status-removing items too; in particular, purchase a good supply of Handerkerchiefs for removing Oil status. (These will be important when you fight the Elder Wyrm.) You can also buy a cheap Eruyt Village map from his partner Lulucce and use the Save Crystal. When you're ready, head east into Eruyt Village.

Eruyt Village

Action Checklist

1. Enter the village and seek Mjrn.

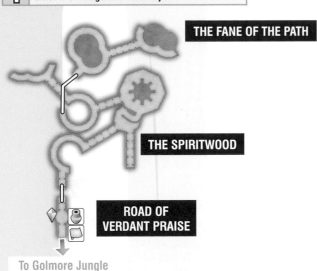

THE FANE OF THE PATH

THE SPIRITWOOD

ROAD OF VERDANT PRAISE

To Golmore Jungle

Look for Mjrn

Follow the winding path past the viera guards and into the central garden. Talk to the villagers to learn you are unwelcome in the Wood. Follow the winding route up to the next area, the Fane of the Path, and follow it to the end to trigger another event. A priestess named Jote indicates that Mjrn is not here and explains that she left the Wood and headed west.

You can learn much by asking questions of the viera in the Eruyt Village, but remember that Mjrn is the one you seek.

After this event, walk back to the entrance area, the Road of Verdant Praise. Another event occurs in which Larsa interprets Jote's cryptic clue to mean Mjrn is somewhere in the Henne Mines. Unfortunately, the mine region is a colony of the Empire, and most likely crawling with soldiers. This brings up a new objective.

Fran enters the village to seek help. Jote indicates to head west if you seek Mjrn.

OBJECTIVE
Find Mjrn in the Henne Mines

World Map

Golmore Jungle

Action Checklist
1 Return to the Sunlit Path in Ozmone Plain.

2 Ride to the hidden Henne Mines via secret chocobo trails.

Enemies do not attack when riding a chocobo, which you must do to reach the Henne Mines.

Ride the Chocobo

Again, the overall objective is to reach Mt Bur-Omisace. However, you cannot get past the magick barriers of Golmore Jungle until you find the viera, Mjrn. She's somewhere in the Henne Mines just south of Ozmone Plain.

Golmore Jungle/Ozmone Plain

FIELD OF LIGHT WINDS

To the Golmore Jungle

SUNLIT PATH

THE GREENSNAKE

To the Ozmone Plain

THE SHRED

= Magick Barrier

PATHS OF CHAINED LIGHT

To the Henne Mines

Map Urn

Chocobo Only

* Please see map of Ozmone Plain for treasure chest locations and drop percentages.

THE NEEDLEBRAKE

* Please see map of Golmore Jungle (West) for treasure chest locations and drop percentages.

Return to Ozmone Plain

Your next move is to retrace your route back out of Golmore Jungle. Starting at Eruyt Village, exit south across the bridge and then proceed northwest out of the forest, bearing right at every intersection or crossing. At the Sunlit Path (the clearing with the Save Crystal) back

in Ozmone Plain, the party finds two wounded Imperial soldiers on the ground with their chocobo walking around loose.

Help out this Imperial, showing him that you're all just humes when you get down to it. He has a chocobo you can borrow.

Talk to the soldier with the Talk Icon above his head and he asks for a Potion for his badly wounded friend. Select "Give him a Potion" to help. This revives his friend, making him grateful. He states that he just came from the Henne Mines. He then offers you the use of his mount, saying that there is terrain nearby that is only accessible via chocobo.

Talk to the standing Imperial again and select "Borrow one." You end up on top of a rather large bird, ready to ride. It isn't far to the chocobo path, but you have only 180 seconds of game time, so don't dally.

Exit southwest to the Field of Light Winds and stay close to the left wall. After just a few steps, you reach an opening with a tree, white flowers, and other foliage, plus a yellow chocobo feeding. Run directly into this area to the left of the tree to enter a chocobo trail.

Here's the spot in the Field of Light Winds where the chocobo trail begins. Just run right into it!

After crossing the zone line, the party ends up in the southern part of an area called The Shred. Continue to the south exit, which leads to the entrance to the Henne Mines. Your approach triggers a quick event. In it, the party comes upon a grim discovery: dead bodies strewn outside the mine entrance. Press the ⊙ button and select "Yes" to dismount the chocobo, then walk into the tunnel entrance to the Henne Mines.

Researchers from the Draklor Laboratory met an unpleasant end here at Henne Mines. What were they looking for?

The Henne Mines

Action Checklist
1. Get through the Henne Mines gates.
2. Survive the Jelly ambush.
3. Defeat Tiamat.

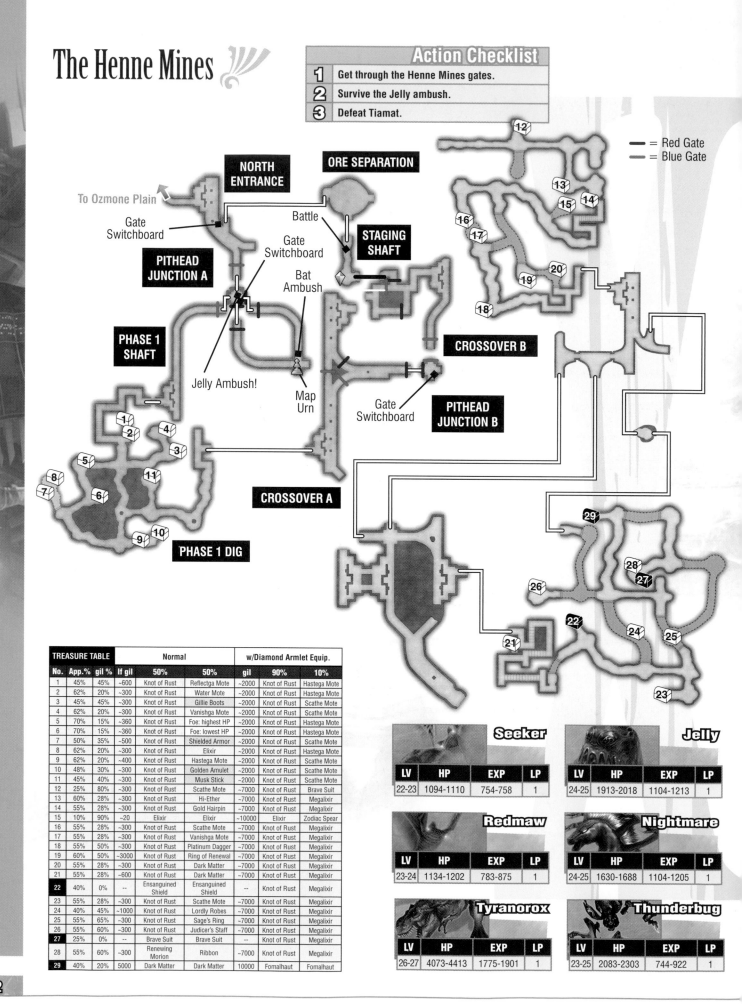

= Red Gate
= Blue Gate

NORTH ENTRANCE

ORE SEPARATION

To Ozmone Plain

Gate Switchboard

Battle

STAGING SHAFT

Gate Switchboard

PITHEAD JUNCTION A

Bat Ambush

PHASE 1 SHAFT

Jelly Ambush!

Map Urn

CROSSOVER B

Gate Switchboard

PITHEAD JUNCTION B

CROSSOVER A

PHASE 1 DIG

TREASURE TABLE		Normal		w/Diamond Armlet Equip.		
No.	App.%	gil %	If gil	50%	50%	gil	90%	10%
1	45%	45%	~600	Knot of Rust	Reflectga Mote	~2000	Knot of Rust	Hastega Mote
2	62%	20%	~300	Knot of Rust	Water Mote	~2000	Knot of Rust	Hastega Mote
3	45%	45%	~300	Knot of Rust	Gillie Boots	~2000	Knot of Rust	Scathe Mote
4	62%	20%	~300	Knot of Rust	Vanishga Mote	~2000	Knot of Rust	Scathe Mote
5	70%	15%	~360	Knot of Rust	Foe: highest HP	~2000	Knot of Rust	Hastega Mote
6	70%	15%	~360	Knot of Rust	Foe: lowest HP	~2000	Knot of Rust	Hastega Mote
7	50%	35%	~500	Knot of Rust	Shielded Armor	~2000	Knot of Rust	Scathe Mote
8	62%	20%	~300	Knot of Rust	Elixir	~2000	Knot of Rust	Hastega Mote
9	62%	20%	~400	Knot of Rust	Hastega Mote	~2000	Knot of Rust	Scathe Mote
10	48%	30%	~300	Knot of Rust	Golden Amulet	~2000	Knot of Rust	Scathe Mote
11	45%	40%	~300	Knot of Rust	Musk Stick	~2000	Knot of Rust	Scathe Mote
12	25%	80%	~300	Knot of Rust	Scathe Mote	~7000	Knot of Rust	Brave Suit
13	60%	28%	~300	Knot of Rust	Hi-Ether	~7000	Knot of Rust	Megalixir
14	55%	28%	~300	Knot of Rust	Gold Hairpin	~7000	Knot of Rust	Megalixir
15	10%	90%	~20	Elixir	Elixir	~10000	Elixir	Zodiac Spear
16	55%	28%	~300	Knot of Rust	Scathe Mote	~7000	Knot of Rust	Megalixir
17	55%	28%	~300	Knot of Rust	Vanishga Mote	~7000	Knot of Rust	Megalixir
18	55%	50%	~300	Knot of Rust	Platinum Dagger	~7000	Knot of Rust	Megalixir
19	60%	50%	~3000	Knot of Rust	Ring of Renewal	~7000	Knot of Rust	Megalixir
20	55%	28%	~300	Knot of Rust	Dark Matter	~7000	Knot of Rust	Megalixir
21	55%	28%	~600	Knot of Rust	Dark Matter	~7000	Knot of Rust	Megalixir
22	40%	0%	--	Ensanguined Shield	Ensanguined Shield	--	Knot of Rust	Megalixir
23	55%	28%	~300	Knot of Rust	Scathe Mote	~7000	Knot of Rust	Megalixir
24	40%	45%	~1000	Knot of Rust	Lordly Robes	~7000	Knot of Rust	Megalixir
25	55%	65%	~300	Knot of Rust	Sage's Ring	~7000	Knot of Rust	Megalixir
26	55%	60%	~300	Knot of Rust	Judicer's Staff	~7000	Knot of Rust	Megalixir
27	25%	0%	--	Brave Suit	Brave Suit	--	Knot of Rust	Megalixir
28	55%	60%	~300	Renewing Morion	Ribbon	~7000	Knot of Rust	Megalixir
29	40%	20%	5000	Dark Matter	Dark Matter	10000	Fomalhaut	Fomalhaut

Seeker

LV	HP	EXP	LP
22-23	1094-1110	754-758	1

Jelly

LV	HP	EXP	LP
24-25	1913-2018	1104-1213	1

Redmaw

LV	HP	EXP	LP
23-24	1134-1202	783-875	1

Nightmare

LV	HP	EXP	LP
24-25	1630-1688	1104-1205	1

Tyranorox

LV	HP	EXP	LP
26-27	4073-4413	1775-1901	1

Thunderbug

LV	HP	EXP	LP
23-25	2083-2303	744-922	1

Navigate the Mine Maze

Step forward into the shaft, turn right, and proceed south until you find a glowing blue Gate Switchboard on the left side of the shaft. The following notes explain the gate system in the Henne Mines.

All mine gates are red or blue, as indicated by the glowing lights above each gate. (You can also see the gates marked by their color on the maps in this section.)

Each Gate Switchboard glows with either red or blue phosphor. The current color indicates which gates are closed.

Thus, if the switchboard glows blue, all of the blue gates are closed and all of the red gates are open. If the switchboard glows red, all of the red gates are closed and all of the blue gates are open.

Press the switch on the first Gate Switchboard to change it from blue to red, thus opening the blue gate just down the shaft.

When you first approach the switchboard in the North Entrance, it glows blue—blue gates close, red gates open. Press the switch to reverse this; the switchboard glows red—red gates close, blue gates open.

This opens the first gate just down the tunnel to the south, a blue gate. (It opens during a brief event.) Go through the open gate and proceed into the next area, Pithead Junction A.

A wounded Imperial warns the party about danger in the mines. Another Gate Switchboard is on the wall nearby. Press its switch to change it from red to blue. Suddenly, grotesque Jelly beasts drop from the ceiling and attack! They drop in two waves, three at a time. They're weak against Fire, so cast Fire at them, or wipe them out with a Quickening chain.

A Jelly ambush drops from above (two waves, with three Jellies in each wave) each time you press the switch in Pithead Junction A.

After eliminating the Jellies, exit the junction south or east and follow the bat-infested tunnel to the Map Urn for a full map of the mines. Near the urn, a flock of Seeker and Redmaw bats attack. Now return to Pithead Junction A.

Press the gate switch to close the red gates and open the blue gates again, then exit west. Follow the Phase 1 Shaft around into another big bat swarm; decimate the foes and proceed to the platform at the tunnel's end. A doorway here leads to a staircase that descends into a large excavated cavern, the Phase 1 Dig.

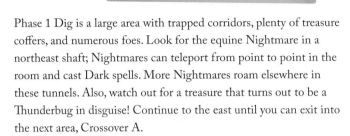

After wiping out the Jellies in the junction, you face quite a few Seekers and Redmaws in a row. Try to string together a nice, long Battle Chain.

Chain the Bats

Phase 1 Dig is a large area with trapped corridors, plenty of treasure coffers, and numerous foes. Look for the equine Nightmare in a northeast shaft; Nightmares can teleport from point to point in the room and cast Dark spells. More Nightmares roam elsewhere in these tunnels. Also, watch out for a treasure that turns out to be a Thunderbug in disguise! Continue to the east until you can exit into the next area, Crossover A.

Solve the Gate Puzzle

Now you must open the gates in the correct order to get north into the Staging Shaft. In Crossover A, move north to where the tracks split; take the left fork heading north through an open blue gate to meet a big dinosaur, a Tyranorox. Don't worry—his bite is bad,

but he's easier to drop than he looks. Hit him with a few Aero spells to take him down a notch; Tyranoroxes are weak versus Wind magick. Continue north, then exit east into Crossover B.

Be ready for this Tyranorox! Don't let the bats distract you from a focused attack against this large creature.

In Crossover B, go left (north) and through the open blue gate. Follow the mine shaft until you reach another junction area, Pithead Junction B. Ready for more Jellies than you ever thought possible? Press the Gate Switchboard switch to change it from red to blue—that is, closed blue gates and open red gates. After doing so, a total of eight Jellies drop from the ceiling, with a lot more on the way! If you have any characters with Quickening spells and a Mist Charge to get a Quickening started, give that a try. If not, you may want to run out of there, fast.

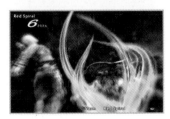

Boy, that's a lot of Jelly. Use a Quickening on them, or just run like crazy.

Now head east back into Crossover A, take the right fork to veer north (fighting another Tyranorox en route), and then exit into Crossover B. This time the red gates are open instead of the blue, so turn right and then go left around three corners until you can exit north and veer into the Staging Shaft.

This triggers a dramatic event in which Larsa notes the rich veins of magicite in this mine, and then Mjrn suddenly appears, staggering and disoriented. She calls Ashe a "power-hungry hume" and then rushes up a mine shaft to the north. A Save Crystal, at last! Save your game and follow Mjrn up that shaft.

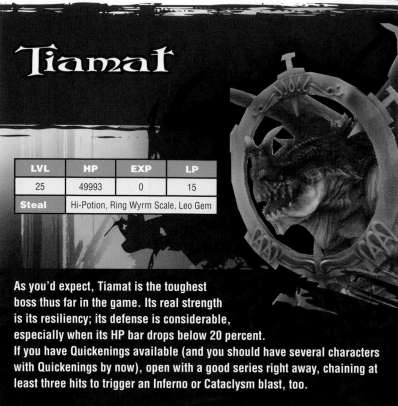

Tiamat

LVL	HP	EXP	LP
25	49993	0	15
Steal	Hi-Potion, Ring Wyrm Scale, Leo Gem		

As you'd expect, Tiamat is the toughest boss thus far in the game. Its real strength is its resiliency; its defense is considerable, especially when its HP bar drops below 20 percent. If you have Quickenings available (and you should have several characters with Quickenings by now), open with a good series right away, chaining at least three hits to trigger an Inferno or Cataclysm blast, too.

Tiamat will focus its attention almost exclusively on one target at a time, as most of its attacks are physical. That target will need a load of healing from his/her comrades. If you have the Curaga spell, set up characters with a gambit that casts it on any HP Critical ally, and be ready with Hi-Potions. Finally, it's a good idea for each party member to have a gambit that casts Raise or uses Phoenix Down on any ally, so that if someone gets KO'd, he or she gets revived automatically.

Note that just one good shield can make the difference against an enemy like Tiamat, who deals out primarily physical damage and focuses on single targets. Make sure your "heavy" fighter (best Strength and armor) has the best shield available, then send him or her in to trade blows toe to toe with Tiamat using a powerful melee weapon like an axe or hammer. Have your other two controllable characters hang back with ranged weapons loaded mainly for support (status effect bolts/arrows/bullets).

KEEP LARSA WHOLE

Like other guest characters, Larsa is a deadly and efficient ally to have in a boss fight. His quick and unlimited use of Hi-Potions alone makes him invaluable, and his attacks are quite effective. Make sure he stays healed! If he goes down, revive him immediately. After all, you can't swap him out.

Tiamat likes to munch on one target until that one falls, then turn to the next lucky victim. Have two characters focus primarily on healing while the other two (one of whom is Larsa) focus on pounding away at the boss.

After Tiamat finally goes down, Mjrn emerges in a state of collapse. Fran goes to her and learns why Mjrn came to investigate the hume activity in the mines. The party returns the stricken viera to her village. In return, Jote hands over **Lente's Tear**, a key item that will grant the party access through the magickal barriers in the woods.

Golmore Jungle (East)

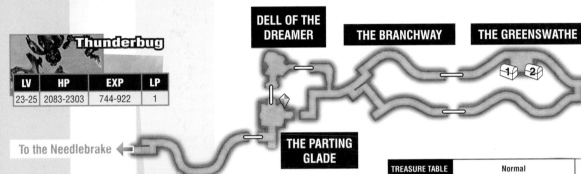

DELL OF THE DREAMER

THE BRANCHWAY

THE GREENSWATHE

To the Paramina Rift

To the Needlebrake

THE PARTING GLADE

WHISPERLEAF WAY

Thunderbug			
LV	HP	EXP	LP
23-25	2083-2303	744-922	1

Walkthrough

TREASURE TABLE				Normal		w/Diamond Armlet Equip.		
No.	App.%	gil %	If gil	50%	50%	gil	90%	10%
1	75%	20%	~200	Potion	Eye Drops	~500	Knot of Rust	X-Potion
2	75%	20%	~200	Potion	Battle Bamboo	~500	Knot of Rust	X-Potion

Action Checklist

The enemies here are the same as Golmore Jungle (West) except for Diresaur.

1 Navigate through eastern Golmore Jungle.

2 Defeat the Elder Wyrm.

3 Proceed to the Paramina Rift.

Diresaur			
LV	HP	EXP	LP
27-28	5281-5621	2891-3017	2

Move into the Dragon's Dell

Exit Eruyt Village into Golmore Jungle and go left to the magick seal. Sure enough, it dissipates when the party approaches and they pass through it safely into Whisperleaf Way. Fight past the Malboros and Gargoyles along the path and enter The Parting Glade to find another Save Crystal. Use it! Just to the north, in the Dell of the Dreamer, another powerful boss is about to awaken.

Lente's Tear enables the party to pass right through the magickal barriers in Golmore Jungle.

Elder Wyrm

LVL	HP	EXP	LP
27	71692	0	14
Steal	Succulent Fruit, Feystone, Emperor Scale		

This guy's big, and he's mad. He has two Treant minions and an arsenal of nasty status magicks like Slow, Blind, Silence, Sleep, Confuse, and Poison. He also uses Oil, then follows up later with Fireball, which can inflict over 1,000 HP of damage a pop. Ouch!

But overall, the Elder Wyrm doesn't inflict big damage with his physical attacks. What makes this battle tough is the onslaught of ailments caused by his Sporefall ability. If you don't come to this battle well-prepared, you will spend much of the fight removing status ailments instead of inflicting damage on the beast.

So, how do you prepare for the Elder Wyrm? First, make sure Esuna is in your gambits somewhere. It consumes a good chunk of MP to cast, but considering the multiple status ailments the Elder Wyrm inflicts, Esuna relief is well worth it. You should also try to keep the party from bunching up. If the party is spread out enough, there is a good chance that Sporefall will not hit everyone and you will have at least one character ailment-free and ready to cast Esuna. Finally, be prepared with with items like Handkerchief, Echo Herbs, Antidote, and so on, for removing bad status effects.

 ESUNA OR LATER

Cast Esuna on allies to remove status ailments. It won't remove Oil, however; that only comes off with the Handkerchief item. Remove Oil immediately before the Elder Wyrm can launch a Fireball attack.

The Elder Wyrm spews evil status magick.

Start with a Quickening chain, if possible. With a good chain that triggers an area attack like Inferno or Cataclysm, you can hurt the Elder Wyrm and seriously degrade his two Treant minions. Finish up the Treants quickly and focus on the boss. Watch for those status ailments, especially the ones that are immediately debilitating, like Sleep (removed by Esuna or Alarm Clock) or Silence (removed by Vox, Esuna, or Echo Herbs). Use non-afflicted characters to remove these first.

If your active characters get overwhelmed by the ailments, make a wholesale party change. If the fresh reserve members have Quickenings available, unleash a Quickening sequence right away. Keep the pressure on the wyrm!

After the fight, go south into The Parting Glade and use the Save Crystal. Next, continue the journey east through the jungle, pushing into the Branchway where a flock of Gargoyles await. Continue east through the Greenswathe until you finally reach the Paramina Rift.

Dire Sore

If you take the northern path across the Branchway and the Greenswathe, you run into a powerful Level 27 Diresaur protecting treasure on a platform.

Paramina Rift (North)

Action Checklist

1 Cross the northern edge of the Paramina Rift to Mt Bur-Omisace.

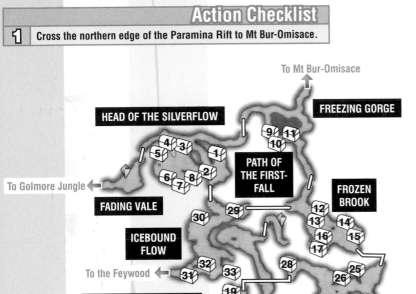

To Mt Bur-Omisace

HEAD OF THE SILVERFLOW

FREEZING GORGE

PATH OF THE FIRST-FALL

To Golmore Jungle

FADING VALE

FROZEN BROOK

ICEBOUND FLOW

To the Feywood

SPINE OF THE ICEWORM

KARYDINE GLACIER

SILVERFLOW'S END

To the Stilshrine of Miriam

White Wolf			
LV	HP	EXP	LP
24-25	1498-1608	894-987	1

Wild Onion			
LV	HP	EXP	LP
25-27	1496-1736	699-907	1

Slaven Warder			
LV	HP	EXP	LP
27-28	2623-2743	1124-1225	1

Skull Knight			
LV	HP	EXP	LP
25-26	1873-1933	1235-1328	1

Lizard			
LV	HP	EXP	LP
24-26	2342-2562	1172-1358	1

Cross the Rift to Mt Bur-Omisace

The Paramina Rift is a snowy, dangerous place, but you don't have to spend much time here. After saving at the crystal in the Fading Vale, exit via the northeast canyon. Fight through the the Head of the Silverflow area. Move across the rock bridge heading east until you reach a fork in the path.

The right fork leads down into an area filled with Skull Knights and other cold-weather creatures; you can explore this area, fighting and looking for treasure. Or you can just skip it for now and take the left fork instead up the northeast canyon into the next area, Freezing Gorge.

Larsa leads your party across the white wasteland of the Paramina Rift toward the holy mountain. Will it be worth it?

				Normal		w/Diamond Armlet Equip.		
TREASURE TABLE								
No.	App.%	gil %	If gil	50%	50%	gil	90%	10%
1	45%	55%	~220	Phoenix Down	Betelgeuse	~750	Knot of Rust	X-Potion
2	60%	40%	~190	Phoenix Down	Blue Fang	~800	Knot of Rust	X-Potion
3	60%	40%	~240	Phoenix Down	Ether	~700	Knot of Rust	X-Potion
4	60%	40%	~160	Phoenix Down	Blue Fang	~800	Knot of Rust	X-Potion
5	60%	40%	~210	Phoenix Down	Foe: highest max HP	~770	Knot of Rust	X-Potion
6	60%	40%	~210	Phoenix Down	Blue Fang	~700	Knot of Rust	X-Potion
7	60%	40%	~210	Phoenix Down	Foe: lowest max HP	~800	Knot of Rust	X-Potion
8	45%	55%	~200	Phoenix Down	Osafune	~800	Knot of Rust	X-Potion
9	60%	40%	~200	Phoenix Down	Blue Fang	~700	Knot of Rust	X-Potion
10	50%	50%	~200	Golden Armor	Serpent Rod	~800	Knot of Rust	X-Potion
11	60%	40%	~200	Phoenix Down	Foe: highest MP	~700	Knot of Rust	X-Potion
12	70%	30%	~200	Phoenix Down	Blue Fang	~700	Knot of Rust	X-Potion
13	50%	40%	~200	Phoenix Down	Quasimodo Boots	~700	Knot of Rust	X-Potion
14	50%	40%	~200	Golden Helm	Blue Fang	~800	Knot of Rust	X-Potion
15	75%	30%	~200	Phoenix Down	Foe: lowest MP	~700	Knot of Rust	X-Potion
16	60%	35%	~200	Bangle	Bangle	~700	Knot of Rust	Elixir
17	50%	40%	~200	Phoenix Down	Musk Stick	~800	Knot of Rust	X-Potion
18	60%	40%	~200	Phoenix Down	Blue Fang	~700	Knot of Rust	X-Potion
19	60%	40%	~200	Phoenix Down	Blue Fang	~800	Knot of Rust	X-Potion
20	60%	40%	~200	Phoenix Down	Ether	~800	Knot of Rust	X-Potion
21	40%	50%	~200	Thief's Cuffs	Thief's Cuffs	~700	Knot of Rust	Nishijin Belt
22	45%	50%	~200	Phoenix Down	Burgonet	~700	Knot of Rust	X-Potion
23	30%	70%	~200	Phoenix Down	Shielded Armor	~800	Knot of Rust	X-Potion
24	60%	40%	~200	Phoenix Down	Foe: ice-weak	~700	Knot of Rust	X-Potion
25	45%	55%	~200	Phoenix Down	Glacial Staff	~800	Knot of Rust	X-Potion
26	60%	40%	~200	Phoenix Down	Blue Fang	~700	Knot of Rust	X-Potion
27	60%	40%	~200	Phoenix Down	Foe: ice-vulnerable	~800	Knot of Rust	X-Potion
28	65%	40%	~200	Phoenix Down	Ether	~700	Knot of Rust	X-Potion
29	50%	50%	~200	Phoenix Down	Glacial Staff	~700	Knot of Rust	X-Potion
30	60%	40%	~200	Phoenix Down	Blue Fang	~800	Knot of Rust	Ice Shield
31	40%	50%	~200	Phoenix Down	Ice Shield	~700	Knot of Rust	X-Potion
32	60%	40%	~200	Phoenix Down	Foe: HP ≥ 2000	~700	Knot of Rust	X-Potion
33	60%	40%	~200	Phoenix Down	Foe: HP < 2000	~800	Knot of Rust	X-Potion

The party's entrance into Freezing Gorge triggers a pair of short events. Balthier and Larsa have a brief exchange about knowing the heart of one's own father. Then the scene shifts to Archadia for a meeting between the Emperor Gramis and his recently returned son, Vayne. When control returns, move up the Freezing Gorge, veering left at the fork to follow the canyon to the northeast. This takes the party into the Sand-Strewn Pass of Mt Bur-Omisace.

Father and son discuss the future of House Solidor. Will it live on? And by what means?

Mt Bur-Omisace

Action Checklist

1 | Speak to the Gran Kiltias.

Explore and Restock

Here you can buy maps for both the Paramina Rift and Mt Bur-Omisace from the Cartographers' Guild moogle, then shop with the two traveling merchants. One sells weapons, armor, and items; the other sells accessories, ammo, and magick.

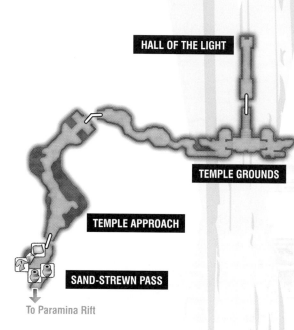

HALL OF THE LIGHT

TEMPLE GROUNDS

TEMPLE APPROACH

SAND-STREWN PASS

To Paramina Rift

Buy the Haste spell and, if you can afford it, Golden Amulets. When equipped with a Golden Amulet, the amount of LP you earn doubles! Keep in mind that while reserve party members do not earn EXP, they do earn LP, so consider equipping even reserve allies with Golden Amulets.

Golden Goods

Meet with the Gran Kiltias

Now walk to the Hall of Light in the main temple. To get there, work your way through the Temple Approach and Temple Grounds. Talk to people along the way. You can learn plenty of interesting things about the sense of safety and refuge here and how generous the Kiltias are.

The temple is a spectacular place and a refuge for all who come to the holy mountain of the Kiltias.

Climb these stairs up into the Hall of Light.

Climb the temple stairs up to the huge doors, called the Gate of the Holy Circle. Open the doors and approach the altar to trigger an event in which the Gran Kiltias meets with your party. Larsa has invited a visitor to the meeting, as well: Al-Cid Margrace, member of the ruling family of Rozarria, who arrives with some shocking news. This causes the Lady Ashe to change her request of the Gran Kiltias.

The scene switches to a grim new situation unfolding in the Imperial Palace of Archadia. Can war still be averted?

As the long event draws to a close, the Gran Kiltias sends your party back across the Paramina Rift to the Stilshrine of Miriam for a new relic that can counter Vayne's dark power growing in the east. Larsa leaves your party, and your next destination lies to the south.

OBJECTIVE

Find the Sword of Kings in the Stilshrine of Miriam

World Map

Paramina Rift (South)

Action Checklist

1 Cross the Paramina Rift to find the Stilshrine of Miriam.

The Gran Kiltias made mention of a great sword that can destroy nethicite. It is hidden in a vast underground sanctuary south of the frigid hoarfrost of the Paramina Rift.

Paramina Rift (South)

To Mt Bur-Omisace

HEAD OF THE SILVERFLOW

FREEZING GORGE

PATH OF THE FIRST-FALL

To Golmore Jungle

FADING VALE

FROZEN BROOK

ICEBOUND FLOW

To the Feywood

SPINE OF THE ICEWORM

KARYDINE GLACIER

SILVERFLOW'S END

To the Stilshrine of Miriam

Enemies here are the same as Paramina Rift (North), plus the following:

Baritine Croc

LV	HP	EXP	LP
26-28	4448-4668	1562-1748	1

Dark Skeleton

LV	HP	EXP	LP
25-26	1488-1548	1164-1257	1

Yeti

LV	HP	EXP	LP
27-29	4237-4477	1660-1862	2

Twintania

LV	HP	EXP	LP
27-28	4917-5257	2051-2177	2

Garuda-Egi

LV	HP	EXP	LP
26-27	2997-3065	1416-1508	2

Emperor Aevis

LV	HP	EXP	LP
27-28	5900-6240	2255-2381	2

Ice Elemental

LV	HP	EXP	LP
25	14830	5583	4

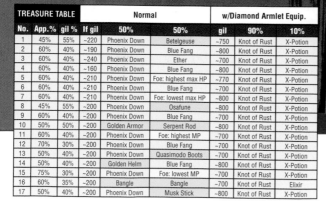

TREASURE TABLE				Normal		w/Diamond Armlet Equip.		
No.	App.%	gil %	If gil	50%	50%	gil	90%	10%
1	45%	55%	~220	Phoenix Down	Betelgeuse	~750	Knot of Rust	X-Potion
2	60%	40%	~190	Phoenix Down	Blue Fang	~800	Knot of Rust	X-Potion
3	60%	40%	~240	Phoenix Down	Ether	~700	Knot of Rust	X-Potion
4	60%	40%	~160	Phoenix Down	Blue Fang	~800	Knot of Rust	X-Potion
5	60%	40%	~210	Phoenix Down	Foe: highest max HP	~770	Knot of Rust	X-Potion
6	60%	40%	~210	Phoenix Down	Blue Fang	~700	Knot of Rust	X-Potion
7	60%	40%	~210	Phoenix Down	Foe: lowest max HP	~800	Knot of Rust	X-Potion
8	45%	55%	~200	Phoenix Down	Osafune	~800	Knot of Rust	X-Potion
9	60%	40%	~200	Phoenix Down	Blue Fang	~700	Knot of Rust	X-Potion
10	50%	50%	~200	Golden Armor	Serpent Rod	~800	Knot of Rust	X-Potion
11	60%	40%	~200	Phoenix Down	Foe: highest MP	~700	Knot of Rust	X-Potion
12	70%	30%	~200	Phoenix Down	Blue Fang	~700	Knot of Rust	X-Potion
13	50%	40%	~200	Phoenix Down	Quasimodo Boots	~700	Knot of Rust	X-Potion
14	50%	40%	~200	Golden Helm	Blue Fang	~800	Knot of Rust	X-Potion
15	75%	30%	~200	Phoenix Down	Foe: lowest MP	~700	Knot of Rust	X-Potion
16	60%	35%	~200	Bangle	Bangle	~700	Knot of Rust	Elixir
17	50%	40%	~200	Phoenix Down	Musk Stick	~800	Knot of Rust	X-Potion

TREASURE TABLE				Normal		w/Diamond Armlet Equip.		
No.	App.%	gil %	If gil	50%	50%	gil	90%	10%
18	60%	40%	~200	Phoenix Down	Blue Fang	~700	Knot of Rust	X-Potion
19	60%	40%	~200	Phoenix Down	Blue Fang	~800	Knot of Rust	X-Potion
20	60%	40%	~200	Phoenix Down	Ether	~800	Knot of Rust	X-Potion
21	40%	50%	~200	Thief's Cuffs	Thief's Cuffs	~700	Knot of Rust	Nishijin Belt
22	45%	50%	~200	Phoenix Down	Burgonet	~700	Knot of Rust	X-Potion
23	30%	70%	~200	Phoenix Down	Shielded Armor	~800	Knot of Rust	X-Potion
24	60%	40%	~200	Phoenix Down	Foe: ice-weak	~700	Knot of Rust	X-Potion
25	45%	55%	~200	Phoenix Down	Glacial Staff	~800	Knot of Rust	X-Potion
26	60%	40%	~200	Phoenix Down	Blue Fang	~700	Knot of Rust	X-Potion
27	60%	40%	~200	Phoenix Down	Foe: ice-vulnerable	~800	Knot of Rust	X-Potion
28	65%	40%	~200	Phoenix Down	Ether	~700	Knot of Rust	X-Potion
29	50%	50%	~200	Phoenix Down	Glacial Staff	~700	Knot of Rust	X-Potion
30	60%	40%	~200	Phoenix Down	Blue Fang	~800	Knot of Rust	Ice Shield
31	40%	50%	~200	Phoenix Down	Ice Shield	~700	Knot of Rust	X-Potion
32	60%	40%	~200	Phoenix Down	Foe: HP ≥ 2000	~700	Knot of Rust	X-Potion
33	60%	40%	~200	Phoenix Down	Foe: HP < 2000	~800	Knot of Rust	X-Potion

Cross the Paramina Rift

Leave Mt Bur-Omisace and head back into Paramina Rift. The map and walkthrough describe the most direct route south to the Stilshrine of Miriam, but note that nearly half of the rift isn't on that route. There is a map of that half in the side quest sidebar, if you want to just explore or take a peek at the Feywood via the western exit from the Icebound Flow area. At this point in the game, though, the Feywood beasts are likely many levels higher than your characters. Also, avoid the extremely powerful Anchag creature that roams in the Karydine Glacier. This foe can KO a party member with a single hit!

If you wander west into these Icebound Flow canyons, you'll run into Level 29 Yetis.

When It's Snowing

Sometimes after you transition into a new area of the Paramina Rift, it will be snowing. A snowfall can bring out the powerful Ice Elemental, so be careful. Remember, an elemental is not aggressive unless you use magick in its presence.

SIDE QUEST

! Paramina Exploration

To try the side quest/exploration route in the Paramina Rift, start at the Frozen Brook and head either east into the Icebound Flow or south into the Karydine Glacier. Explore the areas shown on this map, but don't exit Icebound Flow to the west into the Feywood yet! Fierce foes at level 40 and higher roam that area.

There are a number of hunts in this area: Befoulment of the Beast, Wyrm Wrath's Renewal, and Paramina Run. Paramina Run is a fight against a white chocobo named "Trickster," and it is especially difficult. It does, however, earn you a new character in the Sky Pirate's Den.

For purposes of the story walkthrough, the most direct route to the Stilshrine starts at Freezing Gorge and heads south to Frozen Brook, then southwest to the Path of the Firstfall where you find a Save Crystal. From the crystal, go west and then south to exit into the Spine of the Icewyrm area, where some new enemies make an appearance. In particular, you must cross an ice bridge guarded by a trio of flying Garuda-Egi (weak against Dark magick) and filled with explosive traps. Use your ranged-weapon allies and magick attackers against them.

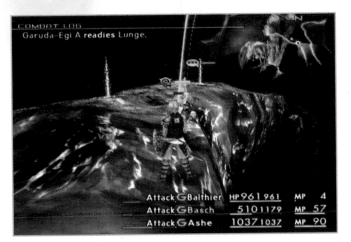

This ice bridge is the "Spine of the Icewyrm"; it is filled with traps and big birds.

Continue south through Silverflow's End, but watch out for a Level 29 Emperor Aevis lurking in this area. Hit it with a few Thunder spells to soften it up, then take it down. Finally, exit south to reach the Stilshrine of Miriam.

Beware the Emperor Aevis in Silverflow's End.

Stilshrine of Miriam

Action Checklist

1. Navigate the maze to find the sword's location.
2. Solve the Stone Brave statue puzzle.
3. Defeat Vinuskar.
4. Defeat Mateus.

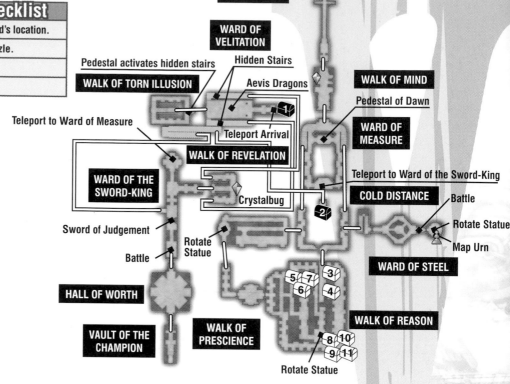

- WALK OF SKY
- WARD OF VELITATION
- Pedestal activates hidden stairs
- Hidden Stairs
- WALK OF TORN ILLUSION
- Aevis Dragons
- WALK OF MIND
- Pedestal of Dawn
- Teleport to Ward of Measure
- Teleport Arrival
- WARD OF MEASURE
- WALK OF REVELATION
- Teleport to Ward of the Sword-King
- WARD OF THE SWORD-KING
- COLD DISTANCE
- Battle
- Crystalbug
- Rotate Statue
- Sword of Judgement
- Rotate Statue
- Map Urn
- Battle
- WARD OF STEEL
- HALL OF WORTH
- WALK OF REASON
- VAULT OF THE CHAMPION
- WALK OF PRESCIENCE
- Rotate Statue

Redmaw

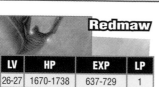

LV	HP	EXP	LP
26-27	1670-1738	637-729	1

Miriam Guardian

LV	HP	EXP	LP
28	6827	1602	1

Zombie

LV	HP	EXP	LP
27-28	2254-2260	0-3	0

Dragon Aevis

LV	HP	EXP	LP
29-31	5479-6159	2549-2801	2

Miriam Facer

LV	HP	EXP	LP
29	5540	1508	1

Crystalbug

LV	HP	EXP	LP
26	2326	0	10

Ghast

LV	HP	EXP	LP
27-29	2348-2468	891-1077	1

Blood Gigas

LV	HP	EXP	LP
27-29	2609-2849	1456-1658	1

Balloon

LV	HP	EXP	LP
28-29	1878-1936	1122-1223	1

Darkmare

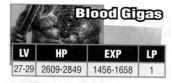

LV	HP	EXP	LP
30-31	4680-4738	1456-1557	1

Facer

LV	HP	EXP	LP
26-29	3026-3356	1151-1610	1

Negalmuur

LV	HP	EXP	LP
31-32	18910-18970	2625-2718	7

Zombie Warrior

LV	HP	EXP	LP
27-29	1878-1998	891-1077	1

TREASURE TABLE				Normal		w/Diamond Armlet Equip.		
No.	App.%	gil %	If gil	50%	50%	gil	90%	10%
1	100%	0%	--	Elixir	Megalixir	--	Megalixir	Megalixir
2	100%	0%	--	Dark Matter	Shell Shield	--	Shell Shield	Dark Matter
3	60%	45%	~50	Knot of Rust	Steel Poleyns	~200	Knot of Rust	Elixir
4	60%	45%	~50	Knot of Rust	Lamia's Tiara	~200	Knot of Rust	Elixir
5	70%	30%	~50	Knot of Rust	Chronos Tear	~200	Knot of Rust	Elixir
6	55%	45%	~50	Knot of Rust	Firefly	~200	Knot of Rust	Elixir
7	60%	45%	~50	Knot of Rust	Sorcerer's Hat	~200	Knot of Rust	Elixir
8	60%	40%	~50	Knot of Rust	Gold Needle	~200	Knot of Rust	Elixir
9	55%	30%	~50	Knot of Rust	Pirate Hat	~200	Knot of Rust	Elixir
10	80%	40%	~50	Knot of Rust	Foe: HP ≥ 3000	~200	Knot of Rust	Elixir
11	80%	40%	~50	Knot of Rust	Foe: HP < 3000	~200	Knot of Rust	Elixir

Find the Way to the Sword

Proceed down the long Walk of Sky into the next area, the Walk of Mind, which has a Save Crystal. Use it and continue south to enter the shrine proper. In the Ward of Measure, find the Pedestal of the Dawn and equip your party leader with the Dawn Shard *before* you touch the pedestal to teleport to a new area. (If you touch the pedestal *without* the Dawn Shard equipped, the teleport won't work and three Zombies will arise from the ground to attack.)

Equip the Dawn Shard before operating the Pedestal of the Dawn, as otherwise it won't teleport the party and three Zombies will appear and attack.

The party's teleportation into the Ward of Velitation awakens a huge stone Miriam Guardian. Pound this foe with Wind spells like Aero, or just hack at it with weapons. There is a rare beneficial "trap" in front of the treasure chest here, so grab the chest and get a nice little boost in HP or MP.

Now comes a brutal fight, one where Quickenings or Time magicks can really come in handy. The only way forward is through a large room where powerful Dragon Aevis monsters stomp around angrily. These are Level 30 beasts! One tactic is to rush right into the middle of them to draw all three closer together, then unleash a Quickening chain. (If you don't have Quickenings or a spell like Disable, it's probably best to simply flee past the dragons for now.) Additionally, try using the spell Blizzara to really inflict some damage!

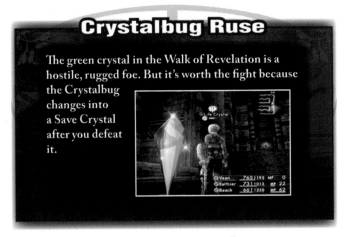

One Dragon Aevis is bad enough, but three of them may be too much unless you Disable them first, or you have multiple characters with Quickenings to cast.

The Dragon Aevis is one type of foe that is susceptible to most Time magicks (most importantly Disable and Immobilize). Use those spells and manually target attacks until all the monsters are disabled. After that, you'll find that the dragons are much easier to KO.

Disable the Dragons

Even if you eliminate a couple of dragons with the Quickening chain, you may still need to flee. So if the situation gets desperate, just run due west past the two Miriam Facers at the doorway and escape into the next room, the Walk of Torn Illusion.

Climb the first staircase and defeat the Miriam Facer at the top. Then climb either set of side stairs and fight through Miriam Guardians to another Pedestal of the Dawn. As noted earlier, make sure your party leader is equipped with the Dawn Shard, then touch the pedestal to activate two hidden staircases back in the Ward of Velitation—yes, you must go back downstairs to the dragon room. When you arrive, go down either one of the newly opened stairs (there's a staircase on either side of the room) to descend into the next room, the Walk of Revelation.

Tame the Crystalbug

This room features a tough, tricky crystal. The green "Life Crystal" in this room resembles a Save Crystal, but it's actually a Crystalbug. After touching it, the Crystalbug will attack your party! Its magick attacks are brutal, so you may need to retreat and recharge your party at some point. Fortunately, the Crystalbug remains stationary, so you can quickly get out of its range. After defeating it, the Crystalbug turns into a blue Save Crystal. Use it and move on.

Crystalbug Ruse

The green crystal in the Walk of Revelation is a hostile, rugged foe. But it's worth the fight because the Crystalbug changes into a Save Crystal after you defeat it.

Go downstairs and enter the next room, the Ward of the Sword-King. As you move forward, two Blood Gigas guards step forward ready to fight. Defeat them and move down the hall to fend off another Miriam Guardian. You can't go north yet, since the ancient door is locked. Therefore, fight your way south to the massive stone Sword of Judgement that blocks the path. Examine it to open the north passage to a Way Stone. Go north to the Way Stone and touch it to teleport to the Ward of Mcasure, which takes you back to where you started.

Beware the Negalmuur

A ghastly and powerful creature called the Negalmuur may appear in the Ward of the Sword-King hallway. His magick creates foul undead minions called Ghasts. Killing the peripheral monsters he summons, whether for fun, EXP, LP, or chains, sounds like a good idea, but he stacks them up way too quickly and you'll almost certainly be overwhelmed. If you do choose to fight, unload everything you have on Negalmuur—remember, a Save Crystal is just one room away!

The doors at the bottom of the stairways are unlocked now. Go to the northwest corner of the room and head down the west stairs. Open the now unlocked door and enter Cold Distance.

Rotate the Three Statues

The party's next task is to find the three Stone Brave statues and rotate them to face the center of the Stilshrine. From Cold Distance, go down the corridor and take the first right into the next room, Walk of Prescience.

West Statue

Turn right and go to the northernmost aisle, turn left, and head west to the wall. Fight through Balloons (weakness: Water), Facers (weakness: Wind), and Zombie Warriors (weakness: Cure) to reach a statue called a Stone Brave. Rotate it to face toward the center of the shrine. To do so, select "Examine the statue" and then "Rotate the statue."

Find the three Stone Brave statues and turn each toward the center of the shrine.

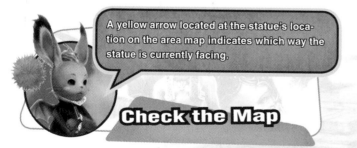

A yellow arrow located at the statue's location on the area map indicates which way the statue is currently facing.

Check the Map

Head south and go downstairs into the next room, called Walk of Reason. This is a huge, maze-like area with treasure tucked into several corners. You may want to spend some time here, exploring and racking up undead KOs. You can put together quite a Battle Chain in this area, what with all the Zombies, Ghasts, and Ghouls about.

Refer to the map for this section to find the statue in the south. (It is a maze, sort of, so check the map.) When you finally reach the Stone Brave statue, rotate it so that it faces north toward the center of the shrine.

Go Save Your Game!

A boss stands between the party and the last Stone Brave statue, so now would be a good time to return to a Save Crystal, heal up, and save your game. From the statue go east, then north to head into the next area, Cold Distance. From here you can go north through the ancient door into the Ward of Measure, then climb the stairs and exit the shrine north via the main door to save at the orange Save Crystal.

Retrace your route back down the east side of the shrine to Cold Distance and take the east exit into the Ward of Steel and go downstairs. Before you go through the door at the bottom, though, here's a tip. The next room holds a boss and a magnetic field that makes everyone wearing metal equipment suffer from the Slow effect. Before engaging this boss, make sure that your active party members are wearing light or mystic armor.

Vinuskar waits with its magnetic field ready to weigh you down.

Vinuskar

LVL	HP	EXP	LP
27	15138	0	19
Steal	Knot of Rust, Thief's Cuffs, Damascus Steel		

Vinuskar casts Slow to compound the sluggishness wrought by the magnetic field on party members wearing metal armor.

This boss fight is tough enough without a magnetic field adding an extra challenge. Any metal–wearing party members will be sluggish to start and then Vinuskar will cast Slow, making some of your characters excruciatingly slow. The good news is that Vinuskar isn't particularly speedy. You should be able to inflict damage to this boss with strong physical attacks.

This fight will seem like it's in slow motion at times, so make sure your status-healing gambits are in good shape, because Vinuskar will toss other spells at the party as well. Every once in a while it will also prepare to launch Sword Dance, its multi-sword super attack.

✦ GO LIGHT AND MYSTIC

This was mentioned before this fight, but it is worth mentioning again. Start with a threesome wearing light or mystic armor, if at all possible.

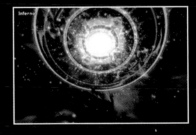

Try to chain together enough Quickening attacks so that you trigger your bonus area attack, Inferno

One tactic to try is to hold allies with Quickenings in reserve. When Vinuskar's health bar drops to about 50 percent, or if your frontline fighters are worn down, swap in the entire reserve party and launch a Quickening mist chain. If you put together a good chain, you can knock out Vinuskar in one shot.

After Vinuskar falls, proceed to the ancient door behind it and enter the back room. Here you find the last of the three Stone Brave statues. Rotate it until it faces west. After doing so, a message indicates that the "Colossus" (the huge statue in the center of the shrine) has undergone some change.

There's also a Map Urn here containing a map of the Stilshrine of Miriam. You've been almost everywhere, so it doesn't reveal too much, but you can see two areas way down on the southern end of the shrine, south of the Sword of Justice that was blocking the hall earlier. It's time to check out those areas.

Find the Sword of Kings

Upon exiting the Ward of Steel, a brief event shows the Colossus raise its massive stone sword, thus unblocking the passage down south in the Ward of the Sword-King.

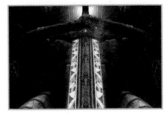

When you turn the third statue toward the center of the shrine, the Colossus raises its sword to open a new passage south.

Go north into the Ward of Measure and use the Way Stone to teleport down to the Ward of the Sword-King. Then take the first left and go upstairs to use the Save Crystal in the Walk of Revelation. Finally, turn around and go back west to the Ward of the Sword-King and head down to the door at the south end of the corridor.

Mateus

LVL	HP	EXP	LP
30	34259	0	27
Steal	Pisces Gem, Ether, High Arcana		

This boss battle really starts off in a frenzy of fighting. The first goal, as in most boss fights, is to eliminate any lesser enemies supporting the boss. Mateus immediately casts Reflect on himself and spawns six swarming Ice Azers that are difficult to beat in their own right. A powerful opening strategy to use is to launch a Quickening attack immediately on an Ice Azer in the middle of the swarm. A good Mist chain will eliminate or seriously debilitate the minions of Mateus.

If you don't have any Quickening spells at your party's disposal, then try Lightning magic: Thunder and Thundara can also cause serious damage to Ice Azers. Be careful about casting magic that might hit Mateus, as it will be reflected back to the party.

> ### ⚠ EQUIP ICE SHIELDS
>
> If you have Ice Shields in your inventory, equip them on your melee fighters. They reduce Ice damage by half, which helps against the Ice Azers and when Mateus unleashes the frigid super attack, Blizzaja.

Once the Azers are melted down into puddles of cold water, unleash your party's weapons on Mateus. If you used Quickenings, you have some characters

Mateus has a Blizzaja area attack that doles out Ice pain to everyone in the area. Ice Shields help mitigate the damage.

with very low MP, so don't use magick attacks; keep MP for healing. Alternatively, you can swap out the characters involved in the opening Quickening for those with full MP. Mateus likes to cast spells that Sap, so make sure you're ready to remove it with Regen or Esuna, whether in a gambit or manually.

Just keep hammering away and keep healing! A gambit that casts Cura when one ally's HP gets low (say, down to 40 percent) keeps everybody healthy. Aside from his huge Blizzaja attacks, Mateus doesn't strike with any real power.

One tactic is to give your party leader a ranged weapon like a gun or bow. Then just keep them running in circles at a distance around Mateus, stopping only when it is time to attack or cast a healing spell. The constant movement is a way to boost the leader's MP without consuming precious Ethers. Another tactic is to assign party leadership to the character currently bearing the brunt of the foe's attention, then have that character run away from Mateus. Running away not only builds MP but also delays the enemy's attacks as the foe is forced to give chase. "Spreading the field" like this can also cause multiple-target enemy attacks like White Breath or Blizzaga to hit only one or two characters.

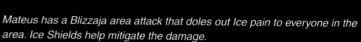

After your victory, continue south through the door into the Vault of the Champion. Walk forward to the spinning gear mechanism to trigger an event in which Ashe seizes the Sword of Kings at last. The sword appears in your weapon inventory, but we don't recommend that you use it. It certainly has its special uses, but fighting isn't one of them. Beyond the storyline and aesthetic purposes, it is mostly notable for being the first Greatsword you're likely to happen upon, as well as one of the few pieces of gear that doesn't require a license to use!

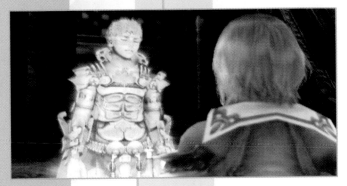

Return to Mt Bur-Omisace

After the event, head north to the Way Stone. Use it to return to the Ward of Measure, then exit the shrine. Next, head for the Save Crystal to trigger another chilling event. The Imperial fleet passes overhead yet again, but they don't stop this time. Looks like their business is finished.

What was it? And what's that smoke ahead in the distance? Go to the Save Crystal and use it to teleport back to Mt Bur-Omisace.

Mt Bur-Omisace

Action Checklist

1	Find the Gran Kiltias Anastasis.
2	Defeat Judge Bergan.
3	Get to Nalbina Fortress.

Stock Up and Upgrade

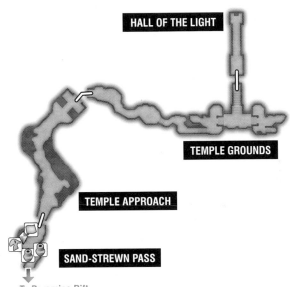

HALL OF THE LIGHT

TEMPLE GROUNDS

TEMPLE APPROACH

SAND-STREWN PASS

To Paramina Rift

Yes, your primary objective is complete, but there is one last boss to face before you can move on to the next objective. It's raining here, and if you talk to some of the wounded Kiltias, you learn that Imperial forces have desecrated the holy mountain.

Before you investigate, visit the traveling merchants and upgrade everything. You should have a lot of loot to sell and plenty of LP to

license new gear, so do it now. Save your game again and head north into the temple to trigger a particularly grim event.

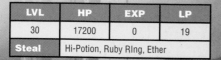

Judge Bergan

LVL	HP	EXP	LP
30	17200	0	19
Steal	Hi-Potion, Ruby RIng, Ether		

As usual, eliminate the minions first. In this case, three minor Judges assist Judge Bergan; they're right behind the party at the start of the fight. Let them catch up with Bergan; you want them all as close together as possible. Once they reach Bergan, nail the boss with a Quickening chain of at least three hits to trigger an Inferno or Cataclysm while his three minions are nearby. This can hurt Judge Bergan and wipe out his minions at the same time.

Bergan will cast random Dark, Water, and Aero spells at the party. However, he lacks a super attack (unlike most other bosses) that can wipe out your characters in a single hit. He does have vicious combo attacks that get faster and deadlier as his HP drops to critical levels. One tip is to send in two strong, well-armored melee sluggers with big hitting weapons, but make your party leader a ranged fighter with good healing gambits. Keep the party leader as far away from Judge Bergan's blades as possible. The temple path is narrow but long, so you can run your healer up and down the path to keep building MP while staying clear of Bergan.

⚡ CHARGE UP

Remember that you can use the Charge technick to replenish any depleted MP.

Judge Bergan gets even more dangerous as he nears KO status.

As mentioned earlier, the Judge goes nuts with combo attacks as his HP dwindles lower. When this occurs, you may want to have only one character, your strongest fighter, trading blows with Bergan while keeping your other two characters slinging health spells and potions at their ally. A shield is essential for this type of role, which still works out nicely for a heavy damage dealer as one-handed weapons like axes and hammers are potentially excellent damage-dealing options. A good shield, especially with the Gauntlets accessory equipped, often reduces previously difficult adversaries to helpless targets.

After the battle, watch the next event to see the fate of the Gran Kiltias and learn what happened to young Lord Larsa. Al-Cid appears and Lady Ashe makes a fateful decision about the Sword of Kings and the Dusk Shard. Balthier then points you toward your next destination: the Draklor Laboratory, where, as he puts it, "the Empire's weapon research begins and ends."

Before you exit the temple area, talk to the "Acolyte" pacing at the bottom of the temple staircase. He will hand over an artifact called the **Stone of the Condemner**. You can use this inside the Stilshrine to find an *optional hidden Esper!* (For more on this, see the "Side Quests" chapter in this guide. This unique battle against Zeromus prevents the use of magicks, and attempting it isn't really reasonable until your party is at least Level 35.) Return to the Save Crystal in the Sand-Strewn Pass. Use the crystal to teleport to Nalbina Fortress if you've already been there and activated its crystal. If not, teleport to Rabanastre and exit the city via Eastgate into the Dalmasca Estersand. Proceed northeast through The Stepping and Outpost into Yardang Labyrinth. From there, exit east to Nalbina Fortress.

OBJECTIVE

Find the Hunters' Camp on the Archadian Border

Action Checklist

1	Stock up on goods and equipment.
2	Enter the Mosphoran Highwaste.

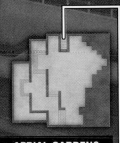

Nalbina Fortress

World Map

The ultimate goal here is the Draklor Laboratory in Archades. You must first reach the Phon Coast hunters' camp, though, traveling on foot from Nalbina Fortress via the Mosphoran Highwaste and the Salikawood.

Nalbina Fortress

LOWER APARTMENTS

THE HIGHHALL

AERIAL GARDENS

Battle

2

1

INNER WARD

Battle

UPPER APARTMENTS

TREASURE TABLE			Normal			w/Diamond Armlet Equip.		
No.	App.%	gil %	If gil	50%	50%	gil	90%	10%
1	100%	0%	-	Potion	Potion	-	-	-
2	100%	0%	-	Potion	Potion	-	-	-

Walkthrough

Prep for the Long Trek

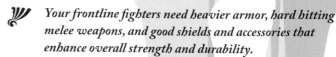

Back on Mt Bur-Omisace Balthier, Fran, and Ashe plot the party's approach to the Draklor Laboratory in Archades. With the air and sea routes sure to be heavily monitored by Imperial eyes, the safest way to go is on foot through Nalbina, the Mosphoran Highwaste, and the Salikawood—and that just gets the party to the border. Before leaving, heed Balthier's words of wisdom: "Better go prepared."

Shop at the finer Nalbina establishments and purchase some upgrades.

By now you should be developing your characters with distinctive roles in mind. This means that each one will have specific needs:

🪶 *Your frontline fighters need heavier armor, hard hitting melee weapons, and good shields and accessories that enhance overall strength and durability.*

🪶 *Your magick casters need new and better spells, mystic armor upgrades, and preferably ranged weapons. This will enable them to heal your party from a distance, while still getting in a few good shots during combat.*

🪶 *Your light armor characters require enhanced speed and vitality, and perhaps technicks that add special twists to their attack capabilities.*

There should be some overlap in roles, of course. You want your brawlers to have the ability to cure a party member and cast an occasional Black Magick spell. You want your mages to have the ability to defend themselves against a close rush of White Wolves or Zombies. Some versatility is good; in general, though, make sure your characters develop well-defined roles.

Dispel is available now at Mysterious Magicks in the Nalbina bazaar area. This is an important spell to purchase. You can remove Haste, Protect, or Shell status among others from enemies by casting Dispel. As an added bonus, you can also cast it on your party members to remove certain negative status effects, like Slow and Reflect.

Buy Dispel!

After you've completed your shopping, you may want to return to the crystal in West Barbican and save your game. Next, head northwest into the Mosphoran Highwaste.

Mosphoran Highwaste

Overview Map

The map of the Mosphoran Highwaste shown here reflects only the areas of the main routes that are directly connected. To learn about access to the secret areas, refer to the "Side Quests" chapter in this guide.

Action Checklist

1 Cross the Mosphoran Highwaste.

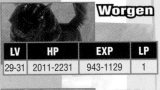

Worgen

LV	HP	EXP	LP
29-31	2011-2231	943-1129	1

Clay Golem

LV	HP	EXP	LP
31-32	6283-6393	1884-2037	2

Slaven Wilder

LV	HP	EXP	LP
30-31	3518-3638	1548-1649	1

Python

LV	HP	EXP	LP
29-32	3016-3346	1749-2028	1

Humbaba

LV	HP	EXP	LP
32-33	5403-5523	2289-2390	2

Vulture

LV	HP	EXP	LP
30-32	4022-4158	1952-2136	2

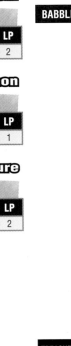

Fire Elemental

LV	HP	EXP	LP
25	14830	5583	4

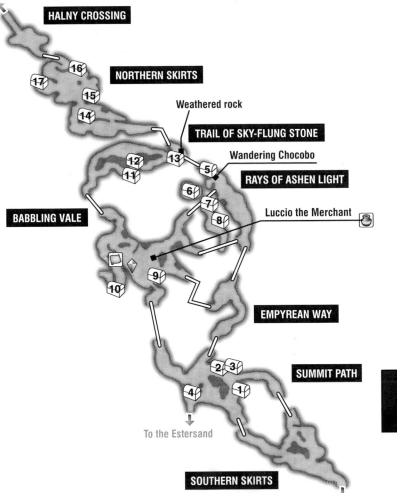

To the Salikawood

HALNY CROSSING

NORTHERN SKIRTS

Weathered rock

TRAIL OF SKY-FLUNG STONE

Wandering Chocobo

RAYS OF ASHEN LIGHT

Luccio the Merchant

BABBLING VALE

EMPYREAN WAY

SUMMIT PATH

To the Estersand

SOUTHERN SKIRTS

To Nalbina Fortress

Walkthrough

Hike Through the Highwaste

Mosphoran Highwaste. Sounds like a fun place, doesn't it? These mountain passes and canyons are crawling with wolf-like Worgens, making it a good place to string together a Battle Chain. The party starts in the Southern Skirts. Move northwest. You can take either one of two exits leading up to the next area, Summit Path, but watch out for the explosive traps blocking the passages. Move up against the ravine walls and carefully move past the traps.

Beware the Fire Elemental floating around this area. Your party may be strong enough to challenge this elemental, but make sure you know where the zone exits are just in case things get out of hand. Keep an eye out for the Wary Wolf on the Summit Path, too; it's a powerful *Rare Game* animal—very rare, in fact!

Lots of Worgens prowl the Highwaste, so try to avoid other species for awhile and put together a Worgen-based Battle Chain. Watch out for the rare Wary Wolf, too.

TREASURE TABLE				Normal		w/Diamond Armlet Equip.		
No.	App.%	gil %	If gil	50%	50%	gil	90%	10%
1	70%	33%	~200	Hi-Potion	Phoenix Down	~390	Knot of Rust	Red Fang
2	70%	33%	~190	Hi-Potion	Bacchus's Wine	~480	Knot of Rust	Elixir
3	70%	33%	~180	Hi-Potion	Foe: character HP ≥ 50%	~480	Knot of Rust	Hi-Ether
4	70%	33%	~250	Hi-Potion	Foe: character HP < 50%	~650	Knot of Rust	Elixir
5	70%	33%	~260	Hi-Potion	Phoenix Down	~390	Knot of Rust	Blue Fang
6	60%	60%	~300	Hi-Potion	Burning Bow	~550	Knot of Rust	Elixir
7	70%	33%	~230	Hi-Potion	Foe: ice-vulnerable	~600	Knot of Rust	Hi-Ether
8	70%	33%	~280	Hi-Potion	Ether	~650	Knot of Rust	Elixir
9	70%	33%	~200	Hi-Potion	Water Mote	~480	Knot of Rust	Elixir
10	50%	60%	~200	Hi-Potion	Embroidered Tippet	~390	Knot of Rust	Blue Fang
11	60%	50%	~300	Hi-Potion	Headband	~390	Knot of Rust	Blue Fang
12	70%	33%	~400	Hi-Potion	Vaccine	~750	Knot of Rust	Elixir
13	70%	33%	~280	Hi-Potion	Hi-Ether	~550	Knot of Rust	Hi-Ether
14	70%	33%	~200	Potion	Foe: highest magick resist	~650	Knot of Rust	Elixir
15	70%	33%	~150	Potion	Foe: highest defense	~480	Knot of Rust	Hi-Ether
16	50%	40%	~400	Potion	Pirate Hat	~500	Knot of Rust	Elixir
17	70%	33%	~150	Hi-Potion	Phoenix Down	~390	Knot of Rust	Blue Fang

Exit from Summit Path to the northwest into Babbling Vale. This area is a caravan rest stop with a Save Crystal, a traveling merchant named Luccio, and a Scout moogle who sells a Mosphoran Highwaste map and tells of a giant Bomb deep in the Salikawood. (This is an *optional* boss you can fight later.)

Remember to swap in party members with ranged weapons against flyers like the Vultures that patrol the Trail of Sky-flung Stone. If Fran is your archer, move her attack gambits higher and let others do the healing.

! The Wind Shrines

SIDE QUEST

If you acquire the Mosphoran Highwaste map from the moogle in the Babbling Vale and examine it, you will see a number of seemingly unconnected areas tucked in and around the main areas of the Highwaste. These are areas that you can reach by finding the hidden paths.

Note the eight wind shrines around the Babbling Vale area of the Mosphoran Highwaste. Talk to the Learned Man looking at the northeast shrine and he gives you some information about what he has learned. Note, however, that you must return later to unlock the shrine puzzle, which leads to an Esper named Exodus. Also, the "Trouble in the Hills" hunt target, Atomos, is located in Northern Skirts.

💥 WHACK THE ROCK

Approach the "Weathered Rock" at the far eastern end of the Trail of Sky-Flung Stone and press the X button to hit it. This action starts a landslide that opens a secret route back to the Rays of Ashen Light area.

Exit the Babbling Vale to the north into the coolest-sounding area so far, the Trail of Sky-flung Stone. Pythons start popping up to attack, so be ready. Near the rock bridge, a flock of Vultures can be seen circling above. Shoot them out of the sky and move to the east exit.

Now fight through the Northern Skirt to a long bridge at Halny Crossing. Run across it to leave the Mosphoran Highwaste behind and enter the Salikawood.

This long bridge at Halny Crossing leads north to the Salikawood.

The Salikawood

Action Checklist

1	Get to the border gate.
2	Round up the moogle apprentices to finish fixing the gate.
3	Exit the Salikawood into the Phon Coast.

Wyrdhare

LV	HP	EXP	LP
33-35	2739-2959	856-1042	1

Pumpkin Head

LV	HP	EXP	LP
32-33	2739-2859	1070-1174	1

Sprinter

LV	HP	EXP	LP
33-34	4070-4138	1569-1661	1

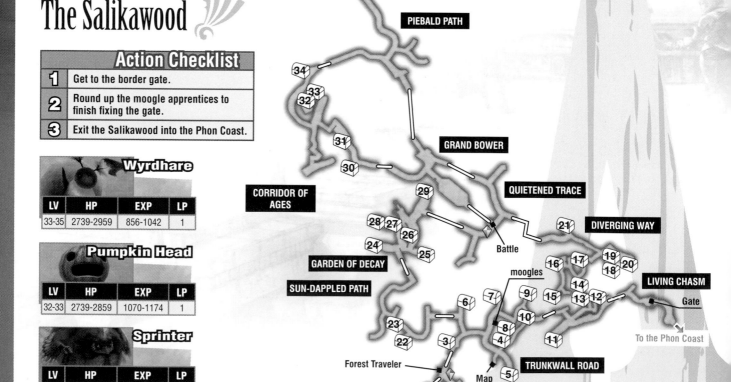

PIEBALD PATH
GRAND BOWER
CORRIDOR OF AGES
QUIETENED TRACE
DIVERGING WAY
Battle
GARDEN OF DECAY
moogles
SUN-DAPPLED PATH
LIVING CHASM
Gate
To the Phon Coast
Forest Traveler
Map Urn
TRUNKWALL ROAD
PATH OF HOURS
THE OMEN-SPUR
To the Mosphoran Highwaste

Malboro King					***Antares**					***Baknamy**					***Brown Chocobo**			
LV	HP	EXP	LP		LV	HP	EXP	LP		LV	HP	EXP	LP		LV	HP	EXP	LP
34-35	4501-4621	2461-2565	1		33-34	6458-6568	2228-2317	1		35-36	4501-4576	1961-2111	1		32-35	3718-3922	1733-2009	1

*Accessible after defeating King Bomb.

TREASURE TABLE			Normal		w/Diamond Armlet Equip.		
No.	App.%	gil %	If gil	50%	gil	90%	10%
2	40%	50%	~220	Hi-Potion	Ether	~500	Knot of Rust	Hi-Ether
1	40%	50%	~220	Hi-Potion	Ether	~540	Knot of Rust	Hi-Ether
3	60%	50%	~180	Hi-Potion	Ether	~500	Knot of Rust	Hi-Ether
4	60%	50%	~180	Hi-Potion	Foe: highest speed	~500	Knot of Rust	Elixir
5	60%	50%	~180	Hi-Potion	Remedy	~540	Knot of Rust	Hi-Ether
6	60%	50%	~180	Hi-Potion	Hi-Ether	~540	Knot of Rust	Elixir
7	60%	50%	~180	Hi-Potion	Remedy	~500	Knot of Rust	Hi-Ether
8	60%	50%	~180	Hi-Potion	Foe: lowest speed	~540	Knot of Rust	Hi-Ether
9	60%	50%	~180	Hi-Potion	Holy Mote	~500	Knot of Rust	Hi-Ether
10	45%	60%	~220	Hi-Potion	Bone Mail	~540	Knot of Rust	Megalixir
11	50%	50%	~190	Hi-Potion	Ether	~500	Knot of Rust	Hi-Ether
12	50%	50%	~250	Hi-Potion	Balance Mote	~540	Knot of Rust	Hi-Ether
13	50%	50%	~190	Hi-Potion	Foe: highest magick power	~500	Knot of Rust	Hi-Ether
14	50%	50%	~220	Hi-Potion	Foe: lowest magick power	~540	Knot of Rust	Hi-Ether
15	50%	50%	~600	Hi-Potion	Remedy	~1000	Knot of Rust	Hi-Ether
16	50%	50%	~200	Hi-Potion	Ether	~500	Knot of Rust	Hi-Ether
17	50%	50%	~200	Hi-Potion	Ether	~500	Knot of Rust	Hi-Ether
18	50%	50%	~220	Hi-Potion	Ether	~500	Knot of Rust	Hi-Ether
19	50%	50%	~190	Hi-Potion	Balance Mote	~540	Knot of Rust	Hi-Ether
20	50%	50%	~300	Hi-Potion	Hi-Ether	~500	Knot of Rust	Elixir
21	40%	50%	~400	Hi-Potion	Bone Helm	~700	Knot of Rust	Elixir
22	70%	40%	~200	Hi-Potion	X-Potion	~500	Knot of Rust	Hi-Ether
23	45%	40%	~500	Hi-Potion	Feathered Boots	~700	Knot of Rust	Hi-Ether
24	40%	50%	~200	Hi-Potion	Ether	~500	Knot of Rust	Elixir
25	40%	50%	~200	Hi-Potion	Aero Mote	~540	Knot of Rust	Elixir
26	40%	50%	~200	Hi-Potion	Hi-Ether	~540	Knot of Rust	Hi-Ether
27	40%	50%	~250	Hi-Potion	Foe: highest strength	~500	Knot of Rust	Hi-Ether
28	40%	50%	~250	Hi-Potion	Foe: lowest strength	~540	Knot of Rust	Elixir
29	40%	50%	~200	Hi-Potion	Water Mote	~500	Knot of Rust	Hi-Ether
30	66%	50%	~200	Hi-Potion	Phoenix Down	~600	Knot of Rust	Hi-Ether
31	45%	90%	~300	Hi-Potion	Fuzzy Miter	~700	Knot of Rust	Elixir
32	66%	50%	~200	Hi-Potion	Foe: lowest level	~700	Knot of Rust	Elixir
33	66%	50%	~200	Hi-Potion	Foe: highest level	~700	Knot of Rust	Hastega Mote
34	66%	50%	~400	Hi-Potion	Hi-Ether	~600	Knot of Rust	Hi-Ether

Get to Salikawood's East Gate

The party arrives in the Omen-Spur area, which contains some odd creatures. Follow the path to the next area, the Path of Hours, where a welcome sight awaits: a Save Crystal. Talk to the pacing Forest Traveler to learn about the hunters' camp on the Phon Coast to the east—the party's interim destination. Unfortunately, the Salikawood's east gate is broken; a moogle crew is doing repairs, but their work ethic is a bit sub-par. He also says he dropped his map of the wood; chances are it's nearby somewhere.

The moogles are resting in their bungalow, but they have a gate to finish…

Approach the nearby forest bungalow and talk to the three "layabout" moogles inside. They indicate that they're working on the gate up ahead. Well… actually, they're resting right now. Now take a moment to find the area map. Exit the Path of Hours, crossing the next bridge north onto Trunkwall Road.

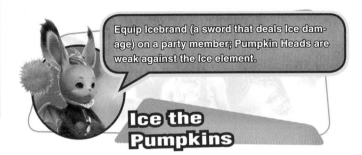

The Pumpkin Head is the dominant species in the southern Salikawood.

Veer right at the first fork, then go right two more times to find the Map Urn that holds the full map of the Salikawood. Next, head straight up the walkway to the northeast; veer east at the intersection to exit into Diverging Way.

There are lots of Pumpkin Heads everywhere, which makes for good Battle Chains. They're tougher than they look, though, especially when they swarm their targets in groups of three or more. Head for the east exit into the next area, Living Chasm.

> Equip Icebrand (a sword that deals Ice damage) on a party member; Pumpkin Heads are weak against the Ice element.

Ice the Pumpkins

While in Living Chasm, you can see the huge gate in the cliff wall up ahead. Approach the moogle Boss pacing at the gate. He explains that the gate leads to the Phon Coast. It will be open as soon as his nine moogle apprentices return from their break in the Salikawood and finish the repair work. He suggests that you look in the Salikawood bungalows scattered throughout the woods. After the conversation ends, talk to him again to get a more complete version of the story.

The great gate lies up ahead. Talk to the moogle Boss to learn that his workers are on break and scattered throughout the Salikawood. Check your map to find their locations.

Round Up the Nine Moogle Apprentices

Talk to the moogles in their forest bungalows to get them back to work. After each conversation, they indicate how many moogles are left to retrieve.

Open up the Area Map to see new flashing icons that indicate where the nine moogles are holed up. Find them and talk to them in their bungalows to get them working on the gate again. A "moogle counter" in the upper-right corner of the screen tracks the number of moogles found. Two of their bungalows are side by side, in the Garden of Decay.

When all nine moogles are back on the job, take them up on their offer to return to the gate with them. The party automatically goes to the east gate to watch the gate open. Walk through and talk to the moogle Boss to get a thank-you gift: a pair of **Quasimodo Boots**, an accessory that makes the wearer immune to Sap status. Next, continue east to the Phon Coast.

Chat with the moogle Boss before moving onward to receive a gift.

The Big Bomb Boss and the Necrohol

An optional boss battle awaits in the Grand Bower in the northwest part of the Salikawood. The King Bomb and three minions prowl this area. This crew may be too tough right now, but you can run away from this boss fight if you get overwhelmed. After defeating the King Bomb, you can continue to the Corridor of Ages and find Braegh, the mark in the "Rodeo to the Death" hunt. Again, check the "Side Quests" chapter for more details on these fights. If you continue northwest from the Salikawood, you will enter the Necrohol of Nabudis. This is quite a grim area with very tough enemies. This is where you can find the **Zodiac Spear** (in a treasure chest located in the Cloister of the Highborn area). Note, however, that you can only obtain it if you do not open the four treasure chests mentioned in our "Don't Touch That Treasure!" tip boxes located in this walkthrough.

NO IMMUNITY AFTER THE FACT

Items like the Quasimodo Boots, which provide immunity to certain status effects, only work if equipped *before* the wearer is hit with the status ailment in question. In this case, for example, equipping the Quasimodo Boots on a character already afflicted with Sap does nothing. Wearing the boots at the moment a foe attempts Sap, however, keeps the wearer immune.

The Phon Coast

Action Checklist

1	Find the Phon Coast hunters' camp.
2	Proceed to the Tchita Uplands.

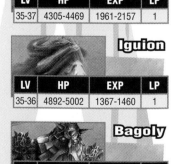

Mandragora

LV	HP	EXP	LP
34-37	2739-3099	607-919	1

Pyrolisk

LV	HP	EXP	LP
36-37	6262-6330	2585-2677	2

Silver Lobo

LV	HP	EXP	LP
34-35	3131-3241	1248-1341	1

Piranha

LV	HP	EXP	LP
35-37	4305-4469	1961-2157	1

Iguion

LV	HP	EXP	LP
35-36	4892-5002	1367-1460	1

Bagoly

LV	HP	EXP	LP
36-38	4500-4720	2051-2237	1

Archaeosaur

LV	HP	EXP	LP
37-38	12251-12592	4457-4583	2

No.	App.%	gil%	If gil	50%	50%	gil	90%	10%
				Normal		w/Diamond Armlet Equip.		
1	50%	75%	~250	Hi-Potion	Metal Jerkin	~500	Knot of Rust	Elixir
2	65%	75%	~200	Hi-Potion	Vanishga Mote	~500	Knot of Rust	Scathe Mote
3	65%	75%	~300	Hi-Potion	Warp Mote	~600	Knot of Rust	Hastega Mote
4	65%	75%	~250	Hi-Potion	Foe: highest max MP	~500	Knot of Rust	Scathe Mote
5	65%	75%	~250	Hi-Potion	Foe: lowest max MP	~500	Knot of Rust	Elixir
6	65%	75%	~250	Hi-Potion	Water Mote	~500	Knot of Rust	Holy Mote
7	65%	75%	~300	Hi-Potion	Riflectga Mote	~600	Knot of Rust	Hastega Mote
8	65%	75%	~250	Phoenix Down	Balance Mote	~500	Knot of Rust	Elixir
9	65%	75%	~250	Hi-Potion	Foe: highest max HP	~500	Knot of Rust	Hastega Mote
10	65%	75%	~250	Phoenix Down	Foe: lowest max HP	~500	Knot of Rust	Elixir
11	45%	75%	~250	Hi-Potion	Murasame	~500	Knot of Rust	Hastega Mote
12	65%	75%	~350	Phoenix Down	Vanishga Mote	~700	Knot of Rust	Scathe Mote
13	65%	75%	~350	Hi-Potion	Float Mote	~700	Knot of Rust	Elixir
14	65%	75%	~350	Hi-Potion	Warp Mote	~700	Knot of Rust	Hastega Mote
15	65%	75%	~350	Hi-Potion	Warp Mote	~550	Knot of Rust	Hastega Mote
16	65%	75%	~340	Hi-Potion	Aero Mote	~600	Knot of Rust	Hastega Mote
17	65%	75%	~300	Hi-Potion	Foe: highest MP	~580	Knot of Rust	Scathe Mote
18	55%	80%	~250	Hi-Potion	Aldebaran	~500	Knot of Rust	Scathe Mote
19	65%	75%	~250	Hi-Potion	Foe: lowest MP	~600	Knot of Rust	Elixir
20	65%	75%	~250	Hi-Potion	Reflectga Mote	~600	Knot of Rust	Hastega Mote
21	65%	75%	~330	Hi-Potion	Float Mote	~550	Knot of Rust	Elixir
22	65%	45%	~300	Hi-Potion	Foe: HP < 5000	~650	Knot of Rust	Elixir
23	65%	75%	~250	Phoenix Down	Vanishga Mote	~500	Knot of Rust	Elixir
24	65%	45%	~300	Hi-Potion	Foe: HP ≥ 5000	~600	Knot of Rust	Hastega Mote
25	65%	75%	~400	Phoenix Down	Warp Mote	~750	Knot of Rust	Hastega Mote
26	40%	80%	~250	Hi-Potion	Black Cowl	~500	Knot of Rust	Scathe Mote
27	40%	80%	~1000	Hi-Potion	Black Garb	~2000	Knot of Rust	Elixir
28	65%	45%	~500	Hi-Potion	Foe: wind-weak	~700	Knot of Rust	Hastega Mote
29	65%	75%	~300	Hi-Potion	Float Mote	~600	Knot of Rust	Hastega Mote
30	65%	45%	~500	Hi-Potion	Foe: wind-vulnerable	~800	Knot of Rust	Scathe Mote
31	65%	75%	~300	Hi-Potion	Hi-Ether	~600	Knot of Rust	Elixir
32	65%	75%	~300	Hi-Potion	Warp Mote	~600	Knot of Rust	Hastega Mote
33	65%	75%	~320	Hi-Potion	Float Mote	~700	Knot of Rust	Elixir
34	60%	80%	~300	Hi-Potion	Diamond Shield	~700	Knot of Rust	Hastega Mote
35	65%	75%	~320	Hi-Potion	Vanishga Mote	~700	Knot of Rust	Scathe Mote
36	60%	80%	~300	Hi-Potion	Halberd	~700	Knot of Rust	Scathe Mote
37	50%	80%	~300	Hi-Potion	Aldebaran	~700	Knot of Rust	Hastega Mote
38	65%	45%	~400	Hi-Potion	Foe: character HP < 50%	~700	Knot of Rust	Elixir
39	65%	45%	~400	Hi-Potion	Foe: character MP ≥ 50%	~700	Knot of Rust	Scathe Mote
40	60%	80%	~300	Hi-Potion	Gokuu Pole	~700	Knot of Rust	Hastega Mote
41	100%	50%	200	Knot of Rust	Knot of Rust	500	Knot of Rust	Dark Matter
42	100%	50%	200	Knot of Rust	Knot of Rust	500	Knot of Rust	Dark Matter
43	100%	50%	2000	Knot of Rust	Knot of Rust	5000	Knot of Rust	Dark Matter
44	100%	50%	200	Knot of Rust	Knot of Rust	500	Knot of Rust	Dark Matter
45	100%	50%	200	Knot of Rust	Knot of Rust	500	Knot of Rust	Dark Matter
46	100%	50%	200	Knot of Rust	Knot of Rust	500	Knot of Rust	Dark Matter
47	100%	50%	200	Knot of Rust	Knot of Rust	500	Knot of Rust	Dark Matter
48	100%	50%	200	Knot of Rust	Knot of Rust	500	Knot of Rust	Dark Matter
49	100%	50%	200	Knot of Rust	Knot of Rust	500	Knot of Rust	Dark Matter
50	100%	50%	200	Knot of Rust	Knot of Rust	500	Knot of Rust	Dark Matter
51	100%	50%	200	Knot of Rust	Knot of Rust	500	Knot of Rust	Dark Matter
52	100%	50%	200	Knot of Rust	Knot of Rust	500	Knot of Rust	Dark Matter
53	100%	50%	200	Knot of Rust	Knot of Rust	500	Knot of Rust	Dark Matter
54	100%	50%	200	Knot of Rust	Knot of Rust	500	Knot of Rust	Dark Matter
55	100%	50%	200	Knot of Rust	Knot of Rust	500	Knot of Rust	Dark Matter
56	100%	50%	200	Knot of Rust	Knot of Rust	500	Knot of Rust	Dark Matter
57	65%	75%	~300	Hi-Potion	Reflectga Mote	~600	Knot of Rust	Hastega Mote
58	55%	75%	~300	Hi-Potion	Thorned Mace	~600	Knot of Rust	Scathe Mote
59	65%	65%	~400	Hi-Potion	Ally: status = Lure	~800	Knot of Rust	Elixir
60	65%	65%	~400	Hi-Potion	Ally: status = Berserk	~800	Knot of Rust	Scathe Mote
61	45%	80%	~200	Hi-Potion	Adamant Hat	~700	Knot of Rust	Hastega Mote
62	65%	50%	~350	Hi-Potion	Ally: status = Reflect	~700	Knot of Rust	Scathe Mote
63	65%	50%	~340	Hi-Potion	Ally: status = Stop	~700	Knot of Rust	Elixir
64	65%	70%	~200	Hi-Potion	Reflectga Mote	~700	Knot of Rust	Hastega Mote
65	65%	70%	~200	Hi-Potion	Vanishga Mote	~700	Knot of Rust	Scathe Mote
66	50%	80%	~180	Hi-Potion	Recurve Crossbow	~700	Knot of Rust	Elixir
67	65%	45%	~400	Hi-Potion	Warp Mote	~700	Knot of Rust	Hastega Mote

Find the Hunters' Camp

At this stage of the game, the party crosses over into Archadia. From the Save Crystal in Kaukula Pass, walk south into The Reseta Strand and then fight your way southeast along the beach. These enemies are quite tough, so come prepared. If you don't have well-equipped party members leveled up to at least 27 or 28, you may have a very difficult time against the Bagoly, Pyrolisk, and Silver Lobo foes.

Continue southeast through the Pora-Pora Sands. (Stay close to the left wall to find a *secret path*, which you can't use yet. A hunter won't allow access.) Now head east across Cape Uahuk to the Hunters' Camp.

This triggers an event in which Balthier tells Lady Ashe a story about nethicite and Doctor Cid, the director of Draklor Laboratories.

After the event, explore the camp a bit. Buy a Phon Coast map from the moogle near the north exit; check out the Vendor of Goods; upgrade equipment and licenses; and then save your game at the Save Crystal.

The hunters' camp is an oasis in a hostile land. Use it as a base for hunts and leveling up in the surrounding monster-filled areas.

Walkthrough

The Hunt Club

If you try talking to the "Shady bangaas" in front of the hut directly across the sand from the Vendor of Goods, you will hear some pretty evasive and threatening responses. These hunters are members of something called the Hunt Club, and this location is where you can start the Hunt Club side quest.

You can't begin the Hunt Club until after you complete the Mandragoras boss fight in Sochen, then return and speak to the Hunt Master (the bangaa at the hut's door). Note the Notice Board with its posted bills is not inside a tavern here, but instead it is located outside not far from the Save Crystal.

If you don't have a few Level 30 characters yet, now would be a good time to explore and do some leveling up. Try heading west into Cape Tialan and then up to the Mauleia Strand, or east to the Vaddu Strand, looking for treasure and conquests.

DON'T TOUCH THAT TREASURE: PART 4

There are four treasure chests connected to a chest found later (in the Necrohol of Nabudis) that holds the most powerful weapon in the game, the **Zodiac Spear**. If you open any of those first four chests, the Zodiac Spear disappears from its chest in Nabudis!

The fourth treasure chest is included amongst the huge stash of 16 chests at the eastern end of the Vaddu Strand in the Phon Coast region. If you want the Zodiac Spear later, do not open these 16 treasure chests. If, however, you've already opened one of the previous three connected chests, you might as well crack open these 16 and reap the gil.

Watch out for the innocent-looking Mandragora foursome on the high pass in Cape Tialan. They're neutral, so they won't do much unless you try to attack or steal from them. If you do, then all four of them will descend on your party with a fury. This would be a good time for a Quickening chain.

Keep stockpiling loot until you can sell enough to get at least three of your characters equipped with the best armor and weapons available from the Vendor of Goods back in Hunters' Camp. When you're ready to move deeper into Archadia, take the northernmost exit from the Hunters' Camp into the next area, the Caima Hills.

SECRET CHOCOBO TRAILS

Look for "Wayward Chocobos" and catch a ride in exchange for some Gysahl Greens. Also, watch for grassy ravines that disappear into the hills. These may be secret chocobo trails that are only accessible when riding a chocobo.

These trails usually provide convenient shortcuts between areas. One of them connects the northern Pora-Pora Sands with the Caima Hills.

Head North to Tchita Uplands

Watch out for a lumbering Archaeosaur in the Caima Hills. Hack and slash up to the northeast exit into the Limatra Hills. Remember to use your ranged weapons when Pyrolisks flap overhead. When you finally reach Rava's Pass, use the Save Crystal to heal up and save your game.

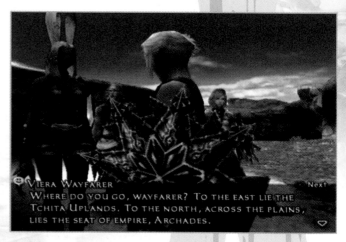

Talk to the viera wayfarer near the crystal in Rava's Pass to get a directional update.

OBJECTIVE
Sneak into the Imperial Capital of Archades

Tchita Uplands

World Map

Action Checklist

1	Cross the Tchita Uplands.
2	Find the Archadian wayfarers who offer a hunt and the Soul Ward Key.
3	Enter the Sochen Cave Palace.

With the main routes into the Imperial city carefully watched, the best way into town is to go through the Tchita Uplands and use a vast underground cavern complex called the Sochen Cave Palace.

Tchita Uplands

THE HIGHLANDS

THE CHOSEN PATH

THE SKYTRAIL

To Sochen Cave Palace

FIELDS OF ETERNITY

To Phon Coast

REALM OF THE ELDER DREAM

SUNDERED EARTH

THE SHADED PATH

OLIPHZAK RISE

THE NAMELESS SPRING

GARDEN OF LIFE'S CIRCLE

THE LOST WAY

UAZCUFF HILLS

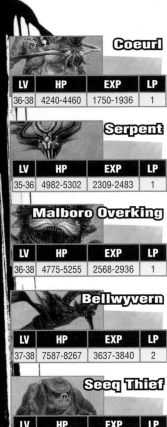

Coeurl

LV	HP	EXP	LP
36-38	4240-4460	1750-1936	1

Serpent

LV	HP	EXP	LP
35-36	4982-5302	2309-2483	1

Malboro Overking

LV	HP	EXP	LP
36-38	4775-5255	2568-2936	1

Bellwyvern

LV	HP	EXP	LP
37-38	7587-8267	3637-3840	2

Seeq Thief

LV	HP	EXP	LP
36-39	5932-6652	2048-2873	1

Walkthrough

TREASURE TABLE

No.	App.%	gil %	Normal If gil	Normal 50%	Normal 50%	w/Diamond Armlet Equip. gil	w/Diamond Armlet Equip. 90%	w/Diamond Armlet Equip. 10%
1	10%	50%	~2000	Hi-Ether	Maduin Gear	~10000	Hi-Ether	Megalixer
2	10%	50%	~2000	Hi-Ether	Gaia Hat	~10000	Hi-Ether	Megalixer
3	10%	50%	~2000	Hi Ether	Battle Harness	~10000	Hi-Ether	Megalixer
4	10%	50%	~2000	Hi-Ether	Diamond Armlet	~10000	Hi-Ether	Megalixer
5	10%	50%	~2000	Hi-Ether	Shell Shield	~10000	Hi-Ether	Megalixer
6	10%	50%	~2000	Foe: highest max HP	Francisca	~10000	Hi-Ether	Megalixer
7	10%	50%	~2000	Foe: lowest max HP	Perseus Bow	~10000	Hi-Ether	Megalixer
8	10%	50%	~2000	Hi-Ether	Armguard	~10000	Hi-Ether	Megalixer
9	10%	50%	~2000	Hi-Ether	Dark Matter	~10000	Hi-Ether	Megalixer

Obtain a Soul Ward Key

Coeurls and Serpents roam the high plains and meadows of the Tchita Uplands. Fight your way east across the Realm of the Elder Dream to the eastern exit. This takes the party into an area called the Skytrail. Cross either bridge into the southern half of the area, then find the exit near the east end.

The Coeurl is a very common foe in the Tchita Uplands.

In the Chosen Path, look for a Save Crystal and an "Archadian wayfarer" next to a bangaa hunter prone on the ground. The wayfarer wants to hire you to deal with a terrible menace in a place called the Sochen Cave Palace. He hands over a bill for the hunt, but note that since it's not an official bill, it won't be listed in the Clan Primer. (*NOTE: You can also get this petition from the wayfarer's father in the "Nameless Spring" area.*)

Select "Yes" to accept the hunt assignment. The wayfarer directs the party to the cave's entrance in the Fields of Eternity to the

northeast. He then hands over the **Soul Ward Key**, which unlocks a door within the entry cavern. Note that the wayfarer's location is now marked by a flashing icon on the Area Map.

BILL?
A TERRIBLE MENACE PLAGUES THE SOCHEN CAVE PALACE. CALLING HALE HUNTERS OF ALL AGES AND RACES TO DEAL WITH THIS SCOURGE UPON US.

The Archadian wayfarer gives you a bill for a hunt in the Sochen Cave Palace to the northeast of the Tchita Uplands.

Continue the trek across the Uplands, but this time with a specific destination in mind. From the Chosen Path, go east across the Highlands, sticking close to the cliff on the left side. Take the north exit up into the Fields of Eternity. So this is the place the wayfarer mentioned! Proceed to the northwest part of the area to find a large cave entrance.

This cave in the Fields of Eternity leads down into the Sochen Cave Palace.

Go inside to enter the Sochen Cave Palace and trigger a quick event. During the event, Balthier explains to the party that this is the "sneaky way" into Archades.

OBJECTIVE
Use the Sochen Cave Palace to Sneak into Archades

World Map

Sochen Cave Palace

Action Checklist

1	Use the Soul Ward Key to enter the boss chamber.
2	Defeat the five bosses.
3	OPTIONAL! Return to the wayfarers in the Tchita Uplands for a reward.
4	Defeat the Crystalbug.

Zombie Knight

LV	HP	EXP	LP
36-38	3693-4053	1427-1747	1

Imp

LV	HP	EXP	LP
37-39	4390-4710	2231-2583	1

Gorgimera

LV	HP	EXP	LP
36-37	5385-5505	1707-1878	1

Iguion

LV	HP	EXP	LP
36-38	5129-5349	2329-2515	1

Zombie Warlock

LV	HP	EXP	LP
36-38	7625-7985	2693-3013	1

Sochen Cave Palace (Entry)

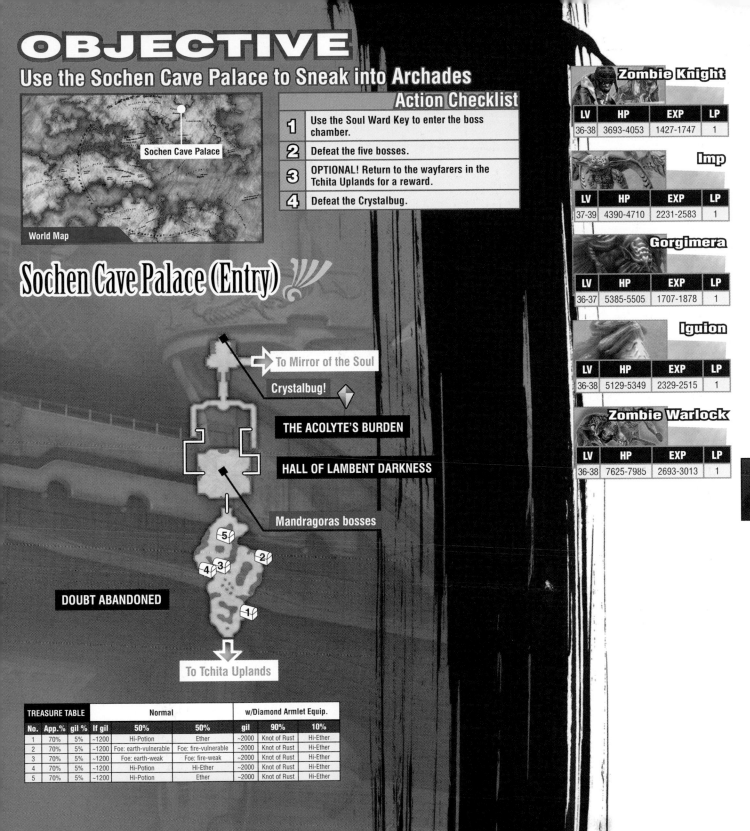

To Mirror of the Soul

Crystalbug!

THE ACOLYTE'S BURDEN

HALL OF LAMBENT DARKNESS

Mandragoras bosses

DOUBT ABANDONED

To Tchita Uplands

TREASURE TABLE			Normal		w/Diamond Armlet Equip.		
No.	App.%	gil %	If gil	50%	50%	gil	90%	10%
1	70%	5%	~1200	Hi-Potion	Ether	~2000	Knot of Rust	Hi-Ether
2	70%	5%	~1200	Foe: earth-vulnerable	Foe: fire-vulnerable	~2000	Knot of Rust	Hi-Ether
3	70%	5%	~1200	Foe: earth-weak	Foe: fire-weak	~2000	Knot of Rust	Hi-Ether
4	70%	5%	~1200	Hi-Potion	Hi-Ether	~2000	Knot of Rust	Hi-Ether
5	70%	5%	~1200	Hi-Potion	Ether	~2000	Knot of Rust	Hi-Ether

Reach the Palace Gate

The cave antechamber, called Doubt Abandoned, isn't actually part of the palace. Fight past the Zombie Warriors and floating Imps while descending the slope. Upon reaching the Gate of the Soul Ward at the north end of the cavern, use the Soul Ward Key to open it. (This is the key you received from the Archadian wayfarer back at the Save Crystal.) Now prepare for a wild boss fight!

Imps and Zombie Knights patrol the dank cavern entrance to the Sochen Cave Palace.

ENTER SOCHEN WITH FULL MP

It is important to enter the fight with the five Mandragora bosses with full Mist Charges on all of your Quickening-equipped characters so you can chain as many Quickening attacks as possible. The best way to do this is to start at the Tchita Crystal in the Chosen Path. Turn off gambits en route, then enter the Highlands and hold down the R2 button to flee. Sprint along the left wall to the exit into the Fields of Eternity.

Hold down the R2 button again and sprint to the cave opening, then flee again through the Doubt Abandoned area. When you reach the Gate of the Soul Ward, use Potions to heal any damage you suffered along the way. Now enter the fight with your party's Mist Charges at 100 percent across the board, ready to sling Quickenings at the bosses. Important: Remember to turn your gambits back on for the three characters who made the run here!

The Mandragoras

Mandragora Prince

LV	HP	EXP	LP
37	9069	0	5

Onion Queen

LV	HP	EXP	LP
37	9069	0	5

Topstalk

LV	HP	EXP	LP
37	9069	0	5

Alraune King

LV	HP	EXP	LP
37	9069	0	5

Pumpkin Star

LV	HP	EXP	LP
37	9069	0	5

When the fight begins, the little bosses scatter in all directions. They have Haste cast on themselves, making them very speedy and difficult to target and counter. If you have active characters without Quickening spells available, use them to cast Dispel on the five foes. Otherwise, hold the R2 button and run around until the Mandragoras re-gather and start chasing the party.

The bosses will form a tight line as they give chase, so this is the moment to trigger a Quickening, targeting the centermost member of the enemy party. As always, try to string together a good Mist chain so you trigger the follow-up area attack that can damage the entire enemy party.

As the fight continues, the Mandragoras follow a pattern. They all attack at once, then when they take damage, they all scatter in multiple directions to regenerate and heal. If your Quickenings didn't wipe them out, cast Dispel on any survivors and wipe them out one by one. You may need to chase the targets a bit, especially when they run off to heal. When this occurs, stay close to them until you can hit them with a series of physical hits.

Overall, the key is to avoid fighting all five Mandragoras at once. Their combined attacks can decimate your party quickly.

Here's what you're looking for—all five Mandragoras in a row giving chase. This is the best time to nail them with a long Quickening chain if possible, triggering an area attack in the process.

Remember, the Mandragora bosses were a mark for a hunt you agreed to do. Return to the Archadian Wayfarer in the Chosen Path of the Tchita Uplands to receive a reward: 1000 gil and three Remedies! Heal and save at the crystal, then return to the Hall of Lambent Darkness (where you fought the Mandragora bosses) in the Sochen Cave Palace.

Remember that after you defeat the Mandragora bosses, you can also join the Hunt Club back at the Phon Coast, if you want.

Join the Club

Defeat the Crystalbug

Exit the Hall of Lambent Darkness via either side door (east or west) into the Acolyte's Burden area. Follow the corridors north to the Save Crystal… except, it *isn't* a Save Crystal! Yes, another sneaky Crystalbug starts slinging Water attacks at the party. If you came here directly from the boss battle, your party may be depleted, so fight carefully. You may want to return to the hall and run around to rebuild MP levels before you battle the bug.

Actually, you can skip the Crystalbug fight if you want and proceed directly east into the main part of the palace. However, this is the last Save Crystal you'll see for a long time, so it's best that you hammer the bug into submission.

Hit this annoying Crystalbug disguised as a Save Crystal.

Sochen Cave Palace (Main)

Action Checklist

1	Navigate through the palace.
2	OPTIONAL! Solve the waterfall puzzle to reach the item in a secret room.
3	Defeat Ahriman.
4	Exit the caves into Old Archades.

The enemies here are the same as Sochen Cave Palace (Entry) plus the following:

Striker

LV	HP	EXP	LP
37-38	5129-5549	2329-2492	1

Focalor

LV	HP	EXP	LP
36-37	4513-4684	2135-2308	1

Wendigo

LV	HP	EXP	LP
37-38	5458-5878	2329-2492	1

Crystalbug

LV	HP	EXP	LP
38	3589	0	10

Pit Fiend

LV	HP	EXP	LP
37-39	4390-4710	2329-2515	1

HALL OF THE WRATH GOD

Optional Boss

12 13

11

14

To Temptation Eluded

HALL OF SHADOWLIGHT

DESTINY'S MARCH

FALLS OF TIME

6 8 9 10
7

4 3 5 1

2

MIRROR OF THE SOUL

Map Urn

To the Acolyte's Burden ←

Find a Palace Map

From the Save Crystal (formerly the Crystalbug) in the Acolyte's Burden area, take the east door to enter the main palace. All sorts of demons prowl the cave corridors, so be ready for combat. In the Mirror of the Soul, go north through the ancient door to the path split. Watch out for a swarm of Imps and a Pit Fiend. Next, turn east and stay close to the easternmost (right) wall as you move toward an alcove with a Map Urn that is guarded by three Gorgimeras. The map will be very helpful in the next areas. Continue to hug the right side wall while moving north across the zone line into the next area, Falls of Time.

Imps and Pit Fiends abound in the palace.

Find the Map Urn right away, especially if you want to solve the waterfall puzzle.

No.	App.%	gil %	If gil	50%	50%	gil	90%	10%
TREASURE TABLE				Normal		w/Diamond Armlet Equip.		
1	45%	50%	~50	Hi-Potion	Gokuu Pole	~1000	Knot of Rust	Hi-Ether
2	70%	5%	~2000	Hi-Potion	Foe: lightning-vulnerable	~3800	Knot of Rust	Hi-Ether
3	70%	5%	~2000	Hi-Potion	Foe: lightning-weak	~3800	Knot of Rust	Hi-Ether
4	75%	10%	~2500	Hi-Ether	Ether	~3800	Knot of Rust	Hi-Ether
5	100%	0%	-	Iga Blade	Koga Blade	-	Knot of Rust	Knot of Rust
6	70%	5%	~30	Hi-Potion	Foe: ice-weak	~1000	Knot of Rust	Hi-Ether
7	50%	50%	~900	Hi-Potion	Officer's Hat	~2000	Knot of Rust	Hi-Ether
8	70%	5%	~30	Hi-Potion	Foe: ice-vulnerable	~1000	Knot of Rust	Hi-Ether
9	80%	10%	7963	Elixir	Dark Matter	28000	Knot of Rust	Megalixir
10	70%	10%	6954	Elixir	Kiku-ichimonji	30000	Knot of Rust	Elixir
11	100%	0%	--	Phoenix Down	Phoenix Down	--	Phoenix Down	Phoenix Down
12	100%	0%	--	Elixir	Elixir	--	Elixir	Elixir
13	100%	0%	--	Elixir	Gaia Hat	--	Elixir	Elixir
14	100%	0%	--	Balance Mote	Holy Mote	--	Balance Mote	Holy Mote

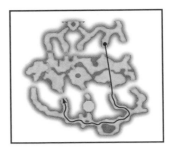

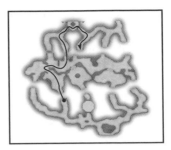

Third move.   *Fourth move.*

OPTIONAL! Solve the Waterfall Puzzle

If you examine the Area Map, you will see a small room in the center of the palace between the southern Mirror of the Soul and the northern Falls of Time. This room holds a treasure chest with an item inside. However, a waterfall blocks the entrance from the north. In fact, numerous waterfalls block passages between the areas. When you move from the Falls of Time area to the Mirror of the Soul area, you trigger magick that actually moves the waterfall locations! (The game states: "The course of the waterfalls seems to have changed.") If you follow the correct route back and forth between the two areas, you can create a path to the secret room.

Several waterfalls block passages between areas of the Sochen Cave Palace, but you can manipulate their locations by simply moving from room to room.

The best way to describe the route is visually with maps, so move from room to room in the order shown here.

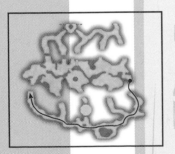

First move.

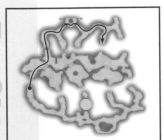

Second move.

When you return south from the Falls of Time to the Mirror of the Soul the last time, you receive a message that a door has opened in the distance. Go across the bridge directly ahead and venture south into the cave. This path leads to the Pilgrim's Door. The inscription on it provides directions for the moves you just completed. After reading it, enter the room and get the treasure.

Head North to Ahriman

Now head north through the Falls of Time and up the middle of Destiny's March. At the far northern edge of the palace is the Hall of Shadowlight, where a boss battle looms.

⚡ RUN AROUND FOR MP

Remember that you build MP by moving around. If you have characters with Mist Charges that aren't full, simply run in a circle around the northern room until their MP fills up.

Consider a Save

There is no Save Crystal near the Hall of Shadowlight where you fight Ahriman. Since you have accomplished quite a bit in the palace, especially if you solved the waterfall puzzle, you may want to return south to the Acolyte's Burden Save Crystal to save your game.

! The Western Menace

You can see the Hall of the Wroth God on your Area Map at this point. This is the home of a mighty (and optional) boss called the Hell Wyrm. You can't get there just yet, however. You must first complete some tasks amongst the Cerobi Steppe windmills, including the hunt for Vyraal. After that, you must solve a directional puzzle here in the Sochen Cave Palace (similar to the waterfall puzzle) to unlock the path to the Hall of the Wroth God. For all the details, check out the "Side Quests" chapter and look for the section on the Hell Wyrm.

Walkthrough

SIDE QUEST

Ahriman

LVL	HP	EXP	LP
38	62149	0	28
Steal	Sky Jewel, Death Powder, Maduin Gear		

The ghostly Ahriman is another one of those maddening foes who keeps the party tied up with status ailments. This boss will toss Doom, Confuse, Blind, and Sleep at the party in combination on occasion. Ahriman also conjures up replicas of itself. At times, you'll find three or four "Ahrimans" in your target selection box.

There are a couple of keys to achieve victory over this boss. First, make sure you heal status ailments immediately. Good status-removing gambits automate this process, but keep an eye on your characters' MP levels. If MP drops to zero, your status-healing spells like Vox and Blindna are worthless. Use the Charge technick, or start using the corresponding items in your inventory such as Echo Herbs and Eye Drops. In any case, you need Remedies available with the License upgrades that allow them to cure Doom as well as other status ailments.

Second, keep moving and swinging away, even when Ahriman's "shadows" (the replicas it spawns) have the party confused. The replicas are weak, so they will drop after one or two good hits. You can also utilize Cura or Bio against the shadows, as these spells will destroy all of the shadows within range with one spell.

Keep everybody's HP above 50 percent, if possible. Ice Shields make good equipment, since Ahriman likes to cast Blizzara at your party. When Ahriman's HP bar hits the 20% mark, watch out for a powerful Maser Eye attack that deals heavy damage. If you have Raise or Phoenix Down gambits set in each ally's number 1 gambit slot (and you *should*), the party can pull through this brutal area attack.

 SWIVEL THAT CAMERA

One of Ahriman's tricks is to disappear and then reappear across the room or sometimes right on top of one of your characters. Keep circling the camera view to spot the boss so you can run your party leader into striking range (if he's a melee fighter) or out of striking range (if he's a magick caster and healer).

Ahriman likes to use Blizzara spells. An Ice Shield will cut down on the damage sustained. Don't panic when you see multiple Ahrimans in your target box; the shadows are weak.

Quickenings will hurt Ahriman, but probably not enough to risk expending all of your MP on them. Consider holding back on Quickenings until Ahriman's HP bar drops below half. Try keeping a reserve party with Mist Charges ready if possible, and swap them in for a Quickening chain when Ahriman's HP drops below one-quarter. After the battle, pick up the treasures around the perimeter of the room and exit via the east door into the Temptation Eluded area.

Survive the Palace Exit

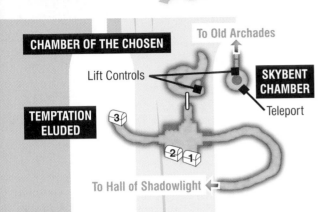

TREASURE TABLE			Normal		w/Diamond Armlet Equip.		
No.	App.%	gil %	If gil	50%	50%	gil	90%	10%
1	70%	5%	~1500	Hi-Potion	Foe: water-vulnerable	~3500	Knot of Rust	Hi-Ether
2	70%	5%	~1500	Hi-Potion	Foe: water-weak	~3500	Knot of Rust	Hi-Ether
3	70%	5%	~1500	Hi-Potion	Ether	~3500	Knot of Rust	Hi-Ether

There is still no Save Crystal in sight yet, so stay alert! Watch out for lots of explosive traps at intervals in the passage ahead. (If you took off your Bangle for the boss fight, equip it now to locate the traps or use Libra.) Fight through the Strikers and Imps guarding the long passage that slopes up into a large room, then exit north into the Chamber of the Chosen.

Find the lift and ride it out of the Sochen Cave Palace once and for all.

Climb the spiral rock ramp to the elevator platform. Activate the Disused Pedestal to ride the lift platform up to the Skybent Chamber, then use the Save Crystal. Open the stone door and exit into Old Archades, the slum on the outskirts of the imperial city, where the party can finally breathe some fresh air. Well, sort of...

! Palace Side Quests

You can return later for the "Shelled Obstruction" hunt for Darksteel and "The Things We Do..." hunt for Overlord. See the "Side Quests" chapter for all the details.

OBJECTIVE
Get Past the City Guards

World Map

Old Archades

Action Checklist	
1	Talk to the Lucky Man near the bridge.
2	Talk to the Imperial guard.
3	Talk to Beasley.

The Imperial City is off-limits to the lowly denizens of Old Archades. Figure out a way to slip past the Imperial soldiers guarding the entrance to the city.

Old Archades

ALLEY OF MUTED SIGHS

Ex-Broker

Lucky Man

Fresh Ardent

Beasley

Stranded Merchant

To the Imperial City

To Sochen Cave Palace

ALLEY OF LOW WHISPERS

Get Past the City Guards

Check out the Stranded Merchant just around the corner. He doesn't have much to sell, but one item is a doozy: the **Embroidered Tippet**, which doubles the amount of EXP you earn by defeating foes. If you have a lot of gil, buy two or three and equip them on your lowest-level active party members. This provides an easy way to balance an unbalanced party.

Now follow the narrow, grimy streets and talk to everybody. Pay attention to the tidbits of information you learn from each NPC; trading info is like gold in the streets. (Several characters tell you as much!)

> In general, any yellow highlighted word or phrase in a character's text dialogue indicates a significant connection to another character or event somewhere. Often, there's a side quest associated with the highlighted clue.

Yellow Word Clues

For example, an Ex-Broker up in the northeast corner of the Alley of Low Whispers is remorseful for all of the former clients he bilked. Not far away, a Fresh Ardent bemoans being bilked by a broker. A connection, perhaps? Also, talk to the "Lucky Man," the one who confides in you how he found a "bag o' money" in a barrel. This information will be very valuable shortly.

Talk to everyone in the streets to pick up juicy bits of info.

Continue to head east, then cross the bridge to the Alley of Muted Sighs. A fellow named Jules sits on a crate and speaks of the "market" for information, offering to pay for good tips. Move on to find the Save Crystal in the southwest alley, then continue up the stairs to the Imperial guards blocking the path.

These guards won't let anyone past without the proper credentials.

Talk to the soldier on the left, who asks for credentials. Regardless of your answer, after you make your way back to the south a little ways, an event follows in which Jules appears and talks to your party. It turns out he knows Balthier, who calls Jules a "streetear"—a peddler of information. When Jules asks for 1500 gil, go ahead and pay up. You can't get into the city without his help.

He asks for any street tips you may have picked up. Vaan tells him about info he's learned. If you talked to the Lucky Man to learn about the bag o' money he took from a barrel, Jules sends the party to report this to Beasley, the man who lost the money. Beasley sits on the ground back near the bridge.

Talk to Beasley and return to Jules to trigger another event. Beasley has started a fight with the Lucky Man! This brings the Imperial guards jogging past to stop the fracas. Now that the coast is clear, Vaan runs upstairs.

After you tell Beasley who took his money, his rage triggers a distraction for the guards.

The party automatically enters the Imperial City of Archades. Watch the brief event in which the party arrives in the busy streets of the capital. At this point, a new objective appears on the Location Map.

OBJECTIVE
Find a Way to Sneak Inside the Draklor Laboratory

World Map

Imperial City of Archades

Action Checklist

1	Shop to upgrade your equipment, gambits, magicks, and technicks.
2	Talk to the Cab Guide.
3	Earn nine chops by passing information between citizens.
4	Take the taxi to Tsenoble.

It's not easy to get inside an Imperial weapons lab. Trade information to earn the "chops" you need to reach Draklor.

The Imperial City of Archades

To Old Archades

MOLBERRY

TRANT

NIBASSE

RIENNA

HIGHGARDEN TERRACE

Taxi ride

GRAND ARCADE

TSENOBLE

Shop for Upgrades

Yes, it's time for more fun consumer frenzy. Before you start throwing your gil around the posh Imperial city stores, however, know that you should keep 2500 gil for a payment to Jules later. If you don't have the gil for Jules, then you can't move on to Draklor Laboratory. Instead, you're forced to go back down to the Sochen Cave Palace to hunt until you get another 2500 gil worth of loot to sell.

Save 2500 gil for Jules

Shop to your heart's content, but if you don't keep 2500 gil for Jules, you won't get the info you need about chops.

First, proceed due west from Trant into Molberry. (On the way, Balthier takes his leave to attend to some business, promising to meet up again later.) Go all the way to Bulward's Technicks in the northwest end of the district. Find the Cartographers' Guild moogle upstairs on the second floor and buy a map of Archades. (You can also buy a map of the Tchita Uplands, if you have the extra gil.)

Buy a map of Archades on the second floor of Bulward's Technicks in the Molberry district.

Now it's time to check out the other establishments in the city. Save the combined Weapons/Armor shop (called Vint's Armaments) in Nilbasse for last, then walk over to the taxi stand directly across the street and talk to the Cab Guide.

The Cab Guide says a taxi ride is a million gil! It's either that, or nine chops. For just 2500 gil (a bargain), Jules explains how to get chops in Archades.

The Cab Guide states that you'll need at least nine "chops" to ride this cab—either that, or a million gil. Fortunately, Jules intervenes again and says that Balthier is waiting for everyone in Central. Jules then demands 2500 gil for the info you need regarding chops.

Select "Pay up." Jules explains that a chop is a mark of status, and it can be used as a writ of transit. You'll need 9 chops to get to Central. The way to earn them, he says, is to talk to people and pass on information.

Play the Archadian Match Game!

Now start talking to people. Each of the four districts in Archades offers opportunities to earn chops. The tactic is to talk to a citizen with a phrase highlighted in yellow in their dialogue text. You can choose to "Commit this tale to memory" or "Do nothing." If you commit it to memory, the highlighted phrase of dialogue appears in the upper-left corner of the screen.

After "memorizing" a phrase, your task is to find the citizen (who is always in the same district) with a matching story. If you find the correct match, you earn one chop. If you talk to someone with an unrelated phrase also highlighted in yellow, you can choose to memorize *that* phrase instead and start looking for the corresponding person. You can only have one phrase "memorized" at a time.

The memorized phrase is listed at the upper-left corner of the screen. If you find the matching person, you can elect to relate the tale and earn a chop.

Each of the four Archadian districts has several pairs of people you can match up to earn one chop. The breakdown is as follows:

- *Molberry: 9 chops*
- *Nilbasse: 6 chops*
- *Rienna: 7 chops*
- *Trant: 6 chops*

Remember that you only need nine chops to buy the ride to the Central area, called Tsenoble. So if you just match up all the pairs available in Molberry alone, you'll have enough for the taxi.

The Molberry Matches

This section lists the nine Molberry dialogue matches, listing the topic and the two citizens who match. IMPORTANT! The first citizen listed is the one you must talk to first, because he or she is the person who provides the topic to "memorize."

1. "The Anniversary" (Poor Husband and Poor Wife)
2. "The Traveler" (Avid Traveler and Traveling Gentleman)
3. "The Mummer" (Reminiscing Lady and Family-Minded Girl)
4. "To Be a Judge" (Would-Be Judge and Judge's Wife)
5. "A Knack for Magick" (Talented Woman and Akademician)
6. "A Trinket from Giza" (Daughter-in-Law and Man from Giza)
7. "The Eight & Twenty Chops" (Ardent Woman and Ardent Man)
8. "The Master of Disguises" (Look-Alike and Look-Alike… yes, they're both the same)
9. "The Tutor" (Proud Mother and Tutor)

When the scene ends, the party appears at the taxi platform. Talk to the Cab Guide and select "You know where to go." Confirm your selection by choosing "Let's go," and you're off to Draklor.

Again, there are other matches in other districts, a grand total of 28 in all. Each successful match earns you a Pinewood Chop. The game will indicate when you have the requisite nine. When this occurs, go to the Cab Guide back in Nilbasse and select "Take me to Tsenoble" to trigger an event.

> ### ! Have You Got the Chops?
>
> If you collect enough Pinewood Chops to trade for a Sandalwood Chop, you can access the elite portions of the city: Grand Arcade and Highgarden Terrace. To get enough chops for the trade, you need to match up all of the pairs of citizens in all four districts (Trant, Molberry, Nilbasse, and Rienna), for a total of 28 matches.
>
> Gaining access to this area is a key part of the "Hunt Club" side quest and the Cockatrice Hunt. You will eventually return here to speak to Otto for part of the hidden medallion quest.

SIDE QUEST

Balthier meets the party in Tsenoble. Save your game at the nearby Save Crystal, then go northeast to the other end of Tsenoble to trigger an event. The Imperials are thinning out, but they are still present.

Go back south to trigger another event. Jules says that a squad of Judges is at Draklor, but his connections are cold as to the actual research being conducted. He's arranged a cab ride, though.

JULES
ALL DEVELOPED WITHOUT THE SENATE'S KNOWLEDGE, OF COURSE. WHY, NOT EVEN THE EMPEROR KNEW THE FULL EXTENT OF DR. CID'S OPERATIONS.

OBJECTIVE
Find Dr. Cid's Lab

World Map

Draklor Laboratory

Action Checklist

1. Use the elevators and bulkhead controls to access the 70th floor.
2. Defeat Dr. Cid.

The urgency is growing. Your goal is to find and confront Dr. Cid before he carries his nethicite experiments too far. The word is, he's somewhere on Draklor's top floor.

Draklor Laboratory

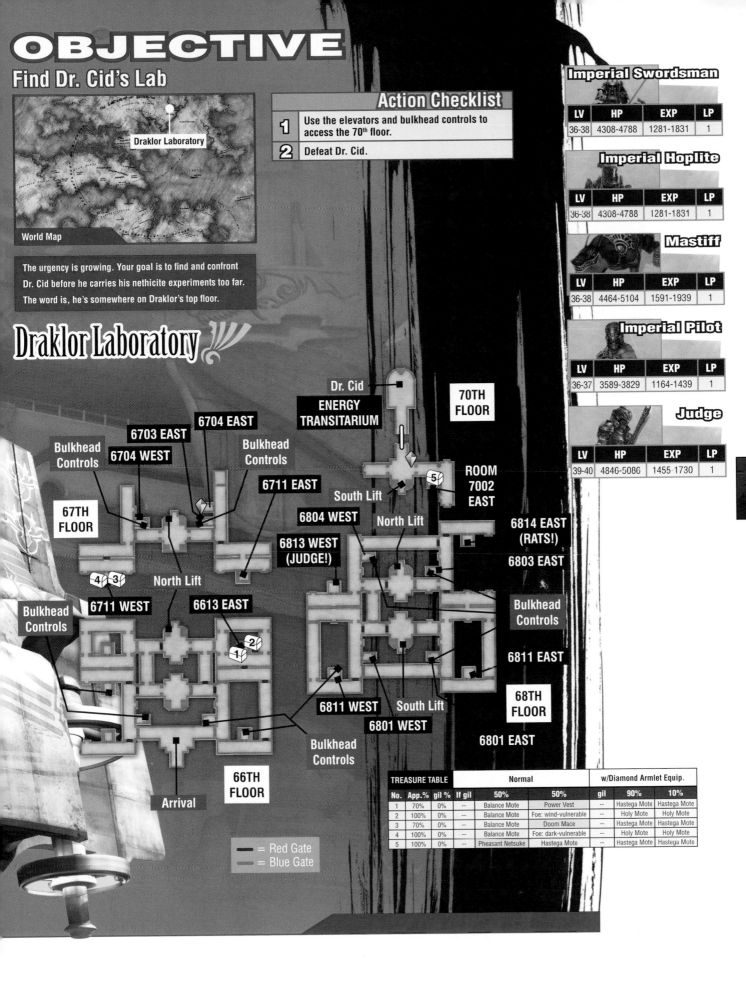

Imperial Swordsman

LV	HP	EXP	LP
36-38	4308-4788	1281-1831	1

Imperial Hoplite

LV	HP	EXP	LP
36-38	4308-4788	1281-1831	1

Mastiff

LV	HP	EXP	LP
36-38	4464-5104	1591-1939	1

Imperial Pilot

LV	HP	EXP	LP
36-37	3589-3829	1164-1439	1

Judge

LV	HP	EXP	LP
39-40	4846-5086	1455-1730	1

Map labels: Dr. Cid · ENERGY TRANSITARIUM · 70TH FLOOR · 6704 EAST · 6703 EAST · Bulkhead Controls · 6704 WEST · Bulkhead Controls · 6711 EAST · South Lift · ROOM 7002 EAST · 67TH FLOOR · 6804 WEST · North Lift · 6814 EAST (RATS!) · 6813 WEST (JUDGE!) · 6803 EAST · North Lift · 6711 WEST · 6613 EAST · Bulkhead Controls · Bulkhead Controls · 6811 EAST · 6811 WEST · South Lift · 68TH FLOOR · 6801 WEST · 6801 EAST · Bulkhead Controls · 66TH FLOOR · Arrival

= Red Gate
= Blue Gate

TREASURE TABLE		Normal			w/Diamond Armlet Equip.		
No.	App.%	gil %	If gil	50%	50%	gil	90%	10%
1	70%	0%	--	Balance Mote	Power Vest	--	Hastega Mote	Hastega Mote
2	100%	0%	--	Balance Mote	Foe: wind-vulnerable	--	Holy Mote	Holy Mote
3	70%	0%	--	Balance Mote	Doom Mace	--	Hastega Mote	Hastega Mote
4	100%	0%	--	Balance Mote	Foe: dark-vulnerable	--	Holy Mote	Holy Mote
5	100%	0%	--	Pheasant Netsuke	Hastega Mote	--	Hastega Mote	Hastega Mote

Get to the Top Floor

Floor 66

When the party arrives on the 66th Floor, head west and work your way north through the corridors (past some dead and wounded Imperial soldiers) to the northernmost lift. Use the control panel, called the "North Lift Terminal," and select 67F as your destination.

Use the North Lift Terminal to take the lift up to 67F.

Floor 67

Head east and then north to the door labeled "C.D.B." (for "Cidolfus Demen Bunansa," Dr. Cid's full name). Enter to trigger a short event showing Balthier examining notes in Dr. Cid's ransacked office. You automatically receive a **Lab Access Card** and a Draklor map. When the scene ends, the party appears back in the hallway. Note that the game's Mini-Map is going haywire, but the Area Map is in good shape.

Go through the first door on the right, marked "Rm 6704 East," to find a Save Crystal. Use it and talk to the Senior Researcher. He explains that the complex features red and blue bulkheads. When red doors are open, blue doors are closed and vice versa.

Exit 6704 East and go next door to 6703 East. Use the Bulkhead Controls in the corner of this room to open the blue bulkheads. (The panel changes from blue to red.) Exit the room and follow the corridor back to the lift, but watch out for an attack by Imperial troops! Fight through the Swordsmen and Hoplite and get to the lift. Note that Imperials will keep arriving via the lift until you actually board it. Take the elevator up to floor 68.

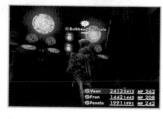

In 6703 East, turn the bulkhead controls from blue to red.

Floor 68

The party arrives in the north lift lobby. Your goal on floor 68 is to reach the south lift on this floor and this goal requires the use of a few bulkhead switches. First, go east and enter 6803 East and switch the bulkhead controls from red to blue, thus opening the red bulkheads. Exit the room, go north, and take the next two lefts around to Room 6804 West. Enter the room and switch the bulkhead controls back to red, thus opening the blue bulkheads.

Now exit and go all the way to the room in the southwest corner of Floor 68, Room 6811 West. Switch the bulkhead controls there from red to blue, opening the red bulkheads again. Now exit the room, go left, and take the first left, heading north up the corridor. Take the first right to find the elevator lobby. Take the lift up to Floor 70.

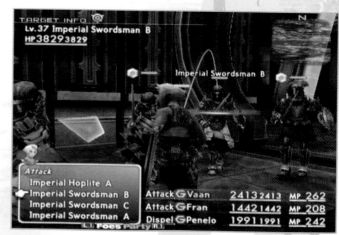

The Imperial presence grows thicker as you move higher up the lab building.

Find Dr. Cid

Finally, a Save Crystal! Before you proceed into Dr. Cid's den, head east and around the corner to Room 7002 East, where a nice item rests inside a treasure coffer. Now return and head north up the stairs toward the Energy Transitarium to trigger the sudden appearance of a foe—or *is* he a foe?

Who is this guy? Once he knows you're not one of Cid's lackeys, he backs off and rushes toward the Energy Transitarium.

Dr. Cid

Dr. Cid			
LVL	**HP**	**EXP**	**LP**
40	72989	0	29
Steal	Knot of Rust, Hi-Potion, X-Potion		

Helm Rook			
LVL	**HP**	**EXP**	**LP**
38	9859	784	5
Steal	Knot of Rust, Potion, Hi-Potion		

Dr. Cid has four floating mechanical Rooks protecting him. These are perhaps the toughest boss minions you've faced so far. It's very difficult to inflict damage to Cid when the Rooks are active, so ignore the doctor and focus your full fury on his minions. You can also target one central Rook (not Dr. Cid!) with a Quickening chain and hope that the follow-up area attack seriously weakens the other three. In any case, you must take out the Rooks before you can have a chance against Dr. Cid. The Rooks will cast Protect, Regen and Reflect on Cid, so don't use any Black magick.

💥 MAKE HASTE

If you have the Haste spell in your arsenal, by all means use it! Have one party member cast Haste on himself/herself and then cast it on the other two allies. Or, you can use a Hastega Mote to speed up the entire party with one toss. The faster you hit the Rooks, the better shape you'll be in.

Dr. Cid's rooks should get your full focus until they are eliminated.

Once the last Rook falls, you'll be in much better shape, even if your party looks depleted. Dr. Cid is powerful but quite slow, so you have time to sling Cure spells, use Potions, Charge up your MP, or use whatever gambit routine has been successful thus far. Try to get the entire party up above 1000 HP as soon as possible, because Cid unleashes a powerful attack that knocks a lot of health out of everyone's HP bar.

You don't actually have to knock Dr. Cid down to zero HP to win this fight. When his health drops low enough, a new ally jumps into the fray and finishes off this particular battle.

After the fight, you see a brief glimpse of what's behind Dr. Cid's maniacal drive for mastery of nethicite. He flies off to Giruvegan, and the man you met on the stairs who jumped into the fight makes his introduction. He's Reddas, a sky pirate based at the Port of Balfonheim.

Meanwhile, in the Border-Skies, the rebel fleet under the command of Marquis Ondore is mustering its strength. From the bridge of the flagship *Garland*, Ondore and his crew discuss the unfolding events. War seems all but inevitable.

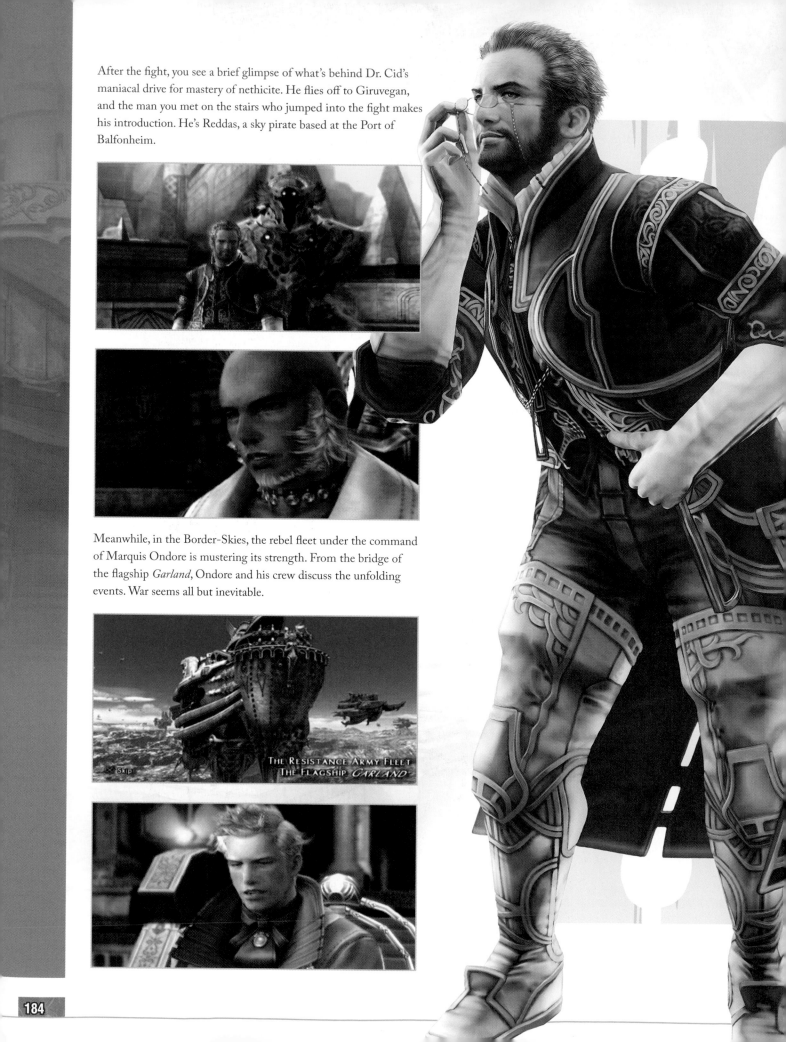

THE RESISTANCE ARMY FLEET
THE FLAGSHIP *GARLAND*

OBJECTIVE
Track Cid to the Ancient City of Giruvegan

Balfonheim Port

World Map

Action Checklist

1 Shop, restock, and upgrade in Balfonheim Port.

2 Teleport to Eruyt Village and head for the Feywood.

3 Solve the Feywood shrine puzzle to reveal the gate.

4 Summon help to open the gate to Giruvegan.

Dr. Cid has the stone—the deifacted nethicite—and it must be destroyed! Track him through the misty, mysterious Feywood to the ancient city of Giruvegan.

Balfonheim Port

CANAL LANE

To the Cerobi Steppe

Map moogle

SEA BREEZE LANE

GALLERINA MARKETPLACE

SACCIO LANE

QUAYSIDE COURT

CHIVANY BREAKWATER

To Reddas Manse

TREASURE TABLE				Normal		w/Diamond Armlet Equip.		
No.	App.%	gil %	If gil	50%	50%	gil	90%	10%
1	100%	0%	-	Elixir	Megalixir	-	Megalixir	Ensanguined Shield
2	100%	100%	5040	--	--	3	--	--

Prep for Giruvegan

As the scene opens in this port city in southeastern Archades, the party gathers at the Reddas Manse, home and sanctuary of the pirate leader. Listen carefully as Ashe, Reddas, and the others discuss the tricky political situation and the threat they all face. More directly, they wonder about Cid's destination: Giruvegan. Reddas knows of a "Mist-storm that surges and seethes" in a corner of the Feywood. This is your party's next destination.

After the event, the party appears outside in the port city, speaking with Rikken, Raz, and Elza, three of Reddas's followers. Rikken speaks of the Feywood, south of the Golmore Jungle. He mentions a gate to the holy land of Giruvegan and a "hidden trial" that must be passed.

Rikken and Elza are the the, uh, "men" Reddas refers to as your contacts regarding the Feywood and the ancient city.

Use the teleport crystal in the northeast to reach Golmore Jungle quickly.

Explore the port city and upgrade anything that you can afford. When you've finished shopping, head to the northeast district, Sea Breeze Lane. First, make sure you find the treasure full of **5000-plus gil** in the trees next to Dyce, the traveling merchant. After doing so, use the orange Save Crystal to teleport to Golmore Jungle.

> ### ! A Good Side Quest Juncture
>
> Several side quests open up at this point in the game, including the "Hunt Loop", "The Great Cockatrice Escape", "Fishing in Nebra River", the "Balfonheim Foot Race", and "Dragon Researcher". Due to the impending difficulty spike in this area, it is important to utilize this lull in the story progression to perform some of these side quests.
>
> It's also important to note that Dyce, the merchant on the Chocobo in Sea Breeze Lane, sells Teleport Stones. These stones make taking a break for side quests, exploration, and free-roaming easier than it's ever been.

> ### !! STEPPE IT UP
>
> You probably haven't accrued much loot since the last time you shopped, so you may want to wander into the Cerobi Steppe to the north and spend some time leveling up and acquiring loot, as the battles ahead will be tough.

Golmore Jungle

Action Checklist

1 Cross the jungle heading south into the Feywood.

The enemies here are the same as your earlier trip through Golmore, plus the following:

Hellhound

LV	HP	EXP	LP
37-39	3570-3790	1591-1777	1

Coeurl

LV	HP	EXP	LP
36-38	3944-4264	1433-1607	1

THE NEEDLEBRAKE

THE PARTING GLADE

To Paths of Chained Light

To the Eruyt Village

To Paths of Chained Light

WHISPERLEAF WAY

To Paths of Chained Light

THE RUSTLING CHAPEL

To the Feywood

Cross Golmore to the Feywood

From the crystal in The Parting Glade, head west through Whisperleaf Way into The Needlebrake, then wind your way south into The Rustling Chapel. Most of the old enemies in this area should drop with one or two hits, if you've been leveling up your characters. When you reach the southern part of the jungle, though, the foes get tougher. In particular, there are some nasty, level 37 Hellhounds roaming the mossy paths. Exit The Rustling Chapel to the south to enter the Feywood.

The jungle isn't quite as forbidding as the first time you passed through. Even the dreaded Diresaur isn't much competition for your buffed-up party now.

The Feywood (North)

Action Checklist

1	Cross the northern half of the Feywood.
2	Defeat Rafflesia.

Deadly Nightshade

LV	HP	EXP	LP
39-41	3167-3647	1262-1630	1

Mu

LV	HP	EXP	LP
40-41	3167-3487	1010-1184	1

Golem

LV	HP	EXP	LP
42-43	11310-11550	2945-3193	2

Cerberus

LV	HP	EXP	LP
38-40	4419-5059	1473-1821	1

Tartarus

LV	HP	EXP	LP
38-40	3619-4259	1473-1821	1

Mirrorknight

LV	HP	EXP	LP
40-42	5202-5842	2419-2767	1

Juggernaut (Rare Game)

LV	HP	EXP	LP
46-47	76251-76491	5145-5393	12

Cross North Feywood

The first thing the party runs into is a swarm of Deadly Nightshades. Although they may look cute, don't underestimate their lethality, especially in large packs. Creatures in the Feywood tend to cast magick such as Haste, Protect, and Shell upon themselves. Make sure your Dispel spell is at the ready.

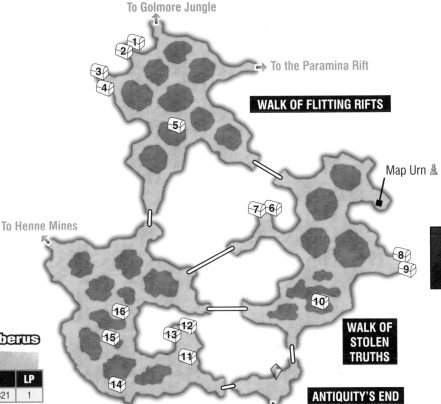

To Golmore Jungle

To the Paramina Rift

WALK OF FLITTING RIFTS

Map Urn

To Henne Mines

WALK OF STOLEN TRUTHS

ANTIQUITY'S END

WALK OF DANCING SHADOW

To Redolent Glade

TREASURE TABLE			Normal			w/Diamond Armlet Equip.		
No.	App.%	gil %	If gil	50%	50%	gil	90%	10%
1	45%	0%	--	Hi-Potion	Foe: character MP ≥ 90%	--	Knot of Rust	Elixir
2	45%	0%	--	Hi-Potion	Foe: character MP ≥ 70%	--	Knot of Rust	Elixir
3	45%	0%	--	Hi-Potion	Foe: character MP ≥ 50%	--	Knot of Rust	Elixir
4	45%	0%	--	Hi-Potion	Foe: character MP ≥ 30%	--	Knot of Rust	Elixir
5	45%	0%	--	Hi-Potion	Foe: character MP ≥ 10%	--	Knot of Rust	Elixir
6	45%	0%	--	Hi-Potion	Foe: character MP < 10%	--	Knot of Rust	Elixir
7	45%	0%	--	Hi-Ether	Foe: character MP < 30%	--	Knot of Rust	Elixir
8	45%	0%	--	Hi-Ether	Foe: character MP < 90%	--	Knot of Rust	Elixir
9	45%	0%	--	Hi-Ether	Foe: character MP < 70%	--	Knot of Rust	Elixir
10	45%	0%	--	Hi-Potion	Foe: character MP < 50%	--	Knot of Rust	Elixir
11	40%	0%	--	Hi-Ether	Foe: character status = Faith	--	Knot of Rust	Elixir
12	45%	0%	--	Hi-Potion	Foe: HP < 10000	--	Knot of Rust	Elixir
13	50%	0%	--	Hi-Potion	Foe: HP < 5000	--	Knot of Rust	Elixir
14	45%	0%	--	Hi-Ether	Foe: HP ≥ 10000	--	Knot of Rust	Elixir
15	50%	0%	--	Hi-Ether	Foe: HP ≥ 5000	--	Knot of Rust	Elixir
16	40%	0%	--	Hi-Potion	Foe: character status = Bravery	--	Knot of Rust	Elixir

You'll find hyena-like creatures like this flaming Cerberus in the east, and massive Mirrorknights in the west.

Proceed to the southeast and cross the zone line into the Walk of Stolen Truths. Now just follow the left cliff wall until you find an alcove with the Map Urn. Your immediate goal is the small area called Antiquity's End to the south, where you'll find a Save Crystal. After saving, head for the dense, swirling mist in the southern exit. It prevents you from advancing, but then the spirit of Rasler appears again and opens a way to the south. Follow him through. He leads the party right into the lair of Rafflesia.

Someone seems to be lending a hand, opening a way through the dense mist.

Rafflesia

LVL	HP	EXP	LP
43	73393	0	31
Steal	Screamroot, X-Potion, Putrid Liquid		

This battle is a status effects nightmare. Rafflesia slings every manner of ailment at the party, plus the MP Drain Field quickly drains your MP down to nothing. That's right—every active character in your party soon loses the ability to cast any magick, including status removal magick!

Thus, it helps if you have plenty of status removal items available. Before you take your first swing (or even before you enter the clearing), you should adjust all of your status-removal gambits so that they use items instead of spells. For example, replace Blindna with Eye Drops, Raise with Phoenix Down, and so on.

Immediately direct a character with either multiple Mist Charges (or none if he has no Quickenings available) to cast Dispel on Rafflesia to remove its Haste, Shell, and Regen status enhancers. The moment that Dispel hits the boss, launch a Quickening chain immediately before your Mist Charges deplete.

When your party has no more magick, just hack away with good old-fashioned weapon attacks. When Rafflesia's HP hits the halfway mark, it spawns a trio of Malboros. Turn your attention to them and wipe them out, then go back to Rafflesia.

Another very effective tactic is to equip as many members of

Magick is useless in the heavy mist, so hit Rafflesia hard with standard weapon attacks. When the big plant drops to half HP, it calls for help from Malboros.

⚡ BE READY FOR CONFUSE AND DISEASE

It helps to have several characters with gambits that remove the Confuse status ailment with Smelling Salts and remove Disease with Vaccine. Rafflesia likes to throw those two ailments at the party.

your party as possible with Mirror Mail. Those allies (like everyone else in your party) will rely on Potions for HP recovery anyway, so they don't really lose out on curing magick. With Mirror Mail, the status ailment spells ricochet harmlessly away and you can hack away at the big stalk boy. Note that you can pick up dropped Mirror Mail from the Mirrorknights that prowl the Walk of Dancing Shadow area to the west if you build up a good Battle Chain against them.

By the way, check out Rafflesia's official classification in your Clan Primer Bestiary: "Aggressive Vegetable." After Rafflesia finally falls, go back north to use the Save Crystal and then move into the southern part of the Feywood.

The Feywood (South)

Action Checklist
1. Solve the "Shrine of the Lost" puzzle.
2. Summon help to open the Gate Gigas.

Preying Mantis

LV	HP	EXP	LP
43-44	7465-7705	2629-2786	1

Basilisk

LV	HP	EXP	LP
42-43	5429-5749	2734-2908	1

Behemoth

LV	HP	EXP	LP
44-45	12199-12619	3834-3997	2

Giruveganus

LV	HP	EXP	LP
46-47	13006-13686	5259-5462	2

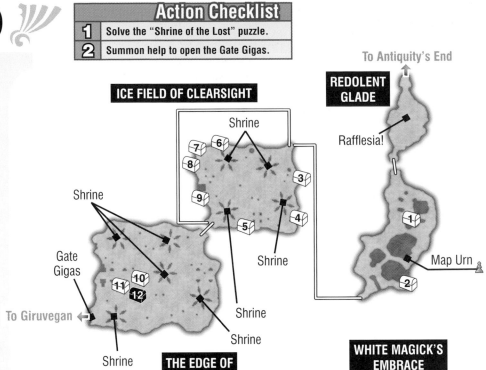

ICE FIELD OF CLEARSIGHT

REDOLENT GLADE

To Antiquity's End

Shrine

Rafflesia!

Shrine

Gate Gigas

To Giruvegan

Shrine

Map Urn

THE EDGE OF REASON

Shrine

WHITE MAGICK'S EMBRACE

TREASURE TABLE			Normal		w/Diamond Armlet Equip.		
No.	App.%	gil %	If gil	50%	50%	gil	90%	10%
1	60%	0%	--	Hi-Potion	Hi-Potion	--	Knot of Rust	Elixir
2	30%	0%	--	Hi-Ether	Elixir	--	Knot of Rust	Elixir
3	30%	0%	--	Hi-Potion	Morning Star	--	Knot of Rust	Elixir
4	45%	0%	--	Hi-Potion	Hi-Ether	--	Knot of Rust	Elixir
5	30%	0%	--	Hi-Potion	Celebrant's Miter	--	Knot of Rust	Elixir
6	30%	0%	--	Hi-Potion	Doom Mace	--	Knot of Rust	Elixir
7	45%	0%	--	Hi-Potion	Hi-Potion	--	Knot of Rust	Elixir
8	45%	0%	--	Hi-Potion	Hi-Potion	--	Knot of Rust	Elixir
9	45%	0%	--	Hi-Potion	Hi-Ether	--	Knot of Rust	Elixir
10	30%	0%	--	Hi-Potion	Deathbringer	--	Knot of Rust	Elixir
11	45%	0%	--	X-Potion	X-Potion	--	Knot of Rust	Elixir
12	25%	0%	--	Ensanguined Shield	Ensanguined Shield	--	Ensanguined Shield	Ensanguined Shield

Cross the South Feywood

From the Redolent Glade, continue south into the next area, White Magick's Embrace. This is where a bunch of creepy Preying Mantises are stalking the countryside, along with Mirrorknights and the snaky Basilisk. Fight through them to the south, looking for another Map Urn with a "Feywood Candle" that reveals the rest of the Feywood map. Finally, exit south into the Ice Field of Clearsight.

The Preying Mantis roams the icy waste in south Feywood.

Solve the "Shrine of the Lost" Puzzle

The map reveals star-shaped figures in the Ice Field of Clearsight. Head for any one of those shapes—it doesn't matter which one you go to first, because the order of the puzzle is generated randomly.

You find that each map star marks a platform structure called a Shrine of the Lost. At the first one you reach, fight off the beasts and step into the the center of the circular platform. If you see an elaborate pattern called a "Feywood Glyph" and an Action Icon pops up, press the ⊗ button and select "Examine the pattern." If you *don't* get an Action Icon, exit the platform and go on to the next star shape on the map. Keep going until you get an Action Icon when you step into the center of the platform.

Walkthrough

A message states that "Illusion betokens the true way." If you lower the camera view and swivel it around, you will see a green, lush forest scene through one of the exits from the platform. That's your "illusion," my friend. Face your party leader in that direction and proceed on to whichever shrine is *directly* ahead of you.

TIP: Before you go very far, check your map to verify exactly which star shape (another Shrine of the Lost) you're pointing toward.

REASON: En route you'll probably run into more monsters to fight and thus get turned around, possibly losing your original bearing. (If that happens, you can always head back to the first shrine and recheck the glyph and the illusion.)

After examining the floor glyph, follow the "illusion" of the forest scene from the shrine structure.

Repeat the process on the floor of the next shrine: examine the Feywood Glyph on the floor and look for the illusory view of a

Here's what the map looks like after you correctly complete your work in both the Ice Field of Clearsight and the Edge of Reason. Note that the game generates the shrine puzzle in a random order, so your map may not look like this one.

beautiful green forest and head in that direction until you reach the third Shrine of the Lost directly ahead. Knock out the beasts protecting the shrine and repeat the process one more time, finding the illusion that leads to the next map area, the Edge of Reason. (NOTE: If you check the map, you will see three icons on the shrines where you examined floor glyphs).

Ice Field Redux

If you don't visit the shrines in the correct sequence in the Ice Field of Clearsight, your exit to the southwest simply leads right back into the Ice Field. In essence, you end up re-entering from the northeast!

After crossing the zone line into the new area, open your map and note that it, too, features star shapes that represent Shrines. Repeat the same process that you used in the previous section to find Feywood Glyphs and activate their "illusions" to determine which shrine you should visit next. In the Edge of Reason area you'll visit *four* shrines before the last one's illusion guides the party to the monumental Gate Gigas.

The gate's very name should provide a vague clue as to the party's next move. Read the inscription to learn that Giruvegan is just on the other side, and that "over the one gate the Gigas holds sway." Got a Gigas? Actually, you do. When you defeated Belias, you gained a Gigas.

The shrine puzzle leads the party to the Gate Gigas.

Summon Belias. If you can't yet, it's because you haven't spent the LP to purchase the Belias license on your License Board; do so now, and then make sure whichever party member licenses Belias has a Mist Charge available to use. *Then* summon Belias and watch the show.

Summon Belias and touch the Gate Gigas to enter the holy city of Giruvegan.

Now watch the event as Balthier balks at going inside, preferring to lie in wait for Cid at Giruvegan's entry. Ashe's vision beckons, however, and the choice seems clear.

OBJECTIVE
Seek Dr. Cid in the Ancient City

Giruvegan

World Map

Action Checklist

1	Defeat Daedalus.
2	Use the correct switches to get through the gate seals in the water-steps.
3	Defeat Tyrant.
4	Navigate through the Great Crystal.
5	Defeat Shemhazai.

Dr. Cid has the nethicite shard, and he has said that he's off to Giruvegan, an ancient city that lies deep within the dense mist of the Jagd Difohr. Answers lie within the Great Crystal, a nethicite motherlode at the heart of Giruvegan.

The Ancient City of Giruvegan

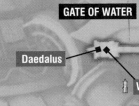

Way Stone

GATE OF WATER

GATE OF EARTH

Daedalus

To the Feywood

Way Stone

Way Stone

THE TRIMAHLA WATER-STEPS

Way Stone

1

2

Avrio Gate Stone

Avrio Gate

Chthes Gate

Chthes Gate Stone

To the Great Crystal

Way Stone

Shemhazai

Way Stone

To the Great Crystal

Way Stone

Tyrant

GATE OF FIRE

Parelthon Gate Stone

Gate Tychi

4

GATE OF WIND

THE HAALMIKAH WATER-STEPS

Paron Gate Stone

Gate Parelthon

3

Paron Gate

Tychi Gate Stone

THE AADHA WATER-STEPS

Behemoth

LV	HP	EXP	LP
44-45	12199-12619	3834-3997	2

Gargoyle Baron

LV	HP	EXP	LP
42-43	6071-6231	2817-2993	1

Mythril Golem

LV	HP	EXP	LP
43-44	17733-17973	3430-3678	2

Vivian

LV	HP	EXP	LP
42-44	6529-7006	3380-3748	1

Ose

LV	HP	EXP	LP
44-45	3739-4059	1887-2061	1

Reaper

LV	HP	EXP	LP
45-46	9931-10111	3185-3345	1

Mom Bomb

LV	HP	EXP	LP
45-46	6384-6544	2263-2439	1

Necrophobe

LV	HP	EXP	LP
46-47	8511-8691	3063-3223	1

Giruveganus

LV	HP	EXP	LP
46-47	13006-13686	5259-5462	2

Crystal Knight (Rare Monster)

LV	HP	EXP	LP
61-62	101390-101570	9973-10133	17

Walkthrough

TREASURE TABLE		Normal			w/Diamond Armlet Equip.		
No.	App.%	gil %	If gil	50%	50%	gil	90%	10%
1	100%	0%	--	White Fang	Elixir	--	Elixir	Megalixir
2	100%	0%	--	White Fang	White Fang	--	X-Potion	Megalixir
3	100%	0%	--	White Fang	Elixir	--	Elixir	Megalixir
4	100%	0%	--	White Fang	White Fang	--	Phoenix Down	Megalixir

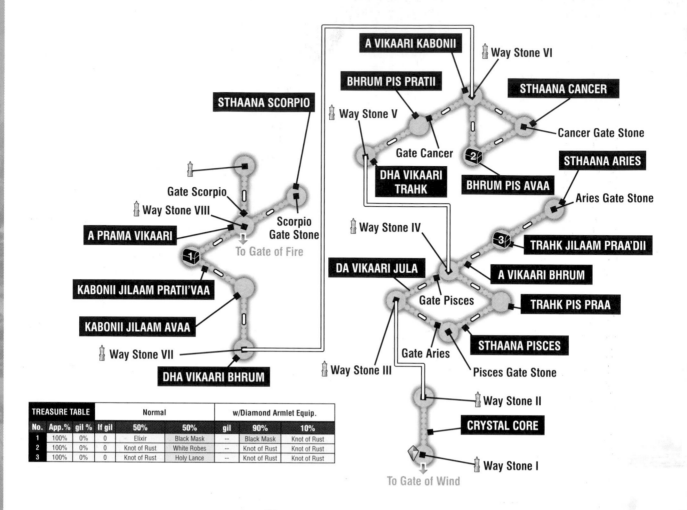

Map labels:
- A VIKAARI KABONII
- Way Stone VI
- BHRUM PIS PRATII
- STHAANA CANCER
- STHAANA SCORPIO
- Way Stone V
- Cancer Gate Stone
- Gate Cancer
- DHA VIKAARI TRAHK
- STHAANA ARIES
- Gate Scorpio
- BHRUM PIS AVAA
- Aries Gate Stone
- Way Stone VIII
- Scorpio Gate Stone
- Way Stone IV
- STHAANA ARIES
- A PRAMA VIKAARI
- To Gate of Fire
- TRAHK JILAAM PRAA'DII
- DA VIKAARI JULA
- A VIKAARI BHRUM
- KABONII JILAAM PRATII'VAA
- Gate Pisces
- TRAHK PIS PRAA
- KABONII JILAAM AVAA
- Gate Aries
- STHAANA PISCES
- Way Stone VII
- Way Stone III
- Pisces Gate Stone
- DHA VIKAARI BHRUM
- Way Stone II
- CRYSTAL CORE
- Way Stone I
- To Gate of Wind

TREASURE TABLE				Normal		w/Diamond Armlet Equip.		
No.	App.%	gil %	If gil	50%	50%	gil	90%	10%
1	100%	0%	0	Elixir	Black Mask	--	Black Mask	Knot of Rust
2	100%	0%	0	Knot of Rust	White Robes	--	Knot of Rust	Knot of Rust
3	100%	0%	0	Knot of Rust	Holy Lance	--	Knot of Rust	Knot of Rust

Get Past the City Guardian

Head west from the Save Crystal to the Way Stone and touch it to teleport across to the Gate of Water. Guess what? You start right off with a boss fight—Daedalus. Proceed west down the walkway to start the battle.

Touch the first Way Stone, if you dare. Giruvegan has a headless entry guardian.

Daedalus

LVL	HP	EXP	LP
42	65644	0	33
Steal	Storm Crystal, Forbidden Flesh, Damascus Steel		

The key here is who's faster, you or him? Haste magick is very important in this battle and Protect helps, too. Daedalus starts by casting Haste on himself, so immediately cast Dispel on him. In fact, it's best if you set up your support characters with a gambit that automatically casts Dispel on any foe with Haste or Protect. This goes a long way toward making this fight easier.

Overall, the basic tactic here is to send in one mauler equipped with good armor to hammer away at Daedalus using physical attacks while your other two allies focus on healing and support. Again, since Daedalus relies heavily on fast-hitting combos, always make sure to dispel his Haste. His combos get faster when his HP drops low, so be ready to switch in a fresh party of reserves.

> ### 💥 MAKE HASTE
> Keep Haste cast on your entire party to offset the speed of Daedalus.

Of course, when you bring in the second string, have them lead off with a powerful chain of Quickening attacks. This may be enough to knock Daedalus down for the count, especially if his HP is below 20 percent or so when the Quickening begins.

Be sure Raise or Phoenix Down is number one in your gambit hierarchy and keep the physical pressure on Daedalus.

After the fight, a new Way Stone appears that can take the party deeper into the holy city. First, you may want to head back east to the last Way Stone. Use it to teleport back to Gate of Earth and use the Save Crystal. Then return to the platform where you just fought Daedalus and use the new Way Stone to teleport into the odd interior of the city.

Work Your Way Down the Water-Steps

Trimahla Water-Steps

The party arrives in an area called the Trimahla Water-Steps, a series of descending ramps guarded by rugged Behemoths. Some of the ramps are blocked by green magickal barriers that can be turned on and off at switches called gate stones. Fight down the first ramp to reach the first barrier, Gate Avrio. It is controlled by the nearby Avrio Gate Stone.

Gate stones activate the gate barriers on the ramps.

> ### 💥 ICE THE BEHEMOTHS
> Behemoths tend to patrol in packs. They are weak against the Ice element, however, so if you have Blizzaga in your arsenal, you can deal big damage to multiple Behemoths.

Grisly Giruvegan

Tough enemies guard each platform and ramp on the ancient water-steps. Behemoths, Gargoyle Barons, and a status-ailment nightmare of the Malboro species known as a Vivian are some of the foes protecting the platforms. It is easy to get overwhelmed in this situation, especially if the Vivians spew Stop, Sleep, or Immobilize on multiple party members. Try to lure single enemies away from the pack and fight them one at a time.

Touch the Avrio Gate Stone to deactivate the Avrio Gate barrier. Next, go south down that ramp and then south again down the next one. Fight through a pair of Mythril Golems and use the Chthes Gate Stone to open the next gate on the ramp system. Go north and climb back up one ramp, then turn left and descend the other side.

Continue working your way down the ramps until you reach what seems like the end of the final platform. Defeat the two Mythril Golems stationed there, then simply walk off the south edge of the platform. Upon doing so, a green walkway appears beneath the party. Follow it over to the next set of ramps, the Aadha Water-Steps.

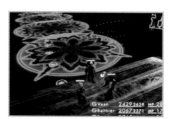

Walk off the ramp at the end of each set of water-steps to trigger a force-field walkway for crossing to the next area.

Aadha Water-Steps

This area is similar to the last area, with magick gates to deactivate, but the Gate Stones are more scattered this time. There are three Gate Stones, but you only need to deactivate one unless you want the treasure in the upper west area.

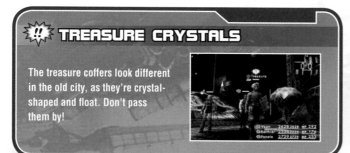

TREASURE CRYSTALS

The treasure coffers look different in the old city, as they're crystal-shaped and float. Don't pass them by!

Fight your way down the first ramp to the Paron Gate Stone, which is protected by two more Mythril Golems. The Paron Gate itself is not the nearby gate, but rather the gate down below to the west. Use the Paron Gate Stone to open the Paron Gate and eventually gain access to the treasure. Descend the ramp heading northeast.

Work your way back and forth down the ramps to the next Golem-guarded switch, the Parelthon Gate Stone. You can switch this one off or not; it opens the gate back up at the top of the area. Continue down the ramp to see the last gate in the area, Gate Tychi. This is the only gate you must open to move onward. Its gate stone is located up the next set of ramps.

Fight your way up to the Tychi Gate Stone and touch it to switch off the gate. If you opened the Paron Gate earlier, you can continue up the ramp to the treasure crystal, then return to the Tychi Gate (now deactivated) and go on through. Upon reaching the end of the last platform, step off again to trigger a green floating walkway. Follow it downward to trigger a short event in which the team considers their ultimate destination in the city as they gaze across the chasm at the Great Crystal.

The next area, the Haalmikah Water-Steps, features a much-needed Save Crystal. Go through the Bulwark Chronos, use the crystal, and open the Bulwark Hemera to enter the next area, called Gate of Fire.

Find the Hidden Ramp

The Gate of Fire area seems like a tricky maze, but there's actually a very simple solution to it. The secret is to trigger another green walkway that leads to a Way Stone. (A quick peek at the maps in this section will save you a lot of time wandering around.) To find it, climb up the second narrow ramp on the left after your arrival in the area, then turn right at the top.

Stay close to the right-hand railing until you reach a section where there's no railing. Doing so triggers the extension of another floating green ramp. It extends to the northeast, toward the Great Crystal.

What comes next isn't so easy. It's another boss battle! Cross the green walkway to a large floating platform, and prepare to meet the Tyrant. He dissolves the walkway while swooping in, leaving the party no choice but to fight.

The ramp from the Gate of Fire extends from the only spot in the area where there's no railing. Follow it out to the Tyrant's platform.

Tyrant

LVL	HP	EXP	LP
43	180428	0	33
Steal	N/A		

Of the utmost importance is the fact that a magick field has negated the use of any technicks! So if you regularly use Charge or some other technick, kiss it goodbye for now. Hopefully, you just saved your game at the Haalmikah Water-Steps so your team should be fully charged. However, Tyrant is a particularly durable boss and it takes a long time to wear him down. Try to rely on movement and license upgrades like Martyr and Inquisitor to boost your MP as the fight wears on.

Start by casting Dispel on Tyrant, then just go into your regular attack patterns. This fight requires patience and careful attention to health bars. Send in one hard-hitting melee fighter and support him with two casters who keep everyone healed and imbued with Haste and Protect. (Or, you can try two melee fighters and one support character, which is riskier but considerably quicker.) Blizzaga attacks are very effective against Tyrant, because of his weakness to the Ice element. Unlike the last boss fight, you won't see many status ailments. Watch out for Sap and be ready with Regen.

RAISE THE HP BAR

Tyrant tends to focus on one target for long stretches and occasionally unleashes brutal attacks that inflict a huge amount of damage. To keep allies from getting KO'd, go into your gambits and raise the curing threshold a bit higher (to "Ally: HP<60%" or even more) to make sure nobody's HP drops too low. It's also worth adding Bubble to the list of buffs, along with staples like Protect and Haste.

Tyrant is difficult to KO. Keep the pressure on with at least one tough fighter and make sure to use Protect, Haste, and Cure on that character.

As always, if you can manage to hold a party in reserve with Quickenings and multiple Mist Charges, you can bring them in when the Tyrant's HP drops below 20 percent. A good Quickening chain at that point can wipe out his health in one fell swoop.

A Way Stone appears on the platform after Tyrant finally falls. As after the last boss fight, you should backtrack to the last Save Crystal to heal up and save your game. After doing so, return to the new Way Stone and use it to teleport to the next area, the Great Crystal.

Navigate the Great Crystal Maze

The party arrives at a place called "A Prama Vikaari." The Way Stone here is numbered VIII. Also note that the Mini-Map disappears and your Location Map displays only a vague image of the Great Crystal! But don't despair, as you can always refer to this area's maps in this guide. The party arrives in the Great Crystal without maps. The first goal is to switch off Gate Scorpio.

Some magick walkways lead up, while some lead down. Take the one leading down from the first platform, A Prama Vikaari, to reach Kabonii Jilaam Pratii'vaa.

Check out the "Secrets" section to learn more about the naming system of the various areas in the Great Crystal.

Crystal Secrets

Now complete the following steps:

🐾 Start by facing the barrier (called Gate Scorpio), then turn left and walk through the gap in the railing to trigger a magick walkway leading down. (The other opening in the platform triggers a walkway leading up; don't take that one.) Continue down the walkway to the next area, the melodiously named Kabonii Jilaam Pratii'vaa.

🐾 Defeat the Ose pair and grab the crystal treasure. You will likely set off explosive traps (or cast Float to avoid the traps), but the treasure is well worth it. Exit via the only other gap, heading down to the next area, Kabonii Jilaam Avaa.

🐾 There's nothing in this area but a couple of more Oses. Take the only other exit down to the next area, Dha Vikaari Bhrum.

🐾 Use Way Stone VII to teleport to the next area, A Vikaari Kabonii. This takes the party to Way Stone VI. There are three openings on one side of the platform. The right path leads down to a closed barrier, Gate Cancer. So take the left path, which leads down to an area called Sthaana Cancer.

🐾 In Sthaana Cancer, defeat the two Mythril Golems and use the Cancer Gate Stone to open Gate Cancer. Go back up the way you just came, returning to A Vikaari Kabonii. Watch out for a lone Reaper on the way.

🐾 Take the other downward path to Bhrum Pis Pratii. Gate Cancer has been switched off, so you can enter the platform. Go straight across and exit the other side, heading downward to Dha Vikaari Trahk.

🐾 Use Way Stone V to teleport to Way Stone IV in the A Vikaari Bhrum area.

🐾 You should see a gate barrier called Gate Pisces. You need to deactivate this gate. Exit via the path that leads down (not up), as it descends to the Trahk Pis Praa.

🐾 Take the only other exit here, leading down to Sthaana Pisces and a gate stone.

🐾 Use the Pisces Gate Stone to deactivate Gate Pisces.

🐾 Now backtrack up to Trahk Pis Praa, then up to A Vikaari Bhrum (where you arrived at Way Stone IV) and turn left. Gate Pisces is gone, so take that exit down to the next area, Dha Vikaari Jula.

🐾 Use Way Stone III to teleport to Way Stone II in the Crystal Core and watch a brief event as the party views the nethicite in the crystal.

The Crystal Core features a motherlode of nethicite.

🐾 Take the only exit down to the platform with the Save Crystal and save your game. After doing so, use Way Stone I to teleport out of the Great Crystal to a new Giruvegan location, the Gate of Wind. (You'll find this location on the first Giruvegan map in this section.)

🐾 Walk forward and open the gate named Bulwark Minas and say hello to the Esper Shemhazai.

Shemhazai, the Whisperer

LVL	HP	EXP	LP
45	91136	0	47
Steal	Sagittarius Gem, Hi-Ether, High Arcana		

The important thing to know in this fight is that, after using the Mana Spring ability, Shemhazai is weak against one element but can absorb all other elements, turning them directly into HP. The problem is that her element of weakness is random. If you tend to focus on physical attacks, this is no problem; just swap out element-imbued weapons, and do not use elemental attack spells (Fire, Water, Wind, etc.).

If you want to cast spells, use Green or Time magicks. A good Quickening chain works wonders, too, especially when Shemhazai is running low on HP.

Shemhazai likes to cast Syphon, which transfers MP from one of your characters to her.

VOX YOUR POPULACE

Make sure everyone has an anti-Silence gambit, whether it's using Vox or Echo Herbs.

By all means, open with a quick cast of Dispel to knock off her Haste. Watch out for her regular attempts to Silence your party. Make sure everyone has a Vox or Echo Herbs gambit set above their attack gambits. Her durability is good but not great, so if you keep up solid attacks and heal properly, this battle can proceed with no major surprises. When Shemhazai's HP drops to critical ranges, she'll cast Silencega, in addition to causing the Disease status with her regular attacks. Be ready to distribute Echo Herbs to at least one ally so he/she can un-Silence the others. A Cleanse/Vaccine gambit is very important for this fight, so set one up.

When you emerge victorious, you gain the ability to summon Shemhazai after you unlock her square on the license board. Proceed south to the Bulwark Aeon and open it. Continue on to the Empyrean Way Stone and read its inscription, then touch the device to trigger a long series of events.

Pay close attention as several deeper truths are revealed to Lady Ashe for the first time in a meeting with the true movers of recent events. Ashe is given the Treaty-Sword, which now appears in your inventory. Lastly, you learn more about Venat, Dr. Cid's "ghostly mentor."

After the event, your next task is to seek a powerful stone called the Sun-Cryst, the mother of all nethicite, source of the Dynast-King's shards. The clue to its whereabouts is simply: "In tower on distant shore it dreams."

Then you see another event in the Imperial City of Archades with two brothers, Judge Gabranth, the good Dr. Cid, and his "spiritual advisor." Now you know who the main players are in this tale and how much is at stake.

Return to Balfonheim

When control returns to you, use the Way Stone to teleport back to the Gate of Earth outside Giruvegan. Walk to the orange Save Crystal and teleport back to the Port of Balfonheim.

OBJECTIVE
Seek Reddas in Balfonheim Port

World Map

Balfonheim Port

Action Checklist

1 Shop to upgrade your party's abilities and equipment.

2 Go to the Reddas Manse.

3 Take the *Strahl* to the Ridorana Cataract.

Beef up your party at the port stores, then visit Reddas at his residence.

Balfonheim Port

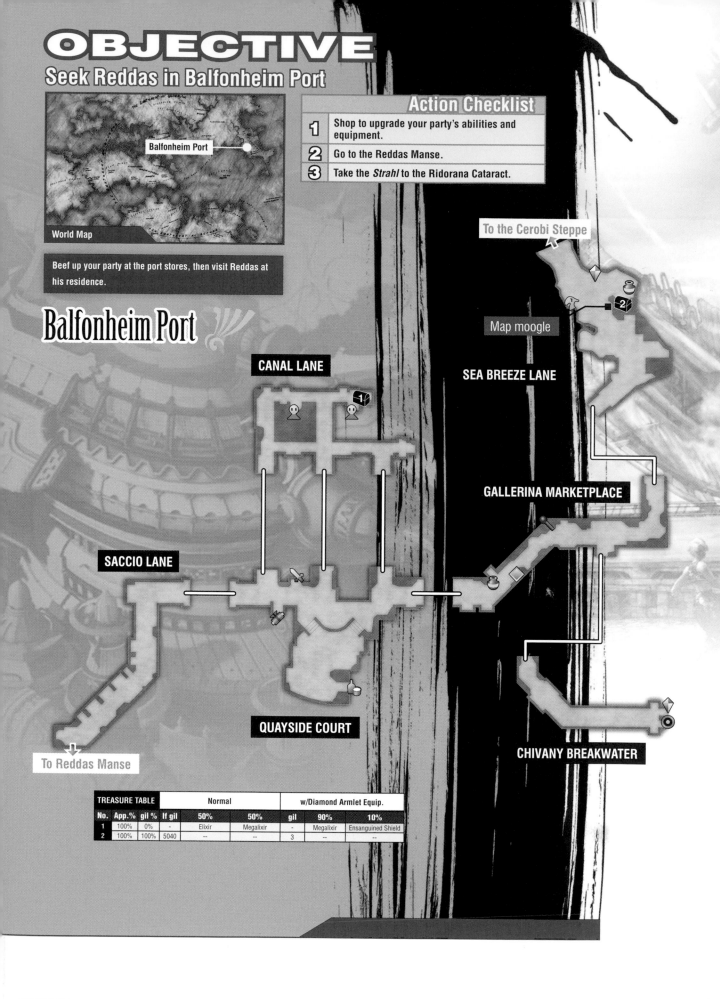

CANAL LANE

To the Cerobi Steppe

Map moogle

SEA BREEZE LANE

SACCIO LANE

GALLERINA MARKETPLACE

QUAYSIDE COURT

To Reddas Manse

CHIVANY BREAKWATER

TREASURE TABLE		Normal			w/Diamond Armlet Equip.		
No.	App.%	gil %	If gil	50%	50%	gil	90%	10%
1	100%	0%	-	Elixir	Megalixir	-	Megalixir	Ensanguined Shield
2	100%	100%	5040	--	--	3	--	--

Shop and See Reddas

You should have a *lot* of LP to use and plenty of loot to sell after the trek across Giruvegan. Check all of the shops and balance out your party with new equipment and magick. When you're finished, head for the red 'X' on the area map in Saccio Lane at the far southwest end of town. When the party arrives, talk to the Manse Watch fellow to gain entrance to Reddas's sanctuary.

The Manse Watch lets the party in to see Reddas.

Reddas issues orders to his team of Rikken, Raz and Elza, sending them out on urgent business. Afterward, Ashe and the rest of your party report to him on what they learned at Giruvegan.

Plans are laid for a journey to the Ridorana Cataract and the towering Pharos lighthouse. These seas are deep in jagd, but Reddas offers Balthier a rare skystone made to resist jagd. It may power an airship through areas that are normally impenetrable.

After the event, Reddas joins your party as a guest. Vaan speaks with Rikken, Raz, and Elza and learns that the *Strahl* is ready for flight at the aerodrome. Raz provides directions to the Pharos, southeast of Balfonheim.

Fly to the Ridorana Cataract

Head for the aerodrome, which is located in the southeast part of town in the Chivany Breakwater district. Inside, talk to the "Private Airships" attendant, the woman in the green dress at the counter next to the Save Crystal. When she asks if you'd like to board, answer "Yes." When the map appears, select "The Ridorana Cataract" in the Jagd Naldoa as your flight destination.

 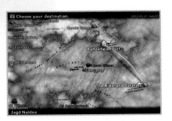

The "Private Airships" attendant at the aerodrome can get you squared away aboard the Strahl. Select your destination: the Ridorana Cataract.

After a stunning flight and arrival sequence, the party approaches the great tower of the Pharos.

OBJECTIVE
Enter the Pharos Lighthouse

World Map

Ridorana Cataract

Action Checklist
1 Get to the Pharos lighthouse.

When the party arrives at the cataract island, proceed across the ruins to the Pharos lighthouse.

Ridorana Cataract

Deathclaw

LV	HP	EXP	LP
46-48	12682-13162	3947-4261	1

Cassie

LV	HP	EXP	LP
46-47	8840-9080	4357-4541	1

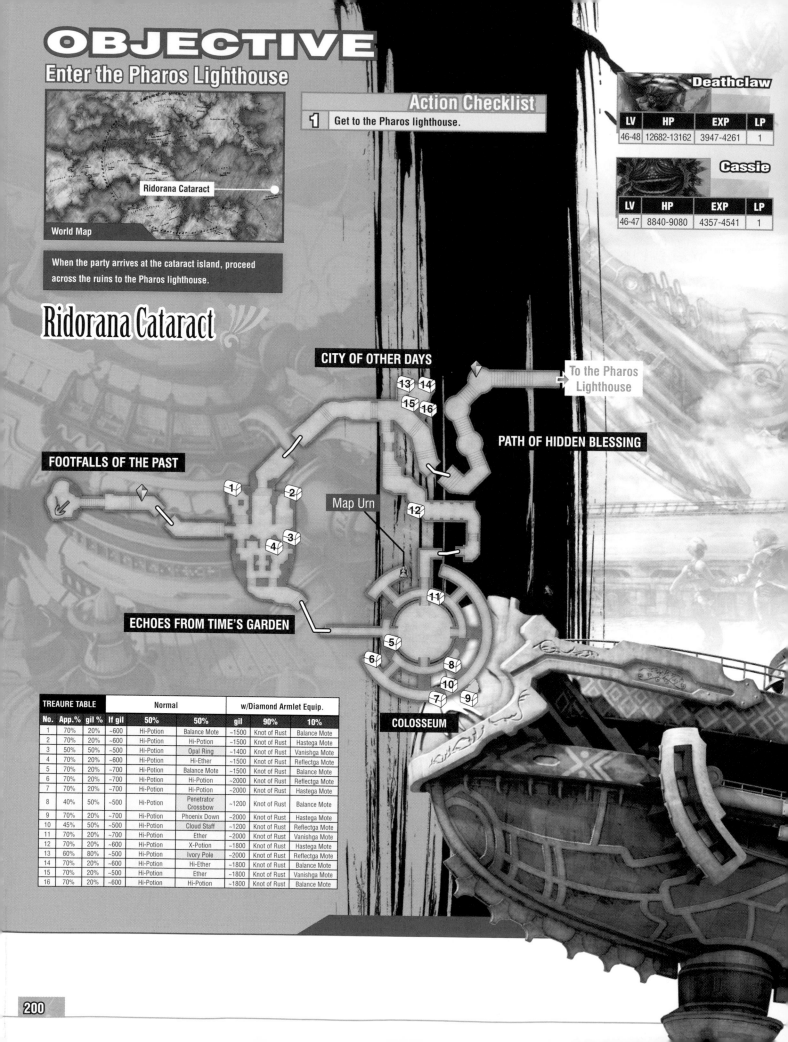

CITY OF OTHER DAYS

To the Pharos Lighthouse

PATH OF HIDDEN BLESSING

FOOTFALLS OF THE PAST

Map Urn

ECHOES FROM TIME'S GARDEN

COLOSSEUM

TREAURE TABLE			Normal		w/Diamond Armlet Equip.		
No.	App.%	gil %	If gil	50%	50%	gil	90%	10%
1	70%	20%	~600	Hi-Potion	Balance Mote	~1500	Knot of Rust	Balance Mote
2	70%	20%	~600	Hi-Potion	Hi-Potion	~1500	Knot of Rust	Hastega Mote
3	50%	50%	~500	Hi-Potion	Opal Ring	~1400	Knot of Rust	Vanishga Mote
4	70%	20%	~600	Hi-Potion	Hi-Ether	~1500	Knot of Rust	Reflectga Mote
5	70%	20%	~700	Hi-Potion	Balance Mote	~1500	Knot of Rust	Balance Mote
6	70%	20%	~700	Hi-Potion	Hi-Potion	~2000	Knot of Rust	Reflectga Mote
7	70%	20%	~700	Hi-Potion	Hi-Potion	~2000	Knot of Rust	Hastega Mote
8	40%	50%	~500	Hi-Potion	Penetrator Crossbow	~1200	Knot of Rust	Balance Mote
9	70%	20%	~700	Hi-Potion	Phoenix Down	~2000	Knot of Rust	Hastega Mote
10	45%	50%	~500	Hi-Potion	Cloud Staff	~1200	Knot of Rust	Reflectga Mote
11	70%	20%	~700	Hi-Potion	Ether	~2000	Knot of Rust	Vanishga Mote
12	70%	20%	~600	Hi-Potion	X-Potion	~1800	Knot of Rust	Hastega Mote
13	60%	80%	~500	Hi-Potion	Ivory Pole	~2000	Knot of Rust	Reflectga Mote
14	70%	20%	~600	Hi-Potion	Hi-Ether	~1800	Knot of Rust	Balance Mote
15	70%	20%	~500	Hi-Potion	Ether	~1800	Knot of Rust	Vanishga Mote
16	70%	20%	~600	Hi-Potion	Hi-Potion	~1800	Knot of Rust	Balance Mote

Find a Map

Climb the stairs and save your game, then continue east into the next section, Echoes from Time's Garden. Climb the stairs to an open courtyard where you face your first foes, Deathclaws and Cassies. The Deathclaws have a Pulsar Wave attack that can Disable party members, while the Cassies spew out status ailments similar to the other Malboros.

This area has two exits. Take the southern one into the Colosseum to find a bunch of treasure, plus a handy map of the area. Don't run across the Colosseum's arena unless you have a Bangle or Libra active, though, because there are eight traps. Turn left and stick to its outer perimeter while moving clockwise to the north exit. Go downstairs, take the first left, then follow the corridor to the Map Urn for a map of the Ridorana Cataract.

Don't walk across the Colosseum arena without a Float spell active, as it's heavily trapped.

Now you can move to the east and south exit passages in search of treasure. (Don't miss the treasure in the secret room that doesn't appear on the Area Map. To access it, go through the Colosseum's east exit and follow the passage around to the southeast corner.) When you're finished, go back through the north exit and keep going north to access the next area, City of Other Days.

Follow the long corridor up to the intersection. (Watch out for a pair of Cassies around the second corner!) Look for treasure across the path and down the stairs in the sunken courtyard. Next, head southeast up the stairs to reach the Path of Hidden Blessing area. Keep climbing up to find another Save Crystal, but watch out for the line of traps. Continue upstairs to enter the Pharos lighthouse.

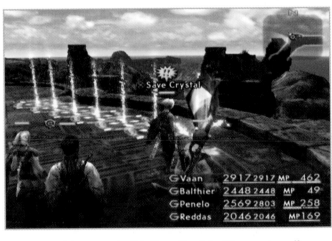

More powerful traps make this Save Crystal a bit precarious. If you set off some of the traps, just touch the Save Crystal and heal your party.

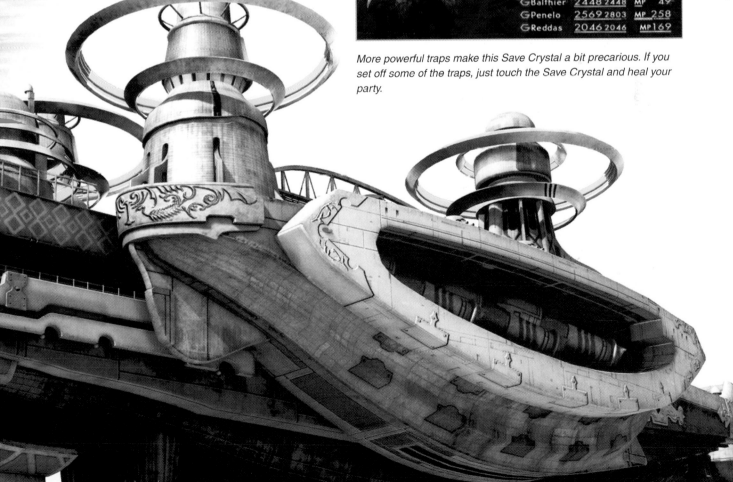

OBJECTIVE
Seek the Sun-Cryst Atop the Pharos at Ridorana

World Map

The Pharos

Travel up all three ascents of the Pharos lighthouse to find the Sun-Cryst.

Action Checklist

1	Defeat Hydro.
2	Collect three Black Orbs from vanquished enemies.
3	Place an orb on each of the three altars on Floor 01 to open an exit door.
4	Defeat Pandaemonium to activate the Way Stone.
5	Teleport to the new area and defeat Brainpans to activate bridges and advance.
6	Defeat Slyt and teleport to the Second Ascent.

First Ascent: Horizon of First Light

WELLSPRING RAVEL - 1ST FLIGHT

Fool's Facade
Carven Pillar
Way Stone
Bridge 10F
To 2nd Flight
Bridge 14F
Carven Pillar

WELLSPRING LABYRINTH

THEY WHO THURST NOT

Hydro
To Path of Hidden Blessing
Way Stone

Altars of Night

Threshold of Night Door

BLACKROCK VAULT

Map Urn

THE WELLSPRING

Arrival

DUNES OF PROFANING WIND

Pandaemonium

TREASURE TABLE		Normal			w/Diamond Armlet Equip.		
No.	App.%	gil %	If gil	50%	50%	gil	90%	10%
1	65%	50%	~1200	Hi-Potion	Gold Hairpin	~2500	Knot of Rust	Elixir
2	65%	20%	~300	Hi-Potion	Giant's Helmet	~600	Knot of Rust	Elixir
3	65%	25%	~300	Hi-Ether	Crystal Shield	~600	Knot of Rust	Elixir
4	65%	65%	~600	Hi-Potion	White Mask	~1000	Knot of Rust	Elixir
5	65%	20%	~800	Hi-Potion	Elixir	~2000	Knot of Rust	Elixir

Chimera Brain

LV	HP	EXP	LP
45-46	9992-10112	2917-3088	1

Mistmare

LV	HP	EXP	LP
45-47	12180-12500	4615-4967	1

Brainpan

LV	HP	EXP	LP
46	15358	3574	1

Mimeo

LV	HP	EXP	LP
46-48	10061-10541	3115-3429	1

Aeronite

LV	HP	EXP	LP
49-50	18004-18684	6156-6359	2

Deidar

LV	HP	EXP	LP
46	15358	3574	1

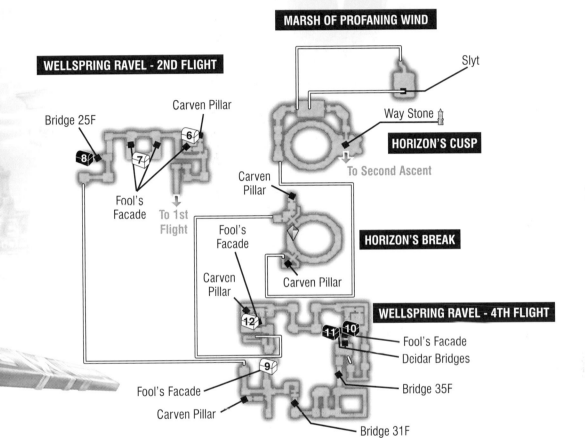

TREASURE TABLE			Normal		w/Diamond Armlet Equip.		
No.	App.%	gil %	If gil	50%	50%	gil	90%	10%
6	65%	78%	~500	Hi-Potion	Black Robes	~800	Knot of Rust	Elixir
7	65%	20%	~1000	Hi-Potion	Hi-Potion	~2000	Knot of Rust	Elixir
8	91%	0%	--	Holy Rod	Holy Rod	--	Holy Rod	Holy Rod
9	65%	20%	~1000	Hi-Potion	Phoenix Down	~3000	Knot of Rust	Elixir
10	70%	0%	--	Dueling Mask	Dueling Mask	--	Dueling Mask	Dueling Mask
11	70%	0%	--	Zeus Mace	Zeus Mace	--	Muramasa	Muramasa
12	65%	20%	~2000	Hi-Potion	Phoenix Down	~5000	Knot of Rust	Elixir

Defeat the Lighthouse Guardian

You know this area is tough when the first thing the party encounters is a boss! Climb the stairs and stop. Before you step forward into the entry hall to meet Hydro, cast Haste and Protect on everyone in your party, and consider adjusting your gambits to switch all healing and status removal from magick to items. Check out the boss section that follows to see why.

Hydro

LVL	HP	EXP	LP
47	203800	0	35
Steal	Maggoty Flesh, Corpse Fly, Wyrm Bone		

Hydro is a classic brawler that has two particularly tough aspects to his attack. First, it likes to hit with some status ailments that are problematic if you're not prepared. Second, Hydro casts a powerful area magick called Fearga that can completely drain your characters' MP. Note that Fearga has a relatively small range. To counteract it, you can fight Hydro with a party using only ranged weapons, causing your characters to spread out naturally or manually keep at least one member at a good distance away from the others.

One obvious tactic if your healers have no MP is to switch in new healers. Make sure you have a Doom-related gambit in place too; that is, one that uses a Remedy if a character is afflicted with Doom. Make sure your characters all have the Remedy 3 license, so their Remedies cure Doom. If Hydro hits with Sap, use a Regen spell to counter it. If your characters' MP gets drained, keep moving and using the Charge technick or Syphon MP from other characters. If you have the Inquisitor and Martyr licenses, you also gain MP simply by inflicting/receiving damage.

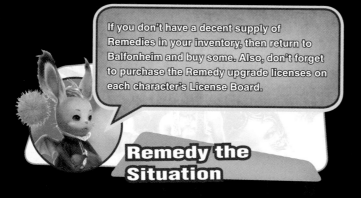

If you don't have a decent supply of Remedies in your inventory, then return to Balfonheim and buy some. Also, don't forget to purchase the Remedy upgrade licenses on each character's License Board.

Remedy the Situation

Hydro is a physical fighter that gets very aggressive with its Lunge attacks when its HP goes critical. Beware of Hydro's fearsome Fearga attack!

After setting up your gambits, wade into battle. Immediately cast Dispel on Hydro and follow up with Slow. After your first team knocks down Hydro's HP to 20 percent or so, bring in the reserves and hit Hydro with a Quickening chain before the boss can rob any characters of their MP. (Spend it or lose it!) Hydro is particularly nasty and fast in its last throes, so it's nice to bypass that phase of the fight by hitting the boss with Quickenings.

After the fight, move forward to the massive gate to trigger an event in which Fran translates an ancient message carved on the nearby wall. It seems to be a message from the Dynast-King to his heir. Sure enough, as Ashe steps forward, the gate opens wide for the party.

Open the First Seal

When you regain control, the party is on the lighthouse's first floor (note the "01F" under the Mini-Map) in an area called The Wellspring. This is a circular corridor that wraps around a huge, mist-filled central chamber. The Wellspring corridor is divided into three arcs. There is a large stone pedestal called an Altar of Night in each arc.

You can't use the Way Stone here yet, so go left to the teleport Save Crystal and save your game. After doing so, follow the Wellspring's curving walkway to find the Altar of Night that faces south. Read it to learn that Pharos beasts "oft possess black orbs." To move above Floor 01 you must do the following:

1	Defeat foes.
2	Pick up three Black Orbs that some fallen foes leave behind.
3	Place one Black Orb on each of the three Altars of Night.

To move to the next level, you must find and collect these glowing Black Orbs left behind by defeated foes.

Altar of Night: South

Exit the Wellspring via the south passage (directly south of the Way Stone) into the Wellspring Labyrinth. Use the maps in this section to navigate the maze east, south, then back west along the southernmost corridor to find the Map Urn of the entire First Ascent area.

Place one Black Orb on the Altar of Night to break its seal.

Along the way, fight enemies and look for a glowing orb hovering in the air after each foe falls. If you see one, walk into it until the words "Black Orb" appear, then press the ✖ button to pick it up. Hurry though, as these orbs only stick around for a few seconds.

Keep felling foes in the southern half of the Wellspring Labyrinth until you obtain three Black Orbs. Now you can focus on reaching the altars. Return to the Altar of Night and use an orb on the altar to break the magicked seal. One down, two to go!

> **!! NO SET ALTAR ORDER**
> You can place the Black Orbs on the Wellspring altars in any order you wish.

Altar of Night: East

As before, exit the Wellspring via the south passage into the Labyrinth. Follow the innermost corridor to the east until you can exit left, back into the Wellspring. This time, though, you step into the eastern arc of the Wellspring. Turn right and approach the Altar of Night, then place a Black Orb to break the second seal. (If you don't have another Black Orb, then KO some foes until you acquire one.)

Altar of Night: North

Now return to the Wellspring Labyrinth. Work your way around the maze to the stairs that connect to the northern half of the labyrinth. At the top, notice the glowing blue door called the Threshold of Night. The magickal seals that you're breaking at the Altars of Night are what bind this door shut. You'll return to this area shortly.

For now, continue downstairs into the northern Labyrinth and navigate (and fight) to the inner corridor. Exit into the northern arc of the Wellspring and place a Black Orb on the third and final Altar of Night. This breaks the third seal and the message "the Seal of Night loses its power" appears on-screen.

Place one Black Orb on the Altar of Night to break its seal.

Walkthrough

The Seal of Night was the magickal seal binding the Threshold of Night door back on the stairs. If you check the Area Map, you will see a flashing icon over that door's location. Navigate back to the Threshold of Night and go through it to reach… a desert?

You may want to trek back through the maze to the Save Crystal in the Wellspring before going through the Threshold of Night doorway, as a powerful boss waits in the desert.

Consider a Save

The Threshold of Night door leads into an odd, desert-like parallel dimension.

Meet the First Watcher

This odd reality is referred to as the Dune of Profaning Wind, and it doesn't appear on the Area Map. Four gray boulders rest in alcoves amongst the sand dunes and darker cliffs. When you try to approach the first three boulders, the party gets sent right back to the bottom. Climb the hill to the topmost "boulder", which turns out to be a giant stone tortoise named Pandaemonium.

Pandaemonium

LVL	HP	EXP	LP
45	116678	0	36
Steal	Ancient Turtle Shell, Aries Gem, Scarletite		

Start by casting Dispel to eliminate the boss's Shell and Protect magick, then start hammering away with your strongest melee fighters. Have a support ally cast Haste and Protect on your attackers, and prepare to remove status effects with Esuna. Pandaemonium is weak against Wind magick, so cast Aeroga if it's in your spell arsenal.

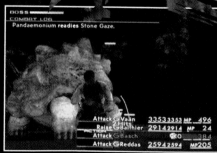

At the halfway point, Pandaemonium becomes immune to all attacks. When this occurs, just bide your time until its Perfect Defense finally dissipates.

When Pandaemonium's HP hits the halfway mark, it casts an impenetrable shield around itself with a "Perfect Defense" spell. There's not much you can do except wait it out. Keep everyone healed, and counter the status ailments (Blind, Petrify) that the big tortoise zaps at the party. Don't waste MP trying to hit the boss with magick, as it's immune to every kind of attack. Just be patient; the shield fades after about a minute, at which time you can get back to punishing Pandaemonium.

After the victory, the party automatically teleports into Blackrock Vault, the small room behind the Threshold of Night door. Exit the vault and return to the Save Crystal in the Wellspring. Next, use the now-active Way Stone to teleport to a new area.

The Way Stone activates after Pandaemonium is defeated.

Wellspring Ravel: 1st Flight

10F Bridge

Go through either of the green, glowing ancient doors and head around the corner to find the Carven Pillar. Read its inscription to learn that the "tongue of stone's green flame your way bespeaks" and "once silenced… its muted form a bridge for you to tread." Broken down, this phrase means that you must hit the green-flame foes to activate bridge mechanisms. (Just kidding: This will become clearer in a minute.) Unfortunately, some flying foes called Aeronites flutter up ahead. Hit them with Telekenesis magick and ranged weapons.

> **!! SECRET TREASURE**
>
> In the 1st Flight of the Wellspring Ravel, go north to the wall to discover that it is called "Fool's Façade." Press the ⊗ button to strike the wall and uncover a secret area with a treasure.

Now climb the stairs to the high platform where two Brainpans spout green flames. After destroying each Brainpan, a section of bridge drops into place just to the east. Cross it and climb upstairs to the next floors.

Each time you destroy a Brainpan, a new section of bridge drops into place.

14F Bridge

Now you must knock out four more Brainpans to drop in all four sections of the next bridge. One Brainpan is on 12F, another is on 14F (where the bridge is located), and there are two of them on 15F—one in an alcove and one in a back room. Cross the newly formed bridge on 14F, then climb up to 17F.

Wellspring Ravel: 2nd Flight

25F Bridge

From 17F, keep climbing and searching for Brainpans. You need six more to form the next bridge, which is on 25F. There are two Brainpans on 20F; one of them is in a back room with another Fool's Façade that you can smash through for a treasure chest. Another Brainpan is on the 21F landing. There is another Fool's Façade on 23F, leading to a staircase that runs up to 24F, where you can bash through another wall that leads back onto the main path. The last three Brainpans are clustered together on 25F near the bridge. Nail them and cross the now-finished bridge, then climb up to 28F to enter a new area.

Wellspring Ravel: 3rd Flight

31F Bridge

You need five Brainpans for the next bridge. Two of them are on the 29F landing, while another one is on 30F behind an ancient door. Read the Carven Pillar there to learn that "the red flame consumes the green, sundering the stair which it has laid." Translation: Don't strike a red-flame guy, called a Deidar, when you have a bridge in progress ahead! If you do, a section of unfinished bridge will actually disappear.

The first Deidar appears on 31F, sitting not far from the next bridge crossing. Press the R2 button and run past it through the portal to find two Brainpans on the other side. Defeat them, then cross the bridge and keep climbing.

35F Bridge

The next bridge calls for the slaughter of 10 more Brainpans. Remember to leave the red Deidars alone! The first Brainpan is on the 32F landing. Two more sit on 34F, while three more are on 35F. Be careful, though, as a Deidar sits not far from the trio of Brainpans on 35F.

Now descend from 35F to find that the duo on 34F has respawned! That makes eight of them. If you do KO a Deidar by accident, look around for some more Brainpans, as they will randomly respawn if the bridge is not finished. Climb the back stairs to find that the trio on 35F has respawned. Keep striking Brainpans until you defeat 10 of them, then cross the bridge.

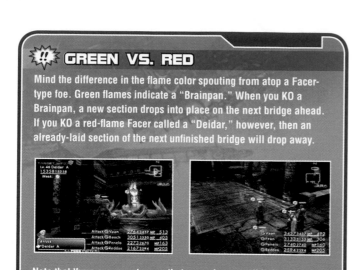
47F Bridge

It takes only four Brainpans to create the next bridge. Defeat two of them on 36F, then run past the red Deidar up to 38F to nail another Brainpan. Another Deidar is close by, so keep your party focused! There are two more Brainpans in the corners of a backroom on 40F. Run past the Deidar on 41F and pound the Brainpan on 42F. Another Brainpan is in a room with a Carven Pillar on 46F, with another fake wall and secret room nearby.

Watch out for a pair of Aeronites on 48F.

After crossing the bridge on 47F, watch out for two powerful Aeronite flyers hovering together on 48F and be ready with your regular flyer-fighters. Nail these foes with Thundaga to quickly clear the skies. After doing so, climb up to the ancient door and open it to enter a new area.

Horizon's Break

Find the Save Crystal as you step into the circular corridor around the mist-filled central chamber of the Pharos. Exit the corridor to the southwest and climb the staircase to an ancient door on 49F. This leads to another new area.

Horizon's Cusp: The Second Watcher

Climb up to another ancient door with an inscription that warns of the "second watcher" waiting ahead. Open the door to enter… a lush green marsh with a waterfall in the distance? This is the Marsh of the Profaning Wind. Step forward to meet the second watcher.

Who is the "watcher" of this marsh?

Slyt

LVL	HP	EXP	LP
47	92661	0	36
Steal	Yensa Scale, Pisces Gem, Yensa Fin		

Slyt is very quick on the attack and has Regen active as well. It will refresh its Regen almost instantly if you try to dispel it, so it's better to ignore it. If you haven't already, use Haste on your party. You can try to Slow and/or Confuse Slyt, but it won't always work. Slyt is weak against Fire, so cast Oil and then light it up with your heavy Fire spells. With Reddas as a melee fighter drawing its attention and two other characters casting Firaga at Slyt, it's possible to take down this foe rather quickly.

After the fight, the party appears right back in Horizon's Cusp. Exit via the east door and climb to the Way Stone on 50F, then use it to teleport to the Second Ascent of the Pharos.

Fish don't like fire, and neither does Slyt.

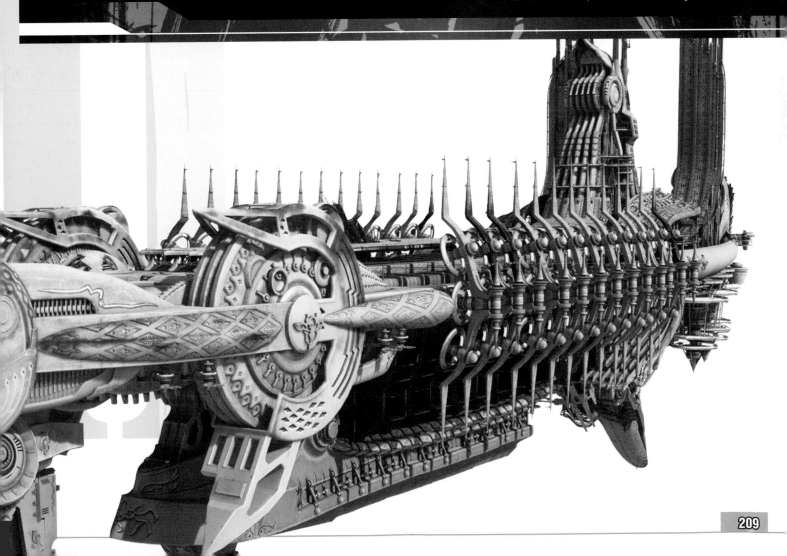

Second Ascent: Reach of Diamond Law

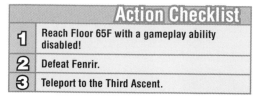

Action Checklist

1 Reach Floor 65F with a gameplay ability disabled!

2 Defeat Fenrir.

3 Teleport to the Third Ascent.

Crusader

LV	HP	EXP	LP
47-48	10592-10772	4868-5028	1

Reaver

LV	HP	EXP	LP
49-50	22771-23191	6539-6702	2

Dragon Lich

LV	HP	EXP	LP
49-51	22241-23601	8078-8484	2

Bune

LV	HP	EXP	LP
48-49	13239-13659	4615-4778	1

Abaddon

LV	HP	EXP	LP
47-49	13239-13879	4615-4963	1

Necrofiend

LV	HP	EXP	LP
48-51	12709-13249	4809-5289	1

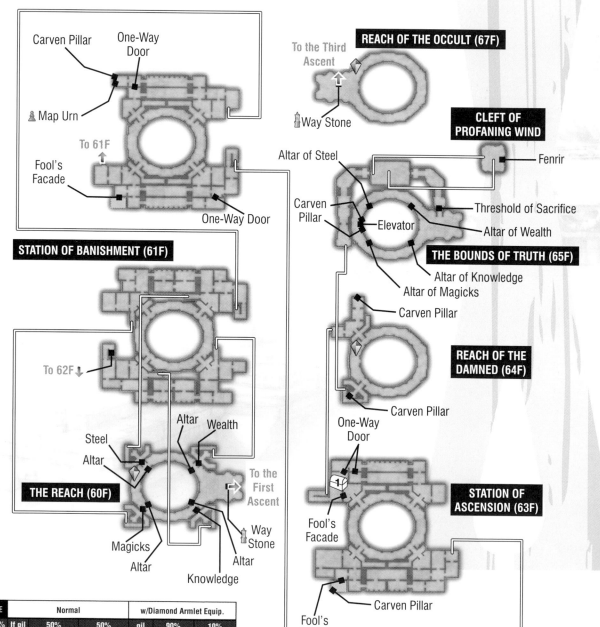

STATION OF SUFFERING (62F)

Carven Pillar
One-Way Door
Map Urn
To 61F
Fool's Facade
One-Way Door

STATION OF BANISHMENT (61F)

To 62F

Altar
Wealth
Steel
Altar

THE REACH (60F)

Magicks
Altar
Knowledge
Altar
Way Stone

To the First Ascent

REACH OF THE OCCULT (67F)

To the Third Ascent
Way Stone

CLEFT OF PROFANING WIND

Altar of Steel
Fenrir
Carven Pillar
Threshold of Sacrifice
Elevator
Altar of Wealth

THE BOUNDS OF TRUTH (65F)

Altar of Knowledge
Altar of Magicks

Carven Pillar

REACH OF THE DAMNED (64F)

Carven Pillar

One-Way Door

Fool's Facade

STATION OF ASCENSION (63F)

Carven Pillar

Fool's Facade

Treasure Table

No.	App.%	gil %	If gil	Normal		w/Diamond Armlet Equip.		
				50%	50%	gil	90%	10%
1	65%	20%	~1500	Hi-Potion	Phoenix Down	~3000	Knot of Rust	Elixir

Choose Your Route—and Your Poison

The party arrives in an area called The Reach, another circular corridor around the mist-filled core. Go to the Save Crystal on the west side of the circle and save your game. Now it's time to make a choice. There are four different exits, each of which leads up to the next floor. Each exit removes a different gameplay tool when you pass through the threshold. Pick your exit based on the following preferences:

 Threshold of Wealth

If you choose this route, the party goes to the Third Ascent without the use of items.

 Threshold of Steel

If you choose this route, the party travels to the Third Ascent without the use of weapons.

 Threshold of Magicks

If you select this route, the party goes to the Third Ascent without the use of magick.

 Threshold of Knowledge

If you select this route, the party travels to the Third Ascent without the use of the game's Mini-Map.

Base your decision about the Threshold you choose and the gameplay tool you elect to forego upon your particular style of play. Some players will rarely use magick and will rely on physical combat and technicks to fight while consuming items to heal. Others will use magick quite often whether it's for combat, combat enhancement, or healing. Give up the thing you use *the least*.

You may want to consider giving up the Mini-Map. Although it is a great orientation tool, when you pass through the Threshold of Knowledge (the southeast exit), you do *not* lose the game's Area Map. If you happen to get disoriented, just press the Select button to get your bearings straight. Another fine option is giving up items, so consider this as an alternative.

60F: Unseal the Door!

This walkthrough now leads you to the southeast exit from The Reach. First, activate the Altar of Knowledge by selecting "Touch the altar" to unseal the Knowledge door (this makes you lose the Mini-Map). Next, go through the door and climb from 60F to 61F. Once on 61F, the actual route upward becomes the same regardless of which choice you made.

To unseal the threshold of your choice, activate the corresponding Altar.

61F: Station of Banishment

Your next goal from all four arrival points is to reach one of the two staircases that lead up to 62F. One is in the northeast corner of this floor, while the other is in the southwest corner. (See the map in this section for exact locations.) You will encounter some nasty new enemies along the way, including ghostly Crusaders, Buncs, powerful Reavers, and the immense Abaddon toads.

62F: Station of Suffering

Your destination here is the staircase in the southeast corner that leads up to 63F. Watch out for a brutal four-foe ambush when the party arrives! Before that occurrence, though, you may want to venture up to the northwest corner and find the map of Pharos Second Ascent. There is also a secret room in the southwest corner, which is only accessible by bashing through a Fool's Façade. The rewards aren't great, though, as all you'll find is three angry Crusaders.

63F: Station of Ascension

Your goal here is to reach the staircase in the northwest corner that leads up to 64F by going through a hallway from the northeast corner. Of the two hallways in that corner, take the northern most route leading west towards the northwest corner. There's a secret room behind a Fool's Façade in the southwest with a nice Rejuvenation trap that heals all nearby allies when it is triggered. Watch out for the powerful Necrofiends near the exit.

Walkthrough

64F: Reach of the Damned

Finally, a Save Crystal! Save your game and head for the only other exit from this area, which is located to the southwest.

65F: The Bounds of Truth

Follow the corridor up to the ancient door and read the inscription. Uh oh, looks like another "watcher" lies in wait up ahead. Select the "Open the door" option. This leads the party right into the clutches of Fenrir.

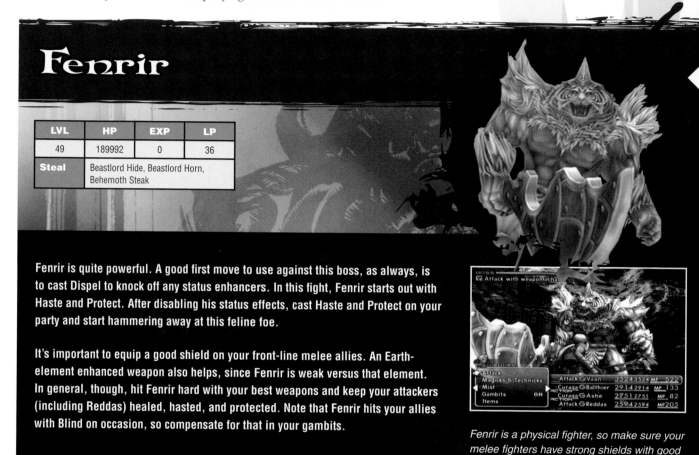

Fenrir

LVL	HP	EXP	LP
49	189992	0	36
Steal	Beastlord Hide, Beastlord Horn, Behemoth Steak		

Fenrir is quite powerful. A good first move to use against this boss, as always, is to cast Dispel to knock off any status enhancers. In this fight, Fenrir starts out with Haste and Protect. After disabling his status effects, cast Haste and Protect on your party and start hammering away at this feline foe.

It's important to equip a good shield on your front-line melee allies. An Earth-element enhanced weapon also helps, since Fenrir is weak versus that element. In general, though, hit Fenrir hard with your best weapons and keep your attackers (including Reddas) healed, hasted, and protected. Note that Fenrir hits your allies with Blind on occasion, so compensate for that in your gambits.

Fenrir is a physical fighter, so make sure your melee fighters have strong shields with good Evade.

After the fight, the party returns to the Bounds of Truth area on 65F. Open the door to the east and follow the big hallway to the next door, the Threshold of Sacrifice. When the party steps through this door, you find four altars that match the four down in The Reach (60F) where you selected the ability to sacrifice. Now you can get that ability back!

Touch the altar that corresponds to that ability you relinquished (Wealth is items; Magicks is magicks; Steel is weapons; and Knowledge is the Mini-Map) to regain that lost ability. This triggers the arrival of an elevator called the Dais of Ascendance. Step aboard and select "67F" as your destination.

67F: Reach of the Occult

Save your game at the Save Crystal, then use the Way Stone to teleport to the Pharos Third Ascent.

When you regain your ability at one of the 66F altars, an elevator arrives for your traveling pleasure.

Third Ascent: Mete of Dynasty

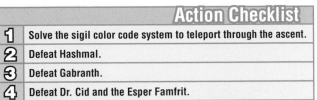

Action Checklist

1. Solve the sigil color code system to teleport through the ascent.
2. Defeat Hashmal.
3. Defeat Gabranth.
4. Defeat Dr. Cid and the Esper Famfrit.

Purobolos

LV	HP	EXP	LP
49-50	9531-9691	3554-3730	1

Necrofiend

LV	HP	EXP	LP
48-51	13709-13249	4809-5289	1

Cataract Aevis

LV	HP	EXP	LP
50-51	23241-23921	8078-8281	2

Aeronite

LV	HP	EXP	LP
49-50	18004-18684	6156-6359	2

Zombie Warlock

LV	HP	EXP	LP
48-50	7598-7958	3838-4158	1

Tower (Rare Game)

LV	HP	EXP	LP
59-60	136638-136878	8484-8732	14

Dead Bones

LV	HP	EXP	LP
49-50	11122-11302	4233-4393	1

TREASURE TABLE			Normal			w/Diamond Armlet Equip.		
No.	App.%	gil %	If gil	50%	50%	gil	90%	10%
1	55%	0%	--	Dragon Whisker	Rubber Suit	--	Dragon Whisker	Dragon Whisker
2	55%	0%	--	Rubber Suit	Dragon Whisker	--	Dragon Whisker	Dragon Whisker
3	35%	50%	999	Elixir	Elixir	9999	Elixir	Elixir
4	100%	0%	--	Circlet	Circlet	--	Ring of Renewal	Circlet

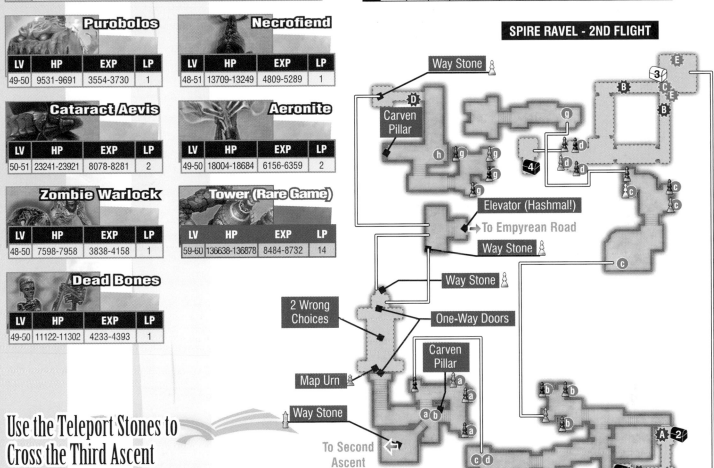

SPIRE RAVEL - 2ND FLIGHT

Way Stone · Carven Pillar · Elevator (Hashmal!) · To Empyrean Road · Way Stone · Way Stone · 2 Wrong Choices · One-Way Doors · Carven Pillar · Map Urn · Way Stone · To Second Ascent

SPIRE RAVEL - 1ST FLIGHT

Use the Teleport Stones to Cross the Third Ascent

80F: Spire Ravel, 1st Flight

Yes, the map in this section looks scary, but this Way Stone transit system is easy to navigate if you just follow these simple steps:

- *When the party arrives from the Second Ascent, watch out for the Purobolos! When these bomb creatures explode, they can take out multiple party members if they aren't at full health. Don't forget to read the Carven Pillar which states, "To seal of night look first."*

- *Night is dark, right? So go up the stairs on either side of the pillar and go to the black Way Stone. It is identified as "Way Stone – Black Sigil" when you approach it. Use the Black Sigil to teleport across the gap to another section of the Spire Ravel, 1st Flight area.*

Two Wrongs Don't Make a Right

In fact, two incorrect choices of the Way Stone sigils gets the party zapped to a truly brutal hidden room with a Map Urn and a seemingly unending supply of undead foes (Zombie Warlocks, Dead Bones, Necrofiends, and the like). They just keep coming, and they like to infect their targets with Disease! If you end up in this place, grab the map right away and desperately fight and heal diseased allies with Vaccine until the door opens.

Proceed east to an intersection.

You have a choice of two paths at the intersection and both work. You can choose to turn left (north) and head up to the next sigil platform, fighting through a painful Purobolos swarm (five of them!) to use the Green Sigil. Instead, let's take the secret path that leads to some treasure!

Watch out for brutal Purobolos swarms around the sigil platforms.

 At the intersection, turn right (south) and walk into what looks like a dead-end alcove. Find the Fool's Façade and smash through it to find a hidden hallway and a Green Sigil. Use it to teleport to another secret hall in the next area.

83F: Spire Ravel, 2nd Flight

You're about halfway through the Third Ascent at this point.

 Step into the first trap. It's a manafont trap and it heals your party! The traps down the two side halls are explosive, though, so carefully maneuver around whichever route you take. You can go down either hall, since both are essentially the same, and meet up around the corner.

 Smash through a pair of fake walls to reach the sigil platform, where an Aeronite hovers. Remember that Thundaga works wonders against these flyers. Also remember that Telekinsis works even better. Use the Way Stone, Red Sigil and not the purple "Sigil of Sacrifice," which is also a reddish color.

 This takes the party to a small platform beneath two more Aeronites. Zap them out of the sky, then examine the four Way Stones.

 The "Sigil of Sacrifice" is on all four stones, but the colors match up with the four altars back in The Reach. Touch the sigil with the color that matches the ability you chose to lose. The color associations are: Yellow-Wealth (items), Purple-Magick (magick), White-Steel (weapons), Pink-Knowledge (map).

 When you select the right color, the party ends up on the northwest platform. Go forward and read the Carven Pillar to receive your last clue in the phrase "untainted by tint or color." When you approach the final sigil platform, you will see the usual four colors—nothing colorless. If you use any one of these, the party gets zapped back to a previous location.

 Instead, go to the northernmost end of the platform and find the Fool's Façade on the left wall. Smash through it to find a clear Way Stone. Use the Way Stone to teleport to one last platform.

Look out! The last Way Stone teleports the party to 88F, which is directly underneath the rare monster, Tower. It's takes time to defeat this foe, so keep everyone hasted and healed if you encounter this hostile golem. Finally, climb the stairs and use the Dais of Ascendance elevator. Select "90F" and take the elevator to another Esper meeting.

Here's the final sigil: a colorless Way Stone behind the fake wall in the extreme northwest part of the map.

WOMB OF THE SUN-CRYST

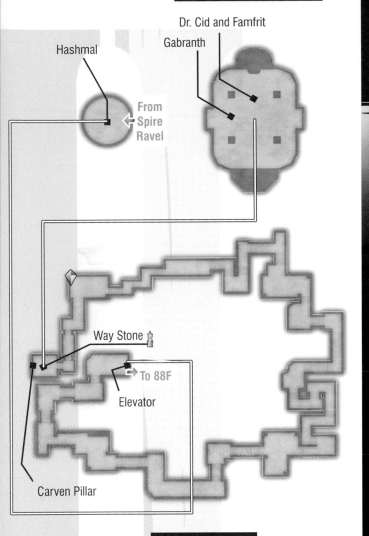

Dr. Cid and Famfrit

Gabranth

Hashmal

From Spire Ravel

Way Stone

To 88F

Elevator

Carven Pillar

EMPYREAN RAVEL

90F: Empyrean Ravel

Just follow the long, linear route up. When you pass 91F, watch the short event with Fran in which she says "the din of the Mist grows greater." The Sun-Cryst must be nearby. Keep climbing all the way to the Save Crystal on 98F, which is truly a welcome sight at this point. Finally, continue to the Way Stone and teleport to trigger a dramatic event.

Here you learn some secrets that we will not reveal in this book. Watch carefully and prepare for a boss fight, which is then followed by *another* boss fight. Yes, the road out of the Pharos lighthouse is a very difficult one.

What will Lady Ashe do?

Hashmal, Bringer of Order

LVL	HP	EXP	LP
50	209060	0	52
Steal	Leo Gem, Hi-Ether, High Arcana		

Hashmal drops right onto your stalled lift platform! Dispel the boss's protection and cast Haste, Protect, and most importantly, Float on your party right away. With his most powerful attacks nullified by the Float status effect, his negative status effects are the only things you will have to worry about. He will hit your party members with Slow several times during the battle, so be ready to recast Haste. You may also want to equip your magick caster with a Sash for this fight to keep him or her immune to the Slow status effect. To counteract the Disease status, make sure you have a Cleanse or Vaccine gambit ready or heal manually.

Hashmal lashes out hard and shields himself magickally as his HP drops.

Hashmal unleashes a powerful area spell when his HP is reduced to about one-quarter. However, characters with the Float status are immune to Hashmal's earth-based attacks. In case you don't have Float, keep everyone's health high to survive Hashmal's Quakeja spell. When his HP drops in HP critical range, Hashmal erects a magickal shield that keeps him immune from attacks for a short period of time. Focus on healing when this occurs until the shield disappears, then finish him off.

When victory is yours, Hashmal appears on the License Board. The party also arrives at a new location.

Judge Gabranth

LVL	HP	EXP	LP
47	64049	0	18
Steal	Potion, Hi-Potion, X-Potion		

As boss fights go, this one isn't complicated. Gabranth is one of the more straightforward foes you'll face in the game. Follow the standard drill: Immediately cast Dispel to remove his protections, then cast Haste and Protect on your party. Normal attacks will bring him down, and it won't take a particularly long time. Watch out for his brutal combo attack, however, as it inflicts massive damage to a single party member.

Once Judge Gabranth goes down, the party receives another happy visit from the good doctor. Cid cruelly dismisses Gabranth and makes his agenda clear, then prepares to teach the lesser humans a godlike lesson.

Dr. Cid and Famfrit, the Darkening Cloud

Dr. Cid

LVL	HP	EXP	LP
50	82093	0	18
Steal	Hi-Potion, Ketu Board, Magepower Shishak		

Famfrit

LVL	HP	EXP	LP
52	149060	0	52
Steal	Aquarius Gem, Elixir, High Arcana		

This boss battle starts out against only Dr. Cid. Cast Dispel on him and Haste/Protect on your party, then commence with your standard attacks. Hack away at Cid until his HP drops to about one-half. When this happens, he conjures up an Esper to aid him: Famfrit!

Now things get more interesting. Focus your attacks on the Esper, as Famfrit has a lot of HP. (Note that the boss HP bar at the top is for Dr. Cid only.) Also, you actually CAN'T hurt Cid while Famfrit's there. Once again, start with the usual routine of casting Dispel on Famfrit, and renew your own Haste and Protect on your party. Consider adding Shell, because Famfrit throws some magickal attacks against the party.

From time to time, Dr. Cid brings down a barrier that makes him immune to magick for a short period of time but stay focused on Famfrit until he falls. Famfrit is weak against Fire, so cast Oil and blast away with multiple shots of Firaga, if at all possible.

Occasionally, Famfrit blasts a powerful area attack that causes damage and inflicts Silence on anyone nearby. Cure that status ailment immediately! When the Esper falls, focus the party's attention back on Dr. Cid. If you're not playing catch-up with healing and raising KO'd allies, you can take him down with case.

It's a two-for-one boss fight at the lighthouse. Dr. Cid is assisted by the Esper Famfrit.

When this titanic battle ends, a spectacular event plays, containing the dramatic resolution of certain matters. Afterward, remember to save your game. Finally, the party automatically returns to Balfonheim to prepare for the great finale of this epic adventure.

OBJECTIVE
Prepare for the Final Confrontation

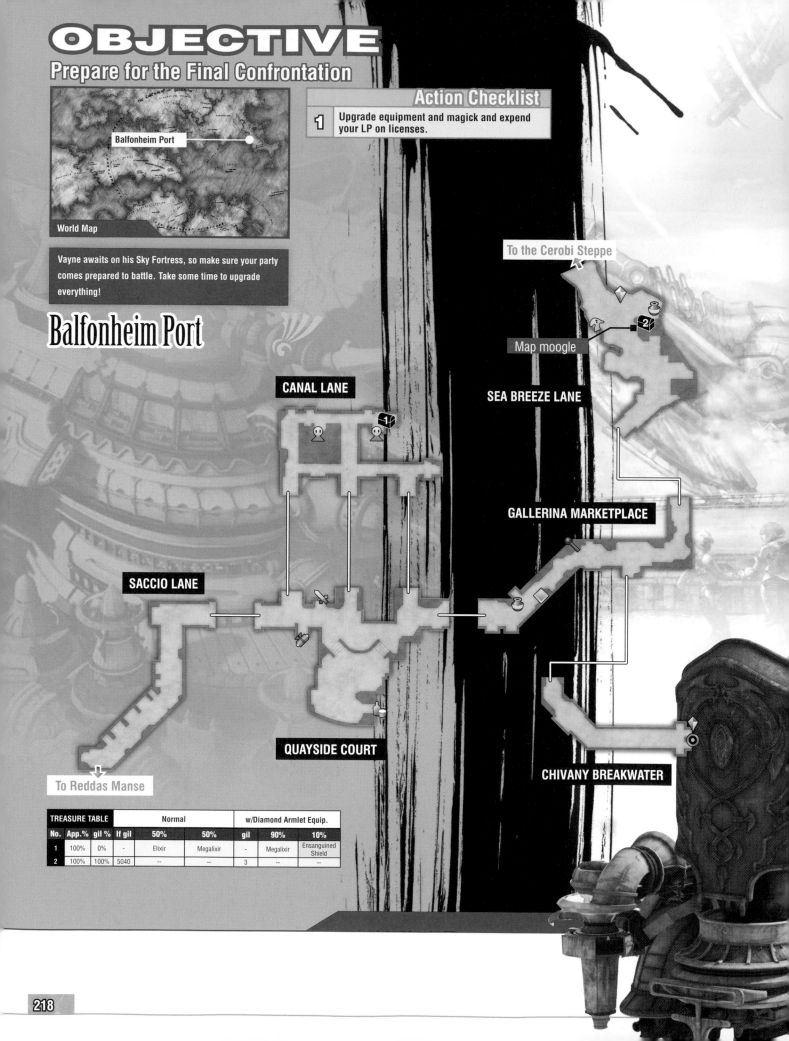

Balfonheim Port

World Map

Action Checklist

1 Upgrade equipment and magick and expend your LP on licenses.

Vayne awaits on his Sky Fortress, so make sure your party comes prepared to battle. Take some time to upgrade everything!

Balfonheim Port

To the Cerobi Steppe

Map moogle

SEA BREEZE LANE

CANAL LANE

GALLERINA MARKETPLACE

SACCIO LANE

QUAYSIDE COURT

CHIVANY BREAKWATER

To Reddas Manse

TREASURE TABLE				Normal		w/Diamond Armlet Equip.		
No.	App.%	gil %	If gil	50%	50%	gil	90%	10%
1	100%	0%	-	Elixir	Megalixir	-	Megalixir	Ensanguined Shield
2	100%	100%	5040	--	--	3	--	--

Buff Up!

There's no reason to hold back now. Once you leave Balfonheim for the Imperial Sky Fortress, there's no turning back. You'll need six strong characters with complementary skills and equipment to survive this upcoming visit to the *Bahamut*. At this point in the game, you should have a balanced party with all members in the 45-level range (preferably higher) with the best weapons, armor, and magicks that gil can buy. If that's not the case, then head out to the Cerobi Steppe or teleport to other hostile areas and level up your characters.

One other suggestion: If you haven't done so already, it is strongly suggested that you read through the chapters on "Gambits" and the "License Board" before you ship off for the sky fortress. If you've gotten this far, you're probably well versed on these gameplay aspects, however, you may be surprised at some of the things you don't know yet.

> ## !! GOOD LICENSES
> Important licenses for all party members include the Martyr and Inquisitor abilities, which keep your MP levels up. You also want all of the Ether upgrades. The Bahamut finale may force you to consume all those Ethers you've been hoarding throughout the game!

Head Out!

When you're ready to roll, go to the Private Airships counter at the aerodrome. Tell the woman that you want to board the *Strahl*, and select "Bahamut" as your destination. (It's flashing right next to Rabanastre.) Note the next message that appears: Once you leave for Bahamut, you can't return. Ready?

Select "Yes" and watch the long event. The great Imperial sky fortress is on the move over Dalmasca. The long-feared final confrontation between the Empire and the Resistance begins and in the midst of the opening salvos, the *Strahl* arrives at a sky dock in the heart of the *Bahamut*…

OBJECTIVE

Stop Vayne!

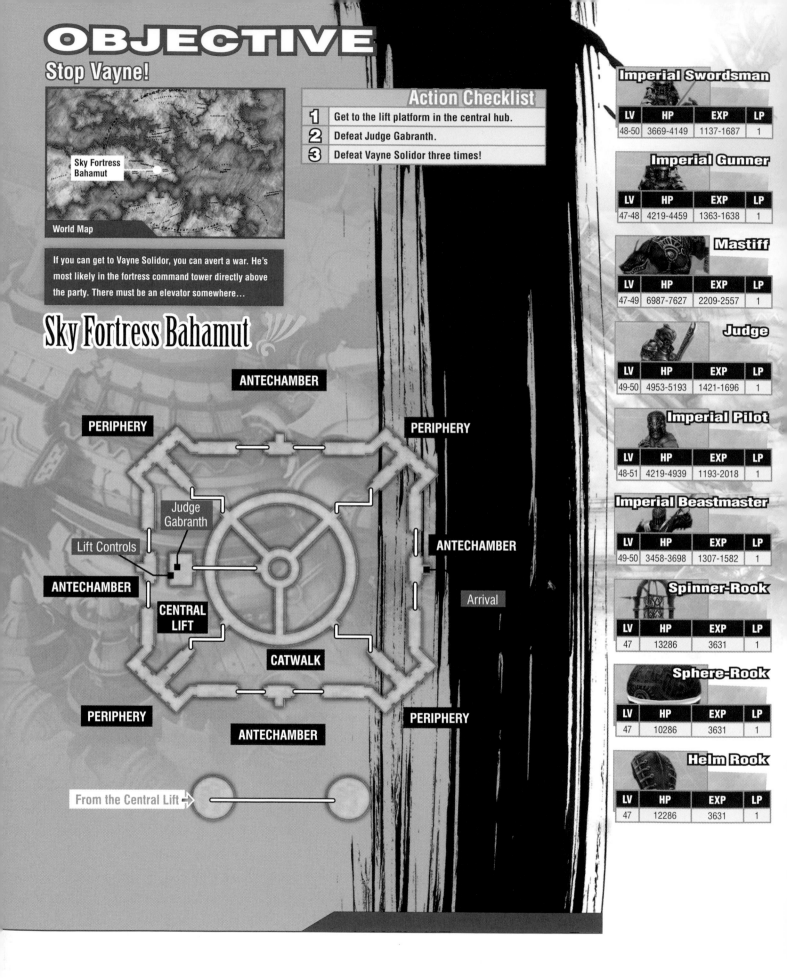

Sky Fortress Bahamut

World Map

If you can get to Vayne Solidor, you can avert a war. He's most likely in the fortress command tower directly above the party. There must be an elevator somewhere…

Action Checklist

1. Get to the lift platform in the central hub.
2. Defeat Judge Gabranth.
3. Defeat Vayne Solidor three times!

Sky Fortress Bahamut

ANTECHAMBER

PERIPHERY

PERIPHERY

Judge Gabranth

Lift Controls

ANTECHAMBER

ANTECHAMBER

CENTRAL LIFT

Arrival

CATWALK

PERIPHERY

PERIPHERY

ANTECHAMBER

From the Central Lift →

Imperial Swordsman			
LV	HP	EXP	LP
48-50	3669-4149	1137-1687	1

Imperial Gunner			
LV	HP	EXP	LP
47-48	4219-4459	1363-1638	1

Mastiff			
LV	HP	EXP	LP
47-49	6987-7627	2209-2557	1

Judge			
LV	HP	EXP	LP
49-50	4953-5193	1421-1696	1

Imperial Pilot			
LV	HP	EXP	LP
48-51	4219-4939	1193-2018	1

Imperial Beastmaster			
LV	HP	EXP	LP
49-50	3458-3698	1307-1582	1

Spinner-Rook			
LV	HP	EXP	LP
47	13286	3631	1

Sphere-Rook			
LV	HP	EXP	LP
47	10286	3631	1

Helm Rook			
LV	HP	EXP	LP
47	12286	3631	1

220

Get to the Central Lift ASAP

The party starts in the Antechamber. Your goal is to reach Vayne while avoiding entanglements that will only sap your strength. Note that there are *no* Save Crystals in the fortress! The key is to get into the central hub as quickly as possible; the longer you take, the more forces will swarm your party's position.

Avoid mixing it up with the fortress guard units, especially the robotic armaments.

There is no Area Map, but the way to the central lift is simple. From the party's arrival point, turn left and go through the south bulkhead. In the next area, called the Periphery, take the first right turn; it leads inward, toward the central hub. When you encounter hostile resistance along the way, you can simply press and hold the R2 button and flee.

When you reach the next area, the circular interior hub called the Catwalk, sit back and watch the party arrive as the battle rages outside the fortress. The Catwalk is patrolled by some extremely powerful Rooks (robotic armaments that can overwhelm your party), so just run away! Veer down any of the three "spokes" leading into the circle's center. You should see the lift platform ahead. Go around the hub and run across the zone line onto the platform.

Oddly enough, the pursuit halts as you cross the zone line into the Central Lift area. Take a breath. Believe it or not, you're safe for now. Take some time to heal up, then run around the lift or use Ethers to recharge your MP to full Mist Charges.

When you reach this zone line to the Central Lift, you're safe—for now, anyway.

When your party reaches 100 percent HP and MP, approach the Lift Controls panel and select "Engage the lift." This brings Judge Gabranth back into the picture.

Activate the lift to trigger your first in a final series of boss battles.

Judge Gabranth

LVL	HP	EXP	LP
49	70719	0	25
Steal	Hi-Potion, X-Potion, Elixir		

Dispel him, then cast Haste and Protect on your main melee fighter(s) and make sure your healing gambits are in order. The first part of the fight will probably go remarkably smoothly, but when Gabranth's HP drops to about one-half, he suddenly regenerates all of his HP and he launches a powerful new sword attack that will likely cause close to 1000 HP damage.

This is a very basic fight, similar to a number you've won in the course of this game already. Keep hitting him and healing your party. Make sure Raise (or better yet, Arise) is the gambit in each character's number one slot.

When Gabranth wields his sword mercilessly like this, get ready to heal.

Vayne Solidor

LVL	HP	EXP	LP
50	76755	0	0
Steal	N/A		

This fight is similar to the other Imperial Judge boss fights in the game (Ghis, Bergan, Gabranth). Vayne unleashes heavy single target attacks/combos that are certainly painful but easily survivable. Deploy your best Heavy Armor melee fighter with a shield and use Decoy on him to draw Vayne's attention, so your support characters can cast Dispel and heal the party.

As with all fights, Dispelling Bravery, Haste, and Protect is absolutely imperative. You can't afford to leave Bravery on against monsters that hit for 1000-plus damage and then combo attack for 4-plus times a turn. Remove buffs, keep Protect, Shell, Haste, and Bubble up on everyone in your party. Conserve MP and consumable items if possible, as two insanely powerful bosses remain with no Save Crystal in sight.

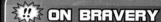

ON BRAVERY

For the game's final stages (starting from about Giruvegan on, through the Pharos and into Bahamut plus all late-game side quests against optional bosses), perhaps nothing is as important as getting Bravery dispelled from foes right away. Even regular enemies like the Bunes in the Pharos can drop your characters in seconds with Bravery on. The same principle applies to Vayne and other bosses.

Vayne Novus/Sephira

LVL	HP	EXP	LP
53	104210	0	0
Steal	N/A		

LVL	HP	EXP	LP
50	12121	0	0
Steal	N/A		

The second incarnation of Vayne is tough enough, but his sword minions flying around can be very troublesome. If you cast Berserk on one party member, that character and Gabranth will focus on the swords. Now you can focus your remaining party members on Vayne Novus.

Another option is to burn a massive Quickening chain or have everyone cast Scathe/Scourge to make the swords go away. Using up Mist Charges for a Quickening might sound like a bad idea with another big boss still left after this fight, but there's no reason to conserve anything at this point. You can throw Megalixirs and Elixirs and Hi-Ethers around like party favors, if the need arises. Vayne is still not excessively hard to beat with standard attacks in this fight, but he is more aggressive and has plenty of help.

The Undying

LVL	HP	EXP	LP
55	228299	0	0
Steal	N/A		

This fight is very difficult. At a minimum, your characters should be around level 40 but levels around 45 and above are recommended. Vayne, infused with the rogue Venat, can become immune to physical/magickal damage, while flying around the arena targeting anyone. Physical attackers can hit him, but that means getting in close and potentially leaving multiple people in the path of Megaflare, powerful area nukes, and The Undying's special attacks.

The Undying has no HP bar or any indication of his health, but at about 75 percent, 50 percent, and 25 percent he pops up different barriers that you need to wait out. Some of them block physical damage, while some prevent magickal damage. For the physical damage barrier, try to use Scathe or Flare over and over. For the magick barrier, you can just cast Bravery on your heavy hitter. Near 25 percent HP, Vayne is completely invulnerable and there's nothing you can do for what seems like a long time. It's best to just run away and heal.

This is the last fight, so don't be shy about using Quickenings, Megalixirs, and busting out Scathe/Holy Motes. Bring Rubber Suits, White Masks, and other status immunity accessories to swap in on the fly in reaction to The Undying's area nukes and status ailments. Keep plugging away, and keep an eye on your active characters' MP and HP levels, always ready to swap in a fresh ally if someone gets too depleted. When Vayne in his final incarnation as The Undying finally falls, you get a treat for the ages in the saga-ending event sequences.

Hunts

As a member of Clan Centurio, you can take on hunts to earn extra experience, gil, and items. The hunts are a very important part of *FINAL FANTASY XII*. They're the keys to unlocking most of the side events throughout the game and even set the stage for finding certain optional bosses and Espers.

Finding a hunt is easy. Go to the local tavern, The Sandsea for instance, and check the Notice Board. New bills are posted all of the time from people in desperate need of a hunter's services. Agree to speak to the petitioner to add the hunt to the Clan Primer.

Finding the hunt is just the first step. You must then seek out the petitioner to learn more about the hunt and actually accept the job. Petitioners can be anywhere, but they're usually located in the major areas and are easy to find. There's even a map in the Clan Primer to help locate them. Agree to take the hunt upon meeting the petitioner and more information is shared. Please note that marks, the target of the hunt, won't appear until the hunt is officially accepted.

Thus, there's no using the guide to cheat a bit and skip over the petitioner. The meeting with the client is critical.

Now it's time to hunt! The petitioner has likely provided the basic information to find the mark, but you'll find the real details in this guide. Petitioners are often a little vague, so expect the information in this section to be of extreme value. You can obtain additional clues by visiting Ma'kenroh in The Clan Hall. Meet all of the requirements to find the mark and defeat it.

It's time to claim the reward. Return to the petitioner to report the mark's defeat. The petitioner provides a reward and may even have an extra bit of information that leads to another event in the game, so pay attention!

That's all there is to it! There are 45 marks in the game. Normal hunts are found on the Notice Board. Montblanc (in The Clan Hall) hands out the elite marks, which are the real challenges. Keep checking the board and visiting Montblanc on a regular basis, as new hunts are added all the time.

Notice Board Hunts

RED & ROTTEN IN THE DESERT

No.01

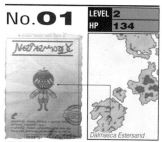

Dalmasca Estersand

| | LEVEL 2 |
| | HP 134 |

ROGUE TOMATO
(Deadly Nightshade)

RANK I-II-III-IV-V-VI-VII-VIII

PETITIONER Tomaj
(Rabanastre/Sandsea Tavern)
REWARD 300 gil, Potion x2,
Teleport Stone (Extra: Handful of Galbana Lilies)

This hunt is given as part of the main storyline when Vaan visits Tomaj in Rabanastre. The battle is fairly simple, so use physical attacks to pound the Rogue Tomato into submission and have Potions ready to heal. Don't take the target too lightly, since it is a little tougher than most enemies at this stage in the game. The mark runs away and heals itself during the first battle. Pursue it down the hill and defeat it again.

WOLF IN THE WASTE

No.02

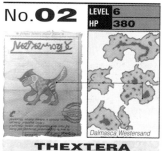

Dalmasca Westersand

| | LEVEL 6 |
| | HP 380 |

THEXTERA
(Mutant Wolf)

RANK I-II-III-IV-V-VI-VII-VIII

PETITIONER Gatsly
(Rabanastre/The Sandsea)
REWARD 500 gil, Headguard,
Teleport Stone

Speak to Gatsly in The Sandsea in Rabanastre to accept this hunt. The mark is located in the Dalmasca Westersand's Galtea Downs section. More specifically, it is located along a cliff wall to the left.

This is a difficult battle, since the mark is never alone. Wait to hunt down this mark until there are at least three people in the party. Eliminate the Wolves around Thextera first. They should fall quickly and it drastically reduces the damage the party will sustain. Although this fight is straightforward, it is important to note that Thextera uses a Saber attack when it nears death that can be lethal. Spread out the party and surround the mark so Saber only hits one or two characters at a time. Thextera also calls for help when it gets low on HP, so expect more wolves to appear near the end of the fight.

No.03 DALMASCA'S DESERT BLOOM

| | LEVEL 4 |
| | HP 755 |

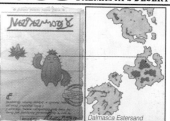

Dalmasca Estersand

FLOWERING CACTOID
(Rare Cactoid)

RANK I-II-III-IV-V-VI-VII-VIII

PETITIONER Dantro
(Dalmasca Estersand/Outpost)
REWARD 500 gil, Potion x10 (Extra: Cactus Flower)

Dantro is located in the small outpost at the south end of the Dalmasca Estersand. A good time to chase this mark is on the way back to Rabanastre while Basch is still in the party as a guest. The Flowering Cactoid is lurking in the Yardang Labyrinth, which is the area just north of the Outpost.

Look for the mark along the north edge of the middle section. The mark is likely to have several lesser Cactoids with it. Expect the beast to flee as it takes damage. This may draw other enemies into the contest, so beware of your surroundings. As the Flowering Cactoid nears defeat, it uses a final attack, 1000 Needles, that causes 1000 HP of damage. Land a finishing blow quickly or this attack will most certainly cause lethal damage.

The party obtains a Cactus Flower at the end of this hunt. Speak to Dantro again after getting the reward and he asks the party to take the flower to his wife in the village to the north (South Bank Village). This begins the "Patient in the Desert" event.

No.04 WATERWAY HAUNTING

| | LEVEL 9 |
| | HP 5146 |

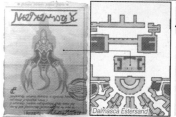

Dalmasca Estersand

WRAITH
(Ghost)

RANK I-II-III-IV-V-VI-VII-VIII

PETITIONER Milha (Lowtown/North Sprawl)
REWARD 500 gil, Ether, Gauntlets

The petitioner, Milha, is in the northeast corner of Lowtown. A Wraith is wandering around in the Garamsythe Waterway in Storehouse 5 near the doors to the sluiceway controls.

Find Storehouse 5 on the northwest side of Lowtown and enter the door, which leads directly to the Overflow Cloaca where the Wraith is hiding. It rises from the ground as the party approaches. This mark uses Doom, which gives the victim till the count of 10 to remove before causing instant death. Use a Remedy to remove the effect, Doom, if you purchased the Remedy Lore 3 license. A Quickening can level this foe immediately.

No.05 MARAUDER IN THE MINES

| | LEVEL 10 |
| | HP 6079 |

Lhusu Mines

NIDHOGG
(Blue Basilisk)

RANK I-II-III-IV-V-VI-VII-VIII

PETITIONER Aekom
(Bhujerba/Lhusu Square)
REWARD 600 gil, Rose Corsage,
Balaclava (Extra: Great Serpentskin)

Seek out Aekom in Bhujerba's Lhusu Square to learn about Nidhogg. The mark is in Lhusu Mines at the point where the shaft splits in two, Transitway 1. This huge snake uses poison, so come prepared and bring a full party with lots of potions and antidotes. The battle is easy at first, but Nidhogg gets faster and gets a significant defense spike as it nears death. At this point, your ability to deal physical damage will really drop, so use magick to tear into him. Black magick does the trick quite well. If you have a Quickening available, you can use it to finish it off at that point. The mark drops a **Great Serpentskin** at the end of the battle, which is used in the "Patient in the Desert" event.

No.06 LOST IN THE PUDDING

LEVEL 15
HP 69469

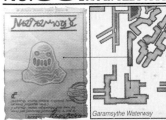

WHITE MOUSSE
(Mutant Flan)

RANK I-II-III-IV-**V**-VI-VII-VIII
PETITIONER Sorbet
(Rabanastre/Westgate)
REWARD 2800 gil, Yoichi Bow
(Extra: Sluice Gate Key)

Garamsythe Waterway

Sorbet is at the moogling station in Westgate. Talk to her to learn about the gelatinous White Mousse. The mark is in the West Sluice Control at the southwest corner of the Garamsythe Waterway. It appears when the party enters the lowered area on the east side.

White Mousse is a caster that uses Toxify and Waterga on a regular basis. It can also blind the party with Flash. Cast Berserk on it to prevent it from casting and force it to rely on physical attacks. Use Decoy to keep its attacks directed on one person while another character heals the victim. Fira also works well, while Shear can increase its effectiveness.

The party claims the **Broken Key** after the battle. Return it to Sorbet to exchange the key for the important **Sluice Gate Key**, which is used in multiple side events and hunts.

No.07 FOR WHOM THE WYRM TOLLS

LEVEL 32
HP 128648

RING WYRM
(Lesser Dragon)

RANK I-II-**III**-IV-VI-VII-VIII
PETITIONER Balzac (Lowtown/ North Sprawl)
REWARD 200 gil, Moon Ring, Icebrand

Dalmasca Westersand

Seek out Balzac in Lowtown's North Sprawl, who recently spotted a very powerful creature in the Windtrace Dunes in the Dalmasca Westersand. Search for the mark south of the central region. It only emerges during sandstorms though, so multiple visits may be necessary. Belias is very handy in this fight, since the Ring Wyrm's powerful breath attacks actually heal the Esper. Dispel the Protect and Haste effects on the mark right away, then Slow the beast to give the party an advantage.

A SCREAM FROM THE SKY

No.08
LEVEL 18
HP 18669

Nam-Yensa Sandsea

WYVERN LORD
(Greater Wyvern)

RANK I-**II**-III-IV-V-VI-VII-VIII
PETITIONER Sherral
(Rabanastre/Amal's Weaponry)
REWARD 1000 gil, Longbow, Shell Shield

Look for an imperial Soldier inside the weapon store in Rabanastre. This is Sherral, the petitioner. A powerful wyvern has been spotted on the west edge of the Nam-Yensa Sandsea. Travel to the north end of Simoon Bluff to locate the mark. This is a flying creature, so equip everyone with ranged weapons or magick. The beast uses Aero, so Windbreakers come in handy.

TINGLING TOAST

No.09
LEVEL 38
HP 54921

Zertinan Caverns

MARILITH
(Crimson Serpent)

RANK I-II-III-IV-**V**-VI-VII-VIII
PETITIONER Tavernmaster
(Rabanastre/The Sandsea)
REWARD 2200 gil, Serpent Eye, Teleport Stone x3 (Extra: Serpentwyne Must)

Talk to the Tavernmaster in The Sandsea in Rabanastre to learn about this powerful serpent in the Zertinan Caverns. Enter the caverns from the Dalmasca Westersand to reach the Zertinan Caverns. The Marilith sits in the rounded bottom-right corner of the largest room. Shut off all Gambits and stay in the room for five minutes. Walk into the corner after that time and the enemy should appear.

Try to Blind and Slow this mark at the start of the battle. That's pretty much all that is needed to make this fight end quickly. Return the **Serpentwyne Must** to the Tavernmaster to complete the hunt.

> **!! A LITTLE EXTRA FUN**
>
> Speak to Migelo later for a bit of added fun at the end of this hunt. There's no reward, but a fun addition to the story.

THE DEFENSE OF OZMONE PLAIN

No.10
LEVEL 22
HP 18709

Ozmone Plain

ENKELADOS
(Slaven)

RANK I-II-III-IV-V-VI-VII-VIII
PETITIONER Low-chief Sugumu (Jahara/Elderknoll)
REWARD 1100 gil, Ether, Golden Amulet (Extra: Errmonea Leaf)

Sugumu is looking for someone to stop an herb-trampling Enkelados in the Ozmone Plain. Warrior Hsernu, the bridge guard, has more info. He says the enkelados detests the creatures known as the "Wu." Travel to The Shred in the eastern section of Ozmone Plain and rid the area of Wu. Leave and return to find the mark. This is a great hunt to take while Larsa is in the party as a guest on the way to Mt Bur-Omisace.

Enkelados begins with Protect and Shell, so hit it with a quick Dispel. Let one person approach the mark while the others attack from range to limit the damage caused by its Spinkick. Have the other two characters support and heal. It's important to mention that Enkelados can and will nullify status afflictions.

The mark drops an **Errmonea Leaf**. Speak to Low-chief Sugumu again after getting the reward to inquire about the mysterious leaf. He asks that the leaf be delivered to Lesina in the Giza Village. She can be found during The Dry and gives the party **two Remedies** for their effort.

A RING IN THE RAIN

No.11
LEVEL 24
HP 19449

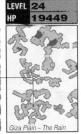

Giza Plain – The Rain

CROAKADILE
(Mutant Lizard)

RANK I-**II**-III-IV-V-VI-VII-VIII
PETITIONER Sadeen (Giza Plains - The Rains/Nomad Village)
REWARD 1200 gil, Serpent Rod, Teleport Stone (Extra: Ring of the Toad)

Visit the Nomad Village during The Rains and speak to the lone man standing in the center. The mark is near the bridge in Starfall Field during The Rains. The battle is straightforward, but near the end of the fight the Croakadile uses Growing Threat to double its level. This is an excellent time to use fire magick or a Quickening to finish it off.

The creature drops the **Ring of the Toad**. Return it to Sadeen, who asks the party to take the Ring of the Toad to a lady in the Nomad Village after The Rains during The Dry. The person you seek is Elder Brunca. Give her the ring and return to Sadeen during the next Rain to see the end of this event.

No.12 THE DEAD OUGHT SLEEP FOREVER

LEVEL 24
HP 22562

Henne Mines

IXTAB
(Undead)

RANK I-II-III-IV-V-VI-VII-VIII
PETITIONER High-chief Zayalu (Jahara/Elderknoll)
REWARD 1300 gil, Ether, Soul Powder

Seek out Zayalu in Jahara's Elderknoll. The mark, Ixtab, is an evil spirit in the Henne Mines. Enter the Henne Mines from the Ozmone Plain to start close to the Phase 1 Shaft and its southeast corner, where the mark is hiding, to make it appear. Ixtab's greatest weapon is Stop. Make sure the leader is equipped with a Power Armlet to block the status and have plenty of Chronos Tears on hand for everyone else. It can also use Doom, but that shouldn't be an issue.

No.13 BEFOULMENT OF THE BEAST

LEVEL 28
HP 22559

Paramina Rift

FERAL RETRIEVER
(Coeurl)

RANK I-II-**III**-IV-V-VI-VII-VIII
PETITIONER Hymms (Mt Bur-Omisace/Sand-strewn Pass)
REWARD 1500 gil, Recurve Crossbow, Teleport Stone

Hymms is in the Sand-strewn Pass in Mt Bur-Omisace. Speak with the petitioner to learn that the mark lurks in the southern part of the Spine of the Icewyrm within the Paramina Rift, near the Stillshrine of Miriam. It has a mass petrify attack at its disposal and uses many different status attacks. Have Esuna ready and protect at least one party member from Sleep with a Nishijin Belt. Note that the Feral Retriever can cast Balance when it's close to death, which can be lethal due to its high HP.

A CHASE THROUGH THE WOODS

No. 14

LEVEL	31
HP	20010

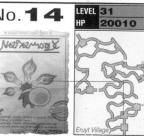

Eruyt Village

VORPAL BUNNY
(Mutant Hare)

RANK I-II-**III**-IV-V-VI-VII-VIII

PETITIONER Nera (Eruyt Village/Spiritwood)

REWARD 2000 gil, Lightning Arrows, Gillie Boots (Extra: Rabbit's Tail)

Locate Nera in the Spiritwood section of the Eruyt Village to learn about the very special creature in the woods. A black dreamhare that appears once every seven years is currently on the loose. The mark is in the Rustling Chapel.

This mark doesn't really want to fight. In fact, it prefers to run away and let the other creatures in the woods do the fighting. Ranged weapons help, but Berserk is better. Cast Berserk on the bunny to force it to stop running and fight. Blind, Silence, and Slow the enemy to make things go smoother. Return the **Rabbit's Tail** to Nera and claim the reward.

No. 15 THE MINE FLAYER

LEVEL	35
HP	31161

Henne Mines

MINDFLAYER
(Mindflayer)

RANK I-II-III-**IV**-V-VI-VII-VIII

PETITIONER Warrior Guromu (Jahara/Lull of the Land)

REWARD 2200 gil, Carmagnole

Seek out Guromu in Jahara to learn what kind of creature could be troubling the mighty hunters. The mark is in the Henne Mines and it's drawn to entities that possess magickal power. It is located where the Mist is densest, which happens to be the south end of the Phase 1 Dig. Enter the mines from Ozmone Plain and bear right.

The mark uses magick freely. While Stop and other harmful status effects are among its arsenal, the most harmful one is Invert, which switches the victim's HP and MP. Use Berserk to control this battle. Cast it on the mark at the start to prevent it from casting magick, then use Slow to keep its speed normal. The first time the mark's HP is critical, it uses a technique that fully heals it and provides it with Haste, Protect, Shell, and other beneficial status effects. This can't be stopped, since it isn't a magick. Slow the boss again and use Berserk again.

Upon returning to Guromu, he mentions that Geomancer Yugelu wishes to speak to the party. Yugelu mentions a power resting at the bottom of the Henne Mines, but says the party isn't ready to face this challenge and won't be until they have gathered many "great beings." This is the introduction to the ultimate Esper, Zodiark.

No. 16 THE DESERTER'S REVENGE

LEVEL	37
HP	41171

Barheim Passage

BLOODWING
(Mutant Steeling)

RANK I-II-III-IV-**V**-VI-VII-VIII

PETITIONER No. 381 (Dalmasca Estersand/South Bank Village)

REWARD 2400 gil, Stun Bombs, Vampyr Fang

Find No. 381 along the beach in South Bank Village. He seeks revenge against a mark in the West Annex of Barheim Passage. The area is full of undead foes, which makes it quite difficult. The mark is in the center of the long stretch along the south. Move through the area slowly to avoid getting in a big battle with several undead and the Bloodwing.

This foe is a flyer, so bring a party with ranged weapons (bows, guns, bombs). The key to this battle is to Silence and Blind the enemy early on. Silence removes its powerful magick attacks and Blind cripples its melee assault. With these two status effects in place, the fight becomes fairly simple. Remember to always immediately attack any undead foes that appear; use Silence on them, too.

TROUBLE IN THE HILLS

No. 17

LEVEL	33
HP	40020

Mosphoran Highwaste

ATOMOS
(Mutant Slaven)

RANK I-II-**III**-IV-V-VI-VII-VIII

PETITIONER Burrogh (Nalbina Fortress/Jajim Bazaar)

REWARD 1800 gil, Gaia Rod, Diamond Shield

Trade is being disrupted by a huge beast in the Mosphoran Highwaste and Burrogh wants the disruption eliminated. Search for the beast at the north end of Nothern Skirts. Dispel the status effects that protect it. Atomos recasts some of them throughout the battle, so use Dispel when necessary. It can also create a White Wind that protects it from harmful status effects. Try using one fighter and two support characters during this fight. Atomos focuses on physical damage, so it's very easy to control which character the mark attacks with Decoy.

ADDING INSULT TO INJURY

No. 18

LEVEL	43
HP	177365

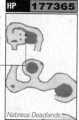

Nabreus Deadlands

ROBLON
(Augmented Automaton)

RANK I-II-III-IV-V-**VI**-VII-VIII

PETITIONER Morgen (Nalbina Fortress)

REWARD 3100 gil, Giant's Helmet, Mythril

The clues for this hunt are a little vague. Morgen points to the Nabreus Deadlands, which is a large area with some very powerful enemies. The only other clue available mentions a place of tall grasses and a bank of thick fog. Look for a hidden path in the northwest corner of the Slumbermead, which leads to The Murmurs and then Overlooking Eternity. This is where you'll find Roblon.

This is a nasty battle. Dead Bones are very common in the area and they pop up throughout the fight. These foes can actually help the party out, if you can defeat enough of them to create a long battle chain. Each time one falls, there's a chance it might drop a bonus that can restore lost HP or MP.

The mark, Roblon, is powerful on its own. It uses multiple elements and can drain the party's MP with Fear. Use Slow to ease the pace of the battle. Have one character repeatedly pound Roblon with Expose to lower its defense to a point where physical attacks become devastating against it. Souleater also works pretty well when there aren't a lot of Dead Bones foes around.

No. 19 RODEO TO THE DEATH

LEVEL	35
HP	43283

Salikawood

BRAEGH
(Mutant Nightmare)

RANK I-II-III-**IV**-V-VI-VII-VIII

PETITIONER Va'Kansa (Mosphoran Highwaste/Babbling Vale)

REWARD 1700 gil, Obelisk, Hi-Ether

Va'Kansa is stuck in the Babbling Vale thanks to Braegh. Track down the beast and defeat it so Va'Kansa can meet up with his partner. The creature is located in the Corridor of Ages of the Salikawood, near the Necrohol of Nabudis. You must fight the optional boss King Bomb in the Grand Bower to reach the mark.

This creature likes to use Immobilizega to pin down the party. This isn't a problem if Decoy is used to make the mark focus on your main fighter. It can also afflict the party with Bleed and Poison, so have Esuna ready at all times. Its Magick Shield can make it immune to magick at times, so focus primarily on physical damage. Silence the enemy as quickly as possible to take the negative statuses out of the fight. Braegh will cast Invert shortly after the fight begins, so cast Reflect on the party to bounce it back at Braegh. After doing so, it will take just a few hits to end the fight.

Talk to Va'Kansa again and he mentions that his partner still hasn't arrived. Go to Phon Chest and look for Hawker near one of the buildings. He provides a message for Va'Kansa. Return to Mosphoran Highwaste and deliver the message to complete the story. There's no reward for this extra need, but it does provide an extra bit of storyline for those willing to do the leg work.

No. 20 SHELLED OBSTRUCTION

LEVEL	38
HP	111331

Sochen Cave Palace

DARKSTEEL
(Titantoise)

RANK I-II-III-**IV**-V-VI-VII-VIII

PETITIONER Homesick Man (Archades/Vint's Armaments)

REWARD 3000 gil, Lead Bolts, Adamantite

The Homesick Man needs a little help clearing his path through Sochen Cave Palace. Seek out Darksteel in the Temptation Eluded area. It's best to enter from Old Archades to shorten the trip.

Use Dispel at the start of the battle to remove Protect, Shell, and Bravery from the mark. It may recast Protect throughout the battle, so keep an eye on its status. Immediately cast Blind and Slow on the beast. Try to keep one character fighting up close while the other two fight from a distance to avoid its area attacks. Near the end of the battle, it goes nuts and casts Darkra over and over. Black Masks, dark absorbing headgear, are very useful in this situation, but a Quickening can finish off the foe before the Bombardment becomes lethal.

GET MY STUFF BACK!

No. 21

LEVEL	41
HP	106616

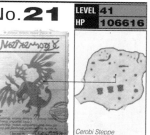

Cerobi Steppe

VYRAAL
(Aevis)

RANK I-II-III-IV-**V**-VI-VII-VIII

PETITIONER Viera Wayfarer (Balfonheim Port/The Whitecap)

REWARD 3500 gil, Halberd, Crystal Shield (Extra: Viera Rucksack, Dragon Scale)

A creature stole the Viera Wayfarer's belongings and she's anxious to get them back. She even decides to join the party for this hunt. Seek the mark in Cerobi Steppe's The Northsward. The Viera Wayfarer uses a bow, so it's fairly easy to keep her healthy. Use Decoy to direct the attacks away from her and she'll pelt the enemy from a safe distance. Cast Slow, Silence, and Blind on the creature to make the battle much easier. You can also use Confuse, which can briefly delay the mark's attacks, but the Viera's attack will quickly break the effect. Confuse is more effective if the Viera falls in battle. Use Magick to avoid breaking the effect.

The creature drops the **Viera Rucksack** and a **Dragon Scale** after the battle. Take the Rucksack back to the Viera in Balfonheim Port. The Dragon Scale is part of the Wyrm Philosopher side event.

OLD LEGENDS, DECAYING BONDS

No. 22

LEVEL	39
HP	228468

Tchita Uplands

LINDWYRM
(Dragon)

RANK I-II-III-IV **V** VI-VII-VIII
PETITIONER Fermon
(Archades/Alley of Muted Sighs)
REWARD 4200 gil, Barrel Coat,
Hi-Ether (Extra: Rusted Scrap of Armor)

Fermon needs someone to hunt a legend in the Tchita Uplands. Seek out the mythical mark in the Garden of Life's Circle. It only appears when the sky is cloudy, which doesn't seem to be very often in this area. If it's sunny, use the Tchita Uplands exit to go in and out of Cerobi Steppe until it's either cloudy or raining. If it's raining when you get to the Garden of Life's Circle, just zone out and back in until it stops raining.

The mark uses Thundara and a variety of status attacks. Come prepared to heal Stone in particular. Shut off all physical attacks and use Shear at the start to lower the boss's magick defense. Also, cast Blind and Silence on the beast. Have the entire party set to put the Lindwyrm to Sleep and use nothing but magick after Blinding and Silencing the toe. The Shades of Black technick works well in this fight, but strong magicks (like Flare) work best.

THE THINGS WE DO...

No. 23

LEVEL	42
HP	64325

Sochen Cave Palace

OVERLORD
(Headless)

RANK I-II-III-IV **VI** VII-VIII
PETITIONER Insecure Seeq
(Archades/Bulward's Technicks)
REWARD 3500 gil, Hi-Ether x2,
Teleport Stone

The Insecure Seeq is looking to defeat a powerful mark-like Overlord. This mark is in Sochen Cave Palace inside the Doubt Abandoned room. The petitioner joins the party for this fight, but don't expect him to be much help. It's unlikely he'll last through the opening moments of the fight.

Dispel Bravery from the Overlord at the start. Cast Slow, Blind, and Silence on the enemy after that to give the party an advantage. The boss uses a powerful fire-based area attack called Pyromania, which may lead to the seeq's early demise. Flame Shields are very effective to counter this attack. Its melee attacks are also quite powerful, but a shield and someone with Curaja can keep the damage from getting too severe.

No. 24 THE CREATURE COLLECTOR

LEVEL	47~48
HP	224294

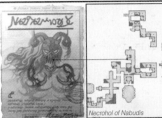

Necrohol of Nabudis

GOLIATH
(Augmented Automaton)

RANK I-II-III-IV **VI** VII-VIII
PETITIONER Barrong (Nalbina Fortress/West Ward)
REWARD 3600 gil, Save the Queen, Einherjarium

Barrong is seeking information for his bestiary. His next entry deals with a beast in the Necrohol of Nabudis. Enter the dungeon from the Nabreus Deadlands to easily reach the Hall of Slumbering Might. Goliath is just around the corner to the left.

Expect a group of Baknamys to surround the mark. Carefully draw them out and eliminate them before challenging the mark. Try to go to the right from the entrance to draw the Baknamys away. The boss comes with Protect in effect, so Dispel it and then cast Slow and Expose against the enemy. This boss only attacks with magick and you can't Silence it. Reflect is pretty handy for dealing with its attacks, but it also pays to have Shell on the entire party, too. Use physical attacks at the start, then switch to Darkga when the boss's Magick Barrier drops. It doesn't hurt to protect the party leader from Disable with a Black Belt either.

No. 25 DEAD CITY WATCH

LEVEL	44
HP	125601

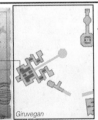

Necrohol of Nabudis

DEATHSCYTHE
(Greater Undead)

RANK I-II-III-IV **VI** VII-VIII
PETITIONER Popol (Nalbina Fortress/Jajim Bazaar)
REWARD 2800 gil, Hi-Ether x2, Soul of Thamasa

Popol needs a cure for bad dreams. Hunt down the mark in the Necrohol of Nabudis. Deathscythe roams the Cloister of the Highborn, but this mark is tricky. It only attacks weak characters and it will make itself immune to physical attacks. Draw it out by wandering around with two characters in the HP Critical state. Be prepared to heal them as soon as the boss appears. This fight isn't difficult, assuming that you can heal the two characters who you use as bait.

VISITOR ON DECK

No. 26

LEVEL	50
HP	184000

Necrohol of Nabudis

DEATHGAZE
(Rare Mutant Aevis)

RANK I-II-III-IV-V-VI **VII** VIII
PETITIONER A Traveler
(Aerodome)
REWARD 3400 gil, Elixir x2

The young Traveler claims to have seen a legendary beast while on the deck of an airship. This mark is hard to draw out and requires a small investment into airship travel. Talk to the petitioner and take an airship to another location. The client will also provide a hint if Deathgaze is close. Check the next aerodome for the Traveler. Talk to the boy to get another tip on the location of Deathgaze. Repeat this process over and over again. Each time it seems that Deathgaze is getting closer until it finally attacks the airship. Speaking to the boy is critical to making Deathgaze appear.

Volunteer to go after Deathgaze when it attacks, then run up to the upper deck. Deathgaze starts the fight by putting up a physical immunity shield. The mark likes to use Poison, Confuse, and HP Sap. It can also instantly kill a party member with its Crushing Fangs. Silence the enemy right away to negate some of its attacks. Scourge works very well against the boss and it will occasionally leave behind the HP Sap effect. Shear and Expose are also good options; use one of the two, depending on which attacks you use the most. If you have the spells Reverse and Renew available, you can kill this mark almost instantly. First, cast Reverse on one character while another starts casting Renew on Deathgaze. If Reverse sticks, the Renew will bring it down to 1HP. Finish it by having the third party member cast Bio or Scourge. Try to time these so they go off one after another because Deathgaze will start to cast Restore on itself as soon as the Reverse/Renew hits.

THE CHILD SNATCHER

No. 27

LEVEL	46
HP	93551

Airship

DIABOLOS
(Mutant Gargoyle)

RANK I-II-III-IV-V-VI **VII** VIII
PETITIONER Miclio (Bhujerba/Miners' End)
REWARD 2600 gil, Demon Shield, Zeus Mace

The unusual boy Miclio has a task for the party. Travel deep into the Lhusu Mines and defeat Diabolos. The mark is found in Site 11 in the southwest corner. The party needs the **Site 11 Key** to reach this area. To obtain the key, you must complete the Antlion Infestation hunt. Then go to the Phon Coast and find the item near a sitting man who fell from the sky.

Cast Slow on the enemy right away. The boss is a fire user and absorbs fire magick, so keep the fire magicks in check. Lower its defenses with Expose and Shear, then spread out the party to avoid taking too much damage from Pyromania at one time.

No. 28 THE BLACK SORCERER

LEVEL	46
HP	49660

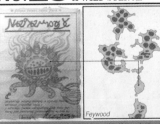

Giruvegan

PISCODAEMON
(???)

RANK I-II-III-IV **V** VI-VII-VIII
PETITIONER Ivaness
(Mt Bur-Omisace/Temple Grounds)
REWARD 3800 gil, Dark Shot, Scathe Mote

Ivaness needs a little help with a family matter. Look for this mark in Giruvegan's Gate of Fire. Search the west side for the enemy and prepare to fight it and possibly a few wandering enemies, too.

Slow the boss immediately. You can also Blind it, but the effect isn't very useful against this caster. The boss will constantly use status effects, so keep Dispel and Esuna ready to use at any moment. It's a good idea to protect one character from Confuse by equipping a Bowline Sash. Physical attacks are very effective. Cast Berserk and Haste on the main damage dealer and let him or her cut the boss to shreds.

No. 29 A WILD STENCH

LEVEL	50
HP	110842

Feywood

WILD MALBORO
(Malboro)

RANK I-II-III-IV-V **VI** VII-VIII
PETITIONER Rena (Eruyt Village/The Spiritwood)
REWARD 4600 gil, Euclid's Sextant

Talk to Rena in the Eruyt Village about a vicious Wild Malboro that threatens their way of life. The mark is in the Feywood's Redolent Glade. When you find the mark, some lesser Malboros will most likely surround it. Eliminate them first and beware of any negative status effects (Bad Breath is particularly nasty). Have Esunaga ready to go at a moment's notice and bring along plenty of status-curing items. Try to use area-of-effect spells at the start of this fight to help deal with the lesser enemies. They don't pose a huge threat, but they can make things difficult.

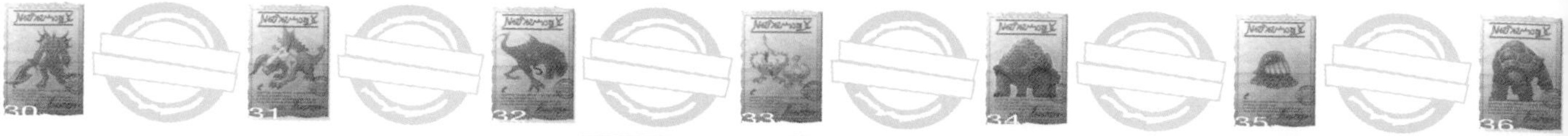

No.30 PAYING FOR THE PAST

LEVEL 46
HP 187991

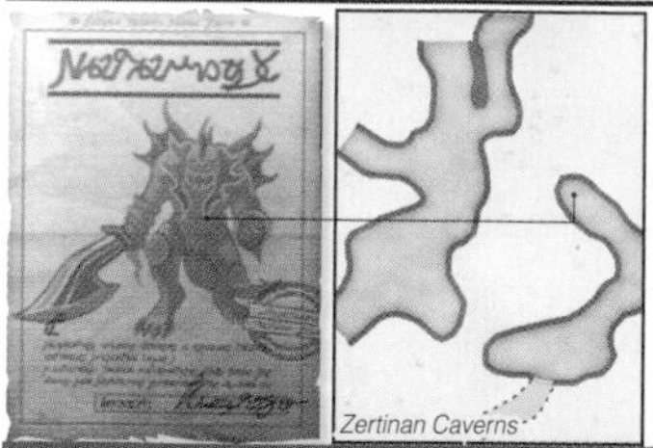

CATOBLEPAS
(Behemoth)

RANK I-II-III-IV-V-**VI**-VII-VIII

PETITIONER War-chief Supinelu (Jahara, Land of the Garif)
REWARD 3200 gil, Volcano, Arctic Wind

Supinelu is seeking a little revenge for a wounded brother. Accompany Supinelu to the Zertinan Caverns. Travel to Hourglass Basin and weave through the hidden passage at the south end to reach the east ledge.

This is a very powerful mark. Cast Dispel on it at the start of the fight to remove Reflect, Bravery, Shell, and Protect. The mark will recast these spells, so stay alert and Dispel them as necessary. Slow and Blind the boss immediately, then attack it normally. Supinelu will attempt to assist in this battle, but it may be difficult to keep him safe given Catoblepas's powerful attacks. Bombard him with physical attacks and magicks until it falls.

No.31 WYRM WRATH'S RENEWAL

LEVEL 68
HP 1390378

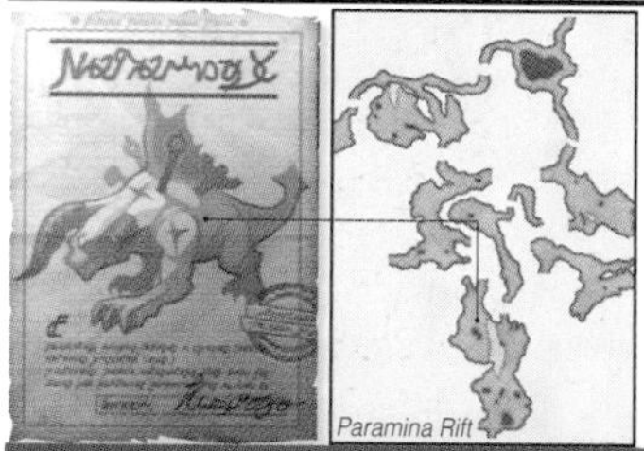

FAFNIR
(???)

RANK I-II-III-IV-V-VI-**VII**-VIII

PETITIONER Ieeha/Relj (Mt Bur-Omisace/Temple Approach)
REWARD 7000 gil, Assassin's Arrows, Teleport Stone (Extra: Ring of Light)

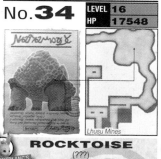

Travel to Mt Bur-Omisace and speak to the Viera Relj to learn that Ieeha seems to be missing. The mark, which is roaming the Paramina Rift, only appears on the west side of Silverflow's End during blizzards. Keep checking back in this area until the snow starts coming down hard.

This will probably be the toughest fight yet. The mark uses some nasty status attacks. Equip a Power Armlet on at least one party member to negate the Stop effect from Fafnir's White Breath, and bring plenty of Chronos Tears and Echo Herbs to the battle. The Bubble spell and the Bubble Belt accessory are absolute musts for this fight, as Fafnir normally hits for a couple of thousand HP and will start using Shock to hit a Decoyed character for 6000-7000 HP once it gets below half of its health. Keep the party spaced out as much as possible to limit the number of party members affected by Silencega and minimize the damage caused by Fafnir's thunder attacks. Again, it's best to have one character focus on melee with Decoy while the other two characters stand back and serve as support characters.

THE CRY OF ITS POWER

No.34

LEVEL 16
HP 17548

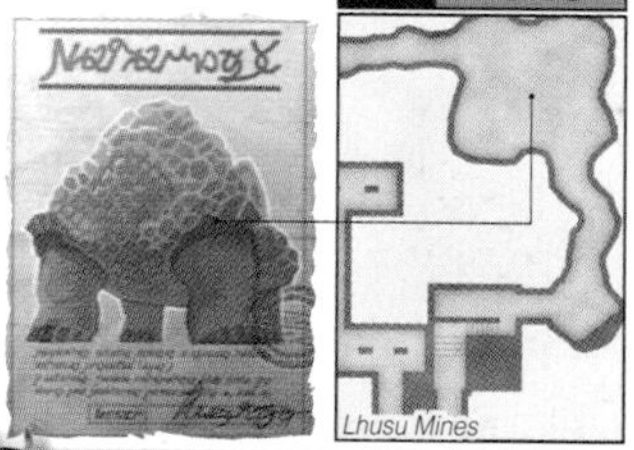

MONTBLANC'S ELITE MARKS

ROCKTOISE
(???)

RANK **I**-II-III-IV-V-VI-VII-VIII

PETITIONER Pilika (Bhujerba/Khus Skygrounds)
REWARD 1200 gil, Hi-Potion x2, Heavy Coat

Seek Pilika out at the south end of Khus Skygrounds in Bhujerba. Her pet is loose in the Lhusu Mines at Site 2 where the Nethicite was found. Bring a full party and maybe even a guest member when you attempt to chase down this target.

Undead foes will occasionally accompany the powerful Rocktoise. When this occurs, use a Quickening right away to eliminate the undead and damage the mark. Spread the party out and keep everyone back except for one character; equip that party member with a shield and Decoy. To avoid the Rocktoise's area attacks, simply use ranged weapons.

CRIME AND PUNISHMENT

No.35

LEVEL 34
HP 87141

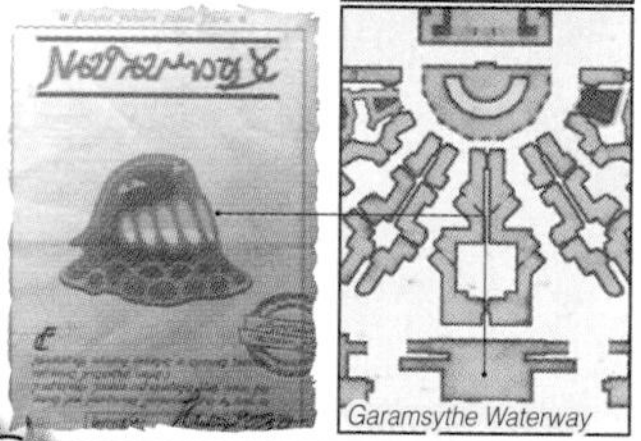

MONTBLANC'S ELITE MARKS

ORTHROS
(???)

RANK I-II-III-IV-**V**-VI-VII-VIII

PETITIONER Contrite Thief (Rabanastre/North Sprawl)
REWARD 3800 gil, Horakhty's Flame, Unpurified Ether (Extra: Stolen Articles, Blackened Fragment)

The Contrite Thief is inside Warehouse #5 and desperate for assistance. Someone must track down the monster that stole her loot and return it to the original owner. The creature is in the south end of the Garamsythe Waterway. Talk to Samal in the South Sprawl courtyard to learn that the creature only attacks females.

Orthros is in the Southern Sluiceway of the Garamsythe Waterway. Lower the water in the No.10 Channel, then go east and then south to find this mark. Enter with Fran, Ashe, and Penelo or the boss won't appear. Note, however, that once Orthros pops, you can switch party members.

Quickly dispel the Shell, Protect, Haste, and Bravery effects from the mark. Blind the boss and use Shear to lower its magick defense. Set all of the characters to use Fira (or better) repeatedly. This may cause approximately 2000-plus HP of damage with each cast.

Return the **Stolen Articles** to the Contrite Thief. Samal makes an appearance and gives the party a **Blackened Fragment**. The fragment is part of the Nabreus's Medal side event.

WHO'S THE STRONGEST!?

No.32

LEVEL 63
HP 493513

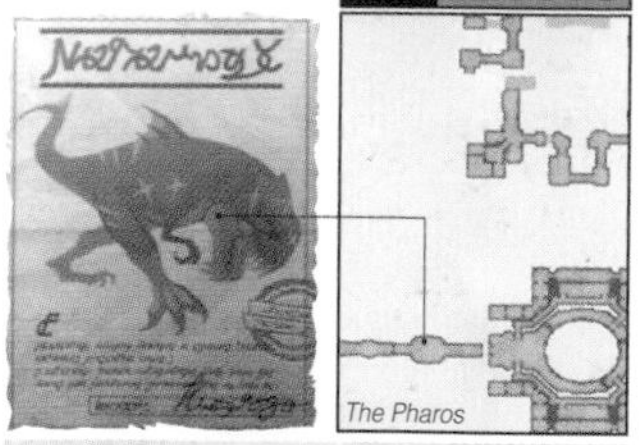

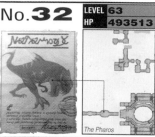

PYLRASTER
(Greater Tyrant)

RANK I-II-III-IV-V-VI-**VII**-VIII

PETITIONER Rikken (Balfonheim Port/Saccio Lane)
REWARD 8000 gil, Grand Mace, Scathe Mote x2

Rikken wants to test Vaan's strength and speed, so visit him on Saccio Lane. He challenges Vaan to a quick footrace before telling him about the mark. The race isn't important to the hunt, but it does introduce the Balfonheim Port Footrace side event. The party can return here and race Rikken and company for prizes.

The mark is located in The Pharos – First Ascent. Use a crystal to reach the area, then head outside to They Who Thirst Not. The Bubble spell and the Bubble Belt accessory also play an important role in this fight. Immediately cast Dispel on the Pylraster and then cast Slow on the beast. Make certain the lead character is equipped with a sword and shield. Pylraster's attacks seem very easy to block, so a shield really helps to reduce damage to your characters. To take this approach a step further, try equipping Gauntlets on your main fighter. Have the support characters bombard the boss with fire magicks and use Shear to lower the boss's magick defense. Note that once Pylraster reaches 50% of his HP, he will use Growing Threat and double in levels. When this occurs, he starts hitting for over 5000 HP per hit and becomes insanely fast.

LITTLE LOVE ON THE BIG PLAINS

No.33

LEVEL 15
HP 7509

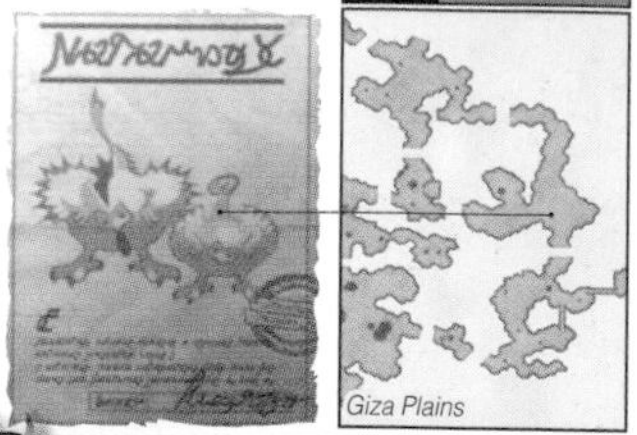

MONTBLANC'S ELITE MARKS

CLUCKATRICE
(???)

RANK **I**-II-III-IV-V-VI-VII-VIII

PETITIONER Dania (Giza Plains)
REWARD 1000 gil, Jackboots, Rainbow Egg

Dania is in the Nomad Village on Giza Plains. She wants someone to eliminate a Cluckatrice and its chicks that are terrorizing the villages. The Cluckatrice is located in Giza's North Bank (southeast of the Nomad Village), but it takes a little work to find it. You must defeat *all* of the enemies in the area, then exit and reenter to force the mark to appear.

This is a very challenging battle early in the game, so you may want to attempt it when you have a party of three or four characters. The three Chickatrices that run with the Cluckatrice cause a great deal of trouble. Although they're less powerful, their attacks can still be overwhelming. A Quickening can do wonders to ease the battle, if one is available, and come prepared to cure Stone attacks. Since this battle may be quite long, make sure you remove the Stone status.

No.36 PARADISE RISEN

LEVEL 37
HP 86956

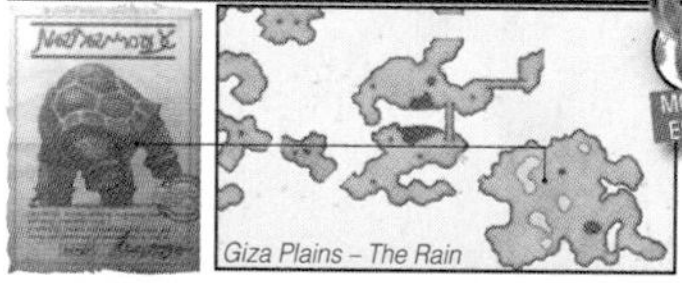

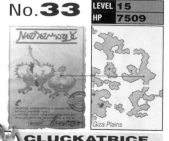

MONTBLANC'S ELITE MARKS

GIL SNAPPER
(???)

RANK I-II-**III**-IV-V-VI-VII-VIII

PETITIONER Nanau (Giza, the Rains/Crystal Glade)
REWARD 3000 gil, Phobos Glaze

FEATHER OF THE FLOCK

Examine the urn in this area to acquire the Feather of the Flock. This item is critical to the Cockatrice side event, which occurs later in the game.

Bansat comments when this hunt is accepted from Montblanc, and he joins the party for the battle. An ancient guardian is on the prowl in Giza Plains. Help Nanau recapture the angry Gil Snapper.

Nanau and Roaklo give the party the **Silent Urn** and mention that you must point it at the beast when the killing blow is landed. (This occurs automatically.) The Gil Snapper is to the east in the Tracks of the Beast, but there's no way into the area. The party must create a bridge to cross the water and reach the Gil Snapper. To do so, you must cut down six dried up trees. Search for them in the following areas: *Toam Hills, Starfall Field, Nomad Village, Giza's North Bank, Throne Road,* and the *Crystal Glade*. Look for leafless white trees along the river and strike them down. After doing so, they float downstream and slowly create a footbridge.

Bansat is there to help with this battle when the party reaches Tracks of the Beast. The mark only appears when the rain is at its strongest; otherwise, the area is occupied by several level 37 Silicon Tortoise. The mark has Protect, Shell, and Haste, so Dispel is handy. Use Slow immediately, then keep casting Silence and Blind until both of them affect the mark and keep recasting Slow whenever it wears off. It's good to have two casters using ranged weapons for this fight. Lastly, use Bettas if at all possible.

Return to Crystal Glade and search the pack that remains to find a **'Soggy Letter'**. The letter asks the party to revisit them during The Dry for the reward. Visit Roaklo and Nanau during The Dry at the Nomad Village at your earliest convenience.

No.37 PARAMINA RUN

LEVEL 44
HP 61321

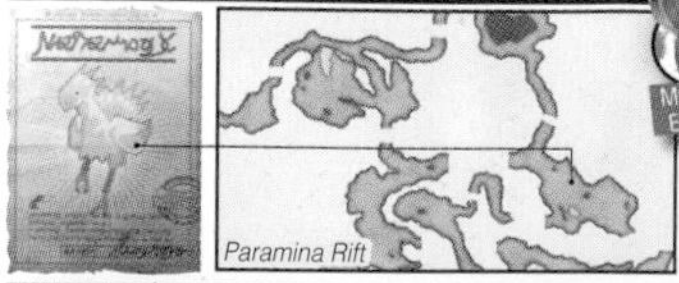

MONTBLANC'S ELITE MARKS

TRICKSTER
(???)

RANK I-II-III-IV-**V**-VI-VII-VIII

PETITIONER Gurdy (Mt Bur-Omisace/Sand-strewn Pass)
REWARD 4800 gil, Deimos Clay

Montblanc... Monid is anxious to go after this target and is quick to speak up when the hunt is accepted from Montblanc. Visit Gurdy at Mt Bur-Omisace's Sand-strewn Pass for the details. Search the area near the Frozen Brook in Paramina Rift to find this mark.

Monid is waiting at Frozen Book when the party arrives and that's a good thing, as this is a challenging fight. The Trickster is always on the move, which makes it difficult to hit. It also uses White Wind to block harmful status effects and a Paling to block physical damage. Trickster puts up the Paling when it has about one-fourth of its HP remaining. When it reaches that point, use a Quickening to finish it off before it can put up the Paling. When the Paling is up, it is only vulnerable to one element, which changes as soon as it is hit with the spell of that element (non-elemental spells work fine while the Paling is up). Also, watch out for Choco-Comet when the Paling goes up; this area attack can cause high damage.

Blind and Silence the enemy at the start of the fight. Have the entire party use Bubble or Bubble Belts to boost HP. Also, be prepared to cast Curaga quite often. The boss's magick attacks are very powerful, so heal after each attack. Try to avoid chasing the enemy around the area; doing so tends to spread the party out too much and makes them more vulnerable. Give the Trickster a few moments and it should run back.

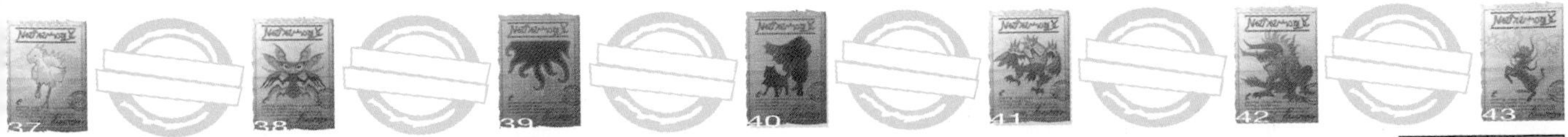

ANTLION INFESTATION

No.38

LEVEL 37
HP 106499

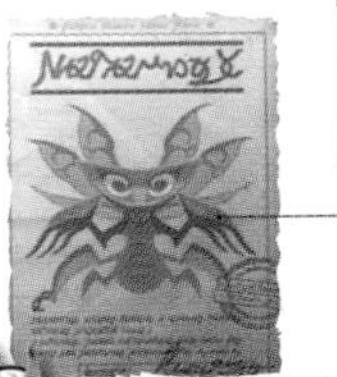

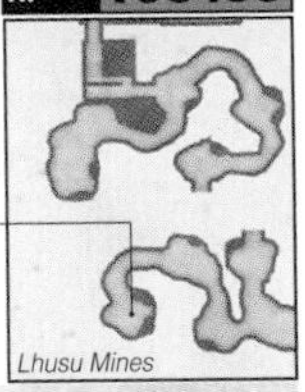
Lhusu Mines

MONTBLANC'S ELITE MARKS

ANTLION
(???)

RANK I-II-III-IV-**V**-VI-VII-VIII
PETITIONER Niray (Bhujerba/The Staras Residence)
REWARD 4300 gil, Bubble Belt, Sickle-Blade

Talk to Niray in Bhujerba about her missing children. It seems that they ran into the Lhusu Mines and took the key to Site 2. She provides the party with the **Site 3 Key** so they can help her out.

Enter the mines and travel to Site 2. Use the Site 3 Key on the Wrought Iron Gate to enter Site 3. Pass through the mines to Site 9 in the southwest corner. The Antlion is surrounded by Killer Mantises. Use a blast or two of Aero to inflict some major damage to them. The Antlion will soon use Cannibalize to feed on a Killer Mantis to raise its level and increase its power! You can survive the battle if the Antlion consumes one Killer Mantis, but run away fast if it consumes more. That said, it's obviously very important to eliminate the Killer Mantises right away.

Cast Silence and Slow on the mark after making a quick attempt to eliminate the Killer Mantises, then keep the mark contained in the area where it begins. Don't let it creep out of the alcove, or it may encounter another Killer Mantis and Cannibalize it. Expect the Antlion to use Disable when its HP gets low. Equip at least one party member with a Black Belt to block the effect and Esuna to cure others.

After the battle, Yrlon mentions something about a key. Unfortunately, the key was dropped and fell into the sea far below. One of the children mentions that it will likely be found on a shore somewhere. The key in question is the **Site 11 Key**, which comes into play later in the game. Look for it on the Phon Coast next to a Fallen Bhujerban. It's the shining **'Small Key'** on the ground next to the man.

CARROT STALK

No.39

LEVEL 49
HP 110842

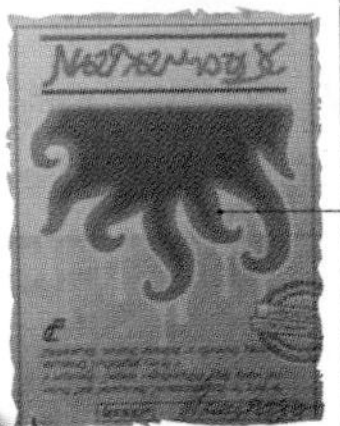

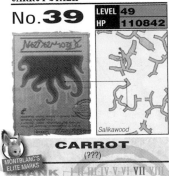

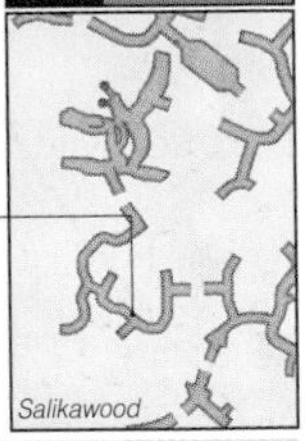
Salikawood

MONTBLANC'S ELITE MARKS

CARROT
(???)

RANK I-II-III-IV-V-VI-**VII**-VIII
PETITIONER Zammadria (Nalbina Fortress/Aerodome)
REWARD 5200 gil, Stink Bombs, Putrid Liquid

Krjn speaks when this hunt is accepted from Montblanc and this time she will take part in the fight. Zammadria says Carrot is hidden in the Salikawood on the Sun-dappled Path. The mark won't appear if any creatures are slain from the time the party enters the woods, so flee from the entrance to the mark's location to avoid contact.

The mark starts with Haste, Shell, Protect, Reflect, Regen, Bravery, and Faith, so Dispel is an absolute must. Carrot's Putrid Breath attack can cause nearly every harmful status effect (e.g., Disable, Sleep, Petrify, Confuse, Disease, Slow, Immobilize, Blind, Poison, and Oil). Have a large stock of Remedy on hand to counteract these effects.

The mark's Time Requiem attack can hit the entire party with Stop. Protect everyone from this effect, or have a healthy supply of Chronos Tears. Those status attacks are the real challenge in this battle. Deal with them quickly and have Remedy on a gambit. When the boss's HP gets low, it uses Growing Threat to double its level. This is an excellent time to use a Quickening to finish off the boss. Slow is effective against the boss, but Putrid Breath clears all negative statuses from the boss each time it's used. Save your MP for something else.

No.40 BATTLE ON THE BIG BRIDGE

LEVEL 45
HP 123103

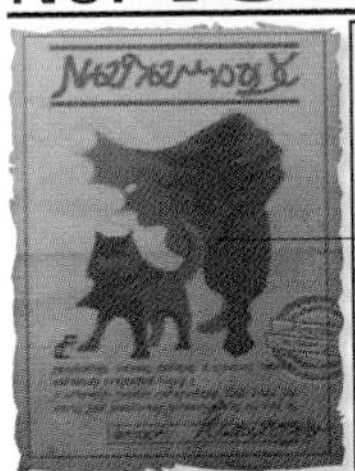

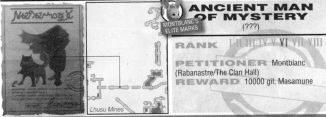

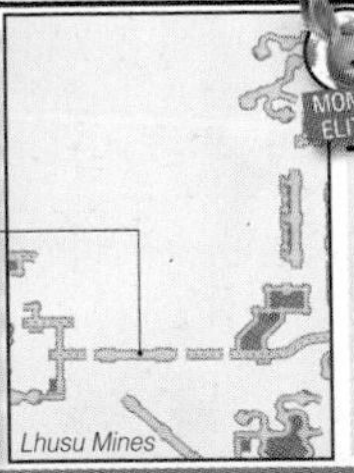
Lhusu Mines

MONTBLANC'S ELITE MARKS

ANCIENT MAN OF MYSTERY
(???)

RANK I-II-III-IV-V-**VI**-VII-VIII
PETITIONER Montblanc (Rabanastre/The Clan Hall)
REWARD 10000 gil, Masamune

Montblanc has a real challenge this time. This mark is located in the Lhusu Mines on the Tasche Span. Target Enkidu, the wolf, and eliminate Shell and Haste with a quick Dispel. Hit the beast with Silence and Blind to cripple its attack. Focus on wiping out Enkidu quickly, so that Gilgamesh is alone.

Keep Slow on Gilgamesh throughout the battle. Use Decoy and a shield to keep his powerful sword attacks under control and let the rest of the party attack from a safe distance. When he gets low on HP, Gilgamesh uses Perfect Defense, which makes him temporarily immune to physical and magick damage. This effect lasts until he performs his Monarch Sword attack twice. Focus on keeping the party healthy and wait for the effects to fade so they can finish him off. There are also five different phases that occur at every one-fifth of his life bar. For the first three phases, you can steal a Potion, X-Potion, 1000 gil, or 2000 gil. During phase 4, you can steal the Genji Shield while in phase 5, it's possible to steal a Genji Glove.

Gilgamesh runs off at the end of the first fight, then enters a deep area in the mines that you can't unlock until the party acquires the Site 11 Key (it's located at The Phon Coast). Search the northwest area to find a Fallen Bhujerban. Look closely for a shining 'Small Key' next to the man and pick it up. Use the key to unlock the Wrought Iron Gate at the south end of the Lhusu Mines' Site 9 area (after the Antlion hunt).

The second battle is much tougher. Enkidu is extremely powerful and the double assault of Enkidu and Gilgamesh is lethal. Do everything you can to eliminate Enkidu right away. Cast Dispel on it, then hit it with Blind immediately. Focus all of the party's attacks on the beast until it drops.

Gilgamesh goes through several forms in this fight. Use Expose to lower his defense and hit him with Darkga and Bio while another character attacks up close. Beware of the boss's Lv.2 Sleep, Lv.3 Disable, and Lv.4 Break. These only affect characters with a level that can be divided by 2, 3, or 4. Don't forget that you can steal the Genji items (Genji Helm and Genji Armor) during phase 4 and 5 from Gilgamesh. If you succeed, equip them immediately!

A DARK RUMOR

No.41

LEVEL 49
HP 115659

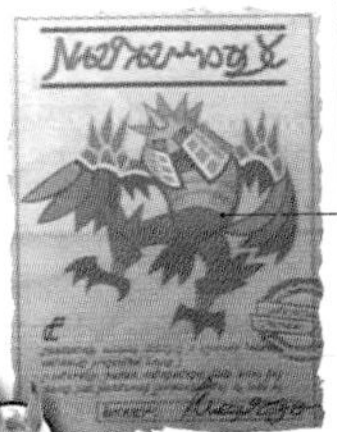

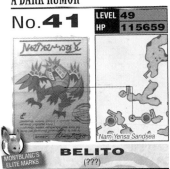

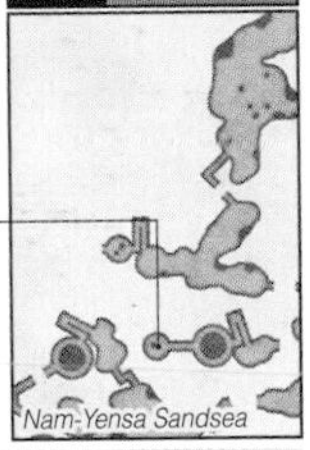
Nam-Yensa Sandsea

MONTBLANC'S ELITE MARKS

BELITO
(???)

RANK I-II-III-IV-**V**-VI-VII-VIII
PETITIONER Montblanc (Rabanastre/The Clan Hall)
REWARD 5100 gil, Megalixir

There's a mysterious mark hiding in the Nam-Yensa Sandsea. Start in the Ogir-Yensa Sandsea and use the exit at the Central Junction to the Zertinan Caverns. Pass through the caverns to the Nam-Yensa Sandsea to reach a secluded section of Withering Shores.

Monid is there when the party arrives and he's fighting alongside the party as the hunter stalkers attack. Bwagi, Ba'Gamnan, Rinok, and Gijuk assault the party from all sides. Ba'Gamnan is the main threat, so eliminate the others first and save him for last. Try to cast Dispelga, then focus on one of the foes at a time. It's important to note that Ba'Gamnan has a very high evasion and he uses powerful area attacks. Make sure your main fighter has Protect, Shell, and Haste. Keep an eye on Ba'Gamnan's status and cast Dispel on him as necessary.

No.42 TRUTH SHROUDED IN MIST

LEVEL 70
HP 1668491

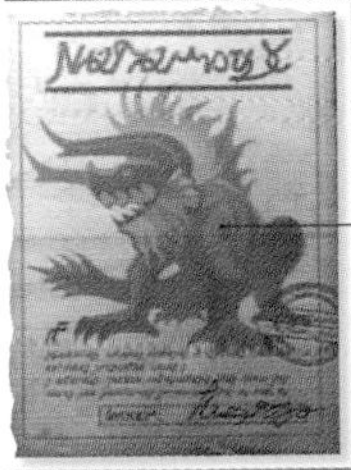

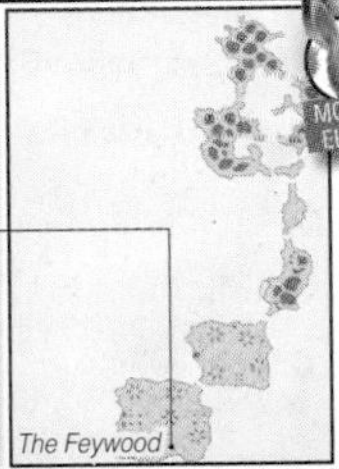
The Feywood

MONTBLANC'S ELITE MARKS

BEHEMOTH KING
(???)

RANK I-II-III-IV-V-VI-**VII**-VIII
PETITIONER Koqmihn (Lowtown/Dalan's House)
REWARD 250 gil, Bacchus's Wine (Extra: 500,000 gil, Rod of Faith)

This mark is located in The Feywood within the Edge of Reason. Getting the creature to appear takes some work. Enter The Edge of Reason and eliminate the monsters there. This can be difficult due to the heavy Mist in the area that tends to hide enemies from view. Travel to the Ice Field of Clearsight and continue to rid the land of creatures. You must clear out everything in both zones. If you stay in one area for too long, the creatures will start respawning. Wander back into The Edge of Reason when the enemies are gone and the Behemoth King should be waiting in the center of the area.

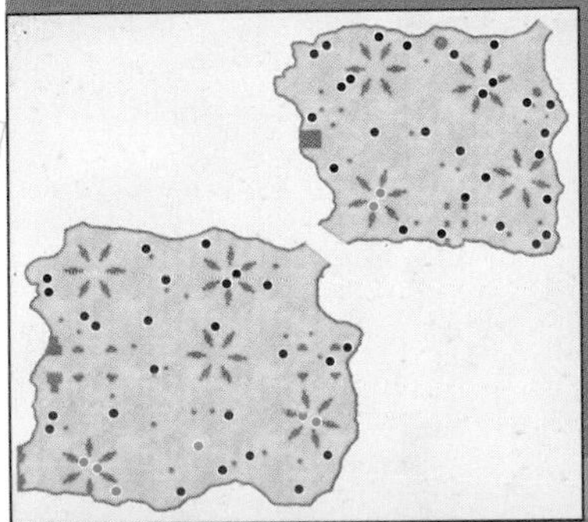

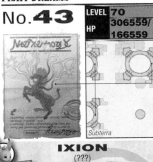

The Behemoth King shifts between Paling and Magick Shield, making it immune to physical damage or magick. Keep the party split up to avoid his area attacks and switch the party's attacks depending on the mark's immunity. Use magick when he's immune to physical damage, and use physical damage when he's immune to magick. Keep Bubble on everyone, along with Shell and Protect.

Koqmihn provides the end of the tale along with the reward. He says "And when the watcher of the deepwood should fall, its slayer shall look to the stone-hewn wyrm and know joy. Though cold stone shall never stir again, a blow struck true by slayer's hand shall find warmth in the wyrm's elation." Go to Temple Approach in Mt Bur-Omisace and look for the **Wyrm Snout** near the center of the path. Strike the snout while empty-handed to claim the loot that hides inside.

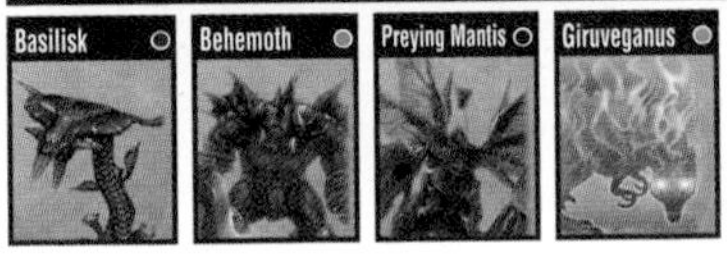
Basilisk
Behemoth
Preying Mantis
Giruveganus

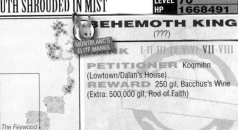

FISHY DREAMS

No.43

LEVEL 70
HP 306559/166559

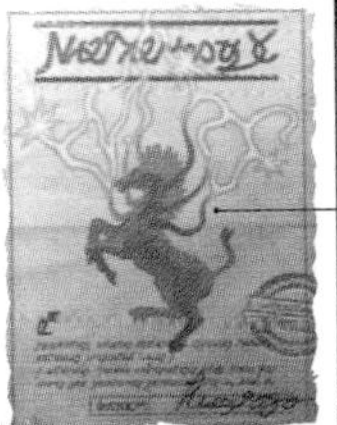

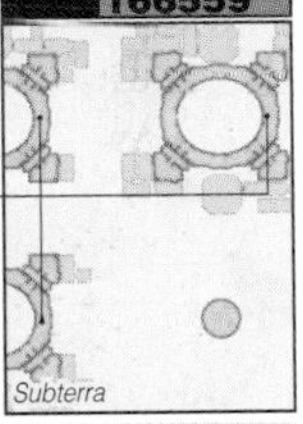
Subterra

MONTBLANC'S ELITE MARKS

IXION
(???)

RANK I-II-III-IV-V-VI-**VII**-VIII
PETITIONER Whitecap Wench (Balfonheim Port/The Whitecap)
REWARD 3000 gil, Sapping Bolts, Ragnarok

The Whitecap Wench asks the party to track down Ixion in The Pharos. Enter First Ascent and use the lift to go down to Subterra. Ixion can appear in any of the mapped rooms in the Penumbra, Umbra, or Abyssal. The easiest way to find it is to pay attention to the surroundings. When Ixion is on the prowl, all of the other monsters in the area disappear. The area is normally swarming with creatures, so this is an easy indicator.

Always attempt to fight Ixion on the ring rather than in one of the side rooms. Ixion's HP is cut in half when it appears on one of the rings, which makes the battle much easier.

The mark uses Sleepga frequently, so protect the party from Sleep effects. It can also cast Silence on the entire party. Have an Echo Herb gambit prepared to quickly remove the effect, if necessary. It likes to use Thundaga, so equip the Rubber Suit armor to absorb thunder. Dispel the boss at the start of the fight, then use physical attacks to beat it into submission.

No.44 GOD OR DEVIL?

	LEVEL	67
	HP	278078

THE SEER

PETITIONER Montblanc

MONTBLANC'S ELITE MARKS

RANK I-II-III-IV-V-VI-VII-VIII

(Rabanastre/The Clan Hall)

REWARD 20000 gil, Megalixir x2

Montblanc wants Vaan to challenge a tough target in The Pharos. Enter The Pharos and use the lift to reach Subterra. The mark is on the bottom floor below Abyssal. To reach that area, you must activate four Pedestals of Night on each floor. Doing so enables the lift to go deeper.

The pedestals are located in the four rooms around each of the central rings. The rooms are pitch-black at first. Placing Black Orbs into the pedestals gradually brightens the rooms until each pedestal is fully activated. Get Black Orbs by defeating the creatures in the hidden halls behind the doors in each room. Stay near the entrance and collect Black Orbs until you have enough to get some light. Then explore the halls fully to gather enough Black Orbs to fully activate each Pedestal of Night. The number of Black Orbs needed is as follows:

LEVEL	NE	NW	SE	SW	TOTAL
Penumbra	18	9	3	6	36
Umbra	15	9	15	18	57
Abyssal	15	21	27	12	75

The Magick Pot

The Magick Pot foe that appears in the basement of the Pharos can be lethal if the party accidentally attacks it while roaming the area. Give the Pot an Elixir (or Megalixir) to render it harmless; you can steal the Elixir back from it, though. If you attack the Magick Pot, it will become invulnerable and start casting very powerful spells like flare and cause lots of physical damage.

> **!! PHOENIX**
>
> There is an optional boss, Phoenix, on the north side of Penumbra. To reach the hall where it resides, use the northeast corner. It is necessary to kill Phoenix to move down to Umbra, though.

The Shadowseer battle is unique. The mark becomes completely immune to damage and begins summoning other foes to fight by its side. Meanwhile, the mark bombards the party with magick as they attempt to deal with the additional threats.

The first three creatures are Pandaemonium, Slyt, and Fenrir. The last summoned creature is Phoenix, which you faced earlier on the way to Shadowseer. All of the summoned creatures are the same as the first time you fought them. The easiest way to deal with these enemies is to use Quickenings to wipe them out. Otherwise, the fights aren't too bad. Be sure to have magick and ranged weapons ready for Phoenix when it appears.

When the four summoned creatures are gone, the shields protecting Shadowseer drop. Attack with physical attacks and use Quickenings as they become available. The boss can drain the party's MP with Fear, so there's no reason to horde it. The Shadowseer's defense increases dramatically at the end, so try to finish it off with magick. This may be tough to accomplish, though, because of the Fear effect.

FAREWELL TO A LEGEND

	LEVEL	73
	HP	50112254

YIAZMAT (???)

MONTBLANC'S ELITE MARKS

RANK I-II-III-IV-V-VI-VII-**VIII**

PETITIONER Montblanc

(Rabanastre/The Clan Hall)

REWARD 30000 gil, Godslayer's Badge

Ridorana Cataract

The ultimate mark, Yiazmat, is in the Ridorana Cataract's Colosseum. This is a very challenging battle that takes a long time to complete, as the mark has 50 million HP! Expect the fight to last for many hours. Fortunately, there's no need to defeat it in one sitting. The party can exit the battle and save at the nearest crystal in Footfalls of the Past or Path of Hidden Blessing.

Work on gambits for this fight. Have your main fighter focus entirely on attacking. Equip him or her with the Masamune, if possible, along with the accessory Genji Glove, and keep Bubble, Haste, Berserk, Decoy, Bravery and Protect on him as much as possible. It should be noted that Katana work well, since they combo often. It's completely possible for a fighter to score a 10-hit combo for 9999 HP of damage with each strike. Have your other two party members focus on support roles. Make one character cast Hastega, Protectga, Shellga, and Bubble, while the other uses Esunaga to cure Petrify and Expose to lower the mark's defense. Both support characters should have *Ally any: Chronos Tear* as their first gambit slot, followed by Arise, Curaja, and Bubble. Yiazmat's regular physical attacks have a chance to KO on hit so expect to raise the Decoy fairly regularly. Also, due to Yiazmat's high combo rate and attack power, set the support characters' Curaja gambit for Ally HP<60% or higher with the Sage Rings equipped to cut down on MP cost by half. Without proper healing, your characters will not survive most of Yiazmat's combos. If a support character runs low on MP, cast Syphon on your Berserked character to replenish a fair amount.

As soon as the fight starts, dispel Yiazmat. Once that is taken care of, get your fighters in their places. There are several stages to this fight and as the fight continues, Yiazmat's attack patterns will change. The first half of this fight is fairly straight-forward. Yiazmat uses Stone Breath, White Breath, and physical attacks with a Cyclone thrown in every now and again. Yiazmat's White Breath does a relatively small amount of damage and has a chance to cause the Stop status effect, which can be problematic for the support characters, so move them to the side of Yiazmat and away from the main fighter. With the Chronos Tear gambit in the top slot, even if multiple people are hit and stopped, the character who gets hit last should be able to throw out a Chronos Tear before he or she is affected by Stop. Cyclone, a major wind attack with a Sap effect, can be quite overwhelming without proper planning. To drastically cut the damage from the attack, equip all of the characters with Windbreakers as soon as you see that Yiazmat is ready to cast it. With Windbreakers and a Curaja gambit in place, this attack shouldn't be too difficult to deal with. When it finishes, switch it out with your normal equipment.

As Yiazmat gets closer to and past the halfway point, his defense rises slightly and he will start using a new attack called Death Strike. As the name implies, the attack is quite deadly and at times he will chain cast this spell. Simply continue to Arise your fallen characters if this happens. Also note that while Death Strike is being cast, Yiazmat cannot and delays all other actions except Attack. Any spells that are being cast will not do so until after the Death Strike has finished casting, so while this is happening, have one of the other characters cast Arise on whoever is being targeted by the spell and it will raise them soon as they die, while attacking with the remaining two characters. Another aspect that changes as Yiazmat draws closer to the halfway point is he will go into his prone position more often and start using Rake, which also has a chance to KO on hit.

The battle gets tougher still when the boss' HP gets down to the last 9 or 10 bars. It uses Growing Threat to double its level (a whopping 146!), which increases its defense and strengthens its attacks. The strategy must change at this point. It may no longer be possible to go toe-to-toe as before, depending on your levels and equipment, and you may have to run in and out of the area more often. Remember to dispel each time you reenter the fight since he will refresh all of his status effects each time you leave the zone. At this point, if your defense is high enough, you may be able to continue the same strategy as before. If not, switch out your accessories with Bubble Belts and start using Reverse on your Decoyed fighter. There is still an instant KO chance with each of Yiazmat's physical attacks so run out immediately if things get bad. Each time you reenter the fight, Yiazmat will cast Growing Threat, followed by Cyclone, so keep those Windbreakers on until after he casts the first one. You may be running in and out of the area often at this point, so make it a point not to stay outside of Yiazmat's range for too long. If after 30 to 60 seconds he can't reach any of your characters while you're in the Colosseum, Yiazmat will begin to heal himself to full health within a matter of seconds.

Finally, as death draws near, Yiazmat will add yet another annoying attack to his arsenal. When he has 4-5 bars remaining, he will cast Reflectga on your party. Be very careful if this if you're using Renew to heal as it will replenish all of the boss' health if it gets reflected! Luckily it is a one time cast per Stage so each time you enter the fight, either cast Dispelga on your party to remove it or temporarily equip Ruby Rings or Mirror Mail as he is casting the spell to make your characters immune to it, then change into your normal equipment. As before, each time you enter, Yiazmat will cast Growing Threat, followed by Cyclone and now Reflectga. You can also try using a Petrified character to summon Zodiark for some quick damage, although, the MP might be better used elsewhere.

Clan Centurio

MONTBLANC
HOW FARES THE HUNT, KUPO?

Clan Provisioner

Vaan has the chance to join a secretive club known as Clan Centurio. Their base, The Clan Hall, is located on the west side of Rabanastre's North End. Take a moment to visit once the party has received an introduction early in the game. The leader of this group is Montblanc. This high-class moogle provides rewards to outstanding members of the clan and also shares information on elite marks. Visit him often to see what's really going on in Ivalice.

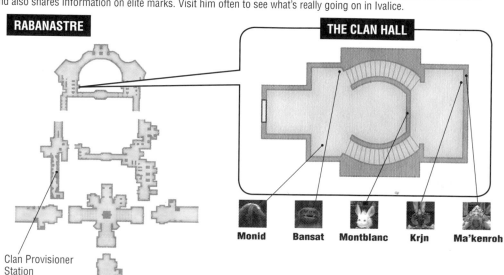

RABANASTRE

THE CLAN HALL

Clan Provisioner Station

Monid   Bansat   Montblanc   Krjn   Ma'kenroh

Being a member of Clan Centurio has its benefits. Vaan can also take on elite marks that only Montblanc knows about. These hunts provide valuable experience, loot, and are often keys to unlocking other events within the game. To fully explore FINAL FANTASY XII, you should try to complete every one of the hunts.

Members of Clan Centurio receive a rank. You can view your current rank at any time by accessing the Clan Primer. Ranks are based on points earned and hunts completed. You receive points for every defeated monster, completed hunt, and every esper that you acquired. Each new rank comes with its rewards. Montblanc always has a nice gift waiting and the Clan Provisioner's stock in the Muthru Bazaar may change.

CLAN CENTURIO RANKS

RANK	MARKS	POINTS	REWARD
Moppet	0	0	Potion x3
Hedge Knight	2	700	Warp Mote x2, Teleport Stone x2
Rear Guard	4	8000	Remedy x3, Teleport Stone x2
Vanguard	8	20000	Hi-Potions x3, Teleport Stone x2
Headhunter	10	30000	Ether x2, Teleport Stone x2
Ward of Justice	12	40000	X-Potion x2, Teleport Stone x2
Brave Companion	14	100000	Hi-Ether x2, Teleport Stone x3
Riskbreaker	16	200000	Elixir x2, Teleport Stone x3
Paragon of Justice	24	250000	High Arcana, Teleport Stones x3
High Guardian	28	300000	Empyreal Soul, Teleport Stone x3
Knight of the Round	32	500000	Megalixir x2, Teleport Stone x3
*Order of Ambrosia	45	1000000	Centurio Hero's Badge, Teleport Stone x3

*The requirements for Order of Ambrosia are: complete all hunts, attain 1 million clan points, and acquire every title in the Sky Pirate's Den (30).

In addition to the bonuses Montblanc provides for new ranks, he also has rewards from third parties when the party achieves certain tasks. The achievements are focused on defeating bosses or obtaining Espers. Here is a list of the specific achievements and rewards.

MONTBLANC'S EVENT-BASED REWARDS

ACHIEVEMENT	REWARD	ACHIEVEMENT	REWARD
Defeat Flans	150 gil	Defeat Tyrant	1900 gil
Defeat Firemane	200 gil	Defeat Hydro	2000 gil
Defeat Mimic Queen	300 gil	Defeat Humbaba Mistant	2100 Gil
Defeat Demon Wall	600 gil & Warp Mote	Defeat Fury	2100 gil & Bacchus's Wine
Defeat 2nd Demon Wall	1200 gil & Electrum	Defeat Hell Wyrm	50000 gil
Defeat Earth Tyrant	1200 gil	Control One Esper	Arcana x2 & Teleport Stone x2
Defeat King Bomb	1300 gil & Mallot	Control Four Espers	High Arcana & Teleport Stone x2
Defeat Ahriman	1600 gil	Control Eight Espers	Gemsteel & Teleport Stone x2
Defeat Mandragoras	1600 gil	Control Thirteen Espers	Serpentarius & Teleport Stone x2
Defeat Rafflesia	1800 gil		
Defeat Daedalus	1900 gil		

Patient in the Desert

WHEN IT'S AVAILABLE

This event is available after the close of the new Consul Inauguration Ceremony. You can't complete it, though, until after you receive the Dawn Shard.

Complete the Dalmasca's Desert Bloom hunt (page ???) to begin this event. Speak to Dantro again after acquiring the hunt reward and he asks the party to take a Cactus Flower to his wife in the village to the north (Dalmasca Estersand/ South Bank Village).

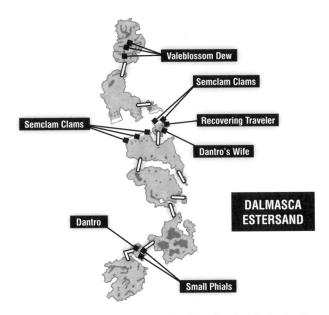

DALMASCA ESTERSAND

Dantro's Wife rewards the party with a **Bundle of Needles** for bringing her the Cactus Flower. Exit and re-enter the village and speak to her again. She asks for Semclam Shells, which are found along the banks of the river. Search the beach in the village for Mysterious Glints, which are actually **Semclam Shells**. There are two of them on the shore inside the South Bank Village, and another three are on the shore in the Banks of the Nebra area. You can move along the event with only one of them, but the more you collect, the better the reward at the end of the event. Return the shells to Dantro's Wife.

She then asks for Nebralim, which Dantro should have. Hike back to Dantro's village to the south (Outpost). Speak to Dantro, then check the supplies scattered around to find two **Small Phials** that contain Nebralim. Return the items to Dantro's Wife.

Something else is needed for the poison in the patient's system. The party must find Valeblossom Dew, which is only found along the cliffs in the Broken Sands area. Note that you must complete this part later in the game (during The Rains) when the ferry is operational. (See the "Ferryman Missing" side quest on page ???.)

Upon gaining access to the northern area, search the Broken Sands section for flowering plants in the ravine. The party can extract a **Drop of Valeblossom Dew** from each of the three trees. Getting into Broken Sands isn't easy, as the area is full of Level 25 Worgen foes and a Wild Saurian blocks the path to Broken Sands from The Yoma.

Return the three Drops of Valeblossom Dew to Dantro's Wife in South Bank Village. Next on the list is a **Great Serpentskin**, which is a reward from the "Marauder in the Mines" hunt (see page ???). Complete the hunt and give the skin to Dantro's Wife. The traveler then needs rest.

Later in the game, return to the village and speak to Dantro's Wife. She indicates that the patient is fully recovered, so speak to the Recovering Traveler behind the house. It turns out the person is a treasure hunter who has found a great treasure in Barheim Passage. The treasure hunter gives the party the **Barheim Key** and mentions an entrance to Barheim in the Estersand. In addition, the treasure hunter hands the party a reward (Balance Mote, Magick Gloves, or Golden Amulet) depending on how many items Dantro's Wife received from the player.

The secret entrance is located at the Murmuring Defile in the Dalmasca Estersand. The Bandit Chief, formerly the recovering patient, is waiting there. The bandit chief mentions the treasure is past Terminus No. 7. Use the Barheim Key to unlock the Weather-beaten Door near them. The passage leads to the Esper Zalera (see page ???).

Jovy the Hero

WHEN IT'S AVAILABLE

This event is available after the Consul Inauguration Ceremony, but you can't complete it until after you visit Draklor Laboratory.

The petitioners for five hunts are on the streets of Nalbina. Whenever the party reports back to the petitioner after one of these hunts, a seeq named Jovy makes a rather curious appearance. His intentions are very unclear. Complete the following hunts:

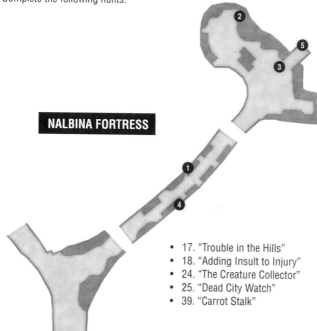

NALBINA FORTRESS

- 17. "Trouble in the Hills"
- 18. "Adding Insult to Injury"
- 24. "The Creature Collector"
- 25. "Dead City Watch"
- 39. "Carrot Stalk"

After completing these hunts, track down Jovy in Nalbina Town's West Ward. He's always on the move, which can make it a little difficult to find him. Speak to him to learn about his new hero and to receive an **Elixir** and a **Knot of Rust**.

Ktjn's Road to Improvement

This event will take place after the party returns to Rabanastre from Barheim Passage.

Ktjn the Viera is sitting mid-way on the stairway leading to the northern part of the city, in the Bazaar area. She will start asking questions as soon as the party talks to her. Note that there is a parameter set involved in this conversation. Her questions are given once per scenario block. If the party fails to answer every question after receiving the Treaty-Blade, she will ask the next question every 15 minutes. The questions and parameter points follow:

RABANASTRE

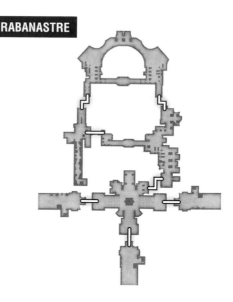

QUESTION 1

Is the city not wonderful? I still lose my way on occasion, but I have come to know some of her walks and alleyways.

But the land, I cannot hear it... Should this not trouble me as a viera?

A: Yes, you should be ashamed. (+1)

A: No, don't be silly. (-1)

QUESTION 2
I knew my choice would bring hardship, yet...

A: You should've thought it through. (+1)

A: Things will get better. (-1)

QUESTION 3
All this time my sister has been making her way through the world, while I lived in the sheltered peace of the Wood.

I would be as she is. Do you think it possible?

A: Sure, if you put your mind to it. (-1)

A: I don't know your sister. (0)

A: It'll never happen. (+1)

QUESTION 4
Perhaps it would be best if I, too, became a warrior like my sister.

What do you think?

A: I think it's a good idea. (+1)

A: I am not sure. (-1)

After the fourth question, she thanks the party and leaves.

KTJN'S PATH

1. +4 => Training at the bottom of the stairs of the clan headquarters. (Reward: Platinum Sword)
2. +3 => Doorkeeper in front of the Clan headquarter. (Reward: Paramina Crossbow)
3. -4 => Shopkeeper in Migelo's shop. (Reward: Firefly)
4. -3 => Barker for Migelo's shop. (Reward: Fuzzy Miter)
5. -2 to +2 => Roaming about Rabanastre. (Reward: Ether, Hi-Potion x3)
   A. Northern part of the city, opposite of the Gambit shop.
   B. Bazaar, sitting
   C. Northern part of the city, outward exit from the bazaar.
   D. Airship terminal, chatting with the bangaas

Ktjn randomly appears in these locations and will remain in the same area while the party stays in Rabanastre. When the party exits Rabanastre, Ktjn will appear in either of the four locations. Loading your game will refresh Ktjn's location. Ktjn will give the party a reward according to the path.

The Seven Sisters

⚠ WHEN IT'S AVAILABLE

This event is available after escaping Barheim Passage and returning to Rabanastre. You can't complete it until after you visit Draklor Laboratory.

Speak to the Chief Steward while traveling between cities by way of the Leisure Craft. Ann and Rande are deep in conversation when Vaan interrupts. Ask about Rande when prompted. A conversation begins that leads to a challenge. Rande proposes that Ann and her sisters collect flowers for mother's name day and she wants Vaan to inform the other sisters of the conditions. He then promises to leave her and her sisters alone if Vaan can deliver the message to all of her sisters. There are seven ships and seven sisters split between them. The chief steward gives Vaan **Ann's Letter**.

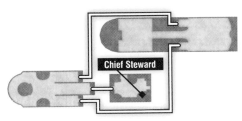

Chief Steward

To complete this quest, you must book flights choosing the leisure craft option. Each sister is on a different route. The order doesn't matter, since the next sister in line always appears on the new route as long as Vaan hasn't already delivered a letter on that route. Deliver all of the messages to the sisters to receive a **Ring of Renewal**. The seven flight paths are:

1. Bhujerba to Balfonheim
2. Bhujerba to Rabanastre
3. Balfonheim to Archades
4. Balfonheim to Nalbina
5. Archades to Nalbina
6. Archades to Rabanastre
7. Nalbina to Rabanastre

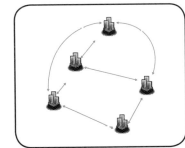

Pilika's Errand

⚠ WHEN IT'S AVAILABLE

This event is available after the party gets attacked by Ba'Gamnan in the Lhusu Mines.

Complete "The Cry of its Power" hunt for Pilika in Bhujerba's Khus Skygrounds, then talk to her again after getting the reward. It seems that she has forgotten her diary on the second floor of Clio's Technicks (south end of the city). She then gives the party a **Merchant's Armband**, which must be worn to enter the shop's second floor.

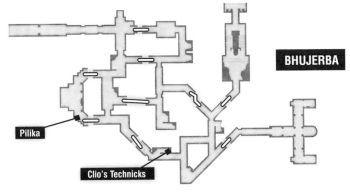

BHUJERBA

Pilika

Clio's Technicks

Enter the shop and search the raised floor on the left to find **Pilika's Diary** in the large bookcase on the wall. You may then opt to read the diary. Reading the diary reveals a second pet that is loose in the store. Return the diary to Pilika and she asks if you read it or not. Choosing the "Read it" option causes Pilika to reward the party with a **Kilimweave Shirt**. If the player answers "I've done nothing" after reading the diary, Pilika rewards the party with a **Shepherd's Bolero**. Whether or not the player has read the diary has no bearing on the outcome.

Making Sunstones

⚠ WHEN IT'S AVAILABLE

This event is available after escaping from Leviathan. You can complete this task an infinite number of times until the end of the game.

Masyua needs help making Sunstones in Giza Plains' Nomad Village. Visit her and inquire about the stones to receive a **Shadestone**.

GIZA PLAINS (THE DRY)

Dark Crystal · Dark Crystal · Masyua · Dark Crystal · Dark Crystal · Dark Crystal

Check the map of Giza Plains. Exclamation points indicate the locations of Dark Crystals that have enough energy to be harvested. Find them and hold the Shadestone up to the Dark Crystals to fill it with energy. Keep visiting Dark Crystals until the Shadestone transforms into a **Sunstone**. Return the completed Sunstone to Masyua for a reward. High grade Sunstones are worth **200 gil**, two **Potions**, and a **Holy Stone**.

Hidden Espers

There are 13 Espers scattered throughout *FINAL FANTASY XII*. You can find five of them in the main storyline, but it takes a little extra work to find the other eight Espers.

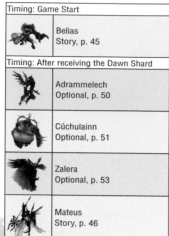
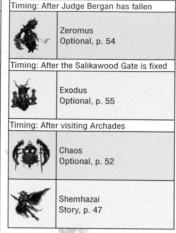
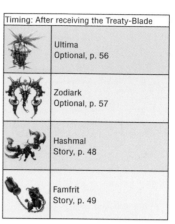
ADRAMMELECH, THE WROTH

Adrammelech is the easiest of the optional Espers to obtain. Its lair, Athroza Quicksands, is within the Zertinan Caverns and it is accessible from Ozmone Plain.

LEVEL	39	EXP	0		
HP	39630	LP	42	STEAL	Pebble, Capricorn Gem, High Arcana

Adrammelech is a flying creature, so come equipped with ranged weapons and magick. Ice is particularly effective. The boss is not alone, though, as Shambling Corpses appear throughout the fight. Let them appear and use either Blizzara or Blizzaga to damage the boss and hopefully eliminate the lesser enemies in the process. Adrammelech uses a Thundaja attack that occasionally causes the Stop affliction. Make sure the party has plenty of Chronos Tears or Remedies (with the Remedy Lore 3 license). Keep Shell up to reduce magick damage and bombard the boss with Ice while trying to keep the Shambling Corpses under control. Try to keep at least one person focused on inflicting damage to Adrammelech, while the others handle the Shambling Corpses. Keep the lesser enemies in check; don't hesitate to use a Quickening if the first group gets wiped out.

Zertinan Caverns

CÚCHULAINN, THE IMPURE

This Esper is located in the Garamsythe Waterway's No. 1 Cloaca under Rabanastre. Getting there isn't easy. You must first complete the "Waterway Haunting" and "Lost in the Pudding" hunts to open the way and obtain the Sluice Gate Key.

With the path open and key in hand, head down to Central Waterway Control. Use the Sluice Gate Key to activate the waterway controls in a specific order, which reveals the path to Cúchulainn. Follow these steps:

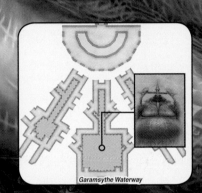

1. Begin by closing the No.3 and No.10 controls in the Central Waterway Control.
2. Enter the No.3 Cloaca Spur and use the No.1 South Waterway Control at the end.
3. Return to the Central Waterway Control and open No.3 and No.10.
4. Close No.4 and No.11, then enter the No.4 Cloaca Spur and use the No.1 North Waterway Control.
5. Return to the Central Waterway Control again and open No.11 and close No.3.
6. Enter the No.1 Cloaca and find the boss at the low point on the south end. Save your game before fighting the boss.

LEVEL	45	EXP	0		
HP	126165	LP	50	STEAL	Scorpio Gem, Elixir, High Arcana

This is a very difficult battle, since there's a constant HP Sap effect on the area that you can't dispel or block. For this reason, it's best to wait for Curaja to become available before challenging this Esper.

Dispel the boss immediately and set two of the characters to heal with Curaja while the other character attacks. Make sure at least one character has a Black Belt equipped to block the boss's Disable attacks. Make sure this character also has an Esuna gambit to free anyone who gets affected.

When the Foobars join the battle, use Firaga to defeat them. Cúchulainn likes to use Invert to quickly wipe out characters. Invert resembles an instant death spell, as HP Sap rapidly drains HP. Revive the victim quickly and immediately trigger a Quickening to turn the battle in the party's favor.

Garamsythe Waterway

ZALERA, THE DEATH SERAPH

The quest to obtain Zalera requires that you complete the Patient in the Desert event to get the Barheim Key. Enter Barheim Passage from the secret entrance in the Dalmasca Estersand and wind through the tunnels to Terminus No. 7. The path isn't an easy one, as many powerful undead creatures appear along the way. This is a great opportunity to level up, but it is also very dangerous. The path through the Zeviah Span seems to be blocked near the south end. Check the west side for an object that can be pushed over to create a path down to West Annex. West Annex is the most challenging area on the way to Terminus No. 7, as the undead appear in groups. Save in Terminus No.7 Adjunct before facing Zalera.

LEVEL	40	EXP	0		
HP	72248	LP	42	STEAL	Pebble, Gemini Gem, High Arcana

This is a very unusual battle. The five-minute timer in this fight really puts things into overdrive! If the timer reaches zero, the party is ejected from the battle, which means starting over from scratch.

Another aspect of the fight revolves around the Dead Bones that join the fracas. Zalera is immune to physical damage whenever a Dead Bones foe is on the field. Kill all of them when they appear, then focus your attacks on the boss.

Check the levels of your party members before battling Zalera. Zalera can cast Lv. 2 Sleep, Lv. 3 Disable, Lv. 4 Break, Lv. 5 Reverse, and Prime Lv. Death. These attacks not only affect those characters with a level divisible by 2,3,4, or 5, but also those of prime numbers. Enter the battle and dispel the status effects on Zalera, then defeat the first set of Dead Bones so that Zalera is vulnerable. When the Dead Bones appear again, quickly dispatch them. As Zalera's HP gets low, he starts casting Sleepga, Stop, and Death. Prepare accordingly. At the end, right before the timer runs out, use another Quickening even if that character is the only one with MP. You can also replace the party with fresh members at this point for a larger, or additional, Quickening.

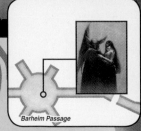

Barheim Passage

ZEROMUS, THE CONDEMNER

Return to Mt Bur-Omisace and speak to the Acolyte at the base of the stairs leading into the Hall of the Light. He instructs the party to seek out a "greater power" in the Stilshrine of Miriam using the Stone of the Condemner that he presents to them.

Enter the Stilshrine of Miriam and activate the Way Stone at the south end of Ward of Measure. Use the Stone of the Condemner at that point to travel to the Throne of Veiled Gods where Zeromus awaits.

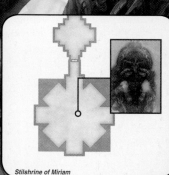

LEVEL	51	EXP	0		
HP	166888	LP	55	STEAL	Cancer Gem, Elixir, High Arcana

All magicks are disabled in this battle, so the party must rely on physical attacks, healing items, and technicks. Change all healing gambits so they use items such as Phoenix Downs. In fact, it's best to equip Pheasant Netsukes and use Phoenix Downs to restore fallen allies rather than using potions. With the augments increasing the effectiveness of Phoenix Downs and the accessory, a party member can fully restore a downed ally, which is far more efficient.

The boss begins with Reflect (nullifying motes), Protect, and Shell. You cannot dispel these effects, so they will be active for the entire battle. The boss is also joined by Dark Lords, which makes things more difficult.

Bring in a melee party, since magick is disabled and use heavy armor and weapons. Shields are a huge help, too. Keep the Dark Lords in check throughout the entire battle, as they can become a nuisance if you ignore them. In fact, make them the priority and only fight Zeromus when the area is clear. Use a Quickening to help level the Dark Lords initially, then use it again whenever the need arises. Keep fighting them to rapidly build a combo. They will eventually drop bonuses, which can restore the party's HP and MP. This is a great way to keep everyone healthy and build more MP for more Quickenings.

Stilshrine of Miriam

EXODUS, THE JUDGE-SAL

Visit the Mosphoran Highwaste and stop at the Babbling Vale. There are two important conversations here. The first one takes place with the Learned Man who explains what has happened to the shrines. The second conversation is with the Caravaner south of the shop, which reveals a hidden path and a wild chocobo in the area.

Begin by touching the Shrine of the South Wind (Babbling Vale/South) to raise the first set of floatweed. Proceed northeast to the Rays of Ashen Light and look for the Wayward Chocobo at the north end. Feed it a Gysahl Green and travel south to Empyrean Way. Look for a floatweed path to the right of the entrance (marked on the area map). Continue all the way to the end and pass through the grassy chocobo area to Skyreach Ridge. Continue toward the west ridge of the Babbling Vale and touch the Shrine of the West Wind. Knock over the Weathered Rock next to the shrine to return to the camp. Revisit the Shrine of the Northwest Wind, next to the Learned Man, and touch it.

LEVEL	46	EXP	0		
HP	119060	LP	52	STEAL	Libra Gem, Elixir, High Arcana

This boss uses Reflect quite often, so beware of casting magick against it. Always make sure you dispel Reflect before attempting any sort of magick attack, or use Opal Rings to cast through the Reflect. This Esper can also cast two very powerful spells: Flare and Scathe. Keep the party separated and Decoy the leader to ensure these spells cause as little damage as possible. Another option to use in this situation is Shell. Note also that Exodus can randomly inflict Stop by using his regular physical attacks.

Items are locked in this fight, but that shouldn't be a problem. Focus on physical damage and technicks like Souleater and 1000 Needles. Use Expose to lower the boss's defense throughout the fight, so physical attacks and technicks inflict as much damage as possible. Near the end of the battle, the boss creates a Paling that makes it immune to physical attacks. This is when Dispel and Darka come into play. Keep a close eye on Exodus and make sure Reflect is dispelled, then bombard it with Darka to finish it off. Otherwise, wait for the Paling to fade and finish it off with a volley of physical attacks.

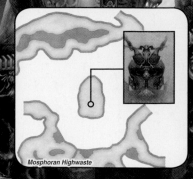

Mosphoran Highwaste

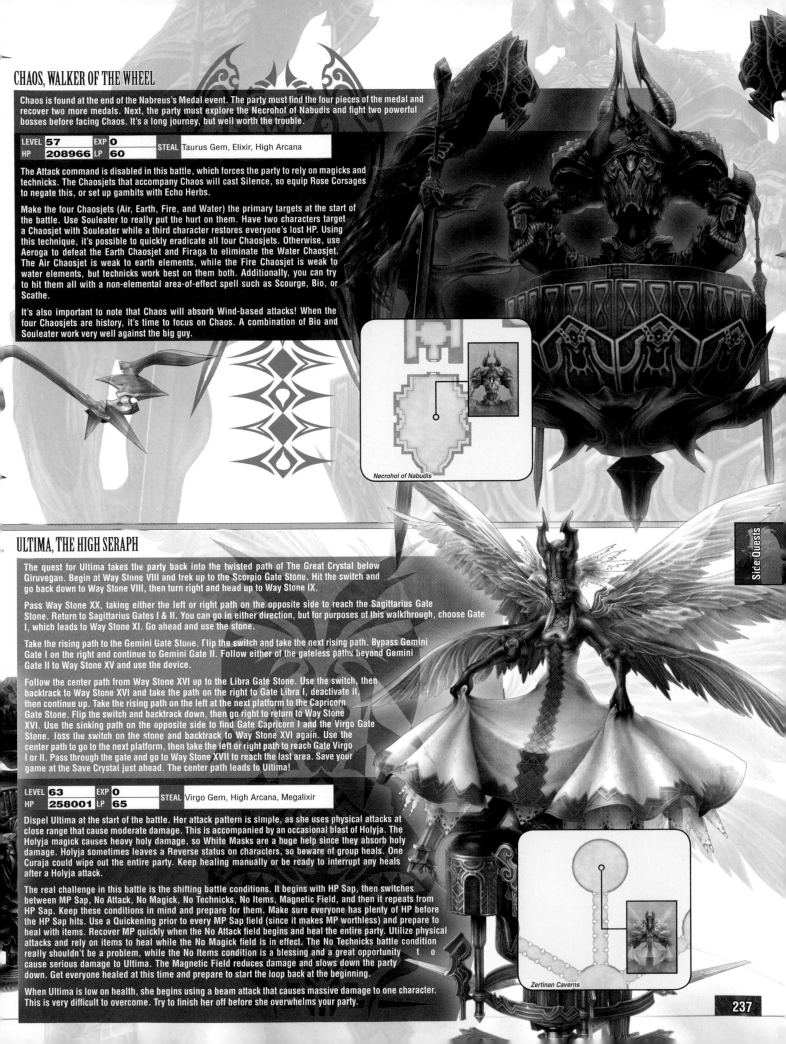

CHAOS, WALKER OF THE WHEEL

Chaos is found at the end of the Nabreus's Medal event. The party must find the four pieces of the medal and recover two more medals. Next, the party must explore the Necrohol of Nabudis and fight two powerful bosses before facing Chaos. It's a long journey, but well worth the trouble.

LEVEL	57	EXP	0	STEAL	Taurus Gem, Elixir, High Arcana
HP	208966	LP	60		

The Attack command is disabled in this battle, which forces the party to rely on magicks and technicks. The Chaosjets that accompany Chaos will cast Silence, so equip Rose Corsages to negate this, or set up gambits with Echo Herbs.

Make the four Chaosjets (Air, Earth, Fire, and Water) the primary targets at the start of the battle. Use Souleater to really put the hurt on them. Have two characters target a Chaosjet with Souleater while a third character restores everyone's lost HP. Using this technique, it's possible to quickly eradicate all four Chaosjets. Otherwise, use Aeroga to defeat the Earth Chaosjet and Firaga to eliminate the Water Chaosjet. The Air Chaosjet is weak to earth elements, while the Fire Chaosjet is weak to water elements, but technicks work best on them both. Additionally, you can try to hit them all with a non-elemental area-of-effect spell such as Scourge, Bio, or Scathe.

It's also important to note that Chaos will absorb Wind-based attacks! When the four Chaosjets are history, it's time to focus on Chaos. A combination of Bio and Souleater work very well against the big guy.

Necrohol of Nabudis

Side Quests

ULTIMA, THE HIGH SERAPH

The quest for Ultima takes the party back into the twisted path of The Great Crystal below Giruvegan. Begin at Way Stone VIII and trek up to the Scorpio Gate Stone. Hit the switch and go back down to Way Stone VIII, then turn right and head up to Way Stone IX.

Pass Way Stone XX, taking either the left or right path on the opposite side to reach the Sagittarius Gate Stone. Return to Sagittarius Gates I & II. You can go in either direction, but for purposes of this walkthrough, choose Gate I, which leads to Way Stone XI. Go ahead and use the stone.

Take the rising path to the Gemini Gate Stone. Flip the switch and take the next rising path. Bypass Gemini Gate I on the right and continue to Gemini Gate II. Follow either of the gateless paths beyond Gemini Gate II to Way Stone XV and use the device.

Follow the center path from Way Stone XVI up to the Libra Gate Stone. Use the switch, then backtrack to Way Stone XVI and take the path on the right to Gate Libra I, deactivate it, then continue up. Take the rising path on the left at the next platform to the Capricorn Gate Stone. Flip the switch and backtrack down, then go right to return to Way Stone XVI. Use the sinking path on the opposite side to find Gate Capricorn I and the Virgo Gate Stone. Toss the switch on the stone and backtrack to Way Stone XVI again. Use the center path to go to the next platform, then take the left or right path to reach Gate Virgo I or II. Pass through the gate and go to Way Stone XVII to reach the last area. Save your game at the Save Crystal just ahead. The center path leads to Ultima!

LEVEL	63	EXP	0	STEAL	Virgo Gem, High Arcana, Megalixir
HP	258001	LP	65		

Dispel Ultima at the start of the battle. Her attack pattern is simple, as she uses physical attacks at close range that cause moderate damage. This is accompanied by an occasional blast of Holyja. The Holyja magick causes heavy holy damage, so White Masks are a huge help since they absorb holy damage. Holyja sometimes leaves a Reverse status on characters, so beware of group heals. One Curaja could wipe out the entire party. Keep healing manually or be ready to interrupt any heals after a Holyja attack.

The real challenge in this battle is the shifting battle conditions. It begins with HP Sap, then switches between MP Sap, No Attack, No Magick, No Technicks, No Items, Magnetic Field, and then it repeats from HP Sap. Keep these conditions in mind and prepare for them. Make sure everyone has plenty of HP before the HP Sap hits. Use a Quickening prior to every MP Sap field (since it makes MP worthless) and prepare to heal with items. Recover MP quickly when the No Attack field begins and heal the entire party. Utilize physical attacks and rely on items to heal while the No Magick field is in effect. The No Technicks battle condition really shouldn't be a problem, while the No Items condition is a blessing and a great opportunity to cause serious damage to Ultima. The Magnetic Field reduces damage and slows down the party down. Get everyone healed at this time and prepare to start the loop back at the beginning.

When Ultima is low on health, she begins using a beam attack that causes massive damage to one character. This is very difficult to overcome. Try to finish her off before she overwhelms your party.

Zertinan Caverns

ZODIARK, KEEPER OF PRECEPTS

Talk to Geomancer Yugelu in Jahara after the party finds at least 10 Espers. Yugelu then unlocks the path within the Henne Mines that leads to Zodiark. The path is just north of the Staging Shaft in the Ore Separation room. The crystal in the Staging Shaft is the closest save point to Zodiark, so use it! The path to Zodiark is very difficult and tricky to navigate. Keep Float on the party at all times to avoid traps.

Secret Stash

Check the west end of the middle path in the Phase 2 Dig area to find a note on the ground. The note makes mention of a hidden stash somewhere in Henne Mines. The stash is at the north end of the Special Charter Shaft in the longest shaft visible on the area map.

LEVEL	66	EXP	0	STEAL	Serpentarius, High Arcana, Megalixir
HP	336847	LP	70		

Henne Mines

To prepare for this fight, ensure everyone has a Black Mask equipped. Enter the battle with only one character and everyone else in reserve. The reason for this is that Zodiark always begins the fight with Darkja and there's no reason to expose the entire party to it. Let one character take the hit, then bring two more characters into the battle.

Zodiark uses Reflect, Protect, Shell, and Haste. Dispel them immediately and be ready to Dispel them again throughout the entire battle.

The boss's big attack is Darkja, which it uses frequently. This powerful attack causes lots of dark damage and it has a good chance of instantly killing its victims. This attack will wipe out your party on occasion. There's simply no way to avoid it, but Black Masks can help.

The trick in this fight involves how you react and recover after Darkja is used. Bring in the reserves and immediately restore the downed allies with Phoenix Downs or Arise. The reserve members can put up a fight for a bit, but chances are they won't be as powerful as the primary party and will quickly fall. Switch in the main party and immediately restore the reserve party with Phoenix Downs (expect to do this often). It becomes even more critical near the end of the battle when Zodiark's attacks are extremely powerful and Darkja isn't the only threat. Keep the party moving and a fair distance from each other to prevent Scathe from hitting all of your characters.

The first half of the fight is pretty simple. Cast Berserk and Bravery on a physical attack specialist and watch him go to work. If you have weapons with the holy element, be sure to use them for now. A powerful fighter can hit for 9999 HP of damage at high speed with Haste and Berserk in play.

The fight gets complicated when Zodiark loses about half of its HP. When this occurs, Zodiark begins casting a Magick Shield that makes it immune to magick. Keep pounding away with physical attacks for the time being. Try to keep Zodiark dispelled, but the Magick Shield occasionally makes this impossible.

As the boss' health starts creeping closer to one-fourth of its total, Zodiark will start to use a skill called Shift which changes its elemental weakness. Replace your holy element weapons with non-elemental weapons. This is also your queue to start a Quickening. You can end the fight here with a large Quickening chain and save yourself some grief with what's coming after Shift. If the Quickening doesn't finish Zodiark off, or if you miss your window, it uses a Paling and a Magick Shield. This means that it will often be completely invulnerable. While the Magick Shield goes down for extended periods, the Paling only ever goes down for a second or less. After this point, physical attacks against Zodiark are not an option and it has only one randomly changing elemental weakness. What to do? Time to put Scathe and the other non-elemental spells to good use. Although Flare also works, avoid using it due to its significant recovery time. One thing you need to be extremely careful about is Reflect. Dispel it off of Zodiark as soon as he casts it. If the Magick Shield is up while it has the Reflect status, sit back and heal up while you wait it out. You don't want your own Scathe wiping out your party.

As the boss's HP gets lower, Zodiark's attacks grow faster and more powerful. It also casts Darkja much more often. The fight really gets dangerous when the boss's HP is almost gone. Take it slow and steady and he will go down eventually.

Cactaur Family

DALMASCA ESTERSAND

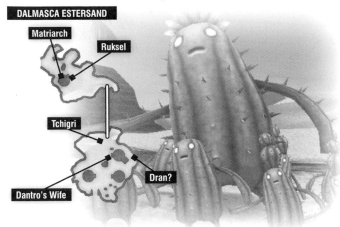

Matriarch
Ruksel
Tchigri
Dran?
Dantro's Wife

WHEN IT'S AVAILABLE

This event is available after receiving the Dawn Shard.

You can start this event after completing the Dalmasca's Desert Bloom hunt and delivering the Cactus Flower to Dantro's Wife in South Bank Village (Dalmasca Estersand). Tchigri in South Bank Village says his dad, the ferry's pilot, is missing. The Village Elder requests that Vaan go with the boy to the North Bank Village to ensure his safety.

Speak to Ruksel at the North Bank Village to make a new Flowering Cactoid appear. The cactoid's eldest son, Dran, is missing. The party automatically returns to the South Bank.

Speak to Dantro's Wife about the Cactus Flower, then check behind her hut to find a flower in the ground marked "Dran?" and inspect it. Return Dran to the Matriarch by speaking with Tchigri.

Dantro gives the party **1000 gil** and some **Wyrmfire Shot**. The ferry is also in running order now, so the party can cross the river at any time.

Bhujerban Madhu

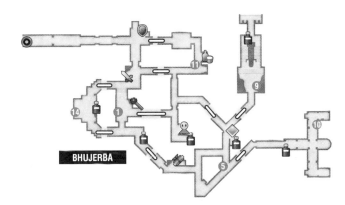

BHUJERBA

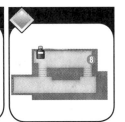

WHEN IT'S AVAILABLE

This event is available after receiving the Dawn Shard.

A famous liquor known as **Bhujerban Madhu** is in short supply. Fans of the popular drink are willing to pay handsomely for a bottle (1000 gil). There are 14 bottles of Bhujerban Madhu hidden throughout the city; one bottle is concealed in every section of the city. There is also a willing buyer somewhere in the same area where a bottle is located. You can sell the bottles to any of the buyers in any order. You can also sell any number of bottles to the same buyer. Here's a list of the bottles and buyers in each section of the city.

① BHUJERBAN AERODOME

Found on a stack of luggage at one end of the hall.

Bhujerban man sitting on the rail next to an Imperial across from the luggage.

② RITHIL'S PROTECTIVES

Inside the cabinet next to the counter.

The elderly Shop Clerk standing by the counter.

③ TARGE'S ARMS

Check between the weapon cases on the upper level.

Lady on the lower level talking to a sitting man.

④ MAIT'S MAGICKS

Sitting amongst the bottles and vases in the raised portion of the shop.

The Bhujerban Guru standing next to the table where the bottle is found.

Side Quests

⑤ TRAVICA WAY

Found on the street next to a Street Kid and young man on the southeast end

Bhujerban leaning on the wall across from Mait's Magicks

⑥ KHUS SKYGROUNDS

On the box with a moogle next to the Street Vendor

Woman leaning on the outside wall across from the Street Vendor.

⑦ CLIO'S TECHNICKS

Inside a box between the counter and the stairs.

Shop Clerk standing in the middle of the main aisle.

⑧ BASHKETI'S GAMBITS

On a bookcase on the upper level.

Seeq Shop Clerk on the upper level.

⑨ MINER'S END

Resting on the crates next to Bashketi's Gambits.

Lhusu Miner at the southeast end of the area talking to a moogle.

⑩ THE CLOUDBORNE

Sitting on the edge of the table closest to the bar.

Magu who is sitting between the tavern's exits.

⑪ THE STARAS RESIDENCE

Hidden between the dressers to the right of the entrance.

Niray who is standing in the middle of the home. Note that you cannot sell the Bhujerban Madhu to Niray until you have completed the Antlion hunt.

⑫ CLOUDBORNE ROW

On the stacked boxes in the alley below the Staras Residence.

Cloudborne Patron across the street from The Cloudborne.

⑬ KAFF TERRACE

Next to the blue Seeq at the top of the stairs.

Bhujerban lady standing near the edge after turning left from the base of the stairs.

⑭ LHUSU SQUARE

On the edge of the pool before the entrance to Lhusu Mines.

The miners next to the Seeq Street Vendor at the top of the stairs.

Earth Tyrant Extermination

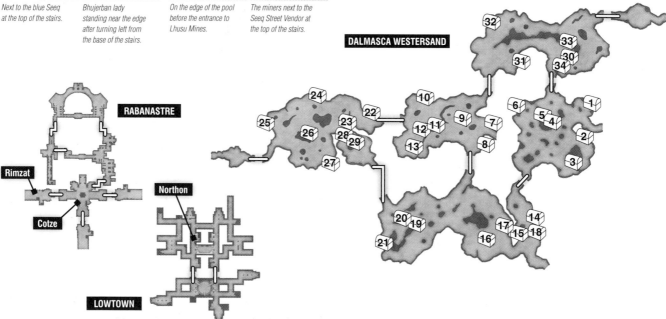

DALMASCA WESTERSAND

RABANASTRE

Rimzat

Cotze

Northon

LOWTOWN

No.	App.%	gil %	If gil	Normal 50%	Normal 50%	gil	w/Diamond Armlet Equip. 90%	w/Diamond Armlet Equip. 10%
1	65%	30%	~110	Potion	Onion Arrow	~1000	Knot of Rust	Hi-Ether
2	65%	30%	~120	Potion	Water Mote	~1000	Knot of Rust	Hi-Ether
3	65%	50%	~130	Potion	Potion	~1000	Knot of Rust	Hi-Ether
4	50%	100%	10	--	--	50	--	--
5	65%	30%	~150	Potion	Onion Arrow	~1000	Knot of Rust	Hi-Ether
6	65%	30%	~160	Potion	Phoenix Down	~1000	Knot of Rust	Balance Mote
7	70%	30%	~70	Potion	Remedy	~500	Knot of Rust	Hi-Ether
8	70%	30%	~70	Hi-Potion	Hi-Potion	~500	Knot of Rust	Hi-Ether
9	70%	30%	~70	Potion	Holy Mote	~500	Knot of Rust	Hastega Mote
10	70%	30%	~70	Potion	Ether	~500	Knot of Rust	Hi-Ether
11	70%	30%	~70	Potion	Remedy	~500	Knot of Rust	Hi-Ether
12	70%	30%	~70	Hi-Potion	Onion Shot	~500	Knot of Rust	Hi-Ether
13	70%	30%	~70	Hi-Potion	Hi-Potion	~500	Knot of Rust	Elixir
14	70%	25%	~600	Remedy	Onion Bolts	~2000	Knot of Rust	Hastega Mote
15	50%	35%	~400	Potion	Hastega Mote	~1600	Knot of Rust	Elixir
16	65%	35%	~80	Hi-Potion	Hi-Potion	~1600	Knot of Rust	Hi-Ether
17	65%	35%	~80	Potion	Ether	~500	Knot of Rust	Hi-Ether

No.	App.%	gil %	If gil	Normal 50%	Normal 50%	gil	w/Diamond Armlet Equip. 90%	w/Diamond Armlet Equip. 10%
18	65%	35%	~80	Potion	Remedy	~500	Knot of Rust	Hi-Ether
19	65%	35%	~80	Hi-Potion	Phoenix Down	~500	Knot of Rust	Hi-Ether
20	65%	35%	~80	Potion	Remedy	~500	Knot of Rust	Hi-Ether
21	70%	30%	~100	Hi-Potion	Ether	~500	Knot of Rust	Elixir
22	68%	30%	~90	Hi-Potion	Hi-Potion	~500	Knot of Rust	Hi-Ether
23	68%	30%	~90	Hi-Potion	Hi-Potion	~500	Knot of Rust	Elixir
24	68%	30%	~90	Potion	Remedy	~500	Knot of Rust	Hi-Ether
25	68%	30%	~90	Potion	Ether	~500	Knot of Rust	Hi-Ether
26	68%	30%	~90	Potion	Remedy	~500	Knot of Rust	Hi-Ether
27	68%	30%	~90	Hi-Potion	Phoenix Down	~500	Knot of Rust	Hi-Ether
28	68%	30%	~350	Potion	Remedy	~2000	Knot of Rust	Elixir
29	68%	30%	~90	Potion	Phoenix Down	~2000	Knot of Rust	Elixir
30	65%	30%	~100	Potion	Balance Mote	~1000	Knot of Rust	Holy Mote
31	65%	30%	~100	Potion	Onion Shot	~1000	Knot of Rust	Holy Mote
32	65%	30%	~120	Potion	Ether	~1000	Knot of Rust	Holy Mote
33	65%	30%	~200	Potion	Potion	~1000	Knot of Rust	Hi-Ether
34	65%	30%	~100	Potion	Echo Herbs	~1000	Knot of Rust	X-Potion

WHEN IT'S AVAILABLE

This event is available after receiving the Dawn Shard.

Find a creature named Rimzat at Rabanastre's Westgate. He was sent from Archadia to study the sandstorms of the Dalmasca Westersand, but the storms' violence makes such study impossible. He requests that the party gather information within Rabanastre on his behalf.

Check the Southern Plaza for a man named Cotze, who is sitting atop the fountain. Speak to him to learn about a man named Northon near Storehouse 5 in Lowtown.

Locate Northon in the North Sprawl of Lowtown. He claims that you need a **Windvane** to get through the storms. The Windvane that Northon and Cotze once used was split into two pieces; Northon's half is in a dead-end section of the Westersand with Giant Dynast Cactuses.

The Dynast-Cactoids are found in the secluded section of the Windtrace Dunes, which is accessible from Shimmering Horizons. Inspect the Dynast-Cactoids in the area to find the **Wind Globe**.

Return to the West Gate and speak to Northon, Cotze and Rimzat. They mention a strange egg in the desert and give the party a completed Windvane. Travel to the Wyrm's Nest in Dalmasca Westersand to face the Earth Tyrant.

EARTH TYRANT

LEV	30	HP	70982	EXP	0		LP	21
STEAL	Hi Potion, Tyrant Hide, Tyrant Bone							

Make sure the party leader has Decoy and a shield equipped to block most of the Earth Tyrant's attacks. Try to keep the other characters back to avoid the boss's area attacks. Immediately hit the boss with Slow to give the party an advantage. A slow physical assault works very well in this fight. The boss's defense increases as it nears defeat, so a little magick can help finish the battle.

July the Streetear 🎐

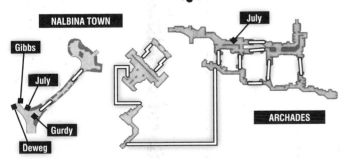

NALBINA TOWN

July · Gibbs · July · Gurdy · Deweg · ARCHADES

WHEN IT'S AVAILABLE

This event is available after receiving the Dawn Shard. You must complete the first half of the event, the portion in Nalbina, before the story moves to the Mosphoran Highwaste. You cannot complete the event until the party visits Archades.

Two imperials stand guard in Nalbina Town at West Barbican, blocking access to the Mosphoran Highwaste. A woman, July, spies on them from nearby. Approach the imperials to discover Gibbs doesn't like chocobos.

Cross the area and rent a chocobo from Gurdy for 800 gil. Ride the chocobo over to Gibbs and Deweg. July thanks the party for their intervention and asks them to visit her in Archades later.

Visit Charlotte's Magickery in the Molberry district of Archades when the area opens up. July then presents the party with a **Salamand Halcyon** for their assistance earlier.

Viera Rendezvous 🎐

WHEN IT'S AVAILABLE

This event is available after speaking with the Garif Elder.

Viera's 2nd position · Yamoora's Gambits · Viera's 3rd position · Viera's 1st position · Lovestruck Man

RABANASTRE

A Viera at Rabanastre's Southgate, near the chocobo stable, is seeking her soul mate. Talk to her and she walks off into the city.

Follow her into the Southern Plaza and look for a Lovestruck Man at the fountain. Speak to him and he mentions seeing the Viera, who was headed to East End.

Actually, she has wandered over to Yamoora's Gambits in North End. Find her there (Wandering Viera) and speak with her again. She mentions getting a drink and leaves the shop.

Travel back to The Sandsea in East End and look for her on the second floor. Speak to her again and she asks if you might know of someone who feels strongly for her.

Return to the Southern Plaza and speak to the Lovestruck Man again. Agree to help him, return to The Sandsea, and tell the Viera about the man's feelings.

Run back to the Southern Plaza once more and look for the duo near the fountain. Speak with them to receive a **Loxley Bow** and **two Hi-Potions**.

Nabreus's Medal 🎐

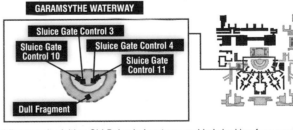

GARAMSYTHE WATERWAY

Sluice Gate Control 3 · Sluice Gate Control 10 · Sluice Gate Control 4 · Sluice Gate Control 11 · Dull Fragment

Roh'kenmou is visiting Old Dalan in Lowtown and he's looking for a medallion that was split into four parts. Old Dalan has one, which he automatically returns to the man. The second part was given to another person, while the third and fourth parts were hidden.

THE DULL FRAGMENT

The man who had the object and split it in four parts used to live in the North Sprawl, but the house is vacant now. Go to the North Sprawl and enter the Private Residence where Deeg was hiding (Deeg from the Waterway Haunting hunt) and speak to him. Note that you actually need to complete the Waterway Haunting hunt before you can speak to him. He mentions a letter on the table from the previous owner. Read the **Dusty Letter** to learn that a valuable item was split into four pieces and hidden. The location of the first piece is mentioned in the note: "Stop the water's flow, then lose it once more. East Southeast East Southwest Southeast I pray that it rest there undisturbed."

Talk to Deeg again. He mentions the letter sounds like it's talking about the waterway gates, but they require a key. He remembers a moogle running around talking about a key. The moogle in question is Sorbet (petitioner for the Lost in the Pudding hunt), who is at the Westgate. Take her hunt and defeat the beast to recover the key.

Go to the Central Waterway Control area in Garamsythe Waterway. Open all of the gates so that the lights are off. Begin by closing gates #11 and #4, then open gate #11 and shut gate #3. Next, open gate #4, then walk around to #3 gate and look on the ground to find a "Shiny Object" that is the **Dull Fragment**.

THE BLACKENED FRAGMENT

The third piece is a reward for successfully completing the Crime and Punishment hunt. Speak to Montblanc to obtain the hunt and complete it to acquire the **Blackened Fragment** from Samal.

THE GRIMY FRAGMENT

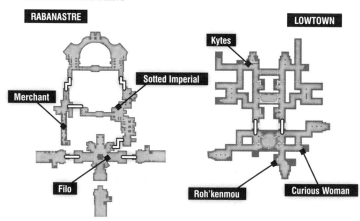

Travel to the Muted Scarp in the Nabreus Deadlands and speak to Ma'kleou about who he is and why he's there. Return to Rabanastre and Lowtown and speak to Roh'kenmou in Old Dalan's Place (this step may be skipped if you have already spoken to Roh'kenmou). Find Filo in the southeast corner of Lowtown's South Sprawl and speak to her. She mentions the city streets are the only place they haven't checked up to this point.

Go to Rabanastre's Southern Plaza and speak to the Curious Woman at the fountain. Head to the Muthru Bazaar and speak to the two "Merchants." One of the merchants mentions selling a necklace to an Imperial.

Cross the city to the East End and visit Yugri's Magicks. Speak to the Sotted Imperial near the door and tell him about the woman at the fountain. She isn't there, so go to Lowtown's North Sprawl and find Kytes near Warehouse #5. Locate Filo at the southeast corner of the South Sprawl and ask to see the woman. Return to Yugri's Magicks and speak with the Sotted Imperial again to receive the **Grimy Fragment**.

THE MOONSILVER MEDALLION

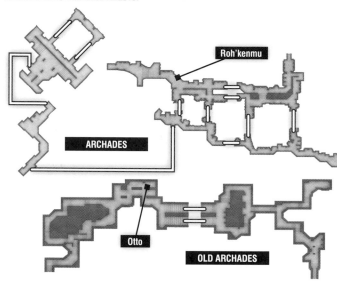

Return all three pieces to Roh'kenmou in Old Dalan's Place within Lowtown's South Sprawl. He instructs Vaan to visit Nabudis later. Travel to Archades and Charlotte's Magickery in Molberry. Speak to Roh'kenmu about the Moonsilver Medallion.

Go into Old Archades and find Otto in the northeast corner of the Alley of Muted Sighs. He turns over the **Moonsilver Medallion**. Return to Charlotte's Magickery and hand the medallion over to Roh'kenmu.

THE MEDALLION OF MIGHT

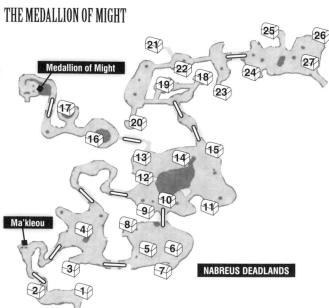

TREASURE TABLE				Normal		w/Diamond Armlet Equip.		
No.	App.%	gil %	If gil	50%	50%	gil	90%	10%
1	80%	15%	~1000	Red Fang	Red Fang	~3000	Knot of Rust	X-Potion
2	80%	15%	~1000	Blue Fang	Blue Fang	~3000	Knot of Rust	X-Potion
3	80%	70%	~1000	Red Fang	Golden Amulet	~3000	Knot of Rust	X-Potion
4	80%	15%	~1000	Blue Fang	Blue Fang	~3000	Knot of Rust	X-Potion
5	80%	15%	~1000	Blue Fang	Blue Fang	~3000	Knot of Rust	X-Potion
6	80%	15%	~1000	Blue Fang	Blue Fang	~3000	Knot of Rust	X-Potion
7	80%	15%	~1000	Red Fang	Elixir	~3000	Knot of Rust	X-Potion
8	80%	15%	~1000	White Fang	White Fang	~3000	Knot of Rust	X-Potion
9	80%	15%	~1000	Blue Fang	Blue Fang	~3000	Knot of Rust	X-Potion
10	80%	15%	~1000	White Fang	White Fang	~3000	Knot of Rust	X-Potion
11	80%	15%	~1000	Blue Fang	Blue Fang	~3000	Knot of Rust	X-Potion
12	80%	15%	~1000	Red Fang	Red Fang	~3000	Knot of Rust	X-Potion
13	80%	15%	~1000	Blue Fang	Blue Fang	~3000	Knot of Rust	X-Potion
14	75%	45%	~1000	Red Fang	Nishijin Belt	~3000	Knot of Rust	X-Potion
15	80%	15%	~1000	White Fang	Red Fang	~3000	Knot of Rust	X-Potion
16	80%	15%	~1000	Red Fang	Red Fang	~3000	Knot of Rust	X-Potion
17	80%	15%	~1000	White Fang	White Fang	~3000	Knot of Rust	X-Potion
18	80%	15%	~1000	Red Fang	Red Fang	~3000	Knot of Rust	X-Potion
19	60%	60%	~1000	White Fang	Gillie Boots	~3000	Knot of Rust	X-Potion
20	80%	15%	~1000	White Fang	White Fang	~3000	Knot of Rust	X-Potion
21	80%	15%	~1000	Red Fang	Red Fang	~3000	Knot of Rust	X-Potion
22	80%	15%	~1000	White Fang	Blue Fang	~3000	Knot of Rust	X-Potion
23	80%	15%	~1000	Red Fang	Red Fang	~3000	Knot of Rust	X-Potion
24	80%	15%	~1000	Blue Fang	Blue Fang	~3000	Knot of Rust	X-Potion
25	80%	15%	~1000	Red Fang	Red Fang	~3000	Knot of Rust	X-Potion
26	80%	15%	~1000	Blue Fang	Blue Fang	~3000	Knot of Rust	X-Potion
27	80%	15%	~1000	White Fang	White Fang	~3000	Knot of Rust	X-Potion

Return to the Muted Scarp in the Nabreus Deadlands and talk to Ma'kleou once more. He mentions the three fell beasts (Humbaba, Fury, and Chaos) and the Medallion of Might, which is in a shrine found at the peak of Overlooking Eternity. Use the secret path just to the right of the northwest corner of the Slumbermead to reach Fog Mutters and Overlooking Eternity. Fight through the undead to reach the shrine and climb the steps to the center. Ma'kleou presents the party with the **Medallion of Bravery, Medallion of Love**, and the **Lusterless Medallion**.

THE NECROHOL OF NABUDIS

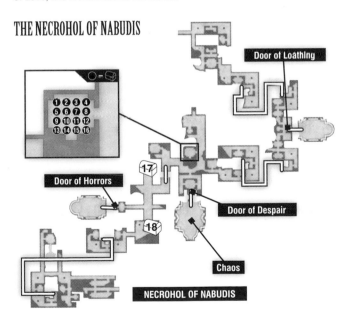

NECROHOL OF NABUDIS

TREASURE TABLE				Normal		w/Diamond Armlet Equip.		
No.	App.%	gil %	If gil	50%	50%	gil	90%	10%
1	100%	0%	--	Knot of Rust	Knot of Rust	--	~3000	Dark Matter
2	100%	0%	--	Knot of Rust	Knot of Rust	--	Dark Matter	Dark Matter
3	100%	0%	--	Knot of Rust	Knot of Rust	--	Dark Matter	Dark Matter
4	100%	0%	--	Knot of Rust	Knot of Rust	--	Dark Matter	Dark Matter
5	100%	0%	--	Knot of Rust	Knot of Rust	--	Dark Matter	Dark Matter
6	100%	0%	--	Knot of Rust	Knot of Rust	--	Dark Matter	Dark Matter
7	100%	0%	--	Knot of Rust	Knot of Rust	--	Dark Matter	Dark Matter
8	100%	0%	--	Knot of Rust	Knot of Rust	--	Dark Matter	Dark Matter
9	100%	0%	--	Knot of Rust	Knot of Rust	--	Dark Matter	Dark Matter
10	100%	0%	--	Knot of Rust	Knot of Rust	--	Dark Matter	Dark Matter
11	100%	0%	--	Knot of Rust	Knot of Rust	--	Dark Matter	Dark Matter
12	100%	0%	--	Zodiac Spear	Zodiac Spear	--	Dark Matter	Dark Matter
13	100%	0%	--	Knot of Rust	Knot of Rust	--	Dark Matter	Dark Matter
14	100%	0%	--	Knot of Rust	Knot of Rust	--	Dark Matter	Dark Matter
15	100%	0%	--	Knot of Rust	Knot of Rust	--	Dark Matter	Dark Matter
16	100%	0%	--	Knot of Rust	Knot of Rust	--	Dark Matter	Dark Matter
17	50%	60%	~600	Knot of Rust	Defender	~1000	Dark Matter	Dark Matter
18	50%	10%	~2000	Knot of Rust	Hi-Ether	~3000	Dark Matter	Dark Matter

Proceed through the Nabreus Deadlands to the Field of the Fallen Lord in the northeast. Enter the Necrohol of Nabudis from this point. There are three chambers within the dungeon that contain bosses. Each chamber can only be unlocked with a particular medallion.

THE MEDALLION OF LOVE & THE DOOR OF LOATHING

Fight past the beasts within the Necrohol of Nabudis to the Hall of the Ivory Covenant. Use the Medallion of Love on the Door of Loathing in the center of the hall to battle Fury.

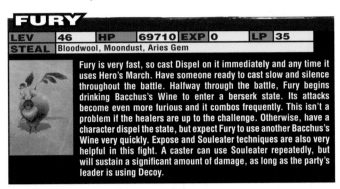

FURY

LEV	46	HP	69710	EXP	0	LP	35

STEAL: Bloodwool, Moondust, Aries Gem

Fury is very fast, so cast Dispel on it immediately and any time it uses Hero's March. Have someone ready to cast slow and silence throughout the battle. Halfway through the battle, Fury begins drinking Bacchus's Wine to enter a berserk state. Its attacks become even more furious and it combos frequently. This isn't a problem if the healers are up to the challenge. Otherwise, have a character dispel the state, but expect Fury to use another Bacchus's Wine very quickly. Expose and Souleater techniques are also very helpful in this fight. A caster can use Souleater repeatedly, but will sustain a significant amount of damage, as long as the party's leader is using Decoy.

THE MEDALLION OF BRAVERY & THE DOOR OF HORRORS

The next stop is the Cloister of Distant Song on the southwest side of Necrohol of Nabudis. Unlock the Door of Horrors with the Medallion of Bravery to battle the Humbaba Mistant.

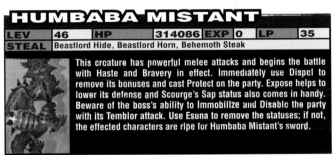

HUMBABA MISTANT

LEV	46	HP	314086	EXP	0	LP	35

STEAL: Beastlord Hide, Beastlord Horn, Behemoth Steak

This creature has powerful melee attacks and begins the battle with Haste and Bravery in effect. Immediately use Dispel to remove its bonuses and cast Protect on the party. Expose helps to lower its defense and Scourge's Sap status also comes in handy. Beware of the boss's ability to Immobilize and Disable the party with its Temblor attack. Use Esuna to remove the statuses; if not, the effected characters are ripe for Humbaba Mistant's sword.

THE MEDALLION OF MIGHT & THE DOOR OF DESPAIR

After defeating both foes, the party obtains a map of the Necrohol of Nabudis and the Lusterless Medallion transforms into the **Medallion of Might**. Go to the Cloister of the Highborn in the center of the dungeon and use the Medallion of Might on the Door of Despair to face the esper Chaos.

THE HIDDEN MERCHANT

There's a merchant hiding in a secret room in the northwest corner of the Hall of Effulgent Light. Check the southeast corner of the room to find his hiding spot.

Hunt Club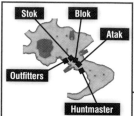

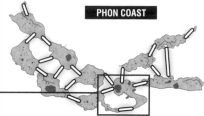

Stok Blok
Atak
Outfitters
Huntmaster

PHON COAST

WHEN IT'S AVAILABLE

This event is not available until after you complete Archades. However, you can't complete it until the *Strahl* becomes available for free travel around the world.

Talk to the Huntmaster at the Phon Coast Hunters' Camp after finishing up Archades. He offers to let Vaan join the Hunt Club if he can prove himself with one small task. The party must track down a Thalassinon on the Vaddu Strand.

The Vaddu Strand is east of the Hunters' Camp. The only way to spot the prey is to look for it from a high elevation. Go to the east end of the Vaddu Strand and climb the small ledge that overlooks the beach. Remain at the peak until the Thalassinon appears. Defeat it and return the **Shelled Trophy** to the Huntmaster.

The Huntmaster orders Vaan to speak to one of the three brothers (formerly Shady Bangaas). Agree to hunt before speaking to the Huntmaster again.

The objective of this event is to find 30 rare monsters located around the world and defeat them. Vaan can then trade their trophies to Atak, Stok, and Blok to unlock items in the Shifty-Eyed Merchant's store. The following section lists the monsters and their locations.

No. 01 ASPIDOCHELON

LV 42~43

HP 63226~63546
DERIVATION Adamantitan
RARITY ☆☆☆☆☆
LOCATION Cerobi Steppe
CONDITION There's a 40% chance for it to appear in the Feddik River area within Cerobi Steppe
STEAL Scarletite
DROP Adamantine Trophy

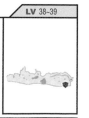

No. 02 THALASSINON

LV 38~39

HP 59868~60188
DERIVATION Emeralditan
RARITY ☆☆☆☆☆
LOCATION Phon Coast
CONDITION Wait at the highest point on the eastern ledge within the Vaddu Strand until the enemy appears on the beach below.
STEAL Adamantite
DROP Shelled Trophy

No. 04 KILLBUG

LV 44~45

HP 28976~29216
DERIVATION Mimic
RARITY ☆☆☆☆☆
LOCATION Ozmone Plain/The Switchback
CONDITION Found on the north edge between exit points near the entrance to Zertinan Caverns
STEAL Knot of Rust
DROP Metallic Trophy

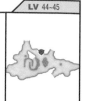

No. 05 GAVIAL

LV 46~47

HP 80511~80871
DERIVATION Baritine Croc
RARITY ☆☆☆☆☆
LOCATION Garamsythe Waterway/No. 10 Channel
CONDITION Appears in the lower section of the No. 10 Channel in the Garamsythe Waterway. Close the No.10 sluice gate, then explore the large room at the west end of the lower section. Gavial appears behind the party at the east end.
STEAL Antarctic Wind
DROP Fur-scaled Trophy

No. 07 KAISER WOLF

LV 41~42

HP 19455~19775
DERIVATION Silver Lobo
RARITY ☆☆☆★★
LOCATION Dalmasca Westersand/Corridor of Sand
CONDITION There's a 40% chance for it to appear in the eastern part of the Corridor of Sand area in the Dalmasca Westersand. However, it only appears after the party defeats the Lindbur Wolf (another rare creature) found in the small valley on the east end of Shimmering Horizons.
STEAL Throat Wolf Blood
DROP Fanged Trophy

No. 09 DREADGUARD

LV 46~47

HP 35074~35394
DERIVATION Mirrorknight
RARITY ☆☆☆☆☆
LOCATION The Feywood/Walk of Dancing Shadow
CONDITION There's a 40% chance for it to appear in the Walk of Dancing Shadow section of the Feywood.
STEAL Mirror Scale
DROP Feathered Trophy

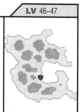

No. 15 RAGECLAW

LV 36~37

HP 39586~39696
DERIVATION Scythe Mantis
RARITY ☆☆☆★★
LOCATION Salikawood/Piebald Path
CONDITION Wait on Piebald Path in the Salikawood for at least one minute without killing anything. This forces Rageclaw to appear from the west or south exit of that area; in essence, it will appear from the exit opposite of where the player entered Piebald Path.
STEAL Sickle-Blade
DROP Sickle Trophy

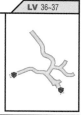

No. 19 GRIMALKIN

LV 38~39

HP 23101~23421
DERIVATION Coeurl
RARITY ☆☆☆☆☆
LOCATION Tchita Uplands/Uazcuff Hills
CONDITION Appears randomly among Coeurls (10% chance).
STEAL Coeurl Whisker
DROP Whiskered Trophy

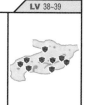

No. 29 NAZARNIR

LV 45~46

HP 39652~39972
DERIVATION Sleipnir
RARITY ☆☆☆☆☆
LOCATION Giza Plains/Starfall Field
CONDITION There's a 40% chance for it to appear in Giza Plain's Starfall Field during The Dry.
STEAL Destrier Mane
DROP Maned Trophy

No.30 VICTANIR
LV 46~47

HP 55114~55434
DERIVATION Shadonir
RARITY ☆☆☆☆☆
LOCATION Nam-Yensa Sandsea/Yellow Sands
CONDITION There's a 40% chance that it will appear in the Yellow Sands portion of Nam-Yensa Sandsea.
STEAL Wargod's Band
DROP Maverick Trophy

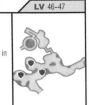

No.35 BULL CHOCOBO
LV 47~48

HP 43263~43383
DERIVATION Chocobo
RARITY ☆☆☆☆☆
LOCATION Ogir-Yensa Sandsea/South Tank Approach
CONDITION There's a 40% chance for it to appear in the South Tank Approach section of the Ogir-Yensa Sandsea.
STEAL Hi-Ether
DROP Beaked Trophy

No.36 SKULLASH
LV 37~38

HP 51065~51745
DERIVATION Cataract Aevis
RARITY ☆☆☆☆☆
LOCATION Phon Coast/Cape Tialan
CONDITION Appears randomly among the Pyrolisks (40% chance).
STEAL Charger Barding
DROP Clawed Trophy

No.37 MYATH
LV 42~43

HP 51065~51745
DERIVATION Dragon Lich
RARITY ☆★★★★
LOCATION Stilshrine of Miriam/Ward of Velitation
CONDITION Eliminate the three Dragon Aevis foes guarding the Ward of Velitation. Exit the room and reenter it to find Myath.
STEAL Leo Gem
DROP Eternal Trophy

No.42 ANUBYS
LV 38~39

HP 19194~19314
DERIVATION Abysteel
RARITY ☆★★★★
LOCATION Sochen Cave Palace
CONDITION It appears in the Mirror of the Soul secret room within the Sochen Cave Palace. To open the door to the room, walk the clockwise spiral through Destiny's March, Falls of Time, and Mirror of the Soul starting at the east entrance into the Falls of Time from Destiny's March.
STEAL Vampyr Fang
DROP Ensanguined Trophy

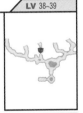

No.46 MELT
LV 48~49

HP 61481~61711
DERIVATION Hecteyes
RARITY ☆☆☆☆☆
LOCATION Henne Mines/Pithead Junction B
CONDITION There's a 50% chance that it will appear in Pithead Junction B within the Henne Mines after you activate the switch inside the room.
STEAL Hastega Mote
DROP Slimy Trophy

No.56 KRIS
LV 38~39

HP 47515~47755
DERIVATION Malboro
RARITY ☆☆☆☆☆
LOCATION Tchita Uplands/The Highlands
CONDITION Appears randomly among the Malboro Overkings (40% chance).
STEAL Putrid Liquid
DROP Odiferous Trophy

No.57 DHEED
LEV 49~50

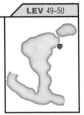

HP 77420~78100
DERIVATION Wyvern
RARITY ☆☆☆☆☆
LOCATION Mosphoran Highwaste/Skyreach Ridge
CONDITION There's a 40% chance that it will appear in the Skyreach Ridge area of the Mosphoran Highwaste. Solve the Floatweed puzzle described in the "Exodus" quest to reach the peak.
STEAL Mirage Vest
DROP Leathern Trophy

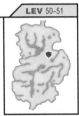

No.59 TERROR TYRANT
LEV 50~51

HP 125704~126384
DERIVATION Wild Saurian
RARITY ☆☆☆☆☆
LOCATION Dalmasca Estersand/Broken Sands
CONDITION There's a 40% chance for it to spawn in Dalmasca Estersand's Broken Sands area after you eliminate the Wild Saurian in the Yoma section.
STEAL Scathe Mote
DROP Hide-covered Trophy

No.60 ABELISK
LEV 49~50

HP 104744~105424
DERIVATION Archaeosaur
RARITY ☆☆☆☆☆
LOCATION Ridorana Cataract/Echoes from Time's Garden
CONDITION There's a 30% chance that it will materialize in the Echoes from Time's Garden area of the Ridorana Cataract
STEAL Eight-fluted Pole
DROP Reptilian Trophy

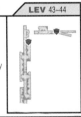

No.62 ISHTEEN
LEV 43~44

HP 34042~34222
DERIVATION Reaper
RARITY ☆☆☆☆☆
LOCATION Barheim Passage/The Zeviah Span & East-West Bypass
CONDITION The odds of Ishteen appearing increase by 2% every 10 seconds that the party spends in the East-West Bypass and Zeviah Span areas within the Barheim Passage. The spawn rate reaches 100% after 8 1/2 minutes.
STEAL Soul of Thamasa
DROP Bony Trophy

No.63 VORRES
LEV 49~50

HP 63758~63938
DERIVATION Gazer
RARITY ☆☆☆☆☆
LOCATION Necrohol of Nabudis/Hall of the Ivory Covenant
CONDITION Find a Dark Elemental in the Hall of the Ivory Covenant within the Necrohol of Nabudis. Lead the elemental from the hallway north of the Cloister of Reason to the hallway on the south side without defeating it. Vorres appears when the elemental reaches the correct spot. Dark Elementals are rare, so be patient and keep reentering the area until one appears.
STEAL Soul Powder
DROP Gravesoil Trophy

No.66 ARIOCH
LEV 47~48

HP 43380~43540
DERIVATION Gargoyle Baron
RARITY ☆☆☆☆☆
LOCATION Nabreus Deadlands/The Slumbermead
CONDITION There's a 40% chance that it will appear in the Slumbermead portion of the Nabreus Deadlands.
STEAL Sage's Ring
DROP Vengeful Trophy

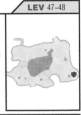

No.68 CRYSTAL KNIGHT
LEV 61~62

HP 101390~101570
DERIVATION Crusader
RARITY ☆★★★★
LOCATION The Great Crystal/A Vikaari Kanbhru Ra
CONDITION Begin at Way Stone XX and run a clockwise loop to the Sagitarius switch and back to Way Stone XX (three zones total). The Crystal Knight should be standing near the Way Stone.
STEAL Glimmering Robes
DROP Skull Trophy

No. 70 ZOMBIE LORD

LEV 38–39

HP 21593~21599
DERIVATION Forbidden
RARITY ★
LOCATION Tomb of Raithwall/Northfall Passage
CONDITION This creature appears in one of the spots in the Northfall Passage section of the Tomb of Raithwall. However, the Zombie Lord only appears after the party has been in the area between 0~29 minutes.
STEAL Close Helmet
DROP Soulless Trophy

No. 73 DISMA

LEV 59–60

HP 99286~99466
DERIVATION Zombie Warlock
RARITY ★★★★★
LOCATION Lhusu Mines/Site 5 & Site 6 South
CONDITION There's a 5% chance that it will appear in one of the marked spots in either Site 5 or Site 6 South. Explore both areas fully.
STEAL Mirage Vest
DROP Accursed Trophy

No. 74 ANCBOLDER

LEV 29–30

HP 14022~14142
DERIVATION Striker
RARITY ★★★
LOCATION Paramina Rift/Karydine Glacier
CONDITION Defeat all 12 enemies in the Karydine Glacier sector of Paramina Rift to force Ancbolder and Anchag, a trophy-less rare creature, to appear.
STEAL Forbidden Flesh
DROP Mind Trophy

No. 75 WENDICE

LEV 38–39

HP 29988~30408
DERIVATION Wendigo
RARITY ★★
LOCATION Sochen Cave Palace/Destiny's March
CONDITION Defeat all of the creatures in the four small rooms that are directly connected to the central hall of Destiny's March. This forces Wendice to appear in the center.
STEAL Gemini Gem
DROP Frigid Trophy

No. 77 BLUESANG

LEV 42–43

HP 30395~30815
DERIVATION Dullahan
RARITY ★★★
LOCATION Cerobi Steppe/Crossfield
CONDITION There's a 40% chance that it will appear in the Crossfield section of Cerobi Steppe.
STEAL Damascus Steel
DROP Cruel Trophy

No. 78 AVENGER

LEV 61~62

HP 105618~106038
DERIVATION Bune
RARITY ★
LOCATION Pharos – Second Ascent/Station of Ascension
CONDITION There's a 40% that it will appear in the Station of Ascension (63F) portion of Pharos - Second Ascent.
STEAL Muramasa
DROP Vile Trophy

No. 79 ALTECI

LEV 41~42

HP 52281~52701
DERIVATION Behemoth
RARITY ★★
LOCATION Zertinan Caverns/The Undershore
CONDITION Defeat at least 11 Mallicants in a row within The Undershore, then step out and reenter the area to trigger Alteci's appearance.
STEAL Behemoth Steak
DROP Fell Trophy

80 RARE MONSTERS!?

There are indeed 80 rare monsters scattered around the world in *FINAL FANTASY XII*. However, only 30 of those rare monsters pertain to this event. Refer to the bestiary to find the other 50 foes. Normal rare monsters reappear each time you meet the appropriate conditions. The 30 rare monsters that appear during this event only appear while the event is in progress and never reappear once you claim their trophy.

ATAK, BLOK, & STOK

When you collect trophies, take them back to the Phon Coast and turn them over to Atak, Blok, or Stok. Upon doing so, the bangaas add items to the Shifty-Eyed Man's store. There are only 30 trophies in the game, so it will be very difficult to claim all of the potential rewards from this event. Refer to the lists below to determine which bangaa you should surrender the trophies to ahead of time.

ATAK (WEAPON PROCURER)

TROPHIES	ITEM UNLOCKED	COST
1	Kogarasumaru	5040 gil
5	Obelisk	6750 gil
10	Murasame	7650 gil
15	Diamond Sword	11250 gil
20	Deathbringer	14400 gil
25	Gastrophetes	18900 gil
30	Gungnir	25500 gil

BLOK (PROTECTIVES PROCURER)

TROPHIES	ITEM UNLOCKED	COST
1	Demon Mail	4410 gil
5	Diamond Armor	6300 gil
10	Mirror Mail	7290 gil
15	Gaia Gear	8370 gil
20	Dragon Mail	11250 gil
25	Magepower Shishak	13500 gil
30	Maximillian	25500 gil

STOK (SUNDRIES PROCURER)

TROPHIES	ITEM UNLOCKED	COST
1	Thief's Cuffs	2700 gil
5	Steel Poleyns	900 gil
10	Winged Boots	450 gil
15	Indigo Pendant	4500 gil
20	Diamond Armlet	18000 gil
25	Reflectga Mote	270 gil
30	Holy Mote	150 gil

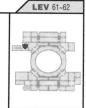

DRUM ROLL, PLEASE!

Vaan is helping Atak, Blok, or Stok win the competition by gaining the most trophies. Speak to the Huntmaster after you collect and turn in all 30 trophies. There is a short awards ceremony for the big winner and Vaan receives a final gift, too. The gift depends on which bangaa wins the contest: Greataxe (Atak wins), Renewing Morion (Blok wins), or Sage's Ring (Stok wins).

HUNT CLUB OWNER

HUNT CLUB OWNER
THEN, ALLOW ME TO PROPOSE A DEAL. WHEN YOU'VE HUNTED DOWN A FAIR SHARE OF MARKS, COME BACK HERE AND REGALE US WITH YOUR TALES OF CONQUEST!

Only the most elite Archadians ever see the Highgarden Terrace. One of those citizens is the Hunt Club Owner, who takes a special interest in the party's exploits. Visit him from time to time to collect additional rewards for finding the 30 rare monsters.

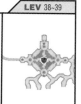

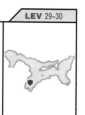

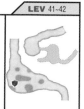

ARCHADIA — Hunt Club Owner

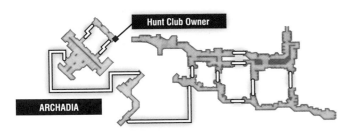

1 Among some leaves on the north side of the tree in the northern loop within Fane of the Path.

2 Between the herbs near Alja on Fane of the Path.

3 On a small tree at the top of the stairs before leaving The Spiritwood and entering the Fane of the Path.

4 On the weapon rack on the west end of The Spiritwood.

5 Near one of the rope anchors in the center or The Spiritwood.

6 In the waters around the courtyard in The Spiritwood. Ask the Wood-dweller to get it.

7 On the edge of the stairs in The Spiritwood, south of the courtyard.

8 Near the screen at the southeast corner of The Spiritwood.

HUNT CLUB OWNER REWARDS

TROPHIES	REWARD
5	Aries Gem & Libra Gem
10	Taurus Gem & Scorpio Gem
15	Gemini Gem & Sagittarius Gem
20	Cancer Gem & Capricorn Gem
25	Leo Gem & Aquarius Gem
30	Virgo Gem & Pisces Gem

The Great Cockatrice Escape

!! WHEN IT'S AVAILABLE

This event is available after finishing the "Little Love on the Big Plains" clan hunt. It can be completed after visiting the Draklor Laboratory.

Visit the Nomad Village in Giza Plains during The Dry to learn that the Cockatrices have all disappeared. Speak to the boy Terra within the pen to learn about a special feather that allows one to communicate with the mystic birds.

The **Feather of the Flock** is inside an urn within the Tracks of the Beast area, which is only accessible during The Rains. Check out the Paradise Risen hunt to learn more about accessing this area. You can't track down the Cockatrices until you acquire the feather.

CHIT (ERUYT VILLAGE/FANE OF THE PATH)

Speak to Chit and then Mjrn, who is standing next to her. Check the ground next to them to find a **Sparkling Light**, then examine it to find a **Dewdrop Pebble**. Offer the Dewdrop Pebble to Mjrn, who asks the party to return more of the pebbles. There are eight more to find:

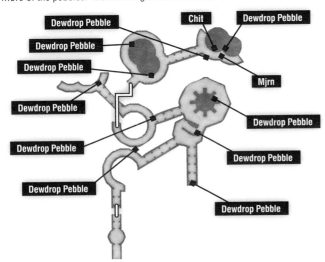

Return the pebbles to Mjrn and speak to Chit again. Pick up the object that falls out of Chit's wing and lands on the ledge. Present the new pebble to Mjrn. Chit leaves for Giza and presents the party with a **Yoichi Bow**.

RENN (RABANASTRE/NORTH END)

Look for this cockatrice in an alcove at the top of North End. After speaking to the cockatrice, it flees the alcove and begins walking a long loop around North End. It runs away any time you attempt to run toward it and just plain walking is too slow. Staying in one spot doesn't work either, since the bird runs away if it spots anyone.

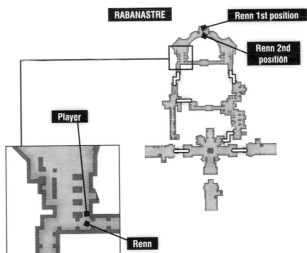

RABANASTRE — Renn 1st position — Renn 2nd position — Player — Renn

Use the entrances around the shops to sneak up on the cockatrice. Get ahead of it and stand behind the pillars by a shop's door, then slowly walk out to the cockatrice's side as it passes and engage it in conversation. Select "Erm… no?" Renn is willing to go home if Chit is already there and presents the party with a **Diamond Sword**. If not, he returns to the top of North End to await word of Chit's arrival in Giza Plains.

SHURRY (JAHARA/LULL OF THE LAND)

Shurry is found on the west side of Lull of the Land. Speak to the Garif Herder next to her and then to Shurry. Speak to the Garif Herder again and tell him that the cockatrice comes from Giza Plains. The Garif Herder then instructs the party to speak to the Great-chief.

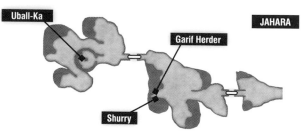

Enter The Elderknoll and tell Great-chief Uball-Ka about the visitor. He presents the party with the **Gift of the Great-chief**. Return the gift to Shurry and speak to the Garif Herder once more. The Garif Herder then presents the party with a **Platinum Dagger**.

SASSAN (DALMASCA ESTERSAND/SOUTH BANK VILLAGE)

Sassan wants to see Torrie in North Bank Village, but won't go near Nathyl, the wolf. Speak to Tchigri about crossing the river to learn more. Select Nathyl when Tchigri asks about taking someone along. Return to South Bank Village and select "no one" when asked. Speak to Tchigri again and choose to cross the river with Arryl. Return to South Bank Village once more while taking "no one" back. Talk to Tchigri one last time and select "Sassan" when crossing the river. Follow Sassan into North Bank Village and speak to him again. He returns to Giza and the party earns a **Koga Blade**.

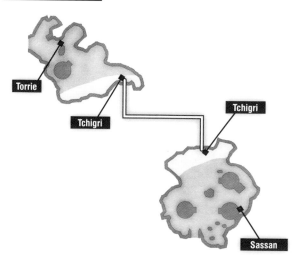

AGYTHA (ARCHADES/GRAND ARCADE)

First, the party must gain access to the Grand Arcade, which requires a **Sandalwood Chop**. To obtain this item, the party must match stories in Archades, then trade Pine Chops for a Sandalwood Chop (see the "Archades Information Exchange").

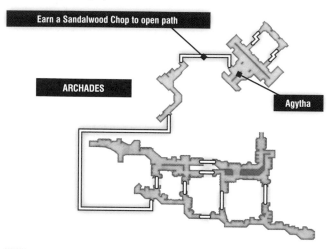

Upon entering the Grand Arcade, the party finds the cockatrice Agytha who is looking for a mate. The mate is in the northeast corner of the Alley of Low Whispers in Old Archades. Tell Agytha about the cockatrice and she leaves immediately, giving the party a **Tumulus** and eventually returning to Giza.

MOOMER (BALFONHEIM PORT/SEA BREEZE LANE)

Speak to the Chocobo Wrangler sitting by the pen and show her the **Feather of the Flock**. Talk to the Miffed Moogle when it approaches the fence, then go to Gurdy after speaking to the Miffed Moogle. The party receives a **Defender** and Moomer returns to Giza.

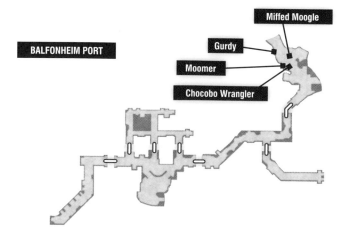

TERRA'S REWARD

Return to the Nomad Village in Giza Plains during The Dry and talk to Terra to obtain a final reward of **two Hi-Ethers**. You can also speak to the cockatrices once more to hear how their adventures turned out.

Fishing Nebra River

WHEN IT'S AVAILABLE

This event begins after the party visits Draklor Laboratory.

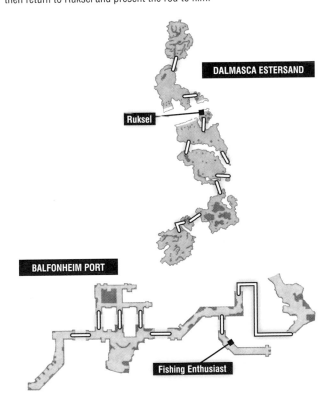

Talk to Ruksel on the west dock in South Bank Village in Dalmasca Estersand. He mentions that he wants to fish, but he doesn't have a rod. Travel to Balfonheim Port and seek out the Fishing Enthusiast in the Chivany Breakwater section. Speak to her twice and ask about her fishing rod. Run to the aerodrome's entrance and then back to where the Fishing Enthusiast was sitting without leaving the area. Check the wall to find the **Muramata** fishing rod, then return to Ruksel and present the rod to him.

DALMASCA ESTERSAND

Ruksel

BALFONHEIM PORT

Fishing Enthusiast

Ruksel is all set to go fishing, but he needs Vaan's help. Vaan must quietly signal to Ruksel the kind of fish that has been hooked so it can be reeled in. A line of four to eight buttons appears on-screen moving from left to right, right to left, top to bottom, or bottom to top. Quickly enter the commands before they reach the opposite side of the screen. Press the buttons in order to capture a fish. Miss a button, or take too long entering the commands, and the fish escapes.

The goal is to catch all six fish in one outing to collect a bonus prize. Downstream is the only fishing spot available at the start, but there are actually five fishing spots in all. Unlock the second location, Midstream, by getting five perfects at Downstream. Unlock the third location, Upstream, by scoring five more perfects at Midstream. The other two locations require some detective work.

DOWNSTREAM

> **GOAL: CLEAR SECTION FIVE TIMES IN A ROW TO UNLOCK MIDSTREAM.**

Downstream is a nice starting area. The commands always appear on the left or right side, so there's plenty of time to enter them as they skip across the screen. Catch all six fish in one outing to earn one of the prizes. Do it five times in a row to unlock Midstream.

POTENTIAL COMMANDS

COMMAND	FISH
○ ○	Common Fish
○ ○ ○ ○	Common Fish
○ ○ ○	Common Fish
○ ○ ○ ○	Common Fish

COMMAND	FISH
○ ○ ○ ○	Common Fish
○ ○ ○ ○	Common Fish
○ ○ ○ ○	Common Fish

COMMAND MOVEMENT

DIRECTION	PROBABILITY
→/←	100%
↑/↓	0%

PERFECT FISHING REWARDS

REWARD	PROBABILITY
100 gil	34%
Hi-Potion	33%
Water Stone	33%

MIDSTREAM

> **GOAL: CLEAR SECTION FIVE TIMES IN A ROW WITH A PERFECT SCORE TO UNLOCK UPSTREAM.**

The fishing gets a little tougher here, as commands begin to appear at the top or bottom of the screen, moving up or down. The commands also get a little longer, plus the shoulder buttons are added into the mix. Clear this section five times with a perfect score to open Upstream.

POTENTIAL COMMANDS

COMMAND	FISH
○ ○ ○ ○	Common Fish
○ ○ ○ ○	Common Fish
○ ○ ○ ○	Common Fish
○ ○ ○ ○	Common Fish

COMMAND	FISH
○ ○ ○ ○	Common Fish
○ ○ ○ ○ ○	Delicious Fish
○ ○ ○ ○ ○	Delicious Fish

COMMAND MOVEMENT

DIRECTION	PROBABILITY
↑↓	40%
↑↓	60%

PERFECT FISHING REWARDS

REWARD	PROBABILITY
Fish Scale	34%
100 Gil	33%
Water Stone	33%

UPSTREAM

Upstream tests your reflexes and controller knowledge. The commands are all five buttons long and a bit trickier. You can't unlock the next area until the party hunts down the Matamune rod and catches the Cactoid Compact. You can only catch the Cactoid Compact once. The reward table changes slightly at that point, adding the Cactoid Compact's extra 10% to the Turtle Shell's drop rate.

COMMAND MOVEMENT

DIRECTION	PROBABILITY
↑↓	40%
↑↓	60%

POTENTIAL COMMANDS

COMMAND	FISH
○ ○ ○ ○	Common Fish
○ ○ ○ ○	Common Fish
○ ○ ○ ○ ○	Delicious Fish
○ ○ ○ ○ ○	Delicious Fish
○ ○ ○ ○ ○	Delicious Fish
○ ○ ○ ○ ○	Delicious Fish
○ ○ ○ ○ ○	Delicious Fish
○ ○ ○ ○ ○	Delicious Fish
○ ○ ○ ○ ○	Delicious Fish

PERFECT FISHING REWARDS

REWARD	PROBABILITY
Fish Scale	30%
Turtle Shell	30%
Frogspawn	30%
Cactoid Compact	10%*

*Requires Matamune; can only be caught once; 10% is added to Turtle Shell once Cactoid Compact is caught.

MATAMUNE HUNT

The Matamune is a legendary cursed fishing rod and finding it isn't easy. To do so, you must solve several puzzles and track down clues all over the world. While fishing in the first three areas, the party will occasionally catch an **Empty Bottle** instead of a fish. When Ruksel hands the bottle over, it may turn out to be one of five special colored bottles. Each of the colored bottles has a note inside that you can view in the Key Items menu. The notes are actually cryptic clues that lead to rewards and additional clues.

If you haven't touched the windmills at this point in the game, you can save some time by heading straight to windmills 2, 3, 5, and 8. To solve the puzzle, stop 3 and 8 and start 2 and 5.

Quick Work

1. BLUE BOTTLE

CLUE: Truth lies just beyond falsehood. CDZCKZMCRANZS

The clue suggests that the real answer is one step beyond the fake. Try adding one letter to each of the letters in the code. The answer is: **DEADLANDS BOAT**. The boat is located in the southeast corner of the Echoes of the Past section of Nabreus Deadlands. Look for a faint glow in the water. Hold the Blue Bottle near the glow to obtain an **X-Potion** and a Wanly-limned Message with "River...unde...o" written on it.

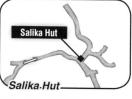

Deadlands Boat

2. GREEN BOTTLE

CLUE: Skip on stones to far bank's shore, by skipping stones return once more. SSADLNIAKLADHAUETDNREA

This puzzle suggests skipping across the clue and then coming back. Start at the left end and read every other letter, then start at the right and read the remaining letters. The answer is: **SALIKA HUT NEAR DEADLANDS**. The hut is in the center of the Piebald Path in The Salikawood. Check the entrance to locate a faint glow. Hold the Green Bottle near the glow to find a **Hastega Mote** and a Green-hued Message with "Forest...rgro...w" written on it.

Salika Hut

3. RED BOTTLE

CLUE: Foothills rise in mountains' shadow. nhliQsTUrEe'

Go to Mosphoran Highwaste's Babbling Vale and search the northwest corner for a Quiet Shrine. Hold the Red Bottle to the Quiet Shrine to receive a **Holy Mote** and a Vermillion Message. The message reads, "Fire...undb...h."

Quiet Shrine

Mosphoran Highwaste

4. YELLOW BOTTLE

CLUE: Dragons stir among the eaters of the wind. 1 2 - - 5 - 7 - 9 -

This is one of the tougher puzzles, since it doesn't provide any info about the location. Note there are 10 numbers, though, which matches the 10 windmills in Cerobi Steppe that are numbered one through ten. 1, 2, and 3 are at North Liavell Hills. 4 and 5 are at The Terraced Bank, while 6 and 7 are in Crossfield. Finally, 8, 9, and 10 are lined up in The Northsward. Turn on (or leave on) windmills 1, 2, 5, 7, and 9 and turn off (or leave off) windmills 3, 4, 6, 8, and 10. The party receives an Auric Message when all of the windmills are adjusted properly. The message reads, "Ash...ridge...e."

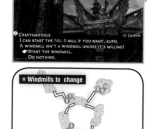

★ Windmills to change

Cerobi Steppe

WYRM PHILOSOPHER

The party may encounter the Wyrm Philosopher at windmill 10, who is seeking the Vyraal Wyrm. Give him the Dragon Scale from the Vyraal Wyrm (which you can find here after finishing the "Get My Stuff Back!" hunt) and he provides an Ageworn Key, which is part of the Wyrm Philosopher side quest.

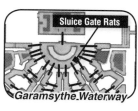

5. BLACK BOTTLE

CLUE: Easy as a, b, c, so count yourself lucky. 19-12-21-9-3-5-7-1-20-5-18-1-20-19

This clue suggests counting letters to solve the puzzle. Write down 1 to 26 on a piece of paper, then place every letter of the alphabet under the numbers starting with 1:A to 26:Z. Next, replace the numbers in the puzzle with the matching letter. The answer is: **SLUICE GATE RATS**. Enter the Central Waterway Control in the Garamsythe Waterway and look for some rats running around the south side of the room. Follow them to the point where they all congregate to find a faint glow. Hold the Black Bottle up to the faint glow to obtain an **Elixir** and an Onyx Message. This message says, "Darkness...eton...e."

Sluice Gate Rats

Garamsythe Waterway

PUTTING THE PIECES TOGETHER

After completing all of these tasks, you have collected five more messages with the following clues:

- River...unde...o
- Forest...rgro...w
- Ash...ridg...e
- Darkness...eton...e
- Fire...undb...h

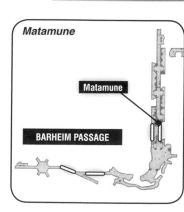

GILGAMESH: ALAS! THERE WAS NO TREASURE. A USELESS STICK I FOUND, AND NOTHING MORE! A WASTE OF PRECIOUS TIME!

Use the five words at the beginning of the messages to determine the logical order: River, Forest, Fire, Ash, Darkness. Next, put the words in the middle together in the same order: unde/rgro/undb/ridg/eton (underground bridge ton). Line up the final five letters in the same order: owhee. The last part is a little cryptic, since it's missing a letter, but the full answer seems to be: underground bridge to nowhere. There's only one place that matches that description.

Matamune

Matamune

BARHEIM PASSAGE

HIDDEN SHOALS

Hidden Shoals is a little tougher than Upstream. Some of the commands are repeats and there's a new six-button command that's a little tricky. The goal here is to keep fishing and getting perfect scores and rewards until you receive the **Cactoid Commendation**. This can take a long time, so be patient and keep practicing. Vaan can fish at the Den of the River Lord after obtaining the Cactoid Commendation.

COMMAND MOVEMENT

DIRECTION	PROBABILITY
↔ ↔	40%
↔ ↔	60%

POTENTIAL COMMANDS

COMMAND	FISH
↔ ▣ ● ⊗ ●	Delicious Fish
↔ ▣ ● ↔ ●	Delicious Fish
▣ ▣ ● ▣ ●	Delicious Fish
↔ ↔ ● ⊗ ▣	Delicious Fish
● ● ↔ ●	Nebra Succulent
▣ ▣	

PERFECT FISHING REWARDS

REWARD	PROBABILITY
Hi-Potion	45%
Adamantite	45%
Cactoid Commendation	10%*

*Requires Matamune; can only be caught once; 10% is added to Adamantite once Cactoid Commendation is caught.

DEN OF THE RIVER LORD

The Den of the River Lord is extremely challenging. The commands get very long, so it pays to learn them all. The most important command is the eight-button command for the King of Nebra. This command appears repeatedly when the player first fishes here. The King of Nebra has nine lives. Catch it 10 times, but note that you don't have to catch them all in a row or even on the same trip to capture the King of Nebra and earn **Lu Shang's Badge**, the ultimate reward for this side quest!

COMMAND MOVEMENT

DIRECTION	PROBABILITY
↔ ↔	40%
↔ ↔	60%

POTENTIAL COMMANDS

COMMAND	FISH
● ● ↔ ● ▣ ▣	Nebra Succulent
↔ ▣ ● ● ↔ ⊗	Nebra Succulent
● ▣ ● ● ⊗ ●	Nebra Succulent
⊗ ▣ ↔ ● ▣ ●	Nebra Succulent
↔ ▣ ↔ ● ⊗ ●	Nebra Succulent
▣ ▣ ↔ ● ● ▣	King of Nebra
⊗ ↔	

Balfonheim Port Footrace

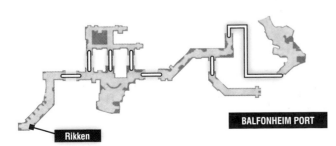

Rikken

BALFONHEIM PORT

Rikken posts a bill for the Who's the Strongest!? hunt, which leads Vaan to the Saccio Lane section of Balfonheim Port. Before he tells Vaan about the hunt, he challenges him to a footrace through the streets. From this point forward, Vaan can race Rikken and his companions endlessly by talking to him again.

The footrace is a simple concept: rhythmically press the ⊗ button and the ● button to run. Keeping an even and steady pace is far more important than quickly mashing the buttons, as Vaan runs the same speed no matter how quickly you press the buttons. Go straight ahead by alternating between the ⊗ and ● buttons. Tap the ⊗ button repeatedly to turn left and the ● button to turn right. If you have trouble keeping a rhythm, you can also tap each button two or three times and still maintain a fairly straight line.

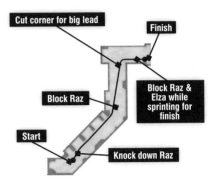

The real trick is in the strategy. There are three opponents: Rikken, the man, Elza, the woman, and Raz, the bird-like creature. Rikken is steady, but sticks to the left side of the track. He's rarely a threat. Elza cuts across the track from left to right. She's tough to beat if she gets all the way to the right. Raz is extremely fast, but clumsy. Vaan can knock him down to keep him from passing.

Keep an even pace at the start until Raz falls, then remain in the middle or slightly to the left to keep Elza to the left side of the track. Raz should make a move and try to come up the middle (preferable) or along the right side. Get in his way immediately if he comes up the middle. Otherwise, wait until after the first turn to cut him off and knock him down by zipping over to the right.

Drift over to the right side of the track after the first turn and stay there until the second turn. With some luck, Elza will get hung up on Rikken and will be unable to cross to the right. Vaan is in trouble if she gets in front of him and to the right side. He can still make up ground at the turn and win, but it isn't easy. The trick to beating Elza is keeping her on the left through the first turn so that Rikken blocks her from moving to the right in the second half of the course.

Cut the second corner as closely as possible, so Vaan just barely scrapes through without getting stuck. You can make up a ton of time with this move and can easily take the lead if Elza and Rikken remain outside and Raz has been held back. Go all out in the final stretch. Get in front of Elza if she's neck-and-neck with Vaan and beware of Raz making a late charge for the lead.

There are 100 tiers to the footrace event. You receive a prize and move up a tier each time you win until you get the ultimate prize at tier 100. There's no penalty for losing and it isn't necessary to clear all the tiers in one sitting, so race with confidence and rest your fingers now and then.

FOOTRACE REWARDS

TIER	REWARD	TIER	REWARD
1	Potion	18	Handkerchief x2
2	Phoenix Down	19	Bacchus's Wine x2
3	Eye Drops	20	300 gil & Float Motes x2
4	Antidote	21	Potion x3
5	10 gil, Echo Herbs	22	Phoenix Down x3
6	Gold Needle	23	Eye Drops x3
7	Alarm Clock	24	Antidote x3
8	Handkerchief	25	30 gil & Echo Herbs x3
9	Bacchus's Wine	26	Gold Needle x3
10	100 gil & Balance Motes x2	27	Alarm Clock x3
11	Potion x2	28	Handkerchief x3
12	Phoenix Down x2	29	Bacchus's Wine x3
13	Eye Drops x2	30	800 gil & Teleport Stones x3
14	Antidote x2	31	Potion x4
15	20 gil & Echo Herbs x2	32	Phoenix Down x4
16	Gold Needle x2	33	Eye Drops x4
17	Alarm Clock x2	34	Antidote x4

TIER	REWARD
35	40 gil & Echo Herbs x4
36	Gold Needle x4
37	Alarm Clock x4
38	Handkerchief x4
39	Bacchus's Wine x4
40	1500 gil & Vanishga Motes x2
41	Potion x5
42	Phoenix Down x5
43	Eye Drops x5
44	Antidote x5
45	50 gil & Echo Herbs x5
46	Gold Needle x5
47	Alarm Clock x5
48	Handkerchief x5
49	Bacchus's Wine x5
50	2500 gil & Reflectga Motes x2
51	Potion x6

TIER	REWARD
52	Phoenix Down x6
53	Eye Drops x6
54	Antidote x6
55	60 gil & Echo Herbs x6
56	Gold Needle x6
57	Alarm Clock x6
58	Handkerchief x6
59	Bacchus's Wine x6
60	3500 gil & Hi-Ethers x2
61	Potion x7
62	Phoenix Down x7
63	Eye Drops x7
64	Antidote x7
65	70 gil & Echo Herbs x7
66	Gold Needle x7
67	Alarm Clock x7
68	Handkerchief x7

TIER	REWARD
69	Bacchus's Wine x7
70	4500 gil & Holy Motes x2
71	Potion x8
72	Phoenix Down x8
73	Eye Drops x8
74	Antidote x8
75	80 gil & Echo Herbs x8
76	Gold Needle x8
77	Alarm Clock x8
78	Handkerchief x8
79	Bacchus's Wine x8
80	6000 gil, Hastega Motes x2, & Caramel
81	Potion x9
82	Phoenix Down x9
83	Eye Drops x9
84	Antidote x9
85	90 gil & Echo Herbs x9

TIER	REWARD
86	Gold Needle x9
87	Alarm Clock x9
88	Handkerchief x9
89	Bacchus's Wine x9
90	8000 gil, Scathe Motes x2, & Slime Oil
91	Potion x10
92	Phoenix Down x10
93	Eye Drops x10
94	Antidote x10
95	100 gil & Echo Herbs x10
96	Gold Needle x10
97	Alarm Clock x10
98	Handkerchief x10
99	Bacchus's Wine x10
100	10000 gil, Elixirs x2, & Unpurified Ether

Wyrm Philosopher

CEROBI STEPPE

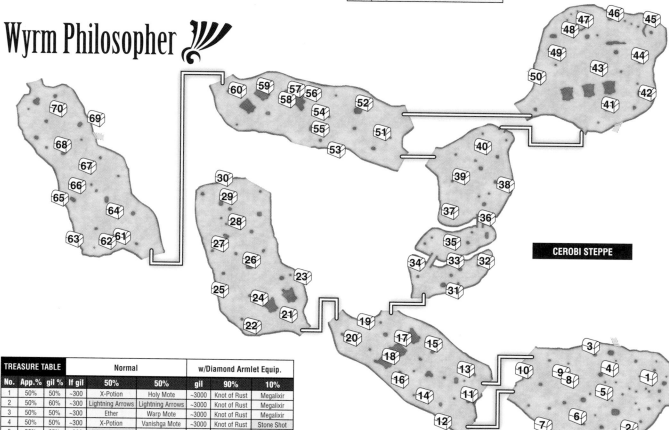

TREASURE TABLE				Normal		w/Diamond Armlet Equip.		
No.	App.%	gil %	If gil	50%	50%	gil	90%	10%
1	50%	50%	~300	X-Potion	Holy Mote	~3000	Knot of Rust	Megalixir
2	50%	60%	~300	Lightning Arrows	Lightning Arrows	~3000	Knot of Rust	Megalixir
3	50%	50%	~300	Ether	Warp Mote	~3000	Knot of Rust	Megalixir
4	50%	50%	~300	X-Potion	Vanishga Mote	~3000	Knot of Rust	Stone Shot
5	50%	65%	~300	Wyrmfire Shot	Hi-Ether	~3000	Knot of Rust	Hastega Mote
6	50%	50%	~300	X-Potion	X-Potion	~3000	Knot of Rust	Sapping Bolts
7	50%	50%	~300	Ether	Aero Mote	~3000	Knot of Rust	Megalixir
8	50%	60%	~300	Leather Gorget	Hastega Mote	~3000	Knot of Rust	Penetrator Crossbow
9	50%	65%	~300	Mud Shot	Hi-Ether	~3000	Knot of Rust	Nishijin Belt
10	50%	60%	~300	Lead Bolts	Reflect Mote	~3000	Knot of Rust	Hastega Mote
11	50%	65%	~300	X-Potion	Gillie Boots	~3000	Knot of Rust	Blazer Gloves
12	50%	50%	~300	Ether	Holy Mote	~3000	Knot of Rust	Megalixir
13	50%	50%	~300	Ether	Aero Mote	~3000	Knot of Rust	Megalixir
14	50%	50%	~300	X-Potion	X-Potion	~3000	Knot of Rust	Kaiser Shield
15	50%	65%	~300	Golden Amulet	Warp Mote	~3000	Knot of Rust	Megalixir
16	50%	80%	~300	Embroidered Tippet	Embroidered Tippet	~3000	Knot of Rust	Celebrant's Miter
17	50%	50%	~300	Ether	Float Mote	~3000	Knot of Rust	Time Bolts
18	50%	50%	~300	X-Potion	Hi-Ether	~3000	Knot of Rust	Megalixir
19	50%	65%	~300	Ether	Quasimodo Boots	~3000	Knot of Rust	Firefly
20	50%	50%	~300	Ether	Reflectga Mote	~3000	Knot of Rust	Dragon Whisker
21	50%	50%	~300	Ether	Holy Mote	~3000	Knot of Rust	Castellanos
22	50%	50%	~300	Ether	X-Potion	~3000	Knot of Rust	Shell Shield
23	50%	50%	~300	Ether	Warp Mote	~3000	Knot of Rust	Artemis Arrows
24	50%	50%	~300	Ether	Reflect Mote	~3000	Knot of Rust	Hastega Mote
25	50%	50%	~300	Ether	X-Potion	~3000	Knot of Rust	Megalixir
26	50%	70%	~300	Ether	Empyrean Rod	~3000	Knot of Rust	Megalixir
27	50%	80%	~300	Ether	Mirror Mail	~3000	Knot of Rust	Megalixir

TREASURE TABLE				Normal		w/Diamond Armlet Equip.		
No.	App.%	gil %	If gil	50%	50%	gil	90%	10%
28	50%	50%	~300	Ether	Megalixir	~3000	Knot of Rust	Euclid's Sextant
29	50%	50%	~300	Ether	Balance Mote	~3000	Knot of Rust	Grand Bolts
30	50%	50%	~300	Ether	Water Mote	~3000	Knot of Rust	Cloud Staff
31	50%	50%	~300	Hi-Ether	Holy Mote	~3000	Knot of Rust	Water Bombs
32	50%	50%	~300	Hi-Ether	X-Potion	~3000	Knot of Rust	Megalixir
33	50%	50%	~300	Hi-Ether	X-Potion	~3000	Knot of Rust	Zwill Crossblade
34	50%	50%	~300	Hi-Ether	Hastega Mote	~3000	Knot of Rust	Nishijin Belt
35	50%	50%	~300	Hi-Ether	Reflectga Mote	~3000	Knot of Rust	Quasimodo Boots
36	50%	65%	~300	Hi-Ether	Leather Gorget	~3000	Knot of Rust	Megalixir
37	50%	50%	~300	Hi-Ether	Aero Mote	~3000	Knot of Rust	Lightning Arrows
38	50%	50%	~300	Hi-Ether	Float Mote	~3000	Knot of Rust	Holy Rod
39	50%	50%	~300	Hi-Ether	Ether	~3000	Knot of Rust	Morning Star
40	50%	50%	~300	Hi-Ether	Warp Mote	~3000	Knot of Rust	Megalixir
41	50%	50%	~300	X-Potion	Warp Mote	~3000	Knot of Rust	Megalixir
42	50%	50%	~300	X-Potion	Holy Mote	~3000	Knot of Rust	Megalixir
43	50%	50%	~300	X-Potion	Float Mote	~3000	Knot of Rust	Black Robes
44	50%	50%	~300	X-Potion	X-Potion	~3000	Knot of Rust	Megalixir
45	50%	50%	~300	X-Potion	X-Potion	~3000	Knot of Rust	Dragon Mail

No.	App.%	gil %	If gil	Normal		w/Diamond Armlet Equip.		
				50%	50%	gil	90%	10%
46	50%	50%	~300	X-Potion	Scathe Mote	~3000	Knot of Rust	Assassin's Arrows
47	50%	50%	~300	X-Potion	Balance Mote	~3000	Knot of Rust	Hastega Mote
48	50%	50%	~300	X-Potion	Hastega Mote	~3000	Knot of Rust	Agate Ring
49	50%	50%	~300	X-Potion	Reflectga Mote	~3000	Knot of Rust	Fomalhaut
50	50%	50%	~300	X-Potion	Vanishga Mote	~3000	Knot of Rust	Megalixir
51	50%	70%	~300	Parallel Arrows	Parallel Arrows	~3000	Knot of Rust	Feathered Boots
52	50%	70%	~300	X-Potion	Scathe Mote	~3000	Knot of Rust	Ribbon
53	50%	50%	~300	X-Potion	X-Potion	~3000	Knot of Rust	Dark Shot
54	50%	60%	~300	Long Bolts	Balance Mote	~3000	Knot of Rust	Fomalhaut
55	50%	50%	~300	X-Potion	Holy Mote	~3000	Knot of Rust	Megalixir
56	50%	50%	~300	X-Potion	Vanishga Mote	~3000	Knot of Rust	Castellanos
57	50%	60%	~300	Poison Bomb	Reflectga Mote	~3000	Knot of Rust	Hastega Mote
58	50%	60%	~300	Silent Shot	Hastega Mote	~3000	Knot of Rust	Icecloud Arrows
59	50%	50%	~300	X-Potion	Warp Mote	~3000	Knot of Rust	Venetian Shield
60	50%	50%	~300	X-Potion	Float Mote	~3000	Knot of Rust	Hastega Mote
61	50%	50%	~300	X-Potion	Warp Mote	~3000	Knot of Rust	Windslicer Shot
62	50%	50%	~300	X-Potion	Float Mote	~3000	Knot of Rust	Magepower Shishak
63	50%	80%	~300	X-Potion	Kiku-ichimonji	~3000	Knot of Rust	Megalixir
64	50%	50%	~300	X-Potion	Aero Mote	~3000	Knot of Rust	Grand Bolts
65	50%	50%	~300	X-Potion	Reflectga Mote	~3000	Knot of Rust	Golden Skullcap
66	50%	70%	~300	X-Potion	Armguard	~3000	Knot of Rust	Megalixir
67	50%	50%	~300	X-Potion	Aero Mote	~3000	Knot of Rust	Megalixir
68	50%	50%	~300	X-Potion	X-Potion	~3000	Knot of Rust	Mirage Vest
69	50%	50%	~300	X-Potion	X-Potion	~3000	Knot of Rust	Megalixir
70	50%	50%	~300	X-Potion	Holy Mote	~3000	Knot of Rust	Castellanos

WHEN IT'S AVAILABLE

This event is available after visiting the Draklor Laboratory.

The Wyrm Philospher is found on a windmill in Cerobi Steppe. Check out windmill #10 in The Northsward to make him appear. He's seeking the Vyraal Wyrm, which the party should have already defeated. Give him the **Dragon Scale** from the Vyraal Wyrm and he provides the party with an **Ageworn Key**.

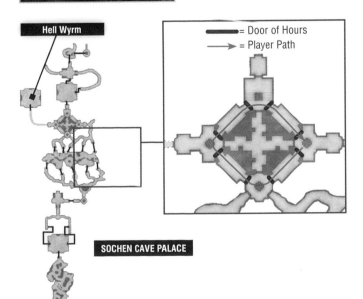

Hell Wyrm

= Door of Hours
→ = Player Path

SOCHEN CAVE PALACE

The Ageworn Key unlocks a secret chamber within the Sochen Cave Palace. The secret chamber is guarded by an ancient puzzle, which mentioned in certain clues scattered around the dungeon. To open the Hall of the Ascetic to the Hall of the Wroth God, you must walk a certain path through Destiny's March.

Enter the Sochen Cave Palace from the south (Tchita Uplands). Proceed up the east side of the dungeon to the far east door into Destiny's March. You must walk a circle around Destiny's March, only opening the doors marked as a '**Door of Hours**'. Go clockwise starting on the east side and heading southwest, then follow the hall all the way around to the starting point. This triggers the Ascetic's Door if done properly.

Go to the west side of Destiny's March and check the Ascetic's Door. Follow the Hall of the Ascetic down to the Hall of the Wroth God and use the Ageworn Key to enter the secret chamber.

HELL WYRM

LEV	60	HP	8930711	EXP	0	LP	150

STEAL Dark Stone, Dark Magicite, Dark Crystal

Begin the battle by casting Dispel on the boss to remove Shell, Protect, and Haste. Have a 'Foe: Status = Faith/Dispel' gambit ready on one character to keep Faith in check throughout the battle. The other status effects never return.

This is a very long battle, but the pattern is fairly easy to follow. The Hell Wyrm mainly uses its Rake attack (a basic physical attack), while throwing in magicks of every elemental type. Throughout the first half of the battle, the boss mainly uses Rake and adds magick as its desperation grows. It also has a powerful Judgement attack that causes dark damage and Stop. Equip at least one character with a Power Armlet to prevent the Stop effect and an 'Ally: Status = Stop/Chronos Tear' gambit to remove the effect from others. It doesn't hurt to put Power Armlets on the entire party, though.

THE LONG HAUL

Since this is a long fight, make sure the party has a 'Self: MP < 10%/Charge' gambit. You can also flee this battle and step into the hall to restore the party, if necessary. This is a good tactic to use if the first party gets wiped out. Don't stick around to fight with the back-up crew. Run into the hall and restore everyone then return to the battle.

Use a strong physical assault through the first part of the battle and summon Zodiark, if possible. Have the summoner in Stone status before summoning Zodiark, so the Esper uses Final Eclipse upon appearing. The Hell Wyrm has a powerful Breakout–Pentagram attack especially designed to wipe out summoned creatures, so watch out.

Magick also works fairly well in this fight. Dark magick heals the boss, so avoid using it. The boss is susceptible to the combination of Shear and Oil, which makes Fire-based magick very effective.

Keep Protect and Lure on the main melee character throughout the battle. Make sure everyone has Bubble and Ensunaga ready to remove Stone effects.

The fight gets much tougher at the end. The Hell Wyrm begins using Invert, which switches victims' HP and MP values, on nearly every other attack. This means that one character is always close to death, but that person also has full MP. Take advantage of this situation and bombard the boss with Quickenings and Zodiark. There are positives and negatives to both strategies. Summoning Zodiark takes the summoner's MP to zero. This isn't a problem early in the fight, but with the Hell Wyrm casting Invert constantly, it becomes deadly. If the summoner gets hit with Invert with zero MP, he will die and the summon will be wasted.

Dealing with Invert

Characters can usually heal themselves quickly enough that Invert doesn't become a problem. However, it doesn't hurt to have an 'Ally: Status = HP Critical/X-Potion' gambit going late in the battle.

There's no item reward for this fight, but that doesn't mean it isn't worthwhile. The party earns a new Sky Pirate's Den award and Montblanc is eager to hand over a large chunk of gil!

OTHER STUFF

Sky Pirate's Den

After completing certain objectives throughout the game, you will receive rewards that are placed into the Sky Pirate's Den. There are a total of 30 rewards. Can you collect them all? If you want to achieve the ultimate rank in Clan Centurio, you must do it!

SKY PIRATE'S DEN REWARDS

CHARACTER	TITLE	ACHIEVEMENT
Ashe	Exemplar	Raised the party's average level above 50
Ba'Gamnan	Scrivener	Completed the Bestiary
Balthier	Assault Striker	Attacked over 300 times
Basch	Blood Dancer	Defeated more than 500 foes
Behemoth King	Lord of the Kings	Defeated Behemoth King
Belias	High Summoner	Obtained 13 Espers
Carrot	Freshmaker	Defeated Carrot
Chocobo	Wayfarer	Took over 50,000 steps
Crystal	Runeweaver	Learned every Magick
Deathgaze	Eagle Eye	Defeated Deathgaze
Fafnir	Wyrmslayer	Defeated Fafnir
Fran	Spellsinger	Cast Magicks over 200 times
Gabranth	Mist Walker	Performed every Concurrence
Gilgamesh	Master Swordsman	Defeated Gilgamesh twice
Gurdy	Spendthrift	Spent more than 1,000,000 gil
Hell Wyrm	Radiant Savior	Defeated Hell Wyrm
Migelo	Privateer	Sold over 1,000 pieces of loot
Mimic	Collector	Obtained rare goods on the bazaar
Montblanc	The Unrelenting	Completed a 50-Chain in battle
Old Dalan	Cartographer	Fully explored every map*
Penelo	Plunderer	Aquired over 100,000 gil
Rasler	Conqueror	Learned every License
Reks	Record Breaker	Obtained over 500,000 Clan Points
Trickster	Sharpshooter	Defeated Trickster
Ultima	Fell Angel	Defeated Ultima
Vaan	Master Thief	Stole successfully over 50 times
Vayne	Premier Prestidigitator	Used Technicks over 100 times
Vossler	Jack-of-All-Trades	Learned every Technick
Yiazmat	Hunter Extraordinaire	Defeated Yiazmat
Zodiark	Zodiac Knight	Defeated Zodiark

*Doesn't include areas that can only be visited once or the final dungeon.

Archades Information Exchange

There are residents in the Molberry, Trant, Rienna, and Nilbasse sections of Archades with valuable information. The party can earn Pine Chops by matching two people's stories. The stories are always contained within one of the four areas. (For example, you won't find one person in Molberry and the other one in Trant.) Match up everyone within the four areas to earn enough Pine Chops to trade them in for a **Sandalwood Chop**. With this item, the party can access the Grand Arcade and Highgarden Terrace sections of Archades.

MOLBERRY

PERSON #1		PERSON #2
Reminiscing Lady	➡	Family-minded Girl
Avid Traveler	➡	Traveling Gentleman
Daughter-in-Law	➡	Man from Giza
Look-Alike	➡	Look-Alike
Talented Woman	➡	Akademician
Ardent Woman	➡	Ardent Man
Proud Mother	➡	Tutor
Poor Husband	➡	Poor Wife
Would-be Judge	➡	Judge's Wife

TRANT

PERSON #1		PERSON #2
Boutiquere	➡	Moneyed Gentleman
Farce-Goer	➡	Girl on an Errand
Music Appreciator	➡	Lutenist
Perceptive Man	➡	Historian
Smitten Woman	➡	Smitten Man
Builder	➡	Artistan Architect

NILBASSE

PERSON #1		PERSON #2
Ex-Researcher	➡	Determined Researcher
Aspiring Starlet	➡	Faded Star
Worried Husband	➡	Materialistic Woman
Senior Researcher	➡	Failed Researcher
Athletic Woman	➡	Avid Reader
Gentleman Onlooker	➡	Eager Crier

RIENNA

PERSON #1		PERSON #2
Dangerous Chef	➡	Philosopher of Cuisine
Lazy Profiteer	➡	Researcher's Wife
Vegetable Seller	➡	Greenseller
Good Brother	➡	Waiting Woman
Tarot Reader	➡	Happy Novelist
Romantic Lady	➡	Lucky Man
Bhujerban Lady	➡	Tour Leader

TAROT'S MISFORTUNE

After matching the Tarot Reader with the Happy Novelist in Rienna, the Tarot Reader offers to reveal the party's misfortune. The misfortune actually tells the player how many matches are left in each section of the city. This is a very helpful way to check your progress when trying to earn the Sandalwood Chop.

King Bomb—OPTIONAL BOSS

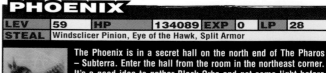

KING BOMB

LEV	34	HP		37596	EXP	0	LP	22
STEAL	Bomb Shell, Fire Crystal, Bomb Fragment							

The King Bomb is in the Salikawood's Grand hall north of the Save Crystal. Although this boss is optional, it will likely come into play the first time the party visits the Salikawood, or when you attempt to complete the Rodeo to the Death hunt.

King Bomb summons lesser Bombs to fight with it and uses powerful Fire magick. Keep a good supply of Handkerchiefs around to remove the Oil status effect, which increase the fire damage the party takes. Blast the enemy with Water elements and use gear that reduces fire damage like Fire Shield. Focus on eliminating the lesser enemies first to prevent them from chain-exploding.

Remember to only attack King Bomb when it's alone. The boss fully restores its HP when it reaches 50%. You can prevent this by using a well-timed Quickening. King Bomb uses the Renew trick several times, but eventually stops using it.

Phoenix—OPTIONAL BOSS

PHOENIX

LEV	59	HP		134089	EXP	0	LP	28
STEAL	Windslicer Pinion, Eye of the Hawk, Split Armor							

The Phoenix is in a secret hall on the north end of The Pharos – Subterra. Enter the hall from the room in the northeast corner. It's a good idea to gather Black Orbs and get some light before facing the enemy. Phoenix is a flying creature, so bring ranged weapons or Telekinesis along for the battle.

Omega Mark XII Extermination

Reaching Omega Mark XII is almost as difficult as fighting the hidden boss. Begin by diving deep into the dungeon following the same route used to reach Ultima. Take a left turn at the Save Crystal to find the Aquarius Gate Stone (1). Backtrack to the previous section and open Gate Aquarius 1 (2), so the path to the Taurus Gate Stone (5) is open. Forget the Taurus Gate Stone for now and go to the nearby Capricorn Gate Stone (3). Flip the switch and run across the area to Gate Capricorn 2 (4). Backtrack to the Taurus Gate Stone (5) and use the switch. Cross the area again passing through Gate Capricorn 2 to reach Gate Taurus 1 (6). The road beyond Gate Taurus 1 leads to Omega Mark XII.

⚡ BE PREPARED

Omega Mark XII is one tough nut to crack. Return to the Save Crystal before moving forward. It may take several tries to fell the boss. Don't take the risk of having to solve the gate puzzle again.

OMEGA MARK·XII

| LEV | 99 | HP | 10370699 | EXP | 0 | LP | 255 |

This is a very challenging enemy. Its attacks are extremely powerful and can typically wipe someone out with a single shot. Those that survive may be stricken with the berserk status, taking them out of the battle unless dispelled.

There's really only one way to fight this creature. It involves the use of Decoy and Reverse. Prepare the party by setting the lead fighter to attack and only attack. It doesn't hurt to equip the character with a Bubble Belt either to ensure his HP stays at the maximum throughout the battle. Also equip armor that lowers the character's Magick Resistance to zero. This is critical, since the other characters in the party will be casting on him constantly.

The other characters go into a strict support role. Set their gambits so that they cast Reverse on the main fighter above everything else. Then make the second command casting Decoy on the same target. Then set one of the two to use Hastega and Protect on Vaan. The two should also have Curaga prepared to cast on them, not on the fighter, if necessary.

Keep it simple. The real goal is just to keep Reverse and Decoy up throughout the entire battle. It pays to take manual control of Decoy. It lasts considerably longer than Reverse and it can be refreshed while the spell is still active on the fighter. Recast it between every two to three casts of Reverse to ensure that it never wears out and the support characters never get hit.

Otherwise Reverse should keep the main fighter healthy throughout the battle. He'll take a hit now and then when Reverse drops, so make sure Bubble stays in effect too. Cast it again before it wears out, or use a Bubble Belt to maintain the effect.

Run if things go wrong. Retreat to the top of the ramp and quickly restore everyone. The boss begins to heal if left alone for too long. It's possible to fully restore everyone and get back into the battle before the boss can completely recover.

100 SECRETS OF FFXII

The following section takes a look at 100 oddities within *FINAL FANTASY XII*. These are subtle things you may not notice while playing through the game, but they're worth mentioning. Have a little fun and check them out for yourself.

Event Related

NO.01: THOUGHTS ON NABREUS DEADLANDS

The first time you enter Nabreus (by either approaching the stone gate or by entering the Hall of Effulgent Light), Basch tells your party about the city. Normally he will simply finish with "We should turn back," but if you visit either places after defeating Judge Bergan but before reaching Archades, a scene in which Ashe talks with Fran about the lost city of Nabreus is added. Furthermore, if you watch Basch's explanation and then visit one of these locations between defeating Judge Bergan and reaching the Imperial City, Fran will be the one who suggests turning back.

NO.02: GETTING THROUGH THE EAST GATE

After setting out to defeat the Rogue Tomato, you will be unable to get back inside Rabanastre. When this occurs, hop into the line of people standing in front of the Dalmascan Soldier guarding the door on the left-hand side. Wait in line. When everyone is gone, speak to the Dalmascan Soldier in front of the gate to get back inside. After sitting through the line once, you can get back in again by simply speaking to the Dalmascan Soldier.

NO.03: THE RABANASTRE PALACE MAP IN OLD ARCHADES

You're only allowed into the Rabanastre Palace when the story sends you there near the beginning of the game. If you miss the map on this trip, you can still pick it up later from the Cartographers' Guild moogle in the Alley of Low Whispers within Old Archades.

NO.04: KTJN'S WELCOME TO THE CLAN HALL

If you influence Ktjn to become a guard for Clan Centurio, you can talk to her outside of the Clan HQ. Avoid visiting the Clan Hall until after defeating Judge Bergan and finishing Ktjn's event and all of the lines that normally belong to the bangaa guard can be heard from Ktjn instead.

NO.05: VISITORS TO THE DALMASCA ESTERSAND OUTPOST

The Outpost in Dalmasca Estersand is visited by different travelers as the story progresses, each taking a rest before continuing their journey. Stop by and see who is visiting every once in a while

TIMING	VISITORS
After the Rogue Tomato hunt	family traveling by chocobo
After escaping the Marquis Ondore's Manor	bangaa and seeq merchants
After obtaining the Dawn Shard	family from the empire
After defeating Judge Bergan	three moogles
After obtaining free flight in the Strahl	a pair of viera

NO.06: THE BUCCANEER'S BATTALION

After completing the Wraith Hunt, you gain access to a house in the Rabanastre Lowtown area that is used by Deeg, the son of the Jovial Seeq. If you can't fulfill certain conditions Kytes, Filo and other children will gather in this house and form the Buccaneer's Battalion. You must meet the following conditions for the children to gather:

- Visit the Draklor Laboratory.
- Return the three medallion pieces to Roh'kenmou in Old Dalan's Place (part of the "Medal of Nabreus" event).
- Return to Charlotte's Magickery and hand the Moonsilver Medallion to Roh'kenmu (part of the "Medal of Nabreus" event).

NO.07: FREE MAPS

Generally, if you do not own the map of an area, you will need to fill the map in manually by walking to every area displayed. However, if your next goal happens to be displayed during the progress of the story or you can check a petitioner's location in the Hunts menu, you can view the entire map, including areas you have never visited.

NO.08: THE REST OF THE STORY...

A few of the side events end with plot points that keep you wondering what happened, but you can fill in some of these loose ends by doing a little research. After finishing the Pilika's Errand side event, read Pilika's diary to find out that her other pet, "Bianca," is hiding above the shelves in the technick shop. You can uncover another storyline after completing the Earth Tyrant Extermination side event. You can meet up again with Rimzat, the investigator, if you travel to the Hunters' Camp on the Phon Coast. He will then return home to his empire hoping for a bonus.

Message Related

NO.09: DALAN'S ADVENTURE TIPS

Dalan provides different bits of advice depending on the progress of the story. If you're ever unsure about where you should go next, seek him out! The following is a list of the type of advice he gives and when you're likely to receive it.

STORY POINT	ADVICE
After the new Consul Inauguration Ceremony	Directions to the Nomad's Camp
After obtaining the Sunstone	How to infiltrate the Rabanastre Royal Palace
After escaping the Barheim Passage	How to deliver the Sword of the Order
After delivering the Sword of Dalmasca	Balthier's location
After talking to Balthier in the Sandsea	Directions to the Lhusu Mines
After escaping the Battleship Leviathan.	How to rescue Penelo
After obtaining the Dawn Shard	Directions to Jahara
After Larsa joins the party	About Mt Bur-Omisace
After visiting Mt Bur-Omisace	Advice on Vaan's worries
After defeating Judge Bergan	Directions to Archades
After visiting the Draklor Laboratory	Directions to Giruvegan
After obtaining the Treaty-Blade	Nothing to say
After the Sky Fortress Bahamut is activated	Offers to provide advice

> DALAN
> FIND YOURSELF IN TROUBLE, YOU CAN ALWAYS COME TO ME, M'BOY. WHO KNOWS? THERE MIGHT BE SOMETHING USEFUL RATTLING ABOUT IN THIS OLD HEAD OF MINE.

NO.10: LEGENDS OF OLD

Paying 1 gil to the Rabanastran boy in the middle of East End across from the stairs to Lowtown allows you to hear stories about Rabanastre's history and several other things. The stories change as the game's story progresses.

STORY POINT	CONTENTS	LEAVING LINE
After Reks' arc ends	The state of Rabanastre after losing the war	"You're not worth his time."
After the close of the new Consul Inauguration Ceremony	How to get to Downtown Rabanastre	"He just wanted to talk."
After Escaping the Barheim Passage	A summary of the Rabanastre Palace attack	"He heard this straight from a fake jailer."
After receiving the Dawn Shard	The connection between King Raithwall and the demon	"He guesses it can't be helped."
After visiting Draklor Laboratory	The connection between a mysterious place and a great power	"To be honest, he's completely out of stories."

NO.11: MIGELO'S CHANGING REACTION

After meeting up with Penelo aboard the Leviathan, talk to Migelo in the item shop in Rabanastre to hear how happy he is that she is safe. This conversation can go one of two ways, depending on whether or not you have obtained the Dawn Shard.

Before obtaining the Dawn Shard

Migelo is happy that Penelo is safe, but angry at Balthier and the others for dragging her into everything.

After obtaining the Dawn Shard

Migelo scolds you for not coming back sooner to tell him that Penelo is safe.

NO.12: WAR-CHIEF SUPINELU'S HEALTH

You can find the Garif warrior, War-chief Supinelu, as an ally in the Haulo Green area of the Ozmone Plains before the party visits Jahara for the first time. Even if he gets knocked out on the plains, he will show up to help your party when they first visit Jahara. If he does happen to perish, you'll notice that the text changes slightly to match his experiences. When he is in good shape, he will explain to the Garif clan at the entrance that Vaan and his party have come across the Ozmone Plains. If he is in bad shape after his fight with the monsters, he will be unable to finish explaining his story to the Garif clan.

NO.13: THE WARRIOR CHIEF'S GOODWILL

When leaving Jahara and heading for Mt Bur-Omisace for the first time, the Garif war-chief Supinelu allows you to use their chocobo rental once, free of charge. If you do not use the rental and visit the Temple Grounds area of Mt Bur-Omisace first, Gurdy will quiz you as to why you haven't taken a chocobo yet.

NO.14: ARROGANT VAAN

After getting nine Pinewood Chops in Archades, you can ride a taxi in the Nilbasse district. For those who don't ride the taxi and continue collecting chops until getting the Sandalwood Chop before talking to the Cab Guide, you can hear a special line and view some very arrogant choices.

NO.15: MOCKED FOR TELEPORTING

Use a teleport stone to visit the Tsenoble area of Archades. Talk to the Prideful Boy nearby to be mocked for using a teleport stone.

> PRIDEFUL BOY
> I SAW YOU COME IN ON THE GATE CRYSTAL. AN ARDENT, AREN'T YOU. NO UPSTANDING GENTRY WOULD USE THE THINGS. WHY LEAVE THE CITY, ANYWAY?

Half the height of Vaan, twice the spunk.

NO.16: INTERESTING AIRSHIP PASSENGERS

Choose the "By leisure craft" option when flying from one of the airship terminals in each region to explore the airship while in flight. There are some nice shops and a variety of other passengers. The passengers depend on the destination, but here are some who are found on the Rabanastre and Archades flights.

> Charming woman in the Sky Saloon on the Rabanastre flight.

> CHARMING WOMAN
> I ALWAYS SEEM TO BE RUNNING INTO YOU. I ENJOY THESE CHANCE MEETINGS.

This girl will speak to you openly after taking the airship to Rabanastre three times or more.

> The innocent girl on the air deck on the Rabanastre flight.

> INNOCENT GIRL
> LOOK HOW HIGH WE ARE! I CAN SEE FOREVER! BUT WHAT IF I FELL... HEY, NO PUSHING!

Stand in front of the innocent young girl on the upper deck and she will charge and send you flying.

> The loving man in the observation parlor on the Archades flight.

> LOVING MAN
> WOULD YOU PLEASE LISTEN TO ME? ONCE I'M IN THE ARMY WE WON'T BE ABLE TO SEE EACH OTHER SO EASILY, AND—PLEASE LOOK AT ME! Please!

These two have times when they get along great and times when they fight. Try talking to him in different zones.

NO.17: THE TRAVEL LOVING FAMILY

The conversations with the family who loves to travel change along with your progress through the story. In essence, it doesn't matter which terminal you talk to them in, but there are some differences between the time when you obtain the Dawn Shard and the moment you defeat Judge Bergan. If the family doesn't appear, try leaving and coming back into the terminal a few times.

STORY POINT	TERMINAL	CONVERSATION
After escaping Barheim Passage and returning to Rabanastre	Everywhere	Reason mother loves to travel by air
After obtaining Dawn Shard	Rabanastre	Chocobo failure
--	Nalbina Fortress	Mother's make-up failure
--	Bhujerba	Rivalry with the neighbors
After defeating Judge Bergan	Everywhere	Dragon attacking public airways

NO.18: CONVERSATION DURING DEATHGAZE'S ATTACK

You can witness different conversations than usual from the passengers on the regular service airship when Deathgaze appears. Once it shows up, don't defeat it right away; instead, keep talking to the passengers and escaping to the Private Cabin.

NO.19: CHANGING MERCHANT RESPONSES

When speaking to the traveling merchant Dyce in Balfonheim Port or to Tetran and Lulucce when first arriving at the Eruyt Village, there are two different sets of lines depending on whether or not you have talked to them before. If you didn't talk to Tetran on the Leviathan, your conversation starts with a self introduction when meeting him in the Eruyt Village. Conversely, if you didn't speak with Dyce in the Ogir-Yensa Sandsea or any of his other potential meeting locations, he won't have much to say when you run into him in Balfonheim Port.

NO.20: CHANGING CONVERSATIONS

The conversations with the people listed in the following table change a great deal depending on who leads the party. Try making each character the party leader, then talk to each person.

CHARACTERS WHOSE CONVERSATIONS CHANGE DEPENDING ON WHO IS LEADER

LOCATION	PERSON
East Spur Stairs (Garamsythe Waterway)	Defeated Soldier (vanishes after escaping from the Nalbina Dungeons)

> RABANASTRAN
> HEY, MISTER. YOU WANNA HEAR SOME OLD LEGENDS FROM RABANASTRE & FOLKLORE? IT WON'T COST YA MUCH. WHAT? I GOTTA EAT, TOO, YA KNOW.

CHARACTERS WHOSE CONVERSATIONS CHANGE DRASTICALLY WHEN FRAN IS LEADER

LOCATION	PERSON
Crystal Glade (Giza Plains)	Viera Wayfarer (vanishes after the Gil Snapper hunt)
Pithead Junction A (Henne Mines)	Wounded Imperial (vanishes after obtaining the Lente's Tear key item)
Rava's Pass (Phon Coast)	Viera Wayfarer

NO.21: CUTTING REMARKS
Attempting to run away from certain bosses or heading in a different direction from where you should be going can lead to unexpected remarks. At the points shown here, head toward the location specified to enjoy a few acidic remarks at your expense.

LOCATION	PLACE TO GO
During the Air Cutter Remora fight in Nalbina Fortress	Aerial Gardens area of Nalbina Fortress
Heading for the Rabanastre Sandsea after hearing Migelo's request	Southern Plaza area of Rabanastre
Heading toward the Crystal Glade (The Dry) area of Giza Plains after hearing Masyua's story	Throne Road area of Giza Plains
Split off from Balthier and in need of a cab in the Imperial City of Archades	Alley of Muted Sighs area of Old Archades

NO.22: CHOCOBO ONLY MESSAGES
Attempting to enter towns or dungeons while riding a chocobo causes a special message to appear saying that you must dismount or turn back. This message changes depending on the location, as shown here.

MESSAGES DISPLAYED WHEN A CHOCOBO WON'T ENTER AN AREA

PLACE	MESSAGE
Any town or village	"You must dismount to proceed."
Dungeon	"The chocobo refuses to go any further."
Esper Zone	"The chocobo is too scared to proceed any further. Something terrifying lies ahead"

NO.23: NO ESPERS, PLEASE
When one of your party members is accompanied by an Esper, you cannot use airships or chocobos. If you are aware of this and attempt to use them while having an Esper, you can hear different lines. Most of these situations require summoning the Esper outside of the city.

WHERE TO GO:
- Try to use a regular service airship.
- Try to ride the Strahl from the airship terminal.
- Try to rent a chocobo from Gurdy (the lines differ depending on whether you are in Nalbina Fortress or another place).
- Try to ride a stray chocobo (the lines differ depending on whether you are trying to ride the chocobo in the Henne Mines or another place).
- Try to borrow the chocobo from the Imperial Soldier in the Ozmone Plains.

According to the girl at the reception desk, there is a chance that the strong magick power exuded by Espers can have a bad influence on an airship's gauges. Sounds like an excuse to me!

System Related

NO.24: SKY PIRATE'S DEN & REKS
The Sky Pirate's Den seems to be Vaan's thing, but during the short amount of time that you play as Reks, it's possible to unlock a few of the Sky Pirate's Den rewards.

GOAL	REWARD
Receive more than 100,000 gil	Penelo
Use the Attack command more than 300 times	Balthier
Use the Magick command more than 200 times	Fran
Defeat more than 500 foes	Basch
Creating a 50-Chain or greater in battle	Montblanc

NO.25: DISTANCE WALKED
A tally of the number of steps taken is kept during the game. The total walked distance can sometimes increase even if you're not actually using the analog stick to move your character. Certain things such as being knocked back when attacked or being pushed around by other characters in towns will increase this number. The distance walked is based on the movements of the party leader.

NO.26: WEAKENED BASCH?!
When first entering the North-South Junction during the escape from the Barheim Passage, Basch obtains a weapon and armor and his appearance changes. At this point, Basch's parameters are actually recalculated as though he had just gained a level. Oddly enough, his MAX HP and MP could actually decrease due to the slightly random nature of these values. This happens most often if your party members have not leveled up during the Barheim Passage section.

NO.27: HIDDEN MEANING ON THE WORLD MAP
Look closely at the isometric location icons displayed on the world map and you'll notice that beneath some of them, there are small colored strips. These strips indicate the different possible ways to warp to those locations.

Blue: A blue strip on the left indicates that a Gate Crystal is present.

Green: If a green strip on the lower-right of the icon is present, an aerodrome is located in that location. After unlocking free movement in the Strahl, the green indicator shows that there's a Strahl Anchor in the area.

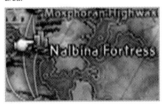

Green and Blue: If both the green and blue strips are present, a Gate Crystal and an aerodrome are in the location.

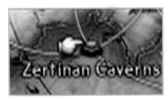

Nothing: If there are no strips underneath the icons, neither a Gate Crystal nor Strahl Anchor can be used to get to that location.

NO.28: STATUS EFFECTS MAXIMUM
Up to 27 different status effects can be applied to a single party member at one time. To do this, you must use items, accessories, spells and even traps. Every status effect aside from X-Zone, KO, Stone, Lure (or Stop) and HP critical (or Disease) can be applied at once!

NO.29: LIMITING AN AREA EFFECT SPELL
If after a character has started to perform an action, his target moves into another zone or the equipment of the character performing the action is changed, the action is interrupted and immediately comes to an end. Making use of this allows you to manipulate area effect actions so that they only hit selected targets. For example, say you are facing a Skeleton and a Steeling in battle. Normally in this situation, casting Curaja would damage the Skeleton but heal the Steeling. However, if you make the Skeleton the

---

target of the Curaja and quickly change equipment immediately after the Skeleton has been damaged, the spell is cut short and doesn't heal the Steeling.

NO.30: ALTERED VIEW
After completing a hunt or immediately after using a Gate Crystal to move to another zone, you cannot move or input commands for a short period of time. However, you can still move around your viewpoint.

NO.31: MERITS OF A LONE WARRIOR
After more than three characters have joined your party, it's likely that you always use the maximum of three, right? Well, there are a few merits to only using one character!

When using an area effect action on allies
> Area effect actions can target all reserve characters. Therefore, if you have only one battle member, you can heal the remaining five reserve characters with a single Curaja spell.

Avoiding traps
> When walking down a narrow passage, other battle members often run into traps. You can avoid this by reducing the number of battle members to one at these points.

Surviving enemy area effect attacks
> Some enemies have area effect attacks, such as Zodiark's Darkja, which they use in a regular pattern or fixed time. Reducing your battle members to one prior to this attack can minimize its effect.

NO.32: MAXIMUM ITEM DROPS
The icons for the items dropped by monsters generally disappear after a set amount of time. If there are already 10 icons in the area before that time runs out, when the 11th icon appears, the oldest symbol will disappear instantly.

NO.33: OBTAINING TRAPPED TREASURE
When a treasure chest appears with a trap underneath it, there is no obvious way to grab the goodies without taking a hit. You could equip the Winged Boots accessory, which provides a constant Float effect, but there is actually an even easier way to get the item. Press lightly on the left analog stick to walk very slowly toward the chest, then as soon as the field sign "!!" appears, press the ✖ button. If there are enemies nearby, make sure the leader's Gambit is in the OFF position.

Slowly make your way to the chest aaaaand, bingo!

NO.34: SWITCHING A TARGETED CHARACTER
When a battle member becomes the target of any kind of action, his name changes to red and he cannot be transferred to the reserve. However, if you use Cure or a potion on a reserve member and then make him a battle member before the action is performed, the character's name remains white, regardless of the fact that he's being targeted. You can also return this character to the reserve.

NO.35: NAME COLORS

When Libra is not in effect on anyone in the battle party, the enemy name displayed in the Target Info box appears as blue, yellow, or red depending on the strength of the targeted enemy compared to the current leader. Unfortunately, boss names are always displayed in white, indicating that the gap between their level and the leader is unknown.

NO.36: STATUS WITHOUT LIBRA

Some allies make it possible to see more than just a target's name and current status effects even if no members of the battle party are using Libra. There are certain ally characters, such as Bansat and Krjn, who only join the party for specific battles. They will make the enemy's Level, HP, and Elemental weakness or just Elemental weakness appear without the use of Libra.

Battle Related

NO.37: REVERSE BATTLE CHAIN

A battle chain ends when you defeat a different type of enemy from that defeated previously, but at that instant another chain actually begins! A hidden, "Reverse Battle Chain" exists, linked by continually defeating different types of monsters. A high Reverse Battle Chain slightly increases the chances of items being dropped, but has few real advantages compared to a regular battle chain.

NO.38: MOVE WHEN IMMOBLIZIED

A character affected by the Immobilize status may not be able to move by himself, but he can still be moved. If the affected character is pushed by another character or knocked back by enemy attacks, he can end up outside of the center of action. Use an attack with a step-in motion to get back into the action.

NO.39: WAIT FOR US!

The only player you can move directly is the leader, while the other battle members follow. So what happens in situations where the leader runs far away while the other members are busy fighting or can't move for some reason? When the party leader is far away, the other battle members' running speed increases by 1.25 times, so they will eventually catch up.

NO.40: BETTER LOOT WITH OMEGA MARK XII

After defeating Omega Mark XII, there is a very small chance that it will drop a **Mythril Sword**. However, you can improve this chance by simply raising your Chain Level prior to the fight. By doing so, the item drop rates improve even though single-mark Omega Mark XII should be unaffected by Chain Level.

NO.41: BATTLE CHAINING ALLIES

A battle chain occurs not only when you defeat monsters, but also when you defeat allies! In some ways, this chain is even easier than a monster chain because you

only need to go to one other zone for an ally to reappear in the same spot. Thus, you can defeat the ally, go to another zone, come back, defeat the ally, and repeat the process over again. You can even attack different allies to build up a chain as long as they're of the same race!

NO.42: MAGICK AND ACTION TIMING EFFECTS

The amount of damage or healing caused by an action along with whether or not status effects take hold are determined the instant the action reaches the target. Knowing this, you can do a couple of things to maximize your defensive prowess. First, if a character with the Serenity license grid unlocked (Serenity increases Magick power when HP are full) uses Curaja to heal all three battle characters, your party benefits the most by selecting the caster as the target of the spell. In this case, Curaja first heals the HP of the target character, bringing his HP back to full and increasing the amount of HP restored on subsequently cured characters.

You can also use attack timing knowledge to protect all of your characters from an enemy area effect status with a single nullification accessory. For example, if the enemy uses an ability such as Disable, select the targeted character first and equip the Black Belt. As soon as "IMMUNE" appears, remove the Black Belt from the targeted character and equip it on the next closest character. Finally, equip the Black Belt onto the final party member to complete your defense.

NO.43: ZERO DAMAGE INDICATORS

If your target is in a counter-attack position, or possesses an attribute that absorbs the attack, their HP will recover by the amount of damage they would normally have received and the attack value will be displayed in green numbers. If absolutely no damage is received or recovered, the number "0" is displayed in red. If an opponent is using "Magic Barrier" or some other neutralization effect, attacks will result in an "IMMUNE" message. If the enemy neutralizes an Esper or Quickening attack, it will also result in a red colored "0".

NO.44: ELEMENTAL DAMAGE AND STATUS EFFECTS

Attacking a monster with an elemental weapon when the foe can nullify or absorb that element will not cause any damage. However, if the weapon has an additional effect, it may still occur at the fixed rate, regardless of the damage being absorbed or healed.

NO.45: COUNTERING DISTANT ENEMIES

A counter enables a character to strike back against an attacking enemy. You may think that you can only counter a ranged attack if the attacking enemy is nearby, but it's actually possible to counter even the most distant enemy. For example, equip a Hand-bomb to an ally and attack another ally with a Sword at long range. If a counter occurs, you will be treated to an awesome display of martial arts.

NO.46: CONTINUOUS "NUMEROLOGY"

The area effect technick Numerology is a special attack technick that doubles in strength each time it is used, so long as it does not miss. Even though there is an initial damage of 1 (2 to surrounding enemies), after 17 consecutive hits the damage will reach 65,536 (131,072 to surrounding enemies). The 18th attack always misses

and returns the damage to 1. After 17 successful hits, if you then attack an enemy using the option "Safety" with Numerology, they will nullify the damage, but you still have a 13% chance of causing 131072 damage to surrounding enemies.

NO.47: MAGICK WITHOUT MP OR A LICENSE

Normally, you need to purchase a magick spell and learn the appropriate license before you can use it. However, there is a way to use Black Magick without fulfilling either of these conditions. The method is simple: use the technick Shades of Black. This technick allows magic to be used regardless of whether you have the license or own the spell.

NO.48: CONFUSION + INVISIBILITY = TOTAL CHAOS

Confused characters will attempt to "fight" an allied character (including themselves). But what happens if all battle members just happen to be Invisible? Unable to find anything to turn their confusion against, the poor character runs off randomly.

Hey guys? Uhh, anybody there? Hello?

NO.49: FAULTY CONCURRENCE?

A Concurrence attack performed after a Quickening will damage all of the enemies around the initially targeted enemy. However, this isn't the case when fighting a boss with minions. If the Quickening damage kills the boss, the battle will end before the surrounding minions are defeated and you won't receive the LP for them.

NO.50: KEEPING INACTIVE CREATURES INACTIVE

You can damage inactive enemies by the surrounding Concurrence damage from a Quickening aimed at a different monster without becoming active. You can use this strategy to defeat powerful inactive monsters, such as the Wild Saurian, even when your party is still quite weak.

NO.51: REPEATEDLY STEAL FROM AN ENEMY

Since you can only steal once from each enemy, after Steal is successful you normally need to go at least two zones away and cause the enemy to respawn before you can steal again. Bosses and marks are an exception to this rule, though. Simply go into a neighboring area to steal from them again. Near the start of the game you can use this technique to repeatedly steal the Glass Jewel (which can be sold for 115 Gil) during the Wraith hunt.

In addition there are some bosses and marks that you can steal from multiple times without having to go to another Zone.

ENEMY	CONDITIONS
Rook x4	Defeat a Rook (only after defeating first Rook)
Dr. Cid (2nd fight)	Reduce HP to less then 50%
Gabranth (1st fight, 2nd fight)	Reduce HP to less then 50%
Gilgamesh (1st time)	Each time HP reduced by 20% of MAX (can steal once at 80%, 60%, 40% and 20%).
Gilgamesh (2nd time)	Each time HP reduced by 20% of MAX (can steal once at 80%, 60%, 40% and 20%).
Shadowseer	When enemy calls Pandemonium

NO.56: LV. 99 RED CHOCOBO

Red and Black Chocobos normally roam the Haulo Green area of the Ozmone Plains. However, if you meet a specific set of requirements, a chocobo called Lv. 99 Red Chocobo may appear. When defeated, this titan can drop valuable items such as a **Ribbon** or **Gemsteel**.

After gaining free use of the *Strahl*, travel to the Ozmone Plains area and defeat six or more Red and Black Chocobos, then enter or reenter the Haulo Green area. Upon arrival there is a 1 in 256 chance for the Lv.99 Red Chocobo to appear. If the enemy does not show up, simply go two zones away (Dagan Flats) and return. Keep in mind this can take a very long time.

NO.57: ONE-TIME ATTACKS REPEATED

The Flowering Cactoid's Thousand Needles or Feral Retriever's Balance are attacks that these monsters should only be able to use once per battle. However, if you move far away from that enemy, or if all current battle members are knocked out after these attacks have been used, the enemy can use the attack again.

NO.58: EXP FROM ALLIES

Fundamentally, there are no merits for defeating the allies who fight with you on the field, such as the Dalmascan soldiers. However, it is possible to garner a few experience points and gil if you defeat certain allies at the following levels.

ALLY	LOCATION	PARTY LEVEL	EXP
Rabanastre Watch	Dalmasca Westersand	4	20
	Dalmasca Estersand	5	
Bangaa Hunter	Giza Plains (The Dry)	4	
Garif Hunter	Giza Plains (The Rains)	22	
Seeq Fisher	Phon Coast	37-38	145-290

NO.59: LEVEL 99 MONSTERS

Some monster actions, such as Cannibalize or Mystery Waltz, raise the monster's level. Furthermore, it is possible for monsters with these actions to use them enough times to reach level 99. Note that the Wild Saurian only consumes nearby wolves while in its inactive "friendly" state.

The Wild Saurian can become level 99 if it uses the Cannibalize ability enough times. Can you defeat it?

NO.60: PUSHY CHOCOBOS

Vaan and the others can push monsters around by walking into them, but some heavier monsters (such as the Clay Golems or Slaven Wilders) only move a small bit. To move them further, simply hop onto a chocobo. When riding a chocobo, it's possible to push around all enemies—no matter how heavy they are.

NO.61: OVERCOME ORTHROS'S DISLIKE OF MEN

Elite Mark Orthros has an affinity for women. Normally, he won't appear unless you have a party consisting of nothing but women. As long as Fran, Penelo, and Ashe are your main party members, bringing either Larsa or Reddas along as a guest member won't cause Orthros to hide.

NO.62: MONSTERS' NATURAL HEALING

Monsters that have lost sight of your party gradually recover HP over time. Even monsters such as Hell Wyrm and Yiazmat, which won't regain HP when the party exits the zone, aren't exceptions to this rule.

NO.63: DECOY AND THE BA'GAMNAN CLAN

Of all the monsters in the game, the only ones incapable of nullifying Decoy status are the Ba'Gamnan Clan (Ba'Gamnan, Bwagi, Gijuk, and Rinok). Cast Decoy on an ally in Reflect status and bounce the spell onto one of them to get things started. In theory, they should now begin to tear each other apart, right? Wrong. They will continue their attack as though nothing has changed. On top of this, your own battle members ignore their Gambits and attack the Decoy enemy.

NO.64: UNIQUE MANDRAGORA ENDINGS

You will fight five monsters called the Mandragoras in the Hall of Lambent Darkness area of the Sochen Cave Palace. You can defeat them in any order, but depending on the one you defeat last, the beginning of the event scene that plays immediately after the battle changes slightly. You can see each of the different Mandragoras' unique personalities depending on which of them goes down last.

NO.65: BASCH AND GABRANTH

The second battle with Judge Gabranth takes place in the Central Lift area of Sky Fortress Bahamut. When his remaining HP falls below 50%, he responds by speaking a few lines. The content can change depending on whether or not Basch is in your party.

If Basch is in your party Gabranth will be mean.

If Basch is not in your party, Gabranth will still be mean—just in a slightly different way.

NO.66: GILGAMESH AND ENKIDU'S BOND

The Elite Mark Gilgamesh spouts some bold lines when his HP falls below 80%, each time you fight him. If you haven't defeated Enkidu at this point, then an additional line is added.

NO.67: GILGAMESH'S WEAPON COLLECTION

Many of the weapons used by Gilgamesh are replicas of those from previous FINAL FANTASY games.

Orichalum Replica
A replica of the Orichalcum, this is a short sword that has been a regular in the FINAL FANTASY series.

Excalibur Replica
A replica of the Excalibur, the moon crest on the hilt is based upon the design from FINAL FANTASY V.

Excalibur XII
This is a replica of the Holy Sword Excalibur. This one is also based on the FINAL FANTASY V model, but this one has a sun emblem on the hilt.

Steel Cutter Replica
A replica of the Steel Cutter blade used by the summon monster Odin. It has a blue-black blade with an unnerving face set into it.

Buster Sword Replica
A replica of the Buster Sword, this mighty blade was used by Cloud, the main character from FINAL FANTASY VII.

Gunblade Replica
This is a replica of the Gunblade used by Squall in FINAL FANTASY VIII. There is a small chocobo printed on the blade.

Brotherhood Replica
This is a replica of the Brotherhood sword used by Tidus in FINAL FANTASY X.

Legendary Sword
A replica of the Legendary Sword found in Dragon Warrior I – III.

NO.68: KNOCK BACK

When using the Attack command, "knock back" can sometimes occur. This means that the enemy is pushed back a little after being hit. If the knock back occurs on the blow that kills an enemy, you will see a special animation of the enemy being sent flying. This does not work on monsters larger than a human, though.

NO.69: PANICKY MALBORO MINIONS

When fighting the Wild Malboro mark, ignore its smaller minions and instead defeat the Wild Malboro first. With their leader history, the other Malboros fall into a panic and simply stop attacking.

NO.70: BESTIARY STAMPS

You can view all monsters you have previously defeated in the Clan Primer Bestiary. Look closely and you'll see that some monsters have a stamp on them.

Mark

Elite Mark

Rare Game

Hunt Club Rare Game

ITEMS

NO.71: VICTORY CELEBRATIONS

After defeating a tricky boss or mark, you will hear the traditional FINAL FANTASY battle victory music. When you hear this sound, watch what your character's reactions very closely. They will celebrate with their favorite weapons.

NO.72: LOST NOTE AND SECRET STASH

In the Phase 2 Dig point area of Henne Mines, you can find a **Discarded piece of paper**. This is actually a fragment from the diary of one of the workers in the mine. Read it to learn that a worker's secret stash is hidden in the mine. The hint states to go "around 4." In other words, go somewhere near the Special Charter Shaft area, which looks like a "4" on the map. Search around here to find the treasure of Bacchus's Wine x3 and Mega Elixir x2.

Well, I guess it kinda looks like a "4."

NO.73: MEGA FANG DAMAGE

The Blue Fang, Red Fang, and White Fang items normally deal damage equivalent to 25% of the target's Max HP. Depending on how it is used, though, it is possible to deal damage that is greater than 100% of the target's HP. To do so, equip a Pheasant Netsuke and a weapon that strengthens the attribute of the Fang you're using, then attack the target's weak point. Doing so deals more damage than 100% of the target's HP and allows you to defeat it in a single attack.

NO.74: NO MIST CHARGE RECOVERY

If one of your characters has the Goddess Tear or Dawn Shard equipped and a different character triggers a Quickening, the character with the MP 0 item equipped cannot participate in the Quickening combo. During the Quickening combo attack, these items deny those characters the ability to select the Mist Charge command to prepare their Mist Charges for attack.

NO.75: THE UNLUCKY MERCHANT

You can find an Unlucky Merchant in the Outpost near Dalmasca Estersand. This merchant's chocobo loves to scatter gil around, and has buried all of his profits around the camp. The "glittering things" scattered around the outpost are actually his profits. Follow the map here to obtain all 17 gil.

After the Inauguration Ceremony, this merchant will move to the South Bank Village part of the Dalmasca Estersand. Even at this new location, his chocobo will bury his profits in the ground. After speaking to the merchant, a "mysterious glint" will randomly appear in one of the locations marked on the map shown here. Each time you leave the zone and return, the random item will reappear.

You can get 1 Gil, 3 Gil, 5 Gil, or a Teleport Stone at one of these random locations.

NO.76: OVERPRICED BAZAAR GOODS?

Among the items you can obtain through the Bazaar are several items that you can find in the shop. In most cases, it is cheaper to obtain these through trading. One of these items, the Large Gloves (Blazer Gloves) is 1300 gil cheaper if you buy it from a shop. Other bazaar goods, such as the Flask of Oily Liquid (Ether) and A Mysterious Substance (Dark Matter) are also cheaper if purchased from the shop, but the conditions for getting them to go on sale are quite tough.

NO.77: ATTACK MOTION AND STANCE VARIETY

Weapons can be used by any character in your party provided they have the license panel opened. Use the same weapon type with more than one character and you'll notice that each character's stance and attack animation differ ever so slightly.

VARIETY

NO.78: TITLE DEMO MONSTERS

FINAL FANTASY XII opens with a beautiful introductory sequence that shows a montage of some of the most impressive imagery the game has to offer. Hang around for the entire introduction and near the end you'll notice that the game flashes through multiple enemies in the span of less than a second each.

1. Chaos   2. Hashmal

3. Humbaba Mistant   4. Fury

5. King Bomb   6. Daedalus

7. Tyrant   8. Shemhazai

9. Ultima   10. Elder Wyrm

11. Flan   12. Firemane

13. Cúchulainn   14. Tiamat

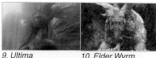

15. Phoenix   16. Rafflesia

17. Mimic Queen   18. Zalera

19. Exodus   20. Vinuskar

21. Mateus   22. Zeromus

23. Fenrir   24. Ahriman

25. Hell Wyrm   26. Yiazmat

27. Garuda   28. Demon Wall

29. Belias   30. Adrammelech

31. Earth Tyrant   32. Hydro

NO.79: A.K.A (CHANGING NAMES)

When you approach characters with whom you can converse, their names appear above their head. For some characters, however, this name will change. In the Highgarden Terrace area of Archades, for example, one of the characters named Archadian Gentry turns out to be the owner of the Hunt Club after you talk to him, and his name switches to Hunt Club Owner.

NO.80: THE JOVIAL SEEQ'S LOST LAUGH

There is a store near the other side of the civilian house in the Northern Area of Rabanastre Lowtown that resembles a weapons shop. Inside you will find a seeq with the name Jovial Seeq. As his name implies, he is almost always laughing loudly. However, if you visit him at a certain time, he won't be laughing. This occurs after you have escaped from the Barheim Passage, but before you have completed the Waterway Haunting hunt. The hiding child mentioned by Milha, the mission's client, is actually Deeg, this seeq's son. After you complete the Wraith hunt, his spirits pick up once again.

The Jovial seeq laughing it up.

NO.81: REUNITE WITH JINN IN RABANASTRE

When the rainy season comes to the Nomad Village in the Giza Plains, move onward. During the story, the rainy season first comes to Giza after you obtain the Dawn Shard. If you go to the Southern Plaza section of Rabanastre at this point, you can meet Jinn. Talk to him and he explains that the rainy season has come, and that there is no one in the nomad settlement.

NO.82: GURDY TAKES TO THE SKY

After obtaining the Sword of Kings but prior to defeating Judge Bergan, the chocobo rental owner Gurdy disappears from the Sand-strewn Pass in the Mt Bur-Omisace. Rotate the camera down and look up into the sky to find out where she is!

NO.83: THE MOOGLES EIGHT

The Moogles Eight are doing their dance near the bridge at Old Archades. What you may not notice, though, is that as you examine the dancing moogles, the camera cycles between three different viewpoints beginning with the view from above and in front, switching the view from above and behind, and finally getting down at their level for a close-up view.

Look at 'em shake their puffballs!

NO.84: THE FACE OF IMPERIALS

Find the Imperial Soldier picking over the wares in front of the weapon shop in the West Ward area of the Nalbina Fortress. Although Archadian Soldier's normally have their visors down, this one's visor is wide open. Rotate the right analog stick to see his face.

Guess they're not all smiling under there.

NO.85: THE CHOCOBO WHO LOVES PEOPLE

Chocobos in rental pens normally ignore Vaan and his friends. However, the friendly chocobos found in the West Barbican area of the Nalbina Fortress are an exception to this rule. If they notice Vaan and his friends, they will move over to them.

Sorry… no carrots today.

NO.86: PSYCHEDELIC CÚCHULAINN

Cúchulainn has a crazy special effect that gives him his unique look. Summon him and cast Vanish on him to make him look even crazier!

Wooah, trippy!

NO.87: PEDESTRIANS AND ESPERS

If you are in Summon Beast mode in the West Barbican area of the Nalbina Fortress, pedestrians may bump into the Summon Beast. You would expect them to go flying away, but they actually just continue on their way.

A seeq tests Zeromus's patience.

NO.88: VIEWING THE ZONE BEYOND

Approach almost any zone break line (the dotted line that separates two zones) and you'll notice that the area on the other side is nearly as detailed as it looks after passing over the zone line. Also, pay attention to the zone line in areas where townspeople are traveling in between zones. You can watch them travel to the other side and actually catch up with them if you follow them through the zone!

Check out the bazaar beyond the line and the strolling patrons.

NO.89: DANGLING MOOGLES

Moogles across the land have a variety of cute poses. Of special note are the moogles hanging from the sides of shop counters and banisters. These little guys are sometimes hanging just a few feet from the ground, but they're kicking their legs as if their life depends on it.

That's a long drop for a moogle.

NO.90: SAVE 1100 GIL!

After escaping Rabanastre and entering the Garamsythe Waterway, Balthier and Fran join the party, bringing with them Cure, Fire and First Aid. As such, you can obtain these for free at this point in the story without purchasing them from a shop.

NO.91: THE ULTIMATE COMBO!

If you select Attack with certain weapons, a combo may occur where multiple attacks are performed one after another. The maximum number of combo attacks is 12, and if all of them connect, the final attack count number will be displayed larger than usual.

NO.92: CHANGING STOPPING ANIMATION

Press the left analog stick for less than three seconds, then release it. You'll notice that your party leader stops suddenly in his tracks. Now try pressing on the left analog stick for longer than three seconds and releasing it. This causes your lead character to bend a bit at the knees upon stopping.

NO.93: AIRSHIP CREW

If you select By Leisure Craft when flying, the names of the crew are announced upon take off. The crew's names are fixed for each possible route. The names of the Captain and Chief Steward are often taken from the names of the cities between which the routes fly. Also note that the coloring of the female crews' uniforms are also different, depending on the route.

NO.94: SECRETS OF THE GREAT CRYSTAL

Each zone in the Great Crystal has a peculiar name. Although they may appear meaningless, each name has a meaning that helps to identify where in the Great Crystal that zone is located.

Let's take the Sirhru Phullam Udiipratii, as an example. "Sirhru" indicates the layer. Use the following chart to determine that Sirhru means Silurian, which indicates that this area is on one of the higher layers away from the core. The "Phullam" section of the name corresponds to Phloem, which indicates the distance from

the core (Phloem is the furthest possible distance away). Lastly, "Udiipratii" indicates North (Udii) and West (Pratii), showing that this area is Northwest from the centre.

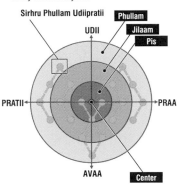

The location map alone doesn't show it, but the Great Crystal is actually comprised of many different layers.

Overview of the Sirhru level within the crystal.

NAME	MEANING	GREAT CRYSTALS DEFINED
Peak	Peak	Crystal Peak is obviously the top.
Kanbhru	Cambrian	Kanbhru, Vikaari, Sirhru, Dhebon, Kabonii, Bhrum, Trahk and Jula are all named after prehistoric periods, with the oldest period coming highest inside Great Crystal. Crystal Core is obviously the central core.
Vikaari	Ordovician	
Sirhru	Silurian	
Dhebon	Devonian	
Kabonii	Carboniferous	
Bhrum	Permian	
Trahk	Triassic	
Jula	Jurassic	
Core	Core	
Prama	Ground	Crystal Ground is where the teleporter links you with Giruvegan.
Pis	Pith	Pis, Jilaam and Phullam indicate the interior, central part, and exterior part of a plant, and are used to show distance from the core inside Great Crystal as indicated on the nearby diagram of the Sirhru region
Jilaam	Xylem	
Phullam	Phloem	
Udii	North	Udii, Avaa, Praa and Pratii indicate North, South, East and West direction in relation to the core.
Avaa	South	
Praa	East	
Pratii	West	
A	Up	A, Dha and Vikaari are used to indicate where a teleporter will take you. "A Vikaari" means move up a layer and Dha Vikaari means to move down a layer.
Dha	Down	
Vikaari	Shift	
Sthaana	Set	Sthaana indicates a location with a wall control switch.

NO.95: A UNIQUE SCENE FOR ASHE

After defeating Gilgamesh, he sneaks up and tries and take the legendary sword that is stuck in the ground. When this occurs, the current party leader senses Gilgamesh's presence and turns around, then gets a puzzled look on his face after

turning back. If Ashe is your party leader, she acts differently than the others. Ashe places her left hand on her chin, then tilts her head as if thinking.

NO.96: SPECIAL BOSS REWARDS

After defeating certain monsters (mainly bosses), Montblanc passes along gil and thanks from across the world that have been entrusted to him by individuals or organizations to hand out as a reward for a job well done.

MONSTER	THANKS RECEIVED FROM...
Flan x4	Rabanastre Rulers
Firemane	Rabanastre Healers
Mimic Queen	Rabanastre Girl
Demon Wall (Front)	Ancient Ruins Study Group
Demon Wall (Interior)	Ancient Ruins Study Group
Earth Tyrant	Merchant Caravan
Tiamat	Henne Miners
Elder Wyrm	Viera Guard
Vinuskar	The Platinum Guild
King Bomb	Salikawoods' Patrol
Ahriman	Barkeep
Mandragora	Mandragora Friends Association
Hell Wyrm	Montblanc
Rafflesia	Garif Warrior
Daedalus	Montblanc
Tyrant	Montblanc
Hydro	Clan Buckaboo
Humbaba Mistant	Nabreus People
Fury	Nabreus People
Belias	Minstrel
4 Espers	Minstrel
8 Espers	Minstrel
All 13 Espers	Minstrel

NO.97: DIFFERENT AIRSHIP SCENES

Both the Strahl and airship terminal methods of transportation include a special takeoff event that lasts just a few moments. Depending on certain factors, these events will vary.

Strahl

Takeoff is shown from three random camera angles. Also, weather affects the takeoff view. If it's raining, the sky will seem cloudy and you can watch the rain bounce off the Strahl as it takes to the skies.

Just one of many cool airship scenes.

Airship Terminal

When flying out of an airship terminal, you may notice that different people on the ground see you off depending on which terminal you're leaving from.

DEPARTURE	DEPARTURE FRIENDS
Rabanastre	Bangaa, hume male, hume female
Nalbina Fortress	Bangaa with a box on his shoulder, Imperial
Bhujerba	Hume male, 1 or 2 moogles, bhujerba guide
Archades	A hume family (father, mother, and son)
Barfonheim Port	2 pirates, hume male waiting for luggage

The pirate departure could use more Ninjas.

NO.98: MOOGLING ATTENDANTS' SPECIAL ACTIONS

In Rabanastre, there is a useful teleport service run by a Moogling Attendant. When you first speak to them, they look up in excitement as you make your selection. Upon choosing a location, the Moogling Attendant bows down, then quickly jumps up, and waves goodbye. When you finally arrive at your destination, the Moogling Attendant there gives you another wave of introduction.

The cutest Moogle yet!

NO.99: CHOCOBO RIDERS

Vaan stands in for your entire party when in a town or city, regardless of who your party leader is. However, this isn't the case when your party is riding chocobos. Select any party member as your leader and hop onto a chocobo. You'll notice that the lead party member you chose is riding the Chocobo instead of Vaan. Once you're on a chocobo, you can't change your lead party member until you hop off the chocobo.

Basch... chocobo wrangler supreme.

NO.100: FIERY-EYED CHOCOBOS

Hop on a chocobo and press the ❌ button to sprint. Swing the camera around to the front and stare into the giant bird's eyes. They're a glowing red color!

This redeye wasn't caused by the camera.

One-Handed Weapons

The most versatile and plentiful weapons in the game, one-handed weapons have one distinct advantage over other classes: they allow the use of a shield. This feature greatly enhances survivability, especially when coupled with the Gauntlets accessory.

Swords

| SMALLSWORDS | SWORDS 1 | SWORDS 2 | SWORDS 3 | SWORDS 4 | BLOOD SWORD | SWORDS 5 | SWORDS 6 | SWORDS 7 |

Swords are perhaps the most basic one-handed weapon, offering a solid mix of speed, consistency, and power. Your character's strength, the sword's attack rating, and the enemy's defense affect a sword's damage potential. All swords except for the Stoneblade add 5 to Evasion.

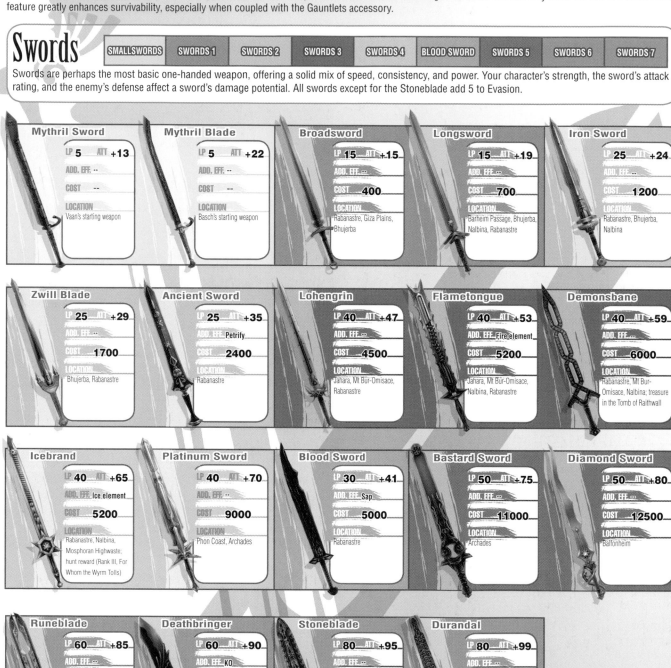

Mythril Sword
LP 5   ATT +13
ADD. EFF. --
COST --
LOCATION: Vaan's starting weapon

Mythril Blade
LP 5   ATT +22
ADD. EFF. --
COST --
LOCATION: Basch's starting weapon

Broadsword
LP 15   ATT +15
ADD. EFF. --
COST 400
LOCATION: Rabanastre, Giza Plains, Bhujerba

Longsword
LP 15   ATT +19
ADD. EFF. --
COST 700
LOCATION: Barheim Passage, Bhujerba, Nalbina, Rabanastre

Iron Sword
LP 25   ATT +24
ADD. EFF. --
COST 1200
LOCATION: Rabanastre, Bhujerba, Nalbina

Zwill Blade
LP 25   ATT +29
ADD. EFF. --
COST 1700
LOCATION: Bhujerba, Rabanastre

Ancient Sword
LP 25   ATT +35
ADD. EFF. Petrify
COST 2400
LOCATION: Rabanastre

Lohengrin
LP 40   ATT +47
ADD. EFF. --
COST 4500
LOCATION: Jahara, Mt Bur-Omisace, Rabanastre

Flametongue
LP 40   ATT +53
ADD. EFF. Fire element
COST 5200
LOCATION: Jahara, Mt Bur-Omisace, Nalbina, Rabanastre

Demonsbane
LP 40   ATT +59
ADD. EFF. --
COST 6000
LOCATION: Rabanastre, Mt Bur-Omisace, Nalbina; treasure in the Tomb of Raithwall

Icebrand
LP 40   ATT +65
ADD. EFF. Ice element
COST 5200
LOCATION: Rabanastre, Nalbina, Mosphoran Highwaste; hunt reward (Rank III, For Whom the Wyrm Tolls)

Platinum Sword
LP 40   ATT +70
ADD. EFF. --
COST 9000
LOCATION: Phon Coast, Archades

Blood Sword
LP 30   ATT +41
ADD. EFF. Sap
COST 5000
LOCATION: Rabanastre

Bastard Sword
LP 50   ATT +75
ADD. EFF. --
COST 11000
LOCATION: Archades

Diamond Sword
LP 50   ATT +80
ADD. EFF. --
COST 12500
LOCATION: Balfonheim

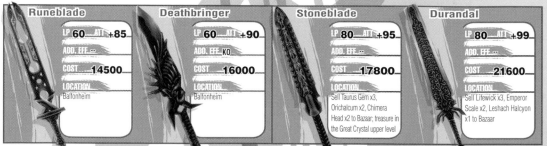

Runeblade
LP 60   ATT +85
ADD. EFF. --
COST 14500
LOCATION: Balfonheim

Deathbringer
LP 60   ATT +90
ADD. EFF. KO
COST 16000
LOCATION: Balfonheim

Stoneblade
LP 80   ATT +95
ADD. EFF. --
COST 17800
LOCATION: Sell Taurus Gem x3, Orichalcum x2, Chimera Head x2 to Bazaar; treasure in the Great Crystal upper level

Durandal
LP 80   ATT +99
ADD. EFF. --
COST 21600
LOCATION: Sell Lifewick x3, Emperor Scale x2, Leshach Halcyon x1 to Bazaar

Daggers

Daggers gain speed over swords at the expense of attack power. Several daggers also have useful additional effects. A dagger's damage is determined by your character's strength and speed compared against the enemy's defense.

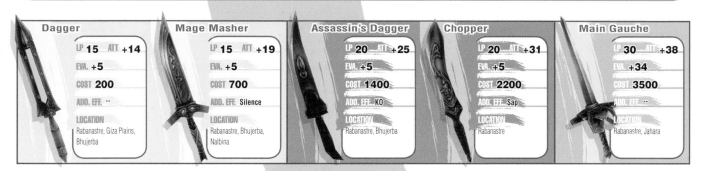

Dagger		Mage Masher		Assassin's Dagger		Chopper		Main Gauche	
LP **15**	ATT **+14**	LP **15**	ATT **+19**	LP **20**	ATT **+25**	LP **20**	ATT **+31**	LP **30**	ATT **+38**
EVA. **+5**		EVA. **+5**		EVA. **+5**		EVA. **+5**		EVA. **+34**	
COST **200**		COST **700**		COST **1400**		COST **2200**		COST **3500**	
ADD. EFF. --		ADD. EFF. Silence		ADD. EFF. KO		ADD. EFF. Sap		ADD. EFF. --	
LOCATION		LOCATION		LOCATION		LOCATION		LOCATION	
Rabanastre, Giza Plains, Bhujerba		Rabanastre, Bhujerba, Nalbina		Rabanastre, Bhujerba		Rabanastre		Rabanastre, Jahara	

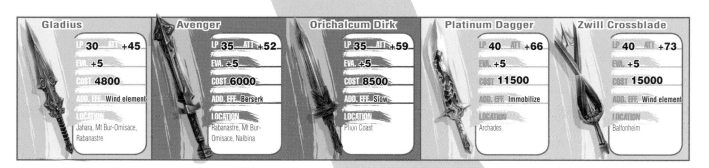

Gladius		Avenger		Orichalcum Dirk		Platinum Dagger		Zwill Crossblade	
LP **30**	ATT **+45**	LP **35**	ATT **+52**	LP **35**	ATT **+59**	LP **40**	ATT **+66**	LP **40**	ATT **+73**
	+5	EVA. **+5**		EVA. **+5**		EVA. **+5**		EVA. **+5**	
COST **4800**		COST **6000**		COST **8500**		COST **11500**		COST **15000**	
ADD. EFF. Wind element		ADD. EFF. Berserk		ADD. EFF. Slow		ADD. EFF. Immobilize		ADD. EFF. Wind element	
LOCATION		LOCATION		LOCATION		LOCATION		LOCATION	
Jahara, Mt Bur-Omisace, Rabanastre		Rabanastre, Mt Bur-Omisace, Nalbina		Phon Coast		Archades		Balfonheim	

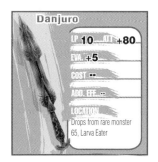

Danjuro	
LP **10**	ATT **+80**
EVA. **+5**	
COST --	
ADD. EFF. --	
LOCATION	
Drops from rare monster 65, Larva Eater	

Axes & Hammers

The axe and hammer class offers huge attack power with a twist: the damage variance is far less consistent than compared to other weapons. Although a sword may consistently strike a foe for 400-500 HP, an axe or hammer may strike that same foe for 800 HP… or 30 HP! For this class of weapons, the weapon damage is determined by the following: your character's strength and vitality, the weapon's attack rating, and the enemy's defense. All axes add 6 to Evasion, while all hammers add 2 to Evasion. Axes also attack slightly faster than hammers.

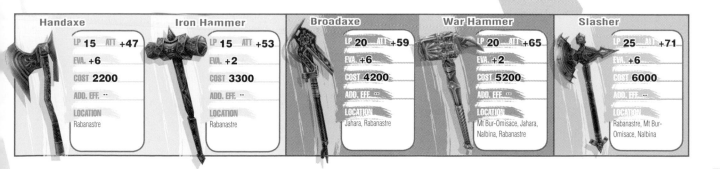

Handaxe		Iron Hammer		Broadaxe		War Hammer		Slasher	
LP **15**	ATT **+47**	LP **15**	ATT **+53**	LP **20**	ATT **+59**	LP **20**	ATT **+65**	LP **25**	ATT **+71**
EVA. **+6**		EVA. **+2**		EVA. **+6**		EVA. **+2**		EVA. **+6**	
COST **2200**		COST **3300**		COST **4200**		COST **5200**		COST **6000**	
ADD. EFF. --		ADD. EFF. --		ADD. EFF. --		ADD. EFF. --		ADD. EFF. --	
LOCATION		LOCATION		LOCATION		LOCATION		LOCATION	
Rabanastre		Rabanastre		Jahara, Rabanastre		Mt Bur-Omisace, Jahara, Nalbina, Rabanastre		Rabanastre, Mt Bur-Omisace, Nalbina	

Equipment

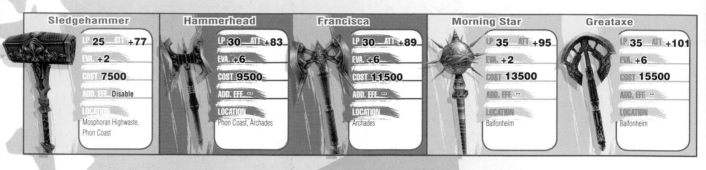

Sledgehammer
LP	25
ATT	+77
EVA.	+2
COST	7500
ADD. EFF.	Disable
LOCATION	Mosphoran Highwaste, Phon Coast

Hammerhead
LP	30
ATT	+83
EVA.	+6
COST	9500
ADD. EFF.	--
LOCATION	Phon Coast, Archades

Francisca
LP	30
ATT	+89
EVA.	+6
COST	11500
ADD. EFF.	--
LOCATION	Archades

Morning Star
LP	35
ATT	+95
EVA.	+2
COST	13500
ADD. EFF.	--
LOCATION	Balfonheim

Greataxe
LP	35
ATT	+101
EVA.	+6
COST	15500
ADD. EFF.	--
LOCATION	Balfonheim

Golden Axe
LP	40
ATT	+110
EVA.	+6
COST	16200
ADD. EFF.	--
LOCATION	Dalmasca Estersand, Bazaar goods

Scorpion Tail
LP	70
ATT	+119
EVA.	+2
COST	60000
ADD. EFF.	--
LOCATION	Sell Charged Gizzard x3, Wyrm Bone x3, Scorpio Gem x4 to Bazaar

Maces

MACES 1	MACES 2	MACES 3	MACES 4	MACES 5

The damage a mace inflicts is based on the weapon's attack power, the magick power of the user, and the enemy's defense. That said, a support character geared entirely for magick power rather than strength or other stats will make good use of a mace. The ability to use a shield also enhances the survivability of those characters. All maces add 4 to Evasion.

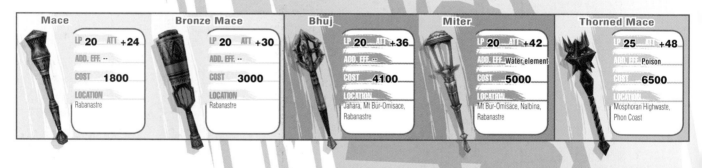

Mace
LP	20
ATT	+24
ADD. EFF.	--
COST	1800
LOCATION	Rabanastre

Bronze Mace
LP	20
ATT	+30
ADD. EFF.	--
COST	3000
LOCATION	Rabanastre

Bhuj
LP	20
ATT	+36
ADD. EFF.	--
COST	4100
LOCATION	Jahara, Mt Bur-Omisace, Rabanastre

Miter
LP	20
ATT	+42
ADD. EFF.	Water element
COST	5000
LOCATION	Mt Bur-Omisace, Nalbina, Rabanastre

Thorned Mace
LP	25
ATT	+48
ADD. EFF.	Poison
COST	6500
LOCATION	Mosphoran Highwaste, Phon Coast

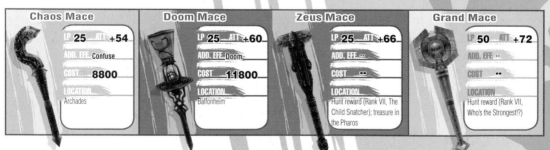

Chaos Mace
LP	25
ATT	+54
ADD. EFF.	Confuse
COST	8800
LOCATION	Archades

Doom Mace
LP	25
ATT	+60
ADD. EFF.	Doom
COST	11800
LOCATION	Balfonheim

Zeus Mace
LP	25
ATT	+66
ADD. EFF.	--
COST	--
LOCATION	Hunt reward (Rank VII, The Child Snatcher); treasure in the Pharos

Grand Mace
LP	50
ATT	+72
ADD. EFF.	--
COST	--
LOCATION	Hunt reward (Rank VII, Who's the Strongest!?)

Measures

| MEASURES 1 | MEASURES 2 | MEASURES 3 |

These peculiar weapons function much like guns in that damage is calculated based solely on the weapon's attack power, completely ignoring the target's defense. They differ greatly, however, in that the target is often inflicted with beneficial status effects like Protect or Shell!

As the attack rating for measures is generally low, they tend to function as a buffing tool. You can target your own party members with low-damage hits that serve to strengthen your party without the use of MP. All measures add 25 to Evasion while still allowing the use of a shield, making those who use measures hard targets indeed. Measures are more useful for those characters who are only used as support and unlikely to ever actually engage the enemy. If MP management is a concern, use measures to buff your party, and then swap them out for more conventional weaponry.

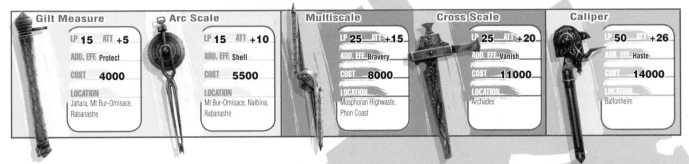

Gilt Measure
LP 15	ATT +5

ADD. EFF. Protect
COST 4000
LOCATION Jahara, Mt Bur-Omisace, Rabanastre

Arc Scale
LP 15	ATT +10

ADD. EFF. Shell
COST 5500
LOCATION Mt Bur-Omisace, Nalbina, Rabanastre

Multiscale
LP 25	ATT +15

ADD. EFF. Bravery
COST 8000
LOCATION Mosphoran Highwaste, Phon Coast

Cross Scale
LP 25	ATT +20

ADD. EFF. Vanish
COST 11000
LOCATION Archades

Caliper
LP 50	ATT +26

ADD. EFF. Haste
COST 14000
LOCATION Balfonheim

Euclid's Sextant
LP 50	ATT +35

ADD. EFF. Bubble
COST --
LOCATION Hunt reward (Rank VI, A Wild Stench)

Two-Handed Weapons

While two-handed weapons do not allow the use of a shield, they compensate for it by consistently inflicting more damage than one-handed weapons. Only axes and hammers approach the damage potential of two-handed weapons, albeit inconsistently. Although it would seem natural that larger weapons would attack less quickly, this is not the case. In fact, most two-handed weapons attack just as quickly, and occasionally more quickly, than their one-handed counterparts.

Greatswords

| STORYLINE ITEM | GREATSWORDS 1 | GREATSWORDS 2 | GREATSWORDS 3 | EXCALIBUR | TOURNESOL |

Greatswords don't start appearing until late in the game, but they are worth the wait. As the most consistently powerful weapons in *Final Fantasy XII*, these swords are at home in any damage-dealing character's hands. Greatsword damage is calculated based on your character's strength, the greatsword's attack rating, and the enemy's defense.

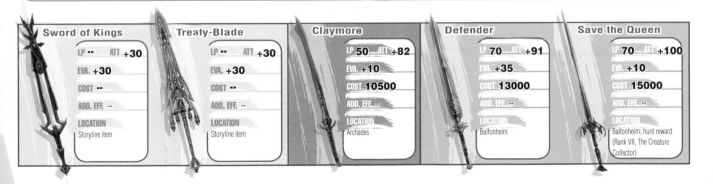

Sword of Kings
LP --	ATT +30

EVA. +30
COST --
ADD. EFF. --
LOCATION Storyline item

Treaty-Blade
LP --	ATT +30

EVA. +30
COST --
ADD. EFF. --
LOCATION Storyline item

Claymore
LP 50	ATT +82

EVA. +10
COST 10500
ADD. EFF. --
LOCATION Archades

Defender
LP 70	ATT +91

EVA. +35
COST 13000
ADD. EFF. --
LOCATION Balfonheim

Save the Queen
LP 70	ATT +100

EVA. +10
COST 15000
ADD. EFF. --
LOCATION Balfonheim; hunt reward (Rank VII, The Creature Collector)

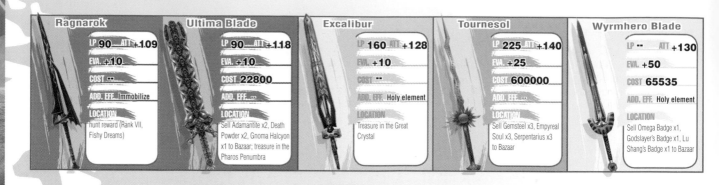

Ragnarok
LP 90 ATT +1.09
EVA. +10
COST --
ADD. EFF. Immobilize
LOCATION
hunt reward (Rank VII, Fishy Dreams)

Ultima Blade
LP 90 ATT +118
EVA. +10
COST 22800
ADD. EFF. --
LOCATION
Sell Adamantite x2, Death Powder x2, Gnoma Halcyon x1 to Bazaar; treasure in the Pharos Penumbra

Excalibur
LP 160 ATT +128
EVA. +10
COST --
ADD. EFF. Holy element
LOCATION
Treasure in the Great Crystal

Tournesol
LP 225 ATT +140
EVA. +25
COST 600000
ADD. EFF. --
LOCATION
Sell Gemsteel x3, Empyreal Soul x3, Serpentarius x3 to Bazaar

Wyrmhero Blade
LP -- ATT +130
EVA. +50
COST 65535
ADD. EFF. Holy element
LOCATION
Sell Omega Badge x1, Godslayer's Badge x1, Lu Shang's Badge x1 to Bazaar

Katana

| KATANA 1 | KATANA 2 | KATANA 3 | KATANA 4 | MASAMUNE |

While katana tend to have lower attack ratings than greatswords, they more than hold their own in damage potential thanks to frequent combo attacks. Katana score two or more hits per combat round far more often than any other weapon type, except for ninja swords and poles. To further take advantage of this, equip either the Genji Gloves (which increases the rate of combo attacks) or the Cat-ear Hood (which increases the character's speed by 50; this more than doubles the amount of turns a character gets, vastly increasing the opportunities for a combo attack to occur).

Katana damage is affected by a character's strength and magick power, the katana's attack rating, and the opponent's defense. Magick power as a factor for a highly powerful weapon adds an interesting twist, allowing a support character geared for magick power to also contribute as a heavy frontline damage dealer. All katana add 5 to Evasion, but make sure that a character in this role (one who deals heavy melee damage with a katana while equipped for magick power rather than, say, defense) does not draw too much of the enemy's attention. Lacking a shield and meaningful Evasion bonuses makes one particularly vulnerable to harsh enemy attacks.

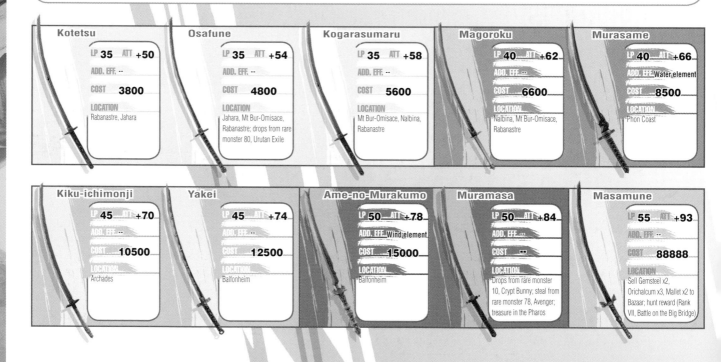

Kotetsu
LP 35 ATT +50
ADD. EFF. --
COST 3800
LOCATION
Rabanastre, Jahara

Osafune
LP 35 ATT +54
ADD. EFF. --
COST 4800
LOCATION
Jahara, Mt Bur-Omisace, Rabanastre; drops from rare monster 80, Urutan Exile

Kogarasumaru
LP 35 ATT +58
ADD. EFF. --
COST 5600
LOCATION
Mt Bur-Omisace, Nalbina, Rabanastre

Magoroku
LP 40 ATT +62
ADD. EFF. --
COST 6600
LOCATION
Nalbina, Mt Bur-Omisace, Rabanastre

Murasame
LP 40 ATT +66
ADD. EFF. Water element
COST 8500
LOCATION
Phon Coast

Kiku-ichimonji
LP 45 ATT +70
ADD. EFF. --
COST 10500
LOCATION
Archades

Yakei
LP 45 ATT +74
ADD. EFF. --
COST 12500
LOCATION
Balfonheim

Ame-no-Murakumo
LP 50 ATT +78
ADD. EFF. Wind element
COST 15000
LOCATION
Balfonheim

Muramasa
LP 50 ATT +84
ADD. EFF. --
COST --
LOCATION
Drops from rare monster 10, Crypt Bunny; steal from rare monster 78, Avenger; treasure in the Pharos

Masamune
LP 55 ATT +93
ADD. EFF. --
COST 88888
LOCATION
Sell Gemsteel x2, Orichalcum x3, Mallet x2 to Bazaar; hunt reward (Rank VII, Battle on the Big Bridge)

Ninja Swords

NINJA SWORDS 1 | NINJA SWORDS 2 | YAGYU DARKBLADE

A less frequently seen partner to katana, ninja swords are even more prone to combo attack than katana, which makes them terrific options for damage dealers. All ninja swords contain the Dark element, so avoid using them against enemies that are immune to Dark (or even worse, absorb it). Ninja sword damage is calculated based on your character's strength and speed, the ninja sword's attack rating, and the enemy's defense. Note that all ninja swords add 20 to Evasion. These factors make ninja swords better suited than katana for characters who are traditional damage dealers. As with katana, Genji Gloves or the Cat-ear Hood serve to make ninja swords far more potent.

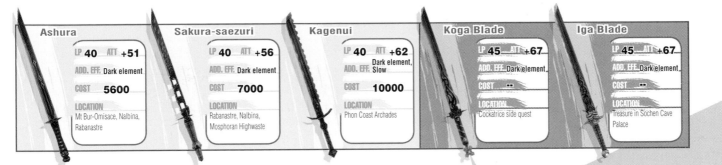

Ashura
LP 40 ATT +51
ADD. EFF. Dark element
COST 5600
LOCATION Mt Bur-Omisace, Nalbina, Rabanastre

Sakura-saezuri
LP 40 ATT +56
ADD. EFF. Dark element
COST 7000
LOCATION Rabanastre, Nalbina, Mosphoran Highwaste

Kagenui
LP 40 ATT +62
ADD. EFF. Dark element, Slow
COST 10000
LOCATION Phon Coast Archades

Koga Blade
LP 45 ATT +67
ADD. EFF. Dark element
COST --
LOCATION Cockatrice side quest

Iga Blade
LP 45 ATT +67
ADD. EFF. Dark element
COST --
LOCATION Treasure in Sochen Cave Palace

Orochi
LP 45 ATT +72
ADD. EFF. Dark element, Disable
COST 15200
LOCATION Sell Coeurl Whisker x2, Sickle-Blade x2, Cancer Gem x3 to Bazaar

Yagyu Darkblade
LP 80 ATT +80
ADD. EFF. Dark element
COST --
LOCATION Drops from rare monster 310, Bombshell

Spears

SPEARS 1 | SPEARS 2 | SPEARS 3 | SPEARS 4 | SPEARS 5 | DRAGON WHISKER | ZODIAC SPEAR

The brute force weapon of *FINAL FANTASY XII*. This group contains perhaps the strongest weapon in the game, the Zodiac Spear. Spears factor in your character's strength, the spear's attack rating, and the enemy's defense when calculating damage dealt. All spears add +8 to Evasion.

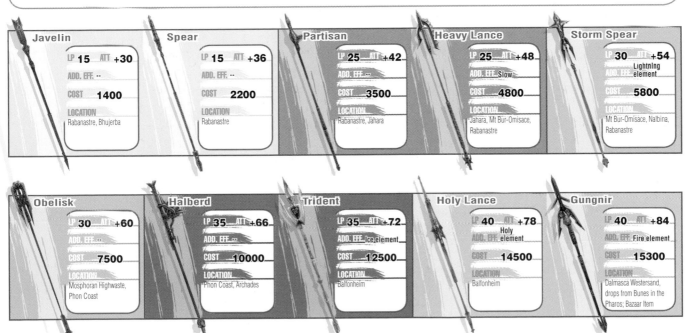

Javelin
LP 15 ATT +30
ADD. EFF. --
COST 1400
LOCATION Rabanastre, Bhujerba

Spear
LP 15 ATT +36
ADD. EFF. --
COST 2200
LOCATION Rabanastre

Partisan
LP 25 ATT +42
ADD. EFF. --
COST 3500
LOCATION Rabanastre, Jahara

Heavy Lance
LP 25 ATT +48
ADD. EFF. Slow
COST 4800
LOCATION Jahara, Mt Bur-Omisace, Rabanastre

Storm Spear
LP 30 ATT +54
ADD. EFF. Lightning element
COST 5800
LOCATION Mt Bur-Omisace, Nalbina, Rabanastre

Obelisk
LP 30 ATT +60
ADD. EFF. --
COST 7500
LOCATION Mosphoran Highwaste, Phon Coast

Halberd
LP 35 ATT +66
ADD. EFF. --
COST 10000
LOCATION Phon Coast, Archades

Trident
LP 35 ATT +72
ADD. EFF. Ice element
COST 12500
LOCATION Balfonheim

Holy Lance
LP 40 ATT +78
ADD. EFF. Holy element
COST 14500
LOCATION Balfonheim

Gungnir
LP 40 ATT +84
ADD. EFF. Fire element
COST 15300
LOCATION Dalmasca Westersand, drops from Bunes in the Pharos; Bazaar Item

Equipment

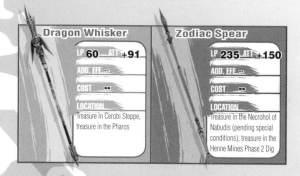

Dragon Whisker
LP 60 **ATT** +91
ADD. EFF. --
COST --
LOCATION
Treasure in Cerobi Steppe, treasure in the Pharos

Zodiac Spear
LP 235 **ATT** +150
ADD. EFF. --
COST --
LOCATION
Treasure in the Necrohol of Nabudis (pending special conditions); treasure in the Henne Mines Phase 2 Dig

Poles

POLES 1   POLES 2   POLES 3   POLES 4   POLES 5   WHALE WHISKER

Like katana and ninja swords, it's easy to combo attack with poles on a frequent basis. Pole damage is calculated based on your character's strength and the pole's attack rating, like most weapons, but instead of checking these factors against an enemy's defense, they are checked against the enemy's magick defense!

Throw high attack ratings and frequent combo attacks on top of this to create a weapon class that completely decimates opponents without Shell or a strong magick defense. All poles add 25 to Evasion as well—not a bad figure for a two-handed weapon. As with katana and ninja swords, accessories that enhance combo attacks or speed are preferred.

Oaken Pole
LP 15 **ATT** +27
ADD. EFF. --
COST 1300
LOCATION
Rabanastre, Bhujerba

Cypress Pole
LP 15 **ATT** +33
ADD. EFF. Earth element
COST 2000
LOCATION
Rabanastre

Battle Bamboo
LP 25 **ATT** +39
ADD. EFF. --
COST 3200
LOCATION
Rabanastre, Jahara

Musk Stick
LP 25 **ATT** +45
ADD. EFF. --
COST 4300
LOCATION
Jahara, Mt Bur-Omisace, Rabanastre

Iron Pole
LP 30 **ATT** +51
ADD. EFF. Slow
COST 5300
LOCATION
Mt Bur-Omisace, Nalbina, Rabanastre

Six-fluted Pole
LP 30 **ATT** +57
ADD. EFF. --
COST 6800
LOCATION
Mosphoran Highwaste, Phon Coast

Gokuu Pole
LP 30 **ATT** +63
ADD. EFF. --
COST 9000
LOCATION
Phon Coast, Archades

Zephyr Pole
LP 35 **ATT** +69
ADD. EFF. Wind element
COST 11200
LOCATION
Balfonheim

Ivory Pole
LP 35 **ATT** +75
ADD. EFF. --
COST 13500
LOCATION
Balfonheim

Sweep
LP 45 **ATT** +81
ADD. EFF. --
COST 16200
LOCATION
Bhujerba

Eight-fluted Pole
LP 45 **ATT** +88
ADD. EFF. --
COST --
LOCATION
Steal from rare monster 357, Vagrant Soul; steal from rare monster 332, Abelisk

Whale Whisker
LP 125 **ATT** +108
ADD. EFF. --
COST 60000
LOCATION
Sell Mythril x3, Corpse Fly x3, Aquarius Gem x1 to Bazaar

Rods

 RODS 1 | RODS 2 | RODS 3 | RODS 4 | ROD OF FAITH

Rods are similar to maces in that they are ideal for support/magick-oriented characters. They differ, however, in that their strength does not lie in actually striking the enemy; rods add magick power and extra MP to characters equipped with them. A few of them also add beneficial status effects on contact. All rods add 6 to Evasion. If you do choose to hit an opponent with a rod, your character's strength, the rod's attack rating, and the enemy's defense are used to determine the damage dealt.

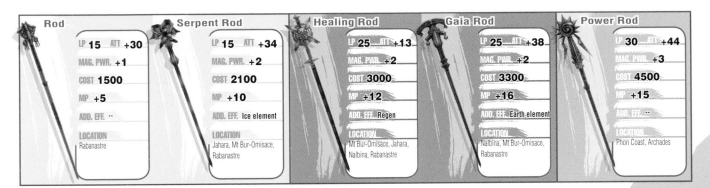

Rod
LP 15 ATT +30
MAG. PWR. +1
COST 1500
MP +5
ADD. EFF. --
LOCATION
Rabanastre

Serpent Rod
LP 15 ATT +34
MAG. PWR. +2
COST 2100
MP +10
ADD. EFF. Ice element
LOCATION
Jahara, Mt Bur-Omisace, Rabanastre

Healing Rod
LP 25 ATT +13
MAG. PWR. +2
COST 3000
MP +12
ADD. EFF. Regen
LOCATION
Mt Bur-Omisace, Jahara, Nalbina, Rabanastre

Gaia Rod
LP 25 ATT +38
MAG. PWR. +2
COST 3300
MP +16
ADD. EFF. Earth element
LOCATION
Nalbina, Mt Bur-Omisace, Rabanastre

Power Rod
LP 30 ATT +44
MAG. PWR. +3
COST 4500
MP +15
ADD. EFF. --
LOCATION
Phon Coast, Archades

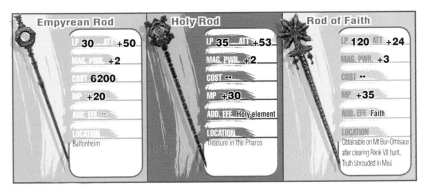

Empyrean Rod
LP 30 ATT +50
MAG. PWR. +2
COST 6200
MP +20
ADD. EFF. --
LOCATION
Balfonheim

Holy Rod
LP 35 ATT +53
MAG. PWR. +2
COST --
MP +30
ADD. EFF. Holy element
LOCATION
Treasure in the Pharos

Rod of Faith
LP 120 ATT +24
MAG. PWR. +3
COST --
MP +35
ADD. EFF. Faith
LOCATION
Obtainable on Mt Bur-Omisace after clearing Rank VII hunt, Truth Shrouded in Mist

Staves

 STAVES 1 | STAVES 2 | STAVES 3 | STAVES 4 | STAFF OF THE MAGI

Staves augment magick users as well, but in a different way. Many staves actually power up certain elements. For example, the spell Blizzaga will cause far more damage when cast with an Ice Staff than without it. When used during melee combat, staves take into account character strength and magick power, staff attack, and enemy defense to determine damage. All staves add 8 to Evasion.

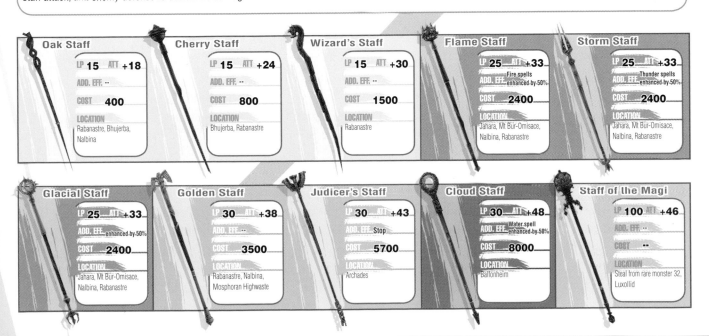

Oak Staff
LP 15 ATT +18
ADD. EFF. --
COST 400
LOCATION
Rabanastre, Bhujerba, Nalbina

Cherry Staff
LP 15 ATT +24
ADD. EFF. --
COST 800
LOCATION
Bhujerba, Rabanastre

Wizard's Staff
LP 15 ATT +30
ADD. EFF. --
COST 1500
LOCATION
Rabanastre

Flame Staff
LP 25 ATT +33
ADD. EFF. Fire spells enhanced by 50%
COST 2400
LOCATION
Jahara, Mt Bur-Omisace, Nalbina, Rabanastre

Storm Staff
LP 25 ATT +33
ADD. EFF. Thunder spells enhanced by 50%
COST 2400
LOCATION
Jahara, Mt Bur-Omisace, Nalbina, Rabanastre

Glacial Staff
LP 25 ATT +33
ADD. EFF. enhanced by 50%
COST 2400
LOCATION
Jahara, Mt Bur-Omisace, Nalbina, Rabanastre

Golden Staff
LP 30 ATT +38
ADD. EFF. --
COST 3500
LOCATION
Rabanastre, Nalbina, Mosphoran Highwaste

Judicer's Staff
LP 30 ATT +43
ADD. EFF. Stop
COST 5700
LOCATION
Archades

Cloud Staff
LP 30 ATT +48
ADD. EFF. Water spell enhanced by 50%
COST 8000
LOCATION
Balfonheim

Staff of the Magi
LP 100 ATT +46
ADD. EFF. --
COST --
LOCATION
Steal from rare monster 32, Luxollid

Equipment

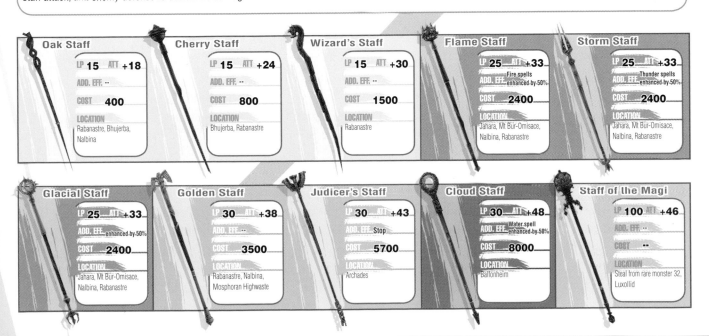

Ranged Weapons

This weapon class offers many benefits over more traditional fare, with a few negatives to balance things out. Ranged weapons prevent a party member from equipping a shield and, for the most part, they do not enhance Evasion in a meaningful way. They also tend to attack less rapidly than melee weapons.

Now for the good news! Ranged weapons allow attacks from a distance, often out of harm's way. Enemies must close the gap to counter-attack. Equipping your party members with ranged weapons also makes it more likely that they will be spread out, causing area-of-effect technicks and magicks (such as Firaga) to hit perhaps just one or two party members rather than the entire party. In some situations (e.g., against enemies that can inflict effects like Disable or Stop to multiple characters at once), this can be a lifesaver.

Ranged weapons require ammunition: arrows for bows, bolts for crossbows, shot for guns, and bombs for hand-bombs. The ammunition will oftentimes inflict status effects on enemies, such as Stop or Disable. The weakening and positional advantages of ranged weapons can more than compensate for the lack of a shield, especially for characters set up as support. Ranged weapons are also required to hit flying monsters as melee weapons cannot strike these enemies without the technik Telekinesis, which does not show up until late in the game.

Bows

| BOWS 1 | BOWS 2 | BOWS 3 | BOWS 4 | BOWS 5 | BOWS 6 | SAGITTARIUS |

Bows provide the most basic ranged damage option. These weapons allow attacks from a distance at the expense of using a shield. They also add no peripheral stats beyond their base attack, and have no additional effects.

However, many arrow types do have additional effects, and the infrequency of crossbow and gun upgrades means that bows are often a good option. Bow accuracy is also affected by the weather in a given region. For example, rain has an adverse effect. Bow damage is determined by the attack power of the bow and arrow, your character's strength and speed, and the enemy's defense. It is also worth remembering that enemies cannot counter bow attacks. Bows do not grant a bonus to Evasion.

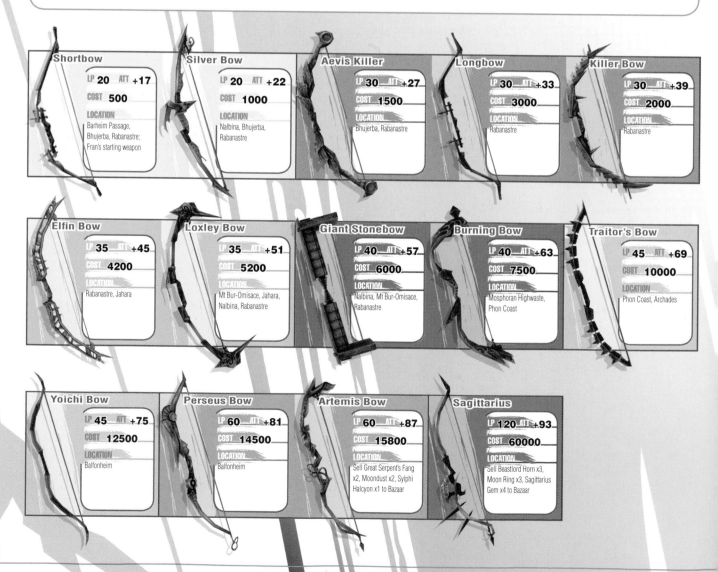

Shortbow — LP 20, ATT +17, COST 500. LOCATION: Barheim Passage, Bhujerba, Rabanastre; Fran's starting weapon

Silver Bow — LP 20, ATT +22, COST 1000. LOCATION: Nalbina, Bhujerba, Rabanastre

Aevis Killer — LP 30, ATT +27, COST 1500. LOCATION: Bhujerba, Rabanastre

Longbow — LP 30, ATT +33, COST 3000. LOCATION: Rabanastre

Killer Bow — LP 30, ATT +39, COST 2000. LOCATION: Rabanastre

Elfin Bow — LP 35, ATT +45, COST 4200. LOCATION: Rabanastre, Jahara

Loxley Bow — LP 35, ATT +51, COST 5200. LOCATION: Mt Bur-Omisace, Jahara, Nalbina, Rabanastre

Giant Stonebow — LP 40, ATT +57, COST 6000. LOCATION: Nalbina, Mt Bur-Omisace, Rabanastre

Burning Bow — LP 40, ATT +63, COST 7500. LOCATION: Mosphoran Highwaste, Phon Coast

Traitor's Bow — LP 45, ATT +69, COST 10000. LOCATION: Phon Coast, Archades

Yoichi Bow — LP 45, ATT +75, COST 12500. LOCATION: Balfonheim

Perseus Bow — LP 60, ATT +81, COST 14500. LOCATION: Balfonheim

Artemis Bow — LP 60, ATT +87, COST 15800. LOCATION: Sell Great Serpent's Fang x2, Moondust x2, Sylphi Halcyon x1 to Bazaar

Sagittarius — LP 120, ATT +93, COST 60000. LOCATION: Sell Beastlord Horn x3, Moon Ring x3, Sagittarius Gem x4 to Bazaar

Bow Ammunition—Arrows

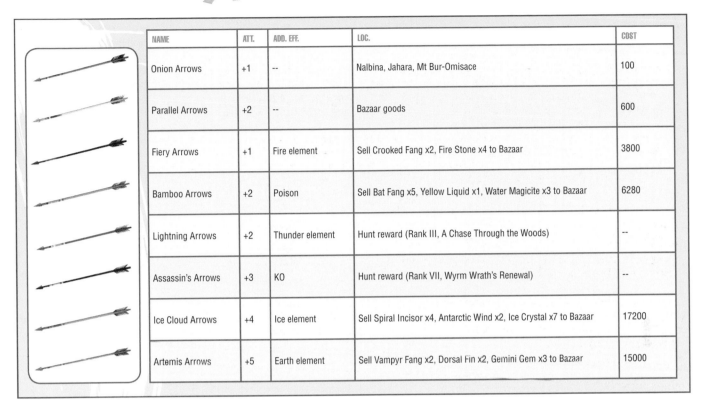

NAME	ATT.	ADD. EFF.	LOC.	COST
Onion Arrows	+1	--	Nalbina, Jahara, Mt Bur-Omisace	100
Parallel Arrows	+2	--	Bazaar goods	600
Fiery Arrows	+1	Fire element	Sell Crooked Fang x2, Fire Stone x4 to Bazaar	3800
Bamboo Arrows	+2	Poison	Sell Bat Fang x5, Yellow Liquid x1, Water Magicite x3 to Bazaar	6280
Lightning Arrows	+2	Thunder element	Hunt reward (Rank III, A Chase Through the Woods)	--
Assassin's Arrows	+3	KO	Hunt reward (Rank VII, Wyrm Wrath's Renewal)	--
Ice Cloud Arrows	+4	Ice element	Sell Spiral Incisor x4, Antarctic Wind x2, Ice Crystal x7 to Bazaar	17200
Artemis Arrows	+5	Earth element	Sell Vampyr Fang x2, Dorsal Fin x2, Gemini Gem x3 to Bazaar	15000

Crossbows

CROSSBOWS 1	CROSSBOWS 2	CROSSBOWS 3	CROSSBOWS 4

All crossbows add 5 to Evasion. While crossbows do not possess additional effects, crossbow ammunition often does. Enemies cannot parry or counter crossbow attacks, although crossbow attacks may simply mlss. Crossbow damage is determined by the attack power of the crossbow and bolt, your character's strength, and the enemy's defense.

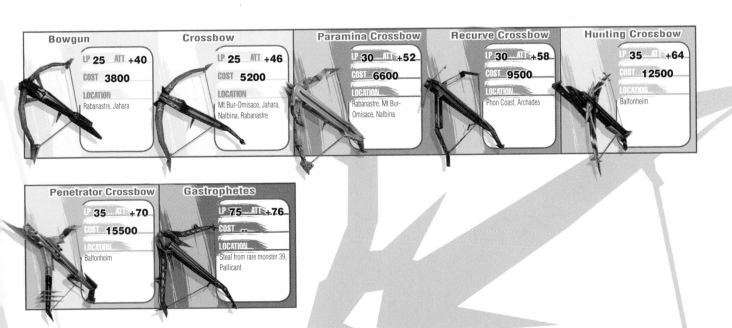

Bowgun
LP 25 ATT +40
COST 3800
LOCATION
Rabanastre, Jahara

Crossbow
LP 25 ATT +46
COST 5200
LOCATION
Mt Bur-Omisace, Jahara, Nalbina, Rabanastre

Paramina Crossbow
LP 30 ATT +52
COST 6600
LOCATION
Rabanastre, Mt Bur-Omisace, Nalbina

Recurve Crossbow
LP 30 ATT +58
COST 9500
LOCATION
Phon Coast, Archades

Hunting Crossbow
LP 35 ATT +64
COST 12500
LOCATION
Balfonheim

Penetrator Crossbow
LP 35 ATT +70
COST 15500
LOCATION
Balfonheim

Gastrophetes
LP 75 ATT +76
COST --
LOCATION
Steal from rare monster 39, Pallicant

Crossbow Ammunition—Bolts

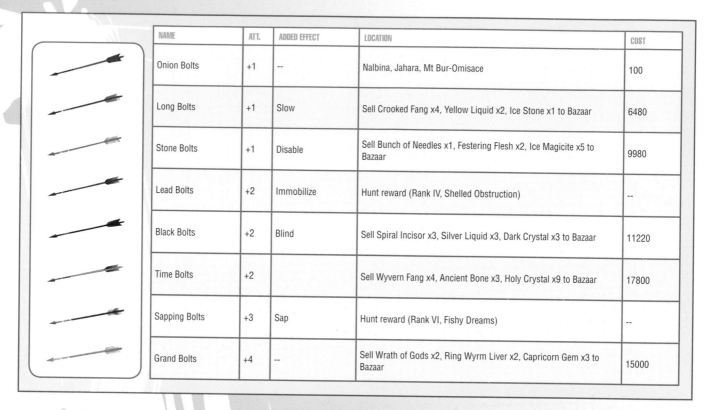

NAME	ATT.	ADDED EFFECT	LOCATION	COST
Onion Bolts	+1	--	Nalbina, Jahara, Mt Bur-Omisace	100
Long Bolts	+1	Slow	Sell Crooked Fang x4, Yellow Liquid x2, Ice Stone x1 to Bazaar	6480
Stone Bolts	+1	Disable	Sell Bunch of Needles x1, Festering Flesh x2, Ice Magicite x5 to Bazaar	9980
Lead Bolts	+2	Immobilize	Hunt reward (Rank IV, Shelled Obstruction)	--
Black Bolts	+2	Blind	Sell Spiral Incisor x3, Silver Liquid x3, Dark Crystal x3 to Bazaar	11220
Time Bolts	+2		Sell Wyvern Fang x4, Ancient Bone x3, Holy Crystal x9 to Bazaar	17800
Sapping Bolts	+3	Sap	Hunt reward (Rank VI, Fishy Dreams)	--
Grand Bolts	+4	--	Sell Wrath of Gods x2, Ring Wyrm Liver x2, Capricorn Gem x3 to Bazaar	15000

Guns

| GUNS 1 | GUNS 2 | GUNS 3 | GUNS 4 | GUNS 5 | GUNS 6 |

Although guns are slow to fire (they take almost twice as long as any other weapon type), they compensate by being 100% accurate! All guns add 10 to Evasion. While guns have no additional effects, their munitions often do. Note that enemies cannot parry, block, or counter gun attacks. Gun damage is determined solely by the attack power of the gun and its ammunition. An enemy's defense is of no consequence when determining damage.

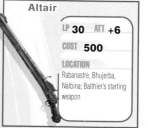

Altair
LP 30 ATT +6
COST 500
LOCATION
Rabanastre, Bhujerba, Nalbina; Balthier's starting weapon

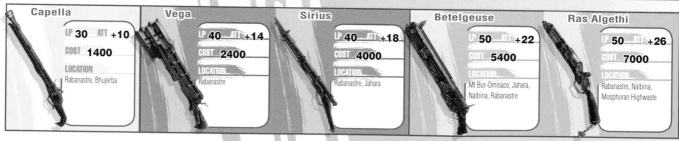

Capella
LP 30 ATT +10
COST 1400
LOCATION
Rabanastre, Bhujerba

Vega
LP 40 ATT +14
COST 2400
LOCATION
Rabanastre

Sirius
LP 40 ATT +18
COST 4000
LOCATION
Rabanastre, Jahara

Betelgeuse
LP 50 ATT +22
COST 5400
LOCATION
Mt Bur-Omisace, Jahara, Nalbina, Rabanastre

Ras Algethi
LP 50 ATT +26
COST 7000
LOCATION
Rabanastre, Nalbina, Mosphoran Highwaste

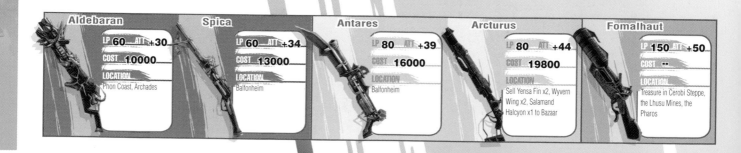

Aldebaran
LP 60 ATT +30
COST 10000
LOCATION
Phon Coast, Archades

Spica
LP 60 ATT +34
COST 13000
LOCATION
Balfonheim

Antares
LP 80 ATT +39
COST 16000
LOCATION
Balfonheim

Arcturus
LP 80 ATT +44
COST 19800
LOCATION
Sell Yensa Fin x2, Wyvern Wing x2, Salamand Halcyon x1 to Bazaar

Fomalhaut
LP 150 ATT +50
COST --
LOCATION
Treasure in Cerobi Steppe, the Lhusu Mines, the Pharos

Gun Ammunition—Bullets

NAME	ATT.	ADDED EFFECT	LOCATION	COST
Onion Shot	+1	--	Nalbina, Jahara, Mt Bur-Omisace	100
Silent Shot	+1	Silence	Sell Fish Scale x2, Green Liquid x1, Dark Stone x3 to Bazaar	1680
Aqua Shot	+3	Water element	Sell Yensa Scale x1, Green Liquid x3, Water Stone x4 to Bazaar	2980
Wyrmfire Shot	+3	Fire element	Back to Barheim side quest reward	--
Mud Shot	+2	Earth element, Blind	Sell Ichthon Scale x4, Silver Liquid x3, Earth Crystal x3 to Bazaar	9080
Windslicer Shot	+4	Wind element	Sell Ring Wyrm Scale x4, Silver Liquid x5, Wind Crystal x7 to Bazaar	15200
Dark Shot	+4	Dark element	Hunt reward (Rank V, The Black Sorcerer)	--
Stone Shot	+3	Petrify	Sell Mirror Scale x2, Tyrant Bone x2, Libra Gem x3 to Bazaar	15000

Hand-Bombs

HAND-BOMBS 1	HAND-BOMBS 2	HAND-BOMBS 3

Hand-bombs serve as the ranged equivalent of the axe and hammer class. They can inflict big-time damage, or they may cause little damage at all. Hand-bombs take into account your character's strength and vitality, the hand-bomb's attack rating, and the enemy's defense when determining damage dealt. The bombs that serve as hand-bomb ammunition often come equipped with useful additional effects. Like bows, hand-bombs do not provide an Evasion bonus.

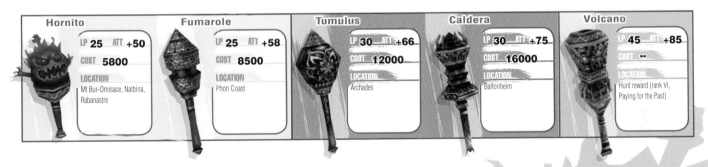

Hornito — LP 25 ATT +50 COST 5800 LOCATION Mt Bur-Omisace, Nalbina, Rabanastre

Fumarole — LP 25 ATT +58 COST 8500 LOCATION Phon Coast

Tumulus — LP 30 ATT +66 COST 12000 LOCATION Archades

Caldera — LP 30 ATT +75 COST 16000 LOCATION Balfonheim

Volcano — LP 45 ATT +85 COST -- LOCATION Hunt reward (rank VI, Paying for the Past)

Hand-Bomb Ammunition—Bombs

NAME	ATT.	ADDED EFFECT	LOCATION	COST
Onion Bombs	+1	--	Nalbina, Jahara, Mt Bur-Omisace	100
Poison Bombs	+2	Poison	Sell Bomb Shell x1, Fire Crystal x3 to Bazaar	9800
Stun Bombs	+2	Stop	Hunt reward (Rank V, The Deserter's Revenge)	--
Stink Bombs	+2	Sap	Hunt reward (Rank VII, Carrot Stalk)	--
Oil Bombs	+3	Oil	Sell Bomb Ashes x3, Book of Orgain x2, Fire Crystal x3 to Bazaar	10625
Chaos Bombs	+4	Confuse	Sell Bomb Shell x4, Book of Orgain-Cent x3, Fire Crystal x7 to Bazaar	17800
Water Bombs	+5	Water element	Sell Book of Orgain x3, Putrid Liquid x3, Water Crystal x10 to Bazaar	7800
Castellanos	+6	-	Sell Bomb Fragment x3, Frog Oil x2, Aries Gem x3 to Bazaar	12000

Shields & Armor

Shields

SHIELDS 1 | SHIELDS 2 | SHIELDS 3 | SHIELDS 4 | SHIELDS 5 | SHIELDS 6 | SHELL SHIELD | ENSANGUINED SHIELD | ZODIAC

Characters equipped with one-handed weapons can and should equip a shield. Shields greatly increase survivability in battle by allowing your characters to block incoming attacks, completely negating the damage they would otherwise sustain. They occasionally provide extra benefits as well; for example, immunity to certain elements or automatic status effects. One shield toward the end of the game even comes equipped with a variety of negative status ailments to compensate for its extremely high evasion rating!

Shields become especially potent when coupled with the Gauntlets accessory. However, one downside to using shields is you lose the option to use two-handed and ranged weapons, which tend to cause more damage than one-handed weapons. This really isn't a huge obstacle when you consider that you could equip one character with a shield and keep the Decoy magick active on that character. This approach forces the character into a "tanking" role and frees up your remaining characters to focus on dealing damage.

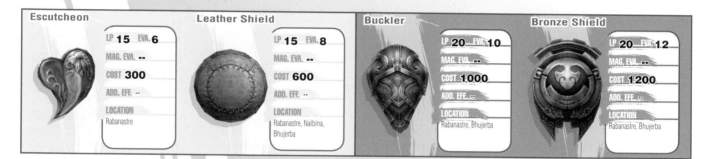

Escutcheon
LP 15 EVA. 6
MAG. EVA. --
COST 300
ADD. EFF. --
LOCATION Rabanastre

Leather Shield
LP 15 EVA. 8
MAG. EVA. --
COST 600
ADD. EFF. --
LOCATION Rabanastre, Nalbina, Bhujerba

Buckler
LP 20 EVA. 10
MAG. EVA. --
COST 1000
ADD. EFF. --
LOCATION Rabanastre, Bhujerba

Bronze Shield
LP 20 EVA. 12
MAG. EVA. --
COST 1200
ADD. EFF. --
LOCATION Rabanastre, Bhujerba

Round Shield
LP 20 EVA. 14
MAG. EVA. --
COST 1600
ADD. EFF. --
LOCATION Rabanastre

Golden Shield
LP 20 EVA. 16
MAG. EVA. --
COST 2100
ADD. EFF. --
LOCATION Rabanastre, Jahara, Mt Bur-Omisace

Ice Shield
LP 20 EVA. 16
MAG. EVA. --
COST 2500
ADD. EFF. 50% Ice resist
LOCATION Rabanastre, Jahara, Mt Bur-Omisace

Flame Shield
LP 20 EVA. 16
MAG. EVA. --
COST 3200
ADD. EFF. 50% Fire resist
LOCATION Rabanastre, Nalbina, Mt Bur-Omisace

Diamond Shield
LP 20 EVA. 18
MAG. EVA. --
COST 3900
ADD. EFF. --
LOCATION Rabanastre, Nalbina

Platinum Shield
LP 20 EVA. 20
MAG. EVA. --
COST 5300
ADD. EFF. --
LOCATION Mosphoran Highwaste, Phon Coast, Archades

Dragon Shield
LP 20 EVA. 23
MAG. EVA. --
COST 6000
ADD. EFF. Immune to earth element
LOCATION Phon Coast, Archades

Crystal Shield
LP 25 EVA. 25
MAG. EVA. 10
COST 7200
ADD. EFF. --
LOCATION Archades, Balfonheim

Kaiser Shield
LP 25 EVA. 27
MAG. EVA. --
COST 8300
ADD. EFF. --
LOCATION Balfonheim

Aegis Shield
LP 25 EVA. 13
MAG. EVA. 50
COST 9600
ADD. EFF. --
LOCATION Balfonheim

Demon Shield
LP 30 EVA. 40
MAG. EVA. --
COST 11200
ADD. EFF. Absorbs Dark element
LOCATION Necrohol of Nabudis

Venetian Shield
LP 30 EVA. 24
MAG. EVA. 25
COST 12420
ADD. EFF. Weak to Lightning element
LOCATION Sell Ancient Turtle Shell x2, Ring Wyrm Liver x2, Undin Halcyon x1 to Bazaar

Shell Shield
LP **90** EVA. **5**
MAG. EVA. --
COST --
ADD. EFF. Equip: Shell
LOCATION
Hunt reward (Rank II, A Scream from the Sky), treasure in the Stilshrine of Miriam

Ensanguined Shield
LP **90** EVA. **90**
MAG. EVA. --
COST --
ADD. EFF. Equip: Poison, Sap, Slow
LOCATION
Treasure in the Henne Mines, treasure in the Feywood

Zodiac Escutcheon
LP **200** EVA. **50**
MAG. EVA. --
COST --
ADD. EFF. Immune to Lightning element
LOCATION
Treasure in the Great Crystal upper layer, treasure in Barheim Passage

Light Armor

Light armor is the most basic armor type and it can be the most useful armor for a large part of the first half of the game. Light armor generally adds a very sizeable bonus to HP as well as moderate defense. When in doubt, light armor is usually a safe bet. Even near the end of the game, when heavy armor and mystic armor provide bonuses that can far outweigh that which light armor offers, the HP bonus can still prove useful when used with the Bubble spell or Bubble Belt accessory.

	NAME	PIECE	LIC. REQ.	LP	HP	MP	DEF.	MAG. RES.	STR.	MAG. PWR.	VIT.	SPD.	ADD. EFF.	LOCATION	COST
	Leather Cap	Head	Light Armor 1	10	10	--	--	4	--	--	--	--	--	Rabanastre	100
	Leather Clothing	Body	Light Armor 1	10	10	--	4	--	--	--	--	--	--	Rabanastre	100
	Headgear	Head	Light Armor 2	15	20	--	--	5	--	--	--	--	--	Rabanastre	200
	Chromed Leathers	Body	Light Armor 2	15	20	--	5	--	--	--	--	--	--	Rabanastre, Barheim Passage	200
	Headguard	Head	Light Armor 2	15	30	--	--	6	--	--	--	--	--	Rabanastre, Nalbina, Bhujerba	300
	Leather Breastplate	Body	Light Armor 2	15	30	--	6	--	--	--	--	--	--	Rabanastre, Nalbina, Bhujerba	300
	Leather Headgear	Head	Light Armor 3	20	40	--	--	8	--	--	--	--	--	Rabanastre, Nalbina, Bhujerba	500
	Bronze Chestplate	Body	Light Armor 3	20	40	--	8	--	--	--	--	--	--	Rabanastre, Nalbina, Bhujerba	500
	Horned Hat	Head	Light Armor 3	20	50	--	--	10	--	--	--	--	--	Rabanastre, Bhujerba	700
	Ringmail	Body	Light Armor 3	20	50	--	10	--	1	--	--	--	--	Rabanastre, Bhujerba	700
	Balaclava	Head	Light Armor 4	25	90	--	--	12	1	--	--	--	--	Rabanastre	1000
	Windbreaker	Body	Light Armor 4	25	100	--	12	--	--	--	--	--	50% Wind resist	Rabanastre	1000
	Soldier's Cap	Head	Light Armor 4	25	110	--	--	14	--	--	--	--	--	Rabanastre, Jahara	1400
	Heavy Coat	Body	Light Armor 4	25	120	--	14	--	--	--	--	--	--	Rabanastre, Jahara	1400

	NAME	PIECE	LIC. REQ.	LP	HP	MP	DEF.	MAG. RES.	STR.	MAG. PWR.	VIT.	SPD.	ADD. EFF.	LOCATION	COST
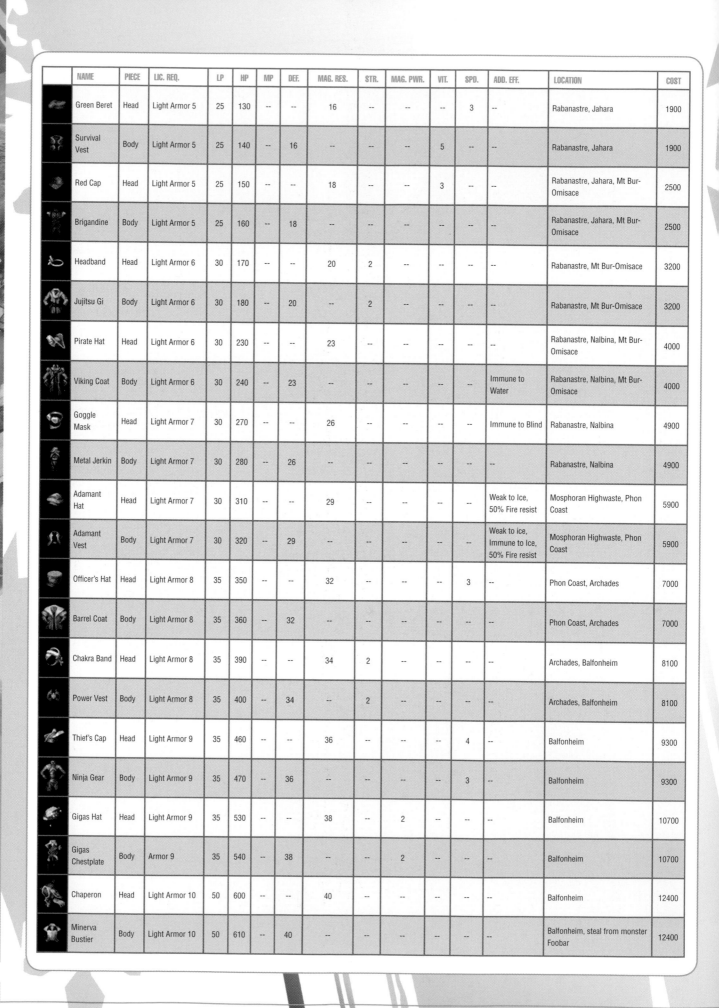	Green Beret	Head	Light Armor 5	25	130	--	--	16	--	--	--	3	--	Rabanastre, Jahara	1900
	Survival Vest	Body	Light Armor 5	25	140	--	16	--	--	--	5	--	--	Rabanastre, Jahara	1900
	Red Cap	Head	Light Armor 5	25	150	--	--	18	--	--	3	--	--	Rabanastre, Jahara, Mt Bur-Omisace	2500
	Brigandine	Body	Light Armor 5	25	160	--	18	--	--	--	--	--	--	Rabanastre, Jahara, Mt Bur-Omisace	2500
	Headband	Head	Light Armor 6	30	170	--	--	20	2	--	--	--	--	Rabanastre, Mt Bur-Omisace	3200
	Jujitsu Gi	Body	Light Armor 6	30	180	--	20	--	2	--	--	--	--	Rabanastre, Mt Bur-Omisace	3200
	Pirate Hat	Head	Light Armor 6	30	230	--	--	23	--	--	--	--	--	Rabanastre, Nalbina, Mt Bur-Omisace	4000
	Viking Coat	Body	Light Armor 6	30	240	--	23	--	--	--	--	--	Immune to Water	Rabanastre, Nalbina, Mt Bur-Omisace	4000
	Goggle Mask	Head	Light Armor 7	30	270	--	--	26	--	--	--	--	Immune to Blind	Rabanastre, Nalbina	4900
	Metal Jerkin	Body	Light Armor 7	30	280	--	26	--	--	--	--	--	--	Rabanastre, Nalbina	4900
	Adamant Hat	Head	Light Armor 7	30	310	--	--	29	--	--	--	--	Weak to Ice, 50% Fire resist	Mosphoran Highwaste, Phon Coast	5900
	Adamant Vest	Body	Light Armor 7	30	320	--	29	--	--	--	--	--	Weak to ice, Immune to Ice, 50% Fire resist	Mosphoran Highwaste, Phon Coast	5900
	Officer's Hat	Head	Light Armor 8	35	350	--	--	32	--	--	--	3	--	Phon Coast, Archades	7000
	Barrel Coat	Body	Light Armor 8	35	360	--	32	--	--	--	--	--	--	Phon Coast, Archades	7000
	Chakra Band	Head	Light Armor 8	35	390	--	--	34	2	--	--	--	--	Archades, Balfonheim	8100
	Power Vest	Body	Light Armor 8	35	400	--	34	--	2	--	--	--	--	Archades, Balfonheim	8100
	Thief's Cap	Head	Light Armor 9	35	460	--	--	36	--	--	--	4	--	Balfonheim	9300
	Ninja Gear	Body	Light Armor 9	35	470	--	36	--	--	--	--	3	--	Balfonheim	9300
	Gigas Hat	Head	Light Armor 9	35	530	--	--	38	--	2	--	--	--	Balfonheim	10700
	Gigas Chestplate	Body	Armor 9	35	540	--	38	--	--	2	--	--	--	Balfonheim	10700
	Chaperon	Head	Light Armor 10	50	600	--	--	40	--	--	--	--	--	Balfonheim	12400
	Minerva Bustier	Body	Light Armor 10	50	610	--	40	--	--	--	--	--	--	Balfonheim, steal from monster Foobar	12400

NAME	PIECE	LIC. REQ.	LP	HP	MP	DEF.	MAG. RES.	STR.	MAG. PWR.	VIT.	SPD.	ADD. EFF.	LOCATION	COST
Crown of Laurels	Head	Light Armor 10	50	680	--	--	42	--	--	--	--	--	Balfonheim	14500
Rubber Suit	Body	Light Armor 10	50	700	--	42	--	--	--	--	--	Immune to Lightning	Balfonheim	14500
Renewing Morion	Head	Light Armor 11	50	370	--	--	44	--	--	4	--	Equip: Regen	Ranabastre Lowtown, drops from Nightwalker in the Stilshrine of Miriam	16000
Mirage Vest	Body	Light Armor 11	50	800	--	45	--	--	--	10	10	--	Rabanastre Lowtown, steal from rare monster 73, Disma	16000
Dueling Mask	Head	Light Armor 12	100	800	--	--	45	2	--	--	--	--	Treasure in the Pharos	--
Brave Suit	Body	Light Armor 12	100	10	--	40	--	--	--	--	--	Equip: Bravery	Treasure in the Great Crystal upper layer, treasure in the Henne Mines eastern section	--

Heavy Armor

Heavy armor is commonly used by frontline fighters. Although it doesn't usually offer the HP bonuses of light armor or the magick power benefits of mystic armor, it does offer plenty of strength and defense. As most weapons primarily factor in strength when determining damage, selecting the right armor class for damage dealers is often a no-brainer. For much of the game, heavy armor doesn't really provide much benefit over light armor. However, toward the end of the game when enemies start striking much harder and offering up increasingly stalwart defense, heavy armor becomes a great option.

Early on in the game, HP is extremely important, so it makes sense to use light armor. However, as your characters level up and gain access to the Bubble spell, raw HP becomes less of a concern and reducing the damage your characters take per hit becomes more important. This is especially true when facing many of the game's strongest adversaries. You should be aware that one specific encounter in the game penalizes the use of heavy armor through greatly increased charge time on actions.

NAME	PIECE	LIC. REQ.	LP	HP	MP	DEF.	MAG. RES.	STR.	MAG. PWR.	VIT.	SPD.	ADD. EFF.	LOCATION	COST
Leather Helm	Head	Heavy Armor 1	20	--	--	--	5	2	--	--	--	--	Rabanastre	500
Leather Armor	Body	Heavy Armor 1	20	--	--	6	--	2	--	--	--	--	Rabanastre	500
Bronze Helm	Head	Heavy Armor 1	20	--	--	--	6	2	--	--	--	--	Rabanastre, Nalbina, Bhujerba	700
Bronze Armor	Body	Heavy Armor 1	20	--	--	7	--	2	--	--	--	--	Rabanastre, Nalbina, Bhujerba	700
Sallet	Head	Heavy Armor 2	25	--	--	--	7	3	--	--	--	--	Rabanastre, Bhujerba	1000
Scale Armor	Body	Heavy Armor 2	25	--	--	9	--	3	--	--	3	--	Rabanastre, Bhujerba	1000
Iron Helm	Head	Heavy Armor 2	25	--	--	--	9	3	--	--	--	--	Rabanastre, Bhujerba	1400
Iron Armor	Body	Heavy Armor 2	25	--	--	11	--	3	--	--	--	--	Rabanastre, Bhujerba	1400
Barbut	Head	Heavy Armor 3	30	--	--	--	11	4	--	--	--	--	Rabanastre	1900

*More Heavy Armor →

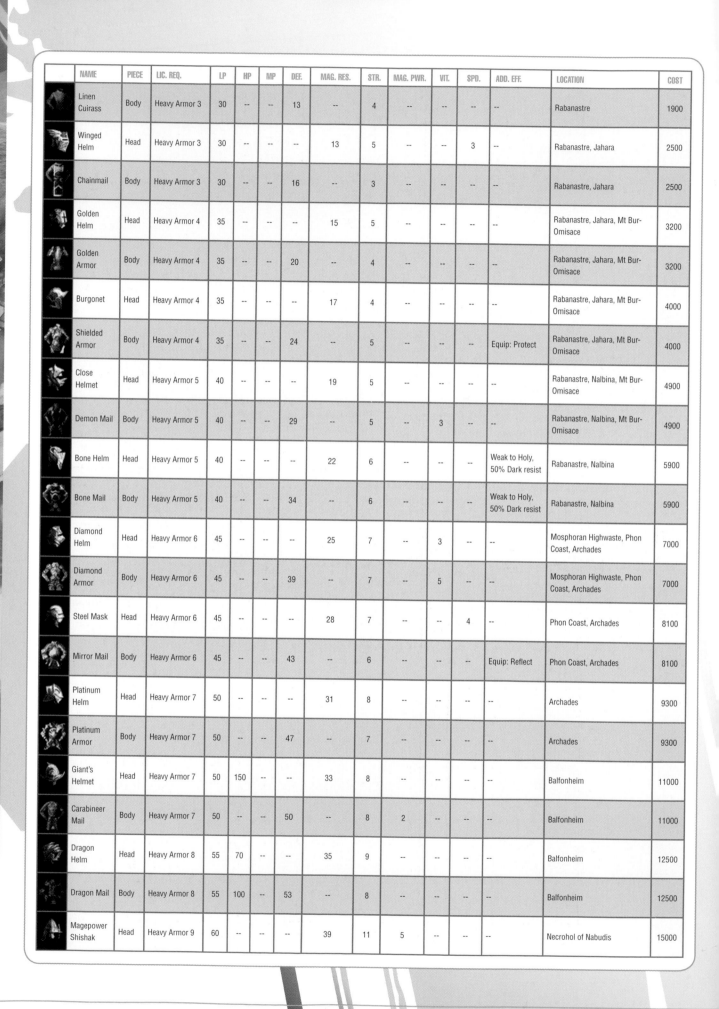

	NAME	PIECE	LIC. REQ.	LP	HP	MP	DEF.	MAG. RES.	STR.	MAG. PWR.	VIT.	SPD.	ADD. EFF.	LOCATION	COST
	Linen Cuirass	Body	Heavy Armor 3	30	--	--	13	--	4	--	--	--	--	Rabanastre	1900
	Winged Helm	Head	Heavy Armor 3	30	--	--	--	13	5	--	--	3	--	Rabanastre, Jahara	2500
	Chainmail	Body	Heavy Armor 3	30	--	--	16	--	3	--	--	--	--	Rabanastre, Jahara	2500
	Golden Helm	Head	Heavy Armor 4	35	--	--	--	15	5	--	--	--	--	Rabanastre, Jahara, Mt Bur-Omisace	3200
	Golden Armor	Body	Heavy Armor 4	35	--	--	20	--	4	--	--	--	--	Rabanastre, Jahara, Mt Bur-Omisace	3200
	Burgonet	Head	Heavy Armor 4	35	--	--	--	17	4	--	--	--	--	Rabanastre, Jahara, Mt Bur-Omisace	4000
	Shielded Armor	Body	Heavy Armor 4	35	--	--	24	--	5	--	--	--	Equip: Protect	Rabanastre, Jahara, Mt Bur-Omisace	4000
	Close Helmet	Head	Heavy Armor 5	40	--	--	--	19	5	--	--	--	--	Rabanastre, Nalbina, Mt Bur-Omisace	4900
	Demon Mail	Body	Heavy Armor 5	40	--	--	29	--	5	--	3	--	--	Rabanastre, Nalbina, Mt Bur-Omisace	4900
	Bone Helm	Head	Heavy Armor 5	40	--	--	--	22	6	--	--	--	Weak to Holy, 50% Dark resist	Rabanastre, Nalbina	5900
	Bone Mail	Body	Heavy Armor 5	40	--	--	34	--	6	--	--	--	Weak to Holy, 50% Dark resist	Rabanastre, Nalbina	5900
	Diamond Helm	Head	Heavy Armor 6	45	--	--	--	25	7	--	3	--	--	Mosphoran Highwaste, Phon Coast, Archades	7000
	Diamond Armor	Body	Heavy Armor 6	45	--	--	39	--	7	--	5	--	--	Mosphoran Highwaste, Phon Coast, Archades	7000
	Steel Mask	Head	Heavy Armor 6	45	--	--	--	28	7	--	--	4	--	Phon Coast, Archades	8100
	Mirror Mail	Body	Heavy Armor 6	45	--	--	43	--	6	--	--	--	Equip: Reflect	Phon Coast, Archades	8100
	Platinum Helm	Head	Heavy Armor 7	50	--	--	--	31	8	--	--	--	--	Archades	9300
	Platinum Armor	Body	Heavy Armor 7	50	--	--	47	--	7	--	--	--	--	Archades	9300
	Giant's Helmet	Head	Heavy Armor 7	50	150	--	--	33	8	--	--	--	--	Balfonheim	11000
	Carabineer Mail	Body	Heavy Armor 7	50	--	--	50	--	8	2	--	--	--	Balfonheim	11000
	Dragon Helm	Head	Heavy Armor 8	55	70	--	--	35	9	--	--	--	--	Balfonheim	12500
	Dragon Mail	Body	Heavy Armor 8	55	100	--	53	--	8	--	--	--	--	Balfonheim	12500
	Magepower Shishak	Head	Heavy Armor 9	60	--	--	--	39	11	5	--	--	--	Necrohol of Nabudis	15000

NAME	PIECE	LIC. REQ.	LP	HP	MP	DEF.	MAG. RES.	STR.	MAG. PWR.	VIT.	SPD.	ADD. EFF.	LOCATION	COST
Maximillian	Body	Heavy Armor 9	60	--	--	58	1	9	--	--	6	--	Necrohol of Nabudis, drops from Elvoret in the Necrohol of Nabudis	17000
Grand Helm	Head	Heavy Armor 10	90	--	--	--	40	12	--	--	--	--	Drops from rare monster 26, Tower	--
Grand Armor	Body	Heavy Armor 10	90	--	--	61	--	12	--	--	--	--	Drops from rare monster 38, Helvinek	--

Mystic Armor

While mystic armor lacks the versatility and HP bonuses of light armor and the defense and strength of heavy armor, it compensates for these deficiencies by offering large bonuses to magick power. This has a marked effect on all magick actions, whether it's using magicks like Firaga to damage the enemy, magicks like Curaja to heal your party, or magicks like Slowga to enfeeble your opponents.

The magick power statistic also comes into play with certain specialized weapon types (staves, katana, and maces) when determining melee damage, so mystic armors can be indirectly useful in this area as well. Several of them also offer terrific bonuses, like the complete absorption of harmful elements. For example, getting hit with Holy while wearing a White Mask will heal instead of harm. This diversity in mystic gear makes different pieces worth carrying around to give you options in counteracting harmful magicks, should the need arise.

The main drawback to mystic armor is its lack of physical defense when compared to heavy or even light armor. To counter this, consider setting one character up specifically as a "tank," using the "Decoy" spell to keep the enemy's attention off the character sporting the mystic armor.

NAME	PIECE	LIC. REQ.	LP	HP	MP	DEF.	MAG. RES.	STR.	MAG. PWR.	VIT.	SPD.	ADD. EFF.	LOCATION	COST
Cotton Cap	Head	Mystic Armor 1	15	--	--	--	4	--	2	--	--	--	Rabanastre	100
Cotton Shirt	Body	Mystic Armor 1	15	--	--	4	--	--	1	--	--	--	Rabanastre	100
Magick Curch	Head	Mystic Armor 1	15	--	5	5	--	2	--	--	--	--	Rabanastre	200
Light Woven Shirt	Body	Mystic Armor 1	15	--	--	5	--	--	2	--	--	--	Rabanastre	200
Pointy Hat	Head	Mystic Armor 2	20	--	--	--	6	--	2	--	--	--	Rabanastre, Nalbina, Bhujerba	300
Silken Shirt	Body	Mystic Armor 2	20	--	--	6	--	--	2	--	--	--	Rabanastre, Nalbina, Bhujerba	300
Topkapi Hat	Head	Mystic Armor 2	20	--	--	8	--	--	3	--	--	--	Rabanastre, Nalbina, Bhujerba	500
Kilimweave Shirt	Body	Mystic Armor 2	20	--	--	8	--	--	3	--	--	--	Rabanastre, Nalbina, Bhujerba	500
Calot Hat	Head	Mystic Armor 3	20	--	--	--	10	--	3	--	--	--	Rabanastre, Bhujerba	700
Shepherd's Bolero	Body	Mystic Armor 3	20	--	--	10	--	--	3	--	--	--	Rabanastre, Bhujerba	700
Wizard's Hat	Head	Mystic Armor 3	20	--	--	--	12	--	4	--	--	--	Rabanastre	1000
Wizard's Robes	Body	Mystic Armor 3	20	--	5	12	--	--	4	--	--	--	Rabanastre	1000

*More Mysitc Armor →

Equipment

	NAME	PIECE	LIC. REQ.	LP	HP	MP	DEF.	MAG. RES.	STR.	MAG. PWR.	VIT.	SPD.	ADD. EFF.	LOCATION	COST
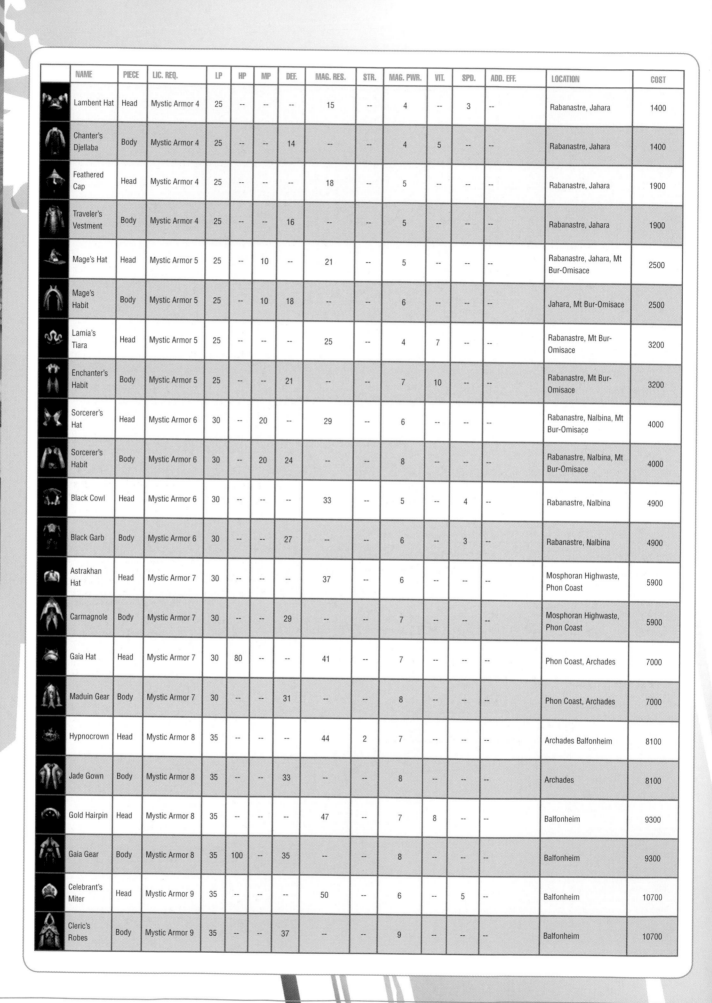	Lambent Hat	Head	Mystic Armor 4	25	--	--	--	15	--	4	--	3	--	Rabanastre, Jahara	1400
	Chanter's Djellaba	Body	Mystic Armor 4	25	--	--	14	--	--	4	5	--	--	Rabanastre, Jahara	1400
	Feathered Cap	Head	Mystic Armor 4	25	--	--	--	18	--	5	--	--	--	Rabanastre, Jahara	1900
	Traveler's Vestment	Body	Mystic Armor 4	25	--	--	16	--	--	5	--	--	--	Rabanastre, Jahara	1900
	Mage's Hat	Head	Mystic Armor 5	25	--	10	--	21	--	5	--	--	--	Rabanastre, Jahara, Mt Bur-Omisace	2500
	Mage's Habit	Body	Mystic Armor 5	25	--	10	18	--	--	6	--	--	--	Jahara, Mt Bur-Omisace	2500
	Lamia's Tiara	Head	Mystic Armor 5	25	--	--	--	25	--	4	7	--	--	Rabanastre, Mt Bur-Omisace	3200
	Enchanter's Habit	Body	Mystic Armor 5	25	--	--	21	--	--	7	10	--	--	Rabanastre, Mt Bur-Omisace	3200
	Sorcerer's Hat	Head	Mystic Armor 6	30	--	20	--	29	--	6	--	--	--	Rabanastre, Nalbina, Mt Bur-Omisace	4000
	Sorcerer's Habit	Body	Mystic Armor 6	30	--	20	24	--	--	8	--	--	--	Rabanastre, Nalbina, Mt Bur-Omisace	4000
	Black Cowl	Head	Mystic Armor 6	30	--	--	--	33	--	5	--	4	--	Rabanastre, Nalbina	4900
	Black Garb	Body	Mystic Armor 6	30	--	--	27	--	--	6	--	3	--	Rabanastre, Nalbina	4900
	Astrakhan Hat	Head	Mystic Armor 7	30	--	--	--	37	--	6	--	--	--	Mosphoran Highwaste, Phon Coast	5900
	Carmagnole	Body	Mystic Armor 7	30	--	--	29	--	--	7	--	--	--	Mosphoran Highwaste, Phon Coast	5900
	Gaia Hat	Head	Mystic Armor 7	30	80	--	--	41	--	7	--	--	--	Phon Coast, Archades	7000
	Maduin Gear	Body	Mystic Armor 7	30	--	--	31	--	--	8	--	--	--	Phon Coast, Archades	7000
	Hypnocrown	Head	Mystic Armor 8	35	--	--	--	44	2	7	--	--	--	Archades Balfonheim	8100
	Jade Gown	Body	Mystic Armor 8	35	--	--	33	--	--	8	--	--	--	Archades	8100
	Gold Hairpin	Head	Mystic Armor 8	35	--	--	--	47	--	7	8	--	--	Balfonheim	9300
	Gaia Gear	Body	Mystic Armor 8	35	100	--	35	--	--	8	--	--	--	Balfonheim	9300
	Celebrant's Miter	Head	Mystic Armor 9	35	--	--	--	50	--	6	--	5	--	Balfonheim	10700
	Cleric's Robes	Body	Mystic Armor 9	35	--	--	37	--	--	9	--	--	--	Balfonheim	10700

	NAME	PIECE	LIC. REQ.	LP	HP	MP	DEF.	MAG. RES.	STR.	MAG. PWR.	VIT.	SPD.	ADD. EFF.	LOCATION	COST
	Black Mask	Head	Mystic Armor 10	50	--	--	--	53	--	8	--	--	Absorbs Dark element	Balfonheim	12400
	Black Robes	Body	Mystic Armor 10	50	--	--	38	--	--	10	--	--	--	Balfonheim	13500
	White Mask	Head	Mystic Armor 10	50	--	--	--	56	--	8	--	--	Absorbs Holy element	Balfonheim	14500
	White Robes	Body	Mystic Armor 10	50	--	--	38	--	--	10	--	--	--	Balfonheim	13500
	Golden Skullcap	Head	Mystic Armor 11	50	--	--	--	58	--	10	--	3	--	Barheim Passage, drops from Dead Bones in the Pharos	16000
	Glimmering Robes	Body	Mystic Armor 11	50	--	--	39	--	--	12	10	--	--	Barheim Passage	16000
	Circlet	Head	Mystic Armor 12	100	--	--	--	60	2	10	--	--	--	Treasure in the Pharos	--
	Lordly Robes	Body	Mystic Armor 12	100	--	--	40	--	5	15	--	--	--	Treasure in the Pharos	--

Genji Armor

A set assembled from legend and belonging to an ancient man of mystery, Genji armor offers many of the benefits of advanced heavy armor sets with a few twists thrown in. The entire set requires only one license and only one set of this armor exists in the game! During your time in Clan Centurio, you may well come across an opportunity to claim this unique set—don't let it slip away!

	NAME	PIECE	LIC. REQ.	LP	DEF.	MAG. RES.	EVA.	MAG. EVA.	STR.	MAG. PWR.	ADD. EFF.	LOCATION
	Genji Shield	Shield	Genji Armor	150	--	--	30	5	--	--	--	Steal during "Battle on the Big Bridge" clan hunt
	Genji Helm	Head	Genji Armor	150	--	--	37	37	9	4	--	Steal during "Battle on the Big Bridge" clan hunt
	Genji Armor	Body	Genji Armor	150	--	--	56	--	9	3	Improves chance to counter.	Steal during "Battle on the Big Bridge" clan hunt
	Genji Gloves	Accessory	Genji Armor	150	--	--	--	--	--	--	Improves chance of scoring multiple hits.	Steal during "Battle on the Big Bridge" clan hunt

Accessories

Rounding out the vast number of equippable items, accessories offer countless benefits for many situations. Whether it's to prevent harmful status effects like Stop and Disable, add permanent beneficial effects like Haste or Bubble, or to enhance damage or defense capabilities, accessories should be an essential part of your party's arsenal.

	NAME	LIC. NEEDED	LP	EFFECTS	LOCATION	COST
	Orrachea Amulet	Accessories 1	5	+25 HP	Giza Plains, given by Tomaj at the Sandsea	250
	Bangle	Accessories 2	15	Equip: Libra	Giza Plains	500
	Steel Gorget	Accessories 2	15	Raises strength when HP Critical.	Dalmasca Westersand	1500
	Armguard	Accessories 3	25	Reduces physical damage taken when HP critical.	Dalmasca Estersand	800
	Tourmaline Ring	Accessories 3	25	Immune: Poison	Dalmasca Westersand	300
	Gauntlets	Accessories 4	35	Improves chance to block with a shield.	Dalmasca Westersand	1200
	Battle Harness	Accessories 4	35	When attacked, automatically counter with weapon in hand.	Dalmasca Westersand	1000
	Leather Gorget	Accessories 5	35	Raises magick power when HP Critical.	Dalmasca Westersand	1500
	Rose Corsage	Accessories 5	35	Immune: Silence	Dalmasca Westersand	800
	Amber Armlet	Accessories 6	35	Increases physical damage dealt while empty-handed.	Eruyt Village	6600
	Sash	Accessories 6	35	Immune: Slow	Eruyt Village	500
	Argyle Armlet	Accessories 7	40	Immune: Blind	Eruyt Village	600
	Blazer Gloves	Accessories 7	40	Raises strength when character has full HP.	Eruyt Village	3200
	Jade Collar	Accessories 7	40	Improves chance of avoiding attacks.	Eruyt Village	3200
	Jackboots	Accessories 8	45	Immune: Immobilize	Rabanastre Lowtown, Mt Bur-Omisace	600
	Black Belt	Accessories 8	45	Immune: Disable, Vitality +8	Rabanastre Lowtown, Mt Bur-Omisace	600
	Golden Amulet	Accessories 8	45	Doubles license points earned.	Rabanastre Lowtown, Mt Bur-Omisace	4500
	Magick Gloves	Accessories 9	30	Increases magick power when HP is full.	Eruyt Village, Mt Bur-Omisace	3200
	Nishijin Belt	Accessories 10	40	Immune: Sleep	Mt Bur-Omisace	800
	Thief's Cuffs	Accessories 10	40	Enables the theft of superior and rare items.	Mt Bur-Omisace	3000
	Gillie Boots	Accessories 11	45	Immune: Oil	Phon Coast, Mt Bur-Omisace	700
	Quasimodo Boots	Accessories 11	45	Immune: Sap	Phon Coast, Mt Bur-Omisace	800

Ruby Ring	Accessories 12	60	Equip: Reflect	Phon Coast, Mt Bur-Omisace	8500
Firefly	Accessories 12	60	Reduces EXP earned to 0, Strength +2.	Phon Coast	5000
Steel Poleyns	Accessories 12	60	Move safely past traps. Defense +1	Phon Coast	1000
Fuzzy Miter	Accessories 13	60	Immune: Petrify	Old Archades	1200
Bowline Sash	Accessories 13	60	Immune: Confuse	Old Archades	1000
Winged Boots	Accessories 13	60	Equip: Float	Old Archades	500
Pheasant Netsuke	Accessories 14	70	Improves potency of restorative items such as potions.	Old Archades	4000
Embroidered Tippet	Accessories 14	70	Doubles EXP earned.	Old Archades	5000
Cameo Belt	Accessories 14	70	Improves chance to hit.	Balfonheim	9000
Power Armlet	Accessories 15	70	Immune: Stop, Strength +2	Balfonheim	5200
Opal Ring	Accessories 15	70	Magicks will not bounce off targets with Reflect status.	Balfonheim	16000
Bubble Belt	Accessories 15	70	Equip: Bubble	Rabanastre Muthru Bazaar	19800
Ring of Renewal	Accessories 16	70	Equip: Regen, Defense +6, Magick Resist +5	Necrohol of Nabudis, complete Air Carrier side quest	18000
Indigo Pendant	Accessories 16	70	Improves chance to strike with magick.	Inside Airship	5000
Turtleshell Choker	Accessories 17	80	Enables casting of magicks with gil, rather than MP.	Bhujerba	9300
Agate Ring	Accessories 17	80	Nullifies weather and terrain effects on elemental damage.	Dalmasca Westersand	3000
Diamond Armlet	Accessories 18	50	Obtain superior items from chests, coffers, and the like.	Dalmasca Estersand	20000
Hermes Sandals	Accessories 18	50	Equip: Haste	Barheim Passage	20000
Sage's Ring	Accessories 19	100	Reduces MP cost by half. Absorb: Holy.	Old Archades	22000
Nihopalaoa	Accessories 20	120	Reverses effects of restorative items such as Potions, Phoenix Downs, and Remedies; affects allies and foes alike.	Rabanastre Muthru Bazaar	30000
Cat-ear Hood	Accessories 20	120	Move with great celerity. Vitality +20, Speed +50.	Rabanastre Muthru Bazaar	30000
Ribbon	Ribbon	150	Immune to all negative status effects.	Drops from rare monster 44, Vishno; treasure in the Henne Mines east section, treasure in the Pharos; drops from level 99 Red Chocobo	--
Genji Gloves	Genji Armor	150	Improves chance of scoring multiple hits.	Steal during "Battle on the Big Bridge" clan hunt	--

Abilities

Technicks

Technicks are abilities that do not require Mist Points to use, although they often have prerequisites for their use. Some technicks can cause damage in unusual ways, or save your character in an emergency when items and MP are strained. A few of them are useful for weakening your foes or judging their weaknesses. To use a technick, follow these two steps: 1. Purchase a technick scroll from a merchant; and 2. Unlock the required license on a character's license board.

Name	LP	Effects	Location	Cost
Steal	15	Steal from one foe.	Rabanastre	1600
Libra	20	Reveal more detailed target information.	Rabanastre	500
First Aid	20	Restore HP to one HP critical ally.	Rabanastre, Nalbina	700
Charge	30	Restore user's MP. If the technick fails, MP is reduced to 0.	Rabanastre, Nalbina, Bhujerba	1700
Poach	30	Capture HP critical foes to obtain loot. No EXP/LP is earned from poached monsters.	Rabanastre, Nalbina, Bhujerba	7000
Souleater	35	Consume HP to deal damage to one foe.	Rabanastre, Nalbina	6400
Horology	55	Deal damage based on a factor of time to all foes in range.	Rabanastre, Nalbina, Bhujerba	2000
Infuse	35	Fully consume user's MP, changing one ally's HP to 10 times that amount.	Rabanastre, Nalbina, Jahara, Archades	2000
Bonecrusher	30	Consume HP to reduce the HP of one foe to 0.	Rabanastre, Archades	7000
1000 Needles	35	Deal 1,000 damage to one foe.	Mosphoran Highwaste	7000
Stamp	40	Inflict one foe with any status effect on the user. Does not remove status effects from user.	Archades	4500
Addle	30	Lower one foe's magick power.	Rabanastre, Archades	3500

Name	LP	Effects	Location	Cost
Shades of Black	40	Cast a random black magick on one foe.	Archades	5000
Expose	35	Lower one foe's defense.	Balfonheim	3800
Achilles	40	Render one foe vulnerable to an additional element.	Rabanastre, Nalbina, Jahara	8800
Gil Toss	35	Throw gil, damaging all foes in range.	Rabanastre, Nalbina, Jahara	2000
Charm	30	Cause one foe to confuse friend with foe.	Rabanastre, Nalbina, Jahara	5000
Sight Unseeing	40	Unleash an attack only available when blind.	Rabanastre, Nalbina, Jahara	6800
Shear	35	Lower one foe's magick resist.	Rabanastre, Nalbina, Jahara	3600
Wither	35	Lower one foe's strength.	Balfonheim	3500
Revive	40	Fully consume user's HP, reviving and fully restoring HP of one KO'd ally.	Balfonheim	10000
Telekinesis	80	Deal ranged damage with melee weapons.	Necrohol of Nabudis	7100
Numerology	40	Deal damage that increases with successive hits.	Rabanastre, Nalbina, Bhujerba	2048
Traveler	65	Deal damage based on total steps taken to all foes in range.	Rabanastre, Nalbina	6700

Magicks

Magicks offer many powerful and unique abilities at the cost of Mist Points (or MP). Having MP as a limiting factor prevents magicks from being too powerful and forces you to carefully manage MP. The difference in how you handle a tough fight will often come down to how well your gambits are utilized to help conserve and maintain MP. Many passive Augment abilities exist only to help generate and maintain MP, and items like the Sage Ring and Turtleshell Choker lessen or alter the cost of casting magick. To cast magick, you must purchase the appropriate magick scroll and unlock the accompanying license.

White Magicks

As the curative school of magick, White Magick enables the caster to restore the health of your party members. It also has a few offensive-minded options for the dark creatures of the world.

Name	Lic. Req.	LP	MP	*MP to Cast	Effects	Location	Cost
Cure	White Magick 1	15	8	5	Restore a small amount of HP to one ally.	Rabanastre, Nalbina	200
Cura	White Magick 3	30	32	22	Restore HP to all allies in range.	Rabanastre, Bhujerba, Dalmasca Westersand, Eruyt Village	1500
Curaga	White Magick 5	45	28	19	Restore a large amount of HP to one ally.	Rabanastre, Nalbina, Eruyt Village, Mt Bur-Omisace	3200
Curaja	White Magick 6	50	68	47	Restore a large amount of HP to all allies in range.	Balfonheim	11700
Renew	White Magick 8	105	98	68	Fully restore the HP of all allies in range.	Dalmasca Westersand	39600
Raise	White Magick 3	30	22	15	Revive one KO'd ally.	Rabanastre, Bhujerba, Dalmasca Westersand, Eruyt Village	1900
Arise	White Magick 6	50	50	35	Revive and fully restore the HP of one KO'd ally.	Balfonheim	9700
Esuna	White Magick 4	35	24	16	Remove harmful status effects from one ally.	Eruyt Village, Mt Bur-Omisace	2800
Esunaga	White Magick 7	55	72	50	Remove harmful status effects from all allies in range.	Balfonheim	14900
Blindna	White Magick 1	15	8	5	Remove Blind from one ally.	Rabanastre, Nalbina	200
Vox	White Magick 2	20	8	5	Remove Silence from one ally.	Rabanastre, Bhujerba	300
Poisona	White Magick 2	20	8	5	Remove Poison from one ally.	Rabanastre, Nalbina	200
Stona	White Magick 3	30	12	8	Remove Stone/Petrify from one ally.	Rabanastre, Bhujerba	800
Cleanse	White Magick 5	45	20	14	Remove Disease from one ally.	Phon Coast	5800
Dispel	White Magick 5	45	16	11	Remove beneficial status effects from one foe.	Rabanastre, Nalbina, Phon Coast	4500
Dispelga	White Magick 6	50	36	25	Remove beneficial status effects from all foes in range.	Balfonheim	8200
Regen	White Magick 4	35	16	11	Restore one ally's HP over time. Removes Sap.	Rabanastre, Eruyt Village, Mt Bur-Omisace	1900
Holy	White Magick 7	55	60	42	Deal heavy holy damage to one foe.	Balfonheim	11200

*MP to Cast w/all Chann. Lic.

Black Magicks

Black magicks exist for one purpose: destruction! With a wide variety of very powerful spells capable of hitting multiple targets, Black magicks are ideal for offensive support characters. Also, use them to great effect in conjunction with the Warmage and Headhunter Augment abilities.

Name	Lic. Req.	LP	MP	*MP to Cast	Effects	Location	Cost
Fire	Black Magick 1	15	8	5	Deal fire damage to one foe.	Rabanastre, Nalbina	200
Thunder	Black Magick 1	15	8	5	Deal lightning damage to one foe.	Rabanastre, Nalbina	200
Blizzard	Black Magick 1	15	8	5	Deal ice damage to one foe.	Rabanastre, Nalbina	200
Water	Black Magick 2	25	12	8	Deal water damage to one foe.	Rabanastre, Bhujerba	800
Aero	Black Magick 2	25	16	11	Deal wind damage to all foes in range.	Rabanastre, Eruyt Village	1200
Fira	Black Magick 3	35	18	12	Deal fire damage to all foes in range.	Rabanstre, Nalbina, Eruyt Village, Mt Bur-Omisace	3000
Thundara	Black Magick 3	35	18	12	Deal lightning damage to all foes in range.	Rabanstre, Nalbina, Eruyt Village, Mt Bur-Omisace	3000
Blizzara	Black Magick 3	35	18	12	Deal ice damage to all foes in range.	Rabanstre, Nalbina, Eruyt Village, Mt Bur-Omisace	3000
Bio	Black Magick 4	40	24	16	Inflict Sap and deal damage to all foes in range.	Rabanastre, Nalbina, Phon Coast	4900
Aeroga	Black Magick 4	40	38	26	Deal heavy wind damage to all foes in range.	Archades	6800
Firaga	Black Magick 5	45	42	29	Deal heavy fire damage to all foes in range.	Balfonheim	8200
Thundaga	Black Magick 5	45	42	29	Deal heavy lightning damage to all foes in range.	Balfonheim	8200
Blizzaga	Black Magick 5	45	42	29	Deal heavy ice damage to all foes in range.	Balfonheim	8200
Shock	Black Magick 6	50	34	23	Deal heavy damage to one foe.	Balfonheim	9400
Scourge	Black Magick 6	50	48	33	Inflict Sap and deal heavy damage to all foes in range.	Balfonheim	11200
Flare	Black Magick 7	70	48	33	Deal massive damage to one foe.	Balfonheim	11200
Ardor	Black Magick 7	70	60	42	Deal massive fire damage to all foes in range.	Barheim Passage	15600
Scathe	Black Magick 8	120	70	49	Deal massive damage to all foes in range.	Necrohol of Nabudis	18100

*MP to Cast w/all Chann. Lic.

Time Magicks

Designed for warping the fabric of time and space, this school of magick allows for the hastening of your allies and the slowing of your foes. There are other options that are designed to press your advantage over your foes by stripping them of abilities.

Name	Lic. Req.	LP	MP	*MP to Cast	Effects	Location	Cost
Haste	Time Magick 5	40	20	14	Speed up one ally's actions by 50%.	Rabanastre, Nalbina, Eruyt Village, Mt Bur-Omisace	3400
Hastega	Time Magick 7	110	70	49	Speed up the actions of all allies in range by 50%.	Dalmasca Estersand	16600
Slow	Time Magick 1	20	8	5	Slow one foe's actions by 50%.	Rabanastre, Nalbina	200
Slowga	Time Magick 7	110	24	16	Slow the actions of all foes in range by 50%.	Balfonheim	10400
Immobilize	Time Magick 1	20	16	11	Immobilize all foes in range.	Rabanastre, Bhujerba	600
Disable	Time Magick 2	25	16	11	Prevent all foes in range from taking action.	Rabanastre, Bhujerba	600
Stop	Time Magick 6	45	20	14	Halt the actions of one foe.	Rabanastre, Nalbina, Mt Bur-Omisace	3700
Reflect	Time Magick 2	25	12	8	Cause magicks to be reflected from one ally	Rabanastre, Bhujerba	800
Reflectga	Time Magick 7	110	24	16	Cause magicks to be reflected from all allies in range.	Archades	6800
Float	Time Magick 5	40	20	14	Allow all allies in range to walk on air. Avoids traps.	Rabanastre, Eruyt Village, Mt Bur-Omisace	2800
Break	Time Magick 3	30	14	9	Turn one foe to stone after a short time.	Rabanastre, Bhujerba, Dalmasca Westersand	900
Countdown	Time Magick 6	45	8	5	Reduce one foe's HP to 0 after a short time.	Rabanastre, Nalbina, Eruyt Village, Mt Bur-Omisace	3100
Balance	Time Magick 4	35	18	12	Area damage equal to difference in caster's current and max HP.	Rabanastre, Eruyt Village	1500
Bleed	Time Magick 4	35	12	8	Heavily damage one foe over time. Inflicts Sap.	Rabanastre, Eruyt Village	1100
Warp	Time Magick 3	30	18	12	Banish all foes in range.	Rabanastre, Eruyt Village	1700

*MP to Cast w/all Chann. Lic.

Green Magicks

Green magick seeks to enhance your character's abilities while weakening those of your enemy. When overwhelmed by multiple foes wielding vicious magicks, rely on spells like Sleepga and Silence to turn the tide of the fight.

Name	Lic. Req.	LP	MP	*MP to Cast	Effects	Location	Cost
Protect	Green Magick 1	25	8	5	Raise one ally's defense by 25%.	Rabanastre, Nalbina, Bhujerba	200
Protectga	Green Magick 7	105	36	25	Raise defense of all allies in range by 25%.	Balfonheim	9400
Shell	Green Magick 2	30	8	5	Raise one ally's magick resist by 25%.	Rabanastre, Bhujerba	300
Shellga	Green Magick 7	105	40	28	Raise magick resist of all allies in range by 25%.	Balfonheim	9900
Bravery	Green Magick 6	50	24	16	Increase one ally's physical attack damage by 30%.	Rabanastre Muthru Bazaar	5800
Faith	Green Magick 6	50	24	16	Augment one ally's magick by 30~50%.	Rabanastre Muthru Bazaar	5800
Blind	Green Magick 1	25	10	7	Lower one foe's chance to hit.	Rabanastre, Nalbina, Bhujerba	200
Blindga	Green Magick 5	45	20	14	Lower the chance to hit of all foes in range.	Archades	6800
Silence	Green Magick 3	35	8	5	Prevent one foe from casting magicks.	Rabanastre, Bhujerba	400
Silencega	Green Magick 5	45	22	15	Prevent all foes in range from casting magicks.	Archades	6800
Sleep	Green Magick 3	35	10	7	Put one foe to sleep.	Rabanastre, Bhujerba	700
Sleepga	Green Magick 7	105	26	18	Put all foes in range to sleep.	Balfonheim	7900
Poison	Green Magick 2	30	10	7	Damage one foe over time.	Rabanastre, Nalbina	500
Toxify	Green Magick 4	40	26	18	Damage all foes in range over time.	Rabanastre, Nalbina, Eruyt Village, Mt Bur-Omisace	4100
Oil	Green Magick 4	40	8	5	Increase fire damage dealt to all foes in range.	Rabanastre, Bhujerba, Dalmasca Westersand	600

*MP to Cast w/all Chann. Lic.

Arcane Magicks

A dark, poorly understood class of magick, the Arcane school offers many unusual options for damaging enemies and enhancing your party members. Many of the game's most powerful tactics are possible due to Arcane magick.

Name	Lic. Req.	LP	MP	*MP to Cast	Effects	Location	Cost
Dark	Arcane Magick 1	25	10	7	Deal moderate dark damage to all foes in range.	Rabanastre, Bhujerba	500
Darkra	Arcane Magick 4	50	20	14	Deal dark damage to all foes in range.	Phon Coast	5800
Darkga	Arcane Magick 7	105	30	21	Deal heavy dark damage to all foes in range.	Balfonheim	9400
Gravity	Arcane Magick 2	30	20	14	Reduce HP of one foe by ¼ of target's max HP.	Rabanastre, Eruyt Village, Mt Bur-Omisace	2800
Graviga	Arcane Magick 7	105	36	25	Reduce HP of one foe by ½ of target's max HP.	Archades	6800
Reverse	Arcane Magick 6	70	50	35	Cause healing and damage to have opposite effect on one foe.	Rabanastre Muthru Bazaar, Phon Coast	7600
Berserk	Arcane Magick 1	25	10	7	Cause one ally to mindlessly attack with weapon in hand.	Rabanastre, Jahara	1000
Confuse	Arcane Magick 2	30	10	7	Cause one foe to confuse friend with foe.	Rabanastre, Eruyt Village	1400
Decoy	Arcane Magick 3	40	10	7	Cause one ally to be the target of all foes.	Rabanastre, Eruyt Village, Mt Bur-Omisace	2500
Death	Arcane Magick 5	60	30	21	Reduce one foe's HP to 0.	Rabanastre, Nalbina, Phon Coast	5200
Vanish	Arcane Magick 4	50	24	16	Render one ally invisible.	Nalbina, Mt Bur-Omisace, Phon Coast	4900
Vanishga	Arcane Magick 6	70	60	42	Render all allies in range invisible.	Rabanastre, Nalbina, Phon Coast	8700
Bubble	Arcane Magick 5	60	32	22	Double max HP of one ally.	Rabanastre Muthru Bazaar, Inside Airship	3300
Drain	Arcane Magick 3	40	18	12	Transfer HP from one foe to the caster.	Rabanastre, Eruyt Village, Mt Bur-Omisace	3200
Syphon	Arcane Magick 4	50	2	1	Transfer MP from one foe to the caster.	Inside Airship	4000

*MP to Cast w/all Chann. Lic.

Augment Abilities

Apart from the licenses for technicks, magicks, armors, and weapons on the license board, there are also licenses for passive abilities that permanently increase your characters' abilities. These bonuses are active for the remainder of the game once you buy them; you need not purchase anything beyond their license. Although they may seem less glamorous than a new ability or weapon, many Augment abilities are among the most useful on the entire board. Whether it's permanently increasing your character's action speed, adding additional Gambit Slots, or permanently increasing HP, Augment abilities are a great way to spend license points.

Name	LP	Effects
Gambit Slot	15	Adds an additional gambit slot.
Potion Lore 1	20	Potions restore more HP.
Gambit Slot	20	Adds an additional gambit slot.
Ether Lore 1	20	Ethers restore more MP.
Remedy Lore 1	20	Remedies remove Sleep, Sap, Immobilize, and Disable.
Magick Lore	25	Increases magick potency.
Battle Lore	25	Increases physical attack damage.
Gambit Slot	25	Adds an additional gambit slot.
Shield Block	25	Increases chance to block with a shield.
+50 HP	30	Increases max HP by 50.
Gambit Slot	30	Adds an additional gambit slot.
Headsman	30	Gain MP after defeating a foe.
Phoenix Lore	30	Phoenix Down restores more HP.
Swiftness	30	Reduces action time by 10%.
Spellbound	30	Increases duration of status effects.
Martyr	30	Gain MP after taking damage.
Channeling	30	Reduces magick MP cost by 10%.
Remedy Lore 2	30	Remedies remove Petrify, Confuse, and Oil.
Inquisitor	30	Gain MP after dealing damage.
Warmage	30	Gain MP after dealing magick damage.
Gambit Slot	35	Adds an additional gambit slot.
Potion Lore 2	35	Potions restore more HP.
Ether Lore 2	35	Ethers restore more MP.
Magick Lore	40	Increases magick potency.
Gambit Slot	40	Adds an additional gambit slot.
Battle Lore	40	Increases physical attack damage.
Shield Block	45	Increases chance to block with a shield.
Gambit Slot	45	Adds an additional gambit slot.
Phoenix Lore	50	Phoenix Down restores more HP.
+100 HP	50	Increases max HP by 100.
Channeling	50	Reduces magick MP cost by 10%.

Name	LP	Effects
Gambit Slot	50	Adds an additional gambit slot.
Swiftness	50	Reduces action time by 10%.
Battle Lore	55	Increases physical attack damage.
Magick Lore	55	Increases magick potency.
Spellbreaker	65	Increases magick power when HP Critical.
Adrenaline	65	Increases strength when HP Critical.
+150 HP	70	Increases max HP by 150.
Potion Lore 3	70	Potions restore more HP.
Last Stand	70	Increases defense when HP Critical.
Focus	70	Increases strength when HP is full.
Ether Lore 3	70	Ethers restore more MP.
Remedy Lore 3	70	Remedies remove Stop, Doom, and Disease.
Serenity	70	Increases magick when HP is full.
Gambit Slot	70	Adds an additional gambit slot.
Shield Block	75	Increases chance to block with a shield.
Channeling	80	Reduces magick MP cost by 10%.
Battle Lore	80	Increases physical attack damage.
Magick Lore	80	Increases magick potency.
Swiftness	80	Reduces action time by 10%.
Phoenix Lore	90	Phoenix Down restores more HP.
Brawler	90	Increases attack power when fighting empty-handed.
+200 HP	100	Increases max HP by 200.
Gambit Slot	100	Adds an additional gambit slot.
Magick Lore	120	Increases magick potency.
Battle Lore	120	Increases physical attack damage.
+500 HP	155	Increases max HP by 500.

Items

Items are quick, disposable, and useable by all party members. Although the use of magicks can duplicate the effect of many items, these goodies take far less time to use. Thus, items can be very handy during emergency situations. The strength of Potions, Phoenix Downs, Remedies, and Ethers are affected by special augmentations on the license board. In fact a few specific items (such as Elixir, Megalixir, and Dark Matter) even perform feats only they can accomplish!

POTION	Restore a small amount of HP to one ally.
HI-POTION	Restore HP to one ally.
X-POTION	Restore a large amount of HP to one ally.

RED FANG	Deal fire damage to all foes in range.
BLUE FANG	Deal ice damage to all foes in range.
WHITE FANG	Deal lightning damage to all foes in range.

ETHER	Restore a small amount of MP to one ally.
HI-ETHER	Restore MP to one ally.
ELIXIR	Fully restore one ally's HP and MP.
MEGALIXIR	Fully restore all allies' HP and MP.

DARK MOTE	A mote containing the power of Dark.
WATER MOTE	A mote containing the power of Water.
AERO MOTE	A mote containing the power of Aero.
HOLY MOTE	A mote containing the power of Holy.
WARP MOTE	A mote containing the power of Warp.
BALANCE MOTE	A mote containing the power of Balance.
SCATHE MOTE	A mote containing the power of Scathe.
HASTEGA MOTE	A mote containing the power of Hastega.

REMEDY	Remove Blind, Poison, Silence, and Slow from one ally.
PHOENIX DOWN	Revive one KO'd ally.
GOLD NEEDLE	Remove Stone/Petrify from one ally.
ECHO HERBS	Removes Silence from one ally.
ANTIDOTE	Remove Poison from one ally.
EYE DROPS	Remove Blind from one ally.
ALARM CLOCK	Remove Sleep from one ally.
HANDKERCHIEF	Remove Oil from one ally.
CHRONOS TEAR	Remove Stop from one ally.
SMELLING SALTS	Remove Confuse from one ally.
VACCINE	Remove Disease from one ally.

REFLECTGA MOTE	A mote containing the power of Reflectga.
VANISHGA MOTE	A mote containing the power of Vanishga.
FLOAT MOTE	A mote containing the power of Float.

| EKSIR BERRIES | A curious item detested by the avion known as the garuda. |

| BACCHUS'S WINE | Cause one ally to mindlessly attack with weapon in hand. |

| DARK MATTER | Deal damage to all foes in range. |

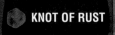

| KNOT OF RUST | Deal damage to one foe. |

The Bazaar

FINAL FANTASY XII has the typical item and gear shops like other RPGs, but this game added something called the Bazaar. All the merchants in the game take part in the Bazaar system. The Bazaar often offers exclusive deals and bargains based upon the amount of loot you've sold to merchants. The loot you sell is used to make item packages that are often cheaper than normal, or exclusive to the Bazaar.

LOOT

While older games in this series usually rely upon gil drops from enemies to build your fortune, a good portion of the money in this game is made by selling a special class of enemy drops that exist for this purpose alone. This item class is referred to as "loot." Whether stolen, poached, or picked up from defeated foes, collecting and selling loot is the key to gaining riches in FINAL FANTASY XII and earning many of the game's rarest items from the Bazaar. Critical pieces of loot, leading to ultimate items or bazaar-exclusive items, appear in a different **typeface**.

Name	Value	Obtained
Adamantite	1479	
Aged Turtle Shell	1075	
Ambrosia	1682	
Ancient Bone	2115	
Ancient Turtle Shell	1337	Drops from Adamantitan in Cerobi Steppe and Nabreus Deadlands; poach from Silicon Tortoise in Giza Plains
Antarctic Wind	1689	
Aquarius Gem	150	Drops from Golem in the Feywood; drops from Deidar in the Pharos
Arcana	10	Drops from rare monsters; drops from all monsters after obtaining key item Canopic Jar
Arctic Wind	1179	
Aries Gem	150	
Bat Fang	105	
Bat Wing	647	
Battlewyrm Carapace	871	
Beastlord Hide	1499	
Beastlord Horn	1334	Drops from Humbaba in Mosphoran Highwaste
Behemoth Steak	1671	
Bent Staff	1194	
Bhujerban Madhu	250	
Black Orb	1	
Blood Wool	871	
Blood-darkened Bone	1435	
Blood-stained Necklace	1663	
Bomb Ashes	200	
Bomb Fragment	1911	
Bomb Shell	896	
Bone Fragment	193	
Book of Orgain	532	
Book of Orgain-Cent	924	
Book of Orgain-Mille	1477	
Braid Wool	465	
Broken Greataxe	1762	
Broken Spear	617	
Broken Sword	1099	

Name	Value	Obtained
Brown Tuft	1	
Bundle of Feathers	833	
Bundle of Needles	92	
Cactus Fruit	59	
Cancer Gem	150	Drops from Preying Mantis in the Feywood
Capricorn Gem	150	Steal from rare monster 340, Negalmuur; steal from rare monster 346, Fideliant
Caramel	276	
Centurio Hero's Badge	1	
Charged Gizzard	945	Drops from Thunderbug in the Henne Mines
Charger Barding	1154	
Chimera Head	2026	Drops from Chimera Brain in the Pharos
Chocobo Feather	480	
Coeurl Pelt	454	
Coeurl Whisker	2076	Drops from Ose in Great Crystal upper layer; steal from rare monster 329, Grimalkin, in Tchita Uplands
Common Fish	10	
Corpse Fly	1798	Drops from Dragon Lich in the Pharos
Crooked Fang	287	
Damascus Steel	2188	Dropped or stolen from Bune in the Pharos; steal from rare monster 300, Vishno, in the Pharos; steal from rare monster 364, Anchag, in Paramina Rift; steal from rare monster 366, Bluesang, in Cerobi Steppe
Dark Crystal	160	
Dark Magicite	80	
Dark Stone	35	
Death Powder	1323	
Death's-Head	653	
Deimos Clay	1000	Reward for the clan hunt "Paramina Run"
Delicious Fish	25	
Demon Drink	1863	
Demon Eyeball	123	
Demon Feather	910	
Demon Tail	1203	
Demon's Sigh	1704	
Destrier Barding	1214	

Name	Value	Obtained
Destrier Mane	808	
Dewdrop Pebble	1	
Diakon Halcyon	1500	
Dorsal Fin	1577	Drops from Focalor in the Nabreus Deadlands
Drab Wool	63	
Earth Crystal	160	
Earth Magicite	80	
Earth Stone	35	
Einherjarium	1682	
Electrum	3563	
Emperor Scale	1395	
Empty Bottle	1	
Empyreal Soul	2000	Sell (High Arcana x1, Soul Powder x1, Wargod's Band x2)
Eye of the Hawk	989	
Festering Flesh	542	
Feystone	1000	Dropped or stolen from Entite monsters
Fine Wool	619	
Fire Crystal	160	
Fire Magicite	80	
Fire Stone	35	
Fish Scale	151	
Forbidden Flesh	1397	
Foul Flesh	143	
Foul Liquid	703	
Four-leaf Clover	1969	
Frog Oil	1826	
Frogspawn	761	
Gemini Gem	150	Drops from Behemoth in the Feywood and Giruvegan; drops from Blood Gigas in the Stilshrine of Miriam; steal from rare monster 362, Wendice
Gemsteel	2000	
Giant Feather	686	
Gimble Stalk	1647	
Glass Jewel	115	
Gnoma Halcyon	1500	
Godslayer's Badge	1	Reward for final clan hunt
Great Serpent's Fang	994	Drops from Python in Mosphoran Highwaste
Great Serpentskin	70	
Green Liquid	206	
Green Tuft	1	
Grimoire Aidhed	1005	
Grimoire Togail	475	
Gysahl Greens	54	
Hell-Gate's Flame	1584	Drops from Cerberus in the Feywood
High Arcana	20	Sell Arcana x10, Soul of Thamasa x1, Feystone x1 to Bazaar; drops from many monsters after obtaining key item Canopic Jar
Holy Crystal	160	
Holy Magicite	80	

Name	Value	Obtained
Holy Stone	35	
Horakhty's Flame	1000	Reward for clan hunt "Crime and Punishment"
Horn	120	
Ice Crystal	160	
Ice Magicite	80	
Ice Stone	35	
Ichthon Scale	1033	
Insect Husk	680	
Iron Carapace	413	
Iron Ore	1043	
Iron Scraps	185	
Jack-o'-Lantern	1888	
Jaya Stick	500	
Ketu Board	1771	
Large Feather	71	
Leamonde Halcyon	1500	
Leo Gem	150	
Leshach Halcyon	1500	Dropped or stolen from Leshach Entite in Paramina Rift during snowstorm
Libra Gem	150	Drops from Ose in Great Crystal upper layer; drops from Tartarus in the Feywood
Lifewick	1740	
Lu Shang's Badge	1	Complete fishing mini-game
Lumber	483	
Maggoty Flesh	741	
Magick Lamp	1753	
Malboro Flower	1043	
Malboro Fruit	612	
Malboro Vine	433	
Mallet	2498	
Mardu Halcyon	1500	
Mirror Scale	1052	Drops from Mirrorknight in the Feywood; drops from rare monster 009, Dreadguard, in the Feywood
Molting	74	
Moon Ring	1647	Drops from Ash Wyrm in Great Crystal upper layer
Moondust	1975	Drops from Mu in the Feywood
Mystletainn	1725	
Mythril	1531	Drops from Mythril Golem in Giruvegan
Nebra Succulent	100	
Nebralim	150	
Omega Badge	1	Drops from Omega MK. XII in Great Crystal upper layer
Onion	2010	
Orange Tuft	1	
Orichalcum	1777	Drops from Deidar in the Pharos; dropped or stolen from rare monster 300, Vishno, in the Pharos
Peach Tuft	1	
Pebble	2	
Phobos Glaze	1000	Reward for clan hunt "Paradise Risen"

Name	Value	Obtained
Pinewood Chop	0	
Pisces Gem	150	
Pointed Horn	706	
Prime Pelt	1124	
Prime Tanned Hide	1372	
Putrid Liquid	1342	
Quality Hide	384	
Quality Lumber	1127	
Quality Pelt	651	
Quality Stone	1425	
Rainbow Egg	538	
Rat Pelt	35	
Rat Tail	224	
Ring Wyrm Liver	1467	Drops from Shield Wyrm in Cerobi Steppe
Ring Wyrm Scale	1285	
Sagittarius Gem	150	Drops from Hecteyes in the Henne Mines east section; dropped or stolen with Thief's Cuffs from Oiling in the Stilshrine of Miriam
Salamand Halcyon	1500	Dropped or stolen from Salamand Entite in the Ogir-Yensa Sandsea during sunny weather, reward for Gibbs & Deweg side quest.
Sandalwood Chop		
Scarletite	1679	Drops from Emeralditan in Nabreus Deadlands; steal from rare monster 293, Aspidochelon, in Cerobi Steppe
Scorpio Gem	150	Steal from Gargoyle Baron in Giruvegan; steal from rare monster 342, Larva Eater, in Great Crystal upper layer
Screamroot	1350	
Semclam Shell	90	
Serpent Eye	1440	Drops from Basilisk in the Feywood
Serpentarius	2000	Clan reward for collecting all 13 Espers; steal from Zodiark in the Henne Mines east section; sell High Arcana x1, Snake Skin x4, Serpent Eye x2 to Bazaar
Sickle-Blade	1878	Drops from Preying Mantis in the Feywood; steal from rare monster 321, Rageclaw, in the Salikawood
Silver Liquid	1376	
Sky Jewel	980	
Slaven Harness	815	
Slime Oil	1717	
Small Feather	49	
Small Package	150	
Snake Skin	53	Dropped or stolen from Wildsnake in Giza Plains; drops from rare monster 345, Grey Molter, in Mosphoran Highwaste; drops from rare monster 347, Midgardsormr, in Golmore Jungle
Snowfly	982	
Solid Horn	1288	
Solid Stone	358	
Soul of Thamasa	1856	Drops from Oversoul in the Necrohol of Nabudis; steal from rare monster 336, Ishteen, in Barheim Passage; reward for rank VI hunt "Dead City Watch"
Soul Powder	2241	Drops from Etém in the Henne Mines east section; steal from rare monster 338, Vorres, in the Necrohol of Nabudis

Name	Value	Obtained
Spiral Incisor	998	
Split Armor	1968	
Stardust	1505	
Storm Crystal	160	
Storm Magicite	80	
Storm Stone	35	
Sturdy Bone	428	
Succulent Fruit	363	
Sylphi Halcyon	1500	Steal from Sylphi Entite in Ozmone Plain during cloudy weather
Tanned Giantskin	672	
Tanned Hide	77	
Tanned Tyrant Hide	802	
Tattered Garment	1470	
Taurus Gem	150	Drops from Vampyr in the Lhusu Mines; drops from Seeker in the Tomb of Raithwall; drops from Pyrolisk on the Phon Coast
Teleport Stone	100	
Throat Wolf Blood	1360	
Tomato Stalk	966	
Turtle Shell	447	
Tyrant Bone	1233	Drops from Archaeoaevis in Zertinan Caverns
Tyrant Hide	549	
Undin Halcyon	1500	Steal from Undin Entite in Cerobi Steppe during rainy or cloudy weather
Unpurified Ether	1783	
Valeblossom Dew	100	
Vampyr Fang	1684	Drops from Abysteel in the Henne Mines
Virgo Gem	150	
Wargod's Band	2214	Drops from Leynir in the Nabreus Deadlands; steal from rare monster 351, Victanir, in the Nam-Yensa Sandsea
Water Crystal	160	
Water Magicite	80	
Water Stone	35	
White Incense	881	
White Tuft	1	
Wind Crystal	160	
Wind Magicite	80	
Wind Stone	35	
Windslicer Pinion	1148	
Wolf Pelt	41	
Wrath of the Gods	2214	Steal from rare monster 312, Minibug, in Barheim Passage
Wyrm Bone	1647	
Wyrm Carapace	739	
Wyvern Fang	1274	
Wyvern Wing	1873	Steal from rare monster 328, Aeros, in Ozmone Plains
Yellow Liquid	531	
Yensa Fin	409	Drops from Urutan-Yensa
Yensa Scale	319	
Zombie Powder	1975	

Grimoires

On occasion, Grimoires appear for sale in the Bazaar when certain conditions are fulfilled. They greatly enhance the frequency and quality of loot from particular kinds of monsters and are worth obtaining as soon as possible. In fact, you may even want to prioritize Grimoire acquisition over new gear, magicks, or technicks. The sooner you get your hands on Grimoires, the sooner your drop quality will improve!

Package Name	Price	Content	Enhances Loot From	Requirements
Forgotten Grimoire	18000	Hunter's Monograph	Beasts/Avions	After finishing the Thextera Hunt, speak with Gatsly in Muthru Bazaar.
Forgotten Grimoire	19000	Knight's Monograph	Giants/Insects	Talk to any weapon merchant more than 30 times.
Forgotten Grimoire	20000	Warmage's Monograph	Amorphs/Undead	Read the hunt bulletin board more than 20 times.
Forgotten Grimoire	21000	Mage's Monograph	Fiends	Talk to any magick merchant over 25 times.
Forgotten Grimoire	22000	Scholar's Monograph	Constructs	Talk to any armor merchant more than 15 times.
Forgotten Grimoire	22000	Dragoon's Monograph	Dragons/Plants	Read the hunt bulletin board more than 40 times.
Forgotten Grimoire	25000	Sage's Monograph	Elementals	Talk to any merchant over 100 times.
Morbid Urn	250000	Canopic Jar	All enemies can drop Arcana	Sell Phobos Glaze, Horakhty's Flame, and Deimos Clay.

BAZAAR PACKAGES

After selling certain combinations of loot to merchants, they are assembled or synthesized into special items and packages. Ultimately, these items become available in the Bazaar. You don't have to sell the required loot combination all at once, and you don't even have to sell the loot to the same merchant because all merchants are connected. To aid in completing loot requirements and obtaining bazaar packages, refer to the Clan Primer Bestiary. Additionally, the monster descriptions often provide clues to completing specific combinations (along with detailing some of the history of Ivalice).

Monsters typically have a common loot drop and a rare loot drop but, in addition, they can also drop special stones and gems imbued with magickal power (such as the Dark Stone, Wind Magicite, Fire Crystal, etc). Later in the game, by fighting rare monsters or obtaining a Canopic Jar in the Bazaar, enemies also begin dropping different magick totems, called Arcana. Bazaar combinations are comprised of any number of common and rare drops and are sometimes coupled with a magickal item to aid the synthesis. Don't worry if this sounds complicated—the Bazaar merchants handle everything! All you need to do is sell loot, after which you are informed when new Bazaar packages are available for purchase!

Name	Loot	Cost	Cost Diff.	Contents
Antidote Set	Drab Wool x2	100	↓50	Antidote x3
Unassuming Surcoat	Wolf Pelt x2, Earth Stone x1	180	↓20	Chromed Leathers x1
Gilt Shield	Molting x1, Fire Stone x1	270	↓30	Escutcheon x1
Tail of the Phoenix	Small Feather x3	400	↓100	Phoenix Down x2
First-aid Kit	Large Feather x3	450	↓100	Phoenix Down x2, Potion x2
Assorted Leathers	Wolf Pelt x2, Tanned Hide x1, Dark Stone x2	680	↓200	Leather Breastplate x1, Leather Headgear x1
Bow & Bodkin	Bat Fang x1, Rat Pelt x2, Dark Stone x2	600	N/A	Parallel Arrows x1, Shortbow x1
Eye Drop Set	Demon Eyeball x2	100	↓50	Eye Drops x3
Marksman's Delight	Fish Scale x2, Green Liquid x1, Dark Stone x3	1680	N/A	Silent Shot x1, Capella x1
Light Spear	Horn x2, Foul Flesh x2, Wind Stone x3	1260	↓140	Javelin x1
Iron-forged Blade	Iron Scraps x3, Foul Flesh x2, Earth Stone x3	1080	↓120	Iron Sword x1
Tinctures & Tonics	Succulent Fruit x4	700	↓100	Potion x5, Handkerchief x3, Gold Needle x3
Arrows Alight	Crooked Fang x2, Fire Stone x4	3800	N/A	Fiery Arrows x1, Long Bow x1
Rain of Tears	Yensa Scale x1, Green Liquid x3, Water Stone x4	2980	N/A	Aqua Shot x1, Vega x1
Wooden Pole	Bone Fragment x5, Succulent Fruit x3, Earth Stone x4	1800	↓200	Cypress Pole x1
Eye Openers	Chocobo Feather x4	1280	↓220	Phoenix Down x5, Alarm Clock x5
Crimson Blade	Solid Stone x2, Glass Jewel x2, Dark Stone x5	4500	↓500	Blood Sword x1
Traveler's Garb	Braid Wool x2, Tanned Hide x2, Water Stone x5	3280	↓520	Feathered Cap x1, Traveler's Vestment x1
Golden Garb	Iron Carapace x3, Tanned Hide x2, Dark Stone x5	6780	↓1790	Golden Helm x1, Golden Armor x1, Golden Shield x1
Matching Reds	Coeurl Pelt x3, Quality Hide x2, Dark Magicite x3	4280	↓720	Red Cap x1, Brigandine x1
Smelling Salts, &c.	Malboro Vine x4	540	↓400	Hi-Potion x4, Smelling Salts x2
Burning Blade	Lumber x2, Malboro Vine x2, Fire Stone x6	4680	↓520	Flametongue x1
Sipping Wine	Tyrant Hide x2	240	↓120	Bacchus's Wine x3
Hollow-shaft Arrows	Bat Fang x5, Yellow Liquid x1, Water Magicite x3	6280	N/A	Bamboo Arrows x1, Loxley Bow x1
Burnished Protectives	Wyrm Carapace x2, Quality Hide x2, Fire Stone x6	8400	↓2100	Burgonet x1, Shielded Armor x1, Ice Shield x1
Burning Fangs	Pointed Horn x2	980	N/A	Red Fang x5
Alluring Finery	Fine Wool x3, Tyrant Hide x1, Ice Magicite x4	5480	↓820	Lamia's Tiara x1, Enchanter's Habit x1
Monk's Garb	Coeurl Pelt x4, Tyrant Hide x2, Ice Magicite x4	5480	↓220	Headband x1, Jujitsu Gi x1
Ranger's Crossbow	Crooked Fang x4, Yellow Liquid x2, Ice Stone x1	6480	N/A	Long Bolts x1, Crossbow x1
Iron-forged Pole	Sturdy Bone x5, Demon Eyeball x3, Fire Magicite x4	4780	↓520	Iron Pole x1
Triage Kit	Giant Feather x3	2980	↓850	Phoenix Down x12, Hi-Potion x3
Magick Shards	Festering Flesh x4	1480	N/A	Water Mote x5
Ninja Garb	Fine Wool x4, Tanned Tyrant Hide x2, Fire Magicite x5	8330	↓1470	Black Cowl x1, Black Garb x1
Light & Sturdy Garb	Coeurl Pelt x6, Tanned Tyrant Hide x2, Storm Magicite x5	9800	↓2000	Adamant Hat x1, Adamant Vest x1
Huntsman's Crossbow	Bundle of Needles x1, Festering Flesh x2, Ice Magicite x5	9980	N/A	Stone Bolts x1, Recurve Crossbow x1
Jag-tooth Ninja Sword	Giant Feather x5, Festering Flesh x4, Dark Magicite x5	9000	↓1000	Kagenui x1

Name	Loot	Cost	Cost Diff.	Contents
Survival Set	Malboro Fruit x4	1500	↓300	Antidote x12, Eye Drops x12, Echo Herbs x12
Soul of the Fire-bird	Bundle of Feathers x3	5980	↓270	Phoenix Down x25
Emboldening Arms	Quality Pelt x6, Tanned Giantskin x4, Fire Crystal x3	13780	↓2420	Chakra Band x1, Power Vest x1
Platinum Gear	Insect Husk x2, Tanned Giantskin x5, Storm Magicite x6	19120	↓4780	Platinum Helm x1, Platinum Armor x1, Platinum Shield x1
Noisome Incendiaries	Bomb Shell x1, Fire Crystal x3	9800	N/A	Poison Bombs x1, Fumarole x1
War Axe	Pointed Horn x2, Malboro Fruit x4, Wind Magicite x6	10350	↓1150	Francisca x1
Warped Blade	Bundle of Feathers x6, Maggoty Flesh x4, Fire Magicite x6	11250	↓1250	Diamond Sword x1
Forked Spear	Pointed Horn x4, Maggoty Flesh x5, Wind Magicite x6	11250	↓1250	Trident x1
Mudslinger	Ichthon Scale x4, Silver Liquid x3, Earth Crystal x3	9080	N/A	Mud Shot x1, Aldebaran x1
Oil-soaked Incendiaries	Bomb Ashes x3, Book of Orgain x2, Fire Crystal x3	10625	N/A	Oil Bombs x1, Tumulus x1
Blindflight Quarrels	Spiral Incisor x3, Silver Liquid x3, Dark Crystal x3	11220	N/A	Black Bolts x1, Hunting Crossbow x1
Phials & Philtres	Malboro Flower x3	1980	↓420	Vaccine x8, Smelling Salts x16
Potion Crate	Screamroot x3	7480	↓5120	Potion x30, Hi-Potion x20, X-Potion x10
Gigas Gear	Prime Pelt x8, Prime Tanned Hide x7, Dark Crystal x7	17800	↓3800	Gigas Hat x1, Gigas Chestplate x1
Armor-piercing Shot	Ring Wyrm Scale x4, Silver Liquid x5, Wind Crystal x7	15200	N/A	Windslicer Shot x1, Spica x1
Permafrost Bow & Quiver	Spiral Incisor x4, Antarctic Wind x2, Ice Crystal x7	17200	N/A	Icecloud Arrows x1, Perseus Bow x1
Befuddling Incendiaries	Bomb Shell x4, Book of Orgain-Cent x3, Fire Crystal x7	17800	N/A	Chaos Bombs x1, Caldera x1
Mystic Staff	Quality Lumber x4, Demon Feather x6, Storm Crystal x7	7200	↓900	Cloud Staff x1
Elegant Pole	Blood-darkened Bone x8, Demon Feather x6, Wind Crystal x7	12150	↓1360	Ivory Pole x1
Phoenix Flight	Windslicer Pinion x5	8750	↓3750	Phoenix Down x50
Black Vestments	Blood Wool x9, Prime Tanned Hide x7, Dark Crystal x8	22800	↓3100	Black Mask x1, Black Robes x1
White Vestments	Blood Wool x9, Beastlord Hide x7, Holy Crystal x8	22800	↓6200	White Mask x1, White Robes x1
Nature's Armory	Prime Pelt x9, Forbidden Flesh x7, Fire Crystal x8	24650	↓4350	Crown of Laurels x1, Rubber Suit x1
Forbidding Shield	Aged Turtle Shell x2, Destrier Barding x8, Leamonde Halcyon x1	9800	↓1400	Demon Shield x1
Sturdy Battle Gear	Charger Barding x4, Split Armor x2, Pisces Gem x3	14800	↓2200	Maximillian x1
Magepower Helm	Charger Barding x5, Chimera Head x2, Feystone x1	12800	↓220	Magepower Shishak x1
Scout's Crossbow	Wyvern Fang x4, Ancient Bone x3, Holy Crystal x9	17800	N/A	Time Bolts x1, Penetrator Crossbow x1
Water-drop Munitions	Book of Orgain x3, Putrid Liquid x3, Water Crystal x10	7800	N/A	Water Bombs x1
Samurai's Katana	Iron Ore x5, Screamroot x7, Water Crystal x9	13800	↓1200	Ame-no-Murakumo x1
Double-bladed Knife	Windslicer Pinion x5, Malboro Flower x7, Wind Crystal x9	13800	↓1200	Zwill Crossblade x1
The Leering Blade	Solid Horn x4, Demon Tail x7, Dark Crystal x10	14800	↓1200	Deathbringer x1
Attenuated Greatsword	Quality Stone x4, Sky Jewel x7, Holy Crystal x10	14000	↓1500	Save the Queen x1
Memories of Yore	Quality Stone x5	999	N/A	Pebble x99
Devastating Incendiaries	Bomb Fragment x3, Frog Oil x2, Aries Gem x3	12000	N/A	Castellanos x1
Darksteel Blade	Orichalcum x2, Chimera Head x2, Taurus Gem x3	17800	N/A	Stoneblade x1
Arrows of the Moon Goddess	Vampyr Fang x2, Dorsal Fin x2, Gemini Gem x3	15000	N/A	Artemis Arrows x1
Serpent Blade	Coeurl Whisker x2, Sickle-Blade x2, Cancer Gem x3	15200	N/A	Orochi x1
Well-forged Blade	Lifewick x3, Emperor Scale x2, Leshach Halcyon x1	21600	N/A	Durandal x1
Comfy Headgear	White Incense x2, Einherjarium x2, Virgo Gem x7	30000	0	Cat-ear Hood x1
Stone Shot	Mirror Scale x2, Tyrant Bone x2, Libra Gem x3	15000	N/A	Stone Shot x1
The Scorpion	Charged Gizzard x3, Wyrm Bone x3, Scorpio Gem x4	60000	N/A	Scorpion Tail x1
Silver Bow	Beastlord Horn x3, Moon Ring x3, Sagittarius Gem x4	60000	N/A	Sagittarius x1
Piercing Bolts	Wrath of the Gods x2, Ring Wyrm Liver x2, Capricorn Gem x3	15000	N/A	Grand Bolts x1
Cursed Necklace	Blood-stained Necklace x3, Death's-Head x2, Leo Gem x3	30000	0	Nihopalaoa x1
Whisker of the Beast	Mythril x3, Corpse Fly x3, Aquarius Gem x4	60000	N/A	Whale Whisker x1
Late-model Rifle	Wyvern Wing x2, Yensa Fin x2, Salamand Halcyon x1	19800	N/A	Arcturus x1

Name	Loot	Cost	Cost Diff.	Contents
Ultimate Blade	Adamantite x2, Death Powder x2, Gnoma Halcyon x1	22800	N/A	Ultima Blade x1
Bow of the Moon Goddess	Great Serpent's Fang x2, Moondust x2, Sylphi Halcyon x1	15800	N/A	Artemis Bow x1
Brilliant Shield	Ancient Turtle Shell x2, Ring Wyrm Liver x2, Undin Halcyon x1	12420	N/A	Venetian Shield x1
Engraved Spear	Ketu Board x2, Broken Spear x2, Mystletainn x2	15300	↓1700	Gungnir x1
Golden Battle Axe	Electrum x2, Broken Greataxe x2, Mardu Halcyon x1	16200	↓1800	Golden Axe x1
Flask of Oily Liquid	Unpurified Ether x2, Caramel x3	4000	↑3775	Ether x1
Flask of Viscous Liquid	Unpurified Ether x2, Foul Liquid x2, Slime Oil x4	12000	N/A	Hi-Ether x1
Saint's Draught	Ambrosia x3, Demon Drink x3, High Arcana x1	36000	N/A	Elixir x1
Esoteric Draught	Onion x3, Rat Tail x3, High Arcana x2	108000	N/A	Megalixir x1
Life Crystal (repeatable)	Arcana x10, Feystone x1, Soul of Thamasa x1	9999	N/A	High Arcana x1
Jewel of the Serpent (repeatable)	Snake Skin x4, Serpent Eye x2, High Arcana x1	19998	N/A	Serpentarius x1
Jewel of Creation (repeatable)	Soul Powder x1, Wargod's Band x2, High Arcana x1	29997	N/A	Empyreal Soul x1
Matchless Metal (repeatable)	Scarletite x1, Damascus Steel x2, Hell-Gate's Flame x2	29997	N/A	Gemsteel x1
Master-crafted Blade	Gemsteel x2, Orichalcum x3, Mallet x2	350000	N/A	Masamune x1
The Sunflower	Gemsteel x3, Empyreal Soul x3, Serpentarius x3	600000	N/A	Tournesol x1
Dragon Crest	Omega Badge x1, Godslayer's Badge x1, Lu Shang's Badge x1	65535	N/A	Wyrmhero Blade x1
Mysterious Substance (repeatable)	Grimoire Togail x3, Grimoire Aidhed x3, Bat Wing x1	14999	↑14997	Dark Matter x1
Magick Shard	Glass Jewel x8, Sky Jewel x8, Diakon Halcyon x1	99	N/A	Holy Mote x1
Magick Shard	Book of Orgain x8, Book of Orgain-Cent x8, Book of Orgain-Mille x8	499	N/A	Scathe Mote x1
Potion Pack (repeatable)	Cactus Fruit x2	70	N/A	Potion x2
Hi-Potion Pack (repeatable)	Rainbow Egg x1	1111	N/A	Hi-Potion x10
Chronos Tear Pack (repeatable)	Eye of the Hawk x1	333	N/A	Chronos Tear x10
Fire-bird's Whisper	Jack-o'-Lantern x1	2222	N/A	Phoenix Down x10
Vaccine Pack	Demon's Sigh x1	999	N/A	Vaccine x10
X-Potion Pack	Behemoth Steak x1	4444	N/A	X-Potion x10
Shell-worked Collar	Bomb Shell x2, Four-Leaf Clover x2	8370	↓930	Turtleshell Choker x1
Ninja Footgear	Slaven Harness x2	450	↓260	Gillie Boots x1
Brawler's Fetish	Gimble Stalk x2	5940	↓560	Amber Armlet x1
Blush of Light	Tomato Stalk x2, Magick Lamp x1, Snowfly x1	4500	↓500	Firefly x1
Shoes of the Dead	Zombie Powder x1, Destrier Mane x1	450	↓360	Quasimodo Boots x1
Back Harness	Wolf Blood x1	800	↓200	Battle Harness x1
Large Gloves	Bent Staff x3	4500	↓1300	Blazer Gloves x1
Chain-link Belt	Battlewyrm Carapace x2, Adamantite x1	17820	↓1080	Bubble Belt x1
Wind Walkers	Gysahl Greens x33, Arcana x15	18000	↓2000	Hermes Sandals x1
Wing Cord	Stardust x2	3600	↓400	Pheasant Netsuke x1
Gilt Phylactery	Tattered Garment x1	3150	↓1350	Golden Amulet x1
Exquisite Ring	Frogspawn x2	14400	↓1600	Opal Ring x1
Feathered Boots	Arctic Wind x1, Broken Sword x1	450	↓50	Winged Boots x1

Merchant Shops

While there is also the Bazaar, operated by and connecting all merchants, the most direct method of acquiring new gear and items is directly through the merchants themselves. When you first happen upon a new merchant, his wares might be limited, but as you progress within the main story more and more of their overall selection will become available. In particular, it is very important to pick up new magicks when they become available, in addition to staying stocked up on curative items like Potions, Echo Herbs, and Phoenix Down. New gambits tend to be very inexpensive and shouldn't dent your coin purse.

A WORD ABOUT GAMBITS

Gambits become available based upon your progress in the game. The further along in the game you are, the more gambits are available for purchase. Once a gambit is for sale, it will be available in any gambit shop.

MERCHANT: ALL GAMBIT MERCHANTS
LOCATION: ANY GAMBIT SHOP

WARES	COST
Ally: any	50
Ally: party leader	50
Ally: lowest HP	50
Ally: strongest weapon	50
Ally: lowest defense	50
Ally: lowest magick resist	50
Ally: HP < 100%	50
Ally: HP < 90%	50
Ally: HP < 80%	50
Ally: HP < 70%	50
Ally: HP < 60%	50
Ally: HP < 50%	50
Ally: HP < 40%	50
Ally: HP < 30%	50
Ally: HP < 20%	50
Ally: HP < 10%	50
Ally: MP < 100%	50
Ally: MP < 90%	50
Ally: MP < 80%	50
Ally: MP < 70%	50
Ally: MP < 60%	50
Ally: MP < 50%	50
Ally: MP < 40%	50
Ally: MP < 30%	50
Ally: MP < 20%	50
Ally: MP < 10%	50
Ally: status = KO	50
Ally: status = Stone	50
Ally: status = Petrify	50
Ally: status = Stop	50
Ally: status = Sleep	50
Ally: status = Confuse	50
Ally: status = Doom	50
Ally: status = Blind	50
Ally: status = Poison	50
Ally: status = Silence	50
Ally: status = Sap	50
Ally: status = Oil	50
Ally: status = Reverse	50
Ally: status = Disable	50
Ally: status = Immobilize	50
Ally: status = Slow	50
Ally: status = Disease	50

WARES	COST
Ally: status = Lure	50
Ally: status = Protect	50
Ally: status = Shell	50
Ally: status = Haste	50
Ally: status = Bravery	50
Ally: status = Faith	50
Ally: status = Reflect	50
Ally: status = Invisible	50
Ally: status = Regen	50
Ally: status = Float	50
Ally: status = Berserk	50
Ally: status = Bubble	50
Ally: status = HP Critical	50
Ally: item AMT > 10	100
Foe: any	50
Foe: targeting leader	100
Foe: targeting self	100
Foe: targeting ally	100
Foe: furthest	50
Foe: nearest	50
Foe: highest HP	50
Foe: lowest HP	50
Foe: highest max HP	50
Foe: lowest max HP	50
Foe: highest MP	50
Foe: lowest MP	50
Foe: highest max MP	50
Foe: lowest max MP	50
Foe: highest level	50
Foe: lowest level	50
Foe: highest strength	50
Foe: lowest strength	50
Foe: highest magick power	50
Foe: lowest magick power	50
Foe: highest speed	50
Foe: lowest speed	50
Foe: highest defense	50
Foe: highest magick resist	50
Foe: HP ≥ 100,000	50
Foe: HP ≥ 50,000	50
Foe: HP ≥ 10,000	50
Foe: HP ≥ 5,000	50
Foe: HP ≥ 3,000	50

WARES	COST
Foe: HP ≥ 2,000	50
Foe: HP ≥ 1,000	50
Foe: HP ≥ 500	50
Foe: HP < 100,000	50
Foe: HP < 50,000	50
Foe: HP < 10,000	50
Foe: HP < 5,000	50
Foe: HP < 3,000	50
Foe: HP < 2,000	50
Foe: HP < 1,000	50
Foe: HP < 500	50
Foe: HP = 100%	50
Foe: HP ≥ 70%	50
Foe: HP ≥ 50%	50
Foe: HP ≥ 30%	50
Foe: status = Petrify	50
Foe: status = Stop	50
Foe: status = Sleep	50
Foe: status = Confuse	50
Foe: status = Doom	50
Foe: status = Blind	50
Foe: status = Poison	50
Foe: status = Silence	50
Foe: status = Sap	50
Foe: status = Oil	50
Foe: status = Reverse	50
Foe: status = Disable	50
Foe: status = Immobilize	50
Foe: status = Slow	50
Foe: status = Disease	50
Foe: status = Protect	50
Foe: status = Shell	50
Foe: status = Haste	50
Foe: status = Bravery	50
Foe: status = Faith	50
Foe: status = Reflect	50
Foe: status = Regen	50
Foe: status = Berserk	50
Foe: status = HP Critical	50
Foe: fire-weak	500
Foe: lightning-weak	500
Foe: ice-weak	500
Foe: earth-weak	500

WARES	COST
Foe: water-weak	500
Foe: wind-weak	500
Foe: holy-weak	500
Foe: dark-weak	500
Foe: fire-vulnerable	250
Foe: lightning-vulnerable	250
Foe: ice-vulnerable	250
Foe: earth-vulnerable	250
Foe: water-vulnerable	250
Foe: wind-vulnerable	250
Foe: holy-vulnerable	250
Foe: dark-vulnerable	250
Foe: undead	100
Foe: flying	100
Foe: character HP = 100%	100
Foe: item AMT ≥ 10	100
Foe: character status = Blind	100
Foe: character status = Silence	100
Foe: character status = Bravery	100
Foe: character status = Faith	100
Foe: character status = HP Critical	100
Foe: character MP ≥ 90%	100
Foe: character MP ≥ 70%	100
Foe: character MP ≥ 50%	100
Foe: character MP ≥ 30%	100
Foe: character MP ≥ 10%	100
Foe: character MP < 90%	100
Foe: character MP < 70%	100
Foe: character MP < 50%	100
Foe: character MP < 30%	100
Foe: character MP < 10%	100
Foe: character HP ≥ 90%	100
Foe: character HP ≥ 70%	100
Foe: character HP ≥ 50%	100
Foe: character HP ≥ 30%	100
Foe: character HP ≥ 10%	100
Foe: character HP < 90%	100
Foe: character HP < 70%	100
Foe: character HP < 50%	100
Foe: character HP < 30%	100
Foe: character HP < 10%	100
Self	50
Self: HP < 100%	50

More Gambits →

WARES	COST
Self: HP < 90%	50
Self: HP < 80%	50
Self: HP < 70%	50
Self: HP < 60%	50
Self: HP < 50%	50
Self: HP < 40%	50
Self: HP < 30%	50
Self: HP < 20%	50
Self: HP < 10%	50
Self: MP < 100%	50
Self: MP < 90%	50

WARES	COST
Self: MP < 80%	50
Self: MP < 70%	50
Self: MP < 60%	50
Self: MP < 50%	50
Self: MP < 40%	50
Self: MP < 30%	50
Self: MP < 20%	50
Self: MP < 10%	50
Self: status = Petrify	50
Self: status = Doom	50
Self: status = Blind	50

WARES	COST
Self: status = Poison	50
Self: status = Silence	50
Self: status = Sap	50
Self: status = Oil	50
Self: status = Reverse	50
Self: status = Immobilize	50
Self: status = Slow	50
Self: status = Disease	50
Self: status = Lure	50
Self: status = Protect	50
Self: status = Shell	50

WARES	COST
Self: status = Haste	50
Self: status = Bravery	50
Self: status = Faith	50
Self: status = Reflect	50
Self: status = Invisible	50
Self: status = Regen	50
Self: status = Float	50
Self: status = Bubble	50
Self: status = HP Critical	50

MERCHANT: BATAHN
LOCATION: RABANASTRE, BATAHN'S TECHNICKS

WARES	COST
Steal	1600
Libra	500
First Aid	700
Poach	7000
Charge	1700
Horology	2000
Souleater	6400
Traveler	6700
Numerology	2048
Shear	3600
Achilles	8800
Gil Toss	2000
Charm	5000
Sight Unseeing	6800
Infuse	2000
Addle	3500
Bonecrusher	700

MERCHANT: YUGRI
LOCATION: RABANASTRE, YUGRI'S MAGICKS

WARES	COST
Cure	200
Poisona	200
Blindna	200
Vox	300
Stona	800
Raise	1900
Cura	1500
Regen	1900
Esuna	2800
Curaga	3200
Dispel	4500
Fire	200
Thunder	200
Blizzard	200
Water	800
Aero	1200
Fira	3000

WARES	COST
Thundara	3000
Blizzara	3000
Bio	4900
Slow	200
Immobilize	600
Disable	600
Break	900
Reflect	800
Warp	1700
Bleed	1100
Balance	1500
Float	2800
Haste	3400
Countdown	3100
Stop	3700
Blind	200
Protect	200

WARES	COST
Poison	500
Shell	300
Silence	400
Sleep	700
Oil	600
Toxify	4100
Dark	500
Berserk	1000
Confuse	1400
Decoy	2500
Gravity	2800
Drain	3200
Vanish	4900
Death	5200
Vanishga	8700

MERCHANT: PANAMIS
LOCATION: RABANASTRE, PANAMIS'S PROTECTIVES

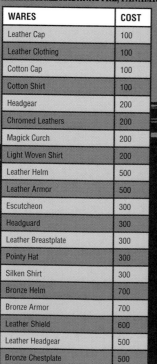

WARES	COST
Leather Cap	100
Leather Clothing	100
Cotton Cap	100
Cotton Shirt	100
Headgear	200
Chromed Leathers	200
Magick Curch	200
Light Woven Shirt	200
Leather Helm	500
Leather Armor	500
Escutcheon	300
Headguard	300
Leather Breastplate	300
Pointy Hat	300
Silken Shirt	300
Bronze Helm	700
Bronze Armor	700
Leather Shield	600
Leather Headgear	500
Bronze Chestplate	500

WARES	COST
Topkapi Hat	500
Kilimweave Shirt	500
Sallet	1000
Scale Armor	1000
Buckler	1000
Horned Hat	700
Ringmail	700
Calot Hat	700
Shepherd's Bolero	700
Iron Helm	1400
Iron Armor	1400
Bronze Shield	1200
Balaclava	1000
Windbreaker	1000
Wizard's Hat	1000
Wizard's Robes	1000
Barbut	1900
Linen Cuirass	1900
Round Shield	1600
Soldier's Cap	1400

WARES	COST
Heavy Coat	1400
Lambent Hat	1400
Chanter's Djellaba	1400
Winged Helm	2500
Chainmail	2500
Green Beret	1900
Survival Vest	1900
Feathered Cap	1900
Traveler's Vestment	1900
Golden Helm	3200
Golden Armor	3200
Golden Shield	2100
Red Cap	2500
Brigandine	2500
Mage's Hat	2500
Mage's Habit	2500
Burgonet	4000
Shielded Armor	4000
Ice Shield	2500
Headband	3200

WARES	COST
Jujitsu Gi	3200
Lamia's Tiara	3200
Enchanter's Habit	3200
Pirate Hat	4000
Viking Coat	4000
Sorcerer's Hat	4000
Sorcerer's Habit	4000
Close Helmet	4900
Demon Mail	4900
Flame Shield	3200
Goggle Mask	4900
Metal Jerkin	4900
Black Cowl	4900
Black Garb	4900
Bone Helm	5900
Bone Mail	5900
Diamond Shield	3900

MERCHANT: AMAL
LOCATION: RABANASTRE, AMAL'S WEAPONRY

WARES	COST	WARES	COST	WARES	COST	WARES	COST
Broadsword	400	Chopper	2200	Serpent Rod	2100	Miter	5000
Dagger	200	Cypress Pole	2000	Lohengrin	4500	Storm Spear	5800
Shortbow	500	Mace	1800	Heavy Lance	4800	Iron Pole	5300
Altair	500	Ancient Sword	2400	Osafune	4800	Hornito	5800
Longsword	700	Vega	2400	Gladius	4800	Arc Scale	5500
Mage Masher	700	Longbow	3000	Musk Stick	4300	Demonsbane	6000
Silver Bow	1000	Wizard's Staff	1500	Gilt Measure	4000	Giant Stonebow	6000
Iron Sword	1200	Rod	1500	Bhuj	4100	Slasher	6000
Oak Staff	400	Iron Hammer	3300	Flame Staff	2400	Avenger	6000
Javelin	1400	Bronze Mace	3000	Storm Staff	2400	Magoroku	6600
Assassin's Dagger	1400	Blood Sword	5000	Glacial Staff	2400	Paramina Crossbow	6600
Capella	1400	Partisan	3500	Flametongue	5200	Gaia Rod	3300
Oaken Pole	1300	Main Gauche	3500	Loxley Bow	5200	Icebrand	7000
Aevis Killer	1500	Battle Bamboo	3200	War Hammer	5200	Ras Algethi	7000
Zwill Blade	1700	Kotetsu	3800	Crossbow	5200	Sakura-saezuri	7000
Cherry Staff	800	Bowgun	3800	Healing Rod	3000	Golden Staff	3500
Killer Bow	2000	Sirius	4000	Betelgeuse	5400		
Spear	2200	Elfin Bow	4200	Kogarasumaru	5600		
Handaxe	2200	Broadaxe	4200	Ashura	5600		

MERCHANT: SHOP CLERK
LOCATION: RABANASTRE, MIGELO'S SUNDRIES

WARES	COST
Potion	70
Antidote	50
Eye Drops	50
Phoenix Down	250
Echo Herbs	50
Gold Needle	100
Alarm Clock	50
Handkerchief	50
Hi-Potion	210
Bacchus's Wine	120
Smelling Salts	50
Remedy	400
Chronos Tear	50

MERCHANT: CLAN PROVISIONER
LOCATION: RABANASTRE, MUTHRU BAZAAR

WARES	COST
Cat-ear Hood	30000
Nihopalaoa	30000
Bubble Belt	19800
Knot of Rust	6
Warp Mote	100
Dark Matter	2
Bravery	5800
Faith	5800
Bubble	3300
Reverse	7600
Teleport Stone	200
Gysahl Greens	108

MERCHANT: TRAVELING MERCHANT
LOCATION: RABANASTRE LOWTOWN, NORTH SPRAWL

WARES	COST
Potion	70
Antidote	50

MERCHANT: ARJIE
LOCATION: GIZA PLAINS, NOMAD VILLAGE

WARES	COST
Broadsword	400
Dagger	200
Orrachea Armlet	250
Bangle	500
Potion	70
Antidote	50
Eye Drops	50

MERCHANT: TRAVELING MERCHANT
LOCATION: RABANASTRE LOWTOWN, SOUTH SPRAWL

WARES	COST
Renewing Morion	16000
Mirage Vest	16000
Jackboots	600
Black Belt	600
Golden Amulet	4500
Potion	70
Eye Drops	50

MERCHANT: PORTENTOUS PROVISIONS
LOCATION: NALBINA TOWN, WEST BARBICAN

WARES	COST
Onion Arrows	100
Onion Bolts	100
Onion Shot	100
Onion Bombs	100
Potion	70
Antidote	50
Eye Drops	50
Phoenix Down	250
Echo Herbs	50
Gold Needle	100
Alarm Clock	50
Handkerchief	50
Hi-Potion	210
Bacchus's Wine	120
Smelling Salts	50
Remedy	400

MERCHANT: TROUBLESOME TECHNICKS
LOCATION: NALBINA TOWN, JAJIM BAZAAR

WARES	COST
First Aid	700
Poach	7000
Charge	1700
Horology	2000
Souleater	6400
Traveler	6700
Numerology	2048
Shear	3600
Achilles	8800
Gil Toss	2000
Charm	5000
Sight Unseeing	6800
Infuse	2000

MYSTERIOUS MAGICKS
NALBINA TOWN, JAJIM BAZAAR

WARES	COST	WARES	COST
Curaga	3200	Countdown	3100
Cure	200	Stop	3700
Poisona	200	Haste	3400
Blindna	200	Slow	200
Dispel	4500	Toxify	4100
Bio	4900	Blind	200
Fira	3000	Protect	200
Thundara	3000	Poison	500
Blizzara	3000	Vanish	4900
Fire	200	Death	5200
Thunder	200	Vanishga	8700
Blizzard	200		

MERCHANT: WEAPONS OF WAR
LOCATION: NALBINA TOWN, WEST WARD

WARES	COST	WARES	COST
Altair	500	Miter	5000
Longsword	700	Storm Spear	5800
Mage Masher	700	Iron Pole	5300
Silver Bow	1000	Hornito	5800
Iron Sword	1200	Arc Scale	5500
Oak Staff	400	Demonsbane	6000
Flame Staff	2400	Giant Stonebow	6000
Storm Staff	2400	Slasher	6000
Glacial Staff	2400	Avenger	6000
Flametongue	5200	Magoroku	6600
Loxley Bow	5200	Paramina Crossbow	6600
War Hammer	5200	Gaia Rod	3300
Crossbow	5200	Icebrand	7000
Healing Rod	3000	Ras Algethi	7000
Betelgeuse	5400	Sakura-saezuri	7000
Kogarasumaru	5600	Golden Staff	3500
Ashura	5600		

MERCHANT: ANTIQUED ARMORS
LOCATION: NALBINA TOWN, WEST WARD

WARES	COST	WARES	COST
Headguard	300	Sorcerer's Hat	4000
Leather Breastplate	300	Sorcerer's Habit	4000
Pointy Hat	300	Close Helmet	4900
Silken Shirt	300	Demon Mail	4900
Bronze Helm	700	Flame Shield	3200
Bronze Armor	700	Goggle Mask	4900
Leather Shield	600	Metal Jerkin	4900
Leather Headgear	500	Black Cowl	4900
Bronze Chestplate	500	Black Garb	4900
Topkapi Hat	500	Bone Helm	5900
Kilimweave Shirt	500	Bone Mail	5900
Pirate Hat	4000	Diamond Shield	3900
Viking Coat	4000		

MERCHANT: RITHIL
LOCATION: BHUJERBA, RITHIL'S PROTECTIVES

WARES	COST	WARES	COST
Leather Headgear	500	Iron Helm	1400
Bronze Chestplate	500	Iron Armor	1400
Topkapi Hat	500	Bronze Shield	1200
Kilimweave Shirt	500	Headguard	300
Sallet	1000	Leather Breastplate	300
Scale Armor	1000	Pointy Hat	300
Buckler	1000	Silken Shirt	300
Horned Hat	700	Bronze Helm	700
Ringmail	700	Bronze Armor	700
Calot Hat	700	Leather Shield	600
Shepherd's Bolero	700		

MERCHANT: TARGE
LOCATION: BHUJERBA, TARGE'S ARMS

WARES	COST	WARES	COST
Iron Sword	1200	Cherry Staff	800
Oak Staff	400	Broadsword	400
Javelin	1400	Dagger	200
Assassin's Dagger	1400	Shortbow	500
Capella	1400	Altair	500
Oaken Pole	1300	Longsword	700
Aevis Killer	1500	Mage Masher	700
Zwill Blade	1700	Silver Bow	1000

MERCHANT: MAIT
LOCATION: BHUJERBA, MAIT'S MAGICKS

WARES	COST	WARES	COST
Raise	1900	Blind	200
Cura	1500	Protect	200
Vox	300	Poison	500
Stona	800	Shell	300
Water	800	Sleep	700
Immobilize	600	Oil	600
Disable	600	Silence	400
Break	900	Dark	500
Reflect	800		

MERCHANT: STREET VENDOR
LOCATION: BHUJERBA, KHUS SKYGROUNDS

WARES	COST
Sweep	16200
Turtleshell Choker	9300
Potion	70
Antidote	50
Eye Drops	50
Phoenix Down	250
Echo Herbs	50
Gold Needle	100
Alarm Clock	50
Handkerchief	50

MERCHANT: CLIO
LOCATION: BHUJERBA, CLIO'S TECHNICKS

WARES	COST
Poach	7000
Charge	1700
Horology	2000
Souleater	6400

MERCHANT: STREET VENDOR
LOCATION: BHUJERBA, LHUSU SQUARE

WARES	COST
Sweep	16200
Turtleshell Choker	9300
Potion	70
Antidote	50
Eye Drops	50
Phoenix Down	250
Echo Herbs	50
Gold Needle	100
Alarm Clock	50
Handkerchief	50

MERCHANT: LOHEN
LOCATION: DALMASCA WESTERSAND, THE WESTERN DIVIDE

WARES	COST
Gungnir	17000
Bangle	500
Steel Gorget	1500
Armguard	800
Tourmaline Ring	300
Gauntlets	1200
Battle Harness	1000
Leather Gorget	1500
Rose Corsage	800
Agate Ring	3000
Renew	30600

MERCHANT: UNLUCKY MERCHANT
LOCATION: DALMASCA ESTERSAND, SOUTH BANK VILLAGE

WARES	COST
Golden Axe	18000
Bangle	500
Steel Gorget	1500
Armguard	800
Tourmaline Ring	300
Gauntlets	1200
Battle Harness	1000
Diamond Armlet	20000
Hastega	16600

MERCHANT: GARIF TRADER
LOCATION: JAHARA, LULL OF THE LAND

WARES	COST	WARES	COST	WARES	COST	WARES	COST
Partisan	3500	Storm Staff	2400	Traveler's Vestment	1900	Eye Drops	50
Main Gauche	3500	Glacial Staff	2400	Golden Helm	3200	Phoenix Down	250
Battle Bamboo	3200	Flametongue	5200	Golden Armor	3200	Echo Herbs	50
Kotetsu	3800	Loxley Bow	5200	Golden Shield	2100	Gold Needle	100
Bowgun	3800	War Hammer	5200	Red Cap	2500	Alarm Clock	50
Sirius	4000	Crossbow	5200	Brigandine	2500	Handkerchief	50
Elfin Bow	4200	Healing Rod	3000	Mage's Hat	2500	Hi-Potion	210
Broadaxe	4200	Betelgeuse	5400	Mage's Habit	2500	Bacchus's Wine	120
Serpent Rod	2100	Soldier's Cap	1400	Burgonet	4000	Smelling Salts	50
Lohengrin	4500	Heavy Coat	1400	Shielded Armor	4000	Shear	3600
Heavy Lance	4800	Lambent Hat	1400	Ice Shield	2500	Achilles	8800
Osafune	4800	Chanter's Djellaba	1400	Onion Arrows	100	Gil Toss	2000
Gladius	4800	Winged Helm	2500	Onion Bolts	100	Charm	5000
Musk Stick	4300	Chainmail	2500	Onion Shot	100	Sight Unseeing	6800
Gilt Measure	4000	Green Beret	1900	Onion Bombs	100	Infuse	2000
Bhuj	4100	Survival Vest	1900	Potion	70		
Flame Staff	2400	Feathered Cap	1900	Antidote	50		

MERCHANT: TETRAN
LOCATION: ERUYT VILLAGE, ROAD OF VERDANT PRAISE

WARES	COST	WARES	COST	WARES	COST	WARES	COST
Amber Armlet	6600	Eye Drops	50	Warp	1700	Drain	3200
Sash	500	Phoenix Down	250	Bleed	1100	Curaga	3200
Argyle Armlet	600	Echo Herbs	50	Berserk	1000	Fira	3000
Blazer Gloves	3200	Gold Needle	100	Aero	1200	Thundara	3000
Jade Collar	3300	Alarm Clock	50	Balance	1500	Blizzara	3000
Jackboots	600	Handkerchief	50	Confuse	1400	Haste	3400
Black Belt	600	Hi-Potion	210	Regen	1900	Toxify	4100
Golden Amulet	4500	Bacchus's Wine	120	Esuna	2800	Countdown	3100
Magick Gloves	3200	Smelling Salts	50	Gravity	2800		
Potion	70	Raise	1900	Float	2800		
Antidote	50	Cura	1500	Decoy	2500		

MERCHANT: HUME TRAVELING MERCHANT
LOCATION: MT BUR-OMISACE, SAND-STREWN PASS

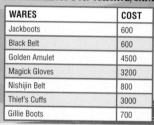

WARES	COST	WARES	COST	WARES	COST	WARES	COST
Serpent Rod	2100	Betelgeuse	5400	Golden Armor	3200	Sorcerer's Habit	4000
Lohengrin	4500	Kogarasumaru	5600	Golden Shield	2100	Close Helmet	4900
Heavy Lance	4800	Ashura	5600	Red Cap	2500	Demon Mail	4900
Osafune	4800	Miter	5000	Brigandine	2500	Flame Shield	3200
Gladius	4800	Storm Spear	5800	Mage's Hat	2500	Potion	70
Musk Stick	4300	Iron Pole	5300	Mage's Habit	2500	Antidote	50
Gilt Measure	4000	Hornito	5800	Burgonet	4000	Eye Drops	50
Bhuj	4100	Arc Scale	5500	Shielded Armor	4000	Phoenix Down	250
Flame Staff	2400	Demonsbane	6000	Ice Shield	2500	Echo Herbs	50
Storm Staff	2400	Giant Stonebow	6000	Headband	3200	Gold Needle	100
Glacial Staff	2400	Slasher	6000	Jujitsu Gi	3200	Alarm Clock	50
Flametongue	5200	Avenger	6000	Lamia's Tiara	3200	Handkerchief	50
Loxley Bow	5200	Magoroku	6600	Enchanter's Habit	3200	Hi-Potion	210
War Hammer	5200	Paramina Crossbow	6600	Pirate Hat	4000	Bacchus's Wine	120
Crossbow	5200	Gaia Rod	3300	Viking Coat	4000	Smelling Salts	50
Healing Rod	3000	Golden Helm	3200	Sorcerer's Hat	4000	Remedy	400

MERCHANT: SEEQ TRAVELING MERCHANT
LOCATION: MT BUR-OMISACE, SAND-STREWN PASS

WARES	COST	WARES	COST	WARES	COST	WARES	COST
Jackboots	600	Quasimodo Boots	800	Esuna	2800	Thundara	3000
Black Belt	600	Ruby Ring	8500	Gravity	2800	Blizzara	3000
Golden Amulet	4500	Onion Arrows	100	Float	2800	Haste	3400
Magick Gloves	3200	Onion Bolts	100	Decoy	2500	Toxify	4100
Nishijin Belt	800	Onion Shot	100	Drain	3200	Countdown	3100
Thief's Cuffs	3000	Onion Bombs	100	Curaga	3200	Stop	3700
Gillie Boots	700	Regen	1900	Fira	3000	Vanish	4900

MERCHANT: LUCCIO
LOCATION: MOSPHORAN HIGHWASTE, BABBLING VALE

WARES	COST	WARES	COST	WARES	COST	WARES	COST
Icebrand	7000	Adamant Hat	5900	Thief's Cuffs	3000	Alarm Clock	50
Ras Algethi	7000	Adamant Vest	5900	Gillie Boots	700	Handkerchief	50
Sakura-saezuri	7000	Astrakhan Hat	5900	Quasimodo Boots	800	Hi-Potion	210
Golden Staff	3500	Carmagnole	5900	Ruby Ring	8500	Bacchus's Wine	120
Burning Bow	7500	Diamond Helm	7000	Potion	70	Smelling Salts	50
Obelisk	7500	Diamond Armor	7000	Antidote	50	Remedy	400
Sledgehammer	7500	Platinum Shield	5300	Eye Drops	50	Chronos Tear	50
Six-fluted Pole	6800	Golden Amulet	4500	Phoenix Down	250	1000 Needles	7000
Thorned Mace	6500	Magick Gloves	3200	Echo Herbs	50		
Multiscale	8000	Nishijin Belt	800	Gold Needle	100		

MERCHANT: STRANDED MERCHANT
LOCATION: OLD ARCHADES, ALLEY OF LOW WHISPERS

WARES	COST	WARES	COST	WARES	COST	WARES	COST
Steel Poleyns	1000	Cameo Belt	9000	Eye Drops	50	Hi-Potion	210
Fuzzy Miter	1200	Power Armlet	5200	Phoenix Down	250	Bacchus's Wine	120
Bowline Sash	1000	Opal Ring	16000	Echo Herbs	50	Smelling Salts	50
Winged Boots	500	Sage's Ring	22000	Gold Needle	100	Remedy	400
Pheasant Netsuke	4000	Potion	70	Alarm Clock	50	Chronos Tear	50
Embroidered Tippet	5000	Antidote	50	Handkerchief	50		

MERCHANT: ARMOR SELLER
LOCATION: ARCHADES, VINT'S ARMAMENTS

WARES	COST	WARES	COST	WARES	COST	WARES	COST
Diamond Helm	7000	Gaia Hat	7000	Chakra Band	8100	Platinum Armor	9300
Diamond Armor	7000	Maduin Gear	7000	Power Vest	8100	Crystal Shield	7200
Platinum Shield	5300	Steel Mask	8100	Hypnocrown	8100		
Officer's Hat	7000	Mirror Mail	8100	Jade Gown	8100		
Barrel Coat	7000	Dragon Shield	6000	Platinum Helm	9300		

MERCHANT: WEAPON SELLER
LOCATION: ARCHADES, VINT'S ARMAMENTS

WARES	COST	WARES	COST
Platinum Sword	9000	Kiku-ichimonji	10500
Power Rod	4500	Claymore	10500
Hammerhead	9500	Chaos Mace	8800
Recurve Crossbow	9500	Bastard Sword	11000
Traitor's Bow	10000	Cross Scale	11000
Halberd	10000	Francisca	11500
Aldebaran	10000	Platinum Dagger	11500
Gokuu Pole	9000	Tumulus	12000
Kagenui	10000	Judicer's Staff	5700

MERCHANT: TECHNICK SELLER
LOCATION: ARCHADES, BULWARD'S TECHNICKS

WARES	COST
Infuse	2000
Addle	3500
Bonecrusher	700
Shades of Black	5000
Stamp	4500

MERCHANT: MAGICKERY PROPRIETOR
LOCATION: ARCHADES, CHARLOTTE'S MAGICKERY

WARES	COST
Aeroga	6800
Reflectga	6800
Silencega	6800
Blindga	6800
Graviga	6800

MERCHANT: GRANCH
LOCATION: ARCHADES, GRANCH'S REQUISITES

WARES	COST	WARES	COST	WARES	COST	WARES	COST
Potion	70	Echo Herbs	50	Hi-Potion	210	Chronos Tear	50
Antidote	50	Gold Needle	100	Bacchus's Wine	120	X-Potion	630
Eye Drops	50	Alarm Clock	50	Smelling Salts	50		
Phoenix Down	250	Handkerchief	50	Remedy	400		

Merchant Shops

301

MERCHANT: DYCE
LOCATION: BALFONHEIM PORT, SEA BREEZE LANE

WARES	COST
Teleport Stone	200
Gysahl Greens	108

MERCHANT: DYCE
LOCATION: THE NAM-YENSA SANDSEA, TRAIL OF FADING WARMTH

WARES	COST	WARES	COST	WARES	COST
Capella	1400	Immobilize	600	Dark	500
Cypress Pole	2000	Disable	600	Potion	70
Rose Corsage	800	Break	900	Antidote	50
Amber Armlet	6600	Reflect	800	Eye Drops	50
Sash	500	Blind	200	Phoenix Down	250
Argyle Armlet	600	Protect	200	Echo Herbs	50
Raise	1900	Poison	500	Gold Needle	100
Cura	1500	Shell	300	Alarm Clock	50
Vox	300	Sleep	700	Handkerchief	50
Stona	800	Oil	600	Hi-Potion	210
Water	800	Silence	400		

MERCHANT: TETRA
LOCATION: THE DREADNOUGHT LEVIATHAN

WARES	COST	WARES	COST	WARES	COST	WARES	COST
Broadsword	400	Headguard	300	Calot Hat	700	Vox	300
Dagger	200	Leather Breastplate	300	Shepherd's Bolero	700	Stona	800
Shortbow	500	Pointy Hat	300	Steel Gorget	1500	Water	800
Altair	500	Silken Shirt	300	Armguard	800	Immobilize	600
Longsword	700	Bronze Helm	700	Tourmaline Ring	300	Disable	600
Mage Masher	700	Bronze Armor	700	Gauntlets	1200	Break	900
Silver Bow	1000	Leather Shield	600	Battle Harness	1000	Reflect	800
Iron Sword	1200	Leather Headgear	500	Leather Gorget	1500	Blind	200
Oak Staff	400	Bronze Chestplate	500	Potion	70	Protect	200
Javelin	1400	Topkapi Hat	500	Antidote	50	Poison	500
Assassin's Dagger	1400	Kilimweave Shirt	500	Eye Drops	50	Shell	300
Capella	1400	Sallet	1000	Phoenix Down	250	Silence	400
Oaken Pole	1300	Scale Armor	1000	Echo Herbs	50	Dark	500
Aevis Killer	1500	Buckler	1000	Gold Needle	100		
Zwill Blade	1700	Horned Hat	700	Alarm Clock	50		
Cherry Staff	800	Ringmail	700	Handkerchief	50		

MERCHANT: QUAYSIDE MAGICKERY
LOCATION: BALFONHEIM PORT, GALLERINA MARKETPLACE

WARES	COST	WARES	COST	WARES	COST	WARES	COST
Curaga	11700	Holy	11200	Shock	9400	Sleepga	7900
Dispelga	8200	Firaga	8200	Scourge	11200	Shellga	9900
Arise	9700	Thundaga	8200	Flare	11200	Protectga	9400
Esunaga	14900	Blizzaga	8200	Slowga	10400	Darkga	9400

MERCHANT: THE LEAPIN' BANGAA
LOCATION: BALFONHEIM PORT, GALLERINA MARKETPLACE

WARES	COST	WARES	COST
Cameo Belt	9000	Alarm Clock	50
Power Armlet	5200	Handkerchief	50
Opal Ring	16000	Hi-Potion	210
Potion	70	Bacchus's Wine	120
Antidote	50	Smelling Salts	50
Eye Drops	50	Remedy	400
Phoenix Down	250	Chronos Tear	50
Echo Herbs	50	X-Potion	630
Gold Needle	100	Vaccine	200

MERCHANT: BERUNY
LOCATION: BALFONHEIM PORT, BERUNY'S ARMAMENTS

WARES	COST	WARES	COST
Diamond Sword	12500	Holy Lance	14500
Yoichi Bow	12500	Caliper	14000
Trident	12500	Deathbringer	16000
Yakei	12500	Greataxe	15500
Zephyr Pole	11200	Ame-no-Murakumo	15000
Hunting Crossbow	12500	Save the Queen	15500
Empyrean Rod	6200	Zwill Crossblade	15000
Defender	13000	Antares	16000
Spica	13000	Ivory Pole	13500
Morning Star	13500	Penetrator Crossbow	15500
Doom Mace	11800	Caldera	16000
Runeblade	14500	Cloud Staff	8000
Perseus Bow	14500		

MERCHANT: EMMA
LOCATION: BALFONHEIM PORT, BERUNY'S ARMAMENTS

WARES	COST	WARES	COST	WARES	COST
Chakra Band	8100	Gaia Gear	9300	Chaperon	12400
Power Vest	8100	Giant's Helmet	11000	Minerva Buster	12400
Hypnocrown	8100	Carabineer Mail	11000	Black Mask	12400
Jade Gown	8100	Gigas Hat	10700	White Robes	13500
Platinum Helm	9300	Gigas Chestplate	10700	Aegis Shield	9600
Platinum Armor	9300	Celebrant's Miter	10700	Crown of Laurels	14500
Crystal Shield	7200	Cleric's Robes	10700	Rubber Suit	14500
Thief's Cap	9300	Dragon Helm	12500	White Mask	14500
Ninja Gear	9300	Dragon Mail	12500	Black Robes	13500
Gold Hairpin	9300	Kaiser Shield	8300		

MERCHANT: ODO
LOCATION: BALFONHEIM PORT, ODO'S TECHNICKS

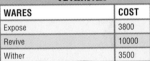

WARES	COST
Expose	3800
Revive	10000
Wither	3500

MERCHANT: VENDOR OF GOODS
LOCATION: PHON COAST, HUNTERS' CAMP

WARES	COST	WARES	COST	WARES	COST	WARES	COST
Burning Bow	7500	Aldebaran	10000	Mirror Mail	8100	Handkerchief	50
Ubelisk	7500	Gokuu Pole	9000	Dragon Shield	6000	Hi-Potion	210
Sledgehammer	7500	Kagenui	10000	Thief's Cuffs	3000	Bacchus's Wine	120
Six-fluted Pole	6800	Adamant Hat	5900	Gillie Boots	700	Smelling Salts	50
Thorned Mace	6500	Adamant Vest	5900	Quasimodo Boots	800	Remedy	400
Multiscale	8000	Astrakhan Hat	5900	Ruby Ring	8500	Chronos Tear	50
Murasame	8500	Carmagnole	5900	Firefly	5000	Vanish	4900
Orichalcum Dirk	8500	Diamond Helm	7000	Steel Poleyns	1000	Bio	4900
Fumarole	8500	Diamond Armor	7000	Potion	70	Dispel	4500
Platinum Sword	9000	Platinum Shield	5300	Antidote	50	Death	5200
Power Rod	4500	Officer's Hat	7000	Eye Drops	50	Vanishga	8700
Hammerhead	9500	Barrel Coat	7000	Phoenix Down	250	Darkra	5800
Recurve Crossbow	9500	Gaia Hat	7000	Echo Herbs	50	Cleanse	5800
Traitor's Bow	10000	Maduin Gear	7000	Gold Needle	100	Reverse	7600
Halberd	10000	Steel Mask	8100	Alarm Clock	50		

MERCHANT: BURROGH
LOCATION: BARHEIM PASSAGE, THE LIGHTWORKS

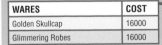

WARES	COST	WARES	COST
Golden Skullcap	16000	Hermes Sandals	20000
Glimmering Robes	16000	Ardor	15600

MERCHANT: BAKNAMY MERCHANT
LOCATION: NECROHOL OF NABUDIS, HALL OF EFFULGENT LIGHT

WARES	COST	WARES	COST
Magepower Shishak	15000	Ether	222
Maximillian	17000	Telekinesis	7100
Demon Shield	11200	Scathe	18100
Ring of Renewal	18000		

Bestiary

Foes are numerous in the world of Ivalice. To keep tabs on them, all of them are contained within this Bestiary. A Bestiary is included with the Clan Primer in the game, but this one is a bit more thorough. The following section indicates how to read the information.

Enemy Name ‹2›

The foe's moniker.

‹3› Genus/Classification

Genus indicates the animal family to which the monster belongs, while Classification determines the type. Enemies must be of the same Classification to create battle chains. Some monsters (particularly Elite Marks and Bosses) defy classification.

‹4› Elemental

The elemental wheel affects different monsters in different ways. Enemies can be weak to a particular element, taking extra damage. Some foes may have no notable weakness or strength toward a particular element, thus taking normal damage. Enemies can have a half-resist versus a particular elemental, always negating half the damage. Elements can also have no effect, in practice a 100% resist, or total immunity. Finally, an enemy may absorb certain elements, with potential damage converted into healing. Certain monsters can shift their elemental properties, making their strengths and weaknesses impossible to pin down.

AB = Causes negative effect by healing monster
NE = Immune to effect
W = Attacks inflict more damage
½ = Attacks inflict half damage

Enemy Number ‹1›

All foes in are assigned a number. This matches the number in the Bestiary within the game's Clan Primer.

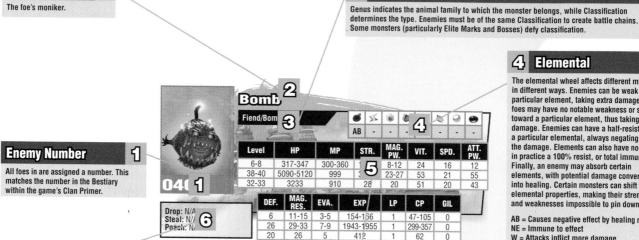

Bomb

Fiend/Bom

AB	-	-	-			-	-

Level	HP	MP	STR.	MAG. PW.	VIT.	SPD.	ATT. PW.
6-8	317-347	300-360	1	8-12	24	16	12
38-40	5090-5120	999	3	23-27	53	21	55
32-33	3233	910	28	20	51	20	43

DEF.	MAG. RES.	EVA.	EXP	LP	CP	GIL
6	11-15	3-5	154-166	1	47-105	0
26	29-33	7-9	1943-1955	1	299-357	0
20	26	5	412	1	62	0

040

Drop: N/A
Steal: N/A ‹6›
Poach: N/A

‹6› Loot

Monsters sometimes drop loot when they are defeated. You can also steal from them before their demise, or poach them when their HP is critical. Monsters become more likely to drop loot during battle chains, and you can enhance the effect of steal by equipping the Thief's Cuffs accessory. Stealing from some monsters (in particular, Rare Game) can be very difficult, sometimes taking literally dozens of tries to get a successful steal. The rewards are often worth the effort, though!

‹5› Statistics

This represents a breakdown of a foe's traits. Level represents the enemy's level range within a certain region. Note that depending on your progression within the storyline or your location within a region, this can vary and affect all other stats. Think of multiple entries in the statistics section as monster version [a], monster version [b], and so on. The same is true for the loot section.

The Dalmasca Sands

Cactite

Plant/Cactus

-	-	-	-	-	-	W	-

Level	HP	MP	STR.	MAG. PW.	VIT.	SPD.	ATT. PW.
4-8	100-136	385-394	9	9	24-27	14	12-15
26-27	1759-1771	999	28	21	43-44	20	41-42
4-6	224-248	112-118	13	7	15-17	12	13-15

DEF.	MAG. RES.	EVA.	EXP	LP	CP	GIL
5-8	11	0	31-40	1	33-60	0
17-18	25	7	2809-2812	1	180-189	0
5-7	7	0	31-37	1	30-48	0

001-A

Drop: Cactus Fruit, Earth Stone, [b] Earth Magicite, Potion, [b] Hi-Potion, Virgo Gem
Steal: Earth Stone, [b] Earth Magicite, Cactus Fruit, Broadsword, [b] Bundle of Needles
Poach Item: Cactus Fruit, Bundle of Needles

Cactoid

Plant/Cactus

-	-	-	-	-	-	W	-

Level	HP	MP	STR.	MAG. PW.	VIT.	SPD.	ATT. PW.
1-4	72-84	50-53	8	5	12-13	9	7-8
2-3	145-157	80-83	11	6	14-15	11	11-12

DEF.	MAG. RES.	EVA.	EXP	LP	CP	GIL
3-4	8	0	7-10	1	13-22	0
4-5	7	0	13-16	1	25-34	0

001-B

Drop: Cactus Fruit, Earth Stone, Potion, Virgo Gem
Steal: Earth Stone, Cactus Fruit, Broadsword
Poach: Cactus Fruit, Bundle of Needles

Ichthon

Ichthian/Pirahna

-	-	-	-	-	-	W	-

Level	HP	MP	STR.	MAG. PW.	VIT.	SPD.	ATT. PW.
9-10	387-398	210-214	12-13	7	24-25	15-17	13-14
26-20	2765-2787	840-848	30-32	18	41-43	20-24	41-43
18-21	1293-1326	490-502	21-24	16	32-35	19-25	25-28
3-4	130-141	140-144	9-10	5	21-22	12-14	11-12

DEF.	MAG. RES.	EVA.	EXP	LP	CP	GIL
5	7	3-4	184-188	1	50-59	0
18	22	5-7	1481-1489	1	198-216	0
13	13	4-7	777-789	1	116-143	0
4	6	0-1	17-21	1	33-42	0

002

Drop: Fish Scale, Water Stone, [b] Water Magicite, [a][d] Light Woven Shirt, [b] Diamond Shield, [c] Traveler's Vestment, Potion, [b] Hi-Potion
Steal: Fish Scale, Eye Drops, Phoenix Down
Poach: Fish Scale, Potion, [b] Hi-Potion

Wolf

Beast/Wolf

-	-	-	-	W	-	-	-

Level	HP	MP	STR.	MAG. PW.	VIT.	SPD.	ATT. PW.
2-7	94-134	30-40	8-10	2	12	10	8-10
3-4, 8-9	135-155	60-65	11-12	5	15	10	11-12

DEF.	MAG. RES.	EVA.	EXP	LP	CP	GIL
4	7	0	9-13	1	15-47	0
5	7	0	16-18	1	26-42	0

003-A

Drop: Wolf Pelt, Wind Stone, Potion, Antidote
Steal: Wind Stone, Wolf Pelt, Pointy Hat
Poach: Wolf Pelt, Eye Drops

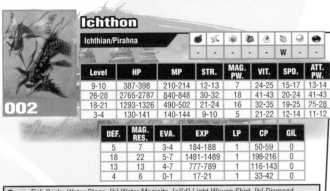

Alpha Wolf

Beast/Wolf

-	-	-	-	W	-	-	-

Level	HP	MP	STR.	MAG. PW.	VIT.	SPD.	ATT. PW.
5-10	113-153	33-43	11-13	5	24	12	11-13
8-9, 12-14	535-575	66-76	16-18	13	31	16	17-19

DEF.	MAG. RES.	EVA.	EXP	LP	CP	GIL
6	8	0	22-26	1	33-65	0
9	9	0	252-256	1	66-98	0

003-B

Drop: Wolf Pelt, Wind Stone, Potion, Antidote
Steal: Wind Stone, Wolf Pelt, [a] Pointy Hat, [b] Wizard's Hat
Poach: Wolf Pelt, Eye Drops

Wild Saurian

Dragon/Tyrant

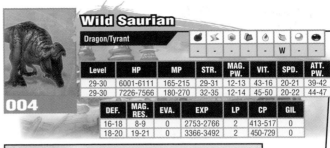

-	-	-	-	-	-	W	-

Level	HP	MP	STR.	MAG. PW.	VIT.	SPD.	ATT. PW.
29-30	6001-6111	165-215	29-31	12-13	43-16	20-21	39-42
29-30	7226-7566	180-270	32-35	12-14	45-50	20-22	44-47

DEF.	MAG. RES.	EVA.	EXP	LP	CP	GIL
16-18	8-9	0	2753-2766	2	413-517	0
18-20	19-21	0	3366-3492	2	450-729	0

004

Drop: Tanned Hide, Earth Crystal, Chronos Tear, Bone Helm, Bone Mail
Steal: Tanned Hide, Hi-Potion, Leo Gem
Poach: Tanned Hide, Tyrant Bone

Cockatrice

Avion/Cockatrice

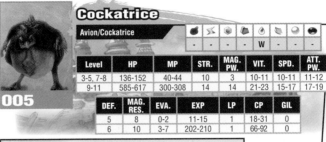

-	-	-	-	-	W	-	-

Level	HP	MP	STR.	MAG. PW.	VIT.	SPD.	ATT. PW.
3-5, 7-8	136-152	40-44	10	3	10-11	10-11	11-12
9-11	585-617	300-308	14	14	21-23	15-17	17-19

DEF.	MAG. RES.	EVA.	EXP	LP	CP	GIL
5	8	0-2	11-15	1	18-31	0
6	10	3-7	202-210	1	66-92	0

005

Drop: Small Feather, Fire Stone, Potion, Phoenix Down
Steal: Small Feather, Potion, Phoenix Down
Poach: Small Feather, Chromed Leathers

Gnoma Entite

Gnoma Entite/Elemental

NE	NE	NE	AB	NE	W	NE	NE

Level	HP	MP	STR.	MAG. PW.	VIT.	SPD.	ATT. PW.
45	48042	999	30	33	38	25	66

DEF.	MAG. RES.	EVA.	EXP	LP	CP	GIL
48	52	2	12627	7	1320	0

006

Drop: Earth Crystal, Feystone, Gnoma Halcyon, Ether
Steal: Earth Crystal, Feystone, Gnoma Halcyon

Dive Talon

Avion/Diver

-	-	-	-	-	-	-	-

Level	HP	MP	STR.	MAG. PW.	VIT.	SPD.	ATT. PW.
27-28	4022-4090	480-489	32-33	16	45-46	17-19	42-44

DEF.	MAG. RES.	EVA.	EXP	LP	CP	GIL
17-18	22	5-7	1952-2044	2	261-311	0

007

Drop: Wind Magicite, Handkerchief, Giant Feather, Burning Bow
Steal: Giant Feather, Large Feather, 120 gil, Taurus Gem
Poach: Giant Feather, Large Feather, Bundle of Feathers

Giza Plains

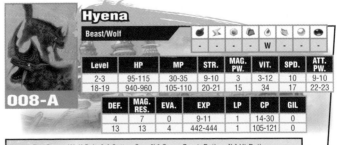

Hyena

Beast/Wolf

-	-	-	-	W	-	-	-

Level	HP	MP	STR.	MAG. PW.	VIT.	SPD.	ATT. PW.
2-3	95-115	30-35	9-10	3	3-12	10	9-10
18-19	940-960	105-110	20-21	15	34	17	22-23

008-A

DEF.	MAG. RES.	EVA.	EXP	LP	CP	GIL
4	7	0	9-11	1	14-30	0
13	13	4	442-444	1	105-121	0

Drop: Fire Stone, Wolf Pelt, [a] Cotton Cap, [b] Green Beret, Potion, [b] Hi-Potion
Steal: Fire Stone, Wolf Pelt, Potion, [b] Festering Flesh
Poach: Pebble, [b] Wolf Pelt, [b] Festering Flesh

Alpha Hyena

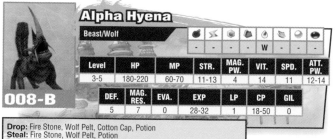

Beast/Wolf — 008-B

Level	HP	MP	STR	MAG. PW.	VIT.	SPD.	ATT. PW.
3-5	180-220	60-70	11-13	4	14	11	12-14

DEF.	MAG. RES.	EVA.	EXP	LP	CP	GIL
5	7	0	28-32	1	18-50	0

Drop: Fire Stone, Wolf Pelt, Cotton Cap, Potion
Steal: Fire Stone, Wolf Pelt, Potion
Poach: Pebble, Wolf Pelt

Wooly Gator

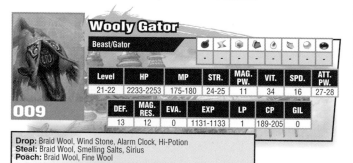

Beast/Gator — 009

Level	HP	MP	STR	MAG. PW.	VIT.	SPD.	ATT. PW.
21-22	2233-2253	175-180	24-25	11	34	16	27-28

DEF.	MAG. RES.	EVA.	EXP	LP	CP	GIL
13	12	0	1131-1133	1	189-205	0

Drop: Braid Wool, Wind Stone, Alarm Clock, Hi-Potion
Steal: Braid Wool, Smelling Salts, Sirius
Poach: Braid Wool, Fine Wool

Happy Bunny

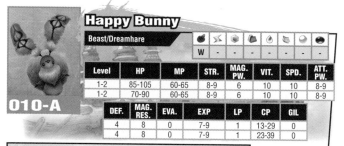

Beast/Dreamhare — 010-A

Level	HP	MP	STR	MAG. PW.	VIT.	SPD.	ATT. PW.
1-2	85-105	60-65	8-9	6	10	10	8-9
1-2	70-90	60-65	8-9	6	10	10	8-9

DEF.	MAG. RES.	EVA.	EXP	LP	CP	GIL
4	8	0	7-9	1	13-29	0
4	8	0	7-9	1	23-39	0

Drop: Drab Wool, Water Stone, Potion, Phoenix Down
Steal: Water Stone, Drab Wool, Antidote
Poach: Drab Wool, Headgear

Ozmone Hare

Beast/Dreamhare — 010-B

Level	HP	MP	STR	MAG. PW.	VIT.	SPD.	ATT. PW.
19-20	823-843	875-880	18-19	18	24	19	22-23

DEF.	MAG. RES.	EVA.	EXP	LP	CP	GIL
13	16	5	339-341	1	84-100	0

Drop: Braid Wool, Water Magicite, Teleport Stone, Aero Mote
Steal: Water Magicite, 150 gil, Golden Helm
Poach: Braid Wool, Balance Mote

Great Tortoise

Beast/Titantoise — 011

Level	HP	MP	STR	MAG. PW.	VIT.	SPD.	ATT. PW.
20-21	3818-3838	999	23-24	17	36	12	25-26

DEF.	MAG. RES.	EVA.	EXP	LP	CP	GIL
17	16	0	1201-1203	2	179-195	0

Drop: Turtle Shell, Water Stone, Phoenix Down, Water Magicite
Steal: Water Stone, Aries Gem, Soldier's Cap
Poach: Turtle Shell, Smelling Salts

Sleipnir

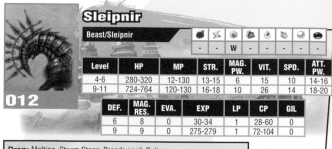

Beast/Sleipnir — 012

Level	HP	MP	STR	MAG. PW.	VIT.	SPD.	ATT. PW.
4-6	280-320	12-130	13-15	6	15	10	14-16
9-11	724-764	120-130	16-18	10	26	14	18-20

DEF.	MAG. RES.	EVA.	EXP	LP	CP	GIL
6	8	0	30-34	1	28-60	0
9	9	0	275-279	1	72-104	0

Drop: Molting, Storm Stone, Broadsword, Potion
Steal: Molting, Storm Stone, 30 gil
Poach: Storm Stone, Molting, Iron Carapace

Silicon Tortoise

Beast/Titantoise — 013

Level	HP	MP	STR	MAG. PW.	VIT.	SPD.	ATT. PW.
36-37	12852-13172	999	32-35	22	50-51	14-16	51-53
37-38	13923-14243	999	33-36	22	57-58	15-17	53-55

DEF.	MAG. RES.	EVA.	EXP	LP	CP	GIL
25-26	26-28	0	3165-3339	2	383-610	0
26-27	27-29	0	3436-3610	2	434-661	0

Drop: Aged Turtle Shell, Water Crystal, Teleport Stone, [a] Aries Gem, [b] Officer's Hat
Steal: 100 gil, [a] Aged Turtle Shell, [b] Aries Gem, [a] Officer's Hat
Poach: Aged Turtle Shell, Ancient Turtle Shell

Wildsnake

Beast/Serpent — 014

Level	HP	MP	STR	MAG. PW.	VIT.	SPD.	ATT. PW.
3-5	210-250	40-50	11-13	3	10	11	12-14

DEF.	MAG. RES.	EVA.	EXP	LP	CP	GIL
5	7	0	16-20	1	27-59	0

Drop: Snake Skin, Wind Stone, Teleport Stone
Steal: Snake Skin, Wind Stone, Leather Breastplate
Poach: Snake Skin, Tanned Hide

Werewolf

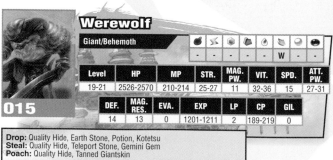

Giant/Behemoth — 015

Level	HP	MP	STR	MAG. PW.	VIT.	SPD.	ATT. PW.
19-21	2526-2570	210-214	25-27	11	32-36	15	27-31

DEF.	MAG. RES.	EVA.	EXP	LP	CP	GIL
14	13	0	1201-1211	2	189-219	0

Drop: Quality Hide, Earth Stone, Potion, Kotetsu
Steal: Quality Hide, Teleport Stone, Gemini Gem
Poach: Quality Hide, Tanned Giantskin

Urstrix

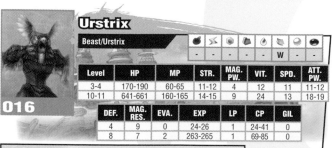

Beast/Urstrix — 016

Level	HP	MP	STR	MAG. PW.	VIT.	SPD.	ATT. PW.
3-4	170-190	60-65	11-12	4	12	11	11-12
10-11	641-661	160-165	14-15	9	24	13	18-19

DEF.	MAG. RES.	EVA.	EXP	LP	CP	GIL
4	9	0	24-26	1	24-41	0
8	7	2	263-265	1	69-85	0

Drop: Large Feather, Earth Stone, Potion, Headguard
Steal: Earth Stone, Large Feather, Echo Herbs
Poach: Large Feather

Storm Elemental

Storm Elemental/Elemental							
NE	AB	W	NE	NE	NE	NE	NE

Level	HP	MP	STR.	MAG. PW.	VIT.	SPD.	ATT. PW.
25	14830	999	25	28	34	20	45

DEF.	MAG. RES.	EVA.	EXP	LP	CP	GIL
42	44	3	5583	4	675	0

Drop: Storm Magicite, Storm Stone, Feystone, Storm Crystal
Steal: Storm Magicite, Feystone, Storm Crystal

017

Slaven

Giant/Slaven							
-	-	-	-	-	-	W	-

Level	HP	MP	STR.	MAG. PW.	VIT.	SPD.	ATT. PW.
4-5	280-302	80-82	13-14	5	14-16	9	13-15
10-11	780-802	80-82	15-16	7	29-31	11	18-20

DEF.	MAG. RES.	EVA.	EXP	LP	CP	GIL
5	8	0	26-31	1	26-41	0
6	5	0	263-268	1	69-84	0

Drop: Earth Stone, Tanned Hide, [a] Shortbow, [b] Aevis Killer, Eye Drops
Steal: Earth Stone, Tanned Hide, 50 gil
Poach: Tanned Hide

018

Mardu Entite

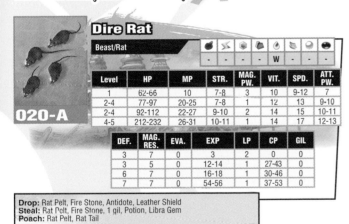

Mardu Entite/Elemental							
NE	AB	W	NE	NE	NE	NE	NE

Level	HP	MP	STR.	MAG. PW.	VIT.	SPD.	ATT. PW.
45	48042	999	30	33	38	25	66

DEF.	MAG. RES.	EVA.	EXP	LP	CP	GIL
48	52	2	12627	7	1320	0

Drop: Storm Crystal, Feystone, Mardu Halcyon, Ether
Steal: Storm Crystal, Feystone, Mardu Halcyon

019

The Garamsythe Waterway

Dire Rat

Beast/Rat							
-	-	-	-	W	-	-	-

Level	HP	MP	STR.	MAG. PW.	VIT.	SPD.	ATT. PW.
1	62-66	10	7-8	3	10	9-12	7
2-4	77-97	20-25	7-8	1	12	13	9-10
2-4	92-112	22-27	10	2	14	15	10-11
4-5	212-232	26-31	10-11	9	14	17	12-13

DEF.	MAG. RES.	EVA.	EXP	LP	CP	GIL
3	7	0	3	2	0	0
3	5	0	12-14	1	27-43	0
6	7	0	16-18	1	30-46	0
7	7	0	54-56	1	37-53	0

Drop: Rat Pelt, Fire Stone, Antidote, Leather Shield
Steal: Rat Pelt, Fire Stone, 1 gil, Potion, Libra Gem
Poach: Rat Pelt, Rat Tail

020-A

Dire Rat

Beast/Rat							
-	-	-	-	W	-	-	-

Level	HP	MP	STR.	MAG. PW.	VIT.	SPD.	ATT. PW.
36-37	3627-3647	180-185	29-30	15	38	24	52-53

DEF.	MAG. RES.	EVA.	EXP	LP	CP	GIL
22	23	8	1023-1025	1	243-259	0

Drop: Rat Pelt, Fire Magicite, Antidote, Rat Tail
Steal: Rat Pelt, 1 gil, Libra Gem
Poach: Rat Pelt, Rat Tail

020-B

Baritine Croc

Beast/Gator							
-	-	-	-	W	-	-	-

Level	HP	MP	STR.	MAG. PW.	VIT.	SPD.	ATT. PW.
40-42	10745-10965	475-505	34-38	17	55-57	18-20	60-62
26-28	4448-4668	250-280	29-33	12	40-42	16-18	36-38

DEF.	MAG. RES.	EVA.	EXP	LP	CP	GIL
25	24	0	3366-3552	1	513-675	0
15	14	0	1562-1748	1	270-432	0

Drop: [a] Blood Wool, [b] Fine Wool, Wind Magicite, [a] X-Potion, [b] Hi-Potion, [a] Wind Crystal, [b] Glacial Staff
Steal: Wind Magicite, Remedy, Blue Fang
Poach: [a] Blood Wool, [b] Fine Wool, Broken Sword

021

Gigantoad

Beast/Toad							
W	-	-	-	-	-	-	-

Level	HP	MP	STR.	MAG. PW.	VIT.	SPD.	ATT. PW.
19-20	1469-1489	455-460	22-23	16	32	15	25-26
5-6	341-361	156-161	12-13	6	21	10	14-15

DEF.	MAG. RES.	EVA.	EXP	LP	CP	GIL
15	15	2	848-850	1	126-142	0
6	8	0	131-133	1	46-62	0

Drop: Water Stone, Horn, Potion, Eye Drops
Steal: Horn, 50 gil, [a] Lambent Hat, [b] Leather Helm
Poach: Horn

022

Malboro Overking

Plant/Malboro							
-	-	-	-	-	-	W	-

Level	HP	MP	STR.	MAG. PW.	VIT.	SPD.	ATT. PW.
38-39	6503-6743	999	30-32	21-24	50-55	20-21	58-61
36-38	4775-5255	999	30-34	20-26	43-53	18-20	52-58

DEF.	MAG. RES.	EVA.	EXP	LP	CP	GIL
24-27	28-30	0	2903-3087	1	314-509	0
20-26	26-30	0	2568-2936	1	248-638	0

Drop: Malboro Fruit, [a] Dark Crystal, [b] Dark Magicite, Vanishga Mote, Virgo Gem
Steal: Dark Magicite, [a] Malboro Flower, [b] Malboro Fruit, [a] Virgo Gem, [b] Adamant Hat
Poach: Malboro Fruit, Putrid Liquid

023

Garchimacera

Fiend/Gargoyle							
-	-	-	-	W	-	-	-

Level	HP	MP	STR.	MAG. PW.	VIT.	SPD.	ATT. PW.
4-6	287-317	180-240	10-12	6-10	17	12	12
37-40	5938-5983	999	31-34	22-28	48	21	57

DEF.	MAG. RES.	EVA.	EXP	LP	CP	GIL
6	8-12	0-2	125-137	1	44-102	0
27	27-33	7-10	2419-2437	1	328-415	0

Drop: Demon Eyeball, [a] Fire Stone, [b] Fire Magicite, [a] Bronze Armor, [b] Fire Crystal, [a] Phoenix Down, [b] Demon Feather
Steal: Demon Eyeball, 10 gil, [a] Dark Mote, [b] Demon Feather
Poach: Demon Eyeball, Demon Tail

024

Gespenst

Undead/Reaper							
-	-	-	-	-	-	W	AB

Level	HP	MP	STR.	MAG. PW.	VIT.	SPD.	ATT. PW.
41-42	7917-8097	999	33-35	24-26	46	19	58-61

DEF.	MAG. RES.	EVA.	EXP	LP	CP	GIL
24-26	25-26	4	2734-2894	1	371-514	0

Drop: Dark Crystal, Book of Orgain, Teleport Stone, Capricorn Gem
Steal: Dark Crystal, Reflectga Mote, Ninja Gear

025

Ghost

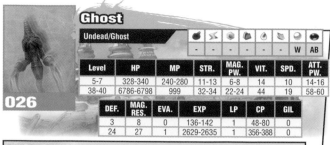

026 · Undead/Ghost

Level	HP	MP	STR.	MAG. PW.	VIT.	SPD.	ATT. PW.
5-7	328-340	240-280	11-13	6-8	14	10	14-16
38-40	6786-6798	999	32-34	22-24	44	19	58-60

DEF.	MAG. RES.	EVA.	EXP	LP	CP	GIL
3	8	0	136-142	1	48-80	0
24	27	1	2629-2635	1	356-388	0

Drop: Glass Jewel, [a] Dark Stone, [b] Dark Magicite, Teleport Stone, [a] Potion, [b] Sky Jewel
Steal: Glass Jewel, Echo Herbs, [a] Silken Shirt, [b] Dark Magicite
Poach: [a] Glass Jewel, [b] Dark Crystal, [a] Phoenix Down, [b] Sky Jewel

Water Elemental

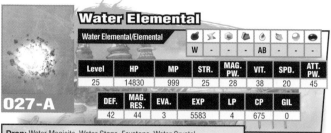

027-A · Water Elemental/Elemental

Level	HP	MP	STR.	MAG. PW.	VIT.	SPD.	ATT. PW.
25	14830	999	25	28	38	20	45

DEF.	MAG. RES.	EVA.	EXP	LP	CP	GIL
42	44	3	5583	4	675	0

Drop: Water Magicite, Water Stone, Feystone, Water Crystal
Steal: Water Magicite, Feystone, Water Crystal

Water Chaosjet

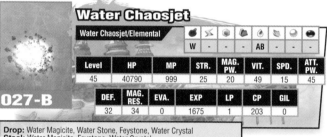

027-B · Water Chaosjet/Elemental

Level	HP	MP	STR.	MAG. PW.	VIT.	SPD.	ATT. PW.
45	40790	999	25	20	49	15	45

DEF.	MAG. RES.	EVA.	EXP	LP	CP	GIL
32	34	0	1675	1	203	0

Drop: Water Magicite, Water Stone, Feystone, Water Crystal
Steal: Water Magicite, Feystone, Water Crystal

The Barheim Passage

Steeling

028 · Avion/Steeling

Level	HP	MP	STR.	MAG. PW.	VIT.	SPD.	ATT. PW.
2-3	94-110	50-54	8	2	17-18	13-14	11-12
4-5	218-234	60-64	9	3	17-18	15-16	13-14
6-7	282-298	75-79	11	4	21-22	16-17	13-14
7-8	446-462	100-104	13	10	23-24	17-18	17-18

DEF.	MAG. RES.	EVA.	EXP	LP	CP	GIL
4	7	0-2	18-22	1	32-45	0
4	7	0-2	57-61	1	40-53	0
5	8	3-5	88-92	1	47-60	0
7	8	3-5	120-124	1	63-76	0

Drop: Wind Stone, [c] Eye Drops, Antidote, Bat Fang, Potion, [c] Phoenix Down
Steal: Bat Fang, [c] Wind Stone, Teleport Stone, Armguard
Poach: Bat Fang

Suriander

029 · Beast/Toad

Level	HP	MP	STR.	MAG. PW.	VIT.	SPD.	ATT. PW.
8-9	410-430	195-200	13-14	7	24	11	13-14
38-39	7069-7089	999	32-33	22	53	19	57-58

DEF.	MAG. RES.	EVA.	EXP	LP	CP	GIL
7	9	2	200-202	1	54-70	0
27	27	4	2525-2527	1	342-358	0

Drop: [a] Storm Stone, [b] Storm Magicite, [a] Horn, [b] Pointed Horn, Teleport Stone, [a] Horned Hat, [b] Indigo Pendant
Steal: [a] Storm Stone, [b] Storm Magicite, [a] Horn, [b] Antidote, Pointed Horn
Poach: [a] Horn, [b] Pointed Horn, Solid Horn

Mimic

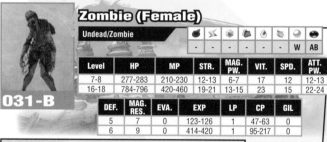

030 · Insect/Mimic

Level	HP	MP	STR.	MAG. PW.	VIT.	SPD.	ATT. PW.
7-8	334-340	105-108	15-16	3	21	14	18-19

DEF.	MAG. RES.	EVA.	EXP	LP	CP	GIL
10-11	5	0	135-138	1	41-46	0

Drop: Earth Stone, Eye Drops, Iron Scraps, Dark Mote
Steal: Iron Scraps, 20 gil, Iron Sword
Poach: Iron Scraps

Zombie (Male)

031-A · Undead/Zombie

Level	HP	MP	STR.	MAG. PW.	VIT.	SPD.	ATT. PW.
7-8	280-286	210-230	12-13	6-7	17	12	13-14
16-18	869-881	390-430	20-22	13-15	23	15	23-25
27-28	2254-2260	847-867	29-30	18-19	34	19	38-39

DEF.	MAG. RES.	EVA.	EXP	LP	CP	GIL
3	7	0	123-126	1	47-63	0
7	9	0	414-420	1	95-217	0
20	23	0	0-3	0	0-16	0

Drop: Dark Stone, Foul Flesh, Antidote, [c] Dark Magicite, Buckler, [c] Festering Flesh
Steal: Foul Flesh, [c] Dark Magicite, 2 gil, 50 gil
Poach: [a][b] Foul Flesh, [a][b] Festering Flesh

Zombie (Female)

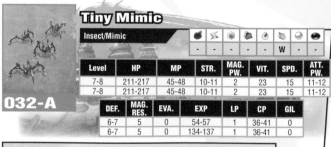

031-B · Undead/Zombie

Level	HP	MP	STR.	MAG. PW.	VIT.	SPD.	ATT. PW.
7-8	277-283	210-230	12-13	6-7	17	12	12-13
16-18	784-796	420-460	19-21	13-15	23	15	22-24

DEF.	MAG. RES.	EVA.	EXP	LP	CP	GIL
5	7	0	123-126	1	47-63	0
6	9	0	414-420	1	95-217	0

Drop: Dark Stone, Foul Flesh, Antidote, Potion
Steal: Dark Stone, Alarm Clock, Kilimweave Shirt
Poach: Foul Flesh, Festering Flesh

Tiny Mimic

032-A · Insect/Mimic

Level	HP	MP	STR.	MAG. PW.	VIT.	SPD.	ATT. PW.
7-8	211-217	45-48	10-11	2	23	15	11-12
7-8	211-217	45-48	10-11	2	23	15	11-12

DEF.	MAG. RES.	EVA.	EXP	LP	CP	GIL
6-7	5	0	54-57	1	36-41	0
6-7	5	0	134-137	1	36-41	0

Drop: [a] Eye Drops, [b] Iron Scraps, Earth Stone, Leather Headgear, Potion
Steal: Earth Stone, 1 gil, Antidote
Poach: Iron Scraps

Tiny Mimic

032-B · Insect/Mimic

Level	HP	MP	STR.	MAG. PW.	VIT.	SPD.	ATT. PW.
7-8	211-217	45-48	10-11	2	23	15	11-12

DEF.	MAG. RES.	EVA.	EXP	LP	CP	GIL
6-7	5	0	54-57	1	36-41	0

Drop: Iron Scraps, Earth Stone, Leather Headgear, Potion
Steal: Earth Stone, 1 gil, Antidote
Poach: Iron Scraps

Skeleton

033

Undead/Skeleton

-	-	-	-	-	-	-	W	AB

Level	HP	MP	STR.	MAG. PW.	VIT.	SPD.	ATT. PW.
7-8	312-318	165-185	13-14	5-6	19	14	12-13
8-9	557-563	220-240	15-16	11-12	21	15	16-17
10-11	798-804	275-295	17-18	12-13	23	16	18-19

DEF.	MAG. RES.	EVA.	EXP	LP	CP	GIL
5	6	3	212-215	1	50-66	0
7	6	3	290-293	1	66-82	0
9	7	3	370-373	1	83-99	0

Drop: Bone Fragment, Dark Stone, Antidote, Iron Helm, [b] Echo Herbs
Steal: Bone Fragment, 20 gil, Dark Mote, [b] Bronze Chestplate
Poach: Bone Fragment, Potion

Battery Mimic

034

Insect/Mimic

-	AB	W	-	-	-	-	-	-

Level	HP	MP	STR.	MAG. PW.	VIT.	SPD.	ATT. PW.
7	520	130	13	8	19	13	14

DEF.	MAG. RES.	EVA.	EXP	LP	CP	GIL
8	7	0	165	2	41	0

Drop: Eye Drops, Iron Scraps, Storm Stone, Mage's Habit
Steal: Iron Scraps, Storm Stone, Alarm Clock

Specter

035

Undead/Ghost

-	-	-	-	-	-	-	W	AB

Level	HP	MP	STR.	MAG. PW.	VIT.	SPD.	ATT. PW.
8-9	402-408	300-320	13-14	7-8	17	11	14-15
36-39	6786-6804	999	32-35	22-25	44	19	58-61

DEF.	MAG. RES.	EVA.	EXP	LP	CP	GIL
4	9	1	209-212	1	56-72	0
24	27	1	2629-2638	1	356-404	0

Drop: [a] Glass Jewel, [b] Dark Stone, [a] Dark Stone, [b] Dark Magicite, [a] Oaken Pole, [b] Sky Jewel, Alarm Clock
Steal: [a] Dark Stone, [b] Dark Magicite, Glass Jewel, [a] Dark Mote, [b] Sky Jewel
Poach: [a] Glass Jewel, [b] Sky Jewel

Tiny Battery

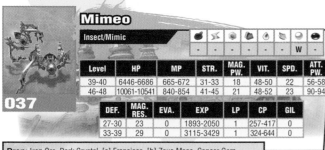

036

Insect/Mimic

-	AB	W	-	-	-	-	-	-

Level	HP	MP	STR.	MAG. PW.	VIT.	SPD.	ATT. PW.
6-7	120	75	11	7	24	20	12

DEF.	MAG. RES.	EVA.	EXP	LP	CP	GIL
5	7	0	76	1	19	0

Steal: Pebble, Knot of Rust, Potion
Poach: Pebble, Knot of Rust

Mimeo

037

Insect/Mimic

-	-	-	-	-	-	-	W	-

Level	HP	MP	STR.	MAG. PW.	VIT.	SPD.	ATT. PW.
39-40	6446-6686	665-672	31-33	18	48-50	22	56-58
46-48	10061-10541	840-854	41-45	21	48-52	23	90-94

DEF.	MAG. RES.	EVA.	EXP	LP	CP	GIL
27-30	23	0	1893-2050	1	257-417	0
33-39	29	0	3115-3429	1	324-644	0

Drop: Iron Ore, Dark Crystal, [a] Fransisca, [b] Zeus Mace, Cancer Gem
Steal: Iron Ore, 500 gil, Cancer Gem
Poach: Iron Ore, Hastega Mote

Flan

038

Amorph/Flan

W	-	-	-	-	-	-	-	-

Level	HP	MP	STR.	MAG. PW.	VIT.	SPD.	ATT. PW.
5	420	100	10	7	20	11	11
6-7	280-294	270-290	14-15	8	21-22	10	12-13

DEF.	MAG. RES.	EVA.	EXP	LP	CP	GIL
10	6	0	0	2	190	0
12-14	2-3	0	200-207	1	54-76	0

Drop: [b] Green Liquid, [b] Water Stone, [b] Water Mote
Steal: [a] Potion, [b] Green Liquid, [a] Caramel, [b] Water Stone, [a] Sagittarius Gem, [b] Gold Needle
Poach: [b] Green Liquid, [b] Caramel

Skull Defender

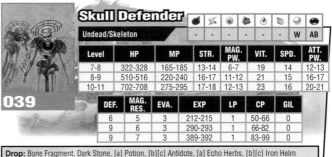

039

Undead/Skeleton

-	-	-	-	-	-	-	W	AB

Level	HP	MP	STR.	MAG. PW.	VIT.	SPD.	ATT. PW.
7-8	322-328	165-185	13-14	6-7	19	14	12-13
8-9	510-516	220-240	16-17	11-12	21	15	16-17
10-11	702-708	275-295	17-18	12-13	23	16	20-21

DEF.	MAG. RES.	EVA.	EXP	LP	CP	GIL
6	5	3	212-215	1	50-66	0
9	6	3	290-293	1	66-82	0
9	7	3	389-392	1	83-99	0

Drop: Bone Fragment, Dark Stone, [a] Potion, [b][c] Antidote, [a] Echo Herbs, [b][c] Iron Helm
Steal: Bone Fragment, [a] Water Mote, [b][c] 20 gil, [a] Bronze Chestplate, [b][c] Dark Mote
Poach: [a] Bone Fragment, [b][c] Potion

Bomb

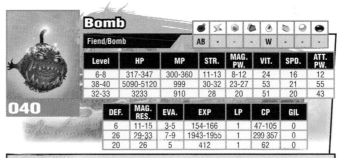

040

Fiend/Bomb

AB	-	-	-	W	-	-	-	-

Level	HP	MP	STR.	MAG. PW.	VIT.	SPD.	ATT. PW.
6-8	317-347	300-360	11-13	8-12	24	16	12
38-40	5090-5120	999	30-32	23-27	53	21	55
32-33	3233	910	28	20	51	20	43

DEF.	MAG. RES.	EVA.	EXP	LP	CP	GIL
6	11-15	3-5	154-166	1	47-105	0
26	29-33	7-9	1943-1955	1	299-357	0
20	26	5	412	1	62	0

Drop: [a] Bomb Ashes, Fire Stone, [b] Fire Magicite, [a] Echo Herbs, [a] Leather Gorget, [b] Bomb Shell
Steal: Fire Stone, [b] Fire Magicite, Bomb Ashes, [a] Gold Needle, [b] Bacchus's Wine, [c] Bomb Fragment
Poach: Bomb Ashes, [c] Pebble, Bomb Shell, [c] Potion

Dead Bones

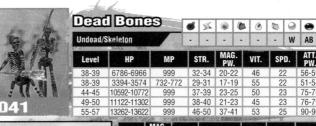

041

Undead/Skeleton

-	-	-	-	-	-	-	W	AB

Level	HP	MP	STR.	MAG. PW.	VIT.	SPD.	ATT. PW.
38-39	6786-6966	999	32-34	20-22	46	22	56-59
38-39	3394-3574	732-772	29-31	17-19	55	22	51-54
44-45	10592-10772	999	37-39	23-25	50	23	75-78
49-50	11122-11302	999	38-40	21-23	45	23	76-79
55-57	13262-13622	999	46-50	37-41	53	25	90-96

DEF.	MAG. RES.	EVA.	EXP	LP	CP	GIL
25-27	24-25	7	2661-2821	1	314-457	0
25-27	24-25	7	799-959	1	94-237	0
28-30	30-31	8	4636-4796	1	396-539	0
26-28	29-30	8	4233-4393	1	396-539	0
30-34	32-34	11	5503-5823	1	437-723	0

Drop: Dark Crystal, Eye Drops, Blood-darkened Bone, [a][b][c] Ancient Bone, [d][e] Golden Skullcap
Steal: Dark Crystal, Blood-darkened Bone, [c] Sturdy Bone, [a][b] Gigas Hat, [c] Golden Skullcap, [d][e] Ancient Bone

The Lhusu Mines

Vampyr

042

Undead/Steeling

-	-	-	-	-	-	-	W	-

Level	HP	MP	STR.	MAG. PW.	VIT.	SPD.	ATT. PW.
41-44	5675-5915	500-528	31-35	19	50-54	24-31	61-65

DEF.	MAG. RES.	EVA.	EXP	LP	CP	GIL
25-29	31-33	8-14	1286-1628	1	315-489	0

Drop: Spiral Incisor, Dark Crystal, Antidote, Zwill Crossblade
Steal: Dark Crystal, Spiral Incisor, Taurus Gem

Headless

043 — Giant/Headless

Level	HP	MP	STR.	MAG. PW.	VIT.	SPD.	ATT. PW.
39-41	8867-9707	500-510	34-38	17-21	48-52	20	63-69

DEF.	MAG. RES.	EVA.	EXP	LP	CP	GIL
27-31	29	0	2939-3265	1	360-912	0

Drop: Earth Crystal, Festering Flesh, Forbidden Flesh, Phoenix Down
Steal: Foul Flesh, Earth Crystal, 500 gil
Poach: Festering Flesh, Forbidden Flesh

Killer Mantis

044 — Insect/Mantis

Level	HP	MP	STR.	MAG. PW.	VIT.	SPD.	ATT. PW.
43-44	11703-11943	500-507	34-36	16	55-57	19	64-66

DEF.	MAG. RES.	EVA.	EXP	LP	CP	GIL
28-31	27	0	3063-3220	1	375-535	0

Drop: Insect Husk, Earth Crystal, Echo Herbs, Cancer Gem
Steal: Earth Crystal, X-Potion, Gigas Hat
Poach: Insect Husk, Charger Barding

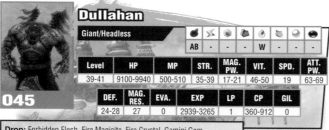

Dullahan

045 — Giant/Headless

Level	HP	MP	STR.	MAG. PW.	VIT.	SPD.	ATT. PW.
39-41	9100-9940	500-510	35-39	17-21	46-50	19	63-69

DEF.	MAG. RES.	EVA.	EXP	LP	CP	GIL
24-28	27	0	2939-3265	1	360-912	0

Drop: Forbidden Flesh, Fire Magicite, Fire Crystal, Gemini Gem
Steal: Fire Magicite, Fire Crystal, 540 gil
Poach: Festering Flesh, Forbidden Flesh

Bug

046 — Insect/Mimic

Level	HP	MP	STR.	MAG. PW.	VIT.	SPD.	ATT. PW.
41-42	6739-6979	700-707	32-34	18	50-52	22	60-62
41-43	6739-7219	700-714	46-50	18	50-54	22	75-79

DEF.	MAG. RES.	EVA.	EXP	LP	CP	GIL
27-30	28	0	1985-2142	1	270-430	0
32-38	28	0	1985-2299	1	270-590	0

Drop: [a] Iron Scraps, [b] Iron Ore, Earth Crystal, [a] Antidote, [b] Teleport Stone, [a] Iron Ore, [b] Perseus Bow
Steal: [a] Earth Magicite, [b] Earth Crystal, [a] 1 gil, [b] Iron Ore, [b] Holy Mote
Poach: [a] Iron Scraps, Iron Ore

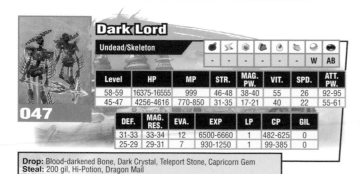

Dark Lord

047 — Undead/Skeleton

Level	HP	MP	STR.	MAG. PW.	VIT.	SPD.	ATT. PW.
58-59	16375-16555	999	46-48	38-40	55	26	92-95
45-47	4256-4616	770-850	31-35	17-21	40	22	55-61

DEF.	MAG. RES.	EVA.	EXP	LP	CP	GIL
31-33	33-34	12	6500-6660	1	482-625	0
25-29	29-31	7	930-1250	1	99-385	0

Drop: Blood-darkened Bone, Dark Crystal, Teleport Stone, Capricorn Gem
Steal: 200 gil, Hi-Potion, Dragon Mail

Pandora

048 — Insect/Mimic

Level	HP	MP	STR.	MAG. PW.	VIT.	SPD.	ATT. PW.
60-62	15557-16037	980-994	60-64	36	57-61	26	120-124
48-49	9366-9606	805-812	42-44	20	53-55	23	91-93

DEF.	MAG. RES.	EVA.	EXP	LP	CP	GIL
35-41	32	0	4161-4475	1	394-714	0
32-35	29	0	2648-2805	1	311-471	0

Drop: Storm Crystal, Hi-Potion, Iron Ore, [a] Cancer Gem, [b] Aegis Shield
Steal: [a] Iron Ore, [b] Storm Stone, [a] Cancer Gem, [b] Iron Ore, [a] Aegis Shield
Poach: Iron Ore, Wrath of the Gods

Gazer

049 — Undead/Reaper

Level	HP	MP	STR.	MAG. PW.	VIT.	SPD.	ATT. PW.
44-45	9931-10111	999	34-36	24-26	48	19	62-65

DEF.	MAG. RES.	EVA.	EXP	LP	CP	GIL
24-26	30-31	4	3185-3345	1	390-533	0

Drop: Dark Crystal, Vaccine, Teleport Stone, Capricorn Gem
Steal: Dark Magicite, Dark Crystal, Book of Orgain-Mille

The Yensan Sandsea

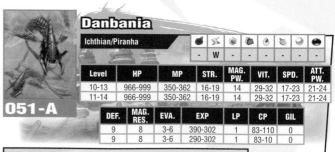

Alraune

050 — Plant/Mandragora

Level	HP	MP	STR.	MAG. PW.	VIT.	SPD.	ATT. PW.
10-11	615-627	875-878	14	17	31-32	17	21-22
11-14	670-694	878-881	14	17	31-33	17	21-23

DEF.	MAG. RES.	EVA.	EXP	LP	CP	GIL
8-9	11	4	285-288	1	75-84	0
8-10	11	4	256-262	1	75-93	0

Drop: Succulent Fruit, Earth Stone, Potion, Alarm Clock
Steal: Succulent Fruit, Handkerchief, Mace
Poach: Succulent Fruit

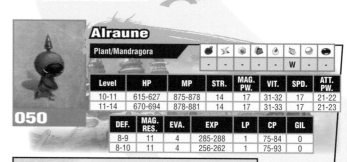

Danbania

051-A — Ichthian/Piranha

Level	HP	MP	STR.	MAG. PW.	VIT.	SPD.	ATT. PW.
10-13	966-999	350-362	16-19	14	29-32	17-23	21-24
11-14	966-999	350-362	16-19	14	29-32	17-23	21-24

DEF.	MAG. RES.	EVA.	EXP	LP	CP	GIL
9	8	3-6	390-302	1	83-110	0
9	8	3-6	290-302	1	83-10	0

Drop: Fish Scale, Water Stone, Echo Herbs, Water Mote
Steal: Water Stone, Fish Scale, Bacchus's Wine
Poach: Fish Scale, Argyle Armlet

Bull Danbania

051-B — Ichthian/Piranha

Level	HP	MP	STR.	MAG. PW.	VIT.	SPD.	ATT. PW.
12-15	1159-1192	385-397	18-21	15	31-34	19-25	22-25

DEF.	MAG. RES.	EVA.	EXP	LP	CP	GIL
11	10	3-6	327-339	1	91-118	0

Drop: Fish Scale, Water Stone, Echo Herbs, Water Mote
Steal: Water Stone, Fish Scale, Bacchus's Wine
Poach: Fish Scale, Argyle Armlet

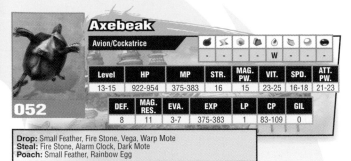

Axebeak

Avion/Cockatrice

Level	HP	MP	STR.	MAG. PW.	VIT.	SPD.	ATT. PW.
13-15	922-954	375-383	16	15	23-25	16-18	21-23

DEF.	MAG. RES.	EVA.	EXP	LP	CP	GIL
8	11	3-7	375-383	1	83-109	0

052

Drop: Small Feather, Fire Stone, Vega, Warp Mote
Steal: Fire Stone, Alarm Clock, Dark Mote
Poach: Small Feather, Rainbow Egg

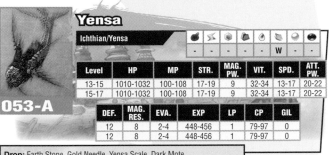

Yensa

Ichthian/Yensa

Level	HP	MP	STR.	MAG. PW.	VIT.	SPD.	ATT. PW.
13-15	1010-1032	100-108	17-19	9	32-34	13-17	20-22
15-17	1010-1032	100-108	17-19	9	32-34	13-17	20-22

DEF.	MAG. RES.	EVA.	EXP	LP	CP	GIL
12	8	2-4	448-456	1	79-97	0
12	8	2-4	448-456	1	79-97	0

053-A

Drop: Earth Stone, Gold Needle, Yensa Scale, Dark Mote
Steal: Yensa Scale, Pisces Gem, Barbut
Poach: Yensa Scale, Yensa Fin

Bull Yensa

Ichthian/Yensa

Level	HP	MP	STR.	MAG. PW.	VIT.	SPD.	ATT. PW.
16-18	1212-1234	110-118	19-21	10	34-36	15-19	21-23

DEF.	MAG. RES.	EVA.	EXP	LP	CP	GIL
14	10	2-4	492-500	1	8/-105	0

053-B

Drop: Earth Stone, Gold Needle, Yensa Scale, Dark Mote
Steal: Yensa Scale, Pisces Gem, Barbut
Poach: Yensa Scale, Yensa Fin

Wyvern

Dragon/Wyvern

Level	HP	MP	STR.	MAG. PW.	VIT.	SPD.	ATT. PW.
14-16	1493-1713	400-500	17-21	15-17	32-38	15-17	22-28
16-18	1493-1713	400-500	17-21	15-17	32-38	15-17	22-28

DEF.	MAG. RES.	EVA.	EXP	LP	CP	GIL
7-11	7-9	0	683-709	2	120-328	0
7-11	7-9	0	683-709	2	120-328	0

054-A

Drop: Fire Stone, Crooked Fang, Linen Cuirass, Hi-Potion
Steal: Fire Stone, Teleport Stone, 300 gil
Poach: Crooked Fang, Bacchus's Wine

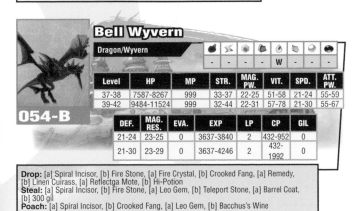

Bell Wyvern

Dragon/Wyvern

Level	HP	MP	STR.	MAG. PW.	VIT.	SPD.	ATT. PW.
37-38	7587-8267	999	33-37	22-25	51-58	21-24	55-59
39-42	9484-11524	999	32-44	22-31	57-78	21-30	55-67

DEF.	MAG. RES.	EVA.	EXP	LP	CP	GIL
21-24	23-25	0	3637-3840	2	432-952	0
21-30	23-29	0	3637-4246	2	432-1992	0

054-B

Drop: [a] Spiral Incisor, [b] Fire Stone, [a] Fire Crystal, [b] Crooked Fang, [a] Remedy, [b] Linen Cuirass, [b] Reflectga Mote, [b] Hi-Potion
Steal: [a] Spiral Incisor, [b] Fire Stone, [a] Leo Gem, [b] Teleport Stone, [a] Barrel Coat, [b] 300 gil
Poach: [a] Spiral Incisor, [b] Crooked Fang, [a] Leo Gem, [b] Bacchus's Wine

Salamand Entite

Salamand Entite/Elemental

AB	NE	NE	NE	W	NE	NE	NE

Level	HP	MP	STR.	MAG. PW.	VIT.	SPD.	ATT. PW.
45	48042	999	30	33	38	25	66

DEF.	MAG. RES.	EVA.	EXP	LP	CP	GIL
48	52	2	12627	7	1320	0

055

Drop: Fire Crystal, Feystone, Salamand Halcyon, Ether
Steal: Fire Crystal, Feystone, Salamand Halcyon

The Tomb of Raithwall

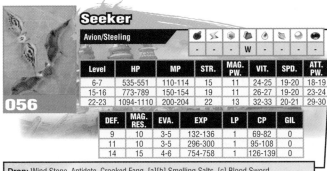

Seeker

Avion/Steeling

Level	HP	MP	STR.	MAG. PW.	VIT.	SPD.	ATT. PW.
6-7	535-551	110-114	15	11	24-25	19-20	18-19
15-16	773-789	150-154	19	11	26-27	19-20	23-24
22-23	1094-1110	200-204	22	13	32-33	20-21	29-30

DEF.	MAG. RES.	EVA.	EXP	LP	CP	GIL
9	10	3-5	132-136	1	69-82	0
11	10	3-5	296-300	1	95-108	0
14	15	4-6	754-758	1	126-139	0

056

Drop: Wind Stone, Antidote, Crooked Fang, [a][b] Smelling Salts, [c] Blood Sword
Steal: Wind Stone, [a] Iron Sword, [b] Taurus Gem, [c] Smelling Salts, [b] Blood Sword
Poach: Smelling Salts, Bat Wing

Lost Soul

Undead/Skeleton

-	-	-	-	-	-	W	AB

Level	HP	MP	STR.	MAG. PW.	VIT.	SPD.	ATT. PW.
17-18	966-972	330-350	21-22	12-13	24	17	22-23

DEF.	MAG. RES.	EVA.	EXP	LP	CP	GIL
11	8	3	713-716	1	99-115	0

057

Drop: Bone Fragment, Dark Stone, Antidote, Teleport Stone
Steal: Dark Stone, 60 gil, Blazer Gloves
Poach: Bone Fragment

Lesser Chimera

Fiend/Cockatrice

Level	HP	MP	STR.	MAG. PW.	VIT.	SPD.	ATT. PW.
15-18	1014-1062	450-462	20	15	24-27	17-20	23-26

DEF.	MAG. RES.	EVA.	EXP	LP	CP	GIL
10	12	3-9	496-508	1	99-138	0

058

Drop: Fire Stone, Handkerchief, Small Feather, Hi-Potion
Steal: Fire Stone, Gold Needle, Taurus Gem
Poach: Small Feather, Main Gauche

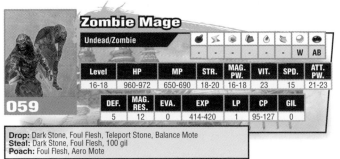

Zombie Mage

Undead/Zombie

-	-	-	-	-	-	W	AB

Level	HP	MP	STR.	MAG. PW.	VIT.	SPD.	ATT. PW.
16-18	960-972	650-690	18-20	16-18	23	15	21-23

DEF.	MAG. RES.	EVA.	EXP	LP	CP	GIL
5	12	0	414-420	1	95-127	0

059

Drop: Dark Stone, Foul Flesh, Teleport Stone, Balance Mote
Steal: Dark Stone, Foul Flesh, 100 gil
Poach: Foul Flesh, Aero Mote

Skull Warrior
Undead/Skeleton

-	-	-	-	-	-	-	W	AB

Level	HP	MP	STR.	MAG. PW.	VIT.	SPD.	ATT. PW.
17-18	876-882	330-350	22-23	12-13	23	18	23-24

DEF.	MAG. RES.	EVA.	EXP	LP	CP	GIL
11	8	4	713-716	1	99-115	0

060

Drop: Bone Fragment, Dark Stone, Alarm Clock, Golden Shield
Steal: Dark Stone, Bone Fragment, 200 gil
Poach: Bone Fragment, Broken Spear

Lich
Undead/Ghost

-	-	-	-	-	-	-	W	AB

Level	HP	MP	STR.	MAG. PW.	VIT.	SPD.	ATT. PW.
18-19	1158-1164	600-620	21-22	14-15	23	14	24-25

DEF.	MAG. RES.	EVA.	EXP	LP	CP	GIL
10	11	1	704-707	1	113-129	0

061

Drop: Dark Stone, Glass Jewel, Aero Mote, Phoenix Down
Steal: Dark Stone, Glass Jewel, Smelling Salts
Poach: Glass Jewel, Chainmail

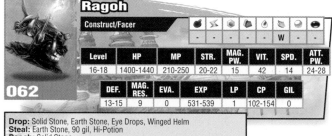

Ragoh
Construct/Facer

-	-	-	-	-	-	W	-

Level	HP	MP	STR.	MAG. PW.	VIT.	SPD.	ATT. PW.
16-18	1400-1440	210-250	20-22	15	42	14	24-28

DEF.	MAG. RES.	EVA.	EXP	LP	CP	GIL
13-15	9	0	531-539	1	102-154	0

062

Drop: Solid Stone, Earth Stone, Eye Drops, Winged Helm
Steal: Earth Stone, 90 gil, Hi-Potion
Poach: Solid Stone

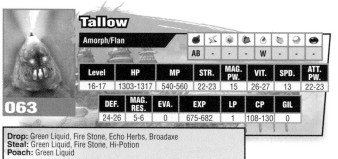

Tallow
Amorph/Flan

AB	-	-	-	W	-	-	-

Level	HP	MP	STR.	MAG. PW.	VIT.	SPD.	ATT. PW.
16-17	1303-1317	540-560	22-23	15	26-27	13	22-23

DEF.	MAG. RES.	EVA.	EXP	LP	CP	GIL
24-26	5-6	0	675-682	1	108-130	0

063

Drop: Green Liquid, Fire Stone, Echo Herbs, Broadaxe
Steal: Green Liquid, Fire Stone, Hi-Potion
Poach: Green Liquid

Ozmone Plain

Mesmenir
Beast/Sleipnir

-	W	-	-	-	-	-	-

Level	HP	MP	STR.	MAG. PW.	VIT.	SPD.	ATT. PW.
20-22	1528-1568	210-220	23-25	13	32	17	25-27

DEF.	MAG. RES.	EVA.	EXP	LP	CP	GIL
15	15	0	848-852	1	126-158	0

064

Drop: Charger Barding, Storm Magicite, Bronze Mace, Echo Herbs
Steal: Charger Barding, Storm Magicite, Aries Gem
Poach: Charger Barding, Destrier Mane

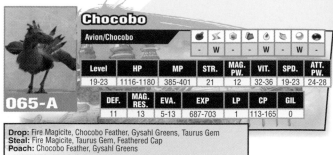

Chocobo
Avion/Chocobo

-	W	-	-	W	-	W	-

Level	HP	MP	STR.	MAG. PW.	VIT.	SPD.	ATT. PW.
19-23	1116-1180	385-401	21	12	32-36	19-23	24-28

DEF.	MAG. RES.	EVA.	EXP	LP	CP	GIL
11	13	5-13	687-703	1	113-165	0

065-A

Drop: Fire Magicite, Chocobo Feather, Gysahl Greens, Taurus Gem
Steal: Fire Magicite, Taurus Gem, Feathered Cap
Poach: Chocobo Feather, Gysahl Greens

Black Chocobo
Avion/Chocobo

-	W	-	-	W	-	W	-

Level	HP	MP	STR.	MAG. PW.	VIT.	SPD.	ATT. PW.
19-23	1116-1180	385-401	21	12	32-36	19-23	24-28

DEF.	MAG. RES.	EVA.	EXP	LP	CP	GIL
11	13	5-13	687-703	1	113-165	0

065-B

Drop: Dark Magicite, Chocobo Feather, Gysahl Greens
Steal: Dark Magicite, Chocobo Feather
Poach: Chocobo Feather, Gysahl Greens

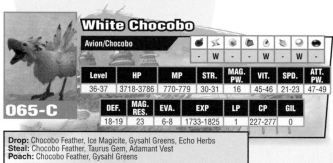

White Chocobo
Avion/Chocobo

-	W	-	-	W	-	W	-

Level	HP	MP	STR.	MAG. PW.	VIT.	SPD.	ATT. PW.
36-37	3718-3786	770-779	30-31	16	45-46	21-23	47-49

DEF.	MAG. RES.	EVA.	EXP	LP	CP	GIL
18-19	23	6-8	1733-1825	1	227-277	0

065-C

Drop: Chocobo Feather, Ice Magicite, Gysahl Greens, Echo Herbs
Steal: Chocobo Feather, Taurus Gem, Adamant Vest
Poach: Chocobo Feather, Gysahl Greens

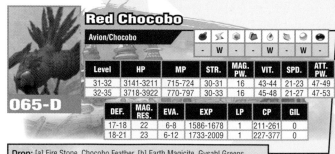

Red Chocobo
Avion/Chocobo

-	W	-	-	W	-	W	-

Level	HP	MP	STR.	MAG. PW.	VIT.	SPD.	ATT. PW.
31-32	3141-3211	715-724	30-31	16	43-44	21-23	47-49
32-35	3718-3922	770-797	30-33	16	45-48	21-27	47-53

DEF.	MAG. RES.	EVA.	EXP	LP	CP	GIL
17-18	22	6-8	1586-1678	1	211-261	0
18-21	23	6-12	1733-2009	1	227-377	0

065-D

Drop: [a] Fire Stone, Chocobo Feather, [b] Earth Magicite, Gysahl Greens, [a] Taurus Gem, [b] Antidote
Steal: [a] Fire Stone, [b] Chocobo Feather, [a] Taurus Gem, [a] Feathered Cap, [b] Fuzzy Miter
Poach: Chocobo Feather, Gysahl Greens

Brown Chocobo
Avion/Chocobo

-	W	-	-	W	-	W	-

Level	HP	MP	STR.	MAG. PW.	VIT.	SPD.	ATT. PW.
32-35	3718-3922	770-797	30-33	16	45-48	21-27	47-53

DEF.	MAG. RES.	EVA.	EXP	LP	CP	GIL
18-21	23	6-12	1733-2009	1	227-377	0

065-E

Drop: Chocobo Feather, Wind Magicite, Gysahl Greens
Steal: Wind Magicite, Smelling Salts, Taurus Gem
Poach: Chocobo Feather, Gysahl Greens

065-F — Lv99 Red Chocobo
Avion/Chocobo

Elemental: - / W / - / - / W / - / W / -

Level	HP	MP	STR.	MAG. PW.	VIT.	SPD.	ATT. PW.
99	239686	999	50	41	71	30	104

DEF.	MAG. RES.	EVA.	EXP	LP	CP	GIL
33	39	19	11949	50	3325	0

Drop: Ribbon
Steal: Elixir, Megalixir, Empyreal Soul
Poach: Pebble

066 — Wu
Beast/Urstrix

Elemental: - / - / - / - / - / W / - / -

Level	HP	MP	STR.	MAG. PW.	VIT.	SPD.	ATT. PW.
20-22	1689-1729	280-290	21-23	12	31	16	25-27

DEF.	MAG. RES.	EVA.	EXP	LP	CP	GIL
14	13	2	813-817	1	121-153	0

Drop: Large Feather, Earth Magicite, Eye Drops, Kogarasumaru
Steal: 40 gil, Large Feather, Aries Gem
Poach: Large Feather, Mage's Hat

067 — Zu
Avion/Diver

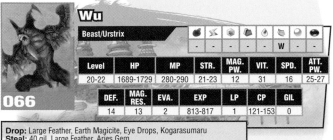

Elemental: - / - / - / W / - / - / - / -

Level	HP	MP	STR.	MAG. PW.	VIT.	SPD.	ATT. PW.
21-22	1880-1896	280-284	23	14	36-37	16-17	25-26

DEF.	MAG. RES.	EVA.	EXP	LP	CP	GIL
12	13	4-6	1025-1029	1	152-165	0

Drop: Large Feather, Wind Magicite, Rod, Remedy
Steal: Wind Magicite, Large Feather, Aero Mote
Poach: Large Feather, Giant Feather

068 — Viper
Beast/Serpent

Elemental: - / - / - / - / - / - / W / -

Level	HP	MP	STR.	MAG. PW.	VIT.	SPD.	ATT. PW.
20-21	1410-1430	140-145	22-23	12	32	18	24-25

DEF.	MAG. RES.	EVA.	EXP	LP	CP	GIL
14	13	4	919-921	1	137-153	0

Drop: Tanned Hide, Dark Magicite, Quality Hide, Serpent Rod
Steal: Dark Magicite, Alarm Clock, Aries Gem
Poach: Tanned Hide, Hi-Potion

069 — Zaghnal
Giant/Behemoth

Elemental: - / - / - / - / - / W / - / -

Level	HP	MP	STR.	MAG. PW.	VIT.	SPD.	ATT. PW.
23-24	3157-3179	210-212	25-26	11	32-34	15	26-28

DEF.	MAG. RES.	EVA.	EXP	LP	CP	GIL
14	13	0	1201-1206	2	189-204	0

Drop: Earth Magicite, Quality Hide, Warp Mote, Hi-Potion
Steal: Earth Magicite, Gemini Gem, Heavy Coat
Poach: Quality Hide, Tanned Giantskin

070 — Hybrid Gator
Beast/Gator

Elemental: - / - / - / - / - / W / - / -

Level	HP	MP	STR.	MAG. PW.	VIT.	SPD.	ATT. PW.
21-23	2233-2273	175-185	24-26	11	34	17	27-29

DEF.	MAG. RES.	EVA.	EXP	LP	CP	GIL
13	12	0	1131-1135	1	189-221	0

Drop: Fire Magicite, Gold Needle, Braid Wool, Fine Wool
Steal: Bacchus's Wine, Aries Gem, Iron Hammer
Poach: Braid Wool, Fine Wool

071 — Sylphi Entite
Sylphi Entite/Elemental

Elemental: NE / NE / NE / W / NE / AB / NE / NE

Level	HP	MP	STR.	MAG. PW.	VIT.	SPD.	ATT. PW.
45	48042	999	30	33	38	25	66

DEF.	MAG. RES.	EVA.	EXP	LP	CP	GIL
48	52	2	12627	7	1320	0

Drop: Wind Crystal, Feystone, Sylphi Halcyon, Ether
Steal: Wind Crystal, Feystone, Sylphi Halcyon

Golmore Jungle

072 — Panther
Beast/Coeurl

Elemental: - / - / W / - / - / - / - / -

Level	HP	MP	STR.	MAG. PW.	VIT.	SPD.	ATT. PW.
21-23	1299-1519	999	22-26	17	36-38	18-20	28-30

DEF.	MAG. RES.	EVA.	EXP	LP	CP	GIL
14	18	4	900-1086	1	132-294	0

Drop: Coeurl Pelt, Storm Magicite, Warp Mote, Quality Pelt
Steal: Coeurl Pelt, Storm Magicite, Libra Gem
Poach: Coeurl Pelt, Quality Pelt

073 — Treant
Plant/Golem

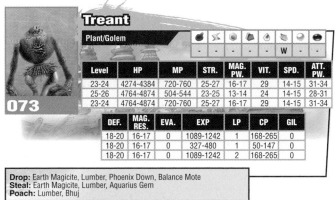

Elemental: - / - / - / - / - / - / W / -

Level	HP	MP	STR.	MAG. PW.	VIT.	SPD.	ATT. PW.
23-24	4274-4384	720-760	25-27	16-17	29	14-15	31-34
25-26	4764-4874	504-544	23-25	13-14	24	14-15	28-31
23-24	4764-4874	720-760	25-27	16-17	29	14-15	31-34

DEF.	MAG. RES.	EVA.	EXP	LP	CP	GIL
18-20	16-17	0	1089-1242	1	168-265	0
18-20	16-17	0	327-480	1	50-147	0
18-20	16-17	0	1089-1242	2	168-265	0

Drop: Earth Magicite, Lumber, Phoenix Down, Balance Mote
Steal: Earth Magicite, Lumber, Aquarius Gem
Poach: Lumber, Bhuj

074 — Hellhound
Beast/Wolf

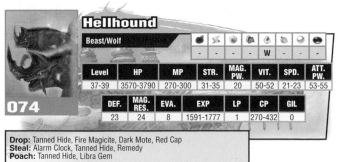

Elemental: - / - / - / - / - / W / - / -

Level	HP	MP	STR.	MAG. PW.	VIT.	SPD.	ATT. PW.
37-39	3570-3790	270-300	31-35	20	50-52	21-23	53-55

DEF.	MAG. RES.	EVA.	EXP	LP	CP	GIL
23	24	8	1591-1777	1	270-432	0

Drop: Tanned Hide, Fire Magicite, Dark Mote, Red Cap
Steal: Alarm Clock, Tanned Hide, Remedy
Poach: Tanned Hide, Libra Gem

Diresaur

075 — Dragon/Tyrant

Level	HP	MP	STR.	MAG. PW.	VIT.	SPD.	ATT. PW.
27-28	5281-5621	165-255	29-32	12-14	43-48	20-22	41-44
27-28	6601-6941	165-255	29-32	12-14	43-48	20-22	41-44

DEF.	MAG. RES.	EVA.	EXP	LP	CP	GIL
16-18	12-14	0	2891-3017	2	413-692	0
16-18	12-14	0	2891-3017	2	413-692	0

Drop: Tyrant Hide, Earth Magicite, Hi-Potion, Float Mote
Steal: Tyrant Hide, Earth Magicite, Leo Gem
Poach: Tyrant Hide, Brigandine

Malboro

076 — Plant/Malboro

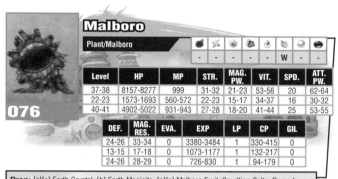

Level	HP	MP	STR.	MAG. PW.	VIT.	SPD.	ATT. PW.
37-38	8157-8277	999	31-32	21-23	53-56	20	62-64
22-23	1573-1693	560-572	22-23	15-17	34-37	16	30-32
40-41	4902-5022	931-943	27-28	18-20	41-44	25	53-55

DEF.	MAG. RES.	EVA.	EXP	LP	CP	GIL
24-26	33-34	0	3380-3484	1	330-415	0
13-15	17-18	0	1073-1177	1	132-217	0
24-26	28-29	0	726-830	1	94-179	0

Drop: [a][c] Earth Crystal, [b] Earth Magicite, [a][c] Malboro Fruit, Smelling Salts, Remedy, [b] Malboro Vine
Steal: Earth Magicite, [a][c] Vaccine, [b] Malboro Vine, [a][c] Earth Crystal, [b] Elfin Bow
Poach: [a][c]Malboro Fruit, [b] Pebble, [a][c] Malboro Flower, [b] Malboro Vine

Gargoyle

077 — Fiend/Gargoyle

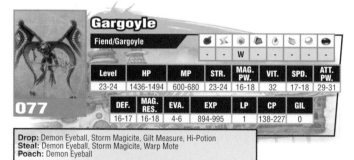

Level	HP	MP	STR.	MAG. PW.	VIT.	SPD.	ATT. PW.
23-24	1436-1494	600-680	23-24	16-18	32	17-18	29-31

DEF.	MAG. RES.	EVA.	EXP	LP	CP	GIL
16-17	16-18	4-6	894-995	1	138-227	0

Drop: Demon Eyeball, Storm Magicite, Gilt Measure, Hi-Potion
Steal: Demon Eyeball, Storm Magicite, Warp Mote
Poach: Demon Eyeball

Great Malboro

078 — Plant/Malboro

Level	HP	MP	STR.	MAG. PW.	VIT.	SPD.	ATT. PW.
22-23	1630-1750	630-642	24-25	16-18	34-37	16	33-35

DEF.	MAG. RES.	EVA.	EXP	LP	CP	GIL
14-16	17-18	0	1141-1245	1	149-234	0

Drop: Malboro Vine, Earth Magicite, Bacchus's Wine, Musk Stick
Steal: Earth Magicite, Malboro Vine, Virgo Gem
Poach: Malboro Vine, Foul Liquid

The Henne Mines

Thunderbug

079 — Insect/Mimic

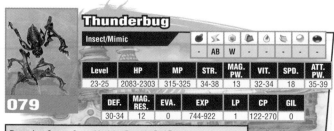

Level	HP	MP	STR.	MAG. PW.	VIT.	SPD.	ATT. PW.
23-25	2083-2303	315-325	34-38	13	32-34	18	35-39

DEF.	MAG. RES.	EVA.	EXP	LP	CP	GIL
30-34	12	0	744-922	1	122-270	0

Drop: Iron Scraps, Storm Magicite, Remedy, Red Fang
Steal: Storm Magicite, Iron Scraps, Cancer Gem
Poach: Iron Scraps, Charged Gizzard

Jelly

080 — Amorph/Flan

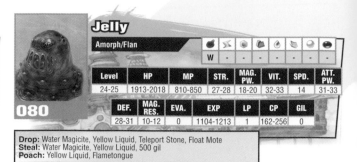

Level	HP	MP	STR.	MAG. PW.	VIT.	SPD.	ATT. PW.
24-25	1913-2018	810-850	27-28	18-20	32-33	14	31-33

DEF.	MAG. RES.	EVA.	EXP	LP	CP	GIL
28-31	10-12	0	1104-1213	1	162-256	0

Drop: Water Magicite, Yellow Liquid, Teleport Stone, Float Mote
Steal: Water Magicite, Yellow Liquid, 500 gil
Poach: Yellow Liquid, Flametongue

Tyranorox

081 — Dragon/Tyrant

Level	HP	MP	STR.	MAG. PW.	VIT.	SPD.	ATT. PW.
26-27	4073-4413	135-225	30-33	11-13	40-45	19-21	35-38

DEF.	MAG. RES.	EVA.	EXP	LP	CP	GIL
15-17	11-13	0	1775-1901	2	338-617	0

Drop: Earth Magicite, Alarm Clock, Tyrant Hide, War Hammer
Steal: Earth Magicite, 60 gil, Leo Gem
Poach: Tyrant Hide, Tanned Tyrant Hid

Hecteyes

082 — Amorph/Flan

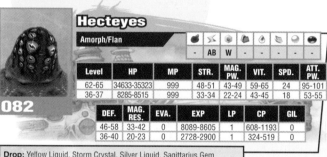

Level	HP	MP	STR.	MAG. PW.	VIT.	SPD.	ATT. PW.
62-65	34633-35323	999	48-51	43-49	59-65	24	95-101
36-37	8285-8515	999	33-34	22-24	43-45	18	53-55

DEF.	MAG. RES.	EVA.	EXP	LP	CP	GIL
46-58	33-42	0	8089-8605	1	608-1193	0
36-40	20-23	0	2728-2900	1	324-519	0

Drop: Yellow Liquid, Storm Crystal, Silver Liquid, Sagittarius Gem
Steal: Chronos Tear, 200 gil, X-Potion
Poach: Silver Liquid, Unpurified Ether

Gizamaluk

083 — Dragon/Plate Wyrm

Level	HP	MP	STR.	MAG. PW.	VIT.	SPD.	ATT. PW.
61-63	53874-55234	999	51-59	40-46	65-79	25-31	98-106

DEF.	MAG. RES.	EVA.	EXP	LP	CP	GIL
37-43	38-42	0	14158-14564	2	1065-2105	0

Drop: Charger Barding, Storm Crystal, Gold Needle, Leo Gem
Steal: Charger Barding, Bacchus's Wine, X-Potion
Poach: Charger Barding, Holy Lance

Etém

084 — Undead/Reaper

Level	HP	MP	STR.	MAG. PW.	VIT.	SPD.	ATT. PW.
64-65	35916-36096	999	48-50	44-46	57	25	97-100

DEF.	MAG. RES.	EVA.	EXP	LP	CP	GIL
32-34	37-38	6	8763-8923	1	659-802	0

Drop: Dark Crystal, Book of Orgain-Mille, Ivory Pole, X-Potion
Steal: Book of Orgain-Mille, Capricorn Gem, Soul Powder

Nightmare

Fiend/Nightmare

| | | | | | | | | W |

085

Level	HP	MP	STR.	MAG. PW.	VIT.	SPD.	ATT. PW.
24-25	1630-1688	900-980	26-27	17-19	31	16-17	31-33

DEF.	MAG. RES.	EVA.	EXP	LP	CP	GIL
15-16	17-19	2-4	1104-1205	1	162-251	0

Drop: Grimoire Togail, Dark Magicite, Smelling Salts, Remedy
Steal: Dark Magicite, Grimoire Togail, Hi-Potion
Poach: Grimoire Togail, Snowfly

Necrofiend

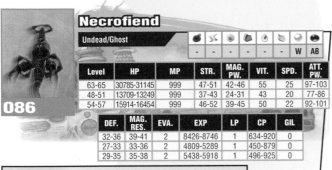

Undead/Ghost

| | | | | | | | W | AB |

086

Level	HP	MP	STR.	MAG. PW.	VIT.	SPD.	ATT. PW.
63-65	30785-31145	999	47-51	42-46	55	25	97-103
48-51	13709-13249	999	37-43	24-31	43	20	77-86
54-57	15914-16454	999	46-52	39-45	50	22	92-101

DEF.	MAG. RES.	EVA.	EXP	LP	CP	GIL
32-36	39-41	2	8426-8746	1	634-920	0
27-33	33-36	2	4809-5289	1	450-879	0
29-35	35-38	2	5438-5918	1	496-925	0

Drop: Sky Jewel, Dark Crystal, Vaccine, Capricorn Gem
Steal: Sky Jewel, Hi-Potion, Lifewick

Paramina Rift

White Wolf

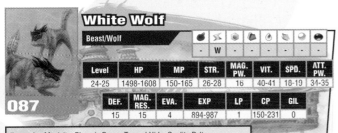

Beast/Wolf

| | W | | | | | | |

087

Level	HP	MP	STR.	MAG. PW.	VIT.	SPD.	ATT. PW.
24-25	1498-1608	150-165	26-28	16	40-41	18-19	34-35

DEF.	MAG. RES.	EVA.	EXP	LP	CP	GIL
15	15	4	894-987	1	150-231	0

Drop: Ice Magicite, Phoenix Down, Tanned Hide, Quality Pelt
Steal: Ice Stone, Quality Pelt, Crossbow
Poach: Tanned Hide, Quality Pelt

Twintania

Dragon/Plate Wyrm

| | W | | | | | | |

088

Level	HP	MP	STR.	MAG. PW.	VIT.	SPD.	ATT. PW.
27-28	4917-5257	500-590	31-34	15-17	40-45	16-18	37-40

DEF.	MAG. RES.	EVA.	EXP	LP	CP	GIL
19-21	16-18	0	2051-2177	2	315-594	0

Drop: Ice Magicite, Antidote, Wyrm Carapace, Smelling Salts
Steal: Ice Stone, Red Fang, Lohengrin
Poach: Wyrm Carapace, Ice Magicite

Lizard

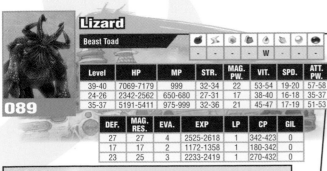

Beast Toad

| | | | | W | | | |

089

Level	HP	MP	STR.	MAG. PW.	VIT.	SPD.	ATT. PW.
39-40	7069-7179	999	32-34	22	53-54	19-20	57-58
24-26	2342-2562	650-680	27-31	17	38-40	16-18	35-37
35-37	5191-5411	975-999	32-36	21	45-47	17-19	51-53

DEF.	MAG. RES.	EVA.	EXP	LP	CP	GIL
27	27	4	2525-2618	1	342-423	0
17	17	2	1172-1358	1	180-342	0
23	25	3	2233-2419	1	270-432	0

Drop: Pointed Horn, [b] Horn, Fire Magicite, [a][c] Fire Crystal, [b][c] Blue Fang
Steal: Fire Magicite, [a][c] Pointed Horn, [b] Float Mote, [a][c] Fire Crystal
Poach: Pointed Horn, Taurus Gem

Emperor Aevis

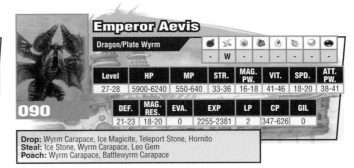

Dragon/Plate Wyrm

| | W | | | | | | |

090

Level	HP	MP	STR.	MAG. PW.	VIT.	SPD.	ATT. PW.
27-28	5900-6240	550-640	33-36	16-18	41-46	18-20	38-41

DEF.	MAG. RES.	EVA.	EXP	LP	CP	GIL
21-23	18-20	0	2255-2381	2	347-626	0

Drop: Wyrm Carapace, Ice Magicite, Teleport Stone, Hornito
Steal: Ice Stone, Wyrm Carapace, Leo Gem
Poach: Wyrm Carapace, Battlewyrm Carapace

Garuda

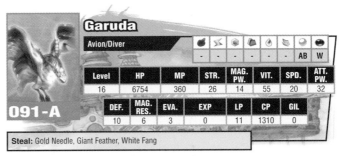

Avion/Diver

| | | | | | | AB | W |

091-A

Level	HP	MP	STR.	MAG. PW.	VIT.	SPD.	ATT. PW.
16	6754	360	26	14	55	20	32

DEF.	MAG. RES.	EVA.	EXP	LP	CP	GIL
10	6	3	0	11	1310	0

Steal: Gold Needle, Giant Feather, White Fang

Garuda-Egi

Avion/Diver

| | | | | | | AB | W |

091-B

Level	HP	MP	STR.	MAG. PW.	VIT.	SPD.	ATT. PW.
26-27	2997-3065	400-409	28-29	15	41-42	17-19	36-38

DEF.	MAG. RES.	EVA.	EXP	LP	CP	GIL
14-15	15	4-6	1416-1508	2	218-268	0

Drop: Large Feather, Holy Magicite, Red Fang, Kogarasumaru
Steal: Holy Stone, Hi-Potion
Poach: Large Feather, White Incense

Dark Skeleton

Undead/Skeleton

| | | | | | | W | AB |

092

Level	HP	MP	STR.	MAG. PW.	VIT.	SPD.	ATT. PW.
37-39	4463-4583	990-999	32-34	19-23	41	22	53-57
35-26	1488-1548	495-525	26-27	15-17	31	18	32-34

DEF.	MAG. RES.	EVA.	EXP	LP	CP	GIL
23-25	28-30	7	2738-2924	1	297-413	0
15-16	13-14	4	1164-1257	1	149-207	0

Drop: [a] Dark Magicite, [b] Dark Stone, Sturdy Bone, Teleport Stone, Burgonet
Steal: Sturdy Bone, [a] Dark Magicite, [b] Dark Stone, Capricorn Gem
Poach: Sturdy Bone, Death's-Head

Slaven Warder

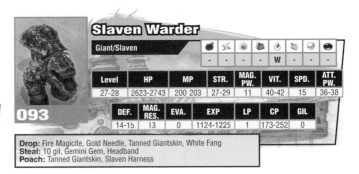

Giant/Slaven

| | | | | | W | | |

093

Level	HP	MP	STR.	MAG. PW.	VIT.	SPD.	ATT. PW.
27-28	2623-2743	200 203	27-29	11	40-42	15	36-38

DEF.	MAG. RES.	EVA.	EXP	LP	CP	GIL
14-15	13	0	1124-1225	1	173-252	0

Drop: Fire Magicite, Gold Needle, Tanned Giantskin, White Fang
Steal: 10 gil, Gemini Gem, Headband
Poach: Tanned Giantskin, Slaven Harness

Skull Knight — 094
Undead/Skeleton

-	-	-	-	-	-	-	W	AB

Level	HP	MP	STR.	MAG. PW.	VIT.	SPD.	ATT. PW.
25-26	1873-1933	550-580	27-28	15-17	32	19	34-36

Drop: Sturdy Bone, Dark Magicite, Hi-Potion, Remedy
Steal: Sturdy Bone, Capricorn Gem, Jujitsu Gi
Poach: Sturdy Bone

Yeti — 095
Giant/Behemoth

-	W	AB	-	-	-	-	-

Level	HP	MP	STR.	MAG. PW.	VIT.	SPD.	ATT. PW.
27-29	4237-4477	300-306	30-34	12	38-42	16	37-41

DEF.	MAG. RES.	EVA.	EXP	LP	CP	GIL
16-18	15	0	1660-1862	2	270-428	0

Drop: Ice Magicite, Tanned Giantskin, Teleport Stone, Demonsbane
Steal: Tanned Giantskin, Remedy, 1000 gil
Poach: Tanned Giantskin, Arctic Wind

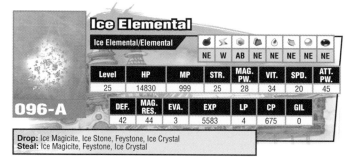

Ice Elemental — 096-A
Ice Elemental/Elemental

NE	W	AB	NE	NE	NE	NE	NE

Level	HP	MP	STR.	MAG. PW.	VIT.	SPD.	ATT. PW.
25	14830	999	25	28	34	20	45

DEF.	MAG. RES.	EVA.	EXP	LP	CP	GIL
42	44	3	5583	4	675	0

Drop: Ice Magicite, Ice Stone, Feystone, Ice Crystal
Steal: Ice Magicite, Feystone, Ice Crystal

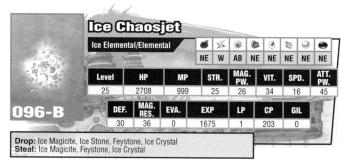

Ice Chaosjet — 096-B
Ice Elemental/Elemental

NE	W	AB	NE	NE	NE	NE	NE

Level	HP	MP	STR.	MAG. PW.	VIT.	SPD.	ATT. PW.
25	2708	999	25	26	34	16	45

DEF.	MAG. RES.	EVA.	EXP	LP	CP	GIL
30	36	0	1675	1	203	0

Drop: Ice Magicite, Ice Stone, Feystone, Ice Crystal
Steal: Ice Magicite, Feystone, Ice Crystal

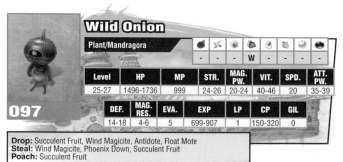

Wild Onion — 097
Plant/Mandragora

-	-	-	-	W	-	-	-

Level	HP	MP	STR.	MAG. PW.	VIT.	SPD.	ATT. PW.
25-27	1496-1736	999	24-26	20-24	40-46	20	35-39

DEF.	MAG. RES.	EVA.	EXP	LP	CP	GIL
14-18	4-6	5	699-907	1	150-320	0

Drop: Succulent Fruit, Wind Magicite, Antidote, Float Mote
Steal: Wind Magicite, Phoenix Down, Succulent Fruit
Poach: Succulent Fruit

Leshach Entite — 098
Leshach Entite/Elemental

NE	W	AB	NE	NE	NE	NE	NE

Level	HP	MP	STR.	MAG. PW.	VIT.	SPD.	ATT. PW.
45	48042	999	30	33	38	25	66

DEF.	MAG. RES.	EVA.	EXP	LP	CP	GIL
48	52	2	12627	7	1320	0

Drop: Ice Crystal, Feystone, Leshach Halcyon, Ether
Steal: Ice Crystal, Feystone, Leshach Halcyon

The Stilshrine of Miriam

Redmaw — 099
Avion/Steeling

-	-	-	W	-	-	-	-

Level	HP	MP	STR.	MAG. PW.	VIT.	SPD.	ATT. PW.
23-24	1134-1202	225-234	24-25	14	32-33	20-22	32-34
26-27	1670-1738	275-284	26-27	15	36-37	21-23	37-39

DEF.	MAG. RES.	EVA.	EXP	LP	CP	GIL
15-16	15	4-6	783-875	1	142-192	0
18-19	22	4-6	637-729	1	173-223	0

Drop: Crooked Fang, Wind Magicite, Red Fang, Ice Shield
Steal: Crooked Fang, 100 gil, Taurus Gem
Poach: Crooked Fang, Remedy

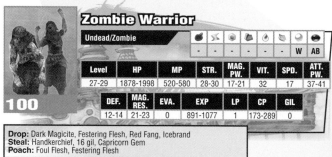

Zombie Warrior — 100
Undead/Zombie

-	-	-	-	-	-	W	AB

Level	HP	MP	STR.	MAG. PW.	VIT.	SPD.	ATT. PW.
27-29	1878-1998	520-580	28-30	17-21	32	17	37-41

DEF.	MAG. RES.	EVA.	EXP	LP	CP	GIL
12-14	21-23	0	891-1077	1	173-289	0

Drop: Dark Magicite, Festering Flesh, Red Fang, Icebrand
Steal: Handkerchief, 16 gil, Capricorn Gem
Poach: Foul Flesh, Festering Flesh

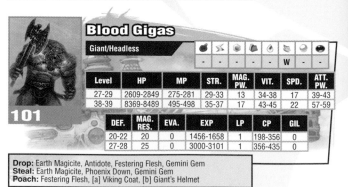

Blood Gigas — 101
Giant/Headless

-	-	-	-	-	W	-	-

Level	HP	MP	STR.	MAG. PW.	VIT.	SPD.	ATT. PW.
27-29	2609-2849	275-281	29-33	13	34-38	17	39-43
38-39	8369-8489	495-498	35-37	17	43-45	22	57-59

DEF.	MAG. RES.	EVA.	EXP	LP	CP	GIL
20-22	20	0	1456-1658	1	198-356	0
27-28	25	0	3000-3101	1	356-435	0

Drop: Earth Magicite, Antidote, Festering Flesh, Gemini Gem
Steal: Earth Magicite, Phoenix Down, Gemini Gem
Poach: Festering Flesh, [a] Viking Coat, [b] Giant's Helmet

Nightwalker — 102-A
Undead/Reaper

-	-	-	-	-	-	W	AB

Level	HP	MP	STR.	MAG. PW.	VIT.	SPD.	ATT. PW.
58-60	18568-18928	999	47-51	41-45	53	22	92-98

DEF.	MAG. RES.	EVA.	EXP	LP	CP	GIL
29-33	33-35	5	5653-5973	1	516-802	0

Drop: Dark Crystal, Book of Orgain-Mille, Renewing Morion, Capricorn Gem
Steal: Dark Crystal, Book of Orgain-Mille, Capricorn Gem

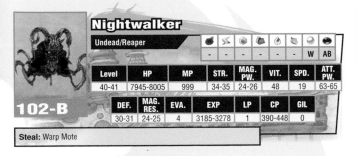

Nightwalker
Undead/Reaper

Level	HP	MP	STR.	MAG. PW.	VIT.	SPD.	ATT. PW.
40-41	7945-8005	999	34-35	24-26	48	19	63-65

DEF.	MAG. RES.	EVA.	EXP	LP	CP	GIL
30-31	24-25	4	3185-3278	1	390-448	0

102-B

Steal: Warp Mote

Nightwalker
Undead/Reaper

Level	HP	MP	STR.	MAG. PW.	VIT.	SPD.	ATT. PW.
40-41	7945-8005	999	24-25	34-36	48	19	63-65

DEF.	MAG. RES.	EVA.	EXP	LP	CP	GIL
24-25	30-31	4	3185-3278	1	390-448	0

102-C

Steal: Warp Mote

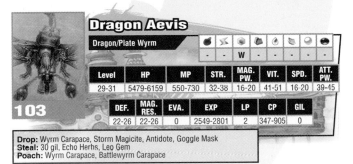

Dragon Aevis
Dragon/Plate Wyrm

Level	HP	MP	STR.	MAG. PW.	VIT.	SPD.	ATT. PW.
29-31	5479-6159	550-730	32-38	16-20	41-51	16-20	39-45

DEF.	MAG. RES.	EVA.	EXP	LP	CP	GIL
22-26	22-26	0	2549-2801	2	347-905	0

103

Drop: Wyrm Carapace, Storm Magicite, Antidote, Goggle Mask
Steal: 30 gil, Echo Herbs, Leo Gem
Poach: Wyrm Carapace, Battlewyrm Carapace

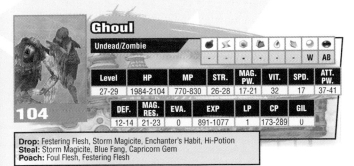

Ghoul
Undead/Zombie

Level	HP	MP	STR.	MAG. PW.	VIT.	SPD.	ATT. PW.
27-29	1984-2104	770-830	26-28	17-21	32	17	37-41

DEF.	MAG. RES.	EVA.	EXP	LP	CP	GIL
12-14	21-23	0	891-1077	1	173-289	0

104

Drop: Festering Flesh, Storm Magicite, Enchanter's Habit, Hi-Potion
Steal: Storm Magicite, Blue Fang, Capricorn Gem
Poach: Foul Flesh, Festering Flesh

Darkmare
Fiend/Nightmare

Level	HP	MP	STR.	MAG. PW.	VIT.	SPD.	ATT. PW.
30-31	4680-4738	999	28-29	18-20	34	17-18	36-38

DEF.	MAG. RES.	EVA.	EXP	LP	CP	GIL
18-19	24-26	2-4	1456-1557	1	198-287	0

105

Drop: Grimoire Togail, Dark Magicite, Demon Mail, Chronos Tear
Steal: Dark Magicite, Grimoire Togail, Scorpio Gem
Poach: Grimoire Togail, Grimoire Aldhed

Facer
Construct/Facer

Level	HP	MP	STR.	MAG. PW.	VIT.	SPD.	ATT. PW.
26-29	3026-3356	385-505	27-33	19-22	52	16-19	38-47

DEF.	MAG. RES.	EVA.	EXP	LP	CP	GIL
20-26	21-24	0	1151-1610	1	186-477	0

106

Drop: Earth Magicite, Solid Stone, Potion, Hi-Potion
Steal: Earth Magicite, Aquarius Gem, Pirate Hat
Poach: Solid Stone, Aquarius Gem

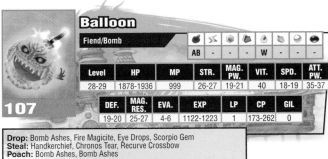

Balloon
Fiend/Bomb

Level	HP	MP	STR.	MAG. PW.	VIT.	SPD.	ATT. PW.
28-29	1878-1936	999	26-27	19-21	40	18-19	35-37

DEF.	MAG. RES.	EVA.	EXP	LP	CP	GIL
19-20	25-27	4-6	1122-1223	1	173-262	0

107

Drop: Bomb Ashes, Fire Magicite, Eye Drops, Scorpio Gem
Steal: Handkerchief, Chronos Tear, Recurve Crossbow
Poach: Bomb Ashes, Bomb Ashes

Miriam Guardian
Construct/Guardian

Level	HP	MP	STR.	MAG. PW.	VIT.	SPD.	ATT. PW.
28	6827	55	31	12	32	13	40

DEF.	MAG. RES.	EVA.	EXP	LP	CP	GIL
21	19	0	1602	1	218	0

108

Drop: N/A
Steal: N/A

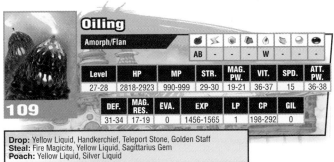

Oiling
Amorph/Flan

Level	HP	MP	STR.	MAG. PW.	VIT.	SPD.	ATT. PW.
27-28	2818-2923	990-999	29-30	19-21	36-37	15	36-38

DEF.	MAG. RES.	EVA.	EXP	LP	CP	GIL
31-34	17-19	0	1456-1565	1	198-292	0

109

Drop: Yellow Liquid, Handkerchief, Teleport Stone, Golden Staff
Steal: Fire Magicite, Yellow Liquid, Sagittarius Gem
Poach: Yellow Liquid, Silver Liquid

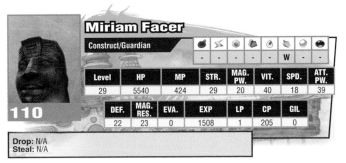

Miriam Facer
Construct/Guardian

Level	HP	MP	STR.	MAG. PW.	VIT.	SPD.	ATT. PW.
29	5540	424	29	20	40	18	39

DEF.	MAG. RES.	EVA.	EXP	LP	CP	GIL
22	23	0	1508	1	205	0

110

Drop: N/A
Steal: N/A

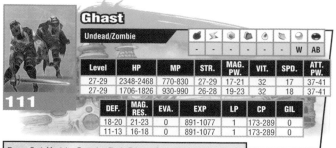

Ghast

Undead/Zombie

Level	HP	MP	STR.	MAG. PW.	VIT.	SPD.	ATT. PW.
27-29	2348-2468	770-830	27-29	17-21	32	17	37-41
27-29	1706-1826	930-990	26-28	19-23	32	18	37-41

DEF.	MAG. RES.	EVA.	EXP	LP	CP	GIL
18-20	21-23	0	891-1077	1	173-289	0
11-13	16-18	0	891-1077	1	173-289	0

111

Drop: Dark Magicite, Festering Flesh, Teleport Stone, Float Mote
Steal: Festering Flesh, Smelling Salts, Paramina Crossbow
Poach: Foul Flesh, Festering Flesh

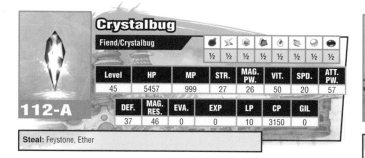

Crystalbug

Fiend/Crystalbug

| ½ | ½ | ½ | ½ | ½ | ½ | ½ | ½ |

Level	HP	MP	STR.	MAG. PW.	VIT.	SPD.	ATT. PW.
45	5457	999	27	26	50	20	57

DEF.	MAG. RES.	EVA.	EXP	LP	CP	GIL
37	46	0	0	10	3150	0

112-A

Steal: Feystone, Ether

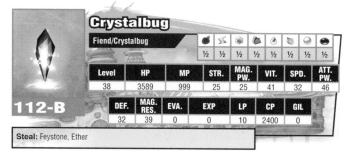

Crystalbug

Fiend/Crystalbug

| ½ | ½ | ½ | ½ | ½ | ½ | ½ | ½ |

Level	HP	MP	STR.	MAG. PW.	VIT.	SPD.	ATT. PW.
38	3589	999	25	25	41	32	46

DEF.	MAG. RES.	EVA.	EXP	LP	CP	GIL
32	39	0	0	10	2400	0

112-B

Steal: Feystone, Ether

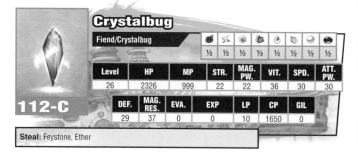

Crystalbug

Fiend/Crystalbug

| ½ | ½ | ½ | ½ | ½ | ½ | ½ | ½ |

Level	HP	MP	STR.	MAG. PW.	VIT.	SPD.	ATT. PW.
26	2326	999	22	22	36	30	30

DEF.	MAG. RES.	EVA.	EXP	LP	CP	GIL
29	37	0	0	10	1650	0

112-C

Steal: Feystone, Ether

The Mosphoran Highwaste

Worgen

Beast/Wolf

Level	HP	MP	STR.	MAG. PW.	VIT.	SPD.	ATT. PW.
25-26	2011-2121	180-195	30-32	17	43-44	18-19	40-41
29-31	2011-2231	180-210	30-34	17	43-45	18-20	40-42

DEF.	MAG. RES.	EVA.	EXP	LP	CP	GIL
18	22	6	943-1036	1	180-261	0
18	22	6	943-1129	1	180-342	0

113-A

Drop: Fire Magicite, Smelling Salts, Quality Pelt, Libra Gem
Steal: Fire Magicite, Hi-Potion, Steel Poleyns
Poach: Quality Pelt, Throat Wolf Blood

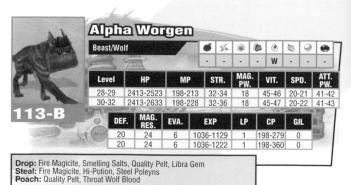

Alpha Worgen

Beast/Wolf

Level	HP	MP	STR.	MAG. PW.	VIT.	SPD.	ATT. PW.
28-29	2413-2523	198-213	32-34	18	45-46	20-21	41-42
30-32	2413-2633	198-228	32-36	18	45-47	20-22	41-43

DEF.	MAG. RES.	EVA.	EXP	LP	CP	GIL
20	24	6	1036-1129	1	198-279	0
20	24	6	1036-1222	1	198-360	0

113-B

Drop: Fire Magicite, Smelling Salts, Quality Pelt, Libra Gem
Steal: Fire Magicite, Hi-Potion, Steel Poleyns
Poach: Quality Pelt, Throat Wolf Blood

Humbaba

Giant/Behemoth

Level	HP	MP	STR.	MAG. PW.	VIT.	SPD.	ATT. PW.
32-33	5403-5523	360-363	34-36	13	41-43	16	43-45

DEF.	MAG. RES.	EVA.	EXP	LP	CP	GIL
19-20	22	0	2289-2390	2	324-403	0

114

Drop: Storm Magicite, Tanned Giantskin, Echo Herbs, Sledgehammer
Steal: Storm Magicite, Teleport Stone, Gemini Gem
Poach: Tanned Giantskin, Beastlord Hide

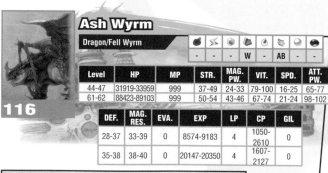

Python

Beast/Serpent

Level	HP	MP	STR.	MAG. PW.	VIT.	SPD.	ATT. PW.
29-32	3016-3346	240-285	31-37	14	41-44	19-22	41-44

DEF.	MAG. RES.	EVA.	EXP	LP	CP	GIL
19	22	5	1749-2028	1	234-477	0

115

Drop: Tanned Hide, Wind Magicite, Gold Needle, Quality Hide
Steal: Wind Magicite, 400 gil, Bone Helm
Poach: Tanned Hide, Great Serpent's Fang

Ash Wyrm

Dragon/Fell Wyrm

Level	HP	MP	STR.	MAG. PW.	VIT.	SPD.	ATT. PW.
44-47	31919-33959	999	37-49	24-33	79-100	16-25	65-77
61-62	88423-89103	999	50-54	43-46	67-74	21-24	98-102

DEF.	MAG. RES.	EVA.	EXP	LP	CP	GIL
28-37	33-39	0	8574-9183	4	1050-2610	0
35-38	38-40	0	20147-20350	4	1607-2127	0

116

Drop: Ring Wyrm Scale, Wind Crystal, Koga Blade, Leo Gem
Steal: Wind Crystal, 800 gil, Leo Gem

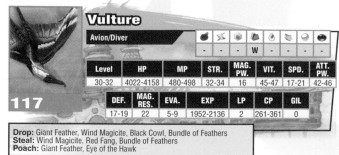

Vulture

Avion/Diver

Level	HP	MP	STR.	MAG. PW.	VIT.	SPD.	ATT. PW.
30-32	4022-4158	480-498	32-34	16	45-47	17-21	42-46

DEF.	MAG. RES.	EVA.	EXP	LP	CP	GIL
17-19	22	5-9	1952-2136	2	261-361	0

117

Drop: Giant Feather, Wind Magicite, Black Cowl, Bundle of Feathers
Steal: Wind Magicite, Red Fang, Bundle of Feathers
Poach: Giant Feather, Eye of the Hawk

Clay Golem

Construct/Golem

118

Level	HP	MP	STR.	MAG. PW.	VIT.	SPD.	ATT. PW.
31-32	6283-6393	999	32-34	18-19	34	15-16	43-46

DEF.	MAG. RES.	EVA.	EXP	LP	CP	GIL
22-24	24-25	0	1884-2037	2	252-349	0

Drop: Earth Magicite, Solid Stone, Iron Pole, Hi-Potion
Steal: Earth Magicite, Gold Needle, Chronos Tear
Poach: Solid Stone, Quality Lumber

Slaven Wilder

Giant/Slaven

119

Level	HP	MP	STR.	MAG. PW.	VIT.	SPD.	ATT. PW.
27-28	3518-3638	240-243	31-33	12	43-45	15	42-44
30-31	3518-3638	240-243	32-34	12	43-45	17	44-46

DEF.	MAG. RES.	EVA.	EXP	LP	CP	GIL
17-18	20	0	1548-1649	1	207-286	0
17-18	20	0	1548-1649	1	207-286	0

Drop: Tanned Giantskin, Earth Magicite, Firefly, Gemini Gem
Steal: Tanned Giantskin, White Fang, Gemini Gem
Poach: Tanned Giantskin

Fire Elemental

Fire Elemental/Elemental

120-A

AB	NE	NE	NE	W	NE	NE	NE

Level	HP	MP	STR.	MAG. PW.	VIT.	SPD.	ATT. PW.
25	14830	999	25	28	34	20	45

DEF.	MAG. RES.	EVA.	EXP	LP	CP	GIL
42	44	3	5583	4	675	0

Drop: Fire Magicite, Fire Stone, Feystone, Fire Crystal
Steal: Fire Magicite, Feystone, Fire Crystal

Fire Chaosjet

Fire Chaosjet/Elemental

120-B

AB	NE	NE	NE	W	NE	NE	NE

Level	HP	MP	STR.	MAG. PW.	VIT.	SPD.	ATT. PW.
45	4079	999	25	20	49	15	45

DEF.	MAG. RES.	EVA.	EXP	LP	CP	GIL
32	34	0	1675	1	203	0

Drop: Fire Magicite, Fire Stone, Feystone, Fire Crystal
Steal: Fire Magicite, Feystone, Fire Crystal

The Salikawood

Wyrdhare

Beast/Dreamhare

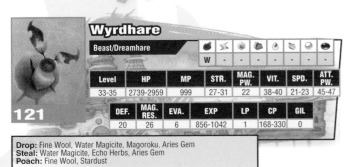

121

W	-	-	-	-	-	-	-

Level	HP	MP	STR.	MAG. PW.	VIT.	SPD.	ATT. PW.
33-35	2739-2959	999	27-31	22	38-40	21-23	45-47

DEF.	MAG. RES.	EVA.	EXP	LP	CP	GIL
20	26	6	856-1042	1	168-330	0

Drop: Fine Wool, Water Magicite, Magoroku, Aries Gem
Steal: Water Magicite, Echo Herbs, Aries Gem
Poach: Fine Wool, Stardust

Pumpkin Head

Plant/Mandragora

122

-	-	W	-	-	-	-	-

Level	HP	MP	STR.	MAG. PW.	VIT.	SPD.	ATT. PW.
32-33	2739-2859	999	28-29	23-25	48-51	21	47-49

DEF.	MAG. RES.	EVA.	EXP	LP	CP	GIL
19-21	26-27	7	1070-1174	1	210-295	0

Drop: Succulent Fruit, Storm Magicite, Handkerchief, Balance Mote
Steal: Storm Magicite, Screamroot, Black Garb
Poach: Succulent Fruit

Sprinter

Avion/Cockatrice

123

-	-	-	-	W	-	-	-

Level	HP	MP	STR.	MAG. PW.	VIT.	SPD.	ATT. PW.
33-34	4070-4138	999	30-31	21	40-41	20-22	49-51

DEF.	MAG. RES.	EVA.	EXP	LP	CP	GIL
19-20	26	26-28	1569-1661	1	231-281	0

Drop: Bundle of Feathers, Fire Magicite, Blue Fang, Astrakhan Hat
Steal: Bundle of Feathers, White Fang, Taurus Gem
Poach: Bundle of Feathers, Chronos Tear

Malboro King

Plant/Malboro

124

-	-	-	-	-	-	W	-

Level	HP	MP	STR.	MAG. PW.	VIT.	SPD.	ATT. PW.
34-35	4501-4621	980-992	29-30	19-21	43-46	18	48-50

DEF.	MAG. RES.	EVA.	EXP	LP	CP	GIL
19-21	26-27	0	2461-2565	1	231-316	0

Drop: Malboro Fruit, Dark Magicite, Thorned Mace, Virgo Gem
Steal: Dark Magicite, Malboro Fruit, Virgo Gem
Poach: Malboro Fruit, Vanishga Mote

Antares

Insect/Mantis

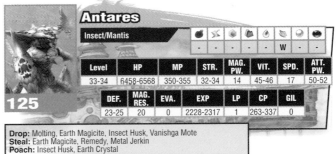

125

-	-	-	-	-	-	W	-

Level	HP	MP	STR.	MAG. PW.	VIT.	SPD.	ATT. PW.
33-34	6458-6568	350-355	32-34	14	45-46	17	50-52

DEF.	MAG. RES.	EVA.	EXP	LP	CP	GIL
23-25	20	0	2228-2317	1	263-337	0

Drop: Molting, Earth Magicite, Insect Husk, Vanishga Mote
Steal: Earth Magicite, Remedy, Metal Jerkin
Poach: Insect Husk, Earth Crystal

Phon Coast

Silver Lobo

Beast/Wolf

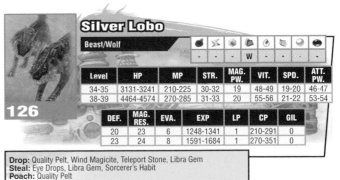

126

-	-	W	-	-	-	-	-

Level	HP	MP	STR.	MAG. PW.	VIT.	SPD.	ATT. PW.
34-35	3131-3241	210-225	30-32	19	48-49	19-20	46-47
38-39	4464-4574	270-285	31-33	20	55-56	21-22	53-54

DEF.	MAG. RES.	EVA.	EXP	LP	CP	GIL
20	23	6	1248-1341	1	210-291	0
23	24	8	1591-1684	1	270-351	0

Drop: Quality Pelt, Wind Magicite, Teleport Stone, Libra Gem
Steal: Eye Drops, Libra Gem, Sorcerer's Habit
Poach: Quality Pelt

Bestiary

Mandragora — 127

Plant/Mandragora

Level	HP	MP	STR.	MAG. PW.	VIT.	SPD.	ATT. PW.
34-37	2739-3099	999	28-31	23-29	48-57	21	47-53

DEF.	MAG. RES.	EVA.	EXP	LP	CP	GIL
19-25	26-29	7	607-919	1	210-465	0

Drop: Succulent Fruit, Water Magicite, Vanishga Mote, Platinum Sword
Steal: Water Magicite, Succulent Fruit, Virgo Gem
Poach: Succulent Fruit, Virgo Gem

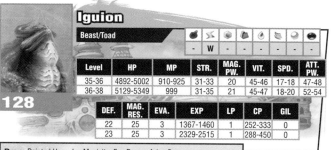

Iguion — 128

Beast/Toad

Level	HP	MP	STR.	MAG. PW.	VIT.	SPD.	ATT. PW.
35-36	4892-5002	910-925	31-33	20	45-46	17-18	47-48
36-38	5129-5349	999	31-35	21	45-47	18-20	52-54

DEF.	MAG. RES.	EVA.	EXP	LP	CP	GIL
22	25	3	1367-1460	1	252-333	0
23	25	3	2329-2515	1	288-450	0

Drop: Pointed Horn, Ice Magicite, Eye Drops, Aries Gem
Steal: Phoenix Down, Aries Gem, Survival Vest
Poach: Pointed Horn, Frogspawn

Archaeosaur — 129

Dragon/Tyrant

Level	HP	MP	STR.	MAG. PW.	VIT.	SPD.	ATT. PW.
37-38	12251-12591	210-300	32-35	14-16	50-55	21-23	50-53

DEF.	MAG. RES.	EVA.	EXP	LP	CP	GIL
20-22	20-22	0	4457-4583	2	525-804	0

Drop: Storm Magicite, Gold Needle, Tanned Tyrant Hide, Leo Gem
Steal: Storm Magicite, Tanned Tyrante Hide, Fumarole
Poach: Tanned Tyrante Hide, Prime Tanned Hide

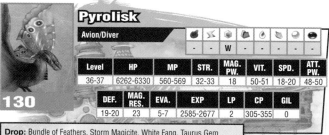

Pyrolisk — 130

Avion/Diver

Level	HP	MP	STR.	MAG. PW.	VIT.	SPD.	ATT. PW.
36-37	6262-6330	560-569	32-33	18	50-51	18-20	48-50

DEF.	MAG. RES.	EVA.	EXP	LP	CP	GIL
19-20	23	5-7	2585-2677	2	305-355	0

Drop: Bundle of Feathers, Storm Magicite, White Fang, Taurus Gem
Steal: Bundle of Feathers, Gold Needle, Balance Mote
Poach: Bundle of Feathers, Murasame

Piranha — 131

Ichthian/Piranha

Level	HP	MP	STR.	MAG. PW.	VIT.	SPD.	ATT. PW.
35-37	4305-4469	980-999	30-32	20	45-47	21-25	47-51

DEF.	MAG. RES.	EVA.	EXP	LP	CP	GIL
20	23-25	5-9	1961-2157	1	231-349	0

Drop: Water Magicite, Eye Drops, Ichthon Scale, Pisces Gem
Steal: Chronos Tear, Remedy, Steel Mask
Poach: Ichthon Scale, Pisces Gem

Bagoly — 132

Fiend/Urstix

Level	HP	MP	STR.	MAG. PW.	VIT.	SPD.	ATT. PW.
14-16	1010-1230	200-230	16-20	10	26-28	14-16	22-24
36-38	4500-4720	560-590	30-34	16	43-45	18-20	48-50

DEF.	MAG. RES.	EVA.	EXP	LP	CP	GIL
10	8	2	490-676	1	86-248	0
21	23	3	2051-2237	1	242-404	0

Drop: [a] Wind Stone, [b] Wind Magicite, [a] Large Feather, [b] Bundle of Feathers, Teleport Stone, Aries Gem
Steal: [a] Large Feather, [b] Bundle of Feathers, [a] Echo Herbs, [b] 480 Gil, [a] 480 Gil, [b] Multiscale
Poach: [a] Large Feather, [b] Bundle of Feathers, [a] Wind Magicite, [b] Bent Staff

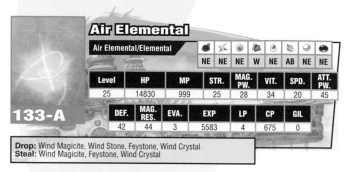

Air Elemental — 133-A

Air Elemental/Elemental

Level	HP	MP	STR.	MAG. PW.	VIT.	SPD.	ATT. PW.
25	14830	999	25	28	34	20	45

DEF.	MAG. RES.	EVA.	EXP	LP	CP	GIL
42	44	3	5583	4	675	0

Drop: Wind Magicite, Wind Stone, Feystone, Wind Crystal
Steal: Wind Magicite, Feystone, Wind Crystal

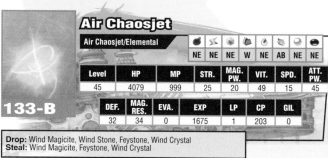

Air Chaosjet — 133-B

Air Chaosjet/Elemental

Level	HP	MP	STR.	MAG. PW.	VIT.	SPD.	ATT. PW.
45	4079	999	25	20	49	15	45

DEF.	MAG. RES.	EVA.	EXP	LP	CP	GIL
32	34	0	1675	1	203	0

Drop: Wind Magicite, Wind Stone, Feystone, Wind Crystal
Steal: Wind Magicite, Feystone, Wind Crystal

Tchita Uplands

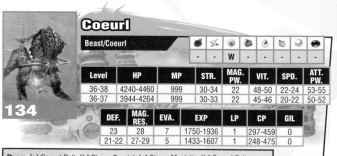

Coeurl — 134

Beast/Coeurl

Level	HP	MP	STR.	MAG. PW.	VIT.	SPD.	ATT. PW.
36-38	4240-4460	999	30-34	22	48-50	22-24	53-55
36-37	3944-4264	999	30-33	22	45-46	20-22	50-52

DEF.	MAG. RES.	EVA.	EXP	LP	CP	GIL
23	28	7	1750-1936	1	297-459	0
21-22	27-29	5	1433-1607	1	248-475	0

Drop: [a] Coeurl Pelt, [b] Storm Crystal, [a] Storm Magicite, [b] Coeurl Pelt, [a] Warp Mote, [b] Quality Pelt, [b] Hi-Potion
Steal: [a] Coeurl Pelt, [b] Storm Stone, [a] Storm Magicite, [b] Quality Pelt, [a] Libra Gem, [b] Embroidered Tippet
Poach: Coeurl Pelt

Feral Croc — 135

Beast/Gator

Level	HP	MP	STR.	MAG. PW.	VIT.	SPD.	ATT. PW.
38-39	9393-9713	375-405	33-36	16	48-49	17-19	54-56

DEF.	MAG. RES.	EVA.	EXP	LP	CP	GIL
21-22	22-24	0	2978-3152	1	405-632	0

Drop: Blood Wool, Wind Magicite, White Fang, Aries Gem
Steal: Blood Wool, Aries GemOrichalcum Dirk
Poach: Blood Wool, Antarctic Wind

136 Serpent

Beast/Serpent

-	-	-	W	-	-	-	-

Level	HP	MP	STR.	MAG. PW.	VIT.	SPD.	ATT. PW.
35-36	4982-5302	300-330	32-35	17	45-46	20-22	53-55

DEF.	MAG. RES.	EVA.	EXP	LP	CP	GIL
22-23	23-25	5	2309-2483	1	293-520	0

Drop: Quality Hide, Wind Magicite, Bacchus's Wine, Aries Gem
Steal: Wind Magicite, Quality Hide, Aries Gem
Poach: Quality Hide, Carmagnole

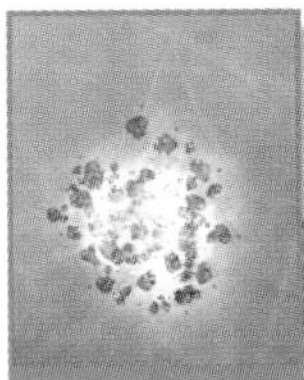

137-A Earth Elemental

Earth Elemental/Elemental

NE	NE	NE	AB	NE	W	NE	NE

Level	HP	MP	STR.	MAG. PW.	VIT.	SPD.	ATT. PW.
25	14830	999	25	28	34	20	45

DEF.	MAG. RES.	EVA.	EXP	LP	CP	GIL
42	44	3	5583	4	675	0

Drop: Earth Magicite, Earth Stone, Feystone, Earth Crystal
Steal: Earth Magicite, Feystone, Earth Crystal

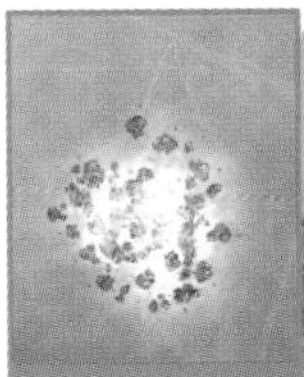

137-B Earth Chaosjet

Earth Chaosjet/Elemental

NE	NE	NE	AB	NE	W	NE	NE

Level	HP	MP	STR.	MAG. PW.	VIT.	SPD.	ATT. PW.
45	4079	999	25	20	49	15	45

DEF.	MAG. RES.	EVA.	EXP	LP	CP	GIL
32	34	0	1675	1	203	0

Drop: Earth Magicite, Earth Stone, Feystone, Earth Crystal
Steal: Earth Magicite, Feystone, Earth Crystal

The Sochen Cave Palace

138 Abysteel

Undead/Steeling

-	-	-	-	-	-	W	-

Level	HP	MP	STR.	MAG. PW.	VIT.	SPD.	ATT. PW.
57-59	13099-13339	700-728	44-48	37	57-61	28-34	93-97
64-65	20524-20644	775-789	45-47	39	59-61	30-33	96-98
35-38	6778-7138	600-642	35-41	22	48-54	25-34	76-82

DEF.	MAG. RES.	EVA.	EXP	LP	CP	GIL
31-35	35-37	12-18	2697-3039	1	460-634	0
33-35	38-39	13-16	9363-9334	1	532-619	0
28-34	32-35	9-18	1924-2437	1	378-639	0

Drop: Dark Crystal, Spiral Incisor, Red Fang, [a][c] Vampyr Fang, [b] Demon Shield
Steal: Spiral Incisor, Teleport Stone[a][c] Demon Shield, [b] Vampyr Fang

139 Imp

Fiend/Gargoyle

-	-	W	-	-	-	-	-

Level	HP	MP	STR.	MAG. PW.	VIT.	SPD.	ATT. PW.
37-39	4390-4710	999	30-34	21-27	41	20-22	52-56

DEF.	MAG. RES.	EVA.	EXP	LP	CP	GIL
23-25	25-33	6-10	2231-2583	1	276-678	0

Drop: Storm Magicite, Blue Fang, Demon Feather, Scorpio Gem
Steal: Remedy, 130 Gil, Storm Crystal
Poach: Demon Feather, Maduin Gear

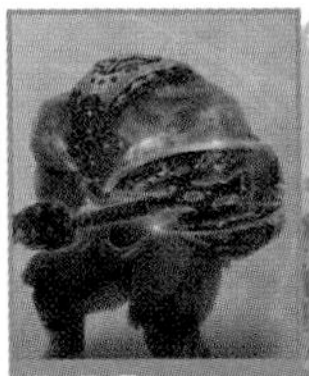

140 Striker

Giant/Headless

-	-	-	-	-	W	-	-

Level	HP	MP	STR.	MAG. PW.	VIT.	SPD.	ATT. PW.
37-38	5129-5549	400-405	32-34	16-18	40-42	19	54-57

DEF.	MAG. RES.	EVA.	EXP	LP	CP	GIL
23-25	22	0	2329-2492	1	288-564	0

Drop: Maggoty Flesh, Earth Magicite, Teleport Stone, Kagenui
Steal: Maggoty Flesh, Earth MagiciteGemini Gem
Poach: Maggoty Flesh, Gemini Gem

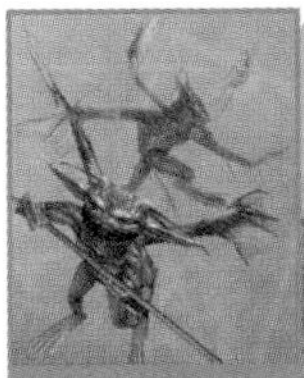

141 Pit Fiend

Fiend/Gargoyle

-	-	-	W	-	-	-	-

Level	HP	MP	STR.	MAG. PW.	VIT.	SPD.	ATT. PW.
37-39	4390-4710	999	29-33	25-31	41	20-22	50-54

DEF.	MAG. RES.	EVA.	EXP	LP	CP	GIL
21-23	27-35	7-11	2231-2583	1	276-678	0

Drop: Wind Magicite, Remedy, Demon Feather, Scorpio Gem
Steal: Eye Drops, Blue Fang, Scorpio Gem
Poach: Demon Feather, Demon Tail

142 Wendigo

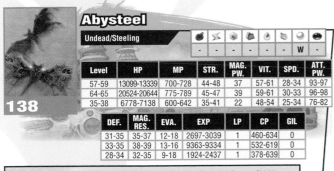

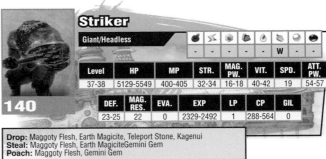

Giant/Headless

-	W	AB	-	-	-	-	-

Level	HP	MP	STR.	MAG. PW.	VIT.	SPD.	ATT. PW.
37-38	5458-5878	300-305	33-35	16-18	38-40	18	55-58

DEF.	MAG. RES.	EVA.	EXP	LP	CP	GIL
22-24	22	0	2329-2492	1	288-564	0

Drop: Maggoty Flesh, Ice Magicite, Hi-Potion, Gemini Gem
Steal: Ice Magicite, Forbidden Flesh, Gokuu Pole
Poach: Maggoty Flesh, Vanishga Mote

143 Zombie Knight

Undead/Zombie

-	-	-	-	-	-	W	AB

Level	HP	MP	STR.	MAG. PW.	VIT.	SPD.	ATT. PW.
36-38	3693-4053	999	30-34	20-24	38	19	52-58

DEF.	MAG. RES.	EVA.	EXP	LP	CP	GIL
14-18	23-25	0	1427-1747	1	252-538	0

Drop: Dark Magicite, Maggoty Flesh, Hypnocrown, Capricorn Gem
Steal: Maggoty Flesh, 80 Gil, Vanishga Mote
Poach: Maggoty Flesh, Capricorn Gem

144 Gorgimera

Fiend/Cockatrice

-	-	-	-	W	-	-	-

Level	HP	MP	STR.	MAG. PW.	VIT.	SPD.	ATT. PW.
36-37	5385-5505	999	30-32	22	44-46	21-24	52-54
38-39	4266-4386	999	30-32	22	40-42	21-24	52-54

DEF.	MAG. RES.	EVA.	EXP	LP	CP	GIL
20-22	26-27	6-9	1707-1878	1	264-351	0
20-22	26-27	6-9	1707-1878	1	264-351	0

Drop: Bundle of Feathers, Fire Magicite, Teleport Stone, [a] Hammerhead, [b] Taurus Gem
Steal: Fire Magicite, Gold Needle, [a] Taurus Gem, [b] Hammerhead
Poach: Bundle of Feathers, Taurus Gem

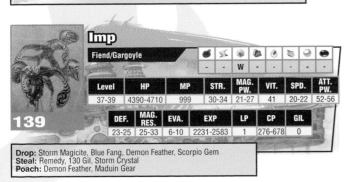

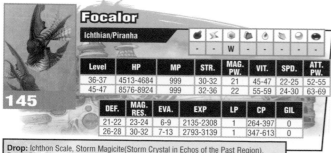

Focalor

145 — Ichthian/Piranha

Elements: - | - | W | - | - | - | - | -

Level	HP	MP	STR	MAG. PW.	VIT.	SPD.	ATT. PW.
36-37	4513-4684	999	30-32	21	45-47	22-25	52-55
45-47	8576-8924	999	32-36	22	55-59	24-30	63-69

DEF.	MAG. RES.	EVA.	EXP	LP	CP	GIL
21-22	23-24	6-9	2135-2308	1	264-397	0
26-28	30-32	7-13	2793-3139	1	347-613	0

Drop: Ichthon Scale, Storm Magicite(Storm Crystal in Echos of the Past Region), Power Rod, Pisces Gem
Steal: Ichthon Scale, Balance Mote, Pisces Gem
Poach: Ichthon Scale, Dorsal Fin

The Feywood

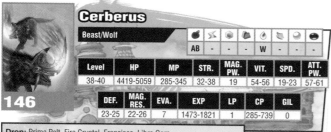

Cerberus

146 — Beast/Wolf

Elements: AB | - | - | - | W | - | - | -

Level	HP	MP	STR	MAG. PW.	VIT.	SPD.	ATT. PW.
38-40	4419-5059	285-345	32-38	19	54-56	19-23	57-61

DEF.	MAG. RES.	EVA.	EXP	LP	CP	GIL
23-25	22-26	7	1473-1821	1	285-739	0

Drop: Prime Pelt, Fire Crystal, Francisca, Libra Gem
Steal: Fire Crystal, Prime Pelt, Festering Flesh
Poach: Prime Pelt, Hell-Gate's Flame

Deadly Nightshade

147 — Plant/Mandragora

Elements: - | - | - | - | W | - | - | -

Level	HP	MP	STR	MAG. PW.	VIT.	SPD.	ATT. PW.
39-41	3167-3647	999	29-33	25-31	50-60	23-25	57-63

DEF.	MAG. RES.	EVA.	EXP	LP	CP	GIL
24-30	28-32	9	1262-1630	1	285-675	0

Drop: Succulent Fruit, Fire Crystal, Chronos Tear, Virgo Gem
Steal: Fire Crystal, Succulent Fruit, Screamroot
Poach: Succulent Fruit, Ring of Renewal

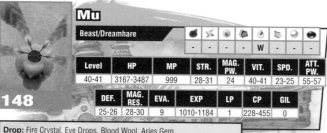

Mu

148 — Beast/Dreamhare

Elements: - | - | - | - | W | - | - | -

Level	HP	MP	STR	MAG. PW.	VIT.	SPD.	ATT. PW.
40-41	3167-3487	999	28-31	24	40-41	23-25	55-57

DEF.	MAG. RES.	EVA.	EXP	LP	CP	GIL
25-26	28-30	9	1010-1184	1	228-455	0

Drop: Fire Crystal, Eye Drops, Blood Wool, Aries Gem
Steal: Blood Wool, Aries Gem, Pheasant Netsuke
Poach: Blood Wool, Moondust

Mandragora Prince

149 — Plant/Mandragora

Elements: W | - | - | - | - | - | - | -

Level	HP	MP	STR	MAG. PW.	VIT.	SPD.	ATT. PW.
37	9069	999	33	25	73	30	54
42-43	3959-4199	999	30-32	25-28	59-64	23-24	57-60

DEF.	MAG. RES.	EVA.	EXP	LP	CP	GIL
26	22	8	0	5	1200	0
25-28	28-30	14	1262-1446	1	285-480	0

Drop: [a] -, [b] Water Crystal, [a] -, [b] Screamroot, [a] -, [b] Teleport Stone, [a] -, [b] Virgo Gem
Poach: [a] -, [b] Screamroot, [a] -, [b] Four-leaf Clover

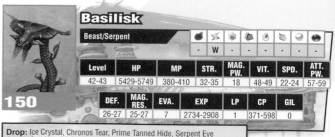

Basilisk

150 — Beast/Serpent

Elements: - | - | W | - | - | - | - | -

Level	HP	MP	STR	MAG. PW.	VIT.	SPD.	ATT. PW.
42-43	5429-5749	380-410	32-35	18	48-49	22-24	57-59

DEF.	MAG. RES.	EVA.	EXP	LP	CP	GIL
26-27	25-27	7	2734-2908	1	371-598	0

Drop: Ice Crystal, Chronos Tear, Prime Tanned Hide, Serpent Eye
Steal: Antidote, 80 Gil, Aries Gem
Poach: Prime Tanned Hide, Serpent Eye

Alraune King

151 — Plant/Mandragora

Elements: - | - | - | - | - | W | - | -

Level	HP	MP	STR	MAG. PW.	VIT.	SPD.	ATT. PW.
37	9069	999	32	26	72	30	53
42-43	3959-4199	999	29-31	26-29	59-64	24-25	57-60

DEF.	MAG. RES.	EVA.	EXP	LP	CP	GIL
25	22	9	0	5	1200	0
24-27	26-28	15	1262-1446	1	285-480	0

Drop: [a] -, [b] Earth Crystal, [a] -, [b] Screamroot, [a] -, [b] Gold Needle, [a] -, [b] Virgo Gem
Steal: [a] -, [b] Screamroot, [a] Gimble Stalk, [b] Virgo Gem, [a] -, [b] Cross Scale
Poach: [a] -, [b] Screamroot, [a] -, [b] Gimble Stalk

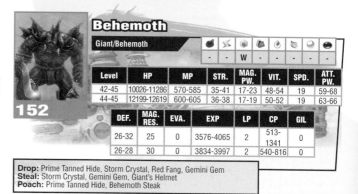

Behemoth

152 — Giant/Behemoth

Elements: - | - | W | - | - | - | - | -

Level	HP	MP	STR	MAG. PW.	VIT.	SPD.	ATT. PW.
42-45	10026-11286	570-585	35-41	17-23	48-54	19	59-68
44-45	12199-12619	600-605	36-38	17-19	50-52	19	63-66

DEF.	MAG. RES.	EVA.	EXP	LP	CP	GIL
26-32	25	0	3576-4065	2	513-1341	0
26-28	30	0	3834-3997	2	540-816	0

Drop: Prime Tanned Hide, Storm Crystal, Red Fang, Gemini Gem
Steal: Storm Crystal, Gemini Gem, Giant's Helmet
Poach: Prime Tanned Hide, Behemoth Steak

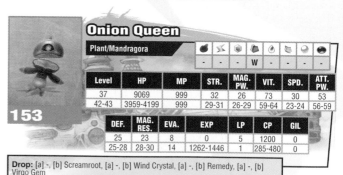

Onion Queen

153 — Plant/Mandragora

Elements: - | - | - | - | W | - | - | -

Level	HP	MP	STR	MAG. PW.	VIT.	SPD.	ATT. PW.
37	9069	999	32	26	73	30	53
42-43	3959-4199	999	29-31	26-29	59-64	23-24	56-59

DEF.	MAG. RES.	EVA.	EXP	LP	CP	GIL
25	23	8	0	5	1200	0
25-28	28-30	14	1262-1446	1	285-480	0

Drop: [a] -, [b] Screamroot, [a] -, [b] Wind Crystal, [a] -, [b] Remedy, [a] -, [b] Virgo Gem
Steal: [a] -, [b] Wind Crystal, [a] Onion, [b] Screamroot, [a] -, [b] Agate Ring
Poach: [a] -, [b] Screamroot, [a] -, [b] Onion

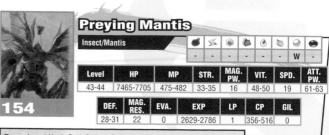

Preying Mantis

154 — Insect/Mantis

Elements: - | - | - | - | - | - | W | -

Level	HP	MP	STR	MAG. PW.	VIT.	SPD.	ATT. PW.
43-44	7465-7705	475-482	33-35	16	48-50	19	61-63

DEF.	MAG. RES.	EVA.	EXP	LP	CP	GIL
28-31	22	0	2629-2786	1	356-516	0

Drop: Insect Husk, Dark Crystal, Reflectga Mote, Cancer Gem
Steal: Dark Crystal, Cancer Gem, Bowline Sash
Poach: Insect Husk, Sickle-Blade

Pumpkin Star

Plant/Mandragora

-		W						-

Level	HP	MP	STR.	MAG. PW.	VIT.	SPD.	ATT. PW.
37	9069	999	33	25	72	31	52
42-43	3959-4199	9999	30-32	25-28	59-64	24-25	57-60

DEF.	MAG. RES.	EVA.	EXP	LP	CP	GIL
26	22	8	0	5	1200	0
24-27	26-28	14	1262-1446	1	285-480	0

155

Drop: [a] -, [b] Storm Crystal, [a] -, [b] Screamroot, [a] -, [b] Traitor's Bow, [a] -, [b] Virgo Gem
Steal: [a] -, [b] Screamroot, [a] Jack-o'-Lantern, [b] Hi-Potion, [a] -, [b] Virgo Gem
Poach: [a] -, [b] Screamroot, [a] -, [b] Jack-o'-Lantern

Golem

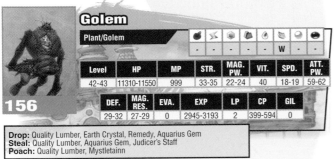

Plant/Golem

-					W			-

Level	HP	MP	STR.	MAG. PW.	VIT.	SPD.	ATT. PW.
42-43	11310-11550	999	33-35	22-24	40	18-19	59-62

DEF.	MAG. RES.	EVA.	EXP	LP	CP	GIL
29-32	27-29	0	2945-3193	2	399-594	

156

Drop: Quality Lumber, Earth Crystal, Remedy, Aquarius Gem
Steal: Quality Lumber, Aquarius Gem, Judicer's Staff
Poach: Quality Lumber, Mystletainn

Topstalk

Plant/Mandragora

-				W				-

Level	HP	MP	STR.	MAG. PW.	VIT.	SPD.	ATT. PW.
37	9069	999	32	25	72	31	53
42-43	3959-4199	999	29-31	25-28	59-64	23-24	58-61

DEF.	MAG. RES.	EVA.	EXP	LP	CP	GIL
25	23	9	0	5	1200	0
24-27	28-30	15	1262-1446	1	285-480	0

157

Drop: [a] -, [b] Fire Crystal, [a] -, [b] Screamroot, [a] -, [b] Echo Herbs, [a] -, [b] Virgo Gem
Steal: [a] -, [b] Screamroot, [a] Tomato Stalk, [b] Virgo Gem, [a] -, [b] Jade Gown
Poach: [a]-, [b]Screamroot, [a]-, [b]Tomato Stalk

Mirrorknight

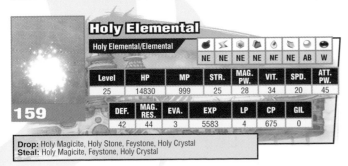

Fiend/Urstrix

1/2	1/2	1/2	W	1/2	1/2	1/2	1/2

Level	HP	MP	STR.	MAG. PW.	VIT.	SPD.	ATT. PW.
40-42	5202-5842	760-820	31-37	18	45-47	20-24	58-62

DEF.	MAG. RES.	EVA.	EXP	LP	CP	GIL
26-28	25-29	4	2419-2767	1	328-782	0

158

Drop: Windslicer Pinion, Wind Crystal, Mirror Mail, Aries Gem
Steal: Wind Crystal, X-Potion, Aries Gem
Poach: Windslicer Pinion, Mirror Scale

Holy Elemental

Holy Elemental/Elemental

NE	NE	NE	NE	NF	NE	AB	W

Level	HP	MP	STR.	MAG. PW.	VIT.	SPD.	ATT. PW.
25	14830	999	25	28	34	20	45

DEF.	MAG. RES.	EVA.	EXP	LP	CP	GIL
42	44	3	5583	4	675	0

159

Drop: Holy Magicite, Holy Stone, Feystone, Holy Crystal
Steal: Holy Magicite, Feystone, Holy Crystal

Tartarus

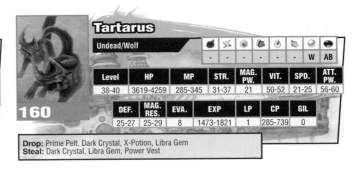

Undead/Wolf

-							W	AB

Level	HP	MP	STR.	MAG. PW.	VIT.	SPD.	ATT. PW.
38-40	3619-4259	285-345	31-37	21	50-52	21-25	56-60

DEF.	MAG. RES.	EVA.	EXP	LP	CP	GIL
25-27	25-29	8	1473-1821	1	285-739	0

160

Drop: Prime Pelt, Dark Crystal, X-Potion, Libra Gem
Steal: Dark Crystal, Libra Gem, Power Vest

The Ancient City of Giruvegan

Ose

Beast/Coeurl

-						W		-

Level	HP	MP	STR.	MAG. PW.	VIT.	SPD.	ATT. PW.
44-45	3739-7059	999	34-37	23	50-51	40-42	63-65

DEF.	MAG. RES.	EVA.	EXP	LP	CP	GIL
25-26	34-36	7	1887-2061	1	330-557	0

161

Drop: Prime Pelt, Dark Crystal, Morning Star, Libra Gem
Steal: Chronos Tear, Prime Pelt, Libra Gem
Poach: Prime Pelt, Coeurl Whisker

Shadonir

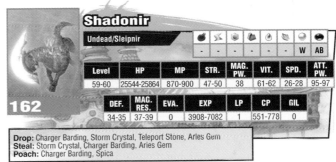

Undead/Sleipnir

-							W	AB

Level	HP	MP	STR.	MAG. PW.	VIT.	SPD.	ATT. PW.
59-60	25544-25864	870-900	47-50	38	61-62	26-28	95-97

DEF.	MAG. RES.	EVA.	EXP	LP	CP	GIL
34-35	37-39	0	3908-7082	1	551-778	0

162

Drop: Charger Barding, Storm Crystal, Teleport Stone, Arles Gem
Steal: Storm Crystal, Charger Barding, Aries Gem
Poach: Charger Barding, Spica

Giruveganus

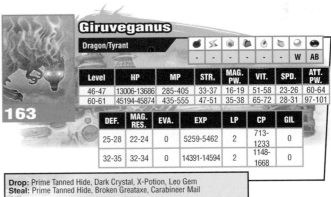

Dragon/Tyrant

-							W	AB

Level	HP	MP	STR.	MAG. PW.	VIT.	SPD.	ATT. PW.
46-47	13006-13686	285-405	33-37	16-19	51-58	23-26	60-64
60-61	45194-45874	435-555	47-51	35-38	65-72	28-31	97-101

DEF.	MAG. RES.	EVA.	EXP	LP	CP	GIL
25-28	22-24	0	5259-5462	2	713-1233	0
32-35	32-34	0	14391-14594	2	1148-1668	0

163

Drop: Prime Tanned Hide, Dark Crystal, X-Potion, Leo Gem
Steal: Prime Tanned Hide, Broken Greataxe, Carabineer Mail

Skulwyrm

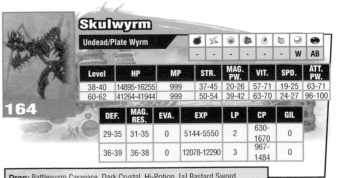

Undead/Plate Wyrm

-							W	AB

Level	HP	MP	STR.	MAG. PW.	VIT.	SPD.	ATT. PW.
38-40	14895-16255	999	37-45	20-26	57-71	19-25	63-71
60-62	41264-41944	999	50-54	39-42	63-70	24-27	96-100

DEF.	MAG. RES.	EVA.	EXP	LP	CP	GIL
29-35	31-35	0	5144-5550	2	630-1670	0
36-39	36-38	0	12078-12290	3	967-1484	0

164

Drop: Battlewyrm Carapace, Dark Crystal, Hi-Potion, [a] Bastard Sword, [b] Charger Barding
Steal: Dark Crystal, [a] Charger Barding, Wyrm Bone, [b]Bastard Sword

Vivian

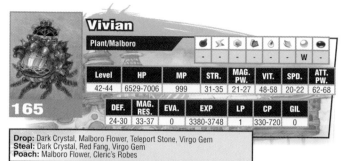

165 — Plant/Malboro

Level	HP	MP	STR	MAG. PW.	VIT.	SPD.	ATT. PW.
42-44	6529-7006	999	31-35	21-27	48-58	20-22	62-68

DEF.	MAG. RES.	EVA.	EXP	LP	CP	GIL
24-30	33-37	0	3380-3748	1	330-720	0

Drop: Dark Crystal, Malboro Flower, Teleport Stone, Virgo Gem
Steal: Dark Crystal, Red Fang, Virgo Gem
Poach: Malboro Flower, Cleric's Robes

Forbidden

166 — Undead/Zombie

Level	HP	MP	STR	MAG. PW.	VIT.	SPD.	ATT. PW.
58-59	17684-17864	999	45-47	40-42	53	25	94-97
58-60	17684-18044	999	45-49	40-44	53	25	94-100

DEF.	MAG. RES.	EVA.	EXP	LP	CP	GIL
21-23	35-36	0	6347-6507	1	482-625	0
32-36	35-37	0	6347-6667	1	482-768	0

Drop: Dark Crystal, Echo Herbs, Forbidden Flesh, Capricorn Gem
Steal: Remedy, X-Potion, Kaiser Shield

Gargoyle Baron

167 — Fiend/Gargoyle

Level	HP	MP	STR	MAG. PW.	VIT.	SPD.	ATT. PW.
42-43	6071-6231	999	32-34	22-25	45	21-22	61-63

DEF.	MAG. RES.	EVA.	EXP	LP	CP	GIL
27-28	32-36	7-9	2817-2993	1	345-546	0

Drop: Dark Crystal, Demon Tail, Doom Mace, Scorpio Gem
Steal: Demon Tail, Dark Crystal, X-Potion
Poach: Demon Tail, Scorpio Gem

Reaper

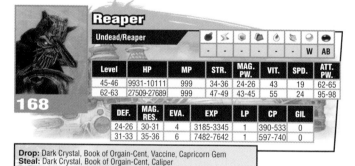

168 — Undead/Reaper

Level	HP	MP	STR	MAG. PW.	VIT.	SPD.	ATT. PW.
45-46	9931-10111	999	34-36	24-26	43	19	62-65
62-63	27509-27689	999	47-49	43-45	55	24	95-98

DEF.	MAG. RES.	EVA.	EXP	LP	CP	GIL
24-26	30-31	4	3185-3345	1	390-533	0
31-33	35-36	6	7482-7642	1	597-740	0

Drop: Dark Crystal, Book of Orgain-Cent, Vaccine, Capricorn Gem
Steal: Dark Crystal, Book of Orgain-Cent, Caliper

Mom Bomb

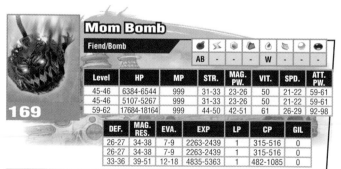

169 — Fiend/Bomb

Level	HP	MP	STR	MAG. PW.	VIT.	SPD.	ATT. PW.
45-46	6384-6544	999	31-33	23-26	50	21-22	59-61
45-46	5107-5267	999	31-33	23-26	50	21-22	59-61
59-62	17684-18164	999	44-50	42-51	61	26-29	92-98

DEF.	MAG. RES.	EVA.	EXP	LP	CP	GIL
26-27	34-38	7-9	2263-2439	1	315-516	0
26-27	34-38	7-9	2263-2439	1	315-516	0
33-36	39-51	12-18	4835-5363	1	482-1085	0

Drop: Bomb Shell, Fire Crystal, Diamond Armlet, Scorpio Gem
Steal: Bomb Shell, Red Fang, Scorpio Gem
Poach: Bomb Shell, Scorpio Gem

Mythril Golem

170 — Construct/Golem

Level	HP	MP	STR	MAG. PW.	VIT.	SPD.	ATT. PW.
43-44	17733-17973	999	34-36	25-27	41	18-19	63-66
45-48	17733-18453	999	34-40	25-31	41	18-21	63-72

DEF.	MAG. RES.	EVA.	EXP	LP	CP	GIL
29-32	32-34	0	3430-3678	2	420-615	0
29-38	32-38	0	3430-4174	2	420-1005	0

Drop: Iron Ore, Fire Crystal, Gaia Gear, Aquaries Gem
Steal: Iron Ore, Fire Crystal, Mythril

Necrophobe

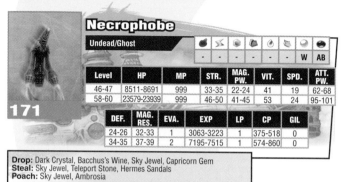

171 — Undead/Ghost

Level	HP	MP	STR	MAG. PW.	VIT.	SPD.	ATT. PW.
46-47	8511-8691	999	33-35	22-24	41	19	62-68
58-60	23579-23939	999	46-50	41-45	53	24	95-101

DEF.	MAG. RES.	EVA.	EXP	LP	CP	GIL
24-26	32-33	1	3063-3223	1	375-518	0
34-35	37-39	2	7195-7515	1	574-860	0

Drop: Dark Crystal, Bacchus's Wine, Sky Jewel, Capricorn Gem
Steal: Sky Jewel, Teleport Stone, Hermes Sandals
Poach: Sky Jewel, Ambrosia

Daikon Entite

172 — Daikon Entite/Elemental

Level	HP	MP	STR	MAG. PW.	VIT.	SPD.	ATT. PW.
25	48042	999	30	33	38	25	66

DEF.	MAG. RES.	EVA.	EXP	LP	CP	GIL
48	52	2	12627	7	1320	0

Drop: Holy Crystal, Feystone, Diakon Halcyon, Ether
Steal: Holy Crystal, Feystone, Diakon Halcyon

The Ridorana Cataract

Deathclaw

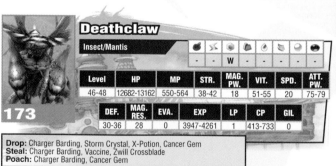

173 — Insect/Mantis

Level	HP	MP	STR	MAG. PW.	VIT.	SPD.	ATT. PW.
46-48	12682-13162	550-564	38-42	18	51-55	20	75-79

DEF.	MAG. RES.	EVA.	EXP	LP	CP	GIL
30-36	28	0	3947-4261	1	413-733	0

Drop: Charger Barding, Storm Crystal, X-Potion, Cancer Gem
Steal: Charger Barding, Vaccine, Zwill Crossblade
Poach: Charger Barding, Cancer Gem

Cassie

174 — Plant/Malboro

Level	HP	MP	STR	MAG. PW.	VIT.	SPD.	ATT. PW.
46-47	8840-9080	999	34-36	23-26	50-55	21-22	73-76

DEF.	MAG. RES.	EVA.	EXP	LP	CP	GIL
26-29	34-36	0	4357-4541	1	363-558	0

Drop: Earth Crystal, Bacchus's Wine, Malboro Flower, Virgo Gem
Steal: Malboro Flower, Virgo Gem, Chaperon
Poach: Malboro Flower, Ketu Board

The Pharos

Abaddon

175-A — Beast/Toad

Level	HP	MP	STR.	MAG. PW.	VIT.	SPD.	ATT. PW.
47-49	13239-13879	999	37-43	25	51-53	20-24	76-80
55-56	16578-16898	999	46-49	39	59-60	22-24	91-93

DEF.	MAG. RES.	EVA.	EXP	LP	CP	GIL
30-32	33-37	4	4615-4963	1	432-686	0
32-33	35-37	5	5221-5395	1	476-703	0

Drop: Dark Crystal, Vaccine, Solid Horn, Aries Gem
Steal: Solid Horn, Teleport Stone, Aries Gem
Poach: Solid Horn, Rubber Suit

Bull Abaddon

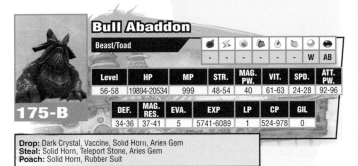

175-B — Beast/Toad

Level	HP	MP	STR.	MAG. PW.	VIT.	SPD.	ATT. PW.
56-58	19894-20534	999	48-54	40	61-63	24-28	92-96

DEF.	MAG. RES.	EVA.	EXP	LP	CP	GIL
34-36	37-41	5	5741-6089	1	524-978	0

Drop: Dark Crystal, Vaccine, Solid Horn, Aries Gem
Steal: Solid Horn, Teleport Stone, Aries Gem
Poach: Solid Horn, Rubber Suit

Chimera Brain

176 — Fiend/Cockatrice

Level	HP	MP	STR.	MAG. PW.	VIT.	SPD.	ATT. PW.
45-46	9992-10112	999	35-37	25	45-47	23-26	72-74

DEF.	MAG. RES.	EVA.	EXP	LP	CP	GIL
26-28	34-35	8-11	2917-3088	1	363-450	0

Drop: Dark Crystal, Hi-Potion, Windslicer Pinion, Taurus Gem
Steal: 60 Gil, Taurus Gem, Celebrant's Miter
Poach: Windslicer Pinion, Chimera Head

Bune

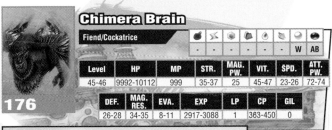

177 — Giant/Headless

Level	HP	MP	STR.	MAG. PW.	VIT.	SPD.	ATT. PW.
48-49	13239-13659	600-605	38-40	20-22	45-47	21	78-81
58-59	16578-16998	650-655	47-49	34-36	53-55	23	93-96

DEF.	MAG. RES.	EVA.	EXP	LP	CP	GIL
30-32	30	0	4615-4778	1	432-708	0
32-34	32	0	5221-5384	1	476-752	0

Drop: Fire Crystal, Forbidden Flesh, Gungnir, Gemini Gem
Steal: Gold Needle, Forbidden Flesh, Gemini Gem
Poach: Forbidden Flesh, Damascus Steel

Magick Pot

178 — Fiend/???

Level	HP	MP	STR.	MAG. PW.	VIT.	SPD.	ATT. PW.
60	30000	999	99	99	21	22	120

DEF.	MAG. RES.	EVA.	EXP	LP	CP	GIL
255	255	10	1	123	1	0

Drop: Ether, Megalixir
Steal: Elixir

Reaver

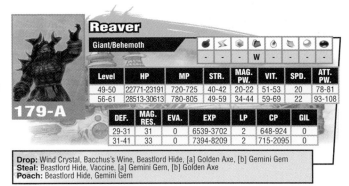

179-A — Giant/Behemoth

Level	HP	MP	STR.	MAG. PW.	VIT.	SPD.	ATT. PW.
49-50	22771-23191	720-725	40-42	20-22	51-53	20	78-81
56-61	28513-30613	780-805	49-59	34-44	59-69	22	93-108

DEF.	MAG. RES.	EVA.	EXP	LP	CP	GIL
29-31	31	0	6539-3702	2	648-924	0
31-41	33	0	7394-8209	2	715-2095	0

Drop: Wind Crystal, Bacchus's Wine, Beastlord Hide, [a] Golden Axe, [b] Gemini Gem
Steal: Beastlord Hide, Vaccine, [a] Gemini Gem, [b] Golden Axe
Poach: Beastlord Hide, Gemini Gem

High Reaver

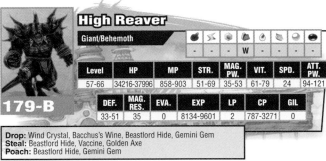

179-B — Giant/Behemoth

Level	HP	MP	STR.	MAG. PW.	VIT.	SPD.	ATT. PW.
57-66	34216-37996	858-903	51-69	35-53	61-79	24	94-121

DEF.	MAG. RES.	EVA.	EXP	LP	CP	GIL
33-51	35	0	8134-9601	2	787-3271	0

Drop: Wind Crystal, Bacchus's Wine, Beastlord Hide, Gemini Gem
Steal: Beastlord Hide, Vaccine, Golden Axe
Poach: Beastlord Hide, Gemini Gem

Crusader

180 — Undead/Skeleton

Level	HP	MP	STR.	MAG. PW.	VIT.	SPD.	ATT. PW.
47-48	10592-10772	999	37-39	23-25	45	23	75-78
44-45	10592-10772	999	37-39	23-25	50	23	75-78

DEF.	MAG. RES.	EVA.	EXP	LP	CP	GIL
28-30	30-31	8	4868-2028	1	396-539	0
28-30	30-31	8	4636-4796	1	396-539	0

Drop: [a] Blood-darkened Bone, [b] Sturdy Bone, Dark Crystal, Crown of Laurels, Capricorn Gem
Steal: [a] Blood-darkened Bone, [b] Sturdy Bone, [a] X-Potion, [b] Capricorn Gem, [a] Capricorn Gem [b] X-Potion

Aeronite

181 — Dragon/Wyvern

Level	HP	MP	STR.	MAG. PW.	VIT.	SPD.	ATT. PW.
59-60	27838-28518	999	46-50	41-44	65-72	25-28	94-98
49-50	18004-18684	999	37-41	26-29	55-62	22-25	77-81

DEF.	MAG. RES.	EVA.	EXP	LP	CP	GIL
29-32	33-35	0	8222-8424	2	701-1221	0
26-29	30-32	0	6156-6359	2	576-1096	0

Drop: Wyvern Fang, Ice Crystal, Dragon Helm, Leo Gem
Steal: Wyvern Fang, Hi-Potion, Leo Gem
Poach: Wyvern Fang, Wyvern Wing

Dragon Lich

182 — Undead/Plate Wyrm

Level	HP	MP	STR.	MAG. PW.	VIT.	SPD.	ATT. PW.
49-51	22241-23601	999	41-49	23-29	53-67	20-26	78-86
59-64	27851-31251	999	50-70	37-52	61-96	22-37	93-113

DEF.	MAG. RES.	EVA.	EXP	LP	CP	GIL
32-38	32-36	0	8078-8484	2	756-1796	0
34-49	34-44	0	9134-10149	2	834-3434	0

Drop: Dark Crystal, Hi-Potion, Charger Barding, Hastega Mote
Steal: Charger Barding, X-Potion, Corpse Fly

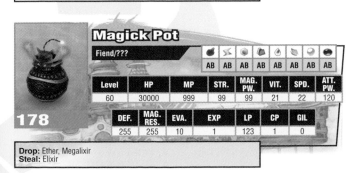

Bestiary

Cataract Aevis

183 — Avion/Diver

Elements: - | W | - | - | - | - | - | -

Level	HP	MP	STR.	MAG. PW.	VIT.	SPD.	ATT. PW.
50-51	23241-23921	999	42-46	23-26	53-60	20-23	77-81

DEF.	MAG. RES.	EVA.	EXP	LP	CP	GIL
33-36	30-32	0	8078-8281	2	756-1276	0

Drop: Charger Barding, Ice Crystal, Holy Mote, Caldera
Steal: Charger Barding, 50 Gil, Leo Gem
Poach: Charger Barding, Leo Gem

Brainpan

184 — Construct/Facer

Elements: - | - | - | - | - | - | W | -

Level	HP	MP	STR.	MAG. PW.	VIT.	SPD.	ATT. PW.
46	15358	840	36	26	63	20	77

DEF.	MAG. RES.	EVA.	EXP	LP	CP	GIL
30	31	0	3574	1	407	0

Drop: Quality Stone, Dark Crystal, Smelling Salts, Aquarius Gem
Steal: Dark Crystal, Chronos Tear, X-Potion
Poach: Quality Stone, Magepower Shishak

Purobolos

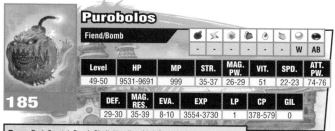

185 — Fiend/Bomb

Elements: - | - | - | - | - | - | W | AB

Level	HP	MP	STR.	MAG. PW.	VIT.	SPD.	ATT. PW.
49-50	9531-9691	999	35-37	26-29	51	22-23	74-76

DEF.	MAG. RES.	EVA.	EXP	LP	CP	GIL
29-30	35-39	8-10	3554-3730	1	378-579	0

Drop: Dark Crystal, Bomb Shell, Handkerchief, Scorpio Gem
Steal: Bomb Shell, Dark Crystal, Scathe Mote
Poach: Bomb Shell, Mallet

Deidar

186 — Construct/Facer

Elements: - | - | - | - | - | - | W | -

Level	HP	MP	STR.	MAG. PW.	VIT.	SPD.	ATT. PW.
46	15358	840	34	26	63	20	75

DEF.	MAG. RES.	EVA.	EXP	LP	CP	GIL
35	36	0	3574	1	407	0

Drop: Quality Stone, Dark Crystal, Antares, Aquarius Gem
Steal: Dark Crystal, Quality Stone, Aquarius Gem
Poach: Quality Stone, Orichalcum

Mistmare

187 — Fiend/Nightmare

Elements: W | - | - | - | - | - | - | -

Level	HP	MP	STR.	MAG. PW.	VIT.	SPD.	ATT. PW.
45-47	12180-12500	999	37-41	25-31	45	21-23	75-79
54-56	15251-15571	999	46-50	39-45	53	23-25	90-94

DEF.	MAG. RES.	EVA.	EXP	LP	CP	GIL
28-30	34-42	5-9	4615-4967	1	432-834	0
30-32	36-44	6-10	5221-5573	1	476-878	0

Drop: Water Crystal, Chronos Tear, Grimoire Aidhed, Scorpio Gem
Steal: Grimoire Aidhed, Water Crystal, Reflectga Mote
Poach: Grimoire Aidhed, Black Robes

Undin Entite

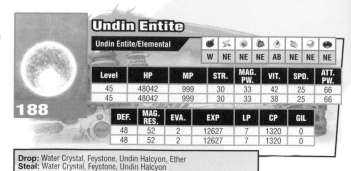

188 — Undin Entite/Elemental

Elements: W | NE | NE | NE | AB | NE | NE | NE

Level	HP	MP	STR.	MAG. PW.	VIT.	SPD.	ATT. PW.
45	48042	999	30	33	42	25	66
45	48042	999	30	33	38	25	66

DEF.	MAG. RES.	EVA.	EXP	LP	CP	GIL
48	52	2	12627	7	1320	0
48	52	2	12627	7	1320	0

Drop: Water Crystal, Feystone, Undin Halcyon, Ether
Steal: Water Crystal, Feystone, Undin Halcyon

Zertinan Caverns

Speartongue

189 — Beast/Toad

Elements: W | - | - | - | - | - | - | -

Level	HP	MP	STR.	MAG. PW.	VIT.	SPD.	ATT. PW.
16-17	1508-1828	390-420	21-24	14	34-35	14-16	23-25
16-17	1792-2112	540-570	23-26	15	29-30	13-15	23-25
11-13	1098-1738	325-385	17-23	14	29-31	13-17	21-25

DEF.	MAG. RES.	EVA.	EXP	LP	CP	GIL
13-14	11-13	2	375-849	1	108-335	0
24-25	5-7	0	675-849	1	108-335	0
11-13	10-14	2	511-859	1	90-544	0

Drop: Water Stone, Horn, Teleport Stone, Aries Gem
Steal: Water Stone, Horn, Potion
Poach: Horn, Frog Oil

Grenade

190 — Fiend/Bomb

Elements: AB | - | - | - | W | - | - | -

Level	HP	MP	STR.	MAG. PW.	VIT.	SPD.	ATT. PW.
35-38	4819-5299	999	30-36	22-31	53	20-23	51-57

DEF.	MAG. RES.	EVA.	EXP	LP	CP	GIL
23-26	28-40	6-12	2337-2862	1	268-871	0

Drop: Fire Crystal, Chronos Tear, Bomb Shell, Scorpio Gem
Steal: Fire Crystal, Scorpio Gem, Opal Ring
Poach: Bomb Shell, Bomb Fragment

Scythe Mantis

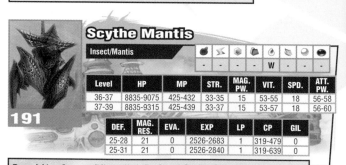

191 — Insect/Mantis

Elements: - | - | - | - | W | - | - | -

Level	HP	MP	STR.	MAG. PW.	VIT.	SPD.	ATT. PW.
36-37	8835-9075	425-432	33-35	15	53-55	18	56-58
37-39	8835-9315	425-439	33-37	15	53-57	18	56-60

DEF.	MAG. RES.	EVA.	EXP	LP	CP	GIL
25-28	21	0	2526-2683	1	319-479	0
25-31	21	0	2526-2840	1	319-639	0

Drop: [a] Iron Carapace, [b]Insect Husk, Fire Crystal, Smelling Salts, Kiku-ichimonji
Steal: Fire Crystal, [a] Iron Carapace, [b] Insect Husk, Cancer Gem
Poach: [a] Iron Carapace, [b] Insect Husk, Tattered Garment

Slime

192 — Amorph/Flan

Elements: - | - | - | - | W | - | AB | -

Level	HP	MP	STR.	MAG. PW.	VIT.	SPD.	ATT. PW.
15-17	1629-2089	540-680	22-24	15-19	29-33	13	22-26
15-17	1659-2119	390-530	22-24	14-18	34-38	14	24-8

DEF.	MAG. RES.	EVA.	EXP	LP	CP	GIL
24-32	5-11	0	675-1019	1	108-498	0
13-21	11-17	2	675-1019	1	108-498	0

Drop: Green Liquid, Wind Stone, Water Mote, Winged Helm
Steal: Green Liquid, Wind Stone, Sagittarius Gem
Poach: Pebble, Yellow Liquid

Archaeoaevis

Dragon/Wyvern

-	-	W	-	-	-	-	-

Level	HP	MP	STR.	MAG. PW.	VIT.	SPD.	ATT. PW.
38-40	11245-12605	850-999	36-44	19-25	55-69	18-24	55-63

DEF.	MAG. RES.	EVA.	EXP	LP	CP	GIL
26-32	25-29	0	4243-4649	2	539-1576	0

193

Drop: Battlewyrm Carapace, Storm Crystal, Cameo Belt, Leo Gem
Steal: Battlewyrm Carapace, Teleport Stone, Leo Gem
Poach: Battlewyrm Carapace, Emperor Scale

Bogey

Undead/Ghost

-	-	-	-	-	-	W	AB

Level	HP	MP	STR.	MAG. PW.	VIT.	SPD.	ATT. PW.
38-39	6426-6606	999	32-34	21-23	44	18	54-57

DEF.	MAG. RES.	EVA.	EXP	LP	CP	GIL
21*-23	26-27	1	2526-2686	1	319-462	0

194

Drop: Sky Jewel, Dark Crystal, Smelling Salts, Iga Blade
Steal: Gold Needle, Vanishga Mote, Capricorn Gem
Poach: Sky Jewel, Death Powder

Mallicant

Fiend/Nightmare

-	-	-	-	-	-	W	-

Level	HP	MP	STR.	MAG. PW.	VIT.	SPD.	ATT. PW.
37-38	6158-6318	999	32-34	21-24	46	19-20	52-54

DEF.	MAG. RES.	EVA.	EXP	LP	CP	GIL
22-23	27-31	4-6	2426-2602	1	306-507	0

195

Drop: Earth Crystal, Eye Drops, Grimoire Aidhed, Gaia Hat
Steal: Phoenix Down, Grimoire Aidhed, Scorpio Gem
Poach: Grimoire Aidhed, Magick Lamp

Shambling Corpse

Undead/Zombie

-	-	-	-	-	-	W	AB

Level	HP	MP	STR.	MAG. PW.	VIT.	SPD.	ATT. PW.
37-38	2892-3072	833-873	28-30	17-19	40	19	48-51

DEF.	MAG. RES.	EVA.	EXP	LP	CP	GIL
15-17	24-25	0	446-606	1	80-223	0

196

Drop: Dark Crystal, Foul Flesh, White Fang, Platinum Dagger
Steal: Foul Flesh, Dark Crystal, Blood-stained Necklace

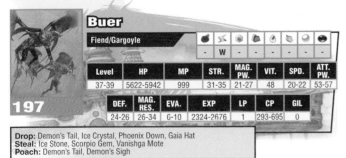

Buer

Fiend/Gargoyle

-	W	-	-	-	-	-	-

Level	HP	MP	STR.	MAG. PW.	VIT.	SPD.	ATT. PW.
37-39	5622-5942	999	31-35	21-27	48	20-22	53-57

DEF.	MAG. RES.	EVA.	EXP	LP	CP	GIL
24-26	26-34	6-10	2324-2676	1	293-695	0

197

Drop: Demon's Tail, Ice Crystal, Phoenix Down, Gaia Hat
Steal: Ice Stone, Scorpio Gem, Vanishga Mote
Poach: Demon's Tail, Demon's Sigh

Cerobi Steppe

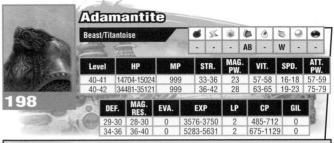

Adamantite

Beast/Titantoise

-	-	-	AB	-	W	-	-

Level	HP	MP	STR.	MAG. PW.	VIT.	SPD.	ATT. PW.
40-41	14704-15024	999	33-36	23	57-58	16-18	57-59
40-42	34481-35121	999	36-42	28	63-65	19-23	75-79

DEF.	MAG. RES.	EVA.	EXP	LP	CP	GIL
29-30	28-30	0	3576-3750	2	485-712	0
34-36	36-40	0	5283-5631	2	675-1129	0

198

Drop: [a] Turtle Shell, [b] Earth Crystal, [a] Water Stone, [b] Hi-Potion, [a] Phoenix Down, [b] Aged Turtle Shell, [a] Water Magicite, [b] Ancient Turtle Shell
Steal: [a] Water Stone, [b] 200 Gil, [a] Aries Gem, [b] Aged Turtle Shell, [a] Soldier's Cap, [b] Aries Gem
Poach: [a] Turtle Shell, [b] Aged Turtle Shell, [a] Smelling Salts, [b] Adamantite

Charybterix

Avion/Diver

-	-	-	W	-	-	-	-

Level	HP	MP	STR.	MAG. PW.	VIT.	SPD.	ATT. PW.
38-40	21219-21459	999	36-40	25	63-67	23-29	76-80

DEF.	MAG. RES.	EVA.	EXP	LP	CP	GIL
29-33	33-35	10-16	4505-4847	2	576-750	0

199

Drop: Wind Crystal, Antidote, Windslicer Pinion, Taurus Gem
Steal: Windslicer Pinion, Taurus Gem, Chaos Mace
Poach: Windslicer Pinion, Split Armor

Bandercoeurl

Beast/Coeurl

-	-	-	W	-	-	-	-

Level	HP	MP	STR.	MAG. PW.	VIT.	SPD.	ATT. PW.
39-40	5300-5620	999	30-33	22	53-54	22-24	53-55

DEF.	MAG. RES.	EVA.	EXP	LP	CP	GIL
23-24	28-30	7	1750-1924	1	297-524	0

200

Drop: Quality Pelt, Storm Crystal, Teleport Stone, Libra Gem
Steal: Storm Crystal, Phoenix Down, Prime Pelt
Poach: Quality Pelt, Zephyr Pole

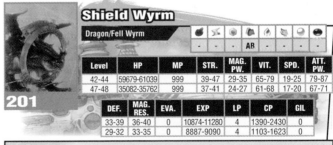

Shield Wyrm

Dragon/Fell Wyrm

-	-	-	AB	-	-	-	-

Level	HP	MP	STR.	MAG. PW.	VIT.	SPD.	ATT. PW.
42-44	59679-61039	999	39-47	29-35	65-79	19-25	79-87
47-48	35082-35762	999	37-41	24-27	61-68	17-20	67-71

DEF.	MAG. RES.	EVA.	EXP	LP	CP	GIL
33-39	36-40	0	10874-11280	4	1390-2430	0
29-32	33-35	0	8887-9090	4	1103-1623	0

201

Drop: [a] Ring Wyrm Scale, [b] Wyrm Carapace, Earth Crystal, Chronos Tear, [a] Leo Gem, [b] Ring Wyrm Scale
Steal: [a] Ring Wyrm Scale, [b] Wyrm Carapace, Hi-Potion, [a] Winged Boots, [b] Leo Gem
Poach: [a] Ring Wyrm Scale, [b] Wyrm Carapace, Ring Wyrm Liver

The Nabreus Deadlands

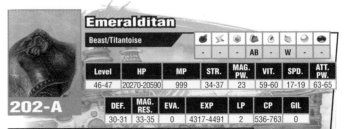

Emeralditan

Beast/Titantoise

-	-	-	AB	-	W	-	-

Level	HP	MP	STR.	MAG. PW.	VIT.	SPD.	ATT. PW.
46-47	20270-20590	999	34-37	23	59-60	17-19	63-65

DEF.	MAG. RES.	EVA.	EXP	LP	CP	GIL
30-31	33-35	0	4317-4491	2	536-763	0

202-A

Drop: Aged Turtle Shell, Earth Crystal, X-Potion, Aries Gem
Steal: Aged Turtle Shell, 800 Gil, Turtleshell Choker
Poach: Aged Turtle Shell, Scarletite

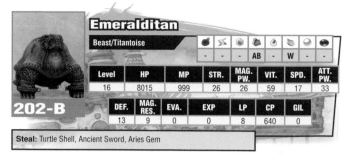

Emeralditan

Beast/Titantoise — #202-B

-	-	-	-	AB	-	W	-	-

Level	HP	MP	STR	MAG. PW.	VIT.	SPD.	ATT. PW.
16	8015	999	26	26	59	17	33

DEF.	MAG. RES.	EVA.	EXP	LP	CP	GIL
13	9	0	0	8	640	0

Steal: Turtle Shell, Ancient Sword, Aries Gem

#203

Undead/Sleipnir

-	-	-	-	-	-	W	AB

Level	HP	MP	STR	MAG. PW.	VIT.	SPD.	ATT. PW.
45-48	10135-11095	630-720	34-43	19	55-58	22-28	64-70

DEF.	MAG. RES.	EVA.	EXP	LP	CP	GIL
28-31	32-38	0	3047-3569	1	378-1059	0

Drop: Storm Crystal, Iron Carapace, Destrier Barding, Defender
Steal: Iron Carapace, Reflectga Mote, Aries Gem
Poach: Iron Carapace, Wargod's Band

Banshee

Undead/Zombie — #204

-	-	-	-	-	-	W	AB

Level	HP	MP	STR	MAG. PW.	VIT.	SPD.	ATT. PW.
44-46	7017-7377	999	32-36	21-25	46	21	63-69

DEF.	MAG. RES.	EVA.	EXP	LP	CP	GIL
17-21	30-32	0	1867-2187	1	331-617	0

Drop: Dark Crystal, Festering Flesh, X-Potion, Black Mask
Steal: Festering Flesh, Dark Crystal, Zombie Powder

Leamonde Entite

Leamonde Entite/Elemental — #205

NE	NE	NE	NE	NE	NE	W	AB

Level	HP	MP	STR	MAG. PW.	VIT.	SPD.	ATT. PW.
45	48042	999	30	33	42	25	66

DEF.	MAG. RES.	EVA.	EXP	LP	CP	GIL
48	52	2	12627	7	1320	0

Drop: Dark Crystal, Feystone, Leamonde Halcyon, Ether
Steal: Dark Crystal, Feystone, Leamonde Halcyon

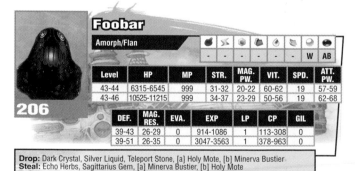

Foobar

Amorph/Flan — #206

-	-	-	-	-	-	W	AB

Level	HP	MP	STR	MAG. PW.	VIT.	SPD.	ATT. PW.
43-44	6315-6545	999	31-32	20-22	60-62	19	57-59
43-46	10525-11215	999	34-37	23-29	50-56	19	62-68

DEF.	MAG. RES.	EVA.	EXP	LP	CP	GIL
39-43	26-29	0	914-1086	1	113-308	0
39-51	26-35	0	3047-3563	1	378-963	0

Drop: Dark Crystal, Silver Liquid, Teleport Stone, [a] Holy Mote, [b] Minerva Bustier
Steal: Echo Herbs, Sagittarius Gem, [a] Minerva Bustier, [b] Holy Mote

The Necrohol of Nabudis

Oversoul

Undead/Reaper — #207

-	-	-	-	-	-	W	AB

Level	HP	MP	STR	MAG. PW.	VIT.	SPD.	ATT. PW.
47-49	20117-20477	2875-2955	59-63	37-41	48	18	75-81
47-49	13802-14162	2875-2955	37-41	26-30	50	20	75-81

DEF.	MAG. RES.	EVA.	EXP	LP	CP	GIL
28-32	29-31	4	3697-4017	1	449-735	0
26-30	31-33	4	4249-4569	1	449-735	0

Drop: Dark Crystal, Grimoire Togail, Teleport Stone, Cloud Staff
Steal: Dark Stone, Grimoire Togail, Capricorn Gem

Babil

Construct/Golem — #208

-	-	-	-	-	-	AB	W

Level	HP	MP	STR	MAG. PW.	VIT.	SPD.	ATT. PW.
47-48	24647-24887	2070-2130	37-39	24-26	48	19-20	76-79

DEF.	MAG. RES.	EVA.	EXP	LP	CP	GIL
31-34	33-35	0	4577-4825	2	483-678	0

Drop: Quality Stone, Holy Crystal, Runeblade, Holy Mote
Steal: Holy Stone, X-Potion, Einerjarium

Elvoret

Fiend/Gargoyle — #209

-	-	-	-	-	W	-	-

Level	HP	MP	STR	MAG. PW.	VIT.	SPD.	ATT. PW.
46-48	10351-10671	1725-2025	35-39	24-30	53	22-24	74-78

DEF.	MAG. RES.	EVA.	EXP	LP	CP	GIL
29-31	33-41	8-12	3760-4112	1	397-800	0

Drop: Demon Eyeball, Earth Crystal, Vaccine, Maxamillian
Steal: Demon Eyeball, 500 Gil, Reflectga Mote
Poach: Demon Eyeball, Demon Drink

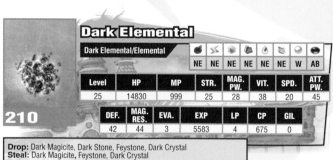

Dark Elemental

Dark Elemental/Elemental — #210

NE	NE	NE	NE	NE	NE	W	AB

Level	HP	MP	STR	MAG. PW.	VIT.	SPD.	ATT. PW.
25	14830	999	25	28	38	20	45

DEF.	MAG. RES.	EVA.	EXP	LP	CP	GIL
42	44	3	5583	4	675	0

Drop: Dark Magicite, Dark Stone, Feystone, Dark Crystal
Steal: Dark Magicite, Feystone, Dark Crystal

Zombie Warlock

Undead/Zombie — #211

-	-	-	-	-	-	W	AB

Level	HP	MP	STR	MAG. PW.	VIT.	SPD.	ATT. PW.
36-38	7625-7985	999	36-40	24-28	43	21	76-82
47-48	8875-9055	999	35-37	23-25	48	21	74-77
48-50	7598-7958	999	32-36	31-35	43	21	70-76
59-60	11935-12115	999	45-47	38-40	50	23	91-94

DEF.	MAG. RES.	EVA.	EXP	LP	CP	GIL
19-23	31-33	0	2693-3013	1	378-664	0
18-20	31-32	0	2403-2563	1	362-505	0
19-23	31-33	0	3838-4158	1	378-664	0
20-22	33-34	0	4584-4745	1	417-560	0

Drop: Dark Crystal, Forbidden Flesh, Alarm Clock, Capricorn Gem
Steal: Dark Crystal, 200 Gil, Capricorn Gem
Poach: Maggoty Flesh, Forbidden Flesh

Marks

Rogue Tomato

▶ Dalmasca Estersand, The Stepping

212

Deadly Nightshade

🔥	⚔	⬦	◈	💧	◗	○	⚡
-	-	-	-	W	-	-	-

Level	HP	MP	STR.	MAG. PW.	VIT.	SPD.	ATT. PW.
2	134	50	9	3	14	12	10

DEF.	MAG. RES.	EVA.	EXP	LP	CP	GIL
7	18	0	0	3	180	0

Rewards: 300 gil, Potion x2, Teleport Stone
Steal: Pebble, Fire Stone, Potion

Atomos
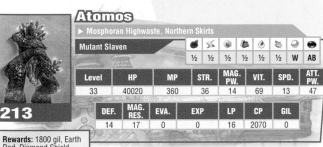
▶ Mosphoran Highwaste, Northern Skirts

213

Mutant Slaven

🔥	⚔	⬦	◈	💧	◗	○	⚡
½	½	½	½	½	½	W	AB

Level	HP	MP	STR.	MAG. PW.	VIT.	SPD.	ATT. PW.
33	40020	360	36	14	69	13	47

DEF.	MAG. RES.	EVA.	EXP	LP	CP	GIL
14	17	0	0	16	2070	0

Rewards: 1800 gil, Earth Rod, Diamond Shield
Steal: Potion, Tanned Giantskin, Gemini Gem

Thextera
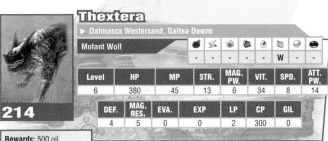
▶ Dalmasca Westersand, Galtea Downs

214

Mutant Wolf

🔥	⚔	⬦	◈	💧	◗	○	⚡
-	-	-	-	-	-	W	-

Level	HP	MP	STR.	MAG. PW.	VIT.	SPD.	ATT. PW.
6	380	45	13	9	34	8	14

DEF.	MAG. RES.	EVA.	EXP	LP	CP	GIL
4	5	0	0	2	300	0

Rewards: 500 gil, Headguard, Teleport Stone
Steal: Pebble, Potion, Wolf Pelt

Roblon
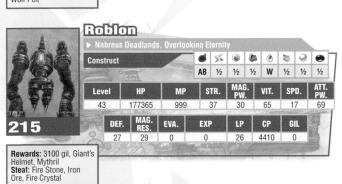
▶ Nabreus Deadlands, Overlooking Eternity

215

Construct

🔥	⚔	⬦	◈	💧	◗	○	⚡
AB	½	½	½	W	½	½	½

Level	HP	MP	STR.	MAG. PW.	VIT.	SPD.	ATT. PW.
43	177365	999	37	30	65	17	69

DEF.	MAG. RES.	EVA.	EXP	LP	CP	GIL
27	29	0	0	26	4410	0

Rewards: 3100 gil, Giant's Helmet, Mythril
Steal: Fire Stone, Iron Ore, Fire Crystal

Flowering Cactoid
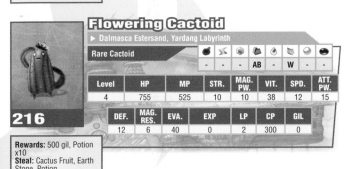
▶ Dalmasca Estersand, Yardang Labyrinth

216

Rare Cactoid

🔥	⚔	⬦	◈	💧	◗	○	⚡
-	-	-	-	AB	-	W	-

Level	HP	MP	STR.	MAG. PW.	VIT.	SPD.	ATT. PW.
4	755	525	10	10	38	12	15

DEF.	MAG. RES.	EVA.	EXP	LP	CP	GIL
12	6	40	0	2	300	0

Rewards: 500 gil, Potion x10
Steal: Cactus Fruit, Earth Stone, Potion

Braegh
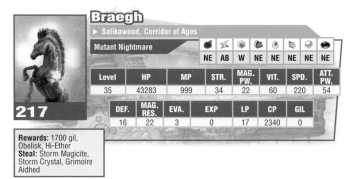
▶ Salikawood, Corridor of Ages

217

Mutant Nightmare

🔥	⚔	⬦	◈	💧	◗	○	⚡
NE	AB	W	NE	NE	NE	NE	NE

Level	HP	MP	STR.	MAG. PW.	VIT.	SPD.	ATT. PW.
35	43283	999	34	22	60	220	54

DEF.	MAG. RES.	EVA.	EXP	LP	CP	GIL
16	22	3	0	17	2340	0

Rewards: 1700 gil, Obelisk, Hi-Ether
Steal: Storm Magicite, Storm Crystal, Grimoire Aidhed

Wraith

▶ Garamsythe Waterway, Central Waterway Control

218

Ghost

🔥	⚔	⬦	◈	💧	◗	○	⚡
-	W	AB	-	-	-	-	-

Level	HP	MP	STR.	MAG. PW.	VIT.	SPD.	ATT. PW.
9	5146	600	18	13	33	15	20

DEF.	MAG. RES.	EVA.	EXP	LP	CP	GIL
7	10	1	0	5	750	0

Rewards: 500 gil, Gauntlets, Ether
Steal: Glass Jewel, Dark Magicite, Hi-Potion

Darksteel

▶ Sochen Cave Palace, Temptation Eluded

219

Titantoise

🔥	⚔	⬦	◈	💧	◗	○	⚡
½	½	½	½	½	½	W	AB

Level	HP	MP	STR.	MAG. PW.	VIT.	SPD.	ATT. PW.
38	111331	999	37	24	77	17	59

DEF.	MAG. RES.	EVA.	EXP	LP	CP	GIL
22	23	0	0	21	4080	0

Rewards: 3000 gil, Adamantite, Lead Bolts
Steal: Eye Drops, Aged Turtle Shell, Ancient Turtle Shell

Nidhogg

▶ Lhusu Mines, Transitway 1

220

Blue Basilisk

🔥	⚔	⬦	◈	💧	◗	○	⚡
W	½	½	½	AB	½	½	½

Level	HP	MP	STR.	MAG. PW.	VIT.	SPD.	ATT. PW.
10	6079	120	21	11	40	13	25

DEF.	MAG. RES.	EVA.	EXP	LP	CP	GIL
12	4	3	0	5	780	0

Rewards: 600 gil, Rose Corsage, Balaclava
Steal: Antidote, Tanned Hide, Aries Gem

Vyraal
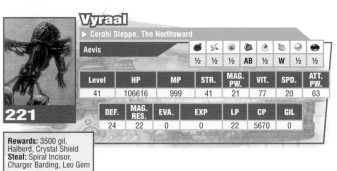
▶ Cerobi Steppe, The Northsward

221

Aevis

🔥	⚔	⬦	◈	💧	◗	○	⚡
½	½	½	AB	½	W	½	½

Level	HP	MP	STR.	MAG. PW.	VIT.	SPD.	ATT. PW.
41	106616	999	41	21	77	20	63

DEF.	MAG. RES.	EVA.	EXP	LP	CP	GIL
24	22	0	0	22	5670	0

Rewards: 3500 gil, Halberd, Crystal Shield
Steal: Spiral Incisor, Charger Barding, Leo Gem

White Mousse

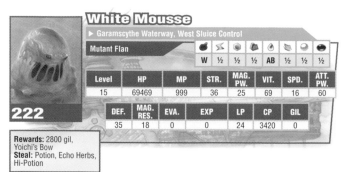

222

▶ Garamscythe Waterway, West Sluice Control

Mutant Flan

W	½	½	½	AB	½	½	½

Level	HP	MP	STR	MAG. PW.	VIT.	SPD.	ATT. PW.
15	69469	999	36	25	69	16	60

DEF.	MAG. RES.	EVA.	EXP	LP	CP	GIL
35	18	0	0	24	3420	0

Rewards: 2800 gil, Yoichi's Bow
Steal: Potion, Echo Herbs, Hi-Potion

Lindwyrm

223

▶ Tchita Uplands, Garden of Life's Circle

Dragon

-	-	-	-	AB	-	W	-

Level	HP	MP	STR	MAG. PW.	VIT.	SPD.	ATT. PW.
39	228468	999	39	25	82	14	62

DEF.	MAG. RES.	EVA.	EXP	LP	CP	GIL
23	24	0	0	22	9450	0

Rewards: 4200 gil, Barrel Coat, Hi-Ether
Steal: Pebble, Ring Wyrm Scale, Ring Wyrm Liver

Ring Wyrm

224

▶ Dalmasca Westersand, Windtrace Dunes

Lesser Dragon

W	½	½	½	AB	½	½	½

Level	HP	MP	STR	MAG. PW.	VIT.	SPD.	ATT. PW.
32	128648	999	38	22	74	11	49

DEF.	MAG. RES.	EVA.	EXP	LP	CP	GIL
18	22	0	0	16	6300	0

Rewards: 200 gil, Moon Ring, Icebrand
Steal: Phoenix Down, Hi-Potion, Water Magicite

Overlord

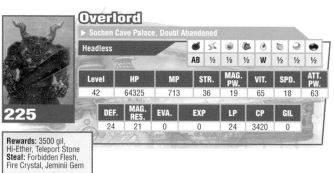

225

▶ Sochen Cave Palace, Doubt Abandoned

Headless

AB	½	½	½	W	½	½	½

Level	HP	MP	STR	MAG. PW.	VIT.	SPD.	ATT. PW.
42	64325	713	36	19	65	18	63

DEF.	MAG. RES.	EVA.	EXP	LP	CP	GIL
24	21	0	0	24	3420	0

Rewards: 3500 gil, Hi-Ether, Teleport Stone
Steal: Forbidden Flesh, Fire Crystal, Jeminii Gem

Wyvern Lord

226

▶ Nam-Yensa Sandsea, Simoon Bluff

Greater Wyvern

-	-	-	-	W	-	AB	-

Level	HP	MP	STR	MAG. PW.	VIT.	SPD.	ATT. PW.
18	18669	720	24	17	55	14	28

DEF.	MAG. RES.	EVA.	EXP	LP	CP	GIL
6	5	0	0	8	1440	0

Rewards: 1000 gil, Longbow, Shell Shield
Steal: Yensa Scale, Crooked Fang, Wyvern Wing

Goliath

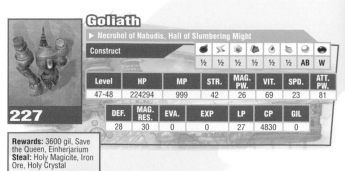

227

▶ Necrohol of Nabudis, Hall of Slumbering Might

Construct

½	½	½	½	½	½	AB	W

Level	HP	MP	STR	MAG. PW.	VIT.	SPD.	ATT. PW.
47-48	224294	999	42	26	69	23	81

DEF.	MAG. RES.	EVA.	EXP	LP	CP	GIL
28	30	0	0	27	4830	0

Rewards: 3600 gil, Save the Queen, Einherjarium
Steal: Holy Magicite, Iron Ore, Holy Crystal

Marilith

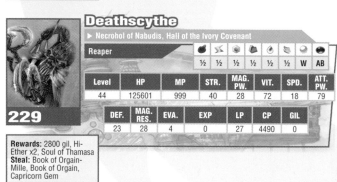

228

▶ Zertinan Caverns, Invitation to Heresy

Crimson Serpent

AB	NE	NE	NE	W	NE	NE	NE

Level	HP	MP	STR	MAG. PW.	VIT.	SPD.	ATT. PW.
38	54921	540	35	19	74	20	58

DEF.	MAG. RES.	EVA.	EXP	LP	CP	GIL
21	21	7	0	22	3510	0

Rewards: 2200 gil, Serpent Eye, Teleport Stone x3
Steal: Fire Stone, Prime Tanned Hide, Fire Crystal

Deathscythe

229

▶ Necrohol of Nabudis, Hall of the Ivory Covenant

Reaper

½	½	½	½	½	½	W	AB

Level	HP	MP	STR	MAG. PW.	VIT.	SPD.	ATT. PW.
44	125601	999	40	28	72	18	79

DEF.	MAG. RES.	EVA.	EXP	LP	CP	GIL
23	28	4	0	27	4490	0

Rewards: 2800 gil, Hi-Ether x2, Soul of Thamasa
Steal: Book of Orgain-Mille, Book of Orgain, Capricorn Gem

Enkelados

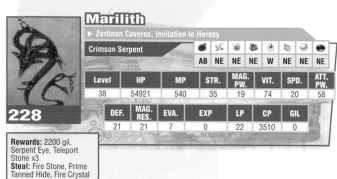

230

▶ Ozmone Plain, The Shred

Slaven

½	½	½	AB	W	½	½	-

Level	HP	MP	STR	MAG. PW.	VIT.	SPD.	ATT. PW.
22	18709	210	27	12	55	12	34

DEF.	MAG. RES.	EVA.	EXP	LP	CP	GIL
12	8	0	0	9	1210	0

Rewards: 1100 gil, Ether, Golden Amulet
Steal: Potion, Earth Magicite, Slaven Harness

Deathgaze

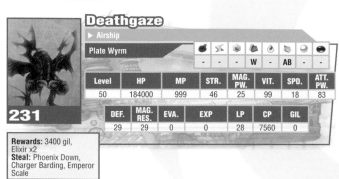

231

▶ Airship

Plate Wyrm

-	-	-	W	-	AB	-	-

Level	HP	MP	STR	MAG. PW.	VIT.	SPD.	ATT. PW.
50	184000	999	46	25	99	18	83

DEF.	MAG. RES.	EVA.	EXP	LP	CP	GIL
29	29	0	0	28	7560	0

Rewards: 3400 gil, Elixir x2
Steal: Phoenix Down, Charger Barding, Emperor Scale

Croakadile

▶ Giza Plains, Starfall Field

Mutant Lizard

W	½	½	½	AB	½	½	½

Level	HP	MP	STR.	MAG. PW.	VIT.	SPD.	ATT. PW.
24	19449	780	29	18	57	13	35

DEF.	MAG. RES.	EVA.	EXP	LP	CP	GIL
13	13	2	0	10	1440	0

232

Rewards: 1200 gil, Snake Rod, Teleport Stone
Steal: Horn, Pointed Horn, Aries Gem

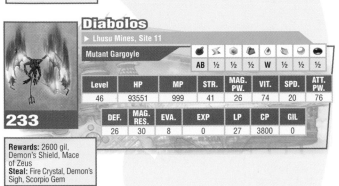

Diabolos

▶ Lhusu Mines, Site 11

Mutant Gargoyle

AB	½	½	½	W	½	½	½

Level	HP	MP	STR.	MAG. PW.	VIT.	SPD.	ATT. PW.
46	93551	999	41	26	74	20	76

DEF.	MAG. RES.	EVA.	EXP	LP	CP	GIL
26	30	8	0	27	3800	0

233

Rewards: 2600 gil, Demon's Shield, Mace of Zeus
Steal: Fire Crystal, Demon's Sigh, Scorpio Gem

Ixtab

▶ Henne Mines, Phase 1 - Shaft

Undead

-	-	-	-	-	-	W	AB

Level	HP	MP	STR.	MAG. PW.	VIT.	SPD.	ATT. PW.
24	22562	999	31	21	49	13	39

DEF.	MAG. RES.	EVA.	EXP	LP	CP	GIL
11	11	2	0	12	1700	0

234

Rewards: 1300 gil, Ether, Soul Powder
Steal: Dark Crystal, Book of Orgain-Mille, Flame Shield

Piscodaemon

▶ Giruvegan, Gate of Fire

???

½	½	½	½	½	½	½	½

Level	HP	MP	STR.	MAG. PW.	VIT.	SPD.	ATT. PW.
46	49660	999	33	27	61	22	64

DEF.	MAG. RES.	EVA.	EXP	LP	CP	GIL
21	33	5	0	26	4730	0

235

Rewards: 3800 gil, Dark Shot, Scathe Mote
Steal: Potion, Reflectga Mote, White Robe

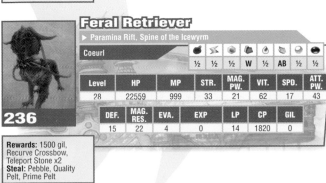

Feral Retriever

▶ Paramina Rift, Spine of the Icewyrm

Coeurl

½	½	½	W	½	AB	½	½

Level	HP	MP	STR.	MAG. PW.	VIT.	SPD.	ATT. PW.
28	22559	999	33	21	62	17	43

DEF.	MAG. RES.	EVA.	EXP	LP	CP	GIL
15	22	4	0	14	1820	0

236

Rewards: 1500 gil, Recurve Crossbow, Teleport Stone x2
Steal: Pebble, Quality Pelt, Prime Pelt

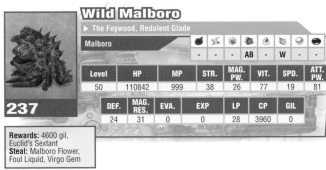

Wild Malboro

▶ The Feywood, Redolent Glade

Malboro

-	-	-	AB	-	W	-	-

Level	HP	MP	STR.	MAG. PW.	VIT.	SPD.	ATT. PW.
50	110842	999	38	26	77	19	81

DEF.	MAG. RES.	EVA.	EXP	LP	CP	GIL
24	31	0	0	28	3960	0

237

Rewards: 4600 gil, Euclid's Sextant
Steal: Malboro Flower, Foul Liquid, Virgo Gem

Vorpal Bunny

▶ Golmore Jungle, The Needlebreak

Dreamhare

½	½	½	½	½	½	W	AB

Level	HP	MP	STR.	MAG. PW.	VIT.	SPD.	ATT. PW.
31	20010	999	35	22	55	25	46

DEF.	MAG. RES.	EVA.	EXP	LP	CP	GIL
15	22	6	0	16	1440	0

238

Rewards: 2000 gil, Lightning Arrows, Gillie Boots
Steal: Drab Wool, Hi-Potion, Blood Wool

Catoblepas

▶ Zertinan Caverns, Hourglass Basin

Behemoth

½	½	½	½	½	½	AB	W

Level	HP	MP	STR.	MAG. PW.	VIT.	SPD.	ATT. PW.
46	187991	990	42	21	79	18	78

DEF.	MAG. RES.	EVA.	EXP	LP	CP	GIL
25	28	0	0	27	5940	0

239

Rewards: 3200 gil, Volcano, Antarctic Wind
Steal: Hi-Potion, Beastlord Hide, Gemini Gem

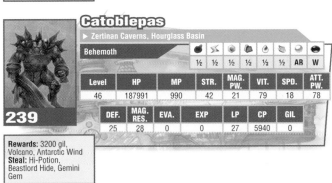

Mindflayer

▶ Henne Mines, Phase 1 - Dig

Mindflayer

½	½	½	½	½	½	½	½

Level	HP	MP	STR.	MAG. PW.	VIT.	SPD.	ATT. PW.
35	31161	999	32	26	74	19	49

DEF.	MAG. RES.	EVA.	EXP	LP	CP	GIL
15	26	4	0	18	3150	0

240

Rewards: 2200 gil, Carmagnole
Steal: Pebble, Float Mote, Vanishga Mote

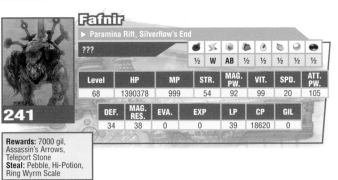

Fafnir

▶ Paramina Rift, Silverflow's End

???

½	W	AB	½	½	½	½	½

Level	HP	MP	STR.	MAG. PW.	VIT.	SPD.	ATT. PW.
68	1390378	999	54	92	99	20	105

DEF.	MAG. RES.	EVA.	EXP	LP	CP	GIL
34	38	0	0	39	18620	0

241

Rewards: 7000 gil, Assassin's Arrows, Teleport Stone
Steal: Pebble, Hi-Potion, Ring Wyrm Scale

Bestiary

Bloodwing

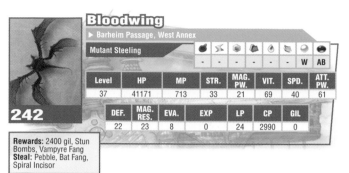

▶ Barheim Passage, West Annex

Mutant Steeling

						W	AB
-	-	-	-	-	-	W	AB

Level	HP	MP	STR	MAG. PW.	VIT.	SPD.	ATT. PW.
37	41171	713	33	21	69	40	61

DEF.	MAG. RES.	EVA.	EXP	LP	CP	GIL
22	23	8	0	24	2990	0

242

Rewards: 2400 gil, Stun Bombs, Vampyre Fang
Steal: Pebble, Bat Fang, Spiral Incisor

Pylraster

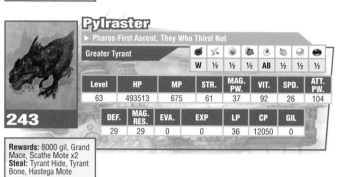

▶ Pharos-First Ascent, They Who Thirst Not

Greater Tyrant

W	½	½	½	AB	½	½	½

Level	HP	MP	STR	MAG. PW.	VIT.	SPD.	ATT. PW.
63	493513	675	61	37	92	26	104

DEF.	MAG. RES.	EVA.	EXP	LP	CP	GIL
29	29	0	0	36	12050	0

243

Rewards: 8000 gil, Grand Mace, Scathe Mote x2
Steal: Tyrant Hide, Tyrant Bone, Hastega Mote

Elite Marks

Chickatrice

▶ Giza Plains, Gizas North Bank

				W	-	AB	-
-	-	-	-	W	-	AB	-

Level	HP	MP	STR	MAG. PW.	VIT.	SPD.	ATT. PW.
13	3067	338	15	10	30	12	17

DEF.	MAG. RES.	EVA.	EXP	LP	CP	GIL
1	7	3	0	1	500	0

244

Rewards: 1000 gil, Jackboots, Rainbow Egg
Steal: Potion, Small Feather, Large Feather

Cluckatrice

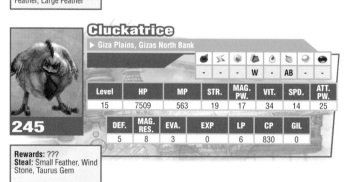

▶ Giza Plains, Gizas North Bank

				W	-	AB	-
-	-	-	-	W	-	AB	-

Level	HP	MP	STR	MAG. PW.	VIT.	SPD.	ATT. PW.
15	7509	563	19	17	34	14	25

DEF.	MAG. RES.	EVA.	EXP	LP	CP	GIL
5	8	3	0	6	830	0

245

Rewards: ???
Steal: Small Feather, Wind Stone, Taurus Gem

Rocktoise

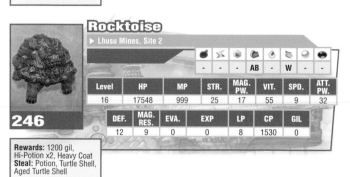

▶ Lhusu Mines. Site 2

-	-	-	AB	-	W	-	-

Level	HP	MP	STR	MAG. PW.	VIT.	SPD.	ATT. PW.
16	17548	999	25	17	55	9	32

DEF.	MAG. RES.	EVA.	EXP	LP	CP	GIL
12	9	0	0	8	1530	0

246

Rewards: 1200 gil, Hi-Potion x2, Heavy Coat
Steal: Potion, Turtle Shell, Aged Turtle Shell

Orthros

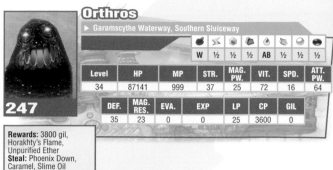

▶ Garamscythe Waterway, Southern Sluiceway

W	½	½	½	AB	½	½	½

Level	HP	MP	STR	MAG. PW.	VIT.	SPD.	ATT. PW.
34	87141	999	37	25	72	16	64

DEF.	MAG. RES.	EVA.	EXP	LP	CP	GIL
35	23	0	0	25	3600	0

247

Rewards: 3800 gil, Horakhty's Flame, Unpurified Ether
Steal: Phoenix Down, Caramel, Slime Oil

Gil Snapper

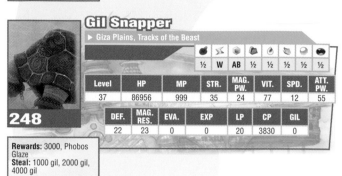

▶ Giza Plains, Tracks of the Beast

½	W	AB	½	½	½	½	½

Level	HP	MP	STR	MAG. PW.	VIT.	SPD.	ATT. PW.
37	86956	999	35	24	77	12	55

DEF.	MAG. RES.	EVA.	EXP	LP	CP	GIL
22	23	0	0	20	3830	0

248

Rewards: 3000, Phobos Glaze
Steal: 1000 gil, 2000 gil, 4000 gil

Trickster

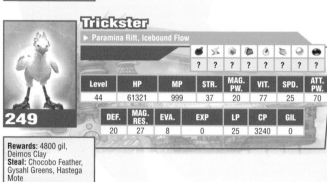

▶ Paramina Rift, Icebound Flow

?	?	?	?	?	?	?	?

Level	HP	MP	STR	MAG. PW.	VIT.	SPD.	ATT. PW.
44	61321	999	37	20	77	25	70

DEF.	MAG. RES.	EVA.	EXP	LP	CP	GIL
20	27	8	0	25	3240	0

249

Rewards: 4800 gil, Deimos Clay
Steal: Chocobo Feather, Gysahl Greens, Hastega Mote

Antlion

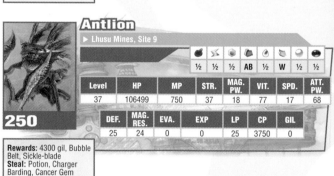

▶ Lhusu Mines, Site 9

½	½	½	AB	½	W	½	½

Level	HP	MP	STR	MAG. PW.	VIT.	SPD.	ATT. PW.
37	106499	750	37	18	77	17	68

DEF.	MAG. RES.	EVA.	EXP	LP	CP	GIL
25	24	0	0	25	3750	0

250

Rewards: 4300 gil, Bubble Belt, Sickle-blade
Steal: Potion, Charger Barding, Cancer Gem

Carrot

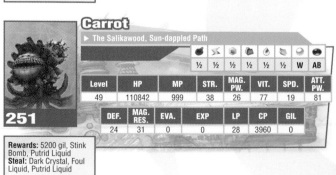

▶ The Salikawood, Sun-dappled Path

½	½	½	½	½	½	W	AB

Level	HP	MP	STR	MAG. PW.	VIT.	SPD.	ATT. PW.
49	110842	999	38	26	77	19	81

DEF.	MAG. RES.	EVA.	EXP	LP	CP	GIL
24	31	0	0	28	3960	0

251

Rewards: 5200 gil, Stink Bomb, Putrid Liquid
Steal: Dark Crystal, Foul Liquid, Putrid Liquid

Gilgamesh

▶ Lhusu Mines, Tasche Span

½	½	½	½	½	½	½	½

Level	HP	MP	STR.	MAG. PW.	VIT.	SPD.	ATT. PW.
45	123103	999	42	25	79	21	76
45	123103	999	44	25	79	21	78

DEF.	MAG. RES.	EVA.	EXP	LP	CP	GIL
26	30	6	0	5	3960	0
26	30	6	0	50	3960	0

252-A

Steal: St.1-Potion, 1000 gil; St.2-Potion, 2000 gil; St.3- Genji Shield; St.4-Genji Gauntlet

Gilgamesh, 2nd Encounter

▶ Lhusu Mines, Site 7

½	½	½	½	½	½	½	½

Level	HP	MP	STR.	MAG. PW.	VIT.	SPD.	ATT. PW.
70	473246	999	55	44	90	27	118
70	473246	999	56	44	90	27	120

DEF.	MAG. RES.	EVA.	EXP	LP	CP	GIL
36	38	10	0	10	6700	0
36	38	10	0	120	6700	0

252-B

Steal: St. 1-Hi-Potion, 3000 gil; St.2-Hi-Potion, 4000 gil; St.3-Genji Helm; St.4-Genji Armor
Rewards: 10000 gil, Masamune

Enkidu

▶ Lhusu Mines

-	-	-	-	-	-	-	-

Level	HP	MP	STR.	MAG. PW.	VIT.	SPD.	ATT. PW.
43	33052	429	38	24	82	21	74
65	140162	644	50	43	92	27	100

DEF.	MAG. RES.	EVA.	EXP	LP	CP	GIL
25	29	10	0	27	1650	0
35	37	17	0	43	2790	0

253

Steal: 1st-Woft Pelt, Beastlord Hide, Throat Wolf Blood; 2nd-Wolf Pelt, Beastlord Hide, Hell's-Gate Flame

Behemoth King

▶ The Feywood, The Edge of Reason

½	½	½	½	½	½	½	½

Level	HP	MP	STR.	MAG. PW.	VIT.	SPD.	ATT. PW.
70	1668491	999	55	47	99	21	107

DEF.	MAG. RES.	EVA.	EXP	LP	CP	GIL
35	39	0	0	10	19530	0

254

Rewards: 250 gil, Bacchus's Wine x2
Steal: Ring Wyrm Scale, Behemoth Steak, Elixir

Ixion

▶ Pharos-Subterra, Penumbra-Interior

½	½	½	½	½	½	W	AB

Level	HP	MP	STR.	MAG. PW.	VIT.	SPD.	ATT. PW.
58	306559	999	48	42	74	25	94
58	166559	999	48	42	74	22	94

DEF.	MAG. RES.	EVA.	EXP	LP	CP	GIL
10	34	7	0	32	5000	0
28	34	7	0	32	5000	0

255

Rewards: 3000 gil, Ragnarok
Steal: Storm Crystal, Grimoire Aidhed, Magick Lamp

Pandaemonium

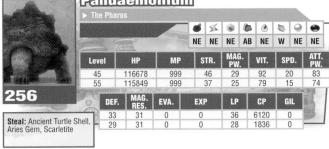

▶ The Pharos

NE	NE	NE	AB	NE	W	NE	NE

Level	HP	MP	STR.	MAG. PW.	VIT.	SPD.	ATT. PW.
45	116678	999	46	29	92	20	83
55	115849	999	37	25	79	15	74

DEF.	MAG. RES.	EVA.	EXP	LP	CP	GIL
33	31	0	0	36	6120	0
29	31	0	0	28	1836	0

256

Steal: Ancient Turtle Shell, Aries Gem, Scarletite

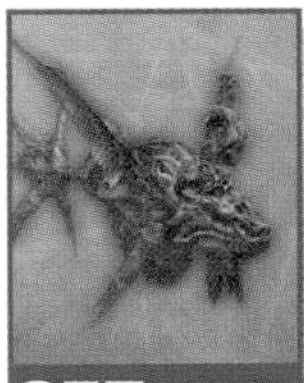

Slyt

▶ The Pharos

W	NE	NE	NE	AB	NE	NE	NE

Level	HP	MP	STR.	MAG. PW.	VIT.	SPD.	ATT. PW.
47	92661	999	45	23	92	25	84
55	66505	504	36	19	79	18	73

DEF.	MAG. RES.	EVA.	EXP	LP	CP	GIL
28	28	3	0	36	3780	0
28	28	4	0	28	1134	0

257

Steal: Yensa Scale, Pisces Gem, Yensa Fin

Fenrir

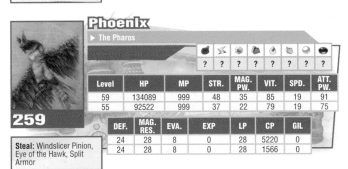

▶ The Pharos

NE	NE	NE	W	NE	AB	NE	NE

Level	HP	MP	STR.	MAG. PW.	VIT.	SPD.	ATT. PW.
49	189992	999	49	23	87	24	85
55	112832	756	39	19	74	18	76

DEF.	MAG. RES.	EVA.	EXP	LP	CP	GIL
27	28	0	0	36	6480	0
26	28	0	0	28	1944	0

258

Steal: Beastlord Hide, Beastlord Horn, Behemoth Steak

Phoenix

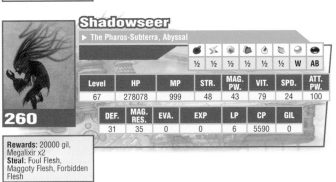

▶ The Pharos

?	?	?	?	?	?	?	?

Level	HP	MP	STR.	MAG. PW.	VIT.	SPD.	ATT. PW.
59	134089	999	48	35	85	19	91
55	92522	999	37	22	79	19	75

DEF.	MAG. RES.	EVA.	EXP	LP	CP	GIL
24	28	8	0	28	5220	0
24	28	8	0	28	1566	0

259

Steal: Windslicer Pinion, Eye of the Hawk, Split Armor

Shadowseer

▶ The Pharos-Subterra, Abyssal

½	½	½	½	½	½	W	AB

Level	HP	MP	STR.	MAG. PW.	VIT.	SPD.	ATT. PW.
67	278078	999	48	43	79	24	100

DEF.	MAG. RES.	EVA.	EXP	LP	CP	GIL
31	35	0	0	6	5590	0

260

Rewards: 20000 gil, Megalixir x2
Steal: Foul Flesh, Maggoty Flesh, Forbidden Flesh

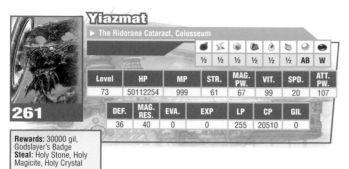

Yiazmat

▶ The Ridorana Cataract, Colosseum

½	½	½	½	½	½	AB	W

Level	HP	MP	STR.	MAG. PW.	VIT.	SPD.	ATT. PW.
73	50112254	999	61	67	99	20	107

DEF.	MAG. RES.	EVA.	EXP	LP	CP	GIL
36	40	0	0	255	20510	0

261

Rewards: 30000 gil, Godslayer's Badge
Steal: Holy Stone, Holy Magicite, Holy Crystal

Espers

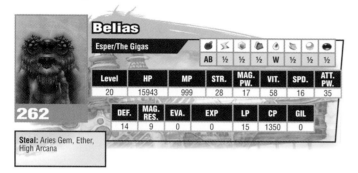

Belias

Esper/The Gigas

AB	½	½	½	W	½	½	½

Level	HP	MP	STR.	MAG. PW.	VIT.	SPD.	ATT. PW.
20	15943	999	28	17	58	16	35

DEF.	MAG. RES.	EVA.	EXP	LP	CP	GIL
14	9	0	0	15	1350	0

262

Steal: Aries Gem, Ether, High Arcana

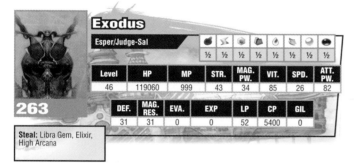

Exodus

Esper/Judge-Sal

½	½	½	½	½	½	½	½

Level	HP	MP	STR.	MAG. PW.	VIT.	SPD.	ATT. PW.
46	119060	999	43	34	85	26	82

DEF.	MAG. RES.	EVA.	EXP	LP	CP	GIL
31	31	0	0	52	5400	0

263

Steal: Libra Gem, Elixir, High Arcana

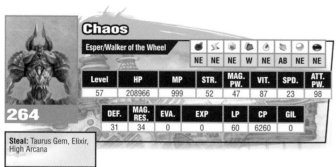

Chaos

Esper/Walker of the Wheel

NE	NE	NE	W	NE	AB	NE	NE

Level	HP	MP	STR.	MAG. PW.	VIT.	SPD.	ATT. PW.
57	208966	999	52	47	87	23	98

DEF.	MAG. RES.	EVA.	EXP	LP	CP	GIL
31	34	0	0	60	6260	0

264

Steal: Taurus Gem, Elixir, High Arcana

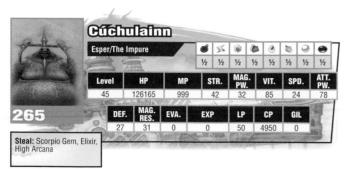

Cúchulainn

Esper/The Impure

½	½	½	½	½	½	½	½

Level	HP	MP	STR.	MAG. PW.	VIT.	SPD.	ATT. PW.
45	126165	999	42	32	85	24	78

DEF.	MAG. RES.	EVA.	EXP	LP	CP	GIL
27	31	0	0	50	4950	0

265

Steal: Scorpio Gem, Elixir, High Arcana

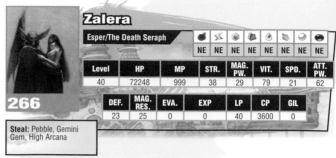

Zalera

Esper/The Death Seraph

NE	NE	NE	NE	NE	NE	NE	NE

Level	HP	MP	STR.	MAG. PW.	VIT.	SPD.	ATT. PW.
40	72248	999	38	29	79	21	62

DEF.	MAG. RES.	EVA.	EXP	LP	CP	GIL
23	25	0	0	40	3600	0

266

Steal: Pebble, Gemini Gem, High Arcana

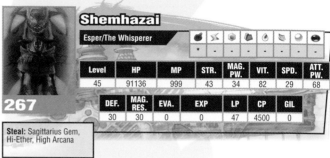

Shemhazai

Esper/The Whisperer

*	-	-	-	-	-	-	-

Level	HP	MP	STR.	MAG. PW.	VIT.	SPD.	ATT. PW.
45	91136	999	43	34	82	29	68

DEF.	MAG. RES.	EVA.	EXP	LP	CP	GIL
30	30	0	0	47	4500	0

267

Steal: Sagittarius Gem, Hi-Ether, High Arcana

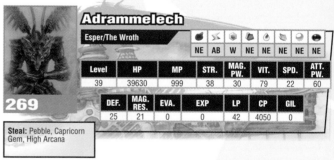

Zeromus

Esper/The Condemner

½	½	½	½	½	½	½	½

Level	HP	MP	STR.	MAG. PW.	VIT.	SPD.	ATT. PW.
51	166888	999	44	35	87	19	86

DEF.	MAG. RES.	EVA.	EXP	LP	CP	GIL
29	33	0	0	55	5670	0

268

Steal: Cancer Gem, Elixir, High Arcana

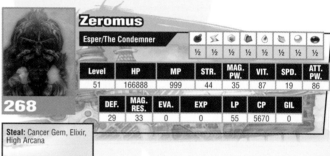

Adrammelech

Esper/The Wroth

NE	AB	W	NE	NE	NE	NE	NE

Level	HP	MP	STR.	MAG. PW.	VIT.	SPD.	ATT. PW.
39	39630	999	38	30	79	22	60

DEF.	MAG. RES.	EVA.	EXP	LP	CP	GIL
25	21	0	0	42	4050	0

269

Steal: Pebble, Capricorn Gem, High Arcana

Hashmal

Esper/Bringer of Order

NE	NE	NE	AB	NE	W	NE	NE

Level	HP	MP	STR.	MAG. PW.	VIT.	SPD.	ATT. PW.
50	209060	999	46	35	85	23	86

DEF.	MAG. RES.	EVA.	EXP	LP	CP	GIL
29	31	0	0	52	5400	0

270

Steal: Leo Gem, Hi-Ether, High Arcana

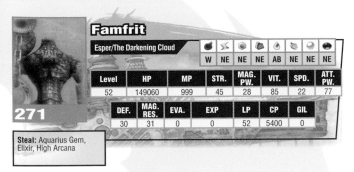

Famfrit — 271
Esper/The Darkening Cloud

W	NE	NE	NE	AB	NE	NE	NE

Level	HP	MP	STR.	MAG. PW.	VIT.	SPD.	ATT. PW.
52	149060	999	45	28	85	22	77

DEF.	MAG. RES.	EVA.	EXP	LP	CP	GIL
30	31	0	0	52	5400	0

Steal: Aquarius Gem, Elixir, High Arcana

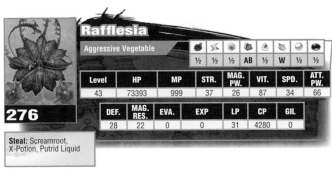

Rafflesia — 276
Aggressive Vegetable

½	½	½	AB	½	W	½	½

Level	HP	MP	STR.	MAG. PW.	VIT.	SPD.	ATT. PW.
43	73393	999	37	26	87	34	66

DEF.	MAG. RES.	EVA.	EXP	LP	CP	GIL
28	22	0	0	31	4280	0

Steal: Screamroot, X-Potion, Putrid Liquid

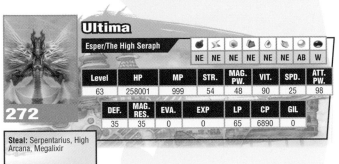

Ultima — 272
Esper/The High Seraph

NE	NE	NE	NE	NE	NE	AB	W

Level	HP	MP	STR.	MAG. PW.	VIT.	SPD.	ATT. PW.
63	258001	999	54	48	90	25	98

DEF.	MAG. RES.	EVA.	EXP	LP	CP	GIL
35	35	0	0	65	6890	0

Steal: Serpentarius, High Arcana, Megalixir

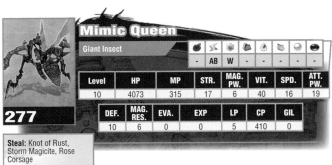

Mimic Queen — 277
Giant Insect

-	AB	W	-	-	-	-	-

Level	HP	MP	STR.	MAG. PW.	VIT.	SPD.	ATT. PW.
10	4073	315	17	6	40	16	19

DEF.	MAG. RES.	EVA.	EXP	LP	CP	GIL
10	6	0	0	5	410	0

Steal: Knot of Rust, Storm Magicite, Rose Corsage

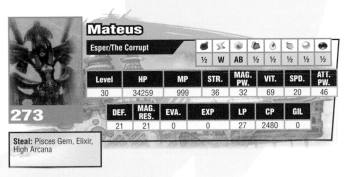

Mateus — 273
Esper/The Corrupt

½	W	AB	½	½	½	½	½

Level	HP	MP	STR.	MAG. PW.	VIT.	SPD.	ATT. PW.
30	34259	999	36	32	69	20	46

DEF.	MAG. RES.	EVA.	EXP	LP	CP	GIL
21	21	0	0	27	2480	0

Steal: Pisces Gem, Elixir, High Arcana

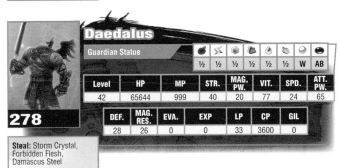

Daedalus — 278
Guardian Statue

½	½	½	½	½	½	W	AB

Level	HP	MP	STR.	MAG. PW.	VIT.	SPD.	ATT. PW.
42	65644	999	40	20	77	24	65

DEF.	MAG. RES.	EVA.	EXP	LP	CP	GIL
28	26	0	0	33	3600	0

Steal: Storm Crystal, Forbidden Flesh, Damascus Steel

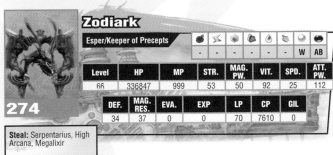

Zodiark — 274
Esper/Keeper of Precepts

-	-	-	-	-	-	W	AB

Level	HP	MP	STR.	MAG. PW.	VIT.	SPD.	ATT. PW.
66	336847	999	53	50	92	25	112

DEF.	MAG. RES.	EVA.	EXP	LP	CP	GIL
34	37	0	0	70	7610	0

Steal: Serpentarius, High Arcana, Megalixir

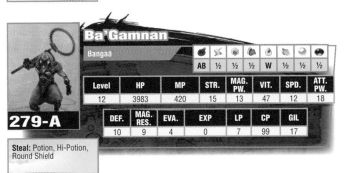

Ba'Gamnan — 279-A
Bangaa

AB	½	½	½	W	½	½	½

Level	HP	MP	STR.	MAG. PW.	VIT.	SPD.	ATT. PW.
12	3983	420	15	13	47	12	18

DEF.	MAG. RES.	EVA.	EXP	LP	CP	GIL
10	9	4	0	7	99	17

Steal: Potion, Hi-Potion, Round Shield

Bosses

Firemane — 275
Flame Spirit

AB	-	-	-	W	-	-	-

Level	HP	MP	STR.	MAG. PW.	VIT.	SPD.	ATT. PW.
7	3571	720	16	11	32	12	18

DEF.	MAG. RES.	EVA.	EXP	LP	CP	GIL
7	7	0	0	3	380	0

Steal: Potion, Phoenix Down, Grimoire Togail

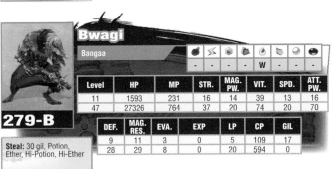

Bwagi — 279-B
Bangaa

-	-	-	-	W	-	-	-

Level	HP	MP	STR.	MAG. PW.	VIT.	SPD.	ATT. PW.
11	1593	231	16	14	39	13	16
47	27326	764	37	20	74	20	70

DEF.	MAG. RES.	EVA.	EXP	LP	CP	GIL
9	11	3	0	5	109	17
28	29	8	0	20	594	0

Steal: 30 gil, Potion, Ether, Hi-Potion, Hi-Ether

Gijuk
Bangaa — 279-C

-	-	-	-	-	W	-	-	-

Level	HP	MP	STR.	MAG. PW.	VIT.	SPD.	ATT. PW.
11	1650	210	15	11	40	14	15
47	27326	764	37	20	74	20	68

DEF.	MAG. RES.	EVA.	EXP	LP	CP	GIL
11	12	4	0	5	109	16
28	29	8	0	20	594	0

Steal: 30 gil, Potion, Ether, Hi-Potion, Hi-Ether

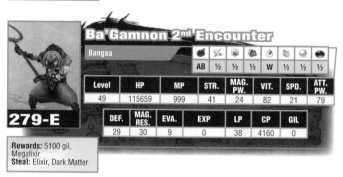

Rinok
Bangaa — 279-D

-	-	-	-	-	W	-	-	-

Level	HP	MP	STR.	MAG. PW.	VIT.	SPD.	ATT. PW.
11	1745	200	16	12	38	12	16
47	27326	764	37	20	74	20	70

DEF.	MAG. RES.	EVA.	EXP	LP	CP	GIL
10	10	3	0	5	109	17
28	29	8	0	20	594	0

Steal: 30 gil, Water Mote, Ether, Potion, Hi-Ether

Ba'Gamnon 2nd Encounter
Bangaa — 279-E

AB	½	½	½	W	½	½	½

Level	HP	MP	STR.	MAG. PW.	VIT.	SPD.	ATT. PW.
49	115659	999	41	24	82	21	79

DEF.	MAG. RES.	EVA.	EXP	LP	CP	GIL
29	30	9	0	38	4160	0

Rewards: 5100 gil, Megalixir
Steal: Elixir, Dark Matter

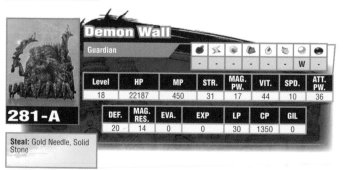

Tyrant
Guardian Beast — 280

½	AB	W	½	½	½	½	½

Level	HP	MP	STR.	MAG. PW.	VIT.	SPD.	ATT. PW.
43	180428	999	42	30	87	28	68

DEF.	MAG. RES.	EVA.	EXP	LP	CP	GIL
28	28	0	0	33	6300	0

Steal: N/A

Demon Wall
Guardian — 281-A

-	-	-	-	-	-	-	W	-

Level	HP	MP	STR.	MAG. PW.	VIT.	SPD.	ATT. PW.
18	22187	450	31	17	44	10	36

DEF.	MAG. RES.	EVA.	EXP	LP	CP	GIL
20	14	0	0	30	1350	0

Steal: Gold Needle, Solid Stone

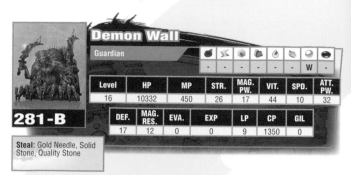

Demon Wall
Guardian — 281-B

-	-	-	-	-	-	-	W	-

Level	HP	MP	STR.	MAG. PW.	VIT.	SPD.	ATT. PW.
16	10332	450	26	17	44	10	32

DEF.	MAG. RES.	EVA.	EXP	LP	CP	GIL
17	12	0	0	9	1350	0

Steal: Gold Needle, Solid Stone, Quality Stone

Hydro
Undead — 282

½	½	½	½	½	½	W	AB

Level	HP	MP	STR.	MAG. PW.	VIT.	SPD.	ATT. PW.
47	203800	999	45	30	90	23	78

DEF.	MAG. RES.	EVA.	EXP	LP	CP	GIL
28	29	0	0	35	6930	0

Steal: Maggoty Flesh, Corpse Fly, Wyrm Bone

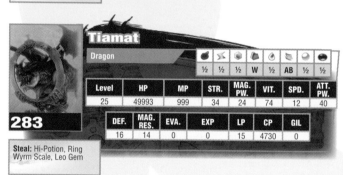

Tiamat
Dragon — 283

½	½	½	W	½	AB	½	½

Level	HP	MP	STR.	MAG. PW.	VIT.	SPD.	ATT. PW.
25	49993	999	34	24	74	12	40

DEF.	MAG. RES.	EVA.	EXP	LP	CP	GIL
16	14	0	0	15	4730	0

Steal: Hi-Potion, Ring Wyrm Scale, Leo Gem

Earth Tyrant
Tyrant — 284

½	½	½	AB	½	W	½	½

Level	HP	MP	STR.	MAG. PW.	VIT.	SPD.	ATT. PW.
30	70982	540	37	15	87	23	51

DEF.	MAG. RES.	EVA.	EXP	LP	CP	GIL
20	24	0	0	21	4500	0

Steal: Hi-Potion, Tyrant Hide, Tyrant Bone

Elder Wyrm
Greater Dragon — 285

-	-	-	-	-	-	W	-	

Level	HP	MP	STR.	MAG. PW.	VIT.	SPD.	ATT. PW.
27	71692	999	33	22	74	9	40

DEF.	MAG. RES.	EVA.	EXP	LP	CP	GIL
16	14	0	0	14	4200	0

Steal: Succulent Fruit, Feystone, Ring Wyrm Scale

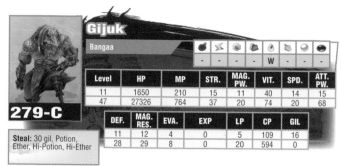

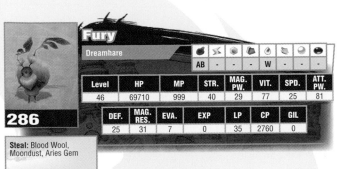

Fury
Dreamhare

AB	-	-	-	W	-	-	-

Level	HP	MP	STR.	MAG. PW.	VIT.	SPD.	ATT. PW.
46	69710	999	40	29	77	25	81

DEF.	MAG. RES.	EVA.	EXP	LP	CP	GIL
25	31	7	0	35	2760	0

286

Steal: Blood Wool, Moondust, Aries Gem

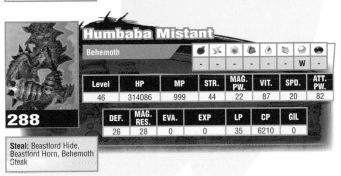

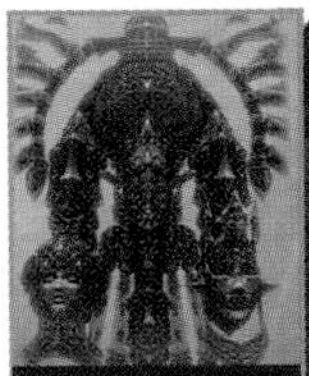

Vinuskar
Manufactured Dragon

-	-	-	-	-	-	-	-

Level	HP	MP	STR.	MAG. PW.	VIT.	SPD.	ATT. PW.
27	15138	999	32	17	60	14	34

DEF.	MAG. RES.	EVA.	EXP	LP	CP	GIL
23	26	0	0	19	2480	0

287

Steal: Knot of Rust, Thief's Cuffs, Damascus Steel

Humbaba Mistant
Behemoth

-	-	-	-	-	-	W	-

Level	HP	MP	STR.	MAG. PW.	VIT.	SPD.	ATT. PW.
46	314086	999	44	22	87	20	82

DEF.	MAG. RES.	EVA.	EXP	LP	CP	GIL
26	28	0	0	35	6210	0

288

Steal: Beastlord Hide, Beastlord Horn, Behemoth Steak

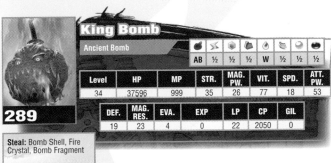

King Bomb
Ancient Bomb

AB	½	½	½	W	½	½	½

Level	HP	MP	STR.	MAG. PW.	VIT.	SPD.	ATT. PW.
34	37596	999	35	26	77	18	53

DEF.	MAG. RES.	EVA.	EXP	LP	CP	GIL
19	23	4	0	22	2050	0

289

Steal: Bomb Shell, Fire Crystal, Bomb Fragment

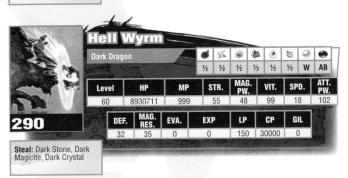

Hell Wyrm
Dark Dragon

½	½	½	½	½	½	W	AB

Level	HP	MP	STR.	MAG. PW.	VIT.	SPD.	ATT. PW.
60	8930711	999	55	48	99	18	102

DEF.	MAG. RES.	EVA.	EXP	LP	CP	GIL
32	35	0	0	150	30000	0

290

Steal: Dark Stone, Dark Magicite, Dark Crystal

Ahriman
Undead Lord

-	-	-	-	-	-	W	AB

Level	HP	MP	STR.	MAG. PW.	VIT.	SPD.	ATT. PW.
38	62149	999	36	30	69	18	56
38	700	999	33	30	69	16	53

DEF.	MAG. RES.	EVA.	EXP	LP	CP	GIL
23	22	3	0	28	3000	0
20	18	2	0	0	10	0

291

Steal: Sky Jewel, Death Powder, Maduin Gear

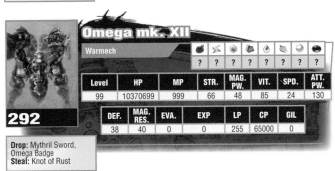

Omega mk. XII
Warmech

?	?	?	?	?	?	?	?

Level	HP	MP	STR.	MAG. PW.	VIT.	SPD.	ATT. PW.
99	10370699	999	66	48	85	24	130

DEF.	MAG. RES.	EVA.	EXP	LP	CP	GIL
38	40	0	0	255	65000	0

292

Drop: Mythril Sword, Omega Badge
Steal: Knot of Rust

Vossler
Humanoid/ Dalmascan Military

-	-	-	-	-	-	-	-

Level	HP	MP	STR.	MAG. PW.	VIT.	SPD.	ATT. PW.
20	9318	693	23	16	49	22	26

DEF.	MAG. RES.	EVA.	EXP	LP	CP	GIL
13	10	4	0	30	1260	0

Steal: Potion, Hi-Potion

Rare Game

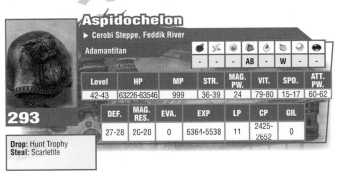

Aspidochelon
▶ Cerobi Steppe, Feddik River
Adamantitan

-	-	AB	-	W	-	-	-

Level	HP	MP	STR.	MAG. PW.	VIT.	SPD.	ATT. PW.
42-43	63226-63546	999	36-39	24	79-80	15-17	60-62

DEF.	MAG. RES.	EVA.	EXP	LP	CP	GIL
27-28	20-20	0	5364-5538	11	2425-2652	0

293

Drop: Hunt Trophy
Steal: Scarletite

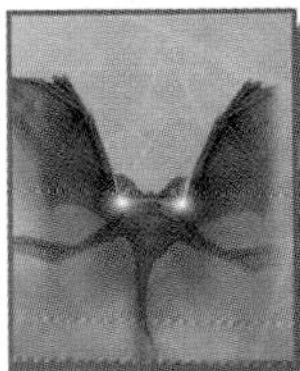

Aerieel
▶ Lhusu Mines, Oltam Span
Vampyr

-	-	-	-	-	-	W	AB

Level	HP	MP	STR.	MAG. PW.	VIT.	SPD.	ATT. PW.
12-13	3017-3033	163-167	18	12	42-43	17-18	24-25

DEF.	MAG. RES.	EVA.	EXP	LP	CP	GIL
7	7	3-5	374-378	3	395-408	0

294

Drop: Bat Fang, Golden Armor
Steal: Bat Wing
Poach: Pebble, Taurus Gem

Thalassinon

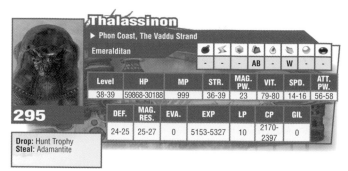

▶ Phon Coast, The Vaddu Strand

Emeralditan

-	-	-	-	AB	-	W	-

295

Level	HP	MP	STR.	MAG. PW.	VIT.	SPD.	ATT. PW.
38-39	59868-30188	999	36-39	23	79-80	14-16	56-58

DEF.	MAG. RES.	EVA.	EXP	LP	CP	GIL
24-25	25-27	0	5153-5327	10	2170-2397	0

Drop: Hunt Trophy
Steal: Adamantite

Vishno

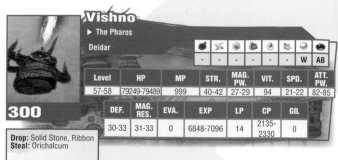

▶ The Pharos

Deidar

-	-	-	-	-	-	W	AB

300

Level	HP	MP	STR.	MAG. PW.	VIT.	SPD.	ATT. PW.
57-58	79249-79489	999	40-42	27-29	94	21-22	82-85

DEF.	MAG. RES.	EVA.	EXP	LP	CP	GIL
30-33	31-33	0	6848-7096	14	2135-2330	0

Drop: Solid Stone, Ribbon
Steal: Orichalcum

Anubys

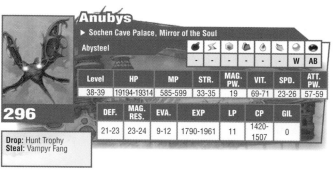

▶ Sochen Cave Palace, Mirror of the Soul

Abysteel

-	-	-	-	-	-	W	AB

296

Level	HP	MP	STR.	MAG. PW.	VIT.	SPD.	ATT. PW.
38-39	19194-19314	585-599	33-35	19	69-71	23-26	57-59

DEF.	MAG. RES.	EVA.	EXP	LP	CP	GIL
21-23	23-24	9-12	1790-1961	11	1420-1507	0

Drop: Hunt Trophy
Steal: Vampyr Fang

Gavial

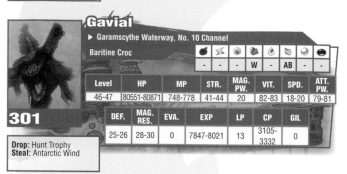

▶ Garamscythe Waterway, No. 10 Channel

Baritine Croc

-	-	-	W	-	AB	-	-

301

Level	HP	MP	STR.	MAG. PW.	VIT.	SPD.	ATT. PW.
46-47	80551-80871	748-778	41-44	20	82-83	18-20	79-81

DEF.	MAG. RES.	EVA.	EXP	LP	CP	GIL
25-26	28-30	0	7847-8021	13	3105-3332	0

Drop: Hunt Trophy
Steal: Antarctic Wind

Greeden

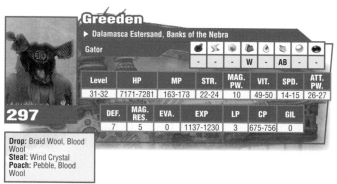

▶ Dalamasca Estersand, Banks of the Nebra

Gator

-	-	W	-	AB	-	-	-

297

Level	HP	MP	STR.	MAG. PW.	VIT.	SPD.	ATT. PW.
31-32	7171-7281	163-173	22-24	10	49-50	14-15	26-27

DEF.	MAG. RES.	EVA.	EXP	LP	CP	GIL
7	5	0	1137-1230	3	675-756	0

Drop: Braid Wool, Blood Wool
Steal: Wind Crystal
Poach: Pebble, Blood Wool

Etherian

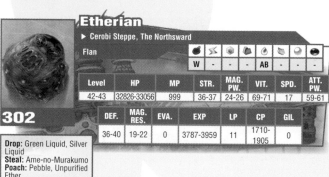

▶ Cerobi Steppe, The Northsward

Flan

W	-	-	-	AB	-	-	-

302

Level	HP	MP	STR.	MAG. PW.	VIT.	SPD.	ATT. PW.
42-43	32826-33056	999	36-37	24-26	69-71	17	59-61

DEF.	MAG. RES.	EVA.	EXP	LP	CP	GIL
36-40	19-22	0	3787-3959	11	1710-1905	0

Drop: Green Liquid, Silver Liquid
Steal: Ame-no-Murakumo
Poach: Pebble, Unpurified Ether

Barmuu

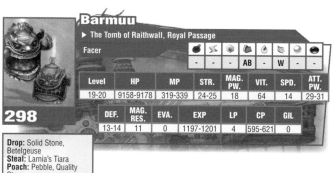

▶ The Tomb of Raithwall, Royal Passage

Facer

-	-	-	AB	-	W	-	-

298

Level	HP	MP	STR.	MAG. PW.	VIT.	SPD.	ATT. PW.
19-20	9158-9178	319-339	24-25	18	64	14	29-31

DEF.	MAG. RES.	EVA.	EXP	LP	CP	GIL
13-14	11	0	1197-1201	4	595-621	0

Drop: Solid Stone, Betelgeuse
Steal: Lamia's Tiara
Poach: Pebble, Quality Stone

Wary Wolf

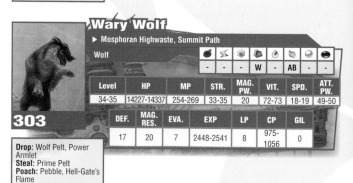

▶ Mosphoran Highwaste, Summit Path

Wolf

-	-	-	W	-	AB	-	-

303

Level	HP	MP	STR.	MAG. PW.	VIT.	SPD.	ATT. PW.
34-35	14227-14337	254-269	33-35	20	72-73	18-19	49-50

DEF.	MAG. RES.	EVA.	EXP	LP	CP	GIL
17	20	7	2448-2541	8	975-1056	0

Drop: Wolf Pelt, Power Armlet
Steal: Prime Pelt
Poach: Pebble, Hell-Gate's Flame

Bull Croc

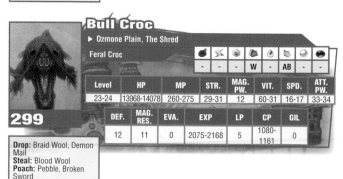

▶ Ozmone Plain, The Shred

Feral Croc

-	-	-	W	-	AB	-	-

299

Level	HP	MP	STR.	MAG. PW.	VIT.	SPD.	ATT. PW.
23-24	13968-14078	260-275	29-31	12	60-31	16-17	33-34

DEF.	MAG. RES.	EVA.	EXP	LP	CP	GIL
12	11	0	2075-2168	5	1080-1161	0

Drop: Braid Wool, Demon Mail
Steal: Blood Wool
Poach: Pebble, Broken Sword

Melt

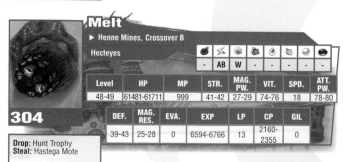

▶ Henne Mines, Crossover B

Hecteyes

-	AB	W	-	-	-	-	-

304

Level	HP	MP	STR.	MAG. PW.	VIT.	SPD.	ATT. PW.
48-49	61481-61711	999	41-42	27-29	74-76	18	78-80

DEF.	MAG. RES.	EVA.	EXP	LP	CP	GIL
39-43	25-28	0	6594-6766	13	2160-2355	0

Drop: Hunt Trophy
Steal: Hastega Mote

Kaiser Wolf

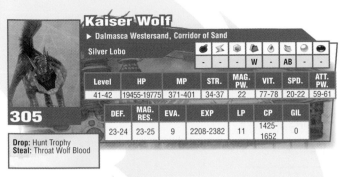

▶ Dalmasca Westersand, Corridor of Sand

Silver Lobo

-	-	-	W	-	AB	-	-

Level	HP	MP	STR.	MAG. PW.	VIT.	SPD.	ATT. PW.
41-42	19455-19775	371-401	34-37	22	77-78	20-22	59-61

DEF.	MAG. RES.	EVA.	EXP	LP	CP	GIL
23-24	23-25	9	2208-2382	11	1425-1652	0

305

Drop: Hunt Trophy
Steal: Throat Wolf Blood

Cubus

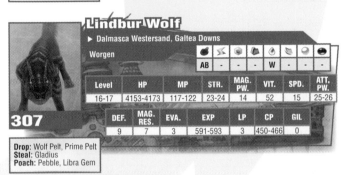

▶ Sochen Cave Palace, Temptation Eluded

Construct

AB	-	-	W	-	-	-	-

Level	HP	MP	STR.	MAG. PW.	VIT.	SPD.	ATT. PW.
37-38	32386-32616	999	36-37	23-25	69-71	17	56-58

DEF.	MAG. RES.	EVA.	EXP	LP	CP	GIL
34-38	18-21	0	4092-4294	11	1620-1815	0

306

Drop: Green Liquid, Holy Mote
Steal: Silver Liquid

Lindbur Wolf

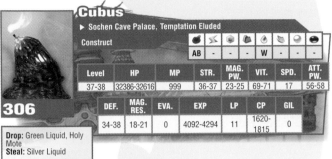

▶ Dalmasca Westersand, Galtea Downs

Worgen

AB	-	-	-	W	-	-	-

Level	HP	MP	STR.	MAG. PW.	VIT.	SPD.	ATT. PW.
16-17	4153-4173	117-122	23-24	14	52	15	25-26

DEF.	MAG. RES.	EVA.	EXP	LP	CP	GIL
9	7	3	591-593	3	450-466	0

307

Drop: Wolf Pelt, Prime Pelt
Steal: Gladius
Poach: Pebble, Libra Gem

Pineapple

▶ Ogir-Yensa Sandsea, Platform 1 - Refinery

Bomb

AB	-	-	-	W	-	-	-

Level	HP	MP	STR.	MAG. PW.	VIT.	SPD.	ATT. PW.
16-18	4668-4698	780-840	22-24	16-20	49	15	24

DEF.	MAG. RES.	EVA.	EXP	LP	CP	GIL
10	11-15	3-5	639-651	3	475-533	0

308

Drop: Bomb Ashes, Storm Staff
Steal: Bomb Shell
Poach: Pebble, Bomb Fragment

Dreadguard

▶ The Feywood, Wall of Dancing Shadow

Mirror Knight

-	-	-	W	-	AB	-	-

Level	HP	MP	STR.	MAG. PW.	VIT.	SPD.	ATT. PW.
46-47	35074-35394	999	35-38	19	74-75	19-21	65-67

DEF.	MAG. RES.	EVA.	EXP	LP	CP	GIL
24-25	28-30	4	4226-4400	12	1725-1952	0

309

Drop: Hunt Trophy
Steal: Mirror Scale

Bombshell

▶ Lhusu Mines, Lasche Span (south segment)

Grenade

AB	-	-	W	-	-	-	-

Level	HP	MP	STR.	MAG. PW.	VIT.	SPD.	ATT. PW.
60-61	76042-76202	999	47-49	43-46	85	25-26	95-97

DEF.	MAG. RES.	EVA.	EXP	LP	CP	GIL
31-32	37-41	13-15	7252-7428	16	2410-2611	0

310

Drop: Yagyu Darkblade, Bomb Ashes
Steal: Mallet

Crypt Bunny

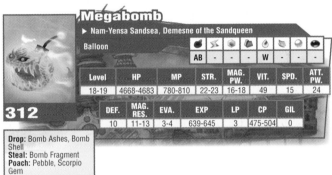

▶ The Feywood, Walk of Stolen Truths

Dreamhare

W	-	-	-	AB	-	-	-

Level	HP	MP	STR.	MAG. PW.	VIT.	SPD.	ATT. PW.
45-46	21348-21668	999	32-35	25	52-53	22-24	62-64

DEF.	MAG. RES.	EVA.	EXP	LP	CP	GIL
23-24	31-33	10	1764-1938	12	1200-1427	0

311

Drop: Drab Wool, Muramasa
Steal: Holy Mote

Megabomb

▶ Nam-Yensa Sandsea, Demesne of the Sandqueen

Balloon

AB	-	-	-	W	-	-	-

Level	HP	MP	STR.	MAG. PW.	VIT.	SPD.	ATT. PW.
18-19	4668-4683	780-810	22-23	16-18	49	15	24

DEF.	MAG. RES.	EVA.	EXP	LP	CP	GIL
10	11-13	3-4	639-645	3	475-504	0

312

Drop: Bomb Ashes, Bomb Shell
Steal: Bomb Fragment
Poach: Pebble, Scorpio Gem

Spee

▶ The Salikawood, Sun-dappled Path

Dreamhare

AB	-	-	-	W	-	-	-

Level	HP	MP	STR.	MAG. PW.	VIT.	SPD.	ATT. PW.
36-37	14725-14835	999	30-32	23	60-61	20-21	48-49

DEF.	MAG. RES.	EVA.	EXP	LP	CP	GIL
18	24	7	1284-1377	9	840-921	0

313

Drop: Drab Wool, Blood Wool
Steal: Stardust
Poach: Pebble, Claymore

Matriarch Bomb

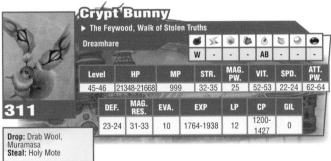

▶ Stilshrine of Miriam, Ward of Measure

Grenade

AB	-	-	-	W	-	-	-

Level	HP	MP	STR.	MAG. PW.	VIT.	SPD.	ATT. PW.
31-32	12156-12214	999	32-33	20-22	65	17-18	42-44

DEF.	MAG. RES.	EVA.	EXP	LP	CP	GIL
17-18	24-26	6-8	1696-1797	7	945-1034	0

314

Drop: Bomb Ashes, Bomb Shell
Steal: Scorpio Gem
Poach: Pebble, Bomb Fragment

Rain Dancer

▶ Giza Plains

Danbania

-	W	-	-	AB	-	-	-

Level	HP	MP	STR.	MAG. PW.	VIT.	SPD.	ATT. PW.
23-24	8084-8166	728-738	26-27	17	57-58	18-20	32-34

DEF.	MAG. RES.	EVA.	EXP	LP	CP	GIL
12	12-13	4-6	1426-1524	5	660-719	0

315

Drop: Fish Scale, Ichthon Scale
Steal: Miter
Poach: Pebble, Dorsal Fin

Ripe Rampager

▶ Dalmasca Estersand, Yardang Labyrinth

Mandragora

W	-	-	-	AB	-	-	-

Level	HP	MP	STR.	MAG. PW.	VIT.	SPD.	ATT. PW.
4-5	357-369	455-458	10	9	38-39	11	14-15

DEF.	MAG. RES.	EVA.	EXP	LP	CP	GIL
1-2	7	0	25-28	2	150-159	0

316

Drop: Pebble, Calot Hat
Steal: Screamroot
Poach: Pebble, Four-leaf Clover

Razorfin

▶ Garamscythe Waterway, North Spur Sluiceway

Piranha

-	W	-	-	AB	-	-	-

Level	HP	MP	STR.	MAG. PW.	VIT.	SPD.	ATT. PW.
4-5	156-167	154-158	11-12	6	33-34	14-16	12-13

DEF.	MAG. RES.	EVA.	EXP	LP	CP	GIL
6	8	0-1	34-38	2	36-45	0

317

Drop: Fish Scale, Iron Sword
Steal: Water Crystal
Poach: Pebble, Ichthon Scale

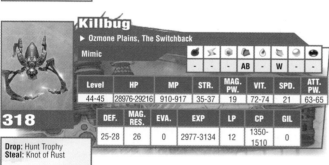

Killbug

▶ Ozmone Plains, The Switchback

Mimic

-	-	-	-	AB	-	W	-

Level	HP	MP	STR.	MAG. PW.	VIT.	SPD.	ATT. PW.
44-45	28976-29216	910-917	35-37	19	72-74	21	63-65

DEF.	MAG. RES.	EVA.	EXP	LP	CP	GIL
25-28	26	0	2977-3134	12	1350-1510	0

318

Drop: Hunt Trophy
Steal: Knot of Rust

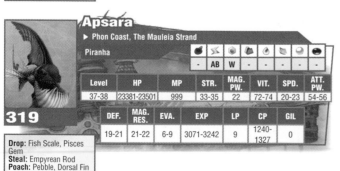

Apsara

▶ Phon Coast, The Mauleia Strand

Piranha

-	AB	W	-	-	-	-	-

Level	HP	MP	STR.	MAG. PW.	VIT.	SPD.	ATT. PW.
37-38	23381-23501	999	33-35	22	72-74	20-23	54-56

DEF.	MAG. RES.	EVA.	EXP	LP	CP	GIL
19-21	21-22	6-9	3071-3242	9	1240-1327	0

319

Drop: Fish Scale, Pisces Gem
Steal: Empyrean Rod
Poach: Pebble, Dorsal Fin

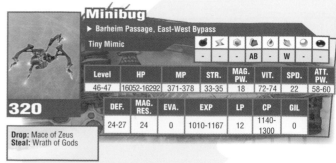

Minibug

▶ Barheim Passage, East-West Bypass

Tiny Mimic

-	-	-	-	AB	-	W	-

Level	HP	MP	STR.	MAG. PW.	VIT.	SPD.	ATT. PW.
46-47	16052-16292	371-378	33-35	18	72-74	22	58-60

DEF.	MAG. RES.	EVA.	EXP	LP	CP	GIL
24-27	24	0	1010-1167	12	1140-1300	0

320

Drop: Mace of Zeus
Steal: Wrath of Gods

Rageclaw

▶ The Salikawood, Piebald Path

Mantis

AB	-	-	-	W	-	-	-

Level	HP	MP	STR.	MAG. PW.	VIT.	SPD.	ATT. PW.
36-37	39586-39696	585-590	36-38	16	74-75	18	60-62

DEF.	MAG. RES.	EVA.	EXP	LP	CP	GIL
24-26	19	0	4263-4352	11	1690-1764	0

321

Drop: Hunt Trophy
Steal: Sickle-Blade

Ithuno

▶ Barheim Passage, Special Op Sector 5

Mimic

-	-	-	-	-	-	W	AB

Level	HP	MP	STR.	MAG. PW.	VIT.	SPD.	ATT. PW.
41-42	23101-23341	865-872	34-36	19	69-71	21	59-61

DEF.	MAG. RES.	EVA.	EXP	LP	CP	GIL
25-28	21	0	2556-2713	11	1285-1445	0

322

Drop: Iron Scraps, Iron Ore
Steal: Deathbringer

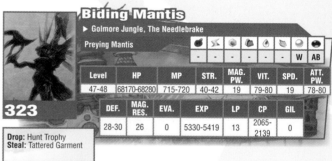

Biding Mantis

▶ Golmore Jungle, The Needlebrake

Preying Mantis

-	-	-	-	-	-	W	AB

Level	HP	MP	STR.	MAG. PW.	VIT.	SPD.	ATT. PW.
47-48	68170-68280	715-720	40-42	19	79-80	19	78-80

DEF.	MAG. RES.	EVA.	EXP	LP	CP	GIL
28-30	26	0	5330-5419	13	2065-2139	0

323

Drop: Hunt Trophy
Steal: Tattered Garment

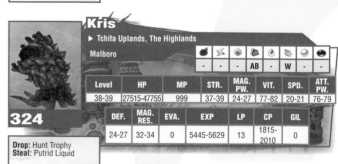

Kris

▶ Tchita Uplands, The Highlands

Malboro

-	-	-	AB	-	W	-	-

Level	HP	MP	STR.	MAG. PW.	VIT.	SPD.	ATT. PW.
38-39	27515-47755	999	37-39	24-27	77-82	20-21	76-79

DEF.	MAG. RES.	EVA.	EXP	LP	CP	GIL
24-27	32-34	0	5445-5629	13	1815-2010	0

324

Drop: Hunt Trophy
Steal: Putrid Liquid

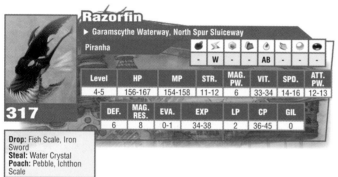

Wood Toad

▶ The Salikawood, Corridor of Ages

Toad

	W	AB					

Level	HP	MP	STR.	MAG. PW.	VIT.	SPD.	ATT. PW.
35-36	51642-51752	999	39-41	25	79-80	19-20	75-76

DEF.	MAG. RES.	EVA.	EXP	LP	CP	GIL
27	31	4	5683-5776	13	1980-2061	0

325

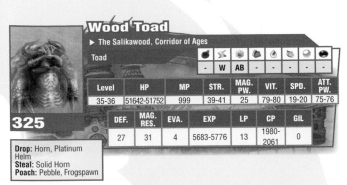

Drop: Horn, Platinum Helm
Steal: Solid Horn
Poach: Pebble, Frogspawn

Dheed

▶ Mosphoran Highwaste, Skyreach Ridge

Plate Wyvern

AB			W				

Level	HP	MP	STR.	MAG. PW.	VIT.	SPD.	ATT. PW.
49-50	77420-78100	999	40-44	27-30	85-92	21-24	80-84

DEF.	MAG. RES.	EVA.	EXP	LP	CP	GIL
24-27	28-30	0	8794-8997	13	2880-3400	0

326

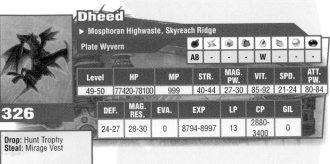

Drop: Hunt Trophy
Steal: Mirage Vest

Tarasque

▶ Tchita Uplands, Garden of Life's Circle

Toad

AB			W				

Level	HP	MP	STR.	MAG. PW.	VIT.	SPD.	ATT. PW.
37-38	27566-27886	999	34-37	22	72-73	17-19	55-57

DEF.	MAG. RES.	EVA.	EXP	LP	CP	GIL
21-22	23-25	3	3492-3666	10	1440-1667	0

327

Drop: Horn, Solid Horn
Steal: Hunting Crossbow
Poach: Pebble, Frog Oil

Aeros

▶ Ozmone Plains, The Shred

Aeronite

	W	AB					

Level	HP	MP	STR.	MAG. PW.	VIT.	SPD.	ATT. PW.
23-24	12497-12837	832-922	27-30	18-20	62-67	16-18	33-36

DEF.	MAG. RES.	EVA.	EXP	LP	CP	GIL
10-12	11-13	0	2075-2201	5	960-1239	0

328

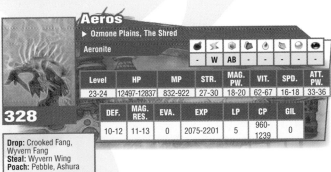

Drop: Crooked Fang, Wyvern Fang
Steal: Wyvern Wing
Poach: Pebble, Ashura

Grimalkin

▶ Tchita Uplands, Uazcuff Hills

Coeurl

	AB	W					

Level	HP	MP	STR.	MAG. PW.	VIT.	SPD.	ATT. PW.
38-39	23101-23421	999	34-37	24	74-75	21-23	59-61

DEF.	MAG. RES.	EVA.	EXP	LP	CP	GIL
23-24	27-29	8	2430-2604	11	1570-1797	0

329

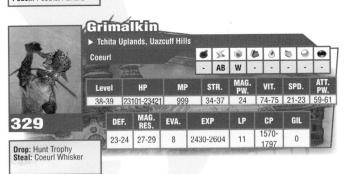

Drop: Hunt Trophy
Steal: Coeurl Whisker

Terror Tyrant

▶ Dalamasca Estersand, Broken Sands

Tyrant

			AB		W		

Level	HP	MP	STR.	MAG. PW.	VIT.	SPD.	ATT. PW.
50-51	125704-126384	488-608	42-46	20-23	87-64	25-28	84-88

DEF.	MAG. RES.	EVA.	EXP	LP	CP	GIL
28-31	28-30	0	14426-14629	14	4725-5245	0

330

Drop: Hunt Trophy
Steal: Scathe Mote

Nekhbet

▶ Dalmasca Estersand, Sand-swept Naze

Cockatrice

AB			W				

Level	HP	MP	STR.	MAG. PW.	VIT.	SPD.	ATT. PW.
5-6	3963-3979	488-492	19	16	38-39	15-16	24-25

DEF.	MAG. RES.	EVA.	EXP	LP	CP	GIL
6	9	3-5	625-629	3	415-428	0

331

Drop: Small Feather, Wizard's Hat
Steal: Rainbow Egg
Poach: Pebble, Small Feather

Abelisk

▶ Ridorana Cataract, Echoes from Time's Garden

Tyrant

Level	HP	MP	STR.	MAG. PW.	VIT.	SPD.	ATT. PW.
49-50	104744-105424	468-588	41-45	20-23	85-92	23-26	82-86

DEF.	MAG. RES.	EVA.	EXP	LP	CP	GIL
26-29	26-28	0	13738-13941	13	4500-5020	0

332

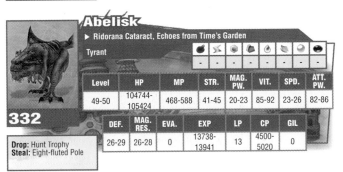

Drop: Hunt Trophy
Steal: Eight-fluted Pole

Glaring Eye

▶ Henne Mines, Phase 2 Shaft

Necrophobe

						W	AB

Level	HP	MP	STR.	MAG. PW.	VIT.	SPD.	ATT. PW.
64 65	175195-175375	999	50-52	43-45	79	24	101-104

DEF.	MAG. RES.	EVA.	EXP	LP	CP	GIL
31-33	38-39	3	13273-13433	18	3325-3468	0

333

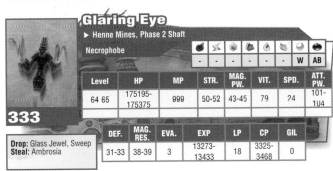

Drop: Glass Jewel, Sweep
Steal: Ambrosia

Dustia

▶ Dalmasca Westersand, Corridor of Sand

Oversoul

						W	AB

Level	HP	MP	STR.	MAG. PW.	VIT.	SPD.	ATT. PW.
17-18	7266-7272	975-995	25-26	17-18	42	13	27-28

DEF.	MAG. RES.	EVA.	EXP	LP	CP	GIL
8	7	2	1098-1101	3	585-601	0

334

Drop: Book of Ordain, Flame Staff
Steal: Book of Ordain-Mille
Poach: Pebble, Capricorn Gem

Cultsworn Lich

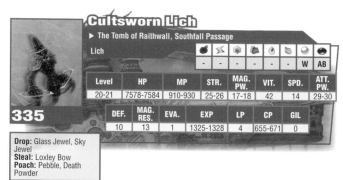

335

▶ The Tomb of Raithwall, Southfall Passage

Lich

Level	HP	MP	STR	MAG. PW.	VIT.	SPD.	ATT. PW.
20-21	7578-7584	910-930	25-26	17-18	42	14	29-30

DEF.	MAG. RES.	EVA.	EXP	LP	CP	GIL
10	13	1	1325-1328	4	655-671	0

Drop: Glass Jewel, Sky Jewel
Steal: Loxley Bow
Poach: Pebble, Death Powder

Negalmuur

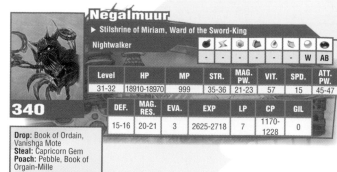

340

▶ Stilshrine of Miriam, Ward of the Sword-King

Nightwalker

Level	HP	MP	STR	MAG. PW.	VIT.	SPD.	ATT. PW.
31-32	18910-18970	999	35-36	21-23	57	15	45-47

DEF.	MAG. RES.	EVA.	EXP	LP	CP	GIL
15-16	20-21	3	2625-2718	7	1170-1228	0

Drop: Book of Ordain, Vanishga Mote
Steal: Capricorn Gem
Poach: Pebble, Book of Orgain-Mille

Ishteen

336

▶ Barheim Passage, The Zeviah Span

Reaper

Level	HP	MP	STR	MAG. PW.	VIT.	SPD.	ATT. PW.
43-44	34042-34222	999	36-38	25-27	65	18	61-64

DEF.	MAG. RES.	EVA.	EXP	LP	CP	GIL
22-24	23-24	4	4101-4261	11	1855-1998	0

Drop: Hunt Trophy
Steal: Soul of Thamasa

Molen

341

▶ Zertinan Cavern, Hourglass Basin

Golem

Level	HP	MP	STR	MAG. PW.	VIT.	SPD.	ATT. PW.
38-39	59976-60216	999	36-38	22-24	62	17-18	59-62

DEF.	MAG. RES.	EVA.	EXP	LP	CP	GIL
25-28	24-26	0	4775-5023	11	1890-2085	0

Drop: Iron Ore, Gigas Chestplate
Steal: Mythril

Evil Spirit

337

▶ The Great Crystal, XIX Teleporter

Necrofiend

Level	HP	MP	STR	MAG. PW.	VIT.	SPD.	ATT. PW.
61-62	121672-121852	999	50-52	42-44	77	23	99-102

DEF.	MAG. RES.	EVA.	EXP	LP	CP	GIL
29-31	35-36	2	11334-11494	17	3015-3158	0

Drop: Glass Jewel, Gungnir
Steal: Lifewick

Larva Eater

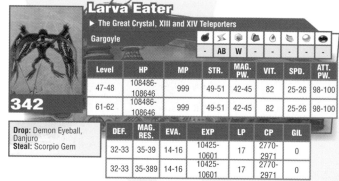

342

▶ The Great Crystal, XIII and XIV Teleporters

Gargoyle

Level	HP	MP	STR	MAG. PW.	VIT.	SPD.	ATT. PW.
47-48	108486-108646	999	49-51	42-45	82	25-26	98-100
61-62	108486-108646	999	49-51	42-45	82	25-26	98-100

DEF.	MAG. RES.	EVA.	EXP	LP	CP	GIL
32-33	35-39	14-16	10425-10601	17	2770-2971	0
32-33	35-389	14-16	10425-10601	17	2770-2971	0

Drop: Demon Eyeball, Danjuro
Steal: Scorpio Gem

Vorres

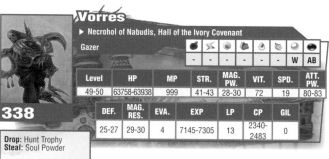

338

▶ Necrohol of Nabudis, Hall of the Ivory Covenant

Gazer

Level	HP	MP	STR	MAG. PW.	VIT.	SPD.	ATT. PW.
49-50	63758-63938	999	41-43	28-30	72	19	80-83

DEF.	MAG. RES.	EVA.	EXP	LP	CP	GIL
25-27	29-30	4	7145-7305	13	2340-2483	0

Drop: Hunt Trophy
Steal: Soul Powder

Tower

343

▶ Pharos-Third Ascent

Babil

Level	HP	MP	STR	MAG. PW.	VIT.	SPD.	ATT. PW.
59-60	136638-136878	999	42-44	26-28	72	20-21	83-86

DEF.	MAG. RES.	EVA.	EXP	LP	CP	GIL
32-35	33-35	0	8484-8732	14	2645-2840	0

Drop: Solid Stone, Grand Helm
Steal: Einherjarium

Juggernaut

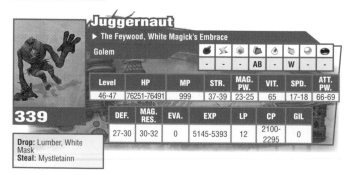

339

▶ The Feywood, White Magick's Embrace

Golem

Level	HP	MP	STR	MAG. PW.	VIT.	SPD.	ATT. PW.
46-47	76251-76491	999	37-39	23-25	65	17-18	66-69

DEF.	MAG. RES.	EVA.	EXP	LP	CP	GIL
27-30	30-32	0	5145-5393	12	2100-2295	0

Drop: Lumber, White Mask
Steal: Mystletainn

Arioch

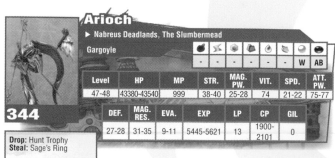

344

▶ Nabreus Deadlands, The Slumbermead

Gargoyle

Level	HP	MP	STR	MAG. PW.	VIT.	SPD.	ATT. PW.
47-48	43380-43540	999	38-40	25-28	74	21-22	75-77

DEF.	MAG. RES.	EVA.	EXP	LP	CP	GIL
27-28	31-35	9-11	5445-5621	13	1900-2101	0

Drop: Hunt Trophy
Steal: Sage's Ring

Grey Moler

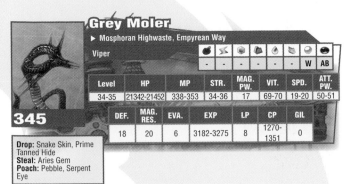

▶ Mosphoran Highwaste, Empyrean Way

Viper

								W	AB
-	-	-	-	-	-	-	-		

Level	HP	MP	STR.	MAG. PW.	VIT.	SPD.	ATT. PW.
34-35	21342-21452	338-353	34-36	17	69-70	19-20	50-51

DEF.	MAG. RES.	EVA.	EXP	LP	CP	GIL
18	20	6	3182-3275	8	1270-1351	0

345

Drop: Snake Skin, Prime Tanned Hide
Steal: Aries Gem
Poach: Pebble, Serpent Eye

Fideliant

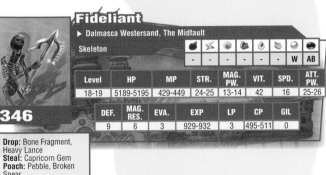

▶ Dalmasca Westersand, The Midfault

Skeleton

								W	AB
-	-	-	-	-	-	-	-		

Level	HP	MP	STR.	MAG. PW.	VIT.	SPD.	ATT. PW.
18-19	5189-5195	429-449	24-25	13-14	42	16	25-26

DEF.	MAG. RES.	EVA.	EXP	LP	CP	GIL
9	6	3	929-932	3	495-511	0

346

Drop: Bone Fragment, Heavy Lance
Steal: Capricorn Gem
Poach: Pebble, Broken Spear

Midgardsormr

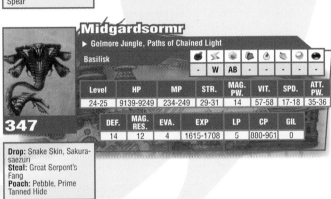

▶ Golmore Jungle, Paths of Chained Light

Basilisk

-	W	AB	-	-	-	-	-

Level	HP	MP	STR.	MAG. PW.	VIT.	SPD.	ATT. PW.
24-25	9139-9249	234-249	29-31	14	57-58	17-18	35-36

DEF.	MAG. RES.	EVA.	EXP	LP	CP	GIL
14	12	4	1615-1708	5	800-961	0

347

Drop: Snake Skin, Sakura-saezuri
Steal: Great Serpent's Fang
Poach: Pebble, Prime Tanned Hide

Crystal Knight

▶ The Great Crystal, XX Teleporter

Crusader

								W	AB
-	-	-	-	-	-	-	-		

Level	HP	MP	STR.	MAG. PW.	VIT.	SPD.	ATT. PW.
61-62	101390-101570	999	50-52	40-42	79	26	97-100

DEF.	MAG. RES.	EVA.	EXP	LP	CP	GIL
30-32	32-33	14	9973-10133	17	2650-2793	0

348

Drop: Hunt Trophy
Steal: Glimmering Robes

Nazarnir

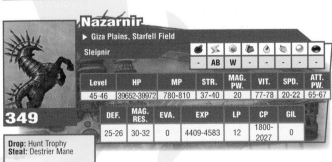

▶ Giza Plains, Starfell Field

Sleipnir

-	AB	W	-	-	-	-	-

Level	HP	MP	STR.	MAG. PW.	VIT.	SPD.	ATT. PW.
45-46	39652-39972	780-810	37-40	20	77-78	20-22	65-67

DEF.	MAG. RES.	EVA.	EXP	LP	CP	GIL
25-26	30-32	0	4409-4583	12	1800-2027	0

349

Drop: Hunt Trophy
Steal: Destrier Mane

Grave Lord

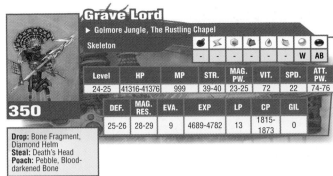

▶ Golmore Jungle, The Rustling Chapel

Skeleton

								W	AB
-	-	-	-	-	-	-	-		

Level	HP	MP	STR.	MAG. PW.	VIT.	SPD.	ATT. PW.
24-25	41316-41376	999	39-40	23-25	72	22	74-76

DEF.	MAG. RES.	EVA.	EXP	LP	CP	GIL
25-26	28-29	9	4689-4782	13	1815-1873	0

350

Drop: Bone Fragment, Diamond Helm
Steal: Death's Head
Poach: Pebble, Blood-darkened Bone

Victanir

▶ Nam-Yensa Sandsea, Yellow Sands

Shadonir

								W	AB
-	-	-	-	-	-	-	-		

Level	HP	MP	STR.	MAG. PW.	VIT.	SPD.	ATT. PW.
46-47	55114-55434	897-927	40-43	22	79-80	21-23	78-80

DEF.	MAG. RES.	EVA.	EXP	LP	CP	GIL
27-28	31-33	0	5296-5470	13	2070-2297	0

351

Drop: Hunt Trophy
Steal: Wargod's Band

Zombie Lord

▶ The Tomb of Raithwall, Northfall Passage

Forbidden

								W	AB
-	-	-	-	-	-	-	-		

Level	HP	MP	STR.	MAG. PW.	VIT.	SPD.	ATT. PW.
38-39	21593-21599	999	34-35	21-22	62	19	57-58

DEF.	MAG. RES.	EVA.	EXP	LP	CP	GIL
21	22	0	2507-2510	11	1420-1436	0

352

Drop: Hunt Trophy
Steal: Close Helmet

Gemhorn

▶ Lhusu Mines, Site 11

Slaven

-	-	-	AB	-	W	-	-

Level	HP	MP	STR.	MAG. PW.	VIT.	SPD.	ATT. PW.
45-46	42701-43121	520-525	36-38	17-19	79-81	17	65-68

DEF.	MAG. RES.	EVA.	EXP	LP	CP	GIL
22-24	26	0	4226-4389	12	1725-2001	0

353

Drop: Tanned Hide, Great Axe
Steal: Slaven Harness

Drowned

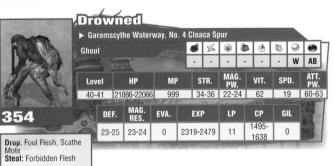

▶ Garamscythe Waterway, No. 4 Cloaca Spur

Ghoul

								W	AB
-	-	-	-	-	-	-	-		

Level	HP	MP	STR.	MAG. PW.	VIT.	SPD.	ATT. PW.
40-41	21886-22066	999	34-36	22-24	62	19	60-63

DEF.	MAG. RES.	EVA.	EXP	LP	CP	GIL
23-25	23-24	0	2319-2479	11	1495-1638	0

354

Drop: Foul Flesh, Scathe Mote
Steal: Forbidden Flesh

Bestiary

355 Luxollid

▶ Pharos-Subterra, Umbra-South — Light Elemental

NE	NE	NE	NE	NE	NE	AB	W

Level	HP	MP	STR.	MAG. PW.	VIT.	SPD.	ATT. PW.
52-53	342179	999	43	50	62	27	89

DEF.	MAG. RES.	EVA.	EXP	LP	CP	GIL
50	53	2	27404	15	8340	0

Drop: Pebble, Elixir
Steal: Staff of the Magi

356 Velelu

▶ Nabreus Deadlands, The Fog Mutters — Banshee

-	-	-	-	-	-	W	AB

Level	HP	MP	STR.	MAG. PW.	VIT.	SPD.	ATT. PW.
46-47	37189-37369	999	38-40	24-26	69	20	75-78

DEF.	MAG. RES.	EVA.	EXP	LP	CP	GIL
25-27	29-30	0	3481-3641	13	1735-1878	0

Drop: Foul Flesh, Save the Queen
Steal: Capricorn Gem

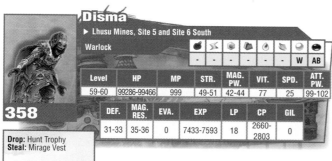

357 Vagrant Soul

▶ Pharos-Subterra, Abyssal-North — Dark Elemental

NE	NE	NE	NE	NE	NE	W	AB

Level	HP	MP	STR.	MAG. PW.	VIT.	SPD.	ATT. PW.
52-53	342179	999	43	50	62	27	89

DEF.	MAG. RES.	EVA.	EXP	LP	CP	GIL
50	53	2	27404	15	8340	0

Drop: Pebble, Elixir
Steal: Eight-fluted Pole

358 Disma

▶ Lhusu Mines, Site 5 and Site 6 South — Warlock

-	-	-	-	-	-	W	AB

Level	HP	MP	STR.	MAG. PW.	VIT.	SPD.	ATT. PW.
59-60	99286-99466	999	49-51	42-44	77	25	99-102

DEF.	MAG. RES.	EVA.	EXP	LP	CP	GIL
31-33	35-36	0	7433-7593	18	2660-2803	0

Drop: Hunt Trophy
Steal: Mirage Vest

359 Imdugud

▶ Nam-Yensa Sandsea, Withering Shores — Zu

-	-	-	W	-	AB	-	-

Level	HP	MP	STR.	MAG. PW.	VIT.	SPD.	ATT. PW.
17-18	8302-8318	312-316	25	13	55-56	14-15	27-28

DEF.	MAG. RES.	EVA.	EXP	LP	CP	GIL
8	7	3-5	1101-1105	3	655-668	0

Drop: Large Feather, Windslicer Pinion
Steal: Shielded Armor
Poach: Pebble, White Incense

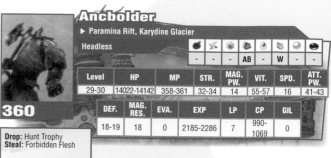

360 Ancbolder

▶ Paramina Rift, Karydine Glacier — Headless

-	-	-	AB	-	W	-	-

Level	HP	MP	STR.	MAG. PW.	VIT.	SPD.	ATT. PW.
29-30	14022-14142	358-361	32-34	14	55-57	16	41-43

DEF.	MAG. RES.	EVA.	EXP	LP	CP	GIL
18-19	18	0	2185-2286	7	990-1069	0

Drop: Hunt Trophy
Steal: Forbidden Flesh

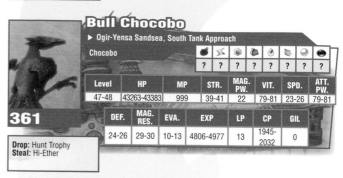

361 Bull Chocobo

▶ Ogir-Yensa Sandsea, South Tank Approach — Chocobo

?	?	?	?	?	?	?	?

Level	HP	MP	STR.	MAG. PW.	VIT.	SPD.	ATT. PW.
47-48	43263-43383	999	39-41	22	79-81	23-26	79-81

DEF.	MAG. RES.	EVA.	EXP	LP	CP	GIL
24-26	29-30	10-13	4806-4977	13	1945-2032	0

Drop: Hunt Trophy
Steal: Hi-Ether

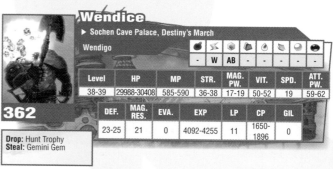

362 Wendice

▶ Sochen Cave Palace, Destiny's March — Wendigo

-	W	AB	-	-	-	-	-

Level	HP	MP	STR.	MAG. PW.	VIT.	SPD.	ATT. PW.
38-39	29988-30408	585-590	36-38	17-19	50-52	19	59-62

DEF.	MAG. RES.	EVA.	EXP	LP	CP	GIL
23-25	21	0	4092-4255	11	1650-1896	0

Drop: Hunt Trophy
Steal: Gemini Gem

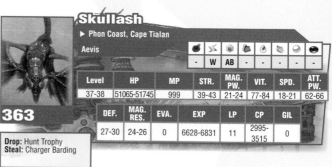

363 Skullash

▶ Phon Coast, Cape Tialan — Aevis

-	W	AB	-	-	-	-	-

Level	HP	MP	STR.	MAG. PW.	VIT.	SPD.	ATT. PW.
37-38	51065-51745	999	39-43	21-24	77-84	18-21	62-66

DEF.	MAG. RES.	EVA.	EXP	LP	CP	GIL
27-30	24-26	0	6628-6831	11	2995-3515	0

Drop: Hunt Trophy
Steal: Charger Barding

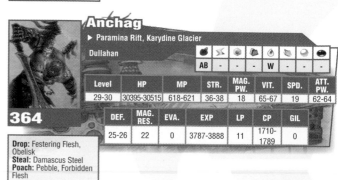

364 Anchag

▶ Paramina Rift, Karydine Glacier — Dullahan

AB	-	-	-	W	-	-	-

Level	HP	MP	STR.	MAG. PW.	VIT.	SPD.	ATT. PW.
29-30	30395-30515	618-621	36-38	18	65-67	19	62-64

DEF.	MAG. RES.	EVA.	EXP	LP	CP	GIL
25-26	22	0	3787-3888	11	1710-1789	0

Drop: Festering Flesh, Obelisk
Steal: Damascus Steel
Poach: Pebble, Forbidden Flesh

Myath

▶ Stilshrine of Miriam, Ward of Velitation

365

Level	HP	MP	STR.	MAG. PW.	VIT.	SPD.	ATT. PW.
42-43	51065-51745	999	39-43	21-24	77-84	18-21	62-66

DEF.	MAG. RES.	EVA.	EXP	LP	CP	GIL
27-30	24-26	0	6628-6831	11	2995-3515	0

Drop: Hunt Trophy
Steal: Leo Gem

Bluesang

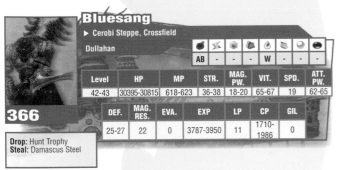

▶ Cerobi Steppe, Crossfield

Dullahan

366

Level	HP	MP	STR.	MAG. PW.	VIT.	SPD.	ATT. PW.
42-43	30395-30815	618-623	36-38	18-20	65-67	19	62-65

DEF.	MAG. RES.	EVA.	EXP	LP	CP	GIL
25-27	22	0	3787-3950	11	1710-1986	0

Drop: Hunt Trophy
Steal: Damascus Steel

Helvinek

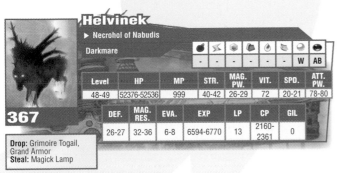

▶ Necrohol of Nabudis

Darkmare

367

Level	HP	MP	STR.	MAG. PW.	VIT.	SPD.	ATT. PW.
48-49	52376-52536	999	40-42	26-29	72	20-21	78-80

DEF.	MAG. RES.	EVA.	EXP	LP	CP	GIL
26-27	32-36	6-8	6594-6770	13	2160-2361	0

Drop: Grimoire Togail, Grand Armor
Steal: Magick Lamp

Avenger

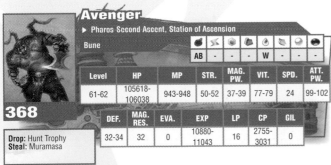

▶ Pharos Second Ascent, Station of Ascension

Bune

368

Level	HP	MP	STR.	MAG. PW.	VIT.	SPD.	ATT. PW.
61-62	105618-106038	943-948	50-52	37-39	77-79	24	99-102

DEF.	MAG. RES.	EVA.	EXP	LP	CP	GIL
32-34	32	0	10880-11043	16	2755-3031	0

Drop: Hunt Trophy
Steal: Muramasa

Pallicant

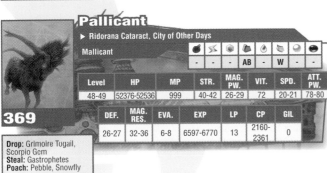

▶ Ridorana Cataract, City of Other Days

Mallicant

369

Level	HP	MP	STR.	MAG. PW.	VIT.	SPD.	ATT. PW.
48-49	52376-52536	999	40-42	26-29	72	20-21	78-80

DEF.	MAG. RES.	EVA.	EXP	LP	CP	GIL
26-27	32-36	6-8	6597-6770	13	2160-2361	0

Drop: Grimoire Togail, Scorpio Gem
Steal: Gastrophetes
Poach: Pebble, Snowfly

Alteci

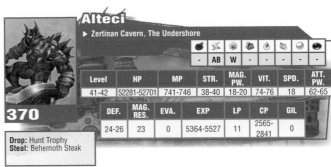

▶ Zertinan Cavern, The Undershore

370

Level	HP	MP	STR.	MAG. PW.	VIT.	SPD.	ATT. PW.
41-42	52281-52701	741-746	38-40	18-20	74-76	18	62-65

DEF.	MAG. RES.	EVA.	EXP	LP	CP	GIL
24-26	23	0	5364-5527	11	2565-2841	0

Drop: Hunt Trophy
Steal: Behemoth Steak

Phyllo

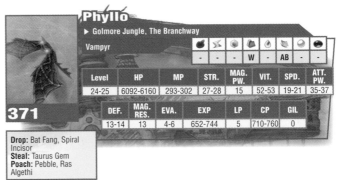

▶ Golmore Jungle, The Branchway

Vampyr

371

Level	HP	MP	STR.	MAG. PW.	VIT.	SPD.	ATT. PW.
24-25	6092-6160	293-302	27-28	15	52-53	19-21	35-37

DEF.	MAG. RES.	EVA.	EXP	LP	CP	GIL
13-14	13	4-6	652-744	5	710-760	0

Drop: Bat Fang, Spiral Incisor
Steal: Taurus Gem
Poach: Pebble, Ras Algethi

Urutan Exile

▶ Ogir-Yensa Sandsea, Platform 2-Refinery

Urutan-Yensa

372

Level	HP	MP	STR.	MAG. PW.	VIT.	SPD.	ATT. PW.
17-18	4153-4161	234-237	22-23	13-14	49-50	18	25-26

DEF.	MAG. RES.	EVA.	EXP	LP	CP	GIL
9	7	3	615-635	3	405-412	0-3

Drop: Earth Stone, Osafune
Steal: Hi-Potion
Poach: Pebble

Humanoids

Seeq Cateran

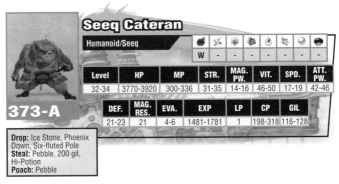

Humanoid/Seeq

373-A

Level	HP	MP	STR.	MAG. PW.	VIT.	SPD.	ATT. PW.
32-34	3770-3920	300-336	31-35	14-16	46-50	17-19	42-46

DEF.	MAG. RES.	EVA.	EXP	LP	CP	GIL
21-23	21	4-6	1481-1781	1	198-318	116-128

Drop: Ice Stone, Phoenix Down, Six-fluted Pole
Steal: Pebble, 200 gil, Hi-Potion
Poach: Pebble

Seeq Thief

Humanoid/Seeq

373-B

Level	HP	MP	STR.	MAG. PW.	VIT.	SPD.	ATT. PW.
36-39	5932-6652	375-495	32-41	17-23	50-56	18-24	52-61

DEF.	MAG. RES.	EVA.	EXP	LP	CP	GIL
24-27	22-25	4-7	2048-2873	1	248-794	168-198

Drop: Dagger, Echo Herbs, Ice Crystal
Steal: 80 gil, Gold Needle, Water Mote
Poach: Pebble

Seeq Explorer

Humanoid/Seeq

Level	HP	MP	STR.	MAG. PW.	VIT.	SPD.	ATT. PW.
41-42	26778-27018	999	37-40	21-23	63-65	23-25	58-61

DEF.	MAG. RES.	EVA.	EXP	LP	CP	GIL
30-31	26-27	15-16	5001-5276	2	1188-1370	215-225

373-C

Drop: Ice Crystal, Smelling Salts, Tumulus
Steal: 160 gil, Teleport Stone, X-Potion

Urutan-Yensa

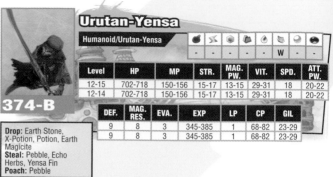

Humanoid/Urutan-Yensa

Level	HP	MP	STR.	MAG. PW.	VIT.	SPD.	ATT. PW.
12-15	702-718	150-156	15-17	13-15	29-31	18	20-22
12-14	702-718	150-156	15-17	13-15	29-31	18	20-22

DEF.	MAG. RES.	EVA.	EXP	LP	CP	GIL
9	8	3	345-385	1	68-82	23-29
9	8	3	345-385	1	68-82	23-29

374-B

Drop: Earth Stone, X-Potion, Potion, Earth Magicite
Steal: Pebble, Echo Herbs, Yensa Fin
Poach: Pebble

Seeq

Humanoid/Seeq

Level	HP	MP	STR.	MAG. PW.	VIT.	SPD.	ATT. PW.
8	232	90	7	6	20	9	7

DEF.	MAG. RES.	EVA.	EXP	LP	CP	GIL
2	8	4	0	2	205	0

373-D

Steal: Potion, 200 gil, Phoenix Down

Urutan-Yensa

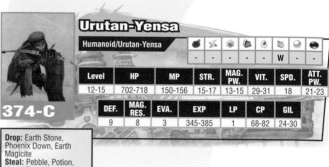

Humanoid/Urutan-Yensa

Level	HP	MP	STR.	MAG. PW.	VIT.	SPD.	ATT. PW.
12-15	702-718	150-156	15-17	13-15	29-31	18	21-23

DEF.	MAG. RES.	EVA.	EXP	LP	CP	GIL
9	8	3	345-385	1	68-82	24-30

374-C

Drop: Earth Stone, Phoenix Down, Earth Magicite
Steal: Pebble, Potion, Yensa Fin
Poach: Pebble

Seeq

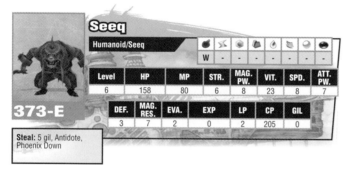

Humanoid/Seeq

Level	HP	MP	STR.	MAG. PW.	VIT.	SPD.	ATT. PW.
6	158	80	6	8	23	8	7

DEF.	MAG. RES.	EVA.	EXP	LP	CP	GIL
3	7	2	0	2	205	0

373-E

Steal: 5 gil, Antidote, Phoenix Down

Garif Warrior

Humanoid/Garif

Level	HP	MP	STR.	MAG. PW.	VIT.	SPD.	ATT. PW.
21	7049	840	28	19	50	20	27

DEF.	MAG. RES.	EVA.	EXP	LP	CP	GIL
13	15	12	1625	2	484	51

375

Drop: Ice Magicite, Potion, Hi-Potion
Steal: Potion, Hi-Potion, 500 gil

Seeq

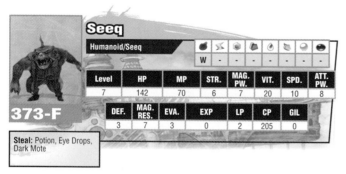

Humanoid/Seeq

Level	HP	MP	STR.	MAG. PW.	VIT.	SPD.	ATT. PW.
7	142	70	6	7	20	10	8

DEF.	MAG. RES.	EVA.	EXP	LP	CP	GIL
3	7	3	0	2	205	0

373-F

Steal: Potion, Eye Drops, Dark Mote

Baknamy

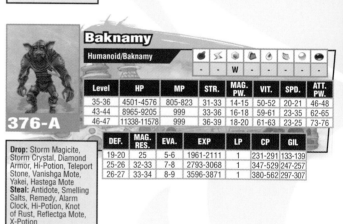

Humanoid/Baknamy

Level	HP	MP	STR.	MAG. PW.	VIT.	SPD.	ATT. PW.
35-36	4501-4576	805-823	31-33	14-15	50-52	20-21	46-48
43-44	8965-9205	999	33-36	16-18	59-61	23-35	62-65
46-47	11338-11578	999	36-39	18-20	61-63	23-25	73-76

DEF.	MAG. RES.	EVA.	EXP	LP	CP	GIL
19-20	25	5-6	1961-2111	1	231-291	133-139
25-26	32-33	7-8	2793-3068	1	347-529	247-257
26-27	33-34	8-9	3596-3871	1	380-562	297-307

376-A

Drop: Storm Magicite, Storm Crystal, Diamond Armor, Hi-Potion, Teleport Stone, Vanishga Mote, Yakei, Hastega Mote
Steal: Antidote, Smelling Salts, Remedy, Alarm Clock, Hi-Potion, Knot of Rust, Reflectga Mote, X-Potion
Poach: Pebble

Urutan-Yensa

Humanoid/Urutan-Yensa

Level	HP	MP	STR.	MAG. PW.	VIT.	SPD.	ATT. PW.
12-14	702-718	150-156	15-17	13-15	29-31	18	20-22

DEF.	MAG. RES.	EVA.	EXP	LP	CP	GIL
9	8	3	345-385	1	68-82	23-29

374-A

Drop: Earth Stone, Phoenix Down, Earth Magicite
Steal: Potion, Echo Herbs, Yensa Fin
Poach: Pebble

Baknamy

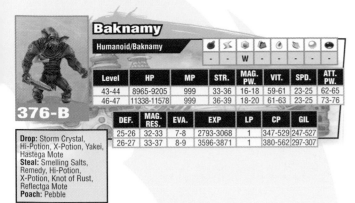

376-B — Humanoid/Baknamy

Level	HP	MP	STR.	MAG. PW.	VIT.	SPD.	ATT. PW.
43-44	8965-9205	999	33-36	16-18	59-61	23-25	62-65
46-47	11338-11578	999	36-39	18-20	61-63	23-25	73-76

DEF.	MAG. RES.	EVA.	EXP	LP	CP	GIL
25-26	32-33	7-8	2793-3068	1	347-529	247-527
26-27	33-37	8-9	3596-3871	1	380-562	297-307

Drop: Storm Crystal, Hi-Potion, X-Potion, Yakei, Hastega Mote
Steal: Smelling Salts, Remedy, Hi-Potion, X-Potion, Knot of Rust, Reflectga Mote
Poach: Pebble

Baknamy

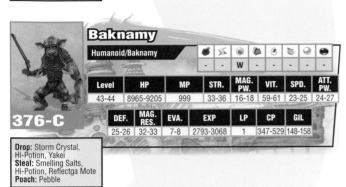

376-C — Humanoid/Baknamy

Level	HP	MP	STR.	MAG. PW.	VIT.	SPD.	ATT. PW.
43-44	8965-9205	999	33-36	16-18	59-61	23-25	24-27

DEF.	MAG. RES.	EVA.	EXP	LP	CP	GIL
25-26	32-33	7-8	2793-3068	1	347-529	148-158

Drop: Storm Crystal, Hi-Potion, Yakei
Steal: Smelling Salts, Hi-Potion, Reflectga Mote
Poach: Pebble

Bangaa Thief

377-A — Humanoid/Bangaa

Level	HP	MP	STR.	MAG. PW.	VIT.	SPD.	ATT. PW.
40-42	6137-6617	630-710	32-38	18-22	53-57	20-24	21-27

DEF.	MAG. RES.	EVA.	EXP	LP	CP	GIL
25-27	24-26	6-8	2500-3050	1	397-661	120-140

Drop: Fire Crystal, X-Potion, Feystone
Steal: Eyedrops, 80 gil, Trident
Poach: Pebble

Bangaa Pirate

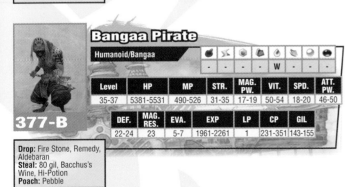

377-B — Humanoid/Bangaa

Level	HP	MP	STR.	MAG. PW.	VIT.	SPD.	ATT. PW.
35-37	5381-5531	490-526	31-35	17-19	50-54	18-20	46-50

DEF.	MAG. RES.	EVA.	EXP	LP	CP	GIL
22-24	23	5-7	1961-2261	1	231-351	143-155

Drop: Fire Stone, Remedy, Aldebaran
Steal: 80 gil, Bacchus's Wine, Hi-Potion
Poach: Pebble

Bangaa Pugilist

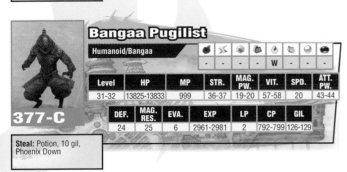

377-C — Humanoid/Bangaa

Level	HP	MP	STR.	MAG. PW.	VIT.	SPD.	ATT. PW.
31-32	13825-13833	999	36-37	19-20	57-58	20	43-44

DEF.	MAG. RES.	EVA.	EXP	LP	CP	GIL
24	25	6	2961-2981	2	792-799	126-129

Steal: Potion, 10 gil, Phoenix Down

The Archadian Empire

Imperial Swordsman

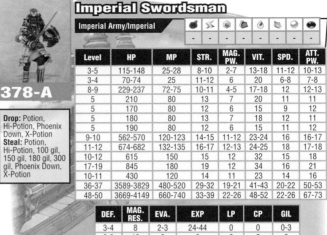

378-A — Imperial Army/Imperial

Level	HP	MP	STR.	MAG. PW.	VIT.	SPD.	ATT. PW.
3-5	115-148	25-28	8-10	2-7	13-18	11-12	10-13
3-4	70-74	25	11-12	6	20	6-8	7-8
8-9	229-237	72-75	10-11	4-5	17-18	12	12-13
5	210	80	13	7	20	11	11
5	170	80	12	6	15	9	12
5	180	80	13	7	18	12	11
5	190	80	12	6	15	11	12
9-10	562-570	120-123	14-15	11-12	23-24	16	16-17
11-12	674-682	132-135	16-17	12-13	24-25	18	17-18
10-12	615	150	15	12	32	15	18
17-19	845	180	19	12	34	16	21
10-11	430	120	14	11	23	14	16
36-37	3589-3829	480-520	29-32	19-21	41-43	20-22	50-53
48-50	3669-4149	660-740	33-39	22-26	48-52	22-26	67-73

DEF.	MAG. RES.	EVA.	EXP	LP	CP	GIL
3-4	8	2-3	24-44	0	0	0-3
2-3	12	0	0	0	0	0
3	5	5	65-85	1	27-34	8-11
6	7	2	0	2	76	6
6	7	3	0	2	76	6
6	7	2	0	2	76	6
6	7	3	0	2	76	6
6	6	3	137-157	1	42-49	8-11
8	8	3	151-171	1	46-53	8-11
6	7	3	285	1	53	9
10	8	3	338	1	63	17
6	6	3	137	1	42	9
20-21	22-23	5-6	1164-1439	1	168-350	84-94
26-28	30-32	7-9	1137-1687	1	231-595	133-153

Drop: Potion, Hi-Potion, Phoenix Down, X-Potion
Steal: Potion, Hi-Potion, 100 gil, 150 gil, 180 gil, 300 gil, Phoenix Down, X-Potion

Imperial Marksman

378-B — Imperial Army/Imperial

Level	HP	MP	STR.	MAG. PW.	VIT.	SPD.	ATT. PW.
7	264	79	10	4	19	15	7

DEF.	MAG. RES.	EVA.	EXP	LP	CP	GIL
4	6	5	65	1	27	6

Drop: Potion, Phoenix Down
Steal: Potion, Phoenix Down, 150 gil
Poach: Pebble

Imperial Hoplite

378-C — Imperial Army/Imperial

Level	HP	MP	STR.	MAG. PW.	VIT.	SPD.	ATT. PW.
8-9	275-283	58-61	12-13	4-5	19-20	12	13-14
10-12	674-682	96-116	16-18	11-13	24-26	16	18-20
36-38	4308-4788	384-464	31-37	19-23	43-47	20-24	52-58

DEF.	MAG. RES.	EVA.	EXP	LP	CP	GIL
5	5	5	72-92	1	30-37	10-13
8	6	3	151-191	1	46-64	9-13
22-24	22-24	5-7	1281-1831	1	185-549	88-108

Drop: Potion, Hi-Potion, Phoenix Down
Steal: Potion, Hi-Potion, 150 gil, 180 gil, Phoenix Down
Poach: Pebble

Imperial Magus

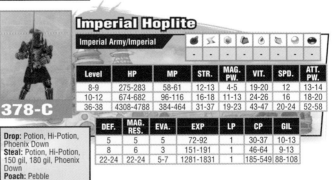

378-D — Imperial Army/Imperial

Level	HP	MP	STR.	MAG. PW.	VIT.	SPD.	ATT. PW.
3-4	110-114	120-130	8-9	5-6	13-14	15	9-10
6-8	197-205	180-200	9-11	8-10	15-17	12	11-13
8-10	481-489	300-320	13-15	15-17	21-23	16	16-18
9-10	384	300	13	15	21	14	15

DEF.	MAG. RES.	EVA.	EXP	LP	CP	GIL
3	11	3	26-46	0	0-9	0-2
4	6	5	65-105	1	27-45	8-12
7	7	2	137-177	1	42-60	7-11
7	7	2	137	1	42	8

Drop: Potion, Dark Mote, Warp Mote, Aero Mote
Steal: Potion, Antidote, Dark Mote, Water Mote, 150 gil
Poach: Pebble

Bestiary

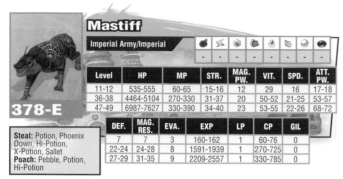

Mastiff

Imperial Army/Imperial — 378-E

Level	HP	MP	STR.	MAG. PW.	VIT.	SPD.	ATT. PW.
11-12	535-555	60-65	15-16	12	29	16	17-18
36-38	4464-5104	270-330	31-37	20	50-52	21-25	53-57
47-49	6987-7627	330-390	34-40	23	53-55	22-26	68-72

DEF.	MAG. RES.	EVA.	EXP	LP	CP	GIL
7	7	3	160-162	1	60-76	0
22-24	24-28	8	1591-1939	1	270-725	0
27-29	31-35	9	2209-2557	1	330-785	0

Steal: Potion, Phoenix Down, Hi-Potion, X-Potion, Sallet
Poach: Pebble, Potion, Hi-Potion

Imperial Beastmaster

Imperial Army/Imperial Elite — 380-D

Level	HP	MP	STR.	MAG. PW.	VIT.	SPD.	ATT. PW.
49-50	3458-3698	999	33-36	29-31	45-47	22-24	68-71

DEF.	MAG. RES.	EVA.	EXP	LP	CP	GIL
28-29	35-36	6-7	1307-1582	1	266-448	134-144

Drop: Phoenix Down, Hi-Potion, Reflecta Mote
Steal: Potion, Hi-Potion, Ether
Poach: Pebble

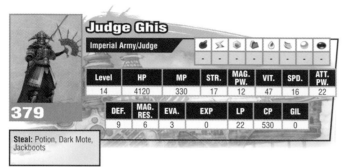

Judge Ghis

Imperial Army/Judge — 379

Level	HP	MP	STR.	MAG. PW.	VIT.	SPD.	ATT. PW.
14	4120	330	17	12	47	16	22

DEF.	MAG. RES.	EVA.	EXP	LP	CP	GIL
9	6	3	0	22	530	0

Steal: Potion, Dark Mote, Jackboots

Judge Bergan

Imperial Army/Judge — 381

Level	HP	MP	STR.	MAG. PW.	VIT.	SPD.	ATT. PW.
30	17200	999	37	23	60	25	49

DEF.	MAG. RES.	EVA.	EXP	LP	CP	GIL
26	22	4	0	19	1980	0

Steal: Hi-Potion, Ruby Ring, Ether

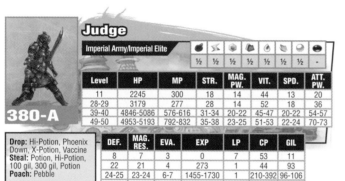

Judge

Imperial Army/Imperial Elite — 380-A

| | ½ | ½ | ½ | ½ | ½ | ½ | ½ |

Level	HP	MP	STR.	MAG. PW.	VIT.	SPD.	ATT. PW.
11	2245	300	18	14	44	13	20
28-29	3179	277	28	14	52	18	36
39-40	4846-5086	576-616	31-34	20-22	45-47	20-22	54-57
49-50	4953-5193	792-832	35-38	23-25	51-53	22-24	70-73

DEF.	MAG. RES.	EVA.	EXP	LP	CP	GIL
8	7	3	0	7	53	11
22	21	4	273	1	44	93
24-25	23-24	6-7	1455-1730	1	210-392	96-106
29-30	31-32	8-9	1421-1696	1	289-471	140-150

Drop: Hi-Potion, Phoenix Down, X-Potion, Vaccine
Steal: Potion, Hi-Potion, 100 gil, 300 gil, Potion
Poach: Pebble

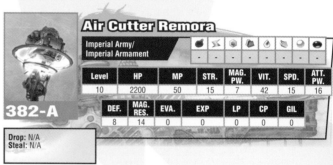

Air Cutter Remora

Imperial Army/Imperial Armament — 382-A

Level	HP	MP	STR.	MAG. PW.	VIT.	SPD.	ATT. PW.
10	2200	50	15	7	42	15	16

DEF.	MAG. RES.	EVA.	EXP	LP	CP	GIL
8	14	0	0	0	0	0

Drop: N/A
Steal: N/A

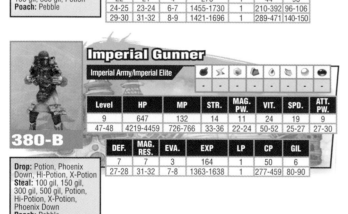

Imperial Gunner

Imperial Army/Imperial Elite — 380-B

Level	HP	MP	STR.	MAG. PW.	VIT.	SPD.	ATT. PW.
9	647	132	14	11	24	19	9
47-48	4219-4459	726-766	33-36	22-24	50-52	25-27	27-30

DEF.	MAG. RES.	EVA.	EXP	LP	CP	GIL
7	7	3	164	1	50	6
27-28	31-32	7-8	1363-1638	1	277-459	80-90

Drop: Potion, Phoenix Down, Hi-Potion, X-Potion
Steal: 100 gil, 150 gil, 300 gil, 500 gil, Potion, Hi-Potion, X-Potion, Phoenix Down
Poach: Pebble

Spinner-Rook

Imperial Army/Imperial Armament — 382-B

| | ½ | ½ | ½ | ½ | ½ | ½ | ½ | ½ |

Level	HP	MP	STR.	MAG. PW.	VIT.	SPD.	ATT. PW.
47	13286	770	33	30	40	20	68

DEF.	MAG. RES.	EVA.	EXP	LP	CP	GIL
28	30	0	3631	1	380	0

Steal: Knot of Rust, Hi-Potion, X-Potion

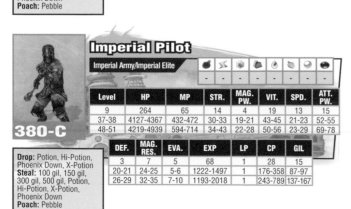

Imperial Pilot

Imperial Army/Imperial Elite — 380-C

Level	HP	MP	STR.	MAG. PW.	VIT.	SPD.	ATT. PW.
9	264	65	14	4	19	13	15
37-38	4127-4367	432-472	30-33	19-21	43-45	21-23	52-55
48-51	4219-4939	594-714	34-43	22-28	50-56	23-29	69-78

DEF.	MAG. RES.	EVA.	EXP	LP	CP	GIL
3	7	5	68	1	28	15
20-21	24-25	5-6	1222-1497	1	176-358	87-97
26-29	32-35	7-10	1193-2018	1	243-789	137-167

Drop: Potion, Hi-Potion, Phoenix Down, X-Potion
Steal: 100 gil, 150 gil, 300 gil, 500 gil, Potion, Hi-Potion, X-Potion, Phoenix Down
Poach: Pebble

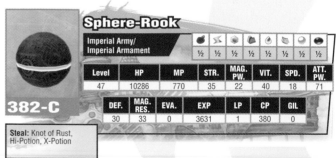

Sphere-Rook

Imperial Army/Imperial Armament — 382-C

| | ½ | ½ | ½ | ½ | ½ | ½ | ½ | ½ |

Level	HP	MP	STR.	MAG. PW.	VIT.	SPD.	ATT. PW.
47	10286	770	35	22	40	18	71

DEF.	MAG. RES.	EVA.	EXP	LP	CP	GIL
30	33	0	3631	1	380	0

Steal: Knot of Rust, Hi-Potion, X-Potion

Helm-Rook — 382-D

Imperial Army/Imperial Armament

½	½	½	½	½	½	½	½

Level	HP	MP	STR.	MAG. PW.	VIT.	SPD.	ATT. PW.
47	12286	770	33	25	40	20	70

DEF.	MAG. RES.	EVA.	EXP	LP	CP	GIL
29	32	0	3631	1	380	0

Steal: Knot of Rust, Hi-Potion, X-Potion

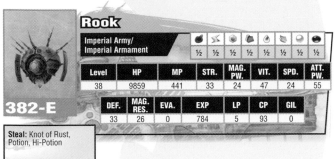

Rook — 382-E

Imperial Army/Imperial Armament

½	½	½	½	½	½	½	½

Level	HP	MP	STR.	MAG. PW.	VIT.	SPD.	ATT. PW.
38	9859	441	33	24	47	24	55

DEF.	MAG. RES.	EVA.	EXP	LP	CP	GIL
33	26	0	784	5	93	0

Steal: Knot of Rust, Potion, Hi-Potion

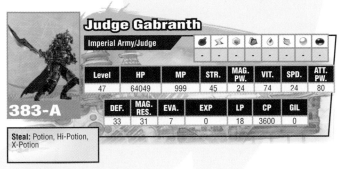

Judge Gabranth — 383-A

Imperial Army/Judge

-	-	-	-	-	-	-	-

Level	HP	MP	STR.	MAG. PW.	VIT.	SPD.	ATT. PW.
47	64049	999	45	24	74	24	80

DEF.	MAG. RES.	EVA.	EXP	LP	CP	GIL
33	31	7	0	18	3600	0

Steal: Potion, Hi-Potion, X-Potion

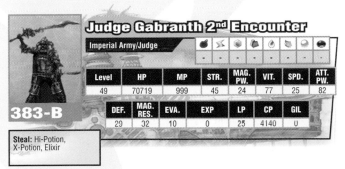

Judge Gabranth 2nd Encounter — 383-B

Imperial Army/Judge

-	-	-	-	-	-	-	-

Level	HP	MP	STR.	MAG. PW.	VIT.	SPD.	ATT. PW.
49	70719	999	45	24	77	25	82

DEF.	MAG. RES.	EVA.	EXP	LP	CP	GIL
29	32	10	0	25	4140	0

Steal: Hi-Potion, X-Potion, Elixir

Doctor Cid — 384-A

Imperial Army/Scientist

½	½	½	½	½	½	W	AB

Level	HP	MP	STR.	MAG. PW.	VIT.	SPD.	ATT. PW.
40	72989	999	36	21	72	30	22

DEF.	MAG. RES.	EVA.	EXP	LP	CP	GIL
83	94	7	0	29	3240	0

Steal: Knot of Rust, Hi-Potion, X-Potion

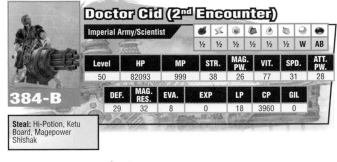

Doctor Cid (2nd Encounter) — 384-B

Imperial Army/Scientist

½	½	½	½	½	½	W	AB

Level	HP	MP	STR.	MAG. PW.	VIT.	SPD.	ATT. PW.
50	82093	999	38	26	77	31	28

DEF.	MAG. RES.	EVA.	EXP	LP	CP	GIL
29	32	8	0	18	3960	0

Steal: Hi-Potion, Ketu Board, Magepower Shishak

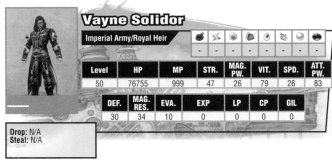

Vayne Solidor

Imperial Army/Royal Heir

-	-	-	-	-	-	-	-

Level	HP	MP	STR.	MAG. PW.	VIT.	SPD.	ATT. PW.
50	76755	999	47	26	79	26	83

DEF.	MAG. RES.	EVA.	EXP	LP	CP	GIL
30	34	10	0	0	0	0

Drop: N/A
Steal: N/A

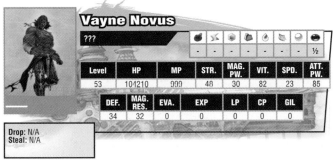

Vayne Novus

???

-	-	-	-	-	-	-	½

Level	HP	MP	STR.	MAG. PW.	VIT.	SPD.	ATT. PW.
53	104210	999	48	30	82	23	85

DEF.	MAG. RES.	EVA.	EXP	LP	CP	GIL
34	32	0	0	0	0	0

Drop: N/A
Steal: N/A

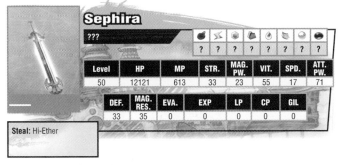

Sephira

???

?	?	?	?	?	?	?	?

Level	HP	MP	STR.	MAG. PW.	VIT.	SPD.	ATT. PW.
50	12121	613	33	23	55	17	71

DEF.	MAG. RES.	EVA.	EXP	LP	CP	GIL
33	35	0	0	0	0	0

Steal: Hi-Ether

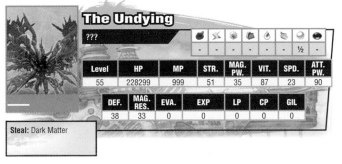

The Undying

???

-	-	-	-	-	-	½	-

Level	HP	MP	STR.	MAG. PW.	VIT.	SPD.	ATT. PW.
55	228299	999	51	35	87	23	90

DEF.	MAG. RES.	EVA.	EXP	LP	CP	GIL
38	33	0	0	0	0	0

Steal: Dark Matter

FINAL FANTASY XII
OFFICIAL STRATEGY VIDEOS

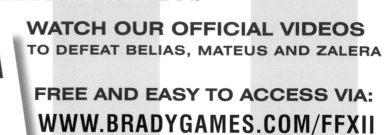

WATCH OUR OFFICIAL VIDEOS
TO DEFEAT BELIAS, MATEUS AND ZALERA

FREE AND EASY TO ACCESS VIA:
WWW.BRADYGAMES.COM/FFXII

This interactive license board gives you:

- Information on the items, spells and abilities you gain with the license

- Where to get these items and their costs

Discover strategy at BradyGames.com!

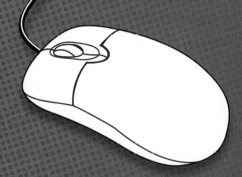

FINAL FANTASY XII

OFFICIAL STRATEGY GUIDE

BradyGames Publishing
An Imprint of DK Publishing, Inc.
800 East 96th Street, 3rd Floor
Indianapolis, Indiana 46240

ISBN: 0-7440-0837-9

Printing Code: The rightmost double-digit number is the year of the book's printing; the rightmost single-digit number is the number of the book's printing. For example, 06-1 shows that the first printing of the book occurred in 2006.

09 08 07 06   4 3 2 1

Manufactured in the United States of America.

BradyGAMES Staff

Publisher
David Waybright

Director of Marketing
Steve Escalante

Licensing Manager
Mike Degler

Editor-In-Chief
H. Leigh Davis

Creative Director
Robin Lasek

Credits

Title Manager
Tim Cox

Book Designers
Keith Lowe
Doug Wilkins

Screenshot Editor
Michael Owen

Layout Designer
Tracy Wehmeyer

Acknowledgments

Rick Barba would like to thank…

First, thanks to the great folks at Bradygames—to Leigh Davis for putting together such a well-balanced project team, and to Tim Cox for the patient, intelligent guidance that kept everything on track. Thanks also to my scary-smart co-writers, David, Wes, and Joe for diligently digging into the guts of this game like true gamers. Finally, special thanks to the folks at Square Enix for all the help and support.

Joe Epstein would like to thank…

To begin, huge gratitude to Craig, James, Brad, and Tommy for their understanding over the last two years, and to Chris "The Hause Always Wins" Hausermann for the shout-out. Big thanks to everyone who worked hard to put this book together, including Tim, Michael, Christian, Rick, Wes, and David. Thanks to the employees at the Hartsfield-Jackson Atlanta Airport for making it about as agreeable a place as any to spend a weekend stranded. Thanks to Frye's Electronics for having the most incredible shipping I've seen from any company, ever. Thanks to pneumonia for making things fun and exciting. Props to Long Tran for moving to Texas for ten seconds and giving me an excuse to take a mini-vacation, and thanks to Jeff Burton for the Chaco's dinners at 4am—good luck in Denver, hoss. And finally, thanks to Yasumi Matsuno and Square Enix for pleasing an old-school cat with the best Final Fantasy since IV.

David Cassady would like to thank…

I'd like to thank my co-authors for their insight and humor. Thanks to the folks at Brady for their hard work and patience on this monster of a project. Square Enix for this superb addition to the Final Fantasy series and wonderful support. But most of all, my family for all the love they give every day and their seemingly endless patience during these gigantic projects, Pastor Chip Bernhard for the inspiration he provides every week, and God for making it all possible. Oh yeah… and Starbucks for all of the Mocha Frappuccino Lights.

Wes Ehrlichman would like to thank…

Many thanks to Yasumi Matsuno and the rest of the Final Fantasy XII team for making the game that reminded me why I love RPGs, my future fiancée Christina for putting up with me during the sleepless months of the guide's creation, and my dog Popper for sitting next to me and keeping me warm while I played.